INFORMATION SYSTEMS ASSURANCE

David C. Chan

INFORMATION SYSTEMS ASSURANCE

ISBN-13: 978-1477561515

INFORMATION SYSTEMS ASSURANCE

Preface

No one would doubt that information systems are playing an increasing role in business operations and our daily lives. The main reason for using computers is to be more efficient. This allows organizations to be more competitive. It also enables individuals to have higher earning power and achieve a better quality of life. Increasingly, organizations are finding it necessary to use technology in order to compete, and survive.

There are risks in using technology. It might be incorrectly applied because of inadequate training or unrealistic expectation on what can be achieved. Computer systems reduce paper and visible audit trail so errors have a higher chance of remaining undetected. There is higher concentration of processing when computers are used and this increases the impact of incorrect functions. Access to computer systems is less noticeable than access to paper files so the risk of unauthorized transactions can increase.

The purpose of this book is to help understand how information technology (IT) affects risks, what controls should be implemented to mitigate risks and how controls can be tested and assessed to provide assurance to management, customers and auditors. This book covers the syllabus of the Certified Information Systems Auditor Examination administered by Information Systems Audit and Control Association.

This book focuses on system assurance, i.e., assurance that risks are adequately mitigated with internal controls. It discusses assurance from the perspectives of management and auditors. Many chapters of this book provide guidelines to auditors in identifying and testing internal controls. How about the auditor's work in testing data to substantiate financial reports and statements? Well, if internal controls are strong, financial reports and statements will tend to be reliable. Auditors, in addition to testing controls, have to perform direct vouching and examination of transactions to ascertain data integrity and completeness. Internal controls vary in complexity in terms of the extent of automation. The nature of transaction data also changes with automation, but it does so to a less extent than internal controls. A bank statement contains the same information whether it is on paper or online. Therefore, this book will not talk at length about how to test transaction data directly, it will focus on assessing risks, implementing internal controls and testing internal controls. Having said that, I want to highlight that the testing of transaction data for integrity and completeness is aided by technology, i.e., auditors can use computers to automate transaction testing. We will discuss audit automation in Chapter Seven.

How about security? Isn't that a hot topic with the increasing use of the Internet and open connectivity of corporate networks? Security is very important and will be covered in Chapter Eight and Chapter Nine. Security is a type of internal controls that are needed to provide information systems assurance, particularly with respect to authorization and proof of occurrence.

The intended users of this book include auditors, managers, students and accountants. In writing this book, I tried to be practical and explain concepts and applications in plain language. This book is divided into two sections. Section One is a summary of all the chapters. Section Two contains individual chapters. Throughout this book, I stress in different ways the importance of ensuring people understand the value they can deliver to their employers and customers. This means the objectives of internal controls should be clearly stated, employees should be thoroughly trained and management should set clear accountabilities and provide useful monitoring and feedback. This makes happy employees and customers.

Resources for this book, including URLs, are referenced throughout the text as much as practical. I have made every attempt to acknowledge sources, although most of the material comes from my own experience and research. It is inevitable to have some errors or omissions, including acknowledgements, in a volume of this size. I would be grateful to any readers who notice such omissions to contact me directly.

David C. Chan, MS, CPA, CA, CISA, CISM, CISSP, CIA, CFE, PMP
August 2012

Toronto, Canada

INFORMATION SYSTEMS ASSURANCE

About the Author

David C. Chan is a highly experienced audit professional who has practiced information technology (IT) auditing and IT security in public accounting, banking and the public sector. He has many years of IT audit and security management experience in Price Waterhouse, Bank of Montreal, Office of the Provincial Auditor of Ontario, Hydro One and Ontario Ministry of Government Services. David has taught information systems auditing in Ontario universities. In addition to his degree of Master of Science in Computer Science, David has earned the following professional designations:

- Certified Public Accountant
- Chartered Accountant
- Certified Information Systems Auditor
- Certified Information Security Manager
- Certified Information Systems Security Professional
- Certified Internal Auditor
- Certified Fraud Examiner
- Project Management Professional

David has been active in professional research with Canadian Institute of Chartered Accountants (CICA), the Institute of Chartered Accountants of Ontario (ICAO) as well as the Information Systems Audit and Control Association (ISACA). He has served on the CICA IT Advisory Committee, the ICAO Course Content Committee and the ISACA Test Enhancement Committee. David has published in CA Magazine and Information Systems Control Journal on the topics of audit scheduling and encryption. David has also taught the preparatory courses for the ICAO Core Knowledge Examination and the Certified Information Systems Auditor Examination.

Table of Contents

This section includes the introduction, management checklist, summary of main points and conclusion of each chapter. It is intended as an executive summary of this book.

This chapter is an overview of the book and discusses why information and information technology are important to businesses. The two terms are used because even when information is not fully attached to IT infrastructure or a system, e.g., a printout, it is important and needs to be controlled. The following topics are covered.

- Information systems stakeholders
- Information system components
- Types of information systems
- Methods of transaction processing and data access
- Database and data structure
- Information and system ownership
- Criteria for information and information technology reliability
- Responsibility for assurance
- How reliability and assurance are achieved
- Types of assurance engagements
- Current IT issues

This chapter discusses what can go wrong in using information and information technology and how new technologies affect what can go wrong. We will examine risks from management and auditors' perspectives. The following topics are covered.

- Inherent risk
- Control risk
- Residual risk
- Detection risk
- Audit risk
- Sampling risk
- Business critical systems

- Responsibility for risk assessment and acceptance
- Risk criteria
- Process of risk assessment
- Corporate risk registry

After risk assessment, management should implement internal controls to mitigate risks. This chapter starts to explore internal controls. It begins with discussing the foundation of internal controls, also called general controls. The following topics are covered.
- Control criteria
- Control risk
- IT governance
- Organizational controls
- Software change controls
- Fundamentals of access controls
- Fundamentals of systems development controls
- Disaster prevention controls
- Disaster recovery controls
- Computer operations controls
- Capacity planning
- IT performance measurement

About half of a large organization's IT budget is spent in developing and upgrading systems. Many organizations have experienced systems development failures which wasted money and led to unreliable systems. This chapter will discuss the methodologies to ensure information systems are developed with adequate internal controls to deliver reliable functions, i.e., making sure quality goes in before the name goes on. The following topics are covered.
- Systems development risks.
- Systems development life cycle and related controls.
- Responsibilities for systems development, testing and implementation.
- Fast path systems development techniques, their pitfalls and how to control them.
- Purchasing systems vs developing systems.
- Project management controls.
- Business process reengineering

eBusiness is widely used. There are concerns about privacy and merchant reliability. This chapter will discuss the risks and controls that organizations should fully understand and reflect in their eBusiness systems. The following topics are covered.

- eBusiness infrastructure
- eBusiness risks
- Privacy concerns
- Controls to ensure reliable eBusiness infrastructure
- Intellectual property
- Electronic data interchange
- eXtensible Business Reporting Language

In this chapter, we will discuss internal controls for specific business systems. We will use an internal control matrix mapping the control criteria of completeness, authorization, accuracy, timeliness, occurrence and efficiency to the transaction stages of input, processing, output and storage, as a frame of reference. We will also talk about database controls. The following topics will be covered.

- Control criteria
- Input controls
- Processing controls
- Output controls
- Controls over data storage
- Database controls
- Enterprise resource planning system controls

The annual doubling of computing power presents a growing opportunity to auditors to automate audit procedures. Audit automation saves time and increases consistency as computers are not sleepy and biased. We will talk about techniques for auditors to use computers to expedite audit work and accurately test financial records. The following topics will be discussed.

- General audit software
- Integrated test facility
- Embedded audit module
- Audit scheduling
- Electronic work papers

Has the Internet changed the world? The opinion is probably split, not 50-50, but more likely in a continuum. There will be more agreement that the Internet has increased the need for information security. Information security means access controls. We will cover the following topics.

- Access control objectives of confidentiality, integrity and availability.
- How are these access control objectives related to the control criteria of completeness, authorization, accuracy, timeliness, occurrence and efficiency?
- Information security policy and procedures.
- Information security techniques.
- Network security.

The access controls we discuss in the previous chapters apply to pretty much all systems and infrastructure. In this chapter, we will go over the access control parameters and architecture at an operating system level and review the security relationship between operating systems and access control software tools. We will cover the following common platforms:

- Windows
- Mac OS X
- Unix
- IBM Z Series (mainframe) servers

Outsourcing is common in large organizations. Banks, utility companies and governments have outsourced. When an organization relies significantly on an IT service provider, risk goes up in terms of authorization, accuracy, availability and completeness. A common analogy is the risk that parents face when taking a baby to a day care center.

We will discuss the following topics.
- Impact of outsourcing on inherent, control and audit risks.
- Impact of outsourcing on the financial statement audit.
- Options to shareholders' auditors to bridge the control assurance gap.
- Independent control assurance opinion on a service organization.
- Options to a service organization if internal control deficiencies are found.

Organizations continue to increase their reliance on information systems. Aside from traditional outsourcing, there are arrangements for organizations to share information systems and trading partners to share information. As a result, there is increasing demand on organizations operating information systems to provide assurance to user organizations. In this chapter, we will discuss two common types of such assurance reports, other than those in an outsourcing agreement, which is discussed in the last chapter. The two types of non-outsourcing IT control assurance engagements we will discuss in this chapter are SysTrust and Payment Card Industry (PCI) security assurance.

We will cover the following topics.
- Drivers for a SystTrust audit
- Types of SysTrust audit
- SysTrust principles
- SysTrust criteria
- SysTrust control procedures
- Process of a SysTrust audit
- Drivers for PCI security assurance requirement
- PCI Security Standard
- PCI Security procedures

Computer crime has increased in volume, impact and variety in the last decade mainly because of the Internet. There are broadly speaking, two types of computer crime: crime causing fairly immediate damage like hacking, and crime that is fraudulent in nature like an email scam. In either case, the crime may be committed on IT resources or it may use IT as a tool to achieve the criminal intent. We will cover the following topics.
- Common computer crime
- Common computer fraud
- Controls against computer crime and computer fraud
- Roles of internal and external auditors
- Computer forensic investigation

SECTION 1 - SUMMARY OF ALL CHAPTERS

CHAPTER ONE – WHO, WHAT, WHEN, WHERE, WHY

Information assurance is the bedrock upon which enterprise decision-making is built. Without assurance, enterprises cannot feel certain that the information upon which they base their mission-critical decisions is reliable, confidential, secure and available when needed. – Information Systems Audit and Control Association

Introduction

There are risks in using technology. It might be incorrectly applied because of inadequate training or unrealistic expectation on what can be achieved. Computer systems reduce paper and also reduce visible audit trail so errors have a higher chance of remaining undetected. There is higher concentration of processing when computers are used and this increases the impact of incorrect functions. Access to computer systems is less noticeable than access to paper files so the risk of unauthorized transactions can increase.

Users of information systems need assurance in order to have faith in what they rely on to perform business transactions and make decisions. They want to have faith in the information to be provided by the organizations they work in or deal with. They have a right to demand that such faith be supported by a rigorous process of system assurance.

Some have said that computing power doubles annually, i.e., information technology (IT) capability costing a dollar today will probably cost fifty cents in a year. We have seen many examples of this in personal computers, storage devices and consumer electronics. That does not mean that consumers and organizations will spend less on IT. What this means is that we can continue to upgrade the use of IT to improve efficiency and our quality of life. To respond to demand, and to generate demand, technology product developers will continue to come up with new gadgets, tools and applications.

The speed of change in IT as well as the seemingly exponential adoption rate by users and organizations sometimes generate a question in one's mind about reliability, just as the speed of driving or the high turnover of staff would cast doubt about safety and quality. How is reliability measured? Who will measure it? Who will assure it?

Management Checklist

To ensure that information systems are reliable and cost effective, senior management should adopt the following practices.

1. Assign business executives to own information systems and infrastructures. Each system should have only one owner. IT infrastructures would logically be owned by the chief information officer (CIO) because an infrastructure usually supports multiple business systems.

2. Establish corporate policies and standards for information risk assessment.

3. Establish a process for periodic risk assessment, internal control formulation and internal control reporting to senior management and the board of directors.

4. Involve the board of directors in IT governance and ensure this is addressed at least twice a year in board meetings.

5. Establish a policy on the use of I & IT in the organization with respect to how to use IT as a business enabler and the approval process for IT investment.

6. Develop an IT strategy to be congruent with the business strategy. The IT strategy should consider the applicability of new technology.

7. Develop a process to continuously assess the cost effectiveness of IT applications.

8. Ensure that the job description and performance contract of each executive include the appropriate information systems assurance accountability.

9. Establish an IT steering committee consisting of a cross section of senior executives including the CIO to carry out IT governance.

10. Establish a process to promptly address IT audit findings.

Chapter One Conclusion

The Internet has changed the world. Large businesses can act small by using the Internet to customize service. Small businesses can act big by using the Internet to reach the world. Although there is still a "digital divide" in the world, the difference between the "have" and the "have not" in knowledge access is narrowing, as information finds its way across continents instantaneously. IT empowers everyone to do constructive things and damage. Successes can be attained and catastrophes can be caused in great magnitude within a short time. Just look at how quickly some of the large IT companies have come about and grown in a few years, and look at how some unauthorized or improper securities transactions that were carried out in only a few days with breaches in IT controls that led to huge financial losses in banks.

Continuing advance in technology makes systems reliability more important. In addition to putting in processes and infrastructure to ensure system reliability, management needs to continuously exemplify and promote a quality culture and hold everyone responsible for quality.

The pace of life is different than it was 10, 20 years ago. Systems undergo more frequent changes. System assurance has to keep pace. Auditors have to keep up; not just to keep up with IT development in terms of knowledge, but to keep pace with "life on the fast lane" in this digital environment, in terms of audit focus, frequency and timeliness. Audit reports should be issued to identify and help fix problems, and less focus should be on reporting history. Don't tell stakeholders at length what they already know. IT can help to automate audit effort so that audits can be more focused and efficient.

Every chief audit executive should strive to build a world class audit organization. Audit quality should not be limited by the size of the enterprise. Research studies indicate that many small organizations have internal audit departments that are superior to large organizations'. Although salary gaps between the private sector and the public sector as well as those between large companies and small companies may be a limiting factor, chief audit executives can work around that using other incentives like job variety and flexible work arrangement. Again, research can indicate that many government auditors are more capable than private sector auditors. The chief internal auditor must continuously seek improvements, promote education, exemplify and hold every auditor accountable for quality.

Auditors have to critically question their findings and recommendations because organizations, to be competitive, have less and less time and resources for "nice to have" recommendations. Auditors have to continuously ask "so what" when finding things they did not expect to see, before the client says "so what". Auditors also have to avoid "just going through the audit program" and avoid being seen as "just going through the motion". They must be innovative to help management mitigate risks, including the risks of overspending. For example, auditors should not just report that a department has a system backlog of transactions, but rather, should analyze what causes the backlog and how management can fix it including shifting resources from less critical tasks. Auditors should try to avoid just being used by line managers to get more resources, but should try diligently to help the organization become more effective, efficient and competitive by recommending internal controls and identifying areas that are over controlled. Although internal controls are owned by management, auditors should not just point out what is wrong and leave management to find the solution. Every employee is an expert in something. The auditor's expertise is internal control, so it is right for management to look to auditors to recommend controls.

Auditors must also be flexible in assessing controls. For example, if a control deficiency is found but management is able to come up with a compensating control that the auditor has tested to be satisfactory, the deficiency in the first control is somewhat just an academic issue. Instead of concluding that the area is weak, the auditor should then just tell management that the failed control may be redundant and management should either fix it to provide stronger control assurance or remove it so as not to waste resource.

Boards of directors have to continuously challenge their management about the sufficiency of IT assurance provided to the boards and customers. Users and customers should be educated to play a constructive role towards such assurance. Regulators need to monitor company system reliability in addition to checking the correctness of filed reports.

Summary of Main Points in Chapter One

System Assurance Criteria

- Completeness
- Authorization
- Accuracy
- Timeliness
- Occurrence
- Efficiency

System Components

- Infrastructure
- Software
- People
- Procedures
- Information

Types of Assurance Engagements

- Financial statement audit
- Value for money audit
- Internal audit
- Third party control assurance audit
- Audit for compliance with specific legislation or contract
- Forensic audit

Types of Systems

- Batch
- Real time
- eBusiness
- Centralized vs distributed processing
- Direct access vs sequential access
- Enterprise resource planning systems

Current IT Issues

American Institute of Certified Public Accountants conducted a survey of top IT priorities in 2012. Here is the list of the top ten topics:

1. Securing the IT environment
2. Managing and retaining data
3. Managing risk and compliance
4. Privacy
5. Leveraging emerging technologies
6. Managing system implementation
7. Enabling decision support and managing performance
8. Governance and managing IT investment/spending
9. Preventing and responding to fraud
10. Managing vendor and service providers

Source:
http://www.aicpa.org/INTERESTAREAS/INFORMATIONTECHNOLOGY/RESOURCES/
TOPTECHNOLOGYINITIATIVES/Pages/2012TTI.aspx

CHAPTER TWO – INFORMATION SYSTEMS RISKS

There are risks and costs to a program of action, but they are far less than the long-range risks and costs of comfortable inaction. – John F. Kennedy

Introduction

- In June 2012, LinkedIn investigated the possible leaking of several million of its users' passwords after a member of a Russian online forum said he managed to hack the popular networking site and upload close to 6.5 million passwords to the internet.

- BlackBerry services returned to normal on October 13, 2011 after four days of global outages, but Research In Motion (RIM) faced a new challenge as it tried to clean up a public relations headache. In a conference call on October 13, RIM explained that the widespread outage was caused by technical glitches linked to a backup switch that did not function as tested, causing a large backlog of emails. Outages started in Europe, then spread to the Middle East, Africa and North America. South America and Asia were also affected.

- In March 2010, hackers flooded the Internet with virus-tainted spam that targeted Facebook's estimated 400 million users in an effort to steal banking passwords and gather other sensitive information.

- The June 2009 subway crash in Washington DC appeared to be linked to a train control system failure.

- One of the biggest frauds in banking history was carried out in Société Générale, a top European bank based in France, by a 31-year-old trader called Jerome Kerviel. He took massive fraudulent directional positions - bets on future movements of European stock indexes, without his supervisors' knowledge. Because he had previously worked in the trading unit's back office, he had in-depth knowledge of the control procedures and evaded them by creating fictitious transactions to conceal his activity. He also breached system access controls.

- A bug in Excel was reported in 2007. For example, multiplying 850 by 77.1 would yield 100,000 instead of the correct product of 65,535.

- Telecommunications throughout Asia were severely disrupted on December 26, 2006, after earthquakes off Taiwan damaged undersea cables, delaying Internet services and hindering financial transactions, particularly in the currency market.

In the last chapter, we talked about the need to assess business risks before developing and implementing internal controls in order to mitigate risks to an acceptable level and therefore provide an acceptable level of assurance on information system reliability. In this chapter, we will discuss the process of risk assessments. We will address risks from the standpoints of management and auditors.

Risk management requires common sense. We manage risk when we walk or drink coffee (a little sip first to see if it is too hot). We turn on the television to check the weather before leaving for work or university.

Computers are fast but they can also make mistakes fast, thus leaving little time to prevent, detect and correct. For example, an electronics retailer mispriced a product a few years ago on its web site as $59.90 when the store price was $599. In a day, the company sold more than 600 units based on the wrong price.

Computers can be consistently right but also consistently wrong. Increasing use of IT means less paper trail. The reduction in hard copy documents may make mistakes more difficult to detect. The concentration of information in computers and electronic media exposes organizations to the risk of "placing all the eggs in one basket". Further, it is more difficult to control who has access. These are some basic risks in using IT. Other less obvious risks include improper use, uneconomical deployment, inadequate capacity and developing systems that do not meet business requirements.

There are basically three types of things that can go wrong with respect to using IT. First, the wrong system may be developed in relation to business requirements, the development of a system may not be well managed and therefore wasting the organization's money, or the system may be developed with significant flaws. Secondly, undesirable things might happen to a system when it is being used; e.g., unauthorized data change may be made, there may be unauthorized use, disasters can happen that damage the hardware and software. Thirdly, system information may be inappropriately used; e.g., users are not trained and therefore misuse some functions, or there may be incorrect interpretation of system information.

The risk of errors occurring because of the nature of the business, organization and system is called inherent risk. To mitigate such risk, management must implement internal controls. However, internal controls are not fool-proof, otherwise they would be too expensive. The risk of internal controls not preventing or detecting significant errors is called control risk. The third type of risk, to an auditor, is the risk of audit procedures failing to detect material errors, and this is called detection risk. Auditors are concerned about all three types of risk. The multiplicative value of inherent risk, control risk and detection risk is called audit risk, which is the risk of providing favorable audit assurance on a system which has major flaws. Management is generally concerned about only inherent risk and control risk. The product of inherent risk and control risk is called "residual risk", i.e., the risk remaining even after implementing internal controls. Management has to assess whether the residual risk is acceptable and organizations should have guidelines and decision limits to ensure consistent application and acceptance of residual risk. The tolerable residual risk should be low for every business critical system.

The term "threat" is often used to refer to risk. A threat is more general and it usually does not bear any quantifiable connotation. For example, a snow storm is a threat. The estimated likelihood of a snow storm is a risk. Another related term is vulnerability. We are vulnerable because we are not well positioned; for example, we are more vulnerable to getting sick if we don't have enough sleep. Vulnerability, therefore, means the extent of risk resulting from a weakness.

Risk Matrix

	Complete	Authorized	Accurate	Timely	Occur	Efficient
Input						
Processing						
Output						
Storage						

Management Checklist

1. Senior management should appoint an executive to coordinate risk assessment throughout the organization.

2. Senior management should develop a risk assessment framework consisting of risk factors, weighting criteria, weight scale, risk assessment scale (e.g., 1 to 10), frequency of risk assessment and a prioritized list of critical systems.

3. Senior management should charge each executive with determining his or her business critical systems.

4. Compile and prioritize the business critical systems for the entire organization.

5. Provide regular risk assessment training to mangers.

6. Provide an annual or quarterly risk profile report to the board of directors.

7. Maintain a risk registry in the organization which details the financial exposure of each business critical system and each business area. A business area may use more than one system and a system may support more than one business area. Financial exposure in the risk registry is supported by quantitative assessment of inherent risk and control risk.

8. Perform annual benchmarking with the industry on the organization's risk profile.

9. Ensure that the risk profile of the organization is appropriately disclosed in the annual report to shareholders and relevant stakeholders.

10. Include a risk assessment section in the business case for every IT project

Chapter Two Conclusion

Because of the uncertainty in audit trail completeness as well as the increased difficulty in understanding and controlling electronic processes and access compared to less automated processes, the overall risk impact of IT is that it generally increases inherent risk, control risk and detection risk. Organizations are increasingly realizing the importance of structured risk management as evidenced by the growing number of chief risk officers in large organizations. There is also a positive and encouraging trend to include IT risk assessment in executive job descriptions.

Summary of Main Points in Chapter Two

- Audit risk = inherent risk x control risk x detection risk (risk of substantive audit procedure failure).
- The risk factors of incompleteness, inadequate authorization, inaccuracy, untimeliness, lack of substantiation and inefficiency apply to inherent risk and control risk.
- Financial statement auditors seek moderate control assurance, whereas internal auditors expect high control assurance.
- Detection risk can be reduced with audit automation.
- Inherent risk = business risk.
- Residual risk = inherent risk x control risk.
- Business function managers own the risks.
- Senior management should set corporate guidelines and approval levels for risk acceptance.
- Outsourcing increases all risks.
- Exposure = risk x materiality
- Threat = a particular risk without the probability quantification, e.g., the threat of terrorism. A threat, once quantified, becomes a risk.
- Vulnerability = exposure resulting from insufficient controls.

CHAPTER THREE – IT GOVERNANCE AND GENERAL CONTROLS

He who controls the present controls the past. He who controls the past controls the future. - George Orwell

Introduction

We have talked about information systems risks in the last chapter. To mitigate risks, organizations should put in place a system of internal controls. The system of internal controls actually is not a stand-alone system, rather, it contains internal controls that work their way into normal transaction processing, in order to be effective on an ongoing basis. *An internal control is an instruction, procedure or tool to mitigate an inherent risk.*

The extent of internal controls to be designed and implemented depends on risk assessments. Based on the result of assessments, internal controls should be implemented to address the five components of a system: infrastructure, software, procedures, people and information. Controls should be implemented to mitigate the risks of incompleteness, inadequate authorization, inaccuracy, untimeliness, fictitious information and inefficient processing. Controls have to span the entire transaction cycle of input, processing, output and information storage.

Management Checklist

1. Develop an IT strategy to be congruent with the business strategy.

2. Develop an information technology directive or policy to provide high level guidance and a structure for information technology practices including IT controls.

3. Develop and keep up to date information technology organization charts that support segregation of duties between the IT functions and user areas as well as within the IT functions.

4. Develop and update information technology and IT related job descriptions.

5. Develop IT policies and procedures to implement segregation of duties, security, software change controls, computer operations controls, privacy protection, disaster recovery controls and network monitoring.

6. Maintain separate libraries and environments for systems development, integration testing, user acceptance testing and production.

7. Establish an IT steering committee to oversee information technology expenditures and review major projects.

8. Develop and regularly test disaster recovery plans.

9. Implement procedures to monitor network reliability and efficiency.

10. Ensure that IT controls are thoroughly documented and assessed annually for effectiveness.

Chapter Three Conclusion

Today's business environment is a lot different from what it was when computers were first used to process transactions. Most business systems in large organizations are now open to the public directly or indirectly. There are more system users and they expect more in terms of system efficiency and reliability. Today's customers are less loyal and have less patience. Just look at the telephone and TV markets. Consumers can switch phone company, TV carrier and Internet service provider with a few clicks. Regulators are more demanding of companies to implement sound internal controls.

Internal controls are not just the interest of auditors. Managers are increasingly convinced and comfortable about their control ownership and responsibilities. They need help, help from industry guidelines, internal control specialists, control systems and auditors. An increasing percentage of business functions are automated. Management and auditors have to continuously keep up with the control implications of technology and use technology to achieve business competitiveness and reliability. Competitiveness and reliability can no longer be separated, and internal controls provide the bridge.

Summary of Main Points in Chapter Three

Although most internal controls operate daily and are at the transaction and data levels, the extent of controls and their responsibilities stem from the control environment and culture that senior management has created and shaped over time. Senior management does that by exercising IT governance. In this chapter, we have focused on those IT controls that are pervasive in the organization across business areas, and they are called general controls.

Internal controls can be preventive, detective or corrective. Preventive controls are preferable to detective controls. However, an organization needs both because it is impractical to prevent all major errors and irregularities. For each detective control, there should be a corresponding corrective control.

General Controls

- Organization controls – including segregation of duties between IT and users as well as within the IT department
- Access controls
- Software change controls
- Systems development controls
- Disaster prevention controls
- Disaster recovery controls
- Computer operation controls
- IT performance measurement controls
- Intellectual property controls

Organization Controls

- IT steering committee
- I&IT strategy
- Policies and standards
- Segregation of duties
- Hiring practices
- Code of business conduct
- Training

Access Controls

- Physical
- Logical (data and software).
- Applies to infrastructure, software, people, information and procedures.

Software Change Control

- Application software change control.
- System software (e.g., operating system) change control.
- Change control policies and procedures.
- Naming conventions.
- Library control.
- Separate environments for development, testing and production (operation).
- Software testing.
- Change approval.
- Change monitoring.
- Procedures to deal with emergency changes to ensure adequate testing, documentation and approval.

Systems Development Controls

- Systems development methodology
- Approval at checkpoints
- Documentation standards

Disaster Prevention Controls

- Data backup
- Software backup
- Hardware and network redundancy
- Fire and water resistant data center
- Locating data centers away from hazardous or high crime areas
- Preventive maintenance schedule and monitoring
- Hardware performance monitoring

Disaster Recovery Controls

- Incident response procedures
- Business impact assessment
- Disaster recovery plan
- Disaster recovery testing

Computer Operation Controls

- Service level agreement
- Operations procedures
- Procedures for hardware purchases and deployment
- Hardware configuration standards and procedures
- Network transmission control
- Operation schedule
- Capacity planning

IT Performance Measurement Controls

- Cost benefit analysis
- Business case methodology
- Cross charging IT cost to avoid waste of resources
- Key performance indicators
- IT score card reporting

CHAPTER FOUR – SYSTEMS DEVELOPMENT CONTROLS

You must be the change you want to see in the world. - Mahatma Gandhi

Introduction

The average organization spends about half of its IT budget in developing systems. Systems development is not trivial and most organizations do not do as well as they would like to. Many systems development projects are not completed on time and on budget and do not meet all user requirements. Organizations need to have a discipline in developing systems. Systems are developed more frequently these days as the life of a system is shorter. The life is shortened in a way by international competition which compels organizations to change to keep up with the industry. eBusiness has empowered small organizations to compete with multinationals. Small companies can change their systems more dynamically as they have less overhead and fewer organizational layers to go through; they are also more adventurous.

Twenty years ago, the average systems development project took two years to complete. Today, if implementation does not start one year from project initiation, the organization may be falling behind its competitors or customer expectation. It is important to maintain discipline and practice controls in systems development while speeding to meet business challenges.

Management Checklist

1. Develop a systems development methodology that addresses systems development, systems acquisition and rapid application options.

2. Develop an end user development policy.

3. Ensure internal audit is involved in systems development.

4. Set procedures to inform the board and the IT steering committee about major projects.

5. Ensure that IT staff and appropriate user areas are trained in the systems development methodology.

6. Develop an annual systems development plan containing planned and active projects.

7. Establish a project management office to monitor and report on systems development projects.

8. Develop quality assurance metrics and procedures for systems testing, documentation, training and acceptance.

9. Include the organization's business case standard practice for capital projects in the systems development methodology.

10. Prepare quarterly status reports on active projects to measure progress, cost and benefit.

Chapter Four Conclusion

Systems development is a major IT activity in most organizations. Even organizations that use purchased software packages often find the need to enhance the systems' functions or tailor the packages to their environments. Systems development may seem straight forward in that users are free to define their requirements and the IT department is expected to write programs to fulfill the requirements. In fact, it is a risky undertaking because of the need to coordinate expectation and understanding between users and stakeholders who may not be IT savvy in working with technical systems development staff, and because of the increasing interaction between systems in today's globally competitive environment. Many organizations have failed to complete systems development projects or they have produced the wrong systems in relation to their business needs. Organizations need to mitigate these risks by implementing a systems development methodology to be used consistently to ensure that the development of systems is authorized, accurate, efficient and complete and that implementation is timely.

Summary of Main Points in Chapter Four

1. Develop a three year systems development plan that is updated every year. This is part of the IT strategy. The systems development plan should include all current and planned projects. The start date, checkpoints, end dates, deliverables and resource requirements should be included for each project. The chief information officer is responsible for this and the IT steering committee should approve the systems development plan. Internal and external auditors should be informed. The project management office should maintain this plan.

2. Problem recognition, a business unit responsibility, must be approved by the business owner before the development of each system. The business owner will then own the system.

3. Feasibility study, a business unit responsibility, must be approved by the business owner before the development of each system.

4. Project proposal, a business unit responsibility, must be approved by the level of management with financial authority to sign off the cost of the project over the life time before netting the cost with operational savings. This is because operational savings may not materialize if circumstances change.

5. System analysis, a project manager responsibility, must be approved by the project sponsor, who should be the executive owner of the system being developed.

6. Project plan, a project management responsibility, must be approved by the project sponsor and the IT department.

7. User requirements, a business unit responsibility, must be approved by the project manager, IT department and project sponsor; should be signed off by internal audit and information technology security. The IT architecture and design units must also sign off to make sure the user requirements can be expanded to architecture and design specifications.

8. System architecture, an IT department responsibility, must be approved by the project manager. It should be signed off by the lead designer, internal audit and IT security.

9. System design can be carried out concurrently with system architecture, and is an information technology department responsibility. It must be approved by the project manager; and it should be signed off by user representatives, the system architects, internal audit and IT security.

10. Programming, an IT department responsibility, must be approved by the programming and project managers.

11. System integration testing, an IT department responsibility, must be approved by the project manager and the information technology department. It should be signed off by internal audit and IT security.

12. User acceptance testing, a business unit responsibility, must be approved by the project manager, IT department and project sponsor. It should be signed off by internal audit.

13. Procedures development, can be carried out concurrently with the above processes after system design. It must be approved by the project manager, IT department and project sponsor; it should also be signed off by internal audit.

14. Disaster recovery plan update, an IT department responsibility, can be carried out concurrently with the above process after system design. It must be approved by the project manager, IT department and project sponsor.

15. Training can be carried out concurrently with the above process after system design. It is a business unit and IT department responsibilities, must be approved by the project manager and the project sponsor. Affected employees should be certified internally or if necessary, externally.

16. Conversion and implementation, a project manager responsibility, must be approved by the IT department and the project sponsor. It should also be signed off by internal audit and the IT department.

17. Post-implementation review, a project sponsor responsibility, must be signed off by the project sponsor and project manager. It should also be signed off by the chief internal auditor.

CHAPTER FIVE – CONTROL AND AUDIT IMPLICATIONS OF E-BUSINESS

The advance of technology is based on making it fit in so that you don't really even notice it, so it's part of everyday life. – Bill Gates

Introduction

In Chapter Two, we discuss the risk impact of information systems. We conclude that generally, business risks increase proportionally with the use of information technology (IT). This relationship applies to inherent risk, control risk and auditors' detection risk. eBusiness involves more IT resources than traditional information systems so we can deduce that eBusiness increases inherent risk, control risk and detection risk.

In addition to discussing the risks of eBusiness, we will cover legal aspects of IT. This is because organizations that engage more in eBusiness will find that they have more IT related intellectual property to protect, e.g., eBusiness model, search engine, proprietary software, software for sale and product information. These properties may be reachable via the Internet and the risk of copyright infringement is higher. Organizations are now more connected through the Internet so their trade secret is at higher risk of unauthorized access.

We will discuss eBusiness controls to mitigate risks. eBusiness is a new way of conducting business, rather than a new type of transactions. So eBusiness controls are classified as general controls. eBusiness differs from traditional computer systems mainly in the area of infrastructure. Organizations must build a strong IT infrastructure before launching eBusiness.

Key eBusiness Controls

When an organization offers eBusiness, it should review the current general and application controls in relation to the increased risks. Usually, the following internal controls have to be expanded or added. These controls are in addition to the existing application controls in transaction processing systems because in most cases, eBusiness is a new or additional way of conducting business but the background transaction processing should not differ significantly whether the order is placed online or in person.

- Boundary checking
- Digital certificate
- Digital signature
- Disaster recovery plan
- Edit checks
- Encryption
- Firewall
- Intrusion detection system
- Intrusion prevention system

- Online backup
- Recalculate transaction amount behind the web server to nullify change made by a hacker
- Redundant communication lines
- Redundant servers
- Web site refresh

Management Checklist

To ensure that eBusiness and electronic data interchange (EDI) are effectively controlled including compliance with privacy legislations, management should consider the following minimum checklist.

1. Develop an eBusiness strategy that is congruent with the overall business strategy.

2. Obtain board approval of the eBusiness strategy.

3. Develop an eBusiness policy and standards that address completeness, authorization, accuracy, information sensitivity and security.

4. Develop an information privacy policy and post it on the web site.

5. Appoint a chief information privacy officer.

6. Review contracts with Internet service providers annually to ensure adequate provision for responsibilities, billing arrangements, security and privacy.

7. Train eBusiness developers, operators and managers on eBusiness and privacy legislations.

8. Ensure the EDI arrangement with each trading partner is documented in a contract.

9. Thoroughly test each new EDI interface.

10. Keep an accurate inventory of its intellectual property and periodically assess whether valuation is realistic and conservative. Periodically assess and test the protection mechanism for intellectual property, including access controls and registration with the respective government offices.

Chapter Five Conclusion

eBusiness is here to grow. Most people do not dispute this. While today's eBusiness customers are more at ease with the Internet than customers ten, twenty years ago, there remain significant risks with respect to transaction authorization, completeness of audit trail and privacy. In fact, the concern about privacy is higher now than ten, twenty years ago because of the increasing power of organizations to store and analyze information. Organizations that offer eBusiness have to be constantly aware of and regularly assess the risks of unauthorized, illegitimate, inaccurate, incomplete and untimely transaction processing, as well as the need to protect information privacy. Those organizations that implement sufficient internal controls to mitigate these risks will not only serve as respectable corporate citizens, but also lay a solid foundation for business growth as eConsumers are increasingly IT savvy and demanding with respect to information reliability, integrity and privacy.

Summary of Main Points in Chapter Five

eBusiness Infrastructure

- The Web server, application server, authentication server and database server require protection with firewalls, anti-virus software and rigorous operating system configuration. The inner servers need more protection.
- The Web master, the person who maintains the web server content, needs to be trained and monitored.
- Routers route traffic from workstations to servers and the Internet; they need to be tightly configured.
- Contracts with Internet service providers should be detailed, and should be reviewed regularly and monitored.
- Domain name servers have to be protected from hacker attack to redirect traffic.

Privacy Principles

1. Accountability – an organization should designate someone to be accountable for privacy.
2. Identifying purpose – When collecting personal information, an organization should state the purpose.
3. Consent – personal information should be collected with consent.
4. Limiting collection – An organization should collect only the personal information needed for the purpose stated.
5. Limiting use, disclosure and retention – in relation to the personal information and the purpose for which it was collected.
6. Accuracy – An organization should put in place a process to ensure the accurate recording and transmission of personal information.

7.   Safeguard – An organization should put in place a process to protect personal information.

8.   Openness – An organization should be open about its privacy policy and practice.

9.   Individual access – An organization should allow the owners of personal information to access the respective information.

10.   Challenging compliance – An organization should be prepared to respond to challenges from privacy regulators, customers and employees.

Uniform Electronic Transaction Act

This act is consistent with most eBusiness legislations in other jurisdictions. It has the following main points.

- It recognizes human-machine interfaces as offer and acceptance.
- It recognizes digital signatures.
- It places the onus on merchants to implement reasonable edit checks to prevent errors.
- It does not recognize biometrics.
- It does not apply to the sale of real estate, negotiable instruments and power of attorney in respect to financial affairs or personal care.

Radio Frequency ID

Radio frequency IDs expedite transactions and help organizations perform better tracking of assets. However, because of their mobility, the risks of unauthorized transactions, device tampering and privacy intrusion increase. To mitigate the above risks, management should consider adopting the following control practices.

1.   Review the radio frequency ID (RFID) application project plans and system functions with the chief privacy officer to ensure compliance with privacy regulations.

2.   Subject RFID systems and devices to rigorous system integration and user acceptance testing.

3.   Periodically perform network penetration testing to assess the exposure to hacker and worm attacks.

4.   Perform regular physical checks of devices.

5.   Perform regular testing of data capture and tracking to ensure accuracy.

6.   Frequently validate the inventory of activated RFIDs.

7. Regularly review reports of activation and deactivation to ensure tag movements are authorized.

8. Regularly review statistics about tag data transfer volume and delay.

9. Ensure servers have adequate intrusion detection and virus detection software.

10. Deploy network transmission integrity checking techniques like redundant data check and parity check.

Electronic Data Interchange (EDI)

- Electronic transfer of accounting documents using the American National Standards Institute Standard (ANSI) in North America, and EDI for Finance, Accounting, Commerce and Transportation (EDIFACT) outside North America.
- Can be used to pay invoices via banks.
- Each organization needs to buy or develop translation software to convert local format to ANSI or EDIFACT format and vice versa.
- Organizations should acknowledge completeness of transfers.
- It needs strong access and reconciliation controls.
- EDI reduces the cost of ordering and therefore also the inventory level and accounts payable, resulting in less obsolescence and lower cost of storage. A smaller balance sheet means less substantive testing but more control testing, mainly EDI and related access controls.

Controls over Intellectual Property

1. Access control.
2. Contracts and service agreements.
3. Confidentiality agreement.
4. User education.
5. Management monitoring.
6. Registration with government office, e.g., registering patents.

CHAPTER SIX – APPLICATION CONTROLS

Drive thy business, let not that drive thee. - Benjamin Franklin

Introduction

Every chief executive officer would agree to the above statement. Driving means moving ahead with a plan. A driver has to know where to go, stop and turn as well as how to control the car. It is the last function, control, that keeps the car on track. Driving a business requires controls to ensure that business goals are met, and met efficiently.

We started our discussion of internal controls in Chapter Three, where we talked about how internal controls should be mapped to inherent risks for management to achieve a tolerable level of business risk. The tolerable level should be set where the cost of an extra control would exceed the cost of the risk materializing, taking into account the probability of the risk. This is called a reasonable level of internal control assurance.

An internal control is an instruction, procedure or tool to mitigate an inherent risk. To ensure that risk mitigation is organized and coordinated effectively, management should correlate internal controls to provide sufficient redundancy to prevent risks from becoming material exposures while avoiding significant duplication of effort. Such correlation is called a plan of internal controls. This plan should be documented and used as a basis for employee training and ongoing risk assessment.

Internal controls may be general in nature or specific to applications. A general control applies to an environment or multiple applications. An application control mitigates the risk of only one application system like payroll. It would appear that general controls are more cost effective. However, because applications differ in risk, organizations cannot implement only general controls. Management should start with general controls until the cost of a control exceeds the monetary impact of the risk being mitigated. Then, if the residual risk is too high and it very much likely will be, application controls should be implemented. Although an application control applies to a specific application (system), the same technique can be used across applications. For example, a credit limit and a check limit both use the same technique, but it is applied in different ways.

MANAGEMENT CHECKLIST

1. Adopt a consistent set of application controls throughout the organization subject to variation between applications because of the nature of transaction processing (e.g., batch vs online) and materiality. For example, there must be monthly reconciliations signed off by managers; the format of a bank reconciliation may differ from that of a credit card reconciliation, but the requirement for extent of documentation and sign-off should be consistent.

2. Require each system owner to submit a control compliance report annually.

3. Document the internal controls in each business critical systems in the same format.

4. Include internal control training as part of new managers' training.

5. Establish a secondment program for people to join the internal audit department for short term assignments and vice versa to increase internal control awareness in the organization.

6. Provide a semi-annual report to the audit committee on overall internal controls reliability in the organization.

7. Ensure that internal control recommendations from auditors are addressed promptly.

8. Include internal control compliance in the performance contracts of executives.

9. Assess the applicability of Six Sigma and initiate a project to achieve it if deemed practical.

10. Include the criteria and measurement of completeness, authorization, accuracy, timeliness and efficiency in each business unit's performance evaluation process.

CHAPTER SIX CONCLUSION

Application controls should be tested on every financial statement audit after testing and gaining assurance on general controls. A moderate level of assurance on general controls and application controls will enable the external auditors to limit substantive testing.

Internal audits mainly focus on internal controls and application controls are usually extensively tested. Other special purpose audits like providing control assurance on a service organization to corporate customers address mainly internal controls including application controls.

Computing power doubles annually. Organizations continue to empower customers and employees with technology by allowing direct access and automated transactions as well as by streamlining the manual review and approval process. This often leads to removing preventive controls to achieve efficiency. To avoid an unacceptable level of risk, management should design and implement rigorous exception reporting system functions and tracking mechanisms for exceptions to be addressed.

Sarbanes-Oxley Act and Canada's Investor Confidence Rules require CEOs to certify internal controls supporting financial statements annually. Application controls are directly related to financial statements. We will therefore see more rigorous documentation of application controls by management and more thorough testing of application controls by the external auditors who are often called on to express an opinion on internal controls for Sarbanes-Oxley and Investor Confidence Rules reporting.

SUMMARY OF MAIN POINTS

- Application controls rest on general controls.
- If general controls are substantially weak, the financial statement auditors may choose to simply walk through application controls instead of detailed testing and adopt a substantive audit approach. Even with a substantive audit approach, auditors place some reliance on internal controls unless the auditors test every transaction. Even if the auditors test every transaction, there is a risk of hidden transactions. So there is always some reliance on internal controls. This is why auditors should at least walk through internal controls. Walkthrough means taking one or two transactions per key control to verify the control. The result of the walkthrough, i.e., presence (with very limited assurance because there is only walkthrough instead of detailed control testing) or absence of controls will influence the auditors in focusing their substantive testing. Even in a substantive audit approach, the extent of substantive testing will differ depending on the result of control walkthrough, e.g., it can range from testing, say 10% of the transactions, to say 25% of the transactions. In other words, a lower detection risk will be tolerated if controls are largely absent as a result of the walkthrough.
- If general controls are reliable, a moderate level of application controls should be sought for the financial statement audit.
- In the audit of a public company in Canada or the United States, the shareholders' auditors are often asked to provide an opinion on internal controls that support the financial statements, in addition to the traditional financial statement audit opinion. In such a case, the shareholders' auditors will seek high control assurance on the internal controls that support the financial statements. The scope of such controls usually includes most general controls and most application controls.
- Internal auditors usually seek a high level of assurance and therefore will do more testing.

- Application controls should include an optimum mix of preventive, detective and corrective controls. Preventive controls are preferred, but not all major risks can practically be mitigated with preventive controls, otherwise, the environment may be too tight and therefore not competitive; e.g., requiring every transaction, regardless of amount, to be pre-approved by management would be impractical. Hence, detective controls should be put in place to detect significant errors or irregularities and corrective controls are necessary to correct these errors and irregularities.

Common Application Controls

- Edit checks – Applied at input stage, e.g., checking for negative amounts.
- Batch total – Comparing one total accumulated to another total accumulated later in the transaction input phase, to check input completeness. Batch total can also be applied by comparing total input to total output.
- Hash total – Similar to batch total, but the total is applied to a field normally not intended for computation, e.g., check number. This avoids offsetting errors, e.g., a $100 check goes missing but another $100 check is recorded as $200.
- Run-to-run control total – Similar to batch total but accumulation and comparison are done by programs within the system, to check the completeness of data passed from one system function to another, applicable to batch systems.
- Reconciliation between sets of records or systems.
- Management review of exceptions.
- Management review of transactions either before or after processing - Some transactions may be impractical or not cost effective for pre-approval, in which case post-approval may mitigate the risk.
- Customer statements of transactions.
- Limit check, e.g., checking customer orders to credit limit.
- Monitoring of open items, such as unbilled shipments.

Edit Checks

Edit checks on data input are critical preventive controls to ensure that data input is correct and complete. The same techniques can be applied in processing. Why do we have to apply the same techniques to processing if input data is correct? Well, in processing, programs perform calculations to update data files. Before data files are updated, the calculated results should be validated to detect errors. For example, an invoice with a negative amount should be reviewed before the sales journal and the accounts receivable subsidiary ledger are updated. Here is a list of common edit checks.

- Check digit to validate data entry of a control number like a product number.
- Data format check, e.g., a date field should be yyyymmdd.
- Limit check.
- Missing data check, i.e., all mandatory fields are filled in.

- Range check.
- Sequence check
- Sign check.
- Validity check, by verifying data input to a table of acceptable values.

Database Controls

More and more systems use databases. In such a system, there need to be internal controls to ensure data integrity when multiple files (tables) are shared by multiple applications. Here are the common database controls.

- Record locking to avoid concurrent update, i.e., two transactions trying to update the same record concurrently leading to a later transaction nullifying the first transaction.
- Referential integrity to avoid null value in critical data fields.
- Detection and resolution of deadlock caused by conflicting record locks to avoid the system being hung.
- Logging of access to database especially changes, to facilitate error recovery.
- Normalization to reduce data redundancy and inconsistency.
- Synchronization between locations and environments to ensure consistency of content and clocks. Clock synchronization is critical to ensure transactions are time stamped correctly for audit trail and for prioritization of updates and interest calculation (e.g., 11:59 pm vs 12:00 am).
- Producing alerts on direct updates, i.e., updating not through an authorized system function like ATM, to detect unauthorized data change.
- Producing alerts on table creation and deletion to detect unauthorized data creation or change.

Common Application Control Test Procedures

- Review and verify bank reconciliation.
- Review the rejected transaction log and follow up for correction.
- Use test data to test input control and processing controls.
- Review the production schedule, i.e., the daily or weekly schedule of batch updates and confirm by reviewing computer operations audit trail.
- Review user procedures for correctness of instructions.
- Ask staff to ascertain their understanding of instructions.
- Observe segregation of duties.
- Review the database management system configuration to assess the adequacy of provision for database integrity.
- Review the data dictionary and confirm with actual table layout.

- Send confirmation to customers to see if they have received the customer statements.
- Observe the mailing of customer statements.
- Perform data correlation to obtain evidence of controls, e.g., cross referencing invoices to receiving reports.

CHAPTER SEVEN – COMPUTER ASSISTED AUDIT TECHNIQUES

The first rule of any technology used in a business is that automation applied to an efficient operation will magnify the efficiency. The second is that automation applied to an inefficient operation will magnify the inefficiency. – Bill Gates

Introduction

In Chapter Two, we discussed inherent risk, control risk and detection risk. We went through the attributes of information technology (IT) as they related to risks. For example, increasing electronic audit trail increases the risk of unauthorized access. Another example is the speed and power of computers, which can decrease the risk of untimeliness. Generally, the factors that affect inherent risk also affect control risk and detection risk in the same direction. We concluded that IT generally increases inherent risk, control risk and detection risk. Detection risk can be decreased with automation, i.e., to use computers to automate the audit process, taking advantage of the accuracy and speed of computers. Further, increasing affordability and portability of storage devices allows auditors to analyze more data and therefore increase audit coverage and correspondingly decrease detection risk. With the use of computer assisted audit techniques (CAAT), the need to sample has gone down.

There are five types of computer assisted audit techniques (CAAT); the first three types receive more attention as they serve to automate audit testing and analysis.

- General audit software (GAS)
- Integrated test facility
- Embedded audit module
- Audit scheduling
- Electronic work papers

This chapter is intended primarily for auditors, so there is no management checklist.

Audit Checklist

1. Document consideration to use CAAT in each audit and justify why CAAT is not used.

2. In systems development auditing, document CAAT requirements in terms of data availability and ensure that these requirements are included in the system development project.

3. For each business critical system, assess CAAT applicability and the types of CAAT.

4. Include CAAT in each auditor's training plan.

5. Build a technical CAAT team in the audit department or the accounting firm.

6. Develop a CAAT documentation standard for each type of CAAT.

7. Use CAAT to perform organization wide analytical review not tied specifically to individual audits to identify risky areas for further audit work and management attention.

8. Include standard confidence levels, tolerable sample error sizes and upper error limits in the organization's audit methodology for different systems.

9. Keep track of CAAT audit hours and audit findings from CAATs to assess CAAT effectiveness.

10. External auditors should use internal auditors as much as practical to apply CAATs as the latter are closer to the organization's systems and have more resources. External auditors should rigorously review the internal audit work papers.

Chapter Seven Conclusion

Our life is increasingly affected by digitization. This helps to enhance consistency, convenience and comfort. Car diagnosis is so computerized today that a mechanic's hands are less dirty and drivers are better educated on what went wrong. Computers facilitate micro surgery to improve precision and limit bleeding. Auditors should consider every meaningful opportunity to automate their work, from electronic work papers to using expert systems to perform analytical review, etc., in order to reduce audit cost and risk.

Summary of Main Points in Chapter Seven

General Audit Software

This is similar to Microsoft Access but tailored for auditors. It allows auditors to perform a variety of data analysis of client's data files. Here are the common functions:
- Data extraction based on criteria (formulae)
- Aging of accounts receivable
- Duplicate transaction identification
- Record gap identification
- Fraud analysis
- Statistical profiling
- Statistical sampling
- Regression analysis

Common CAAT Tests

Here are some common tests of internal controls:
- Compare account balance to credit limit
- Look for negative values to confirm edit checks
- Check access logs for currency
- Compare access profiles to payroll file to identify departed employees still with active access profiles
- Match receiving reports to invoices
- Select pay rate changes and vouch to management approval
- Select loans for vouching to approval and collateral
- Check journal entries and other large transactions for approval
- Check travel expense claims for approval
- Look for credit check confirmation indicator on processed sales
- Check government purchase orders to the list of authorized vendors to ensure that the vendor is approved
- Check write-offs for approval

The quantitative and comparison functions of CAAT tools make them ideal for substantive testing. Further, supporting documents are increasingly electronic and digital which facilitate vouching using a general audit software package. Here are some common substantive tests.
- Age accounts receivable
- Check for inventory obsolescence by looking at date of last sale
- Verify invoice calculation
- Verify medical insurance claims for compliance with policy coverage and regulations
- Verify cost of sales in relation to the costing method like FIFO or LIFO
- Select accounts for customer confirmation
- Compare physical and perpetual inventory file details
- Compare payroll to telephone directory to detect ghost employees
- Verify depreciation calculation
- Check payments for cash discount calculation

Analytical Review

The computational capability of GAS enables a variety of analytical review. Just as increasing computing power makes data mining more practical, financial correlation for audit purpose is easier and easier with automation. Here are some examples.
- Interest revenue over interest expense on a branch by branch basis in a bank.
- Interest revenue over non-interest revenue on a branch by branch basis.
- Non-interest revenue over non-interest expense on a branch by branch basis.
- Budget variance analysis.
- Store sales analysis.
- Inventory turnover.

- Travel expense over payroll expense.
- Sales returns.
- Standard cost variance analysis.
- Benford analysis, analyzing a range of natural numbers to detect the frequency of leading digits. According to Benford Law, the probability of the leading digit(s) being low order digits like 3, 2 or 1 is increasingly higher than the probability of leading digit(s) being high order digits like 7, 8 or 9, in that order. That is, a natural number like population size or an invoice amount most likely starts with 1 regardless of the length of the number. This makes sense, because in the beginning, every number usually starts with 1, then goes to 2, 3, then 10..then 100. 1 always takes precedence over 2. GAS can be used to analyze a range of natural numbers like entertainment expenses in tax returns to see if the frequency of numbers starting with 1 falls within the Benford Law distribution. According to Benford Law, the probability of a number starting with 9 is much less than 10%. Most fraudsters have the mind set of retailers and start faked numbers with a 9 hoping that the number will escape detection because it falls just below a threshold. Retail prices are not natural numbers and don't obey Benford Law.

CHAPTER EIGHT – COMMON ACCESS CONTROLS

The only real security that a man can have in this world is a reserve of knowledge, experience and ability. - Henry Ford

Introduction

In Chapter Two, we discuss the risk factors related to completeness, authorization, accuracy, timeliness, occurrence and efficiency. We also review some examples of what have gone wrong with information systems. One type of mishaps particularly related to authorization is security breach. Here is a common list of security breaches:

- Hacking
- Hardware theft
- Identify theft
- Inappropriate use of IT resources
- Internal breach
- Sniffing
- Software theft
- Spoofing
- Virus
- Worm

To mitigate these threats, an organization must implement preventive and detective access controls tailored to the environment. These controls can take the forms of software, instructions, procedures and physical devices.

Management Checklist

1. Appoint a chief information security officer reporting to the chief information officer.

2. Set up an information security committee as a subordinate committee to the information technology (IT) steering committee. The chief information security officer should be the chair.

3. Develop an information security strategy that supports the IT strategy.

4. Perform annual security risk assessment of the organization to assess inherent risk, control risk and residual risk. This assessment should include security testing such as vulnerability assessments and penetration tests.

5. Ensure that access control assessment is part of the systems development methodology.

6.   Establish an information security policy as a corporate umbrella for access controls.

7.   Develop information security standards for each technology platform such as database management system, eBusiness and cryptography. These standards can be used by individual business units to develop tailored procedures.

8.   Develop corporate information security procedures to ensure consistent handling of security threats and incidents.

9.   Conduct criminal record checks for new hires to sensitive positions and consultants.

10. Establish a security education program to ensure awareness of security policies, standards and procedures. This program should require employees to take annual refresher courses within the organization, e.g., online courses.

11. If the organization hosts eBusiness, it should establish a network security monitoring function to monitor for hacking attempts and network worms.

12. Periodically monitor the Internet traffic generated by employees to prevent inappropriate use including excessive use for personal purpose.

13. Assess the cost effectiveness of each common access control like password, encryption, lock and firewall. The purpose is to determine whether the controls are accepted, complied with, effective and generate the intended risk mitigation. This can be done by surveying users, reviewing system configuration and independent testing.

Chapter Eight Conclusion

Access controls should be implemented at a general level and an application level. Management should assess the inherent risks with respect to authorization, occurrence and timeliness and then design general access controls as much as practical. The remaining risk should be mitigated with application level access controls until the residual risk is tolerable.

Access controls are implemented mainly to address the authorization and occurrence criteria. From the perspective of an IT specialist, the three common access control objectives are confidentiality, integrity and availability. For auditors, these can be tied to authorization and occurrence. Each access control serves one of the following five roles: Identification, Authentication, Authorization, Logging and Monitoring.

Summary of Main Points in Chapter Eight

Access controls should take the forms of policies, standards procedures, system configuration, management review, independent review, exception reporting, system screening, access control rules and systems tools like passwords. Here is a list of common access controls and their functions.

- Access card – identification, authentication and authorization; preventive.

- Access control list – authorization, preventive.

- Access log – logging, detective.

- Anti-virus software – authorization, preventive.

- Biometric – authentication, preventive.

- Boundary checking – authorization, preventive.

- Challenged response – authentication, preventive.

- Compliance scanning – monitoring, detective.

- Cryptography – authentication and authorization; preventive.

- Disabling unnecessary system software features – authorization, preventive.

- Disk wiping – authorization, preventive.

- File blocking – authorization, preventive.

- File integrity monitoring – monitoring, detective.

- Firewall – authorization, preventive.

- Honeypot – authorization, preventive.

- Intrusion detection system – authorization, detective.

- Intrusion prevention system- authorization, preventive.

- Locks – authorization, preventive.

- Management or independent review – monitoring, detective.

- Password – authentication, preventive.

- Patching – authorization, preventive.

- Penetration testing – monitoring, detective.

- Personnel security screening – authorization, preventive.

- Security education – authorization, preventive.

- Single sign-on – identification and authentication, preventive.

- Spam filtering – authorization, preventive.

- Staff termination or transfer checklist – authorization, preventive.

- Standard operating system configuration images – authorization and logging, preventive.

- Two factor authentication – authentication, preventive.

- User profile – authentication and authorization, preventive.

- Virtual private network – authentication and authorization, preventive.

- Vulnerability assessment – monitoring, detective.

- Web filtering – authorization, preventive.

- Web site refresh – authorization, corrective.

CHAPTER NINE – OPERATING SYSTEMS ACCESS CONTROLS

Security is, I would say, our top priority because, for all the exciting things you will be able to do with computers - organizing your lives, staying in touch with people, being creative - if we don't solve these security problems, then people will hold back.

– Bill Gates

Introduction

The access controls discussed in the last chapter apply to all systems and infrastructures. In this chapter, we will go over the access control parameters and architecture at an operating system level and review the security relationship between operating systems and access control software tools. We will cover the following common platforms:

- Windows
- Mac OS X
- Unix
- IBM Z Series (mainframe) servers

For each platform, an organization should have a standard image for each desktop, laptop and server as a baseline. Exceptions should be approved by management. There should be less room for exceptions for desktops and laptops as these devices are not application specific. Common controls in a standard image include disabling certain ports and services and the ability to update the system registry. A common restriction is to take away a user's ability to install software by not giving the user local administration privilege.

Management Checklist

1. Require system administrators to use longer and more complicated passwords than ordinary users. Require them to change passwords more frequently.

2. Secure server rooms with two-factor authentication.

3. Periodically assess the security features and follow a plan to enable and configure them in accordance with risk assessment and the security policy.

4. Develop policies and standard images for security features.

5. Periodically scan operating system and security feature parameters for policy compliance.

6. Establish a policy and procedures for patching.

7. Disable employee access to the administrator account in their workstations.

8. Perform periodic review of the Active Directory configuration for compliance with the security policy.

9. Establish procedures for full disk encryption key recovery.

10. Conduct an annual review of operating system security for each operating system platform and report on overall security policy compliance.

Chapter Nine Conclusion

Personal computer and server security continues to be improved by vendors. Recently made available features include full hard disk encryption (instead of individual files), application firewall (instead of just filtering by IP address and port) and integrated malicious software features including anti-virus. In security, the weakest link is people, including people's commitment to define and comply with strong security policies. Organizations should have a tight operating system image for desktops and servers across the enterprise to comply with their policies. User access rights should be limited to their job functions and ordinary users should not be given administrator privilege to their desktops and laptops. System administrators should be controlled with thorough reference check, criminal record check before hiring and periodically thereafter, rotation of duties among servers, limiting the servers they support, limiting their other duties, and regular management review of the system logs using access control exception analysis software to turn system logs into meaningful management reports.

Summary of Main Points in Chapter Nine

1. Differences between operating systems in terms of access controls mainly have to do with authentication, authorization and logging.

2. Windows salts passwords for offline access. The user name is the salt. A salt is an extra parameter added to the plaintext password to increase the complexity of hashing. A hash is a one-way scrambled form of a password to disguise it from easy viewing by people.

3. Unix salts all passwords with a salt length of 48 to 128 bits, depending on user organization preferences.

4. Unix uses a shadow file to point to the actual password hash, which is stored in a separate file. This reduces the risk of password cracking.

5. An operating system mainly logs the program events, security events and setup events.

6. Ordinary users without local administration privilege can change browser security and privacy settings. This means more monitoring and education are required.

7. Anti-virus software, firewall and full hard drive encryption now come standard with commercial PC operating systems.

8. Ordinary users should not be given local administration privilege so that they cannot install software.

9. Management should install software to decipher system logs to produce meaningful management reports.

10. z/OS has weaker security than Windows and Unix because its predecessors, Multiple Virtual Storage and Virtual Memory, were developed before the Internet and not designed to mitigate the risk of hacking. Resource Access Control Facility should be installed to strengthen security for Z series servers.

CHAPTER TEN – CONTROL AND AUDIT IMPLICATIONS OF OUTSOURCING

If you deprive yourself of outsourcing and your competitors do not, you're putting yourself out of business. – Lee Kuan Yew (founding prime minister of Singapore)

Introduction

Information systems outsourcing has been on the rise in the last twenty years. It has slowed down because there is a finite number of functions in an organization that can be outsourced. The main reason for outsourcing is to cut cost. However, some companies later realize that the short term cost saving has led to long term loss of competitiveness related to disappearing skills within the organizations.

Information technology (IT) is the most common function being outsourced because it is not a core competency in most organizations. Another reason for outsourcing this technical area is that it is harder to build expertise in house, compared to the effort to develop employees in administrative and clerical duties. Other common areas being outsourced are call center operation, payroll and accounting. For example, some banks have outsourced payroll; companies in many industries and some governments outsource systems development, network management and computer operations; many technology companies have outsourced their call centers; some utility companies have outsourced IT, accounting, payroll and accounting.

While outsourcing in most cases brings short and medium term savings, it increases risks. It increases inherent risk because the business process has changed. Even if the changes are all positive, inherent risk can increase because employees have to get used to the new processes. Change, by nature, brings risk, because of uncertainty and the learning curve. Another reason for the increase in inherent risk is that some business processes are now carried out by a vendor and therefore the uncertainty of reliable processing increases.
If inherent risk goes up, so does control risk. This is because control activities are part of business activities. Detection risk also goes up because the auditors have to understand the new processes; secondly, some of the audit trail is now in the service organization and may not be easily accessible to the auditors.

Outsourcing to foreign countries where the cost of labor and professional salaries are lower, is increasing. The CIO Magazine reported the following in July 2012.

Mega-deal outsourcing deals--those contracts with a value of $1 billion or more-picked up in the second quarter of 2012, according to the quarterly Global TPI Index. Five mega-deals were signed during the quarter compared with just one each in the second quarter of 2011 and the first quarter of 2012. All five were awarded outside of the mature U.S. and Western European markets-three of them in India and Brazil. (*Source: http://www.cio.com/article/711727/Mega_IT_Outsourcing_Deals_Move_Offshore?sourc e=CIONLE_nlt_insider_2012-07-24_default*).

If an organization outsources to a foreign company or the subsidiary of a foreign company, the information may be subject to foreign law. The organization has to take into account the implication of foreign legislation in its outsourcing decision.

Management Checklist

1. Perform a risk analysis before deciding to outsource.

2. Perform a cost benefit analysis before deciding to outsource.

3. Obtain approval from the board of directors before outsourcing.

4. Review the outsourcing contract with the legal counsel before committing.

5. Ensure that the outsourcing contract includes at least one of the following:
   - right of audit
   - independent control assurance report
   - written control assurance checklist from the service organization at least semi-annually.

6. Review the service organization's financial stability before committing.

7. Obtain reference checks about the service organization before committing.

8. Follow the organization's signing authority levels before awarding the contract.

9. Designate an executive to own each outsourcing contract and monitor vendor compliance.

10. Perform annual review of each contract for compliance and satisfaction.

Chapter Ten Conclusion

Outsourcing is on the rise and there is no indication that the trend will reverse, although it is slowing down. Management has to balance the risk increase with potential savings. Internal auditors should lend their internal control and risk assessment expertise to help management in outsourcing decisions and in contract management. External auditors need to ensure that management is aware of the effect of outsourcing on audit evidence and audit trail availability.

Summary of Main Points in Chapter Ten

1. A service organization is an organization that provides IT services for a fee.
   A user organization is an organization that procures IT services.
   A service auditor is an accounting firm hired by a service organization to provide an independent control assurance opinion on the services offered.
   A user auditor is the shareholders' auditor of a user organization.

2. When an external audit client has outsourced a financially material function, the external auditors are faced with a control assurance gap. It is only a control assurance gap because a user organization always has access to financial records regardless of the extent of outsourcing. Thus, a substantive audit is always possible.

3. To bridge the control assurance gap, the external auditors should successively consider the following options:
   - Look for compensating in-house controls.
   - Seek to rely on an independent control assurance report.
   - Seek to test controls in the service organization.
   - Resort to a substantive audit.

4. To consider the above options, external auditors in the United States are guided by Statement of Auditing Standards 70.

5. If a service organization offers an independent control assurance report, that report and the audit work to support it must be prepared in accordance with Statement of Standards for Assurance Engagements (SSAE) 16.

6. SSAE16 requires the opinion to address the correctness of system description, the adequacy of internal controls to support each stated control criterion, and the comprehensiveness of internal control objectives.

7. A Type 1 independent control assurance report provides point in time assurance. A Type 2 report covers a period of at least six months.

8 To address a control deficiency in an independent control assurance audit, a service organization has the following options:
   - Correct the control deficiency if the corrected control can be tested by the auditors to cover the majority of the reporting period.
   - Replace the control with another control if the replacement control can be tested by auditors to cover the majority of the reporting period.
   - Stop the audit and deal with the repercussion with the user organizations.
   - Accept a qualified report.

42

9. The independent control assurance report must disclose material changes in internal controls from the previous year and material subsequent events.

10. Internal audit should play a proactive role in helping management assess the risk of outsourcing, preparing clauses in the contract to address risks and control compliance, and regularly assessing the service organization's contract compliance

CHAPTER ELEVEN – SYSTRUST AUDIT AND PAYMENT CARD INDUSTRY SECURITY ASSURANCE

The most important thing for a young man is to establish credit - a reputation and character. - John D. Rockefeller

Introduction

Organizations continue to increase their reliance on information systems. Aside from traditional outsourcing, there are arrangements for organizations to share information systems and trading partners to share information. As a result, there is increasing demand on organizations operating information systems to provide assurance to external stakeholders. In this chapter, we discuss two common types of such assurance reports, other than those in an outsourcing agreement, which was discussed in the last chapter. The two types of non-outsourcing IT control assurance engagements we discuss in this chapter are:

- SysTrust, and
- Payment Card Industry security assurance

Management Checklist

This checklist is intended for the management of an organization that hosts a system to be used by other organizations and also an organization that processes a large volume of credit card transactions.

1. Document the functions and internal controls of systems used by other organizations.

2. Develop a process to monitor system effectiveness regularly in order to assure user organizations.

3. If a SysTrust audit is pursued, assign ownership to an executive.

4. If a SysTrust audit is pursued, consider adopting the optional principles of privacy and confidentiality.

5. If a SysTrust audit is pursued, assess the applicability of control criteria and document control procedures for each criterion.

6. Assess the organization's need to comply with the Payment Card Industry (PCI) Security Standard. This standard applies to all organizations that process credit card transactions electronically. A high volume of credit card transactions will subject the organization to the requirement for external validation of compliance.

7. If the PCI Security Standard is applicable, set up a project to achieve compliance.

8. If the PCI Security Standard is applicable, assign an executive to be accountable for compliance.

9. Perform an internal PCI compliance check regularly.

10. Select the PCI compliance external auditor in accordance with guidelines from the PCI Security Council.

Chapter Eleven Conclusion

Technology trends like cloud computing, edge computing and software as a service increase the need for system operators to provide assurance to users about information reliability. The two commonly comprehensive system assurance frameworks are CSAE 3416 (or the U. S. equivalent, SSAE 16) and SysTrust. The former caters to shareholders' auditors of user organizations, while SysTrust is intended to provide direct assurance to user organization management. SysTrust is highly structured and focuses primarily on policies and monitoring.

PCI Security Standard is also gaining prominence as more merchants, financial institutions and eBusiness service providers realize that they need to be more rigorous in preventing credit card fraud. In the process of complying with the PCI standard, many organizations have come to realize that their networks and security infrastructures have significant holes. The success of the PCI framework can be measured by comparing credit fraud statistics over time as more organizations comply with this standard.

Summary of Main Points in Chapter Eleven

1. A SysTrust audit is intended to provide assurance to user organizations of a system hosted by an external organizations, that the system is reliable from the perspective of security, processing integrity, availability, confidentiality and privacy protection.

2. SysTrust is similar to SSAE 16 in that all three are intended to provide assurance on a system hosted by an organization that is used by other organizations.

3. SysTrust differs from SSAE 16 in that its main audience is management of the user organizations, not shareholders' auditors of the user organizations.

4. SysTrust also differs from SSAE 16 in that it is based on a rigid set of internal control criteria for each of the principles of security, processing integrity, availability, confidentiality and privacy protection, although there is some overlap in control criteria among these principles. CSAE 3416 and SSAE 16 provide the standards for an internal control assurance report to address control objectives set by management in relation to the system description. There is more flexibility in SSAE 16, which focuses on financial statement related controls.

5. The confidentiality and privacy protection principles are optional.

6. A firm must be licensed by Canadian Institute of Chartered Accountants (CICA) or AICPA specifically for SysTrust in order to perform a SysTrust audit.

7. A SysTrust audit can provide point-in-time assurance or assurance over a period.

8. PCI Security Standard applies to all merchants, IT service organizations and financial institutions that accept credit card transactions electronically. Large merchants are required to provide annual independent validation of compliance.

9. The complexity of an organization's networks will affect the extent of details to which the PCI security standard is applied.

10. The PCI Security Standard applies only to the Cardholder Data Environment, a network environment where a substantial quantity of cardholder data is stored or processed.

CHAPTER TWELVE – COMPUTER CRIME

Technological progress is like an axe in the hands of a pathological criminal. –

Albert Einstein

Introduction

Computer crime has increased in volume, impact and variety in the last decade mainly because of the Internet. There are broadly speaking, two types of computer crime: crime causing fairly immediate damage like hacking, and crime that is fraudulent in nature like am email scam. In either case, the crime may be committed on IT resources or it may use IT as a tool to achieve the criminal intent.

Here is a list of recently publicized computer crimes.

- In June 2011, Spanish police reported that it had arrested three members of a local Anonymous group in three separate cities, claiming they were responsible for the hacking attacks against the PlayStation Store. Anonymous is a group initiating active civil disobedience and spread through the Internet while staying hidden. The police alleged that these three individuals were leaders of a the group. In addition to being charged with the PlayStation store hacks, these three are also being accused of leading hacks against government websites of a number of countries, two Spanish banks, an Italian energy company, and the website of the Spanish Electoral Board. The police described the suspects as Spanish men in their early 30s.

- One of the biggest frauds in financial services history was carried out by a 31-year-old trader in Société Générale's Paris headquarters, Jerome Kerviel. The trader took massive fraudulent directional positions – bets on future movements of European stock indices, without his supervisor's knowledge, the Bank said. Because he used to work in the trading unit's back office, he had in-depth knowledge of the control procedures and evaded them by creating fictitious transactions to conceal his activity. The fraud was discovered on January 20, 2008. Société Générale (SocGen), one of the largest banks in Europe, started to unwind the positions the next day just as global equity markets were tanking on fears of a U.S. recession. "It was the worst possible time," says Janine Dow, senior director for financial institutions at the Fitch ratings agency in Paris. SocGen, which also announced a nearly $3 billion 2007 loss related to U.S. mortgage-market woes, had to seek a $5.5 billion capital increase.

- On August 18, 2011, Toronto police arrested and charged a man on 38 charges for Automated teller machine (ATM) skimming. The man identified was arrested after evidence was seized from a house. The suspect was identified on a surveillance tape. According to police, the suspect had installed at least 38 skimming devices on ATMs in financial institutions across the Greater Toronto Area. These skimming devices, installed in the card slots of ATMs, can be used to obtain personal information from ATM cards. The ATM skimming business nets over a billion dollars annually.

Customers should use only ATMs with surveillance cameras. Customers should also notice whether it is difficult to insert the card or whether something sticks out from the ATM card slot.

Here are the common types of computer crime that are not quite fraudulent in nature and that cause immediate damage.

- Altering a public computer system like a bank system without approval – Main control is a firewall.

- Deliberately spreading viruses and worms – Main controls include anti-virus software and patching.

- Email interception – Main control is encryption.

- Hacking – Main control is a firewall.

- Sabotage of computer equipment – Main control is physical security.

- Spreading, uploading or storing child pornography – Main control is web filtering.

- Theft of computer equipment – Main control is physical security.

- Theft of information – Main control is encryption.

- Theft of software – Main controls include access control list, digital rights control and management monitoring.

The following is a list of common computer frauds.

- ATM skimming – Main controls include user education and surveillance cameras.

- Changing computer system information to hide defalcation – Main controls include firewalls and access control lists.

- Computer scam – Main control is user education.

- Email interception – Main control is encryption.

- Gaining unauthorized access to systems to transfer funds – Main control is an access control list.

- Identity theft – Main controls include user education and access control lists.

- Producing fictitious transactions – Main controls include segregation of duties and management review.

These lists are just common examples of information technology (IT) crime. A lot of other crimes can be committed with the aid of computers, e.g., lapping, by adjusting accounts receivable data. This chapter is not intended to discuss all business crime and accounting fraud. It focuses on IT crime and fraud. However, for non-IT crime, many system controls can be used to prevent or detect them. These controls have been discussed in Chapters 3, 6 and 8.

Computer crime is committed because of temptation and opportunity. An opportunity to a criminal is created when internal controls are weak. Temptation is present when vulnerable assets are present.

Internal Controls Against Computer Crime

Here are the common internal controls against computer crime.

- Access control list
- Access log
- Chief ethics officer
- Code of business conduct
- Digital certificate
- Digital signature
- Encryption
- Exception reporting
- File blocking
- File integrity monitoring
- Firewall
- Intrusion detection system
- Intrusion prevention system
- Locks
- Management and independent review
- Password policy
- Password system configuration to comply with the password policy
- Security check for sensitive positions including criminal record check

- Security education

- Segregation of duties

- Web filtering

- Web site refresh

- Whistle blowing policy

Management Checklist

1. Appoint a chief ethics officer.

2. Establish a code of business conduct including a whistle blowing policy.

3. Establish a policy on acceptable use of IT resources.

4. Obtain employee acknowledgement of understanding of the code of business conduct and the policy on acceptable use of IT resources regularly.

5. Establish a policy on reference check for new hires.

6. Establish a policy for conducting security check including criminal record check for positions that handle sensitive information or vulnerable assets.

7. Large organizations should establish a forensic investigation function.

8. Ensure the audit committee is made aware of all computer crime committed against the organization.

9. Ensure that the applicable labor unions are consulted with respect to the development and changes of the code of business conduct.

10. Establish a protocol for informing the police of criminal activities in or against the organization, involving the security and law departments.

Chapter Twelve Conclusion

As people become more computer literate and organizations increasingly rely on computers, cybercrimes and computer related frauds are taking up a larger and larger portion of overall crimes. It doesn't take long for criminals to realize that a few clicks can land them much more money than holding up a bank. Identity theft is growing, which can serve as the portal to other crimes like stealing real estate titles, obtaining business secret, money laundering and transferring money from others' bank accounts.

Shareholders' auditors have to assess the risk of fraud in planning and carrying out every audit. Internal auditors should devote a significant portion of their resources to detecting fraud and responding to management requests to investigate. Internal audit departments of large organizations should be equipped with forensic accounting and auditing tools and selective auditors should receive specialized training. All auditors should have computer forensic awareness as part of their annual training programs. Forensic investigators should use a disciplined investigation program and rigorous tools so that their findings can stand up in court.

Summary of Main Points in Chapter Twelve

1. Opportunity has to be present for computer crime to occur. Opportunity is created by internal control deficiency.

2. Two types of computer crime: crime that is not mainly deceitful like hacking, and computer fraud. Shareholders' auditors are more concerned about computer fraud as it carries more uncertainty.

3. IT resources may be the target of computer crime, or they may be used to commit crime.

4. Preventing computer crime starts with appointing a chief ethics officer as well as educating employees and customers on what behavior and activities are unacceptable.

5. The chief executive officer is ultimately accountable for ethics. The chief ethics officer is a facilitator.

6. Identity theft is a common computer crime that can lead to other crimes.

7. Internal auditors should address the risk of computer crime in every audit.

8. Shareholders' auditors should assess the risk of computer fraud in audit planning and perform analytical review to identify significant computer fraud.

9. Every large organization should establish a computer forensic investigation function to performs forensic investigation based on management requests, suspicions from control deficiencies and proactive scanning of employee IT network activities for anomalies and policy violations.

10. IT forensic assignments should involve obviously technical IT specialists, but also investigators with business and financial experience, the law department and the police (for computer crime).

SECTION 2 – FULL CHAPTERS

CHAPTER ONE – WHO, WHAT, WHEN, WHERE, WHY?

Information technology and business are becoming inextricably interwoven. I don't think anybody can talk meaningfully about one without the talking about the other. – Bill Gates

There are risks in using information technology (IT). It might be incorrectly applied because of inadequate training or unrealistic expectation on what can be achieved. Computer systems reduce paper and visible audit trail so errors have a higher chance of remaining undetected. There is higher concentration of processing when computers are used and this increases the impact of incorrect functions. Access to computer systems is less noticeable than access to paper files so the risk of unauthorized transactions can increase.

Users of information systems need assurance in order to have faith in what they rely on to perform business transactions and make decisions. They want to have faith in the information to be provided by the organizations they work in or deal with. They have a right to demand that such faith be supported by a rigorous process of system assurance.

Some have said that computing power doubles every year, i.e., the IT capability costing a dollar today will probably cost fifty cents in a year. We have seen many examples of this in personal computers, storage devices and consumer electronics. That does not mean consumers and organizations will spend less on IT. What this means is that we can continuously upgrade the use of IT to improve efficiency and our quality of life. To respond to demand, and to generate demand, technology product developers will continue to come up with new gadgets, tools and applications.

The speed of change in IT and the seemingly exponential adoption rate by users and organizations sometimes generate a question in one's mind about reliability, just as the speed of driving or the high turnover of staff would cast doubt about safety and quality. How is reliability measured? Who will measure it? Who will assure it?

I & IT STAKEHOLDERS

The parties with interest in information systems reliability include users, systems developers, management and regulators. Users in turn include customers, employees and trading partners. In the public sector, citizens are customers. These stakeholders have varying degrees of reliance on systems and influence over systems reliability.

WHAT DOES SYSTEM RELIABILITY MEAN?

Reliability in an information system must encompass the following five attributes: completeness, authorization, accuracy, timeliness and occurrence. Occurrence includes existence, e.g., recorded transactions actually occurred, or recorded assets actually exist. One can use the acronym CAATO to memorize these attributes. These attributes should be related to the entire transaction cycle, which includes input, processing, output and storage. This cycle applies to systems that handle and record transactions as well as systems that are used mainly for producing information. In the latter case, a transaction would be a request for information or a system generated report.

Combining the CAATO attributes with the transaction cycle, one would expect a reliable system to have the following performance:

- It processes transactions completely.
- It provides complete and relevant information to users to meet their requirements.
- It has adequate resources and controls to prevent loss of stored information.
- It accepts only authorized transactions.
- It releases information only to authorized parties.
- It changes information only based on authorized requests.
- It processes transactions accurately.
- It performs regular checks and reconciliations to ensure accuracy of stored information.
- It provides accurate information to users.
- It processes transactions promptly.
- It provides current information to users as needed.
- It processes only real transactions (transactions that have actually occurred).
- Its information reflects only real transactions, real assets and real liabilities, i.e., revenue, expenses, assets and liabilities that actually exist.

In addition to satisfying the CAATO attributes, a system should be efficient and cost effective. Efficiency means a high level of performance in relation to the cost required to support the performance. Cost effectiveness means that the benefit of the system must outweigh the cost. Efficiency and cost effectiveness are closely related. If a system is not cost effective, it is not efficient. However, a cost effective system may not be optimal, i.e., there is often room for efficiency improvement. Cost and benefit should be quantified as much as practical. The greater the net benefit the more cost effective the system is. Shareholders' auditors are mainly concerned about CAATO. Management and internal auditors are also concerned about efficiency. For them, CAATO can be expanded to include efficiency (which includes cost effectiveness), to be CAATOE.

How about confidentiality? A system is not reliable if it does not protect confidential information. Well, that is really part of authorization.

How about availability? A system is reliable only if it is available when needed. That is accounted for under timeliness.

A growing concern is security. Security is a type of system assurance and is actually part of authorization. A secured system means that access is always authorized.

HOW IS RELIABILITY ACHIEVED?

A system does not satisfy the above criteria by chance. It needs checks to make sure transactions are processed and information is produced to meet the completeness, authorization, accuracy, occurrence, timeliness and efficiency attributes. These checks are called internal controls. Why do we call them internal controls, rather than just controls? Controls may be external, e.g., monitoring by creditors or regulators. Although external controls serve to mitigate risks, the organization operating the system has little influence over external controls. Therefore, organizations should rely mainly on controls that they can influence, i.e., internal controls implemented by the organizations themselves.

Internal controls may be manual or automated. Implementing internal controls assures stakeholders that systems are reliable, i.e., they have the characteristics of completeness, authorization, accuracy, timeliness, occurrence and efficiency. On an ongoing basis, stakeholders will want assurance that the system continues to be reliable, i.e., internal controls continue to work properly. Such assurance can be delivered by testing controls. Internal controls over a system should address the transaction cycle of input, processing, output and storage.

Internal controls should be applied to the following five system components: infrastructure, software, people, procedures and information.

Infrastructure includes real estate, the network and hardware. They have to have enough capacity, continuously available and be protected from sabotage, abuse, malfunction and unauthorized access. These components need to be configured in such a way that working together, they provide the platform for reliable information processing.

Software includes system software and application software. System software refers to software needed to interface directly with the hardware, e.g., the operating system (Windows is a common product). It also includes database management systems which support multiple transaction processing applications. Application software means systems that process transactions directly or produce end user information. Application software is run on system software which in turn interfaces with hardware directly. Software has to be rigorously developed, tested and documented. It also has to be monitored for unusual behavior and protected from unauthorized changes.

People include management, systems developers, computer operation staff like system administrators as well as business system and information users like employees and customers. A system administrator is someone who controls the software implementation in a computer, usually a server. This person has full control over the computers that s/he services. System administrators have powerful information access and pose a significant risk to organizations. They need to be rigorously controlled. We will discuss this further in Chapter Three. People have to be informed about how to use a system. They have to be screened before system access is granted.

Procedures include policies, standards and procedures for employees and customers. They have to be concise, current and well communicated. Change control should be applied.

Information is the most critical component of a system as without information, a system does not serve its purpose. It is information requirement that determines the extent and type of infrastructure, software, procedures and people. Each system should be tagged to be owned by an executive and it is up to that owner to assess the criticality of information that in turn will affect the amount of money to be invested in the system. Organizations should have guidelines for executives to do such assessment. We will discuss this in more detail in the next chapter. We will discuss information, hardware and software further in the upcoming paragraphs.

Information

Even though this is often the result of computer processing, i.e., the end, it is the most important component of a system. It was an argument I often had with systems developers when I was a young auditor. Hardware and software are no doubt more complicated than information and usually more expensive. However, the type and extent of hardware and software needed depends on what information the system is intended to process and in turn produce. Senior management should assign each system to be "owned" by an executive and charge that owner with assessing the criticality of information as a basis for deciding on the hardware and software as well as the internal controls to be afforded that system.

Traditional Information Structure

Information is organized in a system to describe entities and the attributes within each entity. For example, a payroll master file contains semi-permanent information of each employee such as employee number, name, position, salary, tax deduction code, name of supervisor, work location, inception date, date of birth, year-to-date gross pay, year-to-date deduction for each type of deduction and year-to-date net pay. This file describes the entity called employee. Each record contains the information of each occurrence of the entity, e.g., each employee. The inception date is an attribute about each occurrence of the entity. The term master file refers to a file of semi-permanent information. Each pay period, a transaction file is produced to record, for each employee, the gross pay, deductions and net pay. For each master file, there are usually multiple transaction files, which are used to update the master file. Another example of a transaction file is a file of salary changes during the period.

The above describes a conventional information structure in a system. The data files in each system pertain to only that system and are accessible to only that system. Each file should have a field that is used as the primary key. A primary key is a field that uniquely identifies a record, e.g., student number in the student master file qualifies as a primary key. For human reading, the primary key is positioned as the leftmost field in a table. A table is a data file presented in a human readable format.

Database

A database is a collection of related data files. Databases are increasingly used in organizations to facilitate data sharing for real time transactions and data mining. However, as is common when efficiency is to be gained, risk can go up. The sharing of data files (tables) increases the potential access points and the complexity of software. Thus, organizations need to implement controls to mitigate the additional risks. Modern databases typically use the relational or object oriented relational model. Relational is the most popular model for systems that process primarily numerical and text data. This allows any two tables with a common field name to interrelate and provides a lot of flexibility.

A table is visually identical to an Excel spreadsheet, regardless of the database management system. Common relational database management systems are Microsoft's Structured Query Language (SQL) Server and Oracle. Microsoft also has a mini version of relational database management system called Microsoft Access.

The commercial relational database systems mentioned above also support objects. An object may be a picture, a sound clip or a video clip. It may also be is a piece of reusable object code that often contains standard data like font and color. It can also contain holders for users to input data, thus combining code and data in one object with the data portion being dynamic. When data is changed, a new object can be created. Object code means computer program(s) that have been compiled to machine language understandable to the operating system. Object code is compiled from source code using a compiler (software tool) specific to the source programming language like C++ and an operating system like Windows.

In a relational database, two tables can be related if they have a common alphanumeric field, i.e., a field that can be used as a primary key. This field will be the primary key in one of the tables and will be a field in another table without being a primary key. For example, an inventory table uses the product number as the primary key and among other fields, it has a supplier number. The supplier number is the primary key in the supplier table. These two tables are said to be related which means a transaction can be used to update both tables and also queries can be made on both tables simultaneously. The supplier number field in the inventory table is called a foreign key because it is used as a primary key in another table. The foreign key of a table should not be blank, e.g., a product must have a supplier. Most business applications use the relational database model.

A new model, called non-relational database, NoSQL, is increasingly being adopted for mobile applications involving audio and video streaming. It is less structured and reliable than the relational model but also more dynamic. It is the latter characteristic that makes it attractive for mobile applications. NoSQL is not used for business transaction processing.

Common Reasons for Adopting a Database

1. *Broadening customer service*
   By sharing data between applications, transactions that span different business areas can be processed readily. For example, some bank customers have an automated overdraft protection arrangement with their banks. Under this service, if a customer accidentally overdraws a checking account, the checking account system will check the customer's savings account to see if there is enough money to cover the overdraft plus a

small service charge. If so, without human intervention, the checking account system will move the money into the checking account. This avoids an NSF check. Without a database, the checking account files are "owned" by the checking account system and the savings account files are "owned" by the savings account system. It would be impossible for the checking account system to move money from the savings account system. This sharing of tables (files) between systems is called data program independence.

2. Data sharing to expedite transactions and mitigate risk
Information is power. Organizations can empower systems and people by sharing information. For example, payroll information can be shared with the production system to expedite the accumulation of work-in-progress costs. Similarly, transaction history and holdings about deposits can be accessed by the loan system to decide whether to approve a customer application to increase a line of credit.

3. *Data mining*
Some have said that computing power doubles every year. This is not an overstatement. A one-gigabyte portable hard disk the size of a shoe box cost $400 in 1998. With increasing computing power, organizations are performing more data analysis to know more about their customers, products and the markets. Without databases, analysis would be limited because correlation would require much more manual effort. Data mining is the principle technique in customer relationship management systems that uses mathematical analysis of a mass of data from different systems that share a database.

4. *Reducing data redundancy*
Without a database, a customer's address may be stored in three files if the customer has a checking account, a savings account and a personal line of credit. A database can create a separate file containing non-financial information such as the address which can be accessed by different systems when the address is needed, for, say, statement preparation. This reduces the time to update information, saves storage and avoids data inconsistency, e.g., the address in the savings account system is different from the address in the checking account system, not by customer choice. While one may argue that the above savings will be offset by the increased computer time to search data from different files and in configuring the database management system, such increase in computer time, from experience, is more than offset by the savings in people time and the reduction in risks of data inconsistency.

5. *Increasing Computer Program Flexibility*
Without a database, the data files of a system are "owned" by the system. For example, the checking account data files reside within the checking account system and only checking account programs can use these data files. This way, the computer programs have to keep track of the data file layout, i.e., what fields are in each file as well as the format and order of the fields. A database will alleviate programmers of this tedious work by providing a data dictionary that keeps track of the file layout. A program only has to refer to the file (table) name and field names, instead of specifying the location

and format of the fields when accessing the files. This increases programming efficiency and flexibility, as programs in one system can access the files in another system.

Because a database is just a collection of data files that can he shared by different business systems, software is needed to control the sharing and contention. Such software is called a database management system (DBMS).

Data Organization Structure and Access Methods

A database consists of tables. A table describes an entity. Examples of entities are students and customers. Each table has multiple records which represent occurrences of the entity. For example, in the customer master table, each record represents a unique customer. Each entity has attributes and the attributes are recorded in fields, or columns as we see them. An attribute can vary in value between occurrences. For example, Walmart, being a customer of Coca Cola, will occupy a record in Coca Cola's customer master table. The attributes in that table may include customer name, customer number, credit limit, year-to-date sales etc.

The records in a table may be stored sequentially based on the primary key. This is a controlled way to keep track of records. As records are added or deleted, it may not be necessary to sort the table. However, periodically, each table should be sorted to account for gaps and duplicates.

When a record is updated or needed for reporting, the DBMS or transaction processing system (if a database is not used) will find the record. The traditional method of finding a record is to start with the first record and compare the primary key value of each record to the primary key value of the record that has to be updated, e.g., comparing the customer account number of every record to the customer account number specified by the customer or a customer service representative. This is time consuming and inefficient especially for an online real time system. Data architects many years ago came up with the index sequential method to overcome this inefficiency. It uses an index similar to that in a telephone directory. One column of the index contains the primary key value. The second column contains the physical location of the record, e.g., disk 1, cylinder 5, track 3. This way, instead of searching record by record, the database management or transaction processing system searches only the index and it is faster. Index sequential is mainly used in old legacy systems. I say "old legacy" because the "less old" legacy systems have long been converted to use the direct access method. A common index sequential access software tool is IBM's Virtual Sequential Access Method.

An even faster method is called direct access method. The DBMS uses an algorithm to calculate the physical location of the record based on the primary key. How does this work, because records may be moved from time to time? Well, all record movement is controlled by the DBMS when a database is used. The DBMS uses an algorithm to calculate the location where a record will be placed before placing the record. Thus, using the same algorithm to calculate the location of the record to be updated is almost foolproof. The algorithm uses the primary key of a record and other information about the storage media like number of cylinders and tracks to calculate the physical location. The algorithm has to be sophisticated enough to prevent collision, i.e., two records having the same physical location.

If there is collision, the DBMS can use the algorithm, the primary key value of the existing record and the physical address of the existing record to calculate a new address and move the physical record there. The new address will be designated as a separate region of the database called a chaining region. The address of the new record to be placed will be calculated using the same approach and placed in the chaining region. The original address will be used to store a pointer to the chaining region.

In some business systems, most records are updated periodically at fixed intervals, e.g., payroll. In this case, using the sequential method to update records is acceptable because most of the records have to be accessed in one pass anyway.

Management and auditors should perform checks to account for gaps and duplicates. In addition, checks and tests should be performed to validate the index and the direct access algorithm periodically.

Hardware

Today's information processing hardware can be conveniently classified as servers, personal computers, smart phones, routers, switches and printers. It is important for management to understand the capability of different hardware and its vulnerability in order to make cost effective procurement decisions. It is also important for auditors to be knowledgeable about hardware in order to assess risks and controls. We will describe the different types of hardware from a business perspective.

Servers

Servers come in different sizes; however, the two main types are Z series servers that support legacy systems and local area network (LAN) oriented servers. The former is run on the z/OS operating system. These servers used to be called mainframe computers because of their large size in memory and disk storage. As LAN oriented servers grow in size, the fast computing that was once the monopoly of mainframes is now affordable using LAN oriented servers. Although there is still some difference in speed and power between these two types of computers; the difference is becoming narrower and narrower.

The data architecture is different between PC based servers and Z series servers, as is the data format at the operating system level. For data representation, PC based servers use American Standard Code for Information Exchange (ASCII), which is more user friendly for PC users. Z series servers use Extended Binary Coded Decimal Interchange Code (EBCDIC), which contains a larger character set and therefore can accommodate a keyboard with more special keys. The operating system used in Z series servers is z/OS. Z/OS is viewed by some as a safer operating system than Windows mainly because it is a less popular target for hackers.

Servers should be in locked rooms. There should be a restricted list of computing devices connected to a server. People with direct access to a server, e.g., logging on a server directly to run operating system commands, should be highly limited with explicit management authorization. Servers are often reassigned between business areas and business systems so it is critical for management to keep current inventory by serial number and model as to their location, network connection and supported business systems.

Many organizations are optimizing the use of servers by deploying virtualization technology. This involves using software to dynamically allocate idle server hardware capacity to other busier servers to make the infrastructure more flexible to surging transaction volume. Virtualization also reduces hardware cost and the cost of hiring people to operate servers. It, however, increases the risk of business interruption as there is now more reliance on fewer servers.

Personal Computers

These are often called workstations, desktops, laptops, notebooks, notepads or tablets. They vary in size, speed, memory space and storage capacity. It is critical for management to have an approval process for assigning PCs so that employees are given only what they need. It is not uncommon to find that some employees possess multiple computers that are not all needed. It is also critical to have procedures to ensure that inventory of location, user and network connection of each PC is maintained and regularly updated. A common control is to require managers to sign off the list of computers assigned to their staff members at least annually and subject these lists to independent audits.

Software

There are two broad types of software: system software and application software. System software refers to software needed to interface directly with the hardware, e.g., the operating system. It also includes database management systems which support multiple transaction processing applications. Application software means systems that process transactions directly or produce end user information. Application software is run on system software which in turn interfaces with hardware directly. Software has to be rigorously developed, tested and documented. It also has to be monitored for unusual behavior and protected from unauthorized changes.

Operating System

A computer cannot function without an operating system. This system software interfaces between transaction processing programs and hardware. It manages the allocation of hardware memory, disk space and the central processing unit (CPU). In PCs, the CPU is in a chip. The CPU is the hardware brain of a computer that can perform addition, subtraction, multiplication, division and comparison without the aid of software. The operating system can be configured to log activities and allow only certain activities. It also controls access to transaction processing programs (applications) and data files. The operating system also interfaces between other system software like a DBMS and the CPU. It is important for every organization to have a policy and supporting procedures with respect to the operating systems that should be used in relation to business units and hardware types, version control and how each operating system will be configured for each computer. For example, once an organization has decided to adopt Windows 7 for its PCs, it should also adopt a standard blue print for configuration so that the logging features, allowable types of programs and file controls are consistent from computer to computer within Windows 7. We will discuss this further in Chapter Eight and Chapter Nine.

Applications

An application is a business system, as opposed to system software. There are four types of applications: batch, online real time, online input but batch update, eBusiness (via the Web or an intranet). They differ in terms of responsiveness, cost and risk. Most organizations use all four types of applications.

A batch system records transactions in batches instead of at the time they occur. Almost all organizations use this type of applications. For example, banks are known to have efficient online systems, yet they still use batch applications. Payroll in a bank is a batch system. Check clearing is also a batch system, i.e., if I write a check, the money doesn't come out of my account when the payee deposits the check. My account is debited only on the night the check is deposited. A batch system does not provide instantaneous response to the parties to the transaction mainly because such response is not required. A batch system runs a higher risk of incomplete processing because transactions are batched and input usually only once a day and in that process a transaction may be lost. A batch system, however, is more secure because only a small number of people have access to input transactions, i.e., the parties to the transactions do not perform the data entry. A batch system also has better audit trail because there are usually more source documents. It also allows more time for users to detect errors before the errors are input to the system.

Some systems take data input in real time but the transaction is processed only at the end of the day along with other transactions of the same type that have been input throughout the day. This is because timing within a day is not of the essence. For example, a customer service representative may take my new address on the phone and key it in. The system may just store the data entered and then update my address in the master file at night. This is because my bank does not need to use my address during the day. A system that takes data entry online but updates the master file in a batch gives more assurance about completeness than a batch system as a transaction is accepted by the system as soon as it occurs. It has a greater security risk because there are usually more people who have online access. There are more people with access because the objective of online data entry is to expedite data entry instead of routing the transactions to only a few people to enter in batches.

More and more systems are now online and real time, e.g., banking and point of sales. An online, real time system carries higher assurance of completeness than batch processing because transactions are entered as they occur, however, the security risk is higher because there are a lot of access points. Also, there is less chance to detect errors as there is less paper audit trail. An online system typically uses a database in order to provide comprehensive and real time response to users. Most online users like customer service representatives should not have to sign on to multiple systems to obtain the data when talking to a customer on the phone; this is a common reason most online systems use databases.

Batch and online are the two common ways of processing transactions in terms of immediacy. Another pair of alternatives is centralized vs distributed. Centralized processing means all transactions are processed in a central location, e.g., checks presented in a bank are sent to the data center only once a day for collection from the drawee banks.

Transactions can also be processed in a distributed manner, like ATM, where some functions are handled locally at the ATM, e.g., identification of the bank code for service charge determination; whereas other functions are carried out centrally like checking whether the card has been reported lost. Typically, online real time systems process transactions in a distributed manner. Distributed processing has higher risks of unauthorized access and incorrect processing because more computers are involved in processing and thus software changes have to be implemented in more computers. Also, the system is more complicated as it has to keep track of what is processed centrally and what is processed locally.

An eBusiness system is an online real time system that runs on the Internet or an intranet. The security risk is even higher because there are almost infinite people with access. We will discuss eBusiness in Chapter Five.

Enterprise Resource Planning Systems

This is an integrated accounting system that links the common accounting functions to provide online update to multiple accounting journals and ledgers in recording each transaction. It minimizes data entry and printing by providing real time information to customer service representatives, accounting staff members, managers and system users. This expedites customer service, transaction processing, decision making and management reporting. The needed information comes from the system directly instead of being conveyed in email, phone calls and meetings, thereby also reducing the risk of misunderstanding. Two common commercial products of enterprise resource planning systems (ERP) are SAP and Oracle (not the same as the Oracle DBMS).

Going from more or less "stand alone" accounting systems to an ERP produces efficiency gain for the organization and standardizes the processes for data input, interpretation and output; standardization will help to prevent inconsistency and errors. This is a main reason organizations adopt ERP. However, standardization also calls for change and an organization adopting an ERP has to realize that. The upfront cost is high and payback may not come for several years. Also, business units will give up some control in terms of the way they are used to in inputting certain data, using data and having sole possession of certain data. Such a development project carries a higher risk than developing a stand-alone system. An ERP allows organizations to put in better internal controls because one control can be applied to several business areas. Because of the wide scope of an ERP, an organization planning to implement it should seize the opportunity to review the business processes throughout the enterprise and establish a value chain of functions of activities while at the same time weed out or streamline the functions and activities that do not deliver value. An ERP should be used to automate and integrate efficient processes instead of magnifying inefficiency.

An ERP integrates many accounting systems to provide online update to multiple accounting journals and ledgers in recording each transaction. It minimizes data entry and printing by providing real time information to customer service representatives, accounting staff members, managers and system users. This expedites customer service, transaction processing, decision making and management reporting.

RESPONSIBILITY FOR SYSTEM ASSURANCE

Because internal controls carry a cost, they should be developed and implemented based on risk assessment. Risk assessment, in turn involves understanding the business and assessing the business impact of unreliable systems. Many would agree that the chief information officer is not the best position in an organization to assess the business impact of system failure for every system; in other words, the CIO is not expected to know each business product or service intimately, especially in a large organization.

The person who should be responsible for risk assessment of a system should be the executive responsible for the business affected. For example, if an ATM system goes down, the bank will lose revenue and customer goodwill. The board of directors will not be happy but because they are not employees they cannot carry out line responsibilities, their function is to provide oversight and make strategic decisions; so they cannot be charged with preventing and fixing such a system problem. The chief executive officer and chief operating officer would not be happy but they cannot attend to every problem; they operate at a strategic level. Well, going down the line, it would be logical to turn to the executive responsible for delivering the automated teller machine (ATM) banking service. That person has a business target to meet in terms of ATM revenue and profit. That executive is the "owner" of the ATM business and responsible for sourcing the processes to deliver the business, including the ATM system. This person has to assess the risks of ATM outage and errors and develop internal controls based on such risk assessment. In practice, s/he will use technical people and professionals in the bank to do the risk assessment and control development; but s/he will be the person the CEO turns to for ensuring that the ATM system is reliable.

Some might challenge that the executive accountability for ATM revenue should not own the system but instead, the CIO should own it. Their rationale is that technology advance gave birth to ATM. Well, if we apply this reasoning, the CIO could be charged with owning all business systems. That is impractical and the business executives would likely disagree. Whether it is technology that drives business or business vision that drives technology deployment is like the chicken and egg problem. Instead of fixing a point on this, we should keep in mind that information technology is a business enabler. The CIO is a technical support executive as well as a facilitator, not a business owner.

Once the business owner has assessed risks and implemented internal controls for a system, that person should document and acknowledge that as the business owner for that system, s/he has assessed risks and implemented sufficient internal controls to reduce risk to an acceptable level. This executive should also apply a process to periodically review risks and controls in the system and then update the written acknowledgement. A control conscious organization would require documented risk acceptance from each business owner. The organization should have a framework and criteria to guide executives in risk assessment and acceptance.

Where a system is used to support more than one business unit, the CEO may assign "business ownership" of the system to the executive with the biggest business stake or the highest expertise in the system. For example, the chief financial officer should own the accounting system, and the vice-president of human resources could own the payroll system. Some systems do not process transactions and instead, provide a common service in the organization, e.g., email. Such a system would be logically "owned" by the CIO.

System owners, through technical and operations staff, design, implement and operate internal controls to *ensure* that risks are mitigated to an acceptable level. These owners should also carry out periodic assessment of controls to *assure* senior management and stakeholders that systems are reliable. Auditors periodically carry out audits of controls to independently *assure* their clients and auditees that systems are reliable.

BUSINESS CRITICAL SYSTEMS

Organizations always have limited resources. They should focus assurance effort on business critical systems. The criteria for business criticality for a corporation addresses mainly profitability and customer service. The criteria for a government include safety, health, welfare, revenue and expenditure control. The criteria for a university would include education, faculty support, revenue and expenditure control. We have listed here, for general reference, a list of systems that organizations should consider to be business critical. We will use three types of organizations as examples to show the common business critical systems: retail business, banks and governments. These are by no means complete lists of business critical systems. Each of these systems can be broken into subsystems. The term "mission critical systems" is also commonly used. Some people think that mission critical systems are more critical than business critical systems. However, in closer analysis, a business critical system could cripple an organization if it is out for a few days. Just remember what you did last time the email system was down. By identifying and prioritizing business critical systems, one can address the significance of mission critical systems. In other words, a mission critical system is a business critical system with high priority, or we can call it a tier 1 business critical system.

A large organization should have a registry of systems ranked by business criticality. Each system should be assigned to an executive for ownership. The owner is accountable for the system's reliability.

Common Retail Business Critical Systems

Accounting

Costing

Customer relationship management

eBusiness

Electronic data interchange

Expenditure control

Fixed asset management

Franchising

Inventory

Payroll and human resources

Point of sales

Radio frequency ID interfaces

Sales

Stores profitability

Supply chain management

Treasury

ERP (would encompass a number of the above functions)

Common Business Critical Systems for Banks

ATM

Accounting

Branch profitability

Brokerage

Commercial and government loans

Credit card

Customer relationship management

Deposits

eBanking portal

Expenditure control

Financial derivatives

Financial service regulatory reporting

Fixed asset management

Mortgages

Non-interest revenue

Payroll and human resources

Personal loans

Treasury

Common Government Business Critical Systems

Accounting

Citizenship and residency identification

Court administration

Education

eGovernment portal

Expenditure control

Family support

Fixed asset management

Health insurance

Payroll and human resources

Police

Supply chain management

Taxation

Transportation

Treasury

Water supply

Welfare

INTERNAL AUDIT ASSURANCE

An organization should assign system ownership to executives for system reliability assurance to provide comfort to senior management and the board of directors. Because executives are often pre-occupied with running the business, they and their staff may not always give risk assessment and control assurance the dedicated time and resources required. Even if a system is implemented with adequate internal controls, these controls may deteriorate as a result of ongoing system changes and line management may not be objective enough to detect such deterioration.

To ensure consistent risk assessment and internal control assurance throughout the enterprise, large organizations should have an internal audit function. Internal auditors should provide input to the IT department and business units in developing new systems to make sure adequate internal controls are built in. They should also test internal controls periodically. Internal audit reports will go to management to provide independent system reliability assurance. It is important for organizations to periodically engage accounting firms to assess the quality of internal audits as the work of every employee should be subject to audit.

Internal audit review and testing of internal controls should be guided by professional standards. Common standards include the following:

- American Institute of Certified Public Accountants (AICPA) Statements of Auditing Standards
- Canadian Auditing Standards
- Control Objectives for Information and Related Technology (COBIT) published by ISACA

The internal audit function constitutes a broad internal control in the organization. The chief internal auditor's mandate should include providing an annual opinion to management on the reliability and cost effectiveness of I &IT in the organization.

The above standards include rules for professional conduct. They are very similar. The following is the ISACA Code of Professional Ethics.

ISACA sets forth this Code of Professional Ethics to guide the professional and personal conduct of members of the association and/or its certification holders. Members and ISACA certification holders shall:

1. Support the implementation of, and encourage compliance with, appropriate standards and procedures for the effective governance and management of enterprise information systems and technology, including: audit, control, security and risk management.

2. Perform their duties with objectivity, due diligence and professional care, in accordance with professional standards.

3. Serve in the interest of stakeholders in a lawful manner, while maintaining high standards of conduct and character, and not discrediting the profession or the Association.

4. Maintain the privacy and confidentiality of information obtained in the course of their activities unless disclosure is required by legal authority. Such information shall not be used for personal benefit or released to inappropriate parties.

5. Maintain competency in their respective fields and agree to undertake only those activities they can reasonably expect to complete with the necessary skills, knowledge and competence.

6. Inform appropriate parties of the results of work performed; revealing all significant facts known to them.

7. Support the professional education of stakeholders in enhancing their understanding of the governance and management of enterprise information systems and technology, including: audit, control, security and risk management.

Failure to comply with this Code of Professional Ethics can result in an investigation into a member's or certification holder's conduct and, ultimately, in disciplinary measures.

Source: http://www.isaca.org/Certification/Code-of-Professional-Ethics/Pages/default.aspx, accessed on June 18, 2012.

EXTERNAL AUDIT ASSURANCE

The typical external audit engagement for an organization is the audit of the annual financial statements. In addition, external firms may be hired to perform special audits such as an audit of the internal controls in an IT service organization to provide assurance to the user organizations, an audit of an organization to provide security assurance to a credit card issuer like Visa, an audit of a systems development project or a data conversion project, an audit of a system where controls are in doubt, an audit of information integrity (rather than internal controls), an audit of an organization for compliance with regulatory requirements, or a review of the internal audit department.

Financial Statement Audit

Because every organization uses I & IT, the audit of financial statements has to include testing information system controls. Unless the external auditors confirm every transaction building up to the financial statements, control reliance is necessary and control reliance is based on control testing. It is impractical for the external auditors to confirm every transaction unless the organization is very small, in which case there is probably no requirement for an external audit. Even if the external auditors confirm and substantiate every transaction, control reliance is implicit, i.e., relying on internal controls to ensure that processing is complete, or that every transaction consummated is actually presented to the auditors for confirmation and substantiation. In addition to enhancing financial statement assurance, internal control testing helps the external auditors to understand the client's business processes and that's important for client confidence.

Because the purpose of the audit of financial statements is to express an opinion on the fairness of the financial statements, rather than an opinion on controls, the level of control assurance sought by the external auditors is only moderate. This moderate level of assurance limits the extent of control testing conducted by external auditors. This is why external auditors typically use smaller sample sizes when testing controls compared to internal auditors. In fact, external auditors often rely on the work of internal auditors to further limit the extent of control testing conducted directly.

When the external auditors conclude that internal controls are moderately reliable, they can limit the scope of their substantive testing, i.e., the testing of transactions and account balances for substantiation. Substantive testing is generally more time consuming than internal control testing so it pays for the external auditors to seek a moderate level of internal control reliance. For example, if the external auditors can conclude that internal controls over credit granting and sales processing are reliable, they can limit the scope of account confirmation and vouching to sales and payment details for substantiation.

Some might question why the external auditors would not seek a higher level of control reliance and therefore further reduce substantive testing? A higher level of control assurance means more control testing. In a financial statement audit, because the audit opinion is on the financial statements instead of internal controls, generally accepted auditing standards require a significant extent of substantive testing, i.e., the testing of transactions and account balances for substantiation. Even with a high degree of control reliance, the extent of substantive testing will change little compared to an audit where control reliance is only moderate.

In addition to assessing the reliability of internal controls in order to limit the scope of substantive testing, external auditors will document weaknesses in internal controls and suggest improvements to management, as a value adding service and also with the aim of seeing improved controls which will make the external audits more efficient in the future.

A financial statement audit should be carried out to comply with the American Institute of Certified Public Accountants (AICPA) Statements of Auditing Standards, the standards of the United States Public Company Accounting Oversight Board (PCAOB), and/or Canadian Auditing Standards. PCAOB operates under the authority of Securities Exchange Commission and it sets accounting and auditing standards for public companies.

Accounting institutes in each jurisdiction has rules of professional conduct that they expect members to comply with. The following common topics have more relevance to IT auditing.

Confidentiality of information
Conflict of interest
Disclosure of impaired independence
Documentation
False or misleading documents and oral representations
Firms to ensure compliance by partners and professional employees
Identification of threats and safeguards
Independence
Integrity and due care
Members must disclose prohibited interests and relationships
Objectivity
Professional competence
Retention of documentation and working papers
Unlawful activity

External Audit of Internal Controls

External auditors are increasingly engaged to provide an opinion on the internal controls of an organization or a system as required by regulators, a business acquisition transaction or a contract dispute. In such engagements, the auditors' demand for control reliability will be higher than that in a financial statement audit because the opinion is expressed on internal controls. For example, the United States Sarbanes-Oxley Act and Canada's Investor Confidence Rules require public companies to provide certificates to the securities commissions on the effectiveness of internal controls that support filed financial statements. Public companies in turn, may ask their shareholders' auditors to provide an opinion on internal controls, in addition to the opinion on the financial statements.

Audit of a Service Organization

An IT service organization may be expected by its customers to provide independent assurance that its internal controls are strong. Although such a service organization would likely also need its financial statements to be audited, its customers generally want more assurance than the financial statement audit opinion. The financial statement audit covers internal controls necessary to support the recording of financial transactions, and provides such control assurance only at a moderate level as discussed above. The corporate customers of an IT service organization want a high level of assurance on the internal controls that support the delivery of services to them. For example, The Canadian Depository for Securities Limited (CDS) is subject to an annual audit of its financial statements to be presented to its shareholders; and that audit covers internal controls over the recording of CDS assets, liabilities, revenue and expenses. In addition, the company provides an independent control assurance report to its securities market participants like transfer agents on the internal controls over the processing of securities transactions and the custody of securities. The latter audit includes some controls that do not have to be tested as part of the CDS financial statement audit, or that are tested with smaller sample sizes.

There are two types of audit of a service organization's internal controls for the benefit of user organizations. The first type is carried out to support the financial statement audit of user organizations. It is carried out in accordance with Statement on Standards for Assurance Engagements (SSAE) 16. The second type is carried out in response to the requests of the user organizations directly and it follows the SysTrust model. We will discuss these engagements in Chapter Ten and Chapter Eleven.

Security Control Audit Required by Credit Card Issuers

Concerned about credit card fraud, major credit card issuers have developed information security standards that they expect participating financial institutions, IT service organizations and merchants to comply with. Large IT service organizations processing credit card transactions and large merchants are required to have independent reviews to provide assurance of compliance. Failure to comply may lead to cancellation of the right to accept credit cards from customers. We will discuss this further in Chapter Eleven.

Legislative Audits

Governments appoint their own auditors accountable to the legislatures to provide independent assurance on the public accounts and value-for-money in government operations. Both types of audits include assessing the risks and reliability of I & IT. In large governments, e.g., at the provincial (state) and federal levels, the legislative auditor is independent of the internal audit function within the government. The legislative auditor reports are usually available to the public to help taxpayers assess their government's effectiveness. If the government also has an internal audit function, the legislative auditors can rely on the work of the internal auditors to reduce their direct audit work.

Regulatory Audits

Regulated industries like banking and public utility are also subject to audit by the regulators. These audits typically are of a financial nature to examine the completeness and correctness of financial transactions building up to the filed reports, or to examine the credit positions, fixed asset expenditure to support utility rate increases, capital adequacy and loan reserve. Quite often these financial audits involve assessing system reliability.

Investigative Audits

Auditors are often called on to investigate suspected improper practices, fraud or crimes. Internal control weaknesses present opportunities for carrying out improper activities and crimes. Therefore, the scope of investigative audits should include identifying the relevant control weaknesses and recommending improvements. We will discuss this further in Chapter Twelve.

Audits of Systems Development Projects

Auditors may be called on to audit a systems development project either during development or after implementation. The purpose is to provide assurance that the project is carried out to meet user requirements in a cost effective manner and that adequate internal controls are built into the system. This is not to be confused with systems development consulting where an external firm provides direct assistance and advice on how to develop systems. An accounting firm should be cautious about providing systems development consulting to audit clients as doing so may impair the firm's independence when auditing the client, or may lead to perceived independence impairment. The United States Sarbanes-Oxley Act restricts accounting firms of public companies in performing IT consulting to their audit clients.

INFORMATION TECHNOLOGY AUDITORS

As the general population is more IT literate day by day, so are auditors. Today's auditors can understand and test some IT controls that, twenty years ago, required computer audit specialists. Meanwhile, information technology is becoming more complicated. Hence, there is still a need for IT audit specialists. Large organizations should develop and maintain IT expertise in their audit teams. To help ensure adequate IT audit competence, ISACA administers the Certified Information Systems Auditor (CISA) designation. This is a world wide recognized designation that requires a candidate to pass a universally applicable examination and provide documentation indicating at least three years of experience in IT audit or closely related fields. The examination covers the following areas:

1. Information systems audit process
2. IT governance
3. Systems and infrastructure life cycle
4. IT service delivery and support
5. Protection of information assets
6. Business continuity and disaster recovery

We will cover these areas in the following chapters:

1. Information systems audit process – most chapters
2. IT governance – chapter 3
3. Systems and infrastructure life cycle – chapter 4
4. IT service delivery and support – chapter 3
5. Protection of information assets – chapter 8 and chapter 9
6. Business continuity and disaster recovery – chapter 3

The CISA syllabus focuses more on IT infrastructure and information protection, rather than on applications. This is because infrastructure and access controls are more technical and can seldom be tested with enough expertise by general auditors.

CURRENT IT ISSUES

Earlier this year, American Institute of Certified Public Accountants conducted a survey of top IT priorities. Here is the list of the top ten topics:

1. Securing the IT environment
2. Managing and retaining data
3. Managing risk and compliance
4. Privacy
5. Leveraging emerging technologies
6. Managing system implementation
7. Enabling decision support and managing performance
8. Governance and managing IT investment/spending
9. Preventing and responding to fraud
10. Managing vendor and service providers

Source:
http://www.aicpa.org/INTERESTAREAS/INFORMATIONTECHNOLOGY/RESOURCES/
TOPTECHNOLOGYINITIATIVES/Pages/2012TTI.aspx

Securing the IT Environment

According to the survey report:

"An organization that has not considered all the vulnerabilities and threats related to information technology, and has an inadequate security policy, could be a serious risk. The loss, theft or compromise of a mobile device could disrupt an organization's operations and result in the loss of sensitive or confidential client and customer data. A cyber attack could have the same consequences. Cloud computing has many benefits, but complementary risks include ensuring that the vendor providing the cloud services is appropriately securing and managing the remote environment."

Managing and Retaining Data

We are in the age of information overflow and the Internet is a significant contributing factor. There is no doubt in anyone's mind that information can convey power. However, information can also weaken an organization if it is wrong or irrelevant. Irrelevant information can waste processing resources and lead to inappropriate decisions. Computing power doubles every year. This is a two-edge sword to information management.

With vast computing resources, organizations tend to collect, share and retain increasing information. This can lead to information overflow that results in inefficiency, misuse and mistakes. On the other hand, organizations can use growing computing power to perform more thorough information analysis.

The world is increasingly information intensive. Some people say we are in an information revolution. It is critical for an organization's success to capture the right information, propagate information and knowledge to the right people, codify information for consistent retrieval and interpretation and to classify the risk of information for determining the extent of controls. This requires a formal program of policies, software tools, procedures and training. A large organization should have an information management department whose function is to set the policies and standards for information management, provide the relevant training and coordinate information risk assessment.

Managing Risk and Compliance

Businesses have always had to deal with regulatory compliance. However, in the last 10 to 20 years, these requirements have increased and been drawing more media attention. A number of factors have contributed to this trend. They include the Internet, privacy and increasing public reliance on business financial health. Looking deeper, one can tie all these factors to the Internet. The Internet has changed the world.

The Internet has accentuated privacy concerns, and this has motivated more governments to introduce privacy legislations. The Internet has expedited global data flow and communication, and this makes it easier for investors to learn about public companies and therefore more likely to invest in public companies, and therefore rely more on public companies' financial health. The Internet allows organizations to share their networks and open their systems with affiliates as well as trading partners. This has lowered the cost of computing and made mergers and acquisitions more attractive. Increasing mergers and acquisitions mean larger corporations and that raises concerns about the assurance that transactions, information and business relationships are at arms-length, transparent to investors and reliable.

Here is a common list of legislations, regulations and similar requirements that are imposed on large corporations:

1. Privacy acts – we will discuss this more in Chapter Five.

2. Sarbanes Oxley Act – This U. S. legislation was passed in 2002 soon after the failure of Enron and is intended to provide stronger assurance to investors about reliance on the financial health of public companies. Enron Corporation was an American energy, commodities, and services company based in Houston, Texas. Before its bankruptcy in late 2001, Enron employed approximately 22,000 people and was one of the world's leading electricity, natural gas, communications, and pulp and paper companies, with claimed revenues of nearly $101 billion in 2000. Fortune named Enron America's Most Innovative Company for six consecutive years. At the end of 2001, it was revealed that Enron's reported financial condition was sustained substantially by institutionalized, systematic, and creatively planned accounting frauds. The major features of the Act include requiring public companies to certify internal controls that support the financial statements and restricting the types and extent of consulting services performed by the shareholders' auditors to their audit clients.

    The first requirement helps ensure that frauds are properly prevented and detected and that financial statements are reliable. The second requirement fosters auditor independence and therefore enhances the reliability of the audit opinion. Public companies have to document their internal controls and should engage external auditors to provide an opinion on such controls. There is significant IT impact because internal controls in public companies are increasingly automated.

3. Payment Card Industry Security Standards – This was discussed briefly under External Audits above. We will cover this in more details in Chapter Eleven.

4. Uniform Electronic Transaction Act – This Act recognizes digital signatures and puts the onus on companies to implement reasonable controls to prevent customer input mistakes. We will discuss this further in Chapter Five.

Privacy

The public has never been more concerned about information privacy. The concern has been heightened in recent years by technology advances, identity theft and security breaches. The exponential increase in computing power allows organizations to store more and do more analysis of personal information, potentially breaching privacy.

Hackers are now more entrepreneurial. They are less interested in defacing a web site or sending a worm to bring down a web site without financial gain and running the risk of going to jail. They are more interested in stealing identities and selling to criminals.

Every system that processes or stores personal information is subject to privacy breach. Before such a system is implemented, the organization should conduct a privacy impact assessment and such assessment should be carried out regularly even after system implementation.

Leveraging Emerging Technologies

New technologies are being introduced and adopted at a faster than ever pace by organizations and individuals. These come in the forms of new hardware, more sophisticated and faster software, advanced techniques in hardware virtualization like cloud computing that pull the resources of idle computer resources on the Internet or an intranet, and state-of-the-art consumer oriented tools like iPad and Twitter. New technologies promise productivity gain and more enriched information availability. However, they also present security risk and can lead to incorrect information if the technologies and tools are not properly used.

Organizations should charge their CIOs with keeping in touch with technology development and assessing the applicability of new technologies. Such assessment should include risk analysis, i.e., the risk of not applying a technology and the risk of applying a technology prematurely or incorrectly.

There should be a policy about how to assess the applicability of new technologies and instruct employees not to bring in their own technology tools for connection to organization systems. Letting employees bring in their devices to connect to the employer's network is a trend called "bring your own device" (BYOD). There should be a process for monitoring the use of new tools by employees that have not been rolled out by the organizations. Every large organization should take a position and establish a policy on BYOD that takes into account the impact on risk and productivity. Some employees like BYOD, so, for instance, they can use their phones for just about everything that requires network connections, including activities in the workplace. While allowing BYOD may please some employees, it blurs the line between work and personal life and may increase an employer's exposure to network intrusion, misuse of system and information, legal liability for criminal activities or intellectual infringement, as well as loss of payroll time to personal activities. These have to be considered when deciding to allow BYOD. The media has created too much hype about BYOD; in fact, I have not heard a lot of young workers using this term. I do not believe that a talented employee will quit or refuse to come to work in an organization because it does not allow BYOD. Some smart phones are more like toys than productivity tools. An organization should not allow phones to access the corporate network more so than it allows home PCs to access the corporate network, and the same security measures should be applied to such smart phone connections as those applicable to home PC connections. Further, an organization that tolerates BYOD should have the capability to remotely terminate a connection and prevent a device that does not meet the security requirements or that has breached security, from further connection.

Managing System Implementation

The survey report describes the risk and risk mitigation strategy as follows.

The risks: An organization's strategic goals drive its system implementation. If the goals and the implementation are not aligned, the organization may only partly meet its business goals for implementation – or not meet them at all. It may not realize its return on investment for an implementation project, and it may have other problems such as converting or transferring data inadequately.

Risk management: To manage system implementation, an organization establishes a strong alignment between its strategic goals and IT-related projects. In evaluating new projects, it considers the recommendations of internal advocates who know how to establish a strong business case for such projects. It analyzes and documents the business requirements for such projects, and it evaluates their value based on return on investment, earned value analysis and other criteria. Finally, it ensures the quality and integrity of project data.

Enabling Decision Making and Managing Performance

The survey concludes on this topic as follows.

The reports provided to management should be aligned with an organization's strategic goals. However, this may not be the case if the organization's data architecture does not support an effective reporting system, or management has not supported an investment in business intelligence related projects. As a result, management may receive inaccurate or incomplete reports, and, consequently, may be at risk of making poorly informed business decisions.

Governance and Managing IT Investment/Spending

The term "IT governance" is often used in articles and conferences but many who refer to this term do not understand fully what it entails. Many think this equals the chief information officer's job description, just as many thinking that corporate governance is the CEO's job. A CEO needs the board's support and guidance to "govern" the corporation. S/he also needs the support of the chief operating officer, the chief financial officer, the chief information officer and other executives. Together, they develop and implement strategies and policies to lead and monitor the organization. Similarly, the CIO needs support of all these parties and the CIO's managers to deliver IT governance. IT governance has to be congruent with corporate governance and is a subset of the latter.

The board of directors is also accountable for IT governance to a considerable extent, although not in a hands-on manner. The board carries out its IT governance responsibility by approving major IT projects and monitoring the progress of major projects.

At a management level, an IT steering committee consisting of the C-suite (CEO, COO, CIO, CFO) and senior line executives should oversee and monitor the use of IT including approving major projects, being briefed and demanding corrective actions with respect to major IT audit findings. The objective of IT governance is to ensure that the organization has sufficient IT skills and tools to support its business in the medium to long term and that these skills and resources are used effectively and efficiently. IT governance also ensures IT is used right and the right IT is used. Although management naturally does not always think about internal controls, controls are necessary to ensure effective use of IT resources, and hence effective and reliable systems. It is important for management and auditors to continuously assess whether the governance process adequately addresses risks and includes internal controls. At this stage, the type of internal controls to be included consists of management controls, i.e., controls to be exercised by managers instead of operational controls.

Preventing and Responding to Fraud

Here is the survey summary on this topic.

The risks: Information technology has facilitated the perpetration of fraud in organizations. Those organizations that do not know how to identify IT-related fraud, do not have policies to prevent such fraud, and do not have plans to respond to a fraud, are particularly vulnerable. Likewise, organizations are at greater risk if they do not have policies to prevent management override opportunities within financial-related systems. If a fraud does occur, these organizations may not have plans in place to respond.

Risk management: To prevent and respond to fraud, an organization considers the fraud risks associated with information technology, designs policies and internal controls to mitigate such risks, and establishes policies to detect management override abuse. If a fraud is perpetrated, it is prepared to respond.

Managing Vendors and Service Providers

It is hard to find a large organization that does not outsource. Large organizations that have outsourced in varying degrees include financial institutions, retail giants, software vendors, governments and utility companies, pretty much in every industry. The main reason for outsourcing is to cut cost. But risk always goes up. This is analogous to the decision to hire a baby sitter rather than having the mother staying home to look after the child.

When an organization outsources, it stands to lose skills and in some cases the organization may have to share or give up intellectual property like computer programs. While outsourcing gives the organization short to medium term gain, it may lead to long term pain. Some are blaming the unemployment condition in the United States on companies outsourcing overseas. Offshore outsourcing is also quite prevalent in Canada. For example, a friend of mine working in a large financial services company has told me that most programmers in his team are working for a software service company in India which provides programming resources to this North American financial services company on contract. He worries that one day even he, as the team lead, will lose his job once the consultants in the IT service company have learned enough about how the system interfaces with business processes. There is a concern that over time, large North

American companies may not have a core knowledge base in software development. Management has to consider this risk and also ensure that staff morale remains high by providing training and retaining the needed core competencies within the company.

Outsourcing also increases the risk of confidentiality and privacy as now another organization has access to the outsourcing organization's data. Sometimes a service organization in turn outsources, in which case, the risk of confidentiality breach is compounded.

When assessing and reporting on system reliability, management and auditors have to evaluate the risks of outsourcing and the adequacy of internal controls in the service organization. The latter may be complicated as the service contract may not require the service organization to exercise internal controls, may not give the user organization the right to audit the service organization, or may not specify the service organization's obligation to provide an independent control assurance report. It is important for such arrangement to be made before the contract is finalized.

MANAGEMENT CHECKLIST

To ensure that I & IT is reliable and cost effective, senior management should adopt the following practices.

1. Assign business executives to own information systems and infrastructures. Each system should have only one owner. IT infrastructures would logically be owned by the chief information officer because an infrastructure usually supports multiple business systems.

2. Establish corporate policies and standards for information risk assessment.

3. Establish a process for periodic risk assessment, internal control formulation and internal control reporting to senior management and the board of directors.

4. Involve the board of directors in IT governance and ensure this is addressed at least twice a year in board meetings.

5. Establish a policy on the use of I & IT in the organization with respect to how to use IT as a business enabler and the approval process for IT investment.

6. Develop an IT strategy to be congruent with the business strategy. The IT strategy should consider the applicability of new technology.

7. Develop a process to continuously assess the cost effectiveness of IT applications.

8. Ensure that the job description and performance contract of each executive includes the appropriate I & IT assurance accountability.

9. Establish an IT steering committee consisting of a cross section of senior executives including the CIO to carry out IT governance.

10. Establish a process to promptly address IT audit findings.

INTERNAL AUDIT CHECKLIST

The chief audit executive should take the following steps to provide adequate information systems assurance to management.

1. Establish a dedicated IT audit function with qualified staff members possessing designations such as CISA.

2. Require each IT auditor to undertake annual professional development to keep up with technology and the organization's IT environment.

3. Equip all auditors with up-to-date and efficient IT tools including computer assisted audit techniques.

4. Establish a process for assessing information systems risks and controls.

5. Develop audit programs to test information systems controls.

6. Establish a process for quality control of IT audit.

7. Establish a process to ensure comprehensive, practical and timely reporting of audit findings and recommendations, and ensure that the audit report is fully supported by work papers.

8. Establish a process for following up on internal control recommendations.

9. Educate IT auditors about conflict of interest and applying objectivity in carrying out audits.

10. Educate IT auditors about IT frauds and how to deal with them during an audit.

EXTERNAL AUDIT CHECKLIST

The internal auditor checklist mostly applies also to external auditors such as shareholder's auditors, legislative auditors and auditors carrying out special engagements like SysTrust. In additional, external auditors should ensure that the following high level procedures are included in their audit engagements so that I & IT risks can be adequately assessed in the audit.

1. Obtain a letter of representation from the client about management responsibility for Information systems risks and internal controls.

2. Clearly define the audit scope in an engagement letter.

3. Define the level of acceptable audit risk, i.e., the risk of giving a favorable audit opinion on a system or IT infrastructure when the system or infrastructure is not reliable.

4. Follow up on internal control recommendations from the last audit to ascertain the status of remedy.

5. Clearly define in the engagement letter who the audit report will be directed to.

6. The shareholders' or legislative auditors should conduct an annual assessment of the IT capability of the internal audit department.

7. Build a process to be informed about IT infrastructure and IT organizational changes in the client organization.

8. Ensure that IT specialists hired to perform audits understand the audit objectives and programs and are trained in the respective auditing standards.

9. Ensure that the relevant internal audit work is reviewed before conducting external audit work.

10. Ensure that highly significant findings are reported to the audit committee.

Going forward, we will provide comprehensive discussion of information systems assurance in the following chapters.

CONCLUSION

The Internet has changed the world. Large businesses can act small by using the Internet to customize service. Small businesses can act big by using the Internet to reach the world. Although there is still a "digital divide" in the world, the difference between the "have" and the "have not" in knowledge access is narrowing, as information finds its way across continents instantaneously. IT empowers everyone to do constructive things and damage. Successes can be attained and catastrophes can be caused in great magnitude within a short time. Just look at how quickly some of the large IT companies have grown in a few years, and how some major financial transaction irregularities carried out in a few days involving computer systems that caused huge losses.

Continuing advance in technology makes systems reliability more important. In addition to putting in processes and infrastructure to ensure system reliability, management needs to continuously exemplify and promote a quality culture and hold everyone responsible for quality.

The pace of life is different than it was 10, 20 years ago. Systems undergo more frequent changes. System assurance has to keep pace. Auditors have to keep up; not just to keep up with IT development in terms of knowledge, but to keep pace with "life on the fast lane" in this digital environment, in terms of audit focus, frequency and timeliness. Audit reports should be issued to identify and help fix problems, and less focus should be on reporting history. Don't tell management at length what it already knows. Information technology can be used to help automate audit testing so that audits can be more focused and efficient.

The chief audit executive should work to build a world class audit organization within the enterprise. Audit quality should not be limited by the size of the enterprise. Research studies indicate that many small organizations have internal audit departments that are superior to large organizations. Although salary gaps between the private sector and the public sector as well as those between large companies and small companies may be a limiting factor for audit quality, chief internal auditors can work around that using other incentives like job variety and flexible work arrangement. The chief audit executive must continuously seek improvements, promote education, exemplify and hold every auditor accountable for quality.

Auditors have to critically question their findings and recommendations because organizations, to be competitive, have less and less time and resources for "nice to have" recommendations. Auditors have to ask "so what" when finding things they did not expect to see, before the client says "so what". Auditors also have to avoid "just going through the audit program" and avoid being seen as "just going through the motion". They must be innovative to help management mitigate risks, including the risks of overspending. For example, auditors should not just report that a department has a system backlog of transactions, but rather, should analyze what causes the backlog and how management can fix it including shifting resources from less critical tasks. Auditors should try to avoid just being used by line managers to get more resources, but should try diligently to help the organization to become more effective, efficient and competitive by recommending internal controls and identifying areas that are over controlled or that receive resources and effort that are not warranted by the risks being contained. Although controls are owned by management, auditors should not just point out what is wrong and leave management to find the solutions. Every employee is an expert in something. The auditor's expertise is on internal controls, so it is right for management to look to auditors to recommend controls.

Auditors must also be flexible in assessing controls. For example, if a control deficiency is found but management is able to come up with a compensating control that the auditor has tested to be satisfactory, the deficiency in the first control is somewhat just an academic issue. Instead of concluding that the area is weak, the auditor should tell management that the failed control may be redundant and management should either fix it to provide stronger control assurance or remove it so as not to waste resources.

Boards of directors have to continuously challenge their management about the sufficiency of IT assurance provided to the boards and customers. Users and customers should be educated to play a constructive role towards such assurance. Regulators need to monitor company system reliability in addition to checking the correctness of filed reports.

SUMMARY OF MAIN POINTS

System Assurance Criteria

- Completeness
- Authorization
- Accuracy
- Timeliness
- Occurrence
- Efficiency

System Components

- Infrastructure
- Software
- People
- Procedures
- Information

Types of Assurance Engagements

- Financial statement audit
- Value for money audit
- Internal audit
- Third party control assurance audit
- Audit for compliance with specific legislation or contract
- Forensic audit

Types of Systems

- Batch
- Real time
- eBusiness
- Centralized vs distributed processing
- Direct access vs sequential access
- Enterprise resource planning systems, uses database.

Current IT Issues

1. Securing the IT environment
2. Managing and retaining data
3. Managing risk and compliance
4. Privacy
5. Leveraging emerging technologies
6. Managing system implementation
7. Enabling decision support and managing performance
8. Governance and managing IT investment/spending
9. Preventing and responding to fraud
10. Managing vendor and service providers

REVIEW QUESTIONS

1. Which system component is the most business critical and why?

2. How would you rank the system assurance criteria for a financial statement audit? For an internal audit?

3. Computing power doubles annually. How do you think this affects system assurance?

4. What are the criteria for assessing system criticality in a bank? A large retailer? A government?

5. What is the IT implication of International Financial Reporting Standard?

6. How can IT auditors be proactive to help manage risks?

7. What do you see is the role of a computer audit specialist in a financial statement audit?

8. Which of the current IT issues identified in the AICPA survey do you think affect the financial statement audit more?

9. Which components of the CISA examination do you think are more relevant to the audit of financial statements?

10. What kind of IT knowledge do you expect of the chief auditor of a large bank?

CASE – "Aging Information Technology Systems"

This case study is a direct extract from the Spring 2010 report of the Office of the Auditor General of Canada (OAG). Chapter 1 of the report, titled "Aging Information Technology Systems", is used in this case study. The following is an excerpt of Chapter 1 of the Spring 2010 report, including only the "Main Points" of the "Aging Information Technology Systems" report.

Source: Spring 2010 Report of the Auditor General of Canada – Office of the Auditor General of the Canada. *Reproduced with the permission of the Minister of Public Works and Government Services, Canada, 2012.*

What Was Examined

Aging information technology (IT) systems refers not only to a system's age in years but also to issues that affect its sustainability over the long term, such as the availability of software and hardware support and of people with the necessary knowledge and skills to service these systems. The term also relates to a system's ability to adequately support changing business needs or emerging technologies, such as 24/7 online availability.

The Treasury Board of Canada Secretariat, through its Chief Information Officer Branch (CIOB), is responsible for establishing the federal government's overall strategic direction for IT, in consultation with deputy heads of departments. It is also responsible for identifying areas that offer significant government-wide benefits and for leading initiatives to achieve government-wide solutions. According to the most recent figures available (for 2005), departments and agencies spend about $5 billion a year on IT.

We examined whether five of the government entities with the largest IT expenditures - the Canada Revenue Agency, Public Works and Government Services Canada, Human Resources and Skills Development Canada, the Royal Canadian Mounted Police, and Citizenship and Immigration Canada — have adequately identified and managed the risks related to aging IT systems. The audit also examined whether the Treasury Board of Canada Secretariat, and specifically its Chief Information Officer Branch, has determined if aging IT systems is an area of importance to the government as a whole and to what extent it has provided direction or leadership in developing government wide responses to address the related risks.

We also looked at three major systems that deliver essential services to Canadians — the Employment Insurance Program, the Personal Income Tax and Benefits Return administration system, and the Standard Payment System — to determine how the responsible entities have addressed the risks related to the aging of the IT systems that support these services. The Employment Insurance Program processed more than 3.1 million claims and paid out over $16.3 billion to claimants in the 2008–09 fiscal year. The Personal Income Tax and Benefits Return administration system processed more than 27 million income tax and benefit returns that provided $166 billion of revenue and also distributed $17 billion in payments for benefits and credits in 2008–09. The Standard Payment System (SPS) is the principal system the government uses for issuing payments, including Old Age Security, Canada Pension Plan and Employment

Insurance benefits. It issued more than 250 million payments in 2008. In about 60 percent of cases, these payments are the only income or the main source of income for the people who are receiving them.

Audit work for this chapter was substantially completed on 30 November 2009.

Why It's Important

The federal government relies heavily on IT systems to deliver programs and services to Canadians. Even though these systems are functioning, many of them consist of legacy applications that are supported by old infrastructure and are at risk of breaking down. A breakdown would have wide and severe consequences — at worst, the government could no longer conduct its business and deliver services to Canadians. Even applications that meet current business needs can be difficult and expensive to operate and may not be flexible enough to respond quickly to changes.

The renewal and modernization of IT systems does not happen overnight. It must be planned and budgeted for over the long term. The cost to renew and modernize IT systems are significant and can take many years to fund, and implementation can take five years or longer. Without sufficient and timely investments to modernize or replace aging systems, the ability of departments and agencies to serve Canadians is at risk.

What Was Found

- Aging IT has been identified as a significant risk by the five organizations we examined, and the majority of them consider it sufficiently important to include it in their corporate risk profiles. They state that if these risks are not addressed in a timely manner, the systems may not have the capacity to meet current and future business needs.

- Although the Chief Information Officer Branch of the Treasury Board of Canada Secretariat is aware that the aging of IT systems is an issue, it has not formally identified it as an area of importance for the government. Nor has it assessed the issue from a government-wide perspective or worked with departments and agencies to develop government-wide solutions. Despite the significant funding likely to be needed across government to renew aging systems — estimated at a total of $2 billion in three of the five entities alone — the CIOB has not formulated strategic directions or a plan to address these issues on a government-wide level.

- Citizenship and Immigration Canada, Public Works and Government Services Canada, and Human Resources and Skills Development Canada have taken some steps to manage the risks related to their aging IT systems, but much work remains to be done. The Canada Revenue Agency and the Royal Canadian Mounted Police are farther along. They have both identified the significant risks associated with their aging systems and completed a multi-year investment plan that defines and prioritizes ongoing and future work. Based on their preliminary estimates, they have determined that the costs involved are significant and that presently they lack sufficient resources to complete critical investments.

The departments and agencies have responded. The departments and agencies agree with all of our recommendations. Their detailed responses follow the recommendations throughout the chapter, as applicable.

Introduction

1.1 Canadians expect the government to provide them with many services, such as processing personal income tax returns, issuing pension and benefit payments, and safeguarding personal information. Information technology is now a vital part of service delivery for the government. Government business is supported by a vast array of information technology (IT) systems, some of which have been in use for several decades. However, the term "aging IT systems" refers to more than just how old a system is in years. Many systems that are 10 years old or older were designed to be continuously upgraded. These systems are functioning and are likely to continue to do so for some time.

Risks relating to information technology systems

1.2 For the purposes of this audit, "aging IT systems" refers to applications and infrastructure that may be meeting current needs but are becoming increasingly expensive to operate and may pose certain risks. These risks may affect security or restrict the way the government conducts its business because systems cannot be easily updated to respond to changing business needs flowing from new laws, regulations, or industry standards. The most damaging risk is that an aging critical system could break down and prevent the government from delivering key services to the public — such as issuing income tax refunds and employment insurance and pension cheques. While these risks could apply to any IT system, they are more likely to affect older systems. Exhibit 1.1 describes some of the major factors that drive departments to modernize their aging systems.

Exhibit 1.1—Overview of major factors driving the modernization of aging systems

Factor	Description
Skills shortage	Fewer staff and contractors have the skills and knowledge to use older programming languages and source code structures.
Vendor support	Vendors may no longer exist or no longer support older products.
Regulatory compliance	Outdated systems may be hard to update to comply with changing laws, regulations, and industry standards.
Maintenance costs	Costs go up because aging systems are very complex and difficult to maintain, there are few service providers, and parts are scarce and often very costly.
Access to data	Information becomes increasingly cumbersome to extract and analyze as data structures age.
Meeting client expectations	Older systems cannot be modified to support modern technologies and meet expectations such as 24/7 availability and workflow.
Security	**Legacy systems*** cannot always be modified to conform to changing security requirements (for example, password complexity).
Green IT initiatives	Older IT systems are generally not energy efficient and are hard to modify to reduce their environmental impact.
Disaster recovery	The older the system, the harder it is to recover data after a disaster.
*Legacy systems—Old technology, computer systems or application programs that continue to be used, even though newer technology or more efficient methods of performing a task are now available.	

*** End of OAG report excerpt****

Required

1. What do you think are the causes of aging systems in the public sector?

2. Are these causes common in the private sector?

3. How do the risks of government systems differ from private sector business systems?

MULTIPLE CHOICE QUESTIONS

1. Which system component affects a system's importance the most?

   A. Infrastructure
   B. Information
   C. Software
   D. People
   E. Procedures

2. Who is responsible for ensuring system reliability?

   A. Management
   B. Auditors
   C. CIO
   D. Chief risk officer

3. What should be CEO's main concern about the annual doubling of computing power?
   A. Increasing spending
   B. Impact on audit fee
   C. Inappropriate use by employees
   D. Opportunity and risk

4. What affects an IT strategy the most?

   A. Annual doubling of computing power
   B. Regulatory requirement
   C. Business strategy
   D. Systems development plan

5. Which type of system has benefited the most from fast growth in computing power?
   A. Customer relationship management
   B. ATM
   C. Payroll
   D. Local area network

6. Who should own the customer relationship management system in a major Canadian bank?
   A. Chief financial officer
   B. Chief executive officer
   C. Head of personal banking
   D. Chief information officer

7. Which system component is most critical to ensure system availability?
    A. Information
    B. Infrastructure
    C. People
    D. Software
    E. Procedures

8. Which reliability concern is increased in cloud computing?
    A. Completeness
    B. Accuracy
    C. Timeliness
    D. Authorization

9. The current trouble in European economy has caused the U. S. dollar to fluctuate. What of the following do you think is affected the most?
    A. Cloud computing
    B. Offshore outsourcing
    C. Merger
    D. Cyber warfare

10. In what aspect does the Patriot Act affect Canadian companies?
    A. Outsourcing
    B. Compliance with the Investor Confidence Rules
    C. Intellectual property
    D. Competitiveness

CHAPTER TWO – INFORMATION SYSTEMS RISKS

"There are risks and costs to a program of action, but they are far less than the long-range risks and costs of comfortable inaction." – John F. Kennedy

- In June 2012, LinkedIn was investigating the possible leaking of several million of its users' passwords after a member of a Russian online forum said he managed to hack the popular networking site and upload close to 6.5 million passwords to the Internet.

- BlackBerry services returned to normal on October 13, 2011 after four days of global outage. In a conference call on October 13, Research in Motion explained that the widespread outage was caused by technical glitches linked to a backup switch that did not function as tested, causing a large backlog of emails and texts. Outage started in Europe, then spread to the Middle East, Africa and hit Canada on October 13. Parts of South America, as well as Asian markets were also affected.

- Between April 17 and April 19, 2011, about 100 million Sony PlayStation Network user accounts were hacked into causing compromise to credit card data, email addresses and other personal information. This prompted Sony to temporarily shut down the web site. Sony said the attack may have compromised credit card data, email addresses and other personal information of 77 million user accounts.

- In March 2010, hackers flooded the Internet with virus-tainted spam that targeted Facebook's estimated 400 million users in an effort to steal banking passwords and gather other sensitive information.

- The June 2009 subway crash in Washington DC appeared to have been caused by a train control system failure.

- One of the biggest frauds in Banking was carried out by Jerome Kerviel, a 31-year-old trader in Société Générale's Paris headquarters. He had taken massive fraudulent directional positions - bets on future movements of European stock indices, without his supervisors' knowledge, the Bank said. Because he had previously worked in the trading unit's back office, he had 'in-depth knowledge of the control procedures and evaded them by creating fictitious transactions to conceal his activity. He also breached system access controls.

- A bug in Excel was reported in 2007. For example, multiplying 850 by 77.1 would yield 100,000 instead of the correct product of 65,535.

- Telecommunications throughout Asia were severely disrupted On December 26, 2006, after earthquakes off Taiwan damaged undersea cables, slowing Internet services and hindering financial transactions, particularly in the currency market.

- In 2006, the confidential tax files of almost 2,700 Canadians were missing after a Canada Revenue Agency worker took them home and let a friend download them onto a laptop. The laptop had disappeared, the agency was scrambling to rewrite its security protocols and the privacy commissioner was asking why no one had alerted her to the breach in confidentiality.

In the last chapter, we talked about the need to assess business risks before developing and implementing internal controls in order to mitigate risks to an acceptable level and therefore provide an acceptable level of assurance on information system reliability. In this chapter, we will discuss the process of risk assessment. We will address risks from the standpoints of management and auditors.

A lot about risk management is common sense. We manage risk when we walk and drink coffee (a little sip first to see if it is too hot). We turn on the television to check the weather before leaving for work or university.

Computers are fast but they can also make mistakes fast, thus leaving little time to prevent, detect and correct. For example, an electronics retailer in North America mispriced a product a few years ago on its web site as $59.90 when the store price was $599. In a day, the company sold more than 600 units based at the wrong price.

Computers can be consistently right but also consistently wrong. Increasing use of information technology (IT) means less paper trail. The reduction in hard copy documents may render mistakes and irregularities more difficult to detect. The concentration of information in computers and electronic media exposes organizations to the risk of "placing all the eggs in one basket". Further, it is more difficult to control who has access. These are some basic risks in using IT. Other less obvious risks include improper use, uneconomical deployment, inadequate capacity and systems that do not meet business requirements.

There are basically three types of things that can go wrong with respect to using IT. First, the wrong system may be developed in relation to business requirements, the development of a system may not be well managed and therefore wasting the organization's money, or the system may be developed with significant flaws. Secondly, undesirable things might happen to a system when it is being used; e.g., unauthorized data changes may be made, there may be unauthorized use, disasters can happen that damage the hardware and software. Thirdly, system information may be inappropriately used; e.g., users are not trained and therefore misuse some functions, or there may be incorrect interpretation of system information. We will talk about the risk of inappropriate systems development in Chapter Four. The rest of this chapter will focus on the other two types of unfavorable system occurrences, the degree of which depends on the nature of business, organization and system.

The risk of errors occurring because of the nature of the business, organization and system is called inherent risk. An organization can avoid or reduce inherent risk by engaging in less ambitious business strategy, e.g., by abstaining from eBusiness. To mitigate such risk, management must implement internal controls. However, internal controls are not fool-proof otherwise they would be too expensive. The risk of internal controls not preventing or detecting significant errors is called control risk. The third definition of risk, to an auditor, is the risk of audit procedures failing to detect material errors, and this is called detection risk. Auditors are concerned about all three types of risk. The multiplicative value of inherent risk, control risk and detection risk is called audit risk, which is the risk of providing favorable audit assurance on a system which has a major flaw. Management is generally concerned about only inherent risk and control risk. The product of inherent risk and control risk is called "residual risk", i.e., the risk remaining even after implementing internal controls. Management has to assess whether the residual risk is acceptable and organizations should have guidelines and decision limits to ensure consistent application and acceptance of residual risk. The tolerable residual risk should be low for every business critical system.

The term "threat" is often used to refer to risk. A threat is more general and it usually does not bear any quantifiable connotation. For example, a snow storm is a threat. The estimated likelihood of a snow storm is a risk. Another related term is vulnerability. We are vulnerable because we are not well positioned; for example, we are more vulnerable to getting sick if we don't have enough sleep. Vulnerability, therefore, means the extent of risk resulting from a weakness.

BUSINESS CRITICAL SYSTEMS

Organizations should understand the risks related to every business critical system. A business critical system is one that is needed for the organization to conduct business without significant interruption. These systems can range from common tools like email or a web site to more specific systems like supply chain or automated teller machine (ATM). Often one might question what systems are not business critical. Ideally, those systems should be few. The more systems are not business critical, the less efficient the organization is. Some are inevitable, and although not business critical, are beneficial to the organization, e.g., an employee suggestion system.

Business critical systems should be determined based on the nature of the organization's business mission. For example, banking systems are critical to a bank, a supply chain management system is crucial to a company like Walmart and a water quality system is essential to a city government. In addition to the function of a system, the transaction volume and total value of assets managed by the system should be major criteria in determining business criticality.

INHERENT RISK

The more vulnerable an asset is to errors, loss or damage, the greater is the inherent risk. Similarly, the greater the magnitude of vulnerable assets or transactions processed by a system, the higher is the inherent risk. An extension of this is that the more widespread a system is, e.g., an Internet facing system, the greater is the inherent risk. A wire transfer system that handles a large volume of high dollar transactions daily is more vulnerable than a payroll system because the former involves many user organizations in an online environment and improper transactions can be difficult or too late to reverse. Other factors affecting inherent risk include the legal implications of errors, the potential repercussion in terms of customer goodwill and adverse effect on competitiveness.

Inherent risk has three components: the probability of an unfavorable event, the nature of damage and the extent of damage.

The following factors would be useful in performing inherent risk assessment:
- Age of procedures
- Age of the system
- Method of information storage (on site, off site, network, outsourcing etc.)
- Nature of information processed (e.g., vulnerability, value, frequency of change)
- Nature of people (experienced or inexperienced, consultants vs employees)
- Nature of processes (e.g., batch or online)
- Nature of systems (e.g., complexity, Web enabled, and geographical diversity)
- Past experience
- Stability of system
- Staff turnover
- Transaction volume

Management is responsible for assessing and mitigating inherent risk. The following steps can be followed in risk assessment.

1. Identify the significant and potentially unfavorable events for which a solution requires management decision from event to event. Significance, of course depends on quantitative exposure and probability. Quite often, however, significance can be assessed intuitively based on experience and it is quite easy to rule out far fetched and really trivial exposures. An example of the former is a risk for which the organization has no control, e.g., World War III. An example of something really trivial is an occurrence that can be easily addressed without significant service interruption or loss of assets, e.g., employee tardiness. Some significantly unfavorable events may not be far fetched or trivial but the solution is quite standard across the industry, e.g., the risk of virus infection. In this case, it is a "no brainer" for organizations to deploy commercial anti-virus software on each computer and update the virus detection files as they become available from the anti-virus software vendors. If an event type is within an organization's control, is not trivial and, is not already addressed with an accepted and standard risk mitigating practice, the organization should put it on the list for risk assessment.

2. Assess the damage of each event (not each occurrence). Some events and occurrences are interdependent. For example, when a server breaks down, it increases the probability that another server in the cluster will break if the load is shifted to other servers in the cluster. On the other hand, a broken server cannot be hacked. These chain effects have to be considered in risk assessment. Estimate the average magnitude of each event based on organization and industry experience. For example, how long will it take to fix a server?

3. For damage leading to financial loss, estimate the amount of loss from each occurrence of each event. Take into account the chain effect between events. Damage should be quantified as much as practical. The relevant transaction volume, relevant asset value maintained, contractual obligation as well as organization and industry experience in legal liability should be used to estimate the financial loss. If an estimate is soft, it can be discounted to arrive at a quantified estimate, e.g., if an occurrence of an unfavorable event will likely lead to the loss of a major customer, a subjective likelihood of say, 20%, 30% can be applied to the annual profit from the customer.

4. Estimate the probability of each event (not each occurrence). For example, if the risk of a computer breaking down on a given day is .005%, the annual risk is 365 x .005%, i.e., 1.825%. Well, what period should be used to quantify the risk? It should not be too long like several years, nor should it be too short like daily. The most common time cycle used by organizations to plan and report financial performance is annually. Therefore, it seems practical to express the probability of unfavorable occurrence on an annual basis.

5. Based on probability, estimate the number of occurrences per year. This would also depend on the nature of the event. The denominator unit for the probability should be chosen based on practicality and strong relevance to the event whose risk is being assessed, and it should be clearly stated. Here are some examples:

    a. If the probability of hacking is 0.01% per server per day, the estimated number of hacking incidents would be 3.65% per year per server. This sounds high but the logic is right. A common analogy is our chance of catching a cold. I catch a cold once a year, so on average, my risk of catching a cold is 1/365, or 0.274%.

    b. If the probability of a ghost employee (a recorded employee receiving pay who does not exist) is 1% of the total number of employees, the number of ghost employees on an annual basis would still be 1% of the average number of employees. This is because the first probability is not expressed in relation to a time frame.

    c. If the probability of processing a claim payment in the wrong amount is .01%, the number of incorrect payments in a year would be .01% of the total number of payments in the year. Here, the probability is unchanged because both values are expressed over the same period. However, the number of incorrect claims will change because the annual number of claims is a high number compared to only one claim being processed at a point in time.

6. Multiply the estimated number of occurrences by the estimated financial loss from each occurrence to arrive at the financial exposure from the unfavorable event. The above examples are extended as follows:
    a. If the estimated financial loss of an average hacking incident is $10,000, the financial exposure on an annual basis is $365 per server. This amount should then be multiplied by the number of servers. Some servers are more critical, so the organization can apply a varying degree of granularity in this calculation.

    b. The estimated financial exposure from ghost employees can be calculated as 1% of the average number of employees multiplied by the average salary, or more directly, calculated as 1% of the year's payroll.

    c. The annual financial exposure from incorrect claims payment can be estimated as .005% of the total amount of claims paid in a year. The probability of .01% in step 5 can be converted to .005 % because a mistake can go either way. An overpayment may not be recoverable, whereas an underpayment would most likely be brought to the attention of the organization by the payee. In addition, the cost of reprocessing has to be estimated. These factors have to be considered.

7. Add all the financial exposures for the identified potentially unfavorable events for each business critical system.

8. Rank the business critical systems by financial exposure.

9. Use the financial exposure as a gauge to decide how much internal control to design and implement, taking into account the cost of designing, implementing and operating each internal control. An internal control should be designed and implemented only if the financial impact of the risk to be mitigated outweighs the cost of the control. This means internal controls should be implemented to provide reasonable assurance of system reliability, as opposed to absolute assurance.

10. The financial exposures of all business critical systems can be added to assess the organization's exposure to unreliable systems.

Identifying Potentially Unfavorable Events

Management should use the CAATOE attributes that we talked about in the last chapter to identify potentially unfavourable events.

- Completeness
- Authorization
- Accuracy
- Timeliness
- Occurrence
- Efficiency

The following simple matrix can help to assess inherent risk.

Risk Matrix

	Complete	Authorized	Accurate	Timely	Occur	Efficient
Input						
Processing						
Output						
Storage						

This matrix shows that an unfavorable event can occur at the input, processing, output or information storage phase of a transaction cycle. Such an event may include information change or access that does not reflect a real transaction, incomplete, inaccurate or untimely transaction processing, the processing of an improperly authorized transaction, or processing transactions inefficiently in relation to the cost of processing including the cost of hardware, people and software.

Each cell should be addressed in relation to the system being risk assessed. In addressing each cell, management should consider the five system components, i.e., infrastructure, software, people, procedures and information. Management has to think about what can go wrong with each component during each stage of the transaction cycle (input, processing, output and information storage) with respect to each risk attribute (completeness, authorization, accuracy, timeliness, occurrence and efficiency). To document such risk identification, a number of matrices can be prepared, e.g., one matrix for each system component, one matrix for each subsystem of a system.

Completeness

Incomplete processing will result in incorrect accounting records, loss of revenue, unhappy customers or unhappy users. This can happen because of incomplete input, faulty programs that miss some transactions, invalid data that causes transactions to be rejected and lost, hardware failure, interception of computer processing by hackers, or rogue systems administrators. A system administrator is someone who controls a server. This is a critical IT position and must be rigorously controlled. We will talk about such controls in the next chapter. Here are some examples of incomplete processing.

- An automated banking machine (ATM) fails to capture the last digit of an amount entered although the correct amount is shown on the screen. This can easily occur because of hardware malfunction. Preventive maintenance is a control to mitigate this risk.
- A database fails to record a large amount because of field overflow. This can be a type of buffer overflow which is a common system design flaw. Rigorous system testing can help mitigate this risk.
- Incomplete input procedures resulting in some transaction data not being entered. Detailed user procedures would help mitigate this risk.

- eBusiness customers do not enter all necessary data. The risk is high because people these days are always in a rush. System edit checks should prevent this.
- Incomplete database update because of program flaws. This risk increases as organizations continue to implement enterprise resource planning systems that update multiple database tables based on single data entries. One control that can help mitigate this risk is a database referential integrity check. This means checking that a foreign key is not blank for any record.

Accuracy

Little writing is needed for one to appreciate what inaccurate information can lead to. We live in an information intensive society. Many people have a habit of turning on the TV to check the day's weather forecast, especially in the winter, to decide what to wear and which routes to take to work or school. A store manager will log on to the computer to check the promotions for the day and the sales figures for the previous day, this information will affect how s/he operates the store. A foreign exchange trader will check the rates and trading positions many times a day. When information is wrong, the effect may be minor on a personal basis, or it can be devastating to an organization. Computers have been known to be wrong because of hardware failure, program flaws or human errors in operating the computers or feeding data. Errors may appear in input data, such as in customer names or numbers. Alternatively, they may appear during processing, for example, when a system incorrectly multiplies quantities ordered with unit prices. Some common mistakes are:

- Transposing two digits when entering a social insurance (security) number is a common occurrence. A mitigating control is to use a check digit algorithm, i.e., a system computing the derivative of say, the first 8 digits of a social insurance (security) number to form the last digit and then compares the computed last digit with the input last digit. This control will work if the social insurance (security) system uses this formula when assigning the numbers in the first place.
- A software error leading to wrong calculation, e.g., the Excel bug that was discovered in 2007. Rigorous system testing would be the preventive medicine.
- Entering a wrong amount. For example, accidentally hitting the minus sign. A system edit check can detect this.
- The system looking up the wrong payroll deduction code from the deduction table. System testing would be an effective preventive control.
- Affixing incorrect bar codes on products. Many of us has experienced that when we find out we have been overcharged or when we have to wait at a cashier counter until the correct price is accepted by the system. Verification of bar codes before being rolled out to operation is a preventive control for this type of errors.

Authorization

Unauthorized transactions can cost an organization immensely. For example, Société Générale', a large bank in France, took a significant market loss when it liquidated unauthorized trades in 2008. Unauthorized access to sensitive information can also be damaging to an organization. Imagine a disgruntled employee posting customer credit card numbers on the Internet.

Transactions may be carried out without authorization, or with inadequate authorization. Changes to master files may be made without authorization. There are two elements to this. First, there is no authorization from the person accountable for the transaction or data file. For example, a payroll clerk changes someone's salary without management approval. In this case, the payroll clerk has the system authority to make salary changes, but s/he does so without following documented procedures. Another way transactions are entered without authorization is when someone circumvents system security by say, breaking a password or impersonating an authorized user. Some other examples of unauthorized transactions are:

- Write-off of accounts receivable from a friend.
- A payroll clerk overstates his or her own hours worked.
- An accountant puts through a journal entry that exceeds his or her financial limit.
- A customer accesses another customer's account.
- A programmer changes programs without approval.

A common internal control to mitigate the above risks is restricted access.

Timeliness

To most organizations, information is money. When information is not current, incorrect or ineffective decisions are made. Organizations might even incur liability. The reason for late information may be untimely processing, tardy reporting or a system failure.

Sometimes data may be incompletely input or processed only temporarily. This means although data eventually gets through the system, it is late, and in some cases, too late, resulting in unreliable information or loss to the organization. Here are some examples of untimely transactions:

- Recording sales weeks after shipments leading to cut-off errors. Regular reconciliation can help to detect this.

- Removing employees from payroll long after departure resulting in overpayment. A rigorous exit checklist should be used.

- Late in sending out T4s or W2s, leading to penalty from Canada Revenue Agency or Internal Revenue Service. Regular monitoring of computer processing schedule should be performed.

- Late in recording inventory receipts resulting in an incorrect inventory balance. Regular matching of invoices to receiving reports would help to detect this.

- Late in paying invoices resulting in loss of cash discounts or a supplier. Accounts payable should be aged and reviewed by management.

Occurrence

Information may be processed that does not represent real transactions. This can also mean information being processed by a faked system. Here are some examples of what can go wrong.

- A faked ATM luring customers to insert their ATM cards. The risk is likely to be low because of the significant investment to set up a faked ATM. Regular bank inspection and customer education would help to mitigate this risk.

- A fictitious web site can lure customers to provide identity information and the criminal can then input faked transactions using the stolen identity. A control to mitigate this risk is to use digital certificates, which is a kind of electronic business card downloaded by a browser to verify a web site's identity. We will discuss this more in Chapter Eight.

- An employee downloads a malicious program that appears to be useful software. This is quite common. Anti-virus software can be an effective control.

- A payroll clerk sets up a ghost employee. This is one of the older tricks to commit fraud and is still used. It requires little technical knowledge and can be achieved with just ordinary payroll system privilege if the person doing this is a payroll administrator. A standard control to mitigate this risk is the requirement for management review.

- Entering payroll hours that were not worked. Many organizations would admit that this occurs. Management review can be an effective control.

Efficiency

Even if a system produces information substantiated by authorized transactions in an accurate, complete and timely manner, it is not reliable in the long term because it is too expensive or too slow (a system may be slow and still produces timely information, e.g., users have to wait too long for the screen to refresh). That is, it is not reliable to support the organization's business. Here are some examples.

- Some critics thought that the Canadian Gun Registry system was too expensive and took too long to implement.
- Hiring a highly reliable consultant for $800 a day to import data from text files to Excel spreadsheets for a system conversion. The output would be accurate but the cost is too high.
- Investing in excessively redundant infrastructure without a thorough risk assessment.
- Paying for a corporate software license by overestimating the number of users; e.g., assuming everyone in the organization will use the software but a much lower percentage actually use it.
- Failure to take advantage of the roughly annual doubling of computing power; as a result, the company's systems are falling behind in terms of performance efficiency compared to its competitors.

Common controls over efficiency include developing and enforcing a policy on cost benefit analysis, management review as well as setting up and reporting on system performance indicators.

The Effect of Information Technology on Inherent Risk

Certainly, automation reduces human errors. Replacement of manual functions can make it more difficult to collude to commit fraud, especially for people who are not IT savvy. Computers will not get sick and tired so it is more likely to finish its jobs on time. Computers do not go on strike, although computer staff could. These factors reduce inherent risks. However, one might be under pretence to think that increasing automation will reduce the extent of improper transactions. This theory, as proved by experience, is not true. The reason is that computers are controlled by people. The fewer people are involved, the less cross-checking or observation there is to deter people from carrying out improper activities. Therefore, increasing automation generally increases the risk of fraud.

Electronic transaction trails are less visible and create more uncertainty. Access is more difficult to control. There are more parties having access to corporate information. There is less time to react to errors. There is a higher risk of information loss because of the concentration of storage. Because of the concentration of processing function and connections, power outage or network failures can cause the systems to be unavailable on a massive scale. Such impact would materialize to a lower degree for manual processes. These factors serve to increase inherent risks. Here are the common risk factors in information systems.

Concentrated Processing

In computer systems, the processing is often concentrated within computer facilities. Certain organizational units are bypassed during processing operations. Consequently, less opportunity exists for detecting errors and fraudulent events such as unauthorized transactions, changes in programmed instructions and theft of assets. Current IT practices such as virtualization will concentrate computer processing even further.

Less Reliable Audit Trail

The audit trail is more likely to be fragmented or eliminated. Source documents may not be used, for instance, when sales orders are taken over the phone, they are entered to the system directly. Sometimes there might not even be verbal communication, the transaction initiator puts in to the system what is in the mind; if there is a need to seek justification, where is the audit trail?

Human Judgement Bypassed

Computers perform programmed instructions blindly, i.e., they exercise no judgement. Therefore, fewer opportunities exist for people to spot errors and question data. For example, a pricing error on the web site of a major retailer resulted in the sale of 600 units of a product in a day which were significantly underpriced because of a web price catalog input error.

Data Storage not Visible to Human Eyes

Data stored in computer systems is oriented to the characteristics of digital media. These characteristics differ from the paper oriented and hence human oriented media. Data, when stored in these devices, is not comprehensible to the human eyes. It is necessary for users to take steps to retrieve the data and decipher it using software so it can be interpreted. While this may add to security, the extra steps introduce room for errors.

Data is easily erasable without leaving a trail. A disk can hold millions of records and damage to the disk because of humidity or demagnetization can cause all of these records to be lost. Similarly, if the disk is lost or if an authorized person gets hold of it, a lot of information can be compromised or destroyed.

Other Common Causes of Inherent Risk

Here are some other common causes of information systems risks.

1. Management does not understand IT. It is easier for management to understand business issues and even financial issues. Because of their lack of understanding of information systems, executives often rely on the IT department to tell them how much money is needed. This makes IT investments subject to less scrutiny than other expenditure, and can lead to ineffective spending.

2. Employees do not understand IT. Information technology often facilitates business process reengineering that changes jobs in organizations. Mundane and clerical jobs may be eliminated or replaced with jobs that require higher skills in order to support an organization's goal to expand. Employees who are moved to new jobs may not understand the technology required to do their jobs. Many organizations do not do a good job in training their employees for change. This makes the use of IT more erroneous and ineffective.

3. Increasing use of IT means more processes are integrated. In such a case, the weakest link in the chain can drag down a number of functions. Complicated systems are also more difficult to understand and maintain.

4. More and more organizations are sharing systems and real time information transfers with business partners and vendors. For example, some retail giants open their inventory systems to suppliers to query and automatically send replenishments, avoiding the paper work of purchase orders. The risk of divulging trade secret is higher and organizations may have to rely on systems in which they have no control.

5. Electronic information is easier to steal and there may not be a trail. It is difficult for organizations to know whether an employee has copied sensitive files to memory sticks to be given to competitors.

6. IT changes rapidly and even technical people find it hard to keep up. Computing power doubles every year. Managers are always called by vendors to try new products. Some vendors also use fear tactics to convince management that the options are to upgrade or lose support or competitiveness. Organizations may therefore be talked into making incorrect or excessive purchases. On the other hand, organizations that fail to upgrade may indeed be less competitive. Knowing where to spend IT money is challenging and something managers must pay close attention to.

7. More and more organizations outsource IT functions so they can focus on their core businesses. Governments and large companies have outsourced in order to be more cost effective. Common functions that have been outsourced include payroll, accounting, network support, and call center opeartion. When an organization outsources, it loses some control. If the service provider makes mistakes, it will impact on the user organizations and they sometimes are caught by surprise. Even

without outsourcing, every organization uses an Internet service provider. We hear of ATM failures from time to time; some of them may be the result of system failure of the network service providers.

8. Computers can make managers less productive. Managers who are less technology savvy may spend an inordinate amount of time learning to use systems and this may make them neglect their main function, to manage. On the other hand, more technology oriented managers may really enjoy using technology so much that they treat computers as toys, so as a result, they may spend too much time exploring system functions or surfing the net beyond what is needed to perform their jobs. They may even get a lot of satisfaction in developing their own systems to solve business problems and thus become highly paid programmers who write inefficient or ill-controlled programs.

9. Knowledge management is another common risk factor. To keep up with technology changes, organizations have to invest in training their staff members. A lot of organizations are willing to buy new tools but do not give their staff enough time to attend courses to learn to use the tools; as a result, IT investment is not returning the desired benefits.

10. Many organizations place heavy reliance on long-term IT employees who over the years have accumulated detailed knowledge of the systems used in the organization. When these employees leave, the organization may experience system problems unless there is proper knowledge transfer. For example, many large organizations still rely significantly on systems written in Common Business Oriented Language (COBOL) and Programming Language 1 (PL1), two common mainframe programming languages. Many universities have stopped teaching these languages. Many mainframe programmers have retired or are close to the retirement, so when they leave, there will be a knowledge gap. To some extent, organizations can address this problem by acquiring middleware to bridge web interfaces with legacy systems and make the legacy code (programs) more graphically oriented for younger programmers to maintain. There is still a need to ensure a critical mass of legacy programming skills until organizations replace their mainframe systems. At the other extreme, some organizations are routinely selecting younger workers in hiring and promotion over experienced candidates just to develop a youthful work force. Both of these extreme approaches increase the organization's risk to inaccurate and unauthorized transactions.

11. Because of the high turnover of IT staff, organizations sometimes find it necessary and more flexible to hire consultants, especially when an organization is under a hire freeze for full-time positions. Consultants may not have much knowledge about the organization and its policies. They are more expensive than employees. They may not be as dedicated as employees so in a crisis, the organization may be caught without the necessary staff to solve problems.

12. The needle-in-a-haystack problem will occur more frequently when IT is used. For example, a small program bug can cause erratic information errors. Some program bugs may only be triggered by certain factors and they may take years to be discovered, but when they are active, the impact could be very significant.

Risks of Database Systems

A database improves efficiency and avoids data redundancy. However, data sharing between applications increases the risk of unauthorized access and update errors. The more programs that can update a table, the more likely errors will occur. Also, because more system software is used in a database environment, the risk of incorrect software configuration (incorrect parameters) increases. Database applications often are operated in a distributed network. In that case, there are multiple copies of a database geographically dispersed. It is important to ensure that updates are synchronized. It is just as important to ensure time synchronization, by for example, operating a time server. Because a database consists of many tables that are shared between applications, there is also a risk of data inconsistency between tables when data is repeated unnecessarily, e.g., a customer address shows up in multiple tables but is represented inconsistently. This risk results from data redundancy. There is also the risk of concurrent updates, i.e., one transaction overwriting the result of a previous transaction. We will discuss internal controls to mitigate these risks in Chapter Six.

Risk of Concurrent Updates

In a database environment, programs sometimes contend for the same table and field in terms of reading and writing. Although technically, the hardware will not allow two programs to update a field at the same time, just as it would be impossible for two full size cars to enter a single car garage, there is a risk of updates performed by two programs almost concurrently that could impair data integrity. Here is an example.

I deposit a $1,000 check at an ATM to a joint checking account. Less than a second later, my wife transfers $2,000 from the checking account to a savings account using eBanking. Before these transactions, the checking account balance is $5,000. Here is what could happen.

1.   My transaction reads the $5,000 balance and updates it to $6,000.
2.   My wife's transaction reads the $5,000 balance (after my transaction has read it but before my transaction finishes) and calculates a new balance of $3,000.
3.   My wife's transaction finishes after mine, so it overwrites the new balance as $3,000.
4.   In fact, the correct balance should be $4,000.

This is called concurrent update. That is, two transactions update the same field of the same record without knowing about each other. In other words, the left hand doesn't know what the right hand is doing. To prevent this kind of data inconsistency, organizations should configure database management systems to enforce record locking. We will describe this in further detail in Chapter Six.

CONTROLLING INHERENT RISK

Management can control inherent risk in three ways. Management can avoid inherent risk by refraining from the practice that will generate the risk, e.g., by not offering eBusiness. If risk avoidance is not desirable, management can transfer the risk by buying insurance or engaging a partner to assume all or some of the risk, e.g., an insurance company can sell some insurance policies to a reinsurance company to offload some risk. The third approach is to implement internal controls to mitigate the risks. An internal control is a procedure, instruction or tool to mitigate inherent risk. The procedures may be automated or manual. These three ways are not mutually exclusive.

Inherent risk depends on the nature of business, the nature of assets, as well as the environments in which business is conducted and assets are stored. Management can avoid inherent risk by not going into a certain line of business, staying away from certain products and being more cautious and conservative in choosing locations. Doing so, of course, may limit the organization's growth and profitability and increase cost. There is often a direct relationship between risk and reward. Management wants to strike an optimal balance by doing risk assessment. This is why although large organizations should charge their executives with the responsibility for controlling business risks, these organizations often have separate risk management departments and chief risk officers to coordinate effort in risk management.

To mitigate inherent risk, management should implement internal controls. The remaining risk net of risk reduction by internal controls is called residual risk. Residual risk should be at a level management considers acceptable. The implementation of internal controls should stop at a point where the marginal cost of internal controls will exceed the financial exposure to be reduced. This point is not entirely objective. Organizations should have guidelines to help managers measure the cost and benefit of internal controls. The benefit of internal controls is the extent of inherent risk to be reduced by the controls.

Before deciding whether a risk should be avoided, shared or mitigated, management should assess the significance of the risk. What is significant to one manager may not be to someone else. Therefore, an organization should have a formal risk assessment and acceptance policy in terms of significance. The thresholds should be quantified as much as practical. The degree of granularity of risk quantification and significance assessment should also be indicated in guidelines within the risk assessment and acceptance policy. In other words, should the risk of equipment failure be expressed as per incident, per piece of equipment, per year etc.?

The risk assessment and acceptance policy should specify the monetary levels of risk that can be accepted by each level of manager. Most organizations have documented levels of signing authority for expenditure. For example, a first line manager can make an individual purchase of up to $10,000. However, many organizations don't have a similar policy for risk acceptance. Auditors often get a statement from managers that they are accepting the risks. But can a first line manager accept the risk of asset loss amounting to $1 million, even if this amount is within the annual budget of the manager? Financial service companies have rigorous signing levels for approving loans. More organizations should move towards implementing a policy for risk acceptance for operations risks including IT risks.

Internal auditors should assess inherent risk using the corporate policy. If such a policy does not exist, internal auditors should recommend that it be established. Meanwhile, internal auditors should assess inherent risk in relation to the business strategy for the organization and then for different departments. What is important to management is important to internal auditors.

Shareholders' auditors should assess inherent risk in relation to materiality in the context of the financial statements. Shareholders auditors are concerned about the completeness, accuracy, authorization, timeliness and occurrence of recorded financial information. They are not really concerned about efficiency or lost profit as long as the financial records have integrity. Where a risk is determined to be significant, shareholders' auditors will look for internal controls for mitigation.

CONTROL RISK

Management has to design and implement internal controls to mitigate risk. For an asset or system to be managed, there is a risk that the internal controls will fail to reduce inherent risk to the extent desired. This risk is called control risk. The following control factors contribute to control risk:

- Inadequate assessment of inherent risk resulting in designing the wrong controls or weak controls.
- Designing internal controls that are too hard to follow.
- Designing internal controls that are too vague and subject to inconsistent interpretation.

- Designing internal controls that are carried out too infrequently or that use small samples
- Inadequate or improper implementation of internal controls, e.g., incorrect programming.
- Inadequate compliance with internal controls because of insufficient procedures, training and monitoring.

Most of the factors that affect inherent risk also affect control risks. Here are some examples:

- The speed and inherent accuracy of a computer makes automated controls more reliable than manual controls.
- Increasing automation involves fewer people in transaction processing and therefore makes it harder to segregate duties for cross checking. This increases control risk.
- Electronic trail of transactions also makes the trail of control activities less visible and more prone to being erased. This increases control risk.
- Higher concentration of transaction processing also results in higher concentration of internal controls in fewer servers. This "putting more eggs in a basket" increases the risk of internal controls failure.
- Increasing automation often involves more reliance on trading partners and service providers to carry out internal controls. This increases the risk of controls not being carried out properly because the organization has less control over controls.
- Outsourcing puts some internal controls in the hands of a service organization and because the user organization has no or less influence over the controls, the risk of internal controls being inadequate or ineffective increases.

Management should minimize control risk by involving business units and internal auditors in risk assessment, designing rigorous and redundant internal controls, and monitoring internal control compliance. The level of control risk tolerable to management and internal auditors is low.

Shareholders' auditors generally tolerate a higher level of control risk, it is generally moderate. Moderate does not mean 50%. Accounting firms have a range that they apply to different industries and it can probably range upward to say, 40%. Shareholders' auditors accept a higher level of control risk because their audit opinion is not on internal controls, but rather, on the fairness of presentation in the financial statements. There is an exception, Canadian and U. S. public companies have to report on internal controls supporting the financial statements to securities regulators and shareholders' auditors are usually asked to provide an opinion on the controls. In this case, the shareholders' auditors will tolerate only a low level of control risk.

RESIDUAL RISK

Residual risk is the product of inherent risk and control risk. Assume that in an organization, the inherent risk of setting up a ghost employee in the payroll system is 1%, i.e., without any internal controls, management estimates that the probability of a ghost employee being set up is 1% based on industry and organization experience. Management has now implemented internal controls to mitigate this inherent risk. Assume that management has estimated the risk of the internal controls not being adequate and effective is 5%. The residual risk is now .05%. If this is not acceptable, management will have to improve internal controls to lower the control risk. The inherent risk cannot be changed unless management decides to make structural changes to the payroll system like centralization.

Management should assess and accept residual risk in the same manner as its assessment and acceptance of inherent risk. This is because residual risk is simply a reduced degree of inherent risk. The organization policy on risk assessment acceptance with different sign-off levels should apply to residual risk. That is, when a residual risk exceeds the level of authority of a manager, s/he should implement further internal controls to lower the risk. If the cost of the controls exceeds the amount of the risk to be mitigated, the manager can in theory accept the risk. However, if such a risk exceeds the manager's approval authority, s/he should refer it to a higher level of management to understand, assess and accept the risk.

Internal auditors should assess whether management's tolerable control risk is appropriate given their assessment of inherent risk. If it is not, the internal auditors should raise their objection to management with explanation and raise it with the audit committee if management's tolerable control risk is significantly higher than what the internal auditors think it should be. If management's tolerable control risk is appropriate, the internal auditors will have to confirm that the control risk is actually at that level. Such confirmation will require studying internal controls to assess their reliability on paper and then testing internal controls. The extent of testing will depend on the control risk. The higher the tolerable control risk, the lower the acceptable control reliability, and the smaller the samples will be used in testing.

External auditors of financial statements will take a slightly different approach in assessing control risk. We will discuss that under Detection Risk. Before that, we should talk about audit risk. Detection risk is part of audit risk.

RISK REGISTRY

An organization should maintain a consolidated list of inherent risks and residual risks segmented by lines of business. This registry should indicate the risk owners, risk weights, risk ratings and exposures. The list of inherent risk is used to regularly assess the adequacy and redundancy of internal controls. The list of residual risk points to the actual exposures faced by the organization and it is also used to assess the effectiveness of internal controls in operations. The owner of the risk registry is the chief risk officer, whereas individual risks are owned by the line executives or the CIO depending on whether a risk is related to a business area or the IT infrastructure.

The chief risk officer should develop and maintain the risk assessment and risk acceptance policy as well as supporting procedures to ensure consistent risk assessment in the organization. This executive should also provide a center of excellence in risk assessment. To maintain the risk registry, the chief risk officer has to coordinate periodic risk assessment and ensure that the findings are addressed with internal control improvements. There should be a corporate risk report broken down by business line and types of risks (e.g., IT, credit, market) submitted to senior management at least annually. In a major North American bank, the chief risk officer is a vice-chair responsible for the coordination of assessments of credit risks, IT risks and operation risk. She is also responsible for insurance (to protect bank operation and liability) and internal audit.

AUDIT RISK

Everything in life has risk. Auditors are trained to assess risk. So they are aware that an audit may not deliver the correct assurance. The main force to reduce risk is diligence. For example, Olympians and litigation lawyers know that thorough practice and preparation make them more confident and thereby lowers the risk of not achieving their goals. Auditors should plan and carry out their audits with a high degree of diligence in order to practically minimize the risk that the audit delivers the wrong assurance, i.e., concluding that something is reliable when it is not. That's audit risk. Audit risk should be set to low.

Internal Audit Risk

Internal audit departments should have a documented range of audit risks for different departments and types of audits and these ranges should reflect the nature of the industry, audit committee expectation, shareholders' auditors' expectation, as well as generally accepted internal audit standards published by organizations like the Institute of Internal Auditors and ISACA.

For an internal audit, audit risk = inherent risk x detection risk

Detection risk for internal auditors is defined as the risk of failing to detect a significant internal control deficiency or the risk of failing to detect a significant financial misstatement, depending on the scope of the audit.

External Audit Risk

For an external audit like the audit of financial statements, audit risk is the risk of giving an incorrect audit opinion; e.g., the risk of opining that the financial statements are reliable when they are significantly misleading. Accounting firms should set audit risk in relation to the industry and the audience of the audit report, the latter addresses the nature of reliance placed by the audience. They should also be guided by their national accounting institute audit standards. The range of audit risk for financial statement audits should be quite narrow, e.g., the audit of a small city government should not be substantially less rigorous than the audit of an international bank, although the effort and complexity will no doubt differ significantly.

For an external audit, audit risk = inherent risk x control risk x detection risk

DETECTION RISK

Detection risk is the risk of audit procedures failing to detect significant errors and exceptions. This risk has to be measured by auditors in order to decide what and how many audit procedures to carry out to support the audit report. Detection risk has different meanings for an audit of internal control compliance vs an audit of financial records.

Detection Risk for Control Compliance (Internal) Audit

For an audit with the objective of drawing a conclusion on internal controls, e.g., an internal audit, audit procedures should be carried out to test key internal controls to a sufficient extent for compliance. Detection risk in this case would be the risk of audit procedures failing to detect a significant internal control infraction. If the actual detection risk is higher than the tolerable detection risk, auditors can extend control testing to lower the detection risk. Auditors should have guidelines or software to calculate the actual detection risk.

Detection risk is affected by the quality of auditors and the extent of testing. If an auditor tests every key control, detection risk will go down. Because control testing practically is performed by means of observing transactions or examining transaction documentation, a larger sample of transactions would reduce detection risk. How large should the sample size be and how many procedures should be used to test each critical control? Because management wants to have a low degree of control risk, auditors should conduct enough testing to convince themselves that control risk is indeed low. This means testing has to be extensive, i.e., detection risk is low. What does "low" mean in terms of percentage? Industry practices in auditing and risk management indicate that it means less than 10%. This means management should design controls that will, overall, work, at least 90% of the time. Controls for more critical systems like water quality inspection will merit a much higher reliability and therefore involve much lower control risk. For the auditors, to achieve detection risk of lower than 10%, say 5%, means that audit procedures should be carried out to tell the auditors that 95% of the time, the auditor will have carried out adequate procedures to detect significant internal control infractions if such infractions actually exist. This does not mean that, in the long run, only 95% of audits is effective, because an effective audit still has risk; for the 5% of audits where a significant control deficiency is not detected, the rest of the audit procedures are still likely very reliable. In most cases, it would be impractical for the auditors to close the risk to zero. A 5%

detection risk also does not mean that significant control deficiencies will occur 5% of the time; it just means that a significant control deficiency is not detected by internal auditors 5% of the time. The frequency of control deficiency is control risk and that depends on the effectiveness of control design and implementation. Detection risk in a control compliance audit indicates the risk of audit procedures failing to detect a significant internal control deficiency.

Although detection risk in a control compliance audit is the auditor's risk and control risk is management's risk, they point to the same thing – the risk of controls not working. Therefore, in closer analysis, detection risk is the auditor's estimate of control risk. No matter what the method of estimate, if two parties try to estimate something, their objective is to come to the same estimate. Therefore, detection risk in a control compliance audit is the auditor's confirmation of control risk.

Detection Risk for Financial Attest Audit

This is the risk of audit procedures failing to detect a significant financial error. Significance should be tied to materiality and frequency, including the size of the error in relation to the population. For example, an error that constitutes 1% of the population may be significant if the error is of a recurring nature.

The most common type of financial records audit is the audit of financial statements. Other types of financial records audit include due diligence audit for a stock offering or a business acquisition, audit of financial records for litigation, audit of a database to provide assurance to users before system conversion etc.

Financial Statement Audit Detection Risk

Detection risk in a financial statement audit is the risk of audit procedures failing to detect significant errors that will contribute to financial statement misrepresentation. The significance of errors depends on materiality and frequency. The objective of a financial statement audit is to express an opinion on the fairness of financial statements. Here is an example of an opinion.

Auditors' Report

To the Shareholders of Gerica Limited.

We have audited the balance sheets of Gerica Limited (the Company) as at December 31, 2011 and December 31, 2010 and the statements of earnings, changes in shareholders' equity, comprehensive income and cash flows for the years then ended. These financial statements are the responsibility of the Company's management. Our responsibility is to express an opinion on these financial statements based on our audits.

We conducted our audits in accordance with auditing standards generally accepted in the United States of America. These standards require that we plan and perform an audit to obtain reasonable assurance whether the financial statements are free of material misstatement. An audit includes examining, on a test basis, evidence supporting the amounts and disclosures in the financial statements. An audit also includes assessing the accounting principles used and significant estimates made by management, as well as evaluating the overall financial statement presentation.

In our opinion, these financial statements present fairly, in all material respects, the financial position of the Company as at December 31, 2011 and December 31, 2010 and the results of its operations and its cash flows for the years then ended in accordance with Canadian generally accepted accounting principles.

Feng and Liscio, LLP

Certified Accountants
Phoenix, Arizona
May 25, 2012

As you can see from this audit opinion, internal control is not mentioned. This is because the objective of a financial statement audit is to express an opinion on the fairness of financial statements, rather than on the reliability of internal controls.

As we discussed in the last chapter, the auditors of a financial statement audit have to rely on internal controls. The degree of reliance will determine the extent of substantive testing (testing of transaction details) to be performed. The more reliable internal controls are, the less substantive testing is required. The rationale is that strong internal controls will prevent more errors and irregularities and detect more of them for management to correct before the situation worsens. So before determining the tolerable detection risk, shareholders' auditors should assess control risk.

Tolerable Control Risk

Most internal controls are like smoke detectors. When the detector beeps, we know something is wrong. A little smoke can mean a dangerous fire. Thus, we can draw an analogy that an internal control deviation can mean a larger number of actual mistakes. For example, the result of lack of joint signatures on checks may lead to quite a few unsubstantiated disbursements.

This relationship can be extended to mean that confirmation of one control will equate the value of confirming multiple transactions. Therefore, it is more economical to test internal controls than to do substantive testing (test of transactions for supporting details).

However, because the audit opinion is on the financial statements which are built up with transaction details, auditors cannot perform only control testing to arrive at the opinion. They have to perform substantive testing to a significant extent. They would like to be able to rely on key internal controls to reduce the extent of substantive testing, from say, highly significant to significant. This would allow them to reduce the extent of substantive testing.

Generally accepted auditing standards for financial statements require a significant level of substantive audit procedures to be performed and some procedures like confirmation of accounts receivable, verification of physical stock taking and evaluation of loan reserve. This means regardless of how strong internal controls are, a significant extent of substantive testing has to be performed. Therefore, it does not pay for the financial statement auditors to maximize their reliance on internal controls by doing exhaustive internal control testing. On the other hand, they do not want to do minimal internal control testing. This is because even if internal controls are highly impressive on paper, without adequate testing, auditors cannot confirm that the internal controls are effective.

The extent of internal control reliance to be sought by financial statement auditors should be moderate. This is consistent with the Canadian Audit Standards that indicate that "auditors should assess control risk at below maximum". "Below maximum" means not maximum, nor does it mean minimum. What does that mean in percentage? Practitioners generally agree that it must be lower than 50% but can be higher than 20%. Where it falls in the range depends on factors such as experience with the organization's financial stability, knowledge about the client's operations, management's control consciousness, fraud experience and recent system changes.

Detection Risk

Once the financial statement auditors have conducted enough internal control testing to confirm internal controls reliability at the desired level, i.e., moderate reliability, they can now perform substantive testing to comply with generally accepted auditing standards.

If internal controls are found to be weaker than a moderate level of reliability, auditors will have to perform more extensive substantive audit procedures. This means detection risk will decrease, i.e., the auditors will tolerate a lower probability that audit procedures fail to detect significant financial errors because the auditors now think there are more financial errors resulting from weaker controls.

The above analysis means that higher control risk will have to be offset by lower detection risk, i.e., more assurance that substantive audit procedures are adequate, meaning more substantive audit procedures. Because generally accepted auditing standards require a significant level of substantive testing, meaning a significant level of assurance from substantive testing, detection risk, which is the risk of audit procedures failing to detect a material financial or accounting mistake, cannot be high. This means the detection risk in a financial statements audit must be moderate or low, or the extent of substantive testing must be moderate or high. The range depends on the levels of inherent risk and control risk.

Detection Risk for Other Financial Records Audits

Other financial records audits are typically narrower in scope than financial statement audits and are non-recurring, so reliance on internal controls is less crucial. This makes the formulation of audit procedures more straight forward. The detection risk, however, is not much different than that for a financial statement audit. It is still the risk of audit procedures failing to detect a significant error. Because there is less need to rely on internal controls, more substantive audit procedures are carried out and detection risk is usually lower than that for a financial statements audit. In some financial records audit like one supporting a business acquisition, the suitor might prescribe the exact audit procedures to be carried out.

Detection Risk for Dual Purpose Audits

Some audits, like an internal audit or a value-for-money audit, will produce reports that conclude on internal controls and financial records. In that case, detection risk should first be assessed using the control compliance audit approach. That detection risk, which we can call a stage 1 detection risk, is then used as the control risk in a financial records audit to formulate substantive testing, i.e., testing of transactions for supporting details and cost effectiveness. The stage 1 detection risk is like the assessment of control risk in a financial statements audit.

Sarbanes-Oxley Act requires the CEO of a public company to certify to the securities commissions that internal controls supporting the financial statements are reliable. The CEO may ask the shareholders' auditors to provide an opinion on internal controls. The financial statement audit of a public company will therefore produce two opinions, one on the fairness of the financial statements and the other on internal controls reliability. In such an audit, the control risk demanded by the auditors will be low, because of the opinion on internal controls. However, because auditing standards require a significant extent of substantive testing, low control risk does not mean that little substantive testing can be performed. Substantive testing will be carried out to the extent as if control risk is moderate. This means that such a dual-purpose audit will involve more audit work than a typical financial statements audit, and the increase in audit work is on internal control testing.

The following is an example of the audit opinions from a dual purpose financial statement audit.

We have audited the consolidated balance sheets of Wiletec Inc. ("the Company") as at December 31, 2011, and December 31, 2010, and the consolidated statements of earnings and comprehensive income, changes in shareholders' equity and cash flows for years that ended on December 31, 2011 and December 31, 2010. These financial statements are the responsibility of the Company's management. Our responsibility is to express an opinion on these financial statements based on our audits.

We conducted our audits in accordance with the standards of the Public Company Accounting Oversight Board. These standards require that we plan and perform an audit to obtain reasonable assurance whether the financial statements are free of material misstatement. An audit includes examining, on a test basis, evidence supporting the amounts and disclosures in the financial statements. An audit also includes assessing the accounting principles used and significant estimates made by management, as well as evaluating the overall financial statement presentation.

In our opinion, these consolidated financial statements present fairly, in all material respects, the financial position of the Company as at December 31, 2011 and December 31, 2010 and the results of its operations and its cash flows for each of the years that ended on December 31, 2011 and December 31, 2010, in accordance with Canadian generally accepted accounting principles

We also have audited, in accordance with the standards of the Public Company Accounting Oversight Board, Wiletec's internal control over financial reporting as of December 31, 2011, based on the criteria established in Internal Control — Integrated Framework issued by the Committee of Sponsoring Organizations of the Treadway Commission (COSO), and our report dated April 16, 2012 expresses an unqualified opinion on the effectiveness of the Company's internal control over financial reporting.

Bata, He and Kuhn
Certified Public Accountants
Phoenix, Canada
April 16, 2012

The COSO internal control standard is endorsed by CICA and AICPA.

So what is the scope of internal controls over financial reporting? According to COSO, they include internal controls over the following:
- Financial closing.
- Financial reporting.
- Business process controls over revenue, expenditures, assets and liabilities.
- Information systems controls.

This virtually means all the internal controls over transactions that eventually end up in the financial statements. However, because the focus is on financial reporting, let's keep in mind the financial statement audit opinion. It is about fairness of presentation of financial statements and does not speak to company profitability or efficiency. Therefore, the internal controls that should be addressed in the controls audit opinion should address the control criteria of completeness, authorization, accuracy, timeliness and occurrence, but not efficiency.

Controlling Detection Risk

Detection risk varies inversely with the extent and nature of audit procedures. If the auditor examines all transactions, detection risk is very low. Even if all transactions are vouched and verified, the auditor can make mistakes. The rigor of the audit procedure, i.e., its design, affects detection risk. The knowledge of the auditor also affects detection risk. External auditors can tolerate higher detection risk if internal controls are strong. Auditors have no influence over transaction volume and complexity, have indirect influence over internal controls by recommending improvements, but they have direct influence over the nature and extent of audit procedures. Therefore, detection risk is controlled by auditors.

Effect of IT on Detection Risk

Most of the factors that affect inherent risk also affect control risk and detection risk. Here are some examples:
- Computer assisted audit techniques can be used to reduce detection risk.
- Electronic trail of transactions makes the trail of control activities less visible and more prone to being erased. This increases control risk. It also directly increases detection risk because it is more challenging for auditors to understand electronic audit trail than paper audit trail.
- Increasing automation often involves more reliance on trading partners and service providers to carry out internal controls. This increases the risk of controls not being carried out properly because the organization has less control over controls. This also directly increases detection risk because the testing dimensions have expanded.
- Outsourcing puts some internal controls in the hands of a service organization and because the user organization has no or less influence over the controls, the risks of internal controls being inadequate or ineffective increases. This also directly increases detection risk because the population for testing may now reside in a service organization which makes testing more time consuming and potentially less direct.
- In an enterprise resource planning system, an entry can update several ledgers. This increased system complexity is more challenging to auditors to trace transactions. It puts more burden on auditors to learn the systems.

MANAGEMENT CHECKLIST

1. Senior management should appoint an executive to coordinate risk assessment throughout the organization.

2. Senior management should develop a risk assessment framework consisting of risk factors, weighting criteria, weight scale, risk assessment scale (e.g., 1 to 10), frequency of risk assessment and a prioritized list of critical systems.

3. Senior management should charge each executive with determining his or her business critical systems.

4. Compile and prioritize the business critical systems for the entire organization.

5. Provide regular risk assessment training to mangers.

6. Provide an annual or quarterly risk profile report to the board of directors.

7. Maintain a risk registry in the organization which details the financial exposure of each business critical system and each business area. A business area may use more than one system and a system may support more than one business area. Financial exposure in the risk registry in turn is supported by quantitative assessment of inherent risk and control risk.

8. Perform annual benchmarking with the industry on the organization's risk profile.

9. Ensure that the risk profile of the organization is appropriately disclosed in the annual report to shareholders and relevant stakeholders.

10. Include a risk assessment section in the business proposal for every IT project.

INTERNAL AUDIT CHECKLIST

1. Review the risk assessment framework used by management to assess the soundness of methodology as well as comprehensiveness of criteria, factors and scales.

2. Review the list of business critical systems and the supporting rationale to assess its completeness and appropriateness.

3. Develop an audit universe, which is a list of auditable entities based on assessment of inherent risk. Such assessment should start with management's risk documentation. An auditable entity within an organization may be a system, a project or a business unit.

4. Develop a methodology for scheduling audits based on inherent risk, control risk and time since the last audit.

5. Develop an annual audit plan to ensure that every business critical system is subject to audit over a cycle which should not exceed three years. Riskier systems should be audited more frequently.

6. Develop audit programs for each audit based on assessment of inherent risk as well as control risk assessment from the previous audit of the same system or unit.

7. Provide a quarterly IT risk assessment update to senior management.

8. Provide risk assessment training to auditors and management.

9. Ensure that audit report recommendations are based on and refer to the relevant inherent and control risks.

10. Ensure that every auditor's performance and skills development plan includes annual IT risk training.

EXTERNAL AUDIT CHECKLIST

1. Develop an audit methodology that includes tolerable audit risk, inherent risk, control risk and detection risk.

2. Review the client's risk assessment framework to determine comprehensiveness.

3. Review the list of business critical systems to assess inherent risk for audit planning.

4. Review the client's risk assessment reports in order to reflect the risks in the external audit plan.

5. Review the IT qualifications, audit methodologies, audit coverage and findings of the internal audit department.

6. Provide training to staff on the assessment of inherent, control, detection and audit risks.

7. Provide automated tools to facilitate the assessment of inherent, control, detection and audit risks.

8. Provide a management letter to the audit client to summarize control weaknesses with recommendations for improvements.

9. Establish a quality control function to monitor audit risk by performing quality assurance review of work papers.

10. Ensure every auditor receives IT training every year.

CONCLUSION

Because of the uncertainty in audit trail completeness as well as the increased difficulty in understanding and controlling electronic processes and access compared to less automated processes, the overall risk impact of information technology is that it generally increases inherent risk, control risk and detection risk. Organizations are increasingly realizing the importance of structured risk management as evidenced by the growing number of large organizations that have appointed chief risk officers. There is also a positive and encouraging trend to include IT risk assessment in the job description of the chief risk officer.

SUMMARY OF MAIN POINTS

- Audit risk = inherent risk x control risk x detection risk (risk of substantive audit procedure failure).
- The risk factors of incompleteness, inadequate authorization, inaccuracy, untimeliness, lack of substantiation and inefficiency apply to inherent risk and control risk.
- Financial statement auditors seek moderate control assurance, whereas internal auditors expect high control assurance.
- Detection risk can be reduced with audit automation.
- Inherent risk = business risk.
- Residual risk = inherent risk x control risk.
- Business owner owns the risk.
- Senior management should set corporate guidelines and approval levels for risk assessment and acceptance.
- Outsourcing increases all risks.
- Exposure = risk x materiality
- Threat = a particular risk without the probability quantification, e.g., the threat of terrorism. A threat, once quantified, becomes a risk.
- Vulnerability = a risk magnified by a control deficiency.

REVIEW QUESTIONS

1. How does automation affect segregation of duties?

2. What do you see are the responsibilities of a chief risk officer?

3. What are the risks of an ATM (banking) system?

4. Why are financial statement auditors content with moderate control risk?

5. What is the relationship between sample size and risk?

6. What level of control risk can external auditors tolerate when giving an opinion on a client's compliance with Sarbanes Oxley Act?

7. What risks do consultants cause to an organization?

8. What computer characteristics can both increase and decrease risk?

9. Describe the risk of BYOD to large companies.

10. As an internal auditor, you have been asked by the CIO to develop a risk registry. How should you respond to this request?

CASE - Automotive Parts Incorporated

Automotive Parts Incorporated (API) is a distributor of automotive parts. API believes that its paperless sales system, implemented at the beginning of its current fiscal year, will provide a competitive edge. The paperless sales system includes order entry, invoicing, receivables and collection. Its customers include service shops and retailers.

API operates its information system using a wide area network (WAN) that connects its head office with five branch offices across the country. Each branch office has its own warehouse. The exhibit contains notes from an interview that you, CPA, conducted in with Jim Cook, the chief information officer (CIO), about the overview of the sales system.

The audit partner wants you to prepare an audit planning memo that addresses the risks and audit approach relating to the sales system. Discuss the inherent and control and risks.

EXHIBIT

API CORPORATION
OVERVIEW OF SALES SYSTEM ENVIRONMENT
PREPARED BY CPA

1. The CIO reports to the CFO. There is an IT coordinator in head office and one in each branch. They report to the IT manager. They are specialists in operating systems and networks. In addition, they have been thoroughly trained in the use of the application software packages purchased by API.

2. A service shop or small retailer customer that wants to establish an account would access API's web site to complete a credit application. Besides the standard information normally associated with a credit application, the applicant must provide a valid credit card number or bank account number that will be charged for all purchases. The customer must also supply an email address. The applicant is prompted by the system to select a user ID and a password.

3. The applicant's credit status is verified with a credit rating agency, and the API credit manager approves the applicant as a customer within a week.

4. Using the ID and password, a customer can look up product availability at any of API's five warehouses and place an order.

5. For small customers, when a customer finishes placing an order, API's system connects to the previously identified bank or credit card network that will authorize the transfer of funds, to ensure that sufficient credit or cash on deposit is available. API records this code on an electronic order confirmation that has a unique order number assigned sequentially by API's computer to every order placed within its system. The order confirmation and invoice are emailed to the customer. Large customers are invoiced and they will pay based on the invoices.

6. For small customers, funds are electronically transferred from the credit card or checking account.

7. Using tablet computers attached to hand held scanners wirelessly, the warehouse staff scan the bar-coded shelf labels and enter the quantity they pick.

8. Head office administers all master file updates (e.g., customer and inventory item additions, modifications and deletions). Only the head office IT coordinator has direct access to data files, i.e., access to change without using a regular transaction like a sales order.

MULTIPLE CHOICE QUESTIONS

1. Which database feature increases risk the most?
   a) Maintaining data independence
   b) Reducing data redundancy
   c) Increased accessibility
   d) Expedited transaction processing
   e) Data dictionary

2. Which risk is most affected by social networking sites?
   a) Reliability
   b) Privacy
   c) Integrity
   d) Authorization

3. Which is the right formula for residual risk?
   a) Inherent risk x detection risk
   b) Inherent risk x audit risk
   c) Inherent risk x control risk
   d) Control risk x detection risk
   e) Control risk – audit risk

4. Which risk increases the most with virtualization?
   a) Program errors
   b) Data entry errors
   c) Improper data access
   d) Data redundancy
   e) Data loss

5. What will happen if two bits are altered during data communication, i.e., a 0 becoming a 1 and vice versa?
   a) The transaction will be incorrectly recorded.
   b) Confidentiality will be breached.
   c) The network will be jammed.
   d) The message will be intact because of the offsetting errors.

6. "Passwords may be easily broken." This is a(n):
   a) inherent risk.
   b) weakness.
   c) control risk.
   d) conclusion.

7. "With the current infrastructure, we stand to lose $2 million of business a year as a result of system breakdown." This is a(n):
   a) exposure.
   b) conclusion.
   c) residual risk.
   d) accepted risk.

8. A manager creates an Excel spreadsheet for his staff members to enter hours worked. The spreadsheet is then imported to the payroll system. What is the greatest risk?
   a) Staff getting paid for hours not worked.
   b) Employees may see the numbers of hours worked by others.
   c) Staff do not enter hours worked.
   d) The spreadsheet is not signed by employees.
   e) The spreadsheet cannot be printed properly.

9. Outsourcing increases
   a) audit risk.
   b) control risk.
   c) inherent risk.
   d) detection risk.

10. When the shareholders' auditors find that internal controls are less reliable than expected, they should
    a) assess control risk as lower.
    b) increase materiality.
    c) reduce the planned detection risk.
    d) assess inherent risk as higher.

CHAPTER THREE – IT GOVERNANCE AND GENERAL CONTROLS

"He who controls the present controls the past. He who controls the past controls the future." - George Orwell, author and journalist.

We have talked about information systems risks in the last chapter. To mitigate risks, organizations should put in place a system of internal controls. The system of internal controls actually is not a stand-alone system, rather, it contains internal controls that work their way into normal transaction processing, in order to be effective on an ongoing basis.

The extent of internal controls to be designed and implemented depends on risk assessments. Based on the result of assessments, internal controls should be implemented to address the five components of a system: infrastructure, software, procedures, people and information. Controls should be implemented to mitigate the risks of lack of authorization, inaccuracy, incompleteness, untimeliness, fictitious information and inefficient processing. Controls have to span the entire transaction cycle of input, processing, output and information storage. We repeat here the risk matrix which should be used to ensure controls address the transaction cycle and risks.

	Complete	Authorized	Accurate	Timely	Occur	Efficient
Input						
Processing						
Output						
Storage						

Internal controls to address the above can be manual or automated. Most manual controls also involve system generated information. The Y axis of this control matrix is more useful for developing internal controls that directly address a transaction cycle, i.e., application controls. Application controls are internal controls that apply to a specific business system, e.g., an edit check of a student number. The transaction cycle is less relevant to developing infrastructure controls, also called general controls. A general control applies to multiple systems, e.g., a network password. The matrix, on the whole, is useful for both general and application control development. We will discuss general controls in this chapter and application controls in Chapter Six.

DEFINITIONS OF INTERNAL CONTROL

An internal control is an instruction, tool or procedure to mitigate risk. A procedure may be manual or automated. It is not simply a statement of what should be done, nor does it simply state what the organization wants to achieve. An internal control is specific and should indicate the subject, object, action and when it is to be performed. Although a control often carries the word "ensure", that word is not enough. The objective of a control is to ensure that certain risk is mitigated. A statement containing only the "ensure" clause is a control objective, not the actual control. A control must be action oriented, not just objective oriented.

Strictly speaking, an internal control is not an essential activity to carry out a transaction. However, a transaction without internal control is risky. For example, identifying a customer in an ATM transaction is not an internal control even though "identification" is commonly included by security specialists when designing the "identification, authentication and authorization" model. The ATM has to identify the customer in order to pull up the account information, so identification is an essential activity. Authentication is a control because strictly speaking, a bank can choose not to use authentication. Without authentication, identification is subject to higher risk.

Internal controls should not be a separate set of system functions or procedures. Instead, to ensure that internal controls are carried out consistently with management ownership, management should integrate internal controls in systems and operation procedures. Some controls of a policy nature may be published and communicated on a standalone basis, e.g., a code of business conduct. In addition to forming part of a system's computerized functions and operation procedures, internal controls should be compiled in a separate document, e.g., an internal control manual. This separate compilation is performed to help management to continuously assess risks and get their fingers around what controls are in place in the organization. Internal control objectives should be included in this compilation to help people understand the purpose of the controls. Management can use the internal control manual to organize, coordinate and correlate internal controls to provide sufficient redundancy to prevent risks from being ignored while avoiding significant duplication of effort. Such correlation is called a plan of internal controls. This plan should be documented and be used as a basis for employee training.

Risk always exists. For example, it could rain on any day. But a reasonable person would not carry an umbrella every day. So when is an internal control necessary? It is important to keep in mind that internal controls should be enough to provide reasonable assurance that material risk does not remain. The key words are "reasonable" and "material". For example, I don't have to give much thought to cost effectiveness or whether a favorite chocolate bar has passed the "best before" date by a week if it goes on sale for 25 cents each. That's materiality. "Reasonableness" means the cost of the control must not exceed the amount of risk being mitigated. It also means that the control is not too onerous and is user friendly. A control that is not user friendly, no matter how appealing it is on paper, will run a high risk of non-compliance.

Employees should be trained on internal controls and understand the objectives. This will help ensure compliance. Here is a story that shows the importance of training and understanding objectives.

A computer equipment manufacturer prides itself on communicating its strategies so that every employee is aware of the company goals. An auditor decided to test this claim. She asked a summer student sweeping the factory loading dock how his job related to company goals. The summer student replied as follows.

"My company's goal is to reduce the cost of its products. A major cost is inventory. We recently shifted to just-in-time production to reduce inventory stocking cost. This means our suppliers deliver products to us every two hours. If I don't clean the loading dock before the next load arrives, we are unable to accept delivery. This would set back the production schedule in the plant and increase the cost of production. We would also have the added cost of returning the material to the supplier."

This guy now works in a Big Four accounting firm.

Internal controls and IT controls have been defined and the related objectives and principles have been discussed at length by AICPA, the Institute of Internal Auditors (IIA) and ISACA.

It is the responsibility of the system owner to design and implement internal controls. S/he of course will have to rely on technical staff. For internal controls that apply to the infrastructure instead of a specific transaction processing system, the executive responsible for the infrastructure is responsible for designing and implementing internal controls, i.e., the CIO. The executive responsible for internal controls is also responsible for communicating internal controls to people and monitoring for compliance.

Compliance monitoring can take the following measures:
- Surveying employees.
- Meeting with unit managers.
- Transaction walkthrough, taking one or two transactions to test system and manual controls.
- Monitoring control, i.e., controls over controls e.g., management review of logs.

Compliance monitoring must be structured and disciplined. The chief risk officer should set up a process for compliance monitoring by system owners. This should be a requirement stated in the risk management policy.

AICPA Definition of Internal Control

According to AICPA Statement of Auditing Standard (SAS) 78::

Internal control is a process, effected by an entity's board of directors, management and other personnel, designed to provide reasonable assurance regarding the achievement of objectives in each of the following categories:

127

· *Reliability of financial reporting:* This category relates to the preparation of reliable published financial statements, including interim and condensed financial statements and selected financial data derived from such statements, such as earnings releases, reported publicly.

· *Effectiveness and efficiency of operations:* This category addresses an entity's basic business objectives, including performance and profitability goals and safeguarding of resources.

· *Compliance with applicable laws and regulations:* This category deals with complying with those laws and regulations to which the entity is subject.

SAS 78 adopts the five internal control components in the COSO model: control environment, risk assessment, control activities, information and communication, and monitoring.

COBIT Definition of Internal Control

ISACA has developed Control Objectives for Information and Related Technology (COBIT). COBIT's definition of internal control is:
"The policies, procedures, practices and organizational structures designed to provide reasonable assurance that business objectives will be achieved and that undesired events will be prevented or detected and corrected."

According to COBIT, IT processes fall into four domains: planning and organization, acquisition and implementation, delivery and support, and monitoring. These domains consist of 32 processes facilitated by the following 5 classes of IT resources: data, application systems, technology, facilities and people. COBIT identifies 271 control objectives.

COSO Definition of Internal Control

The report of the Committee of Sponsoring Organizations of the Treadway Commission (COSO) released its report entitled Internal Control - Integrated Framework in September 1992. COSO included representatives of the following organizations: AICPA, IIA, Financial Executives Institute, the Institute of Management Accountants, and the American Accounting Association.

According to COSO, internal control is a process, effected by an entity's board of directors, management and other personnel, designed to provide reasonable assurance regarding the achievement of objectives in each of the following categories:

- Effectiveness and efficiency of operations - This addresses a firm's basic business objectives, such as maintaining performance and profitability goals and safeguarding assets.

- Reliability of financial reporting - This ensures the preparation of reliable financial statements.

- Compliance with applicable laws and regulations - This addresses compliance with laws and regulations to which the firm is subjected.

REGULATORY REQUIREMENTS ON INTERNAL CONTROLS

Organizations should be aware of the relevant legislation, regulation, and business practices in the countries in which they do business – in order to assess the organizational impacts and requirements. The United States Sarbanes-Oxley Act of 2002 (SOX) requires public companies to report on internal controls annually along with their financial statements to Securities Exchange Commission. Canada's Investor Confidence Rules contain a similar provision. Regulators of the financial services and energy industries also have smaller scale requirements for internal control reporting.

Sarbanes-Oxley Act

The Sarbanes-Oxley (SOX) Act was intended to reform public accounting practices and other corporate governance processes and shore up the capital markets in the wake of the Enron, WorldCom, and other corporate governance scandals. Although SOX does not specifically address the issue of IT controls, this does not mean IT can be ignored when performing the compliance reviews required by the Act. The Act is neutral with regard to technology, but the implication is clear that IT controls are critical to the organization's overall system of internal controls. IT controls address the secure, stable, and reliable performance of hardware, software, and personnel to ensure reliability of financial applications, processes, and reporting, they are significant elements of internal controls in any public company.

Some key IT control areas have been interpreted as not included in SOX compliance. These include disaster recovery planning, privacy policy, business continuity and business planning systems. The following is a brief description of the relevant sections of SOX related to auditors and IT Controls.

Sections 103 and 802

These sections establish rules for public accounting firms related to the audit of financial statements. They also require that the auditors test the internal control structures and attest to the strength of those structures. This must include a thorough examination of the IT controls that are fundamental to the system of internal control over financial reporting.

One specific requirement relates to the retention of records "that in reasonable detail accurately and fairly reflect the transactions and dispositions of the assets..." Again, this is strongly influenced by the way in which IT records are maintained and retained.

<u>Sections 302 and 404</u>

Section 302 of the act requires the chief executive officer (CEO) and the chief financial officer (CFO) to evaluate the system of internal controls and report their conclusions and any changes in controls.

They must disclose:

- "all significant deficiencies in the design or operation of internal controls which could adversely affect the issuer's ability to record, process, summarize, and report financial data and have identified for the issuer's auditors any material weaknesses in internal controls";
- "any fraud, whether or not material, that involves management or other employees who have a significant role in the issuer's internal controls".

Section 404 requires that the CEO and CFO must also produce an annual audit report that:

- assesses the effectiveness of the internal control structure over financial reporting,
- discloses all known internal control weaknesses, and
- discloses all known frauds.

This will cover all applicable IT controls including software change controls and application controls.

INTERNAL CONTROL CLASSIFICATIONS

There are two ways to classify internal controls. One is to classify them by function. The other way is to classify them by scope. By function, a control can be preventive, detective or corrective. By scope, a control can be general or application specific.

It is quite obvious that preventive controls are more effective than detective or corrective controls. However, there is a limit to which an organization can implement preventive controls before making the environment inflexible and difficult to operate. Further, preventive controls can break down because of system malfunction or human circumvention. Detective controls, which are less intrusive, are needed. When a problem is detected, corrective measures will have to be taken. Management should implement preventive controls to a point where the cost of additional preventive controls would outweigh the benefit. The remaining risk will still very likely be significant. To mitigate the remaining risk, management should implement detective and corrective controls.

In addition to preventing, detecting and correcting mistakes, controls are also needed to monitor other controls, i.e., to check if other controls are being complied with. For example, a system control to report on delinquent management approval of electronic timesheets is a control over control and it mitigates control risk instead of inherent risk. Another example is management review of bank reconciliations.

Controls can vary in scope. A control that applies to the entire organization is generally desired because it ensures standardization. However, such a control can make operation inflexible and ineffective where business units are exposed to different degrees of risks and a variety of systems are used. Thus, controls specific to environments and applications are also needed. Organizations should adopt a combination of general controls that apply to multiple systems and application controls that apply to specific systems. Both general controls and application controls can fulfill the functions of prevention, detection and correction. General controls should be designed and implemented first. Application controls should then be designed and implemented for each system.

In Chapter One, we discuss the five components of a system as procedures, infrastructure, software, people and information. Internal controls are needed to address all of these components. Internal controls can also take the form of procedures, infrastructure, software and people. Procedures include policies, standards and operation procedures.

Internal controls, whether general or application, start at the policy level. Procedures are instructions for users to interface with a system and interpret system information. Procedures are based on policies, which contain mandatory statements about governance, expected behavior and adopted principles. Policies are less fluid than procedures as the latter are used to guide day to day operation. Procedures are written to comply with policies. Because procedures are for people to use, they do not apply to automated functions. How do automated functions comply with policies? Such compliance is achieved in two ways. First, policy requirements should be included in systems development user requirements and design specifications that we will discuss in the next chapter. The extent of such compliance, however, is often questionable. For example, how long should a password be? To address this, standards can be created. Standards sit between policies and procedures. They also sit between policies and system specifications. Standards are changed more frequently than policies and less frequently than procedures and system requirements.

GENERAL CONTROLS

General controls can be classified as follows:
- Organization controls
- Software change controls
- Access controls
- Systems development controls
- Disaster prevention and recovery controls
- Computer operation controls
- IT performance measurement controls
- Intellectual property controls

ORGANIZATION CONTROLS

The objective of organization controls is to ensure that operations involving I & IT follow best practices that are consistent throughout the organization and compatible with customer and stakeholder expectations. Controls in this category include:

- An I & IT strategy that is congruent with the business strategy.
- A governance structure including a process to keep the board of directors informed of IT direction and major IT projects .
- An IT steering committee that oversees IT investments and provides IT direction.
- An audit committee made up of independent directors that provides oversight on internal audit coverage, external auditor selection as well as management actions to remedy control weaknesses and transaction irregularities. These functions include:
  - Approving the annual internal audit plan.
  - Approving the annual appointment of the financial statement auditors.
  - Approving other appointment of external auditors for special engagements.
  - Reviewing periodic reports on internal audit findings and holding management to correcting the deficiencies and mistakes.
  - Reviewing the annual shareholders' auditors report.
  - Reviewing the annual shareholders' auditors' management letter on internal control recommendations.
- Policies and procedures that address:
  - The responsibilities for IT investment, deployment, monitoring and controls.
  - The approval levels for IT investments.
  - IT risk assessment and acceptance, we discussed this in the last chapter.
  - Systems development, we will discuss this in the next chapter.
  - Procurement of IT products and services.
  - Hiring, including requirements for job posting, interviews, tests, reference checks and criminal record checks (for sensitive positions).
  - Staff development, including mandatory training plans, analysis and reporting of training achieved in relation to job descriptions. Organizations should also encourage and financially support professional memberships that are relevant to employees' responsibilities and help employees keep up with professional development so that their employees are more competitive than those in other organizations in the same sector.
  - Privacy, we will discuss this in Chapter Five.
  - Security, we will discuss this in Chapter Eight and Chapter Nine.
  - Computer operations.
  - Capacity planning.
- Organization charts and job description to cover every IT employee.
- A defined reporting relationship between the chief information officer (CIO) and a senior executive, who should be the chief executive officer or the chief operating officer (COO). If the CIO reports to other executives, the arrangement can make the CIO's role less effective as it sends the message that the organization does not view IT as top corporate priority. For example, if the CIO reports to the chief financial officer, the IT department may receive undue influence in devoting its resources to

support financial systems. A similar problem would occur if the CIO reports to a line executive. Organizations that have CIOs reporting to lower levels than the COO will find it hard to attract top calibre people to fill that role.

- A designated executive accountable for information security.
- Segregation of duties between the IT department and business areas to support a process for independent approval and review of IT expenditure, facilitate the detection of errors, and prevent frauds and improper practices.
- Segregation of duties within the IT department to provide for independent approval and review, facilitate detection of errors and prevent frauds and improper practices. This may be less practical in small organizations, where heavier reliance will have to be placed on application controls to compensate.
- Procedures for hiring consultants to ensure value for money, proper approval and knowledge transfer to staff.
- Staff development procedures and a performance review process to ensure the organization continues to have high quality of IT staff.
- IT budget review procedures.
- Procedures for accounting and cross-charging IT expenditures. This deters unnecessary use of IT and holds managers accountable for effective and optimal IT deployment. The cross-charge rates must be competitive. It would be discomforting and counter-productive if the cross-charge rates are higher than market rates.
- Systems and procedures for IT asset and information inventory control.
- A skills database indicating who have the skills for each position in the organization. There should be enough redundancy built in.

I & IT Strategy

The board of directors should challenge management to develop an I & IT strategy that is congruent with the business strategy. The I & IT strategy should describe the direction of the IT environment in the organization over the time frame of the business strategy. The following information should be included:

- A description of the organization's dependence on I & IT to sustain and grow its business and operation. This will also entail how competitors are using IT. The criticality of IT in each business line should be assessed.
- The approach to managing the investment in and operation of IT. Will there be significant dependence on software and hardware vendors and how will this affect the organization's competitiveness?
- The organization structure for managing the IT investments and information systems.
- The staffing plan for managing and operating information systems. This should include projected attrition and a strategy for succession planning and staff development to ensure that the organization has competent human resources to develop, maintain and operate information systems.
- The cost and justification for annual IT investments including the maintenance of current IT assets and operations.
- IT infrastructure development plan.

- Systems development plan. We will talk more about this in the next chapter.
- eBusiness plan. No organization is immune to the Internet's influence. Most of them cannot compete without offering electronic business services. This global network enables big companies to act small and small companies to act big. For example, multi-nationals can use the Internet to reach individual customers anywhere in the world and use electronic business activities to study the pattern and preferences of retail customers in order to give them tailored attention. Small companies can similarly use the Internet to reach large corporate clients and do business with them.

IT Governance

IT governance is part of corporate governance. While it is clear that the board of directors, the CEO and the COO are directly accountable for corporate governance, it is less obvious as to who are accountable for IT governance. Should it be the CEO or the CIO? IT governance is about making sure that IT is used effectively to support the organization. The same parties accountable for corporate governance are also accountable for IT governance. In addition, the CIO is accountable.

AICPA defines IT governance as follows.

IT governance is a framework that ensures that technology decisions are made in support of the business' goals and objectives. IT governance is the responsibility of the board of directors and executive management. It is derived from corporate governance and is concerned primarily with the connection between business focus and IT management of an organization. The primary goal for IT governance is to assure that the investments in IT generate business value and the mitigation of risks associated with IT.

A steady influx of business regulations is forcing companies to find new strategies that minimize the burdens and maximize the benefits of addressing regulatory compliance. Companies can obtain a range of benefits from regulatory compliance, including more accurate financial reporting, improved visibility of risk, and better IT governance. IT governance is part of corporate governance and it provides the organizational structures to enable the creation of business value within information technology (IT). Part of this process is obtaining assurance that IT investments are only made in beneficial projects and that there are adequate IT control mechanisms. By aligning IT planning with organizational goals, IT becomes a key player in evaluating the business issues that factor into enterprise-wide decision making. Standardized frameworks for IT governance and accounting controls are among the tools available to companies that can be used to link Sarbanes-Oxley documentation activities with corporate IT management procedures. This resource area will provide you with the information and tools to meet the numerous challenges of IT governance and regulation.

Source:
http://www.aicpa.org/INTERESTAREAS/INFORMATIONTECHNOLOGY/RESOURCES/ ITGOVERNANCE/Pages/default.aspx, accessed on July 6, 2012.

IT governance includes mainly a framework to ensure that the right technology is used and technology is used right. This framework is made up of organization charts, staff, policies, standards, corporate procedures (as opposed to local procedures), training and monitoring systems. IT governance is of an assurance and monitoring nature, to assure shareholders that the organization's IT adequately supports the organization's business. It is not the same as the IT infrastructure, which is needed for day to day operations. In other words, if IT governance breaks for a day, business will still be as usual. But if it is absent for a month or a few months, the organization's competitiveness and survival will be in increasing doubt.

The CIO needs support from other executives in carrying out IT governance. Such support should be lent on a frequent basis formally and informally. An effective and common formal support mechanism is an IT steering committee. This should consist of the C-suite of executives and the heads of major business lines. For example, the IT steering committee of a major Canadian bank consists of the CEO, COO, CIO, CFO, chief administrative officer, the treasurer as well as the heads of personal banking, commercial banking, corporate banking, government banking and international banking. The mandate of this committee is to set the IT strategy, approve major IT projects, monitor major IT projects, make major IT risk decisions and provide ongoing senior level guidance in IT risk management.

Responsibility of the Board of Directors

The board is expected by shareholders to set business direction for the organization and monitor operation to ensure that it is in line with the stated direction. Monitoring is performed by means of reviewing information provided by management. Most organizations have board committees to focus on specific areas of corporate significance. Some committees are required by regulations, e.g., the audit committee is usually a requirement of the securities regulator, the industry regulator or legislation for incorporation. Typical committees are audit, compensation, corporate governance as well as health and safety. Why isn't there an IT committee?

The board looks at IT as a means of doing business, i.e., to make business more efficient. Some boards of large companies that have corporate governance committees use them to address IT governance. Some IT companies indeed have technology committees, and this is a favorable trend for all public companies, to show more transparency to shareholders that the companies will continuously review the use of IT to be more competitive.

Segregation of Duties

Employees that can perform a variety of duties are valuable to the organization. However, in reality, there are few, or no supermen and superwomen. Thus, after a certain point, the more different tasks an employee performs, the less good s/he is on any of

135

them. It is important to limit the types of work an employee performs. Such limitation serves the purpose of building expertise and efficiency, as well as preventing mistakes and fraud. It is also important to cross train employees and expand their horizon. Segregation of duties does not work against that. Employees can be cross trained under supervision to build their knowledge in other areas but they don't have to be given the access to information or charged with the expectation to do work in multiple areas regularly. Segregation of duties supports the control criteria of accuracy, authorization, occurrence and efficiency.

The purpose of segregation of duties is to provide opportunities for errors to be detected and to reduce the opportunity for irregular practices or fraud. Incompatible duties should be separated. Two functions are incompatible if they satisfy the following criteria:

- Having one person performing both functions will unduly and significantly increase the risk of fraud.
- Having one person performing both functions will unduly and significantly increase the risk of errors not being detected.
- Assigning the functions to at least two persons will not significantly impair operation effectiveness.
- Assigning the functions to at least two persons will not significantly reduce operation efficiency.

Segregation of duties is therefore based on risk assessment. Where it is impractical to segregate duties because of staff constraint, the organization can mitigate the resultant risk with more rigorous exception reporting and management review.

Segregating IT from Other Functions

The IT department should be separated from business units and other corporate functions. Simply stated, the CIO should have no other responsibilities and IT people should report to the CIO but not to the business units or other corporate functions. The purpose of this segregation is threefold.

First, this allows IT people to focus on IT, which is a specialized area that calls for frequent knowledge upgrade. Letting IT people work on non-IT areas or projects would distract their focus. Similarly, business units and other corporate areas need to develop their own expertise that is not directly related to IT. They view information technology as a set of tools and this is the right attitude. If IT people were to run the business or accounting, there is a danger of letting the tools drive the business instead of the right approach of letting business requirements determine the tools.

Secondly, IT should be separated from the business and other corporate functions in order to establish proper accountability. If IT performs other functions, it would be easier for the users of those other functions to "blame it on the system" when something goes wrong. Business units and corporate executives should take ownership of their functions and results. They should determine how much information technology to use and how many internal controls to implement, instead of letting IT decide.

Thirdly, organizations should distribute functions to avoid one party having extensive control over transaction processing. The information technology department has full control over information and significant damage can result from mistakes or rouge behavior. Organizations should not add to this risk by giving IT people the responsibility for initiating accounting entries or business transactions. By separating this from IT, there is more assurance that system information is adequately supported by legitimate business transactions and accounting decisions.

Segregation of Information Technology Functions

For the same reasons as above, IT functions should be segregated to the extent practical. Obviously, segregation of duties has to stop somewhere, otherwise the organization will become extremely bureaucratic and people will spend more time communicating and seeking approval than actually doing the work. Research as well as industry experience in IT effectiveness and reliability indicate that systems development and computer operations should be separated. In addition to helping people focus, this separation would mitigate the risks of:
- systems developers implementing programs without approval,
- systems developers changing business information and
- computer operations people developing systems without approval.

In other words, separating systems development from computer operations prevents improper changes to systems and information. Within systems development, the following functions should be further separated to facilitate expertise development and prevent improper activities:
- Systems analysis (business interfaces)
- Systems architecture development
- Systems design
- Programming
- Testing
- Quality assurance
- Project management office

Similarly, the computer operations function of the IT department can be further separated as follows:
- Network operations
- Database administration
- Server administration
- Desktop administration
- Mobile technologies support

- Disaster recovery planning and maintenance
- Capacity planning
- IT research
- Information security

In large organizations, the following functions should be moved out of the systems development and computer operations areas to provide better focus and reduce the exposure to undue or biased influence from systems development and computer operations. These functions should report directly to the CIO.

- Information security
- IT research
- Quality assurance
- Project management office

Information security is increasingly important to organizations because of eBusiness and expanding reliance on trading partners. To some companies, customers and suppliers are treated as partners in that there is almost open system access between these parties. For example, a world retail leader lets some of its suppliers query its inventory database to find out what needs to be replenished. Such open connectivity raises the importance of information security. Further, cybercrime is an increasing threat to every organization and this heightens the importance of information security.

If information security reports to the executive in charge of computer operations, it may not receive adequate emphasis. When there is a crunch or financial pressure, computer operations may sacrifice security in favor of efficiency; and that can present an unacceptable risk to the organization. By aligning the information security function to report to the CIO, there is more assurance that information security will receive adequate emphasis in the organization.

Organizations need to keep up its competitiveness by using the right technology. Focused effort and a high degree of expertise are needed. An increasing number of organizations have established the position of chief technology officer reporting to the CIO to focus the effort of IT research and assessment.

The purpose of quality assurance is to ensure systems reliability by developing policies and standards, training IT people and performing independent testing before implementation. This is not to be confused with the assurance responsibilities of line executives and internal audit. Line executives should carry out periodic risk assessment of their own systems currently used in transaction processing. Internal audit tests and assesses systems periodically to provide independent control assurance. The main reason for the quality assurance function is to ensure that new systems are developed and implemented properly. In addition, this unit should be responsible for developing IT policies and procedures. Because of the somewhat independent nature of this function, i.e., independent of system design and programming, it should report directly to the CIO.

The role of the project management office (PMO) is to monitor IT projects to ensure timely and proper completion. Proper completion includes completion on target and budget. Because of the monitoring role of this function, it should report to the CIO.

In a large Canadian bank, the executive vice-president and CIO has the following direct reports:
- Senior vice-president of systems development
- Senior vice-president of computer operations
- Vice-president and chief information security officer
- Vice-president and chief technology officer
- Director of quality assurance
- Director of project management office

The chief technology officer (CTO) title is increasingly common in large organizations. This person is often viewed as the "technical CIO". S/he is actually the technical advisor to the CIO. This job serves to ensure that the organization uses the right IT, i.e., using modern IT to support the business effectively. Effective use also includes consistency and scalability across the organization. The CTO has a staff of technical IT specialists who perform research and beta testing.

Segregation of duties should be implemented using organization charts, job descriptions, procedures and access control.

Code of Business Conduct

Every organization should have a code of business conduct that instructs employees about what is acceptable and what is not acceptable in their dealings with customers, colleagues and other external parties. The code should also tell employees what is not acceptable in using organization resources such as email. We will discuss the relevance to IT resources in more detail in Chapter Eight and Chapter Twelve. Employees should be asked to acknowledge this code upon acceptance of a job offer and should be reminded periodically by means of email or a pop-up screen upon network logon.

Management of Consultants

IT consultants are commonly used to fill the gap between business requirements for IT support and available staff resources or expertise. Consultants are more fluid and expensive and therefore should be subject to rigorous justification to hire and close monitoring. They may not be as familiar with the organization's rules of dos and don'ts so may need more guidance than employees. Usually, an advantage they have over employees is their IT expertise. The following is a checklist that should be followed in hiring and managing consultants.

139

1. Follow the organization's procurement policy with respect to sending out requests for proposals. Establish a list of requirements and factors for assessing proposals to include technical requirements, reference checks, criminal record checks, desirable skills, knowledge and prices etc.
2. Inform the chosen and declined vendors in writing.
3. Obtain management signoff for the chosen vendor before the contract is signed.
4. Use the organization's standard contract which has been approved by the law department. Add information about the assignment.
5. Require proof of malpractice and liability insurance.
6. Include a statement of work that details the deliverables in the contract.
7. Require the consulting company to sign the following agreements:
    - confidentiality agreement to keep the client's non-public information confidential during or after the engagement, unless otherwise directed by the client;
    - assignment of copyright, giving the client copyright to all material developed by the consulting company or the assigned consultants during the engagement;
    - waiver of moral rights, therefore giving the client the right to use the developed work in any way it sees fit without breaking the law and to alter the work.
    - an agreement that discloses all inventions during the term of the contract within the scope of the statement of work and that grants the ownership of invention to the client at no additional cost other than the consulting fee covered in the contract.
8. Approve invoices based on examination of deliverables rather than just time sheets.
9. Meet with the consultant at least weekly to monitor progress.
10. Document a performance appraisal at the end of the contract. If the contract goes beyond six months, an interim performance appraisal should be documented.

SOFTWARE CHANGE CONTROL

Changes are always risky. Even obviously favorable changes are risky. A salary increase may be calculated incorrectly thereby short changing employees or causing unnecessary payroll expense. Change management is the process of mitigating the risk of changes. If you win a lottery jackpot, you will be riskier in the short term. You will be at a higher risk of being robbed and your driving may be less focused while your mind wanders to world wide travel.

Software changes are made from time to time, even for new systems. This is because no matter how much a system has been tested before implementation, there will be bugs discovered during operation, and the bugs require correction. Another reason is that business requirements change from time to time. Software changes need to be managed with approval, documentation, cost justification, testing and conversion. There also have to be controls to prevent unauthorized changes.

Internal controls are needed to ensure that software changes are implemented:
- only based on written management requests,
- completely,
- accurately,
- with authorization,
- on a timely basis, and
- efficiently.

Software change controls should include the following:
- Software change control policy and procedures
- Testing procedures
- Software library controls
- Software change tracking
- Code (program) comparison

Software Change Management Policy and Procedures

Almost all internal controls start with policies and procedures. Management states the control objectives and accountabilities in policies. Procedures tell people what controls to carry out, how and who should carry them out.

Every organization should have a software change policy. This policy will define who are authorized to request and approve changes. It will also set thresholds for approval in terms of the amount of human, software and hardware resources required to design and implement the change. In other words, every change request should be accompanied with a business case, no matter how simple the change is. A change request should state the benefit, quantifiable where practical, of the change. Requests should be generated by user area management and approved based on a schedule of signing authorities depending on the magnitude of the change in terms of resources required. The change management policy and procedures should address the following:

- Definition of what constitutes a software change. Basically, this means any change to a computer program instruction.
- Criteria for estimating the magnitude of the change, e.g., in terms of person days and human resources cost required to complete the change. Also, software and hardware resources should be estimated.
- A change request form that states the identity and rank of the requester, the identity and rank of the approver and the project manager for the change. No matter how small a change is, it should be assigned to a project manager who will likely manage a number of small projects concurrently. The project manager can be assigned by the requester, the approver or the CIO department. The required delivery date should also be specified. In organizations that cross charge IT cost, the cost center of the requester

141

should be stated. This means every change request should be a project or part of a project to enable tracking and ensure compliance with the software change policy and procedures.
- Criteria for justifying a change request based on cost and benefit.
- Criteria for ranking and approving change requests.
- Types of testing required and the responsibilities. Many large organizations use a change control board made up of IT management and a cross-section of managers from the organization. This board is similar in composition to the IT steering committee but at a lower level. Its mandate is to review and approve changes. There should be criteria for referring change requests to this board and criteria for the board to use to approve. The criteria should include the cost and benefit of the change, impact on current systems and the risk of the change. Risk assessment of a change request should be made in accordance with the organization's risk assessment and acceptance policy that we discussed in the last chapter.
- Naming conventions for programs, e.g., if this is 101st program in the system, how is it numbered and named?
- Stages of approval and approvers.
- List of approvers.
- Criteria for and extent of system testing.
- Separation of development, testing and production (operation) libraries. A library is a collection, like a folder, of programs.
- Tracking of source and object code (programs).
- Tracking of change requests.
- Forms and related documentation for closing a change request.

Software Library Controls

A system library is a collection of computer programs for a system. It is like a folder of files, except that the files are computer programs. It is not the same as the system itself, which consists of an integrated set of computer programs that have been compiled and linked and is fully operational. The purpose of a system library is to keep track of the versions of computer programs during development and in operation. A library consists of the source code and object code to keep track of completeness and facilitate changes.
Access to system libraries should be restricted. Large organizations should use automated tools to track and control program movement during development, testing and implementation. Such a tool is commonly called a software change management system.

Source Code vs Object Code

The word "code" is commonly used to collectively refer to computer programs. A program in the form of the chosen programming language is called source code. Common examples of programming languages include C and Java. Source code is understandable to programmers but not the operating system. For computer programs to be operable, they must be translated to computer languages (machine languages). A program translated to a computer language is called object code. This translation process is called compilation. Compilation is an automated process. Once a programmer highlights the source programs and clicks "compile", the programs will be compiled to a big object code file. An example of such a file is a .exe file that we sometimes download from a Web site.

A source code instruction (a line of code) is often compiled to several lines in object code. This is because a programmer does not have to worry about how much hardware resource like real memory to allocate and how to keep track of real time calculation and intermediary results in RAM and the central processing unit. At the end of compilation, the lines of code are usually linked to one object file, like a .exe file.

What is a computer language? It is the collection of terms including nouns and verbs that are understandable to the computer's operating system. The operating system (e.g., Windows) in turn interacts with the central processing unit (CPU, the computer's brain) and peripheral devices like input, storage, output and memory. In the 1940's and 1950's, computer programs were often written in computer languages. Programmers had to understand the operation of the CPU and peripheral in order to program and a program could take days to write. As computers became more powerful and programs grew in functionality and length, it became inefficient for programmers to write programs in computer languages. Programming languages of a more narrative nature like PL/1, C++ and Common Business Oriented Language (COBOL) were invented to make programming more user oriented and efficient. However, even today, software that interacts directly with the CPU like an operating system and electronic circuit control functions still has to be written in computer (machine) languages.

Programs written in programming languages are also more portable. That is, a program written to run on a Mac computer can quite easily be modified to run in Windows by recompiling it using a Windows compiler for that programming language. However, a program in object code for a Mac computer cannot be run on a personal computer because of the different architectures of these computers.

Programmers' Personal Library (program writing and programmer's own testing)

When a programmer is assigned a change request, s/he needs the current version of the programs to be changed or interfaced. S/he can go fetch the programs directly or obtain them through a change control coordinator. The change control coordinator is part of the quality assurance department described earlier in this chapter. In a large organization, there may be several change control coordinators who are assigned responsibilities for different business areas. The latter is a more desirable approach as it ensures proper segregation of duties. The programmer then makes the changes and writes new programs. While s/he is doing that, no one should have access to the "work-in-progress". Such work-in-progress should be in the programmer's own library. In this library, the programmer will also conduct testing. When a programmer is satisfied that the programs work, s/he will ask the programming manager to review and approve. It is impractical for

143

the programming manager to review all the programs. In practice, the manager will peruse the programming documentation (narrative description in the form of comments instead of the actual program steps) and review selected and critical code. To supplement his or her limited review, the programming manager usually asks other programmers to review the code and conduct peer testing. Each programmer should have full access to his or her own library and read access to a common development library.

Development Library (peer testing or string testing)

When the programs undergo peer review and testing, they should be located in the development library. Every programmer in the group can have read access to this library but only the change control coordinator should have write access. When programs are ready for peer review and testing, the programming manager will inform the change control coordinator who will then take the programs from the programmers' personal libraries and put them in the development library. The actual fetch and deposit of programs will likely be via the software change management system. The peer testing should use more data and be more rigorous. It is also called string testing because a string of programs is tested together including their interfaces.

Only the change control coordinator should have the access right to move programs into the development library. No one else should have update access to the programs. What happens if the peer testing identifies program flaws? The programming manager will be notified and the programs will be returned to the authors or reassigned to another programmer to fix. In either case, the programs will be transferred to a programmer's personal library via the software change management system.

System Integration Test Library (system integration testing)

Once the programs have passed peer testing, they should be subjected to more rigorous testing in an integrated manner. This means testing the programs along with the rest of the system or major module and including even the programs that have not been changed. This is called system integration testing (SIT). It is the change control coordinator's job to move the programs from the development library and the related but unchanged programs from the production library to the test library. In large organizations, there may be different coordinators that control different libraries, e.g., one coordinator controlling the development library and another coordinator controlling the test library. We will discuss production library in a few minutes. Integration testing is more rigorous than peer programmer testing because it includes interfaces with the entire system or module. A module is a major section of a system consisting of a lot of functions. Whether the entire system has to be tested or only certain modules are tested depends on the extent of programs being changed. The criteria should be stated in the change control procedures.

Only the change control coordinator should have the access right to move programs into the test library. No one else should have update access to the programs. There should be backup change control coordinators.

Who should perform integration testing? These testers should not be programmers in order to maintain objectivity. They should be dedicated testers. Their background does not have to be in IT. In fact, some large organizations have hired liberal arts graduates or transferred business unit employees to be testers. A tester has to be meticulous and good in documentation. The former CEO of a major North American bank was a system tester for a year soon after he graduated with a bachelor degree in history. Testers have no access to source code and have only the access right to run object code.

What happens when program flaws are revealed in system integration testing? The programming manager is informed and the programs are sent back to the authors or reassigned to be fixed. The programs then have to go through programmers' own testing and peer testing before returning to the test library for system integration testing. In other words, a flawed program has to go back to square one instead of being corrected midway in the process (which is dangerous because the correction will then tend to be haphazard).

Where do the change control coordinators work? They are part of the Quality Assurance area.

User Acceptance Test Library

After system integration testing, the system changes are subjected to user acceptance testing (UAT). The testers are user representatives. This is the last phase of the iterative test cycle. It is a little less time consuming and extensive than system integration testing because at this stage, the system changes have been tested exhaustively in terms of reliability. UAT will repeat the functional tests in a smaller scale, e.g., using less extensive test data. In addition, it will include testing for system performance efficiency, user friendliness as well as comprehensiveness of the system reports and user procedures.

Only the change control coordinator should have the access right to move programs into the UAT library. No one else should have update access to the programs. What happens when program flaws are revealed in UAT? The programming manager should be notified and the programs are sent back to the authors or reassigned to be fixed. The programs then have to go through programmers' own testing, peer testing and SIT before returning to UAT. Testers have no access to source code and have only the access right to run object code but not to update object code.

Production Library

Once programs are signed off by users as having passed UAT, they are ready for implementation. A change control coordinator will move these programs from UAT to the production library. No one else should have update access to the production library. The production library consists of programs that are used in transaction processing, i.e., live programs. Because of the importance of the production library, movement into this library should require actually two change control coordinators, i.e., the change management system should require dual logon to implement any change.

The production library should use different servers for source code and object code. This is because source code is not needed for transaction processing. Keeping object code in a separate server helps prevent version mix-up and unauthorized access. The server used to store source code should be offline and subject to very limited access.

Movement of Source Code and Object Code?

A common question is whether the source code only or the object code only should be moved between libraries or both? Let's explore the pros and cons of these three options.

Option 1: Moving Source Code Only – This means that the source code has to be recompiled in the destination library because in order for the programs to be used for testing, they have to operate in a computer (machine) language.

Option 2: Moving the Object Code Only – There is no recompilation needed.

Option 3: Moving Both Object Code and Source Code – There is no recompilation needed.

On surface, option 1 seems to be the least desirable.

Even though source code, if everything goes well, is not needed in the common development, SIT and UAT libraries, it is needed in the production library. This is because when a programmer begins working on a changed request, s/he needs the current source code, which resides in the production library. The production library consists of programs that have been fully signed off and are working. This is the official version of the programs. Therefore, to maintain continuity and ensure completeness of transferring programs at each stage, source code should be moved between libraries throughout the cycle. Now option 2 does not look attractive. Further, when testing reveals a program bug, the software change management system will need the associated source code to tell the change control coordinator which source programs have to be fixed. So it is important to have source code in all libraries.

Option 3 moves the source code and object code between libraries. This introduces the risk of source code not compatible with object code because the wrong versions were moved. For example, the change control coordinator may have moved version 3 of object code but version 2 of source code. Moving is prone to losing things.

Under option 1, although only the source code is moved between libraries, object code can be created in each library by compiling from the source code. This ensures that object code is compatible with the source code. Option 1 seems to be the most desirable method to ensure synchronization between source code and object code. However, one would argue that if the wrong version of source code is moved, the compiled object code will be wrong. Well, let's adopt another option, option 4, which is the safest.

Option 4 – Move the source code and the object code to the next library. Once moved, recompile the source code and compared the compiled object code with the moved object code. This will make sure the correct versions of source code and object code have been moved.

Software Change Environments

For each library discussed above, there should be a hardware environment. The purpose of the environment is to hold the library and restrict access. In a large organization like a bank, an environment may be a data center. In smaller organizations, it may be local area network or even just a server.

A word of caution about the production environment is that the source code should be kept offline. Many production environments are online and even Web enabled. The source code, however, does not have to be online, in order to avoid unauthorized change.

Emergency Changes

Emergency system changes are inevitable. A common purpose is to fix a system problem to prevent or avoid prolonged outage. There is usually not enough time for the rigorous testing or documentation of testing normally performed. It is important that emergency changes be thoroughly tested after implementation and documentation should be brought up to date. To ensure that emergency changes are properly documented, tested and approved, the change management system should track these changes and report to the appropriate manager for actions. In fact, today's change management systems should automate documentation in terms of version control and audit trail as much as possible and prevent alteration or deletion of the audit trail. It should also send automated notifications to management and the quality assurance department.

Source Code and Object Code Comparisons

Periodically, IT management should use software tools to compare the current source code with the backup or with yesterday's source code to identify changes. Changes should then be reconciled to the approval audit trail. Both source code and object code can be compared between versions. Source code comparison is more informative as it is easier to reconcile to audit trail; this is because there are more source code modules than object code modules. Many source code modules are usually compiled to one object code module; e.g., when you download software (object code), there is one executable file which is the compiled result of many programs. So if object code is compared between days, a difference in size won't give the quality assurance people much clue as to which functions have changed. If an organization does not have the source code, such as using SAP, an integrated accounting system purchased from a software vendor, it should still perform object code comparison.

ACCESS CONTROLS

Access controls are increasingly important as organizations expand their use of eBusiness and open their networks to the world. Organizations need to secure access to the computing environments and specific systems. Access controls support software change controls and organizational controls such as segregation of duties because for example, without access controls, a programmer can install programs without approval. Access controls can be general in nature or specific to applications. Many techniques are equally applicable in a general scope and a specific environment, e.g., a password can restrict access to the general network, another password can be used to access the payroll system.

Physical Access Controls

In spite of the increasing use of technology in all organizations, basic physical security is still important. In fact, it is becoming more and more important as computing devices are smaller and can hold a growing quantity of data. Here are some examples of key physical access controls.

- A system to record access.
- Access cards
- Access control procedures for premises that house hardware or software.
- Biometrics for granting physical access
- Fire and flood protection.
- Locks for portable hardware.
- Mantraps
- Restricted zones within a building
- Security guards
- Unmarked data centers.
- Video surveillance for multiple levels of access restriction for sever rooms and data centers.

Information Access Controls

Here are some examples of key information access controls. Information access controls take the form of policies, procedures, independent review and software functions. The last category is also called logical access controls.

- An information security policy that defines accountability and responsibilities.
- A process for assessing the sensitivity of information and linking sensitivity to security tools.
- Security standards to address:
  - Appropriate use of information systems.
  - Confidentiality agreement with employees and contractors.
  - Cryptography
  - eBusiness
  - Email
  - Incident response.
  - Intrusion prevention and detection.
  - Investigation.
  - Privacy
  - Remote access.
  - Security check as part of hiring process.
  - Server and workstation administration.
  - System security updates.
  - User authentication including password controls.
  - Virus detection and removal.
  - Vulnerability assessment.
  - Wireless security.
- A repository of information owners which contains names and titles of designated owners of systems. There should be one owner of each system. The owner will decide who can have access to the system and information stored in the system.
- Procedures for:
  - access granting and disabling.
  - access violation review.
  - investigating anomalies.
- Access logs

General access controls are increasingly automated and these include:
- Anti-virus detection tools
- Encryption software
- Firewall to protect the organization's network from the Internet
- Intrusion detection system
- Intrusion prevention system
- Passwords
- Single sign on
- Two-factor authentication
- Virtual private network

SYSTEMS DEVELOPMENT AND ACQUISITION CONTROLS

Studies show that the average organization spends about half of its IT budget to acquire and develop systems. A large percentage of IT projects fail to be implemented or fail to deliver the promised benefit. Common reasons for project failures include the following:

- Lack of senior management attention and review
- Unclear user requirement
- Incorrect or inaccurate user requirement
- Incorrect design
- Inadequate testing
- Unrealistic business case that understates cost and overstates benefit
- Incorrect or incomplete conversion
- Inadequate infrastructure

To mitigate these risks, an organization should have a systems development methodology that includes criteria for initiating and approving IT projects, documentation and testing standards as well as requirements for checkpoints and signoffs. We will discuss this in more depth in the next chapter.

DISASTER PREVENTION CONTROLS

We experience or see mishaps almost every day. Earthquakes, tornados, floods, fires, "break and enter" and terrorist attacks are common occurrences. These events can damage buildings, offices, files, computers and information storage media. Some of these are not within the control of most organizations. For example, earthquakes and tornados are beyond business organizations and even some governments to predict, let alone controlling. However, incidents of a smaller scale can be controlled by organizations.

Incidents such as fire, flood, "break and enter" or overheating are well within the capability of most organizations to prevent. Disaster prevention controls for these events include the following:

- Alarm systems.
- Close circuit TV and monitoring stations.
- Fire extinguishing devices.
- Hardware performance and capacity monitoring.
- High capacity air conditioner in the server and storage media rooms to prevent damage from heat and humidity.
- Locate the data center away from hazardous or high crime areas.
- Preventive maintenance monitoring.
- Preventive maintenance schedule.
- Redundant communication lines, servers and storage media, e.g., redundant array of independent disks (RAID). RAID is a technology to write the same data to multiple disk drives. It is not a substitute for backup because the drives are controlled by the same server. Malfunction of the server can cause erasure of written data. RAID mainly

provides short term redundancy whereas backup provides long term redundancy. Servers should be configured to use RAID. For online systems that process a high transaction volume like banking and point-of-sales systems, redundant servers and communication lines are used. In many cases, the redundant servers and communication lines are actually used to record multiple copies of each transaction, for contingency. More organizations are moving towards virtualization, i.e., using software to pull servers together to tap unused hardware resources. Generally, this means putting more eggs in a basket. This increases the importance of redundancy planning and provision.

- Strong locks with multi-level barriers.
- Uninterrupted power supply including diesel battery and generator.
- Use fire retardant material for data center construction.
- Use raised floor construction to avoid floods.

For incidents that are beyond the control of organizations to prevent, reliance will be mainly on recovery controls. Such recovery controls will also be useful to recover from incidents that could have been prevented but were not prevented because of flawed preventive measures or because they were too expensive to prevent.

INCIDENT AND DISASTER RECOVERY CONTROLS

To ensure that operation is not significantly interrupted in the event of computer incidents and disasters, organizations should have internal controls in the form of policies, procedures, response teams, hardware, software and information. These controls should be formulated with coordination of the user areas and periodically validated. Recovery controls are really of a corrective nature. One might wonder why we have skipped detective controls. Controls to detect incidents that affect system performance will be discussed below under Network Monitoring Controls. Disasters do not need controls to be detected because their occurrence and impact are usually felt immediately.

Data Retention and Backup

A common risk in information systems is the loss of data. A rigorous backup schedule should be followed. The backup files must be kept offsite to avoid total data loss when the site that holds the original files is unreachable. Organizations should use automated backup tools such as electronic vaulting or storage access networks to ensure regular backup and avoid physical transfer of disks and tape. Backup logs should be reviewed periodically and backed up data should be retrieved for testing to ensure it is comprehensible. Employees should be given network folders to store their work files and be reminded not to store work files on local hard disks. Electronic vaulting uses online transfer of data to backup servers without using computer tape. A storage access network provides cross-departments and cross-locations storage of backup with online access; i.e., it is a LAN or WAN used only for backup.

Software Backup

Source code and object code should be backed up as it is changed. Because organizations tend to implement system changes only at night so as not to contend for system time with transaction processing, backing up source code and object code daily is enough. Smaller organizations may adopt even a weekly or monthly backup schedule, or when it is known that source code or object code has been changed.

Data Backup for Batch Systems

A batch system is one that updates data files at fixed intervals instead of when every transaction occurs. Examples of transactions that are processed on a batch basis are bill payments by customers, payroll and deposited checks. Even if we pay bills online and the money is deducted from our bank accounts right away, the payee does not get the money from our bank until the end of the day and therefore our account with the payee company will only be updated at the end of the day or the next day. Data backup for a batch system should be performed daily.

In every transaction system, there are two types of data files, master file and transaction file. A transaction file contains every transaction processed within a period. A daily transaction file consists of the transactions processed that day. Tomorrow, a new transaction file will be started.

A master file contains permanent and semi-permanent information. An example is a credit card account file. This file contains the cardholder name, card number, balance, interest rate, address, credit rating and recent transactions. This file is updated periodically by transactions.

Backed up transaction files should be kept long enough to satisfy the Canada Revenue Agency or Internal Revenue Service requirements as appropriate. That usually means seven years. To save space, the backup software usually compresses the backed up files. The backed up file should not be confused with the archived original files which are also compressed. The backed up file is an extra copy and should be kept off site.

The backed up master files do not have to be kept as long. A master file is not a file of history; instead it evolves. Yesterday's master file has been superseded by today's. Therefore, the importance of old master files is less than that of old transaction files. If an old master file is lost, it can be recreated using the transaction files and the master file previous to the one that has been lost. An organization should keep the original master file versions long enough to satisfy financial statement audit requirements. How long should the backup copy of old master files be kept? Industry standard indicates that the minimum should be three versions, i.e., the backup of the last three master files should be kept. This is often called the grandparent-parent-child approach. This approach involves a shorter cycle than that normally used to keep the original master files because the backup files are needed only if the original files are lost or damaged. In practice, most organizations surpass the grandparent-parent-child standard for backup retention. Grandparent-parent-child is more a concept than a limit in terms of the number of generations of backup master files to be kept.

How long should the original master files be kept? Even though a master file can be recreated from transactions, such recreation can be time consuming and prone to errors. The time it takes to recreate a master file may make the recreated file too late to satisfy business requirements. It is therefore important to keep the master file versions for a safely long period. The general convention is to keep them for two years, to allow enough time for financial reporting for the fiscal year to complete. After two years, old master files are seldom needed.

Data Backup for Online Systems

The requirement for transaction file backup is the same as that for batch systems because after a transaction is processed, the criticality of transaction data is the same between a batch system and an online system. As indicated earlier, because of the high frequency of online transactions and the higher likelihood that they are paperless, large companies can use redundant servers and disks to write every transaction to multiple devices and this satisfies the back-up requirement, because the multiple recording will also update multiple copies of the master file. If this redundancy method is not used, the master file should be backed up more frequently than once a day because the master file is updated when every transaction occurs. The master files change throughout the day, so backing it up only at the end of the day presents a major risk. For example, if the master file is damaged at noon, the organization will operate with significantly non-current master file information. Although the master file can be recreated from yesterday's master file and today's transaction file, that will take time and until it is completed, the organization will be operating with non-current balances. It is therefore critical to back up the master file several times a day. The end of day master file and transaction file should also be backed up.

Data backup should not be confused with data retention. Data should be retained sufficiently long to meet operational, financial reporting and statutory requirements. Backup is done to mitigate the risk of business interruption caused by the loss, damage or destruction of the original data files. Organizations should have a retention schedule. Also, data file labels should have a retention date indicating that the data cannot be erased before that date.

Incident Response Procedures

Although computers are fast and inherently accurate, its interface with people is not without glitches. Human to human interface is easier to comprehend and problems can be detected more interactively than computer to human interface. In the last chapter, we talked about the risks of computers going down, computer programs being wrong and people misusing information systems etc. These incidents can lead to unreliable information and financial loss. Organizations must have a set of procedures to address incidents.

A large number of incidents are security related. This is why the incident response procedures in many organizations are developed and maintained by the security department. However, the impact on the organization and the urgency for action are often the same between security incidents and non-security incidents. The escalation and remedial action depend on the incident's severity.

Incident response procedures should guide management in determining an incident's severity. For example, it is common in governments to rate an incident as severity level 1, 2, 3 etc. The severity level would call for different amount of resources and different layers of management to be involved in investigation and resolution.

Incident handling usually starts with the IT help desk. In cases where the incident cannot be resolved, procedures should be followed to escalate it to level 2 support. Level 2 support is staffed by subject matter experts. If the incident cannot be resolved there, it should be escalated to level 3 and so on. It is rare for an organization to have more than five levels in terms of technical support because the more levels there are the more bureaucratic the process will become. Meanwhile, the procedures should guide staff to keep management informed on an escalating scale.

Sample Information Systems Incident Response Procedures

1) An incident may be discovered by any of the following areas.
   a) Help desk
   b) Intrusion detection monitoring personnel
   c) A system administrator
   d) A firewall administrator
   e) A business partner
   f) A manager
   g) Information Protection Centre (IPC)
   h) An employee
   i) A customer
   j) Another outside party

2) If the initial discovery is made by someone other than a security administrator, the help desk or the IPC, it should be reported to the following units in the order of availability.
   A. IPC at 9054972882 and ipc@wiletec.com.
   B. Help desk at 9054644751 and ithelp@wiletec.com.

Reporting should be done by email and telephone, with email following the phone call. If the IPC does not answer, leave a voice mail and call the help desk. In either case, an email must be sent to the IPC following each incident reported by phone. If an incident is discovered by a security administrator or the help desk, it must be reported to the IPC by phone and email.

3) The help desk and IPC should log the following.

   a) The name of the caller.
   b) Time of the call.
   c) Contact information about the caller.
   d) The nature of the incident.
   e) What equipment or persons were involved?
   f) Location of equipment or persons involved.
   g) How the incident was detected.
   h) When the event was first noticed that supported the idea that the incident occurred.

4) The IPC will gather the following information:

   a) Is the equipment affected business critical?
   b) What is the severity of the potential impact?
   c) Name of system being targeted, along with operating system, Internet Protocol (IP) address, and location.
   d) IP address and any information about the origin of the attack.

The IPC will contact the business division incident response manager.

5) The IPC and the business division incident response manager will meet (eConference is fine) to discuss the situation and determine a response strategy. The following questions will have to be answered.

   a) Is the incident real or perceived?
   b) Is the incident still in progress?
   c) What data or property is threatened and how critical is it?
   d) What is the impact on the business should the attack succeed? Minimal, serious, or critical?
   e) What system or systems are targeted, where are they located physically and on the network?
   f) Is the incident inside the trusted network?
   g) Is the response urgent?
   h) Can the incident be quickly contained?
   i) Will the response alert the attacker?
   j) What type of incident is this? Exampled are virus, worm, intrusion, abuse and damage. An incident ticket will be created.

The incident will be categorized as follows:
Category one - A threat to safety or life.
Category two - A threat to sensitive data
Category three - A major threat to computer system reliability
Category four - A minor threat to computer system reliability

6) Team members will follow one of the following procedures as needed to formulate their response on the incident assessment:

a) Worm response procedure
b) Virus response procedure
c) System failure procedure
d) Intrusion response procedure - is critical data at risk?
e) System abuse procedure
f) Property theft response procedure
g) Website denial of service response procedure
h) Database or file denial of service response procedure

7) Team members will use forensic techniques, including reviewing system logs, looking for gaps in logs, reviewing intrusion detection logs, and interviewing witnesses and the incident victim to determine how the incident was caused.

8) If hacking has been determined to be successful or there is internal compromise, the IPC will contact the Forensic Team.

9) The Forensic Team will seek advice from the Forensic Manager and if a formal investigation is deemed necessary, seek the approval of the Vice-president of Information Security to start an investigation.

10) Team members will recommend changes to prevent recurrence.

11) Upon management approval, the changes will be implemented.

12) Team members will work with IT operations to restore the affected system. They may do any or more of the following:

a) Re-install the affected system(s) from scratch and restore data from backups if necessary. Preserve evidence before doing this.
b) Make users change passwords if passwords.
c) Be sure the system has been hardened by turning off or uninstalling unused services.
d) Be sure the system is fully patched.
e) Be sure real time virus protection and intrusion detection are running.
f) Be sure the system is logging events.

13) Documentation - the following shall be documented:

   a) How the incident was discovered.
   b) The category of the incident.
   c) How the incident occurred, whether through email, firewall, etc.
   d) Where the attack came from, such as IP addresses and other related information about the attacker.
   e) What the response plan was.
   f) What was done in response?
   g) Whether the response was effective.

14) Evidence preservation—make copies of logs, email and other communication. Keep lists of witnesses. Keep evidence for seven years after resolution.

15) Notify proper external agencies - notify the police if there is criminal implication.

16) Assess damage and cost - assess the damage to the organization and estimate both the damage and the cost of the containment efforts.

17) Review response and update policies - plan and take preventive steps:

   a) Consider whether an additional policy could have prevented the intrusion.
   b) Consider whether a procedure or policy was not followed which allowed the intrusion, and then consider what could be changed to ensure that the procedure or policy is followed in the future.
   c) Was the incident response appropriate? How could it be improved?
   d) Was every appropriate party informed in a timely manner?
   e) Were the incident response procedures detailed and did they cover the entire situation? How can they be improved?
   f) Have changes been made to prevent a re-infection? Have all systems been patched, locked down, passwords changed, and anti-virus updated?
   g) What lessons have been learned from this experience?

Disaster Recovery Plan

The 9/11 attack reminds us of the importance of disaster recovery. Every organization that relies on information systems should have a plan to help it recover from accidents and disasters. This plan should be more extensive than incident response procedures. To prepare the plan, an organization needs to first understand its information systems risks and business critical systems. A business impact analysis (BIA) should be performed for each mission critical system. The list of business critical systems discussed in the first chapter would be a strong basis for determining the complexity of the plan and the priority of recovery.

The disaster recovery plan should consist of the following:
- Types of disasters.
- Criteria for calling an incident a disaster and ranking disasters.
- Authority for calling disasters.
- The disaster recovery team, i.e., the people who will be called on to manage disasters. Key contact information should be kept current.
- Automated tool to contact the team, e.g., an organization can use an automated tool that has stored multiple contact points for each team member and at one click, the tool will send online notification to the team members within seconds.
- Disaster recovery procedures to include:
    - damage control
    - moving people and equipment
    - locating backup data and equipment
    - protecting systems that are still operating
    - resuming broken systems.
- Provision for alternate processing facilities, which may be a hot, warm or cold site.
- Priority of systems for recovery.
- Process and responsibilities for communication to executives, stakeholders and customers.
- Procedures for recovering from the disaster.
- Common scenarios and case studies on how they are responded to.
- Schedule of testing.
- Test criteria.

Some organizations call this a contingency plan. A contingency plan is actually wider in scope. It addresses more than just IT resources, e.g., space for office workers, how to deal with the press. In this book, we will study disaster recovery planning instead of contingency planning.

The disaster recovery plan (DRP) should be tested annually and a copy must be kept at an alternate location that is reachable to the team. The disaster recovery plan needs to be supported by regular data backup procedures, as without backup, it would be difficult to recover from a disaster.

The DRP should be developed based on a comprehensive BIA. BIAs should be performed by business unit executives who will charge their teams with preparing the assessment. The IT department can provide technical assistance in terms of the effect of IT disasters on business units. The process for system ownership and risk assessment discussed in Chapter Two should be applied to BIA. The business unit BIAs should be rolled up by the chief risk officer, and in the absence of that function, by the CIO. The business unit executives, chief risk officer and CIO will work together to prioritize the list of systems to be recovered in situations of limited resources. This list should be approved by the IT steering committee and in the absence of that committee, by the CEO.

The DRP is then developed by the IT department to ensure that there are significant IT resources to resume operation of the business critical systems within the tolerable periods of system outage. These systems are generally classified as tier 1, tier 2 and tier 3 etc. For example, a tier 3 system may be a system whose outage is tolerable up to a month. Subsidiary to the corporate DRP, there is a separate DRP for each business critical system. The system specific DRPs should be approved by the system owners. The overall DRP should be approved by the IT steering committee and the CEO, after the CIO's approval.

The DRP should be tested at least annually. Often, regular testing may take several rounds, e.g., when testing reveals a deficiency in the DRP or associated procedures, the deficiency must be fixed and testing will be reperformed. A successful test is one that reveals deficiency in the disaster recovery plan, that means a test must be comprehensive. Tests should be reviewed by the people who developed the DRP and DR team representatives. Test results should be signed off by the CIO.

Alternate Data Center

A DRP has to be supported by an alternate data center. Such an alternate data center can be a hot site, a warm site or a cold site. It may be sourced internally or contracted. The type of site and the extent of equipment in each site depend on risk assessment, i.e., the business criticality of systems and the risk that the organization wants to take. The organization's budget also affects the type of sites.

A hot site is one that is immediately available. It has hardware and software available, although not necessarily with the same capacity as the primary data center. A warm site usually has hardware but not software and documentation, so in the event of a disaster, it may take a few days to activate. A cold site has the premises but no hardware and software; the organization will have to make arrangement or call vendors to honor an existing agreement to install hardware and software in order to make the site functional. For each type of site, the site provider may be a company that specializes in disaster recovery facilities or a trading partner. The site may also be an internal facility. The backup site should be reasonably apart from the primary site to make the former easily reachable while minimizing the risk of both sites being destroyed by an accident. A rule of thumb is forty miles. An organization may use a combination of hot, warm and cold sites. For example, it may operate a hot site for its tier 1 systems and a warm site for its tier 2 systems.

COMPUTER OPERATIONS CONTROLS

These are controls to ensure that information systems are operated as scheduled and as needed. They include the following.
- Procedures to cover IT purchases
- Processing schedule
- IT deployment procedures
- Computer operations procedures
- Network documentation
- Server and network configuration
- Network transmission controls
- Service level agreements

Controls over IT Purchases

Every organization should have purchasing policies and procedures to ensure approval and value for money. These policies and procedures should apply to IT procurement. The risk presented by IT purchases goes beyond cost. Management should be aware of the total cost of ownership (TCO) of hardware and software, even if software is leased or paid for as annual licenses. TCO includes the purchase, lease or license cost, the maintenance charges by vendors, maintenance cost incurred internally, the cost of training and the disposition cost. Therefore, the approval levels for initial purchase, lease or license should be determined by considering TCO. For example, if TCO is $100,000, approval should be obtained from a manager with signing authority of $100,000.

Aside from cost, organizations should control the acquisition of software to ensure that the software is compatible with the organization's IT platform. A company using Windows throughout will not want people to go to a store to buy computers using other operating systems to connect to the company network without approval.

The acquisition policy and procedures should define who can request hardware and software, who will do the actual procurement and who will approve. The criteria for approval and justification should be stated. There should be periodic verification of inventory.

It is increasingly common for large organizations to set up a portal for employees to request hardware and software and for such requests to be routed to management for approval. The approved requests will then be sent by the portal to the procurement department; i.e., employees are not allowed to go to a retail store or an online vendor to buy hardware or software.

An organization should negotiate bulk discounts with hardware and software vendors. The discounted prices may be grossed up to include the organization's staff and overhead cost for managing the central IT procurement and related IT life cycle support like installation and ongoing technical support. However, such grossed up internal prices

160

should not exceed market prices for purchases, warranty and technical support, otherwise end user departments may be tempted to purchase computers, software and services directly from retailers; and that would defeat the procurement controls discussed above.

Controls over IT purchases support the control criteria of accuracy, authorization, occurrence and efficiency.

Processing Schedule

There should be management approved schedules to control network and system availability as well as when batch processing is to be carried out. The schedules should be monitored using software and deviations should be reported for explanations. The schedule should also be periodically reviewed to ensure that it meets business requirements and use hardware resources optimally. Process scheduling controls support the criteria of completeness, accuracy, timeliness and efficiency.

Hardware and Software Deployment Procedures

In addition to controls over IT purchases, organizations should have a policy and procedures to make sure staff are aware that installation of hardware and software must be approved by management and performed by designated specialists. This prevents inappropriate use of hardware and software which can violate maintenance agreements or licenses and cause system instability. These procedures will also help ensure that the organization knows exactly what computers are connected to the network, which is important for network monitoring.

The organization should have standard configuration parameters for hardware and software to ensure consistency throughout the organization. There are network tools that allow organizations to audit such configuration from server to server and from desktop to desktop. Staff should be prevented by the network from changing the configuration of their desktops or laptops. For example, a bank employee's office network ID gives that person ordinary user access to his or her computer, instead of "administrator" access, so s/he cannot install software.

Hardware and software deployment procedures support the control criteria of completeness, accuracy, authorization and efficiency.

Network and Hardware Operation Procedures

There should be procedures to guide system and network administrators to perform routine maintenance and respond to user questions. These procedures should be consistent with the processing schedule described earlier and the configuration procedures. Network and hardware operation procedures should be stored away from the servers to which the procedures apply to prevent losing a server and the procedures for running that server simultaneously. Network and hardware operation controls support the criteria of completeness, accuracy, authorization and efficiency.

In Chapter One, we mention the roles of the system administrator and database administrator. The former has full control of the assigned server and can change data and programs. The latter has full control over the database. These two functions must be separated because either one is powerful enough to cause significant damage if the employee is careless, not well trained, or rogue. Also, the operating system should be configured to log all database activities carried out by the database administrator (DBA) and the DBMS should then be configured to produce management reports on the DBA activities for regular review. Operating systems have the default setting of logging all system administrator activities and IT management should install software to take the operating system log and produce management reports for regular review.

Network Documentation

Network documentation is critical for an organization to plan and implement network changes, move servers and troubleshoot. Such documentation should include a minimum of network topology diagrams and related narrative description. It should be developed when the network is built and updated as necessary, especially after a network relocation or major system implementation. The documentation should be periodically verified to ensure currency. It should be protected from unauthorized access especially access through the Internet. Network documentation supports the criteria of completeness and accuracy.

Server and Network Configuration

Organizations should have a policy and set of procedures to guide such configuration, including a standard checklist compiled based on risk assessment. Configuration should be periodically reviewed to ensure it reflects the current policy, standards and procedures. The standard configuration should be saved as a software image for deployment on multiple servers and workstations to ensure consistency. Server and network configuration controls support the criteria of completeness, accuracy, authorization and efficiency.

Network Transmission Controls

It is preferable to prevent errors rather than to rely on error detection and correction. Preventing errors involves choosing physical media with low inherent data error rates and taking suitable care in designing physical and logical circuit configurations. For example, wires should be properly shielded, voice and data lines should be reasonably apart to avoid cross-interruption (cross talk). The choice of circuit also affects the error rate. Fiber is less susceptible to environmental interruption than telephone line and copper. Network transmission controls support the criteria of completeness and accuracy.

Networks should be monitored continuously to ensure availability, stability and efficiency. Organizations should have redundant servers and dynamic load balancers to minimize outage and bottleneck. Network tools should be run to identify bottlenecks. Network reports should be reviewed by management and an audit trail of corrective actions should be maintained. Data transmission redundancy should be built in to avoid data loss. A variety of methods of transmission redundancy should be deployed depending on the reliability of the communication circuit, the sensitivity of data and the cost of error correction. The common methods are parity check, redundant data check and echo check.

The ability to detect errors depends on the inclusion of extra data at the sender's end that can be verified at the receiver's end. The extra data is used only for error detection and will be discarded after the detection process. This extra data is called error detection value. You should understand the trade-off between using more or less error-detection value. Including more data increases the ability to detect errors, but also slows data transmission because of the extra data needed to be sent with the message. This is analogous to airport security.

Computer data is in bits and bytes. There are usually 8 bits in a byte. A byte can represent a character or a number. A byte usually can accommodate a maximum number of 256. Therefore a large number usually takes several bytes. Bytes are combined into a packet. An organization will adopt a packet size that is optimal for data transmission. The purpose of packetization is to allow a transaction or message to be broken into smaller strings of bytes (packets) so that the packets can travel in different routes to avoid bottle neck, i.e., finding the fastest combination of routes to the destination. It is similar to dividing an army into groups so they can find small openings to get through to the destination and once at the destination, they will be regrouped. We will discuss this more in Chapter Five.

Parity Check

This simple and old form of data transmission check method can detect about 50% of errors. This does not mean that data transmission using this method of detection is only reliable half of the time, because errors, in the first place, may seldom occur depending on the quality of circuit. Parity checking involves using the last bit of every byte as the check bit. A network can adopt the even parity mode or the odd parity mode. In even parity, the number of "1" bits in a byte, including the check bit, must be even; in odd parity, the number of "1" bits in a byte, including the check bit, must be odd.

If the network adopts the even parity mode, it will inspect every byte before transmission. If the number of "1" bits is even, the network will assign an additional bit as the check bit and make that bit 0. If the number of "1" bits is odd, the check bit will be assigned the value of 1. By so doing, the number of "1" bits in every byte, including the check bit, will be even. The receiving node (network point) can then count the number of "1" bits in each byte to make sure it is even. If it is odd, that means one or more bits have been changed along the way by a system software glitch, hardware malfunction, environmental condition or hacker.

For example, if the organization uses a 7-bit byte before assigning the check bit and an even parity mode, and the first 7 bits of a byte are 0101011, the check bit will then be assigned a value of 0, so that the number of "1" in the full byte will be even; if the first 7 bits are 0101001, the check bit will be assigned the value of 1.

The receiving node must be programmed to discard the check bit after checking for transmission accuracy. The receiving node may be in another organization, in which case, the sending organization will have to make that kind of agreement with the receiving organization, i.e., adopting even parity or odd parity.

If an even number of bits in a byte are off (either from 0 to 1 or vice versa), parity checking will not detect it, because of offsetting errors.

Redundant Data Check

This method is applied to a message, transaction or packet, instead of individual bytes. A packet contains a number of bytes. A standard packet contains 1,024 bytes. In applying this method, the message or packet to be transmitted is treated as a long binary number. A fixed number is then divided into the message to obtain a remainder. Common lengths of the divisor are 8 bits, 16 bits, 24 bits and 32 bits. The longer the divisor, the more reliable the method is, up to the point where the divisor reaches half of the value of the dividend.

The remainder is added to the message as the error detection value. The receiving node will repeat the calculation and compare the calculated error detection value with the received error detection value. A divisor of 16 bits will detect almost 100% of errors.

Echo Check

This means the receiving node returns what it receives for the sending node to check that it equals what was sent. This is usually done at a packet level. This is expensive as it doubles the traffic. However, it is very reliable as any missed bits will be detected. A node is a network connection point like a router, switch or server. Echo check is more reliable than parity check and redundant data check that uses a divisor that has fewer than sixteen bits.

Error Correction

If an error is detected by the receiver, it is usually corrected by retransmitting all or part of the message. However, when the distance is great such as in satellite transmission, retransmission can be too costly and the retransmitted data may be too late and affects usefulness, e.g., critical video or financial data. In such a case, the network should send enough data to facilitate error correction to take place automatically. This is called forward error correction. The extra data to be sent for error correction usually amounts to 50% to 100% of the original data. The use of the forward correction method should be based on comparison of the cost of extra data transmission and the delay involved in retransmission.

Service Level Agreement

The IT department of an organization often receives more requests for services than its resources can accommodate. It is important for the CIO to adopt a consistent methodology to review and prioritize user requests and communicate the response to such requests clearly and on a timely basis. Part of the methodology should be a costing mechanism that will be used to charge users for the cost of providing the services. When a user department is charged with cost, it will think carefully before requesting service. Once a service is promised for delivery, the users should know when to expect delivery, the basic quality expected and how to escalate problems. The above information, e.g., deliverables, cost, deadlines and problem escalation channels, should be documented in a service level agreement between the IT department and each major user department. These agreements will be similar but tailored to the business needs of individual user departments. However, the IT department should not charge market rates because it is not supposed to make a profit. A service level agreement supports the control criteria of completeness, accuracy, authorization, timeliness and efficiency.

Capacity Planning

Organizations should continuously monitor their infrastructure to assess stability and adequacy to support the IT strategy. Current technologies like cloud computing and virtualization should be considered to increase scalability. The capacity plan should be updated at least annually and should cover, hardware, network and the alternate data center.

IT PERFORMANCE MEASUREMENT CONTROLS

IT expenditure represents a very significant portion of an organization's budget and it seems to be increasing. It is estimated that a large North American bank spends about $2.5 billion a year on information technology. IT accounts for about 50% of capital spending in North America. Organizations invest in IT for two reasons. The more common reason is to increase efficiency. The second reason is to comply with regulatory requirement, e.g., a new tax. A question often in the mind of management is whether the desired efficiency is achieved. In other words, is the organization getting enough value from IT investment?

While it is widely accepted that IT can increase competitiveness, the question is how much. Will the next dollar spent generate more than one dollar of value? Can lower IT spending generate the same benefit? Can the money be better spent elsewhere in the organization? A number of research studies show that as much as 40% of IT projects fail to deliver promised business results.

Here are a few "failure stories".

- An insurance company hired a large system development firm to develop an integrated system. After spending $15 million, the company was unhappy with the project progress and replaced the developer; the project cost estimate was revised to $100 million.

- A Canadian city hired a system consulting firm to develop a $1.2 million billing and information system for its water and gas utilities over a three-year period. After paying close to $1 million, the city cancelled the project on the ground that no system had been delivered. The consulting firm filed a $2 million breach of contract suit.

- After more than four years of hard work and half a billion dollars spent in the early 2000's, Trilogy, FBI's project to modernize its technology infrastructure, had little impact on the Bureau's case management efficiency. (Source: InfoWorld, March 21, 2005)

Although inadequate project management is a common reason for project failure, it is also often evident that management underestimated the project costs. Many IT projects are undertaken based on economic justification that fails to materialize.

It is not enough to justify the cost of developing a system at the proposal stage. The basis for approving the undertaking a development project has to be followed through to avoid cost overrun and make sure the expected benefits are delivered. This process does not end when the project is completed. It will go on as long as the system is in use. Ensuring value for money is not just the responsibility of the project manager, IT management and systems developers, it is up to everyone who has a part in developing, maintaining, operating and using a system. Achieving value for money requires informed decisions, rigorous project management and a conscientious culture.

The following are measures that organizations should adopt to ensure that IT investments generate satisfactory returns to the organization.

Cross Charge IT Cost

This is an incentive for both the IT department and business units. Business units will expect the IT department to be cost competitive. Similarly, being charged for the IT resources they use, business units will be motivated to closely align system use and change requests with business plans. The internal charge rates should be lower than market rates; otherwise business units will go outside instead of using the IT department. If the internal cross-charge rates are not lower than market rates, it speaks to the inefficiency of the IT department.

Establish Key Performance Indicators

Ensuring value for money invested in IT is a continuous process and it applies to new and existing technologies. There are a number of indicators organizations can use to measure the value of the use of technology, or the value of information systems. A best practice is to generate annual report cards on the business critical systems. Here are some common key performance indicators.

Accuracy - The error rates in transaction processing and information generation should be recorded and reviewed. It is believed that 20% of the program code generates 80% of the system errors. The payback from identifying these programs is high. Such identification and remedies are an ongoing exercise, and over time, although this 80-20 rule still applies, the magnitude and number of errors should go down. If not, the system is probably too old or obsolete to warrant ongoing maintenance, and should be replaced. Accuracy also depends on the skills of people using the system, e.g., data entry skills. Keeping track of errors will help identify areas and staff members that need training or additional procedures.

Simple and seamless - Systems should be easy to use and complicated functions should be carried out behind the scene with minimal user interference. Manual adjustments and overrides cause inconvenience to customers and delay transaction processing; they should be kept to a low frequency of occurrence while still providing adequate checks for unusual and inappropriate transactions. Systems designers should strike a balance between richness of information on a screen and the ease of comprehension and navigation. For example, it is believed that each additional click customers have to make discourages them from completing a purchase.

The IT department should keep track of help desk calls, such a number is a good indicator of the ease of system use. A high volume of help desk calls is not necessarily negative, it at least shows significant system usage. The nature of the calls should be tracked to identify problems and trends.

Availability, capacity and responsiveness – Money is yours only if you can spend it. A system is useless if availability is uncertain or if it always keeps users on hold. IT departments should keep track of system availability and response time to troubleshoot and improve. Response time statistics should also address the system's ability to process transactions within prescribed timeframes. In addition, the reactivity of operations staff including the help desk should be tracked and reviewed.

System availability – System failures and down time should be tracked and reported to senior management periodically. Failures have to be investigated with action plans to prevent recurrence.

IT incidents – IT incidents should be tracked and reported monthly to senior management. Reports should include trend analysis of duration, losses, cost of resolution, types of root causes and status of corrective actions.

Usage rate – A frequently used system indicates value. However, the type of use should also be tracked. A system may be excessively used by certain groups and as a result is not always available to other users; or a high volume of usage may be confined to a subset of functions leaving a significant part of the system idle most of the time.

Rate of change - In today's globally competitive environment, change is the norm and change management is a day-to-day challenge. System changes are often implemented to make systems more useful. Quite often, a system could have been made more useful with more detailed design, better articulated user requirements and more thorough testing. It is therefore important to keep track of system changes to ascertain the extent of bug fixing and rework. Metrics should be maintained about the frequency and magnitude of changes. A system that undergoes constant changes, especially emergency changes, may be nearing the end of its useful life.

Redundant systems - As organizations grow and mature, users are always finding that existing systems do not meet their needs. In environments where systems changes are slow to implement, user areas may develop or procure their own solutions. It is important to identify and prevent duplicating systems between business units. To prevent and reduce unproductive overlaps, organizations should periodically review the inventory of systems with business units. How do you know the inventory is complete? Well, surveys and dialogs with business unit managers are important. Transparency will also help. For example, a repository of systems listed alphabetically and by function can be posted on the corporate intranet with contact names.

User satisfaction - User feedback is just as reliable as metrics that are collected from systems data. It is objective as long as the sample is unbiased. Feedback should address the indicators listed above and the quality of information, e.g., richness and relevance. An organization should collect data to measure the above metrics and report periodically to management including the CIO and the IT steering committee.

Staff turnover – A reasonable level of turnover is unavoidable and in fact healthy for an organization. Turnover allows an organization to bring in new blood and recruit from campuses to demonstrate its corporate citizenship. However, high turnover will lead to instability and it might be the symptoms of inequitable human resources policies, incompetent management or unreliable systems. Inadequate compensation can cause high caliber staff members to flee to competitors. IT management should track the turnover rate from period to period and between IT functions.

Training – It is critical for IT staff members to keep up with technology and system changes in the organization. A large organization should devote at least two weeks per year to training each employee. An annual training budget should be established to ensure people receive continuing education of a high quality. IT management should receive periodic reports on training statistics and types of courses attended to assess whether training is widely taken by IT staff members throughout the organization and also to assess the relevance of training to the organization's IT deployment.

Staff survey – Management has to listen to staff on an ongoing basis. To ensure that staff morale is high and there is candid two way communication, the IT organization should conduct an annual staff survey to identify significant issues with respect to communication, training, bureaucracy, system reliability and system performance.

User survey Some users often tend to blame mistakes on "the systems" or the IT department. It is important for the IT organization to find out how users feel about computer systems and services. A survey may reveal inadequate user training, inadequate user procedures, substandard system performance or unsatisfactory IT services. An annual survey should be conducted with users. Further, it is increasingly common for the IT help desk to ask the user to respond to a simple survey after each help desk ticket is resolved. Staff members who don't work in the IT areas of an organization sometimes criticize that IT people are not cost conscious and tend to use the scare tactic to obtain resources from senior management to build empires. Some even criticize that IT people are not disciplined, don't have a sense of urgency and seldom finish projects on time. Well, these perceptions in many cases are probably biased. However, to many people, perception is reality.

Performance appraisal - It is important for the IT organization to train its staff members, set high standards, monitor compliance with IT operation procedures, measure IT performance, understand user concerns and develop action plans to address user concerns. These practices should be applied to IT staff members at all levels. Lower level IT staff members are assessed more on their technical skills and deliverables. IT staff members at the management level should be assessed based on their administrative skills, leadership and deliverables. The more senior the level, the more non-IT skills should be measured. For example, a large Canadian bank includes financial control in every IT manager's performance appraisal.

There should be monthly report cards to inform senior management of the organization's effectiveness using the above performance indicators. Unfavorable trends should be discussed in senior management meetings and action plans should be formulated to charge all managers with reversing such trends that are within their control.

Return on investments in information systems is always more challenging to achieve than that for brick-and-mortar projects, partly because of technological advances and the perceived consequence of inaction. The increasing use of outsourcing, sometimes driven by short-term considerations, can heighten the risk of IT governance. Although there is no silver bullet, adopting the above measures can help to increase the value for money invested in IT.

Decisions help us start. Discipline helps us finish!

169

INTELLECTUAL PROPERTY CONTROLS

Information technology enables organizations to be more innovative. As a result, there is increasing reliance on intellectual property purchased or developed. Intellectual property purchased such as software should be protected from unauthorized use and this can be done mainly with access controls.

Intellectual property developed warrants more attention. It must be protected from unauthorized use and infringement of the property ownership. Access controls are critical. Also important are license contracts, contract compliance audits, non-disclosure agreements with employees and contractors, as well as registration with the appropriate intellectual property government offices under legislations such as the Copyright Act.

We will discuss intellectual property in more detail in Chapter Five.

MANAGEMENT CHECKLIST

1. Develop an IT strategy to be congruent with the business strategy.

2. Develop an IT directive or policy to provide high level guidance and a structure for IT practices including IT controls.

3. Develop and keep up to date IT organization charts that support segregation of duties between the IT functions and user areas as well as within the IT functions.

4. Develop and update job descriptions.

5. Develop IT policies and procedures to implement segregation of duties, security, software change controls, computer operations controls, privacy protection, disaster recovery controls and network monitoring.

6. Maintain separate libraries and environments for systems development, integration testing, user acceptance testing and production.

7. Establish an IT steering committee to oversee IT expenditures and review major projects.

8. Develop and regularly test a disaster recovery plan.

9. Implement procedures to monitor network reliability and efficiency.

10. Ensure that IT controls are thoroughly documented and assessed annually for effectiveness.

AUDIT COVERAGE

External Audit Approach

General controls must be tested as part of a financial statement audit. Today's audits are control based, i.e., the auditor expects to rely on internal controls and perform limited substantive testing. The external auditor should strive to obtain moderate assurance on general controls. While high assurance is possible, it would take a lot more control testing. Even if high assurance is obtained, the auditor still has to perform a significant amount of substantive testing of transactions and account balances to meet generally accepted auditing standards. Therefore, moderate assurance is the target for external auditors.

When one or more categories of general controls are found to be weak, the auditor has to assess the impact on application controls. Usually, that does not mean that moderate assurance cannot be derived from application controls at all. For example, if software change controls are found to be weak, the auditor may still be able to derive moderate assurance on application controls for a system where the client has no source code and by supplementing with targeted testing of other general controls surrounding that system.

Although all general controls are important to the auditors, we should mention that software change controls are very critical to the audit of the financial statements. In a financial statement audit, the auditors typically conduct internal control testing (general controls and application controls) at around mid-year and perform substantive testing close to and after year end. Control testing is performed around mid-year for two reasons. First, it evens out the work load. Secondly and actually more important in terms of audit effectiveness, is that, if controls are found to deserve moderate reliance, the auditors can plan to perform limited substantive testing. If the auditors wait until close to year end to perform control testing and controls are found to be weak, the auditors have little time to expand their substantive testing in order to keep audit risk at the acceptable level.

Because the external auditors conduct control testing at mid-year, in order to conclude that internal controls deserve moderate reliance throughout the year, auditors should update their control testing at year end. However, at year end, auditors are preoccupied with substantive testing so little resource can be devoted to control testing. Because of the focus on substantive testing at the year end period, the update of control testing will be less extensive than the original testing. It doesn't take a statistician to question the validity of the basis for placing moderate reliance on internal controls throughout the year if control testing is skewed towards the first half of the year. Well, the external auditors have an answer.

The external auditors, by testing software change controls and finding that change controls deserve moderate reliance, will also get assurance that there are no significant unauthorized changes. With this assurance at hand, the external auditors will ask for a list of software changes from management when they return close to year end to start their update of control testing. The auditors will review the changes for significance to the financial statements. For any significant changes, the auditors will audit the changes and conduct more extensive testing in those systems. For the systems that have not been significantly affected, the auditors will just perform limited update of control testing. How do the external auditors know the list of system changes is complete? This is where software change controls come in. If software change controls are reliable, the list should be reliable because management would know about significant software changes.

A challenger would then ask, "how can you place moderate reliance on software change controls throughout the year if you skewed your testing towards the first half of the year?" Well, it is necessary to update the testing of software change controls to the same extent as that carried out during the earlier (interim) stage of the audit. If the software change control testing update towards year end reveals that change control does not warrant moderate reliance, the list of system changes used to determine significant changes may not be reliable and the auditors will have to assess the need for more extensive application control testing update and increased substantive testing.

Control Deficiency

How does the auditor deal with control deficiencies? Here are the common steps.

1. Look for compensating controls. In an organization, seldom are only the needed controls implemented. By design or as processes evolve, some redundant or complementary internal controls have been implemented. This provides room for the external auditors to find compensating controls. An example of a compensating control is that the IT steering committee includes the CEO, CIO, CFO and the most senior line executives and that it meets monthly with a formal agenda and documented minutes. The control deficiency being compensated for is that the CIO reports to the CFO.

2. If there are insufficient compensating controls, the auditor should assess the need to rate general controls in that area, e.g., software change control, as low.

3. This means the auditor will conduct much more extensive testing of application controls.

4. In some cases, where general controls are extremely weak, e.g., both software change controls and access controls are rated low, there is not much point in testing application controls and the auditors might just resort to a mainly substantive audit approach.

5. The control deficiency should be included in the management letter with recommendations for improvements. In making recommendations, the auditor should keep in mind cost effectiveness at a general level without doing detailed analysis.

Internal Audit Approach

Internal auditors often test only general controls in an audit. For example, a data center audit would address only general controls. On the other hand, a payroll audit would address application controls. Compensating controls should be sought to mitigate the effect of control deficiencies. Deficiencies should be reported with recommendations for remedy. In making recommendations, the auditor should keep in mind cost effectiveness.

Audit Evidence

Audit evidence about internal control existence, effectiveness and compliance can be obtained in a number of ways. Common methods are:

1. Observation – to ascertain control existence and compliance. This is easy to carry out, but the effectiveness is limited to the instance of observation, i.e., compliance assurance is only at a point-in-time.

2. Surveys – to ascertain control effectiveness. The limitation is that the survey questions and sample size may be inadequate. Also, this provides somewhat subjective evidence.

3. Interviews – to ascertain control effectiveness and compliance. The limitation is similar to that of surveys, but evidence is more direct as you know who you are talking to. Interviewing a large group of people about a control provides fairly strong evidence about the control's compliance.

4. Testing – to ascertain control effectiveness. The limitation is similar to that of observation. Within the time period of testing, this technique provides direct and credible evidence.

5. Review of policies and procedures – Easy to carry out, but it does not address compliance.

6. Review of system configuration like operating system parameters – This provides more direct evidence than policies and procedures but narrower in scope. The review has to be conducted on many servers. It provides only point in time assurance.

7. Reviewing audit trail – This can cover a large period and provides strong evidence.

8. Confirming with external parties if an external party is a recipient or a part of a control. For example, if an organization confirms transactions with customers periodically, auditors can independently confirm with some customers about whether they have received the auditee's or client's confirmation requests and responded. This provides very direct evidence, but may be challenging in coordinating with the auditee or client. Generally, external evidence is more reliable than internal evidence.

Generic Audit Program

The following generic audit procedures can be used in both internal and external audits.

1. Review the previous audit file for weaknesses identified and notes about changing IT environment.

2. Meet with the CIO to find out about changes that have taken place and will take place in the current year, in order to assess the impact on business risks.

3. Review the IT policies and procedures and document controls and weaknesses.

4. Assess the appropriateness of the CIO reporting relationship and his or her interfaces with the board of directors. Directors should be informed of IT directions and major problems. The CIO does not have to have a direct line to the board, but there should be a process for directors to be informed.

5. Review the IT department organization charts and job descriptions to assess the clarity of responsibility definition and segregation of duties.

6. Observe IT operations, interview staff and review work files to assess segregation of duties.

7. Review IT procedures to assess segregation of duties.

8. Review minutes of the IT steering committee to assess the adequacy of senior management oversight and identify any weaknesses noted.

9. Review the control parameters for network access, remote connectivity and wireless connections to assess their adequacy in protecting the client's systems.

10. Review the system maintenance and change control procedures.

11. Select a sample of software changes from the change log and check for management approval and user acceptance. Review the testing audit trail.

12. For the sample of software changes, review system documentation to assess whether it is up-to-date.

13. Perform source code and/or object code comparison to identify changes and cross reference to management approval.

14. Review management's audit trail of source and/or object code comparison for frequency and resolution of discrepancies.

15. Review the DRP and backup procedures for comprehensiveness and approval. Correspond the disaster recovery plan to the list of business critical systems and the business impact assessments.

16. Review the audit trail for testing the disaster recovery plan.

17. Review the backup log to assess whether backup is done regularly and whether offsite storage is sufficient.

CONCLUSION

Today's business environment is a lot different from what it was when computers were first used to process transactions. Most business systems in large organizations are now open to the public directly or indirectly. There are more system users and they expect more in terms of system efficiency and reliability. Today's customers are less loyal and patient. Just look at the telephone and TV markets. Consumers can switch phone company, TV carrier and Internet service provider with a few clicks. Regulators are more demanding on companies to implement sound internal controls.

Internal controls are no longer just the interest of auditors. Managers are increasingly convinced and comfortable about their control ownership and responsibilities. They need help, help from industry guidelines, internal control specialists, control systems and auditors. An increasing percentage of business functions are automated. Management and auditors have to continuously keep up with the control implications of technology and using technology to achieve business competitiveness and reliability. Competitiveness and reliability can no longer be separated, and internal controls provide the bridge.

SUMMARY OF MAIN POINTS

Although most internal controls operate daily and are at the transaction and data levels, the extent of controls and their responsibilities stem from the control environment and culture that senior management has created and shaped over time. Senior management does that by exercising IT governance.

In this chapter, we have focused on those IT controls that are pervasive in the organization across business areas, and they are called general controls. There are IT controls that are specific to individual business systems. Those are called application controls and we will discuss them in Chapter Six.

Internal controls can be preventive, detective or corrective. Preventive controls are preferable to detective controls. However, an organization needs both because it is impractical to prevent all major errors and irregularities. For each detective control, there should be a corresponding corrective control.

General Controls

- Organization controls – including segregation of duties between IT and users as well as within the IT department.
- Access controls – we will discuss them in detail in Chapters Eight.
- Software change controls.
- Systems development controls – to be discussed in the next chapter.
- Disaster prevention controls.
- Disaster recovery controls.
- Computer operation controls.
- IT performance measurement controls.
- Intellectual property controls.

Organization Controls

- I&IT strategy.
- IT steering committee.
- Policies and standards.
- Segregation of duties.
- Hiring practices.
- Code of business conduct.
- Training.

Access Controls

- Physical
- Logical (data and software).
- Applies to infrastructure, software, people, information and procedures.

Software Change Control

- Application software change control.
- System software (e.g., operating system) change control.
- Change control policies and procedures.
- Naming conventions.
- Library control.
- Separate environments for development, testing and production (operation).
- Software testing.
- Change approval.
- Change monitoring.
- Procedures to deal with emergency changes to ensure adequate testing, documentation and approval.

Systems Development Controls

- Systems development methodology.
- Approval at checkpoints.
- Documentation standards.

Disaster Prevention Controls
- Hardware and network redundancy.
- Backup testing.
- Fire and water resistant data centers.
- Locating data centers away from hazardous or high crime area.
- Preventive maintenance schedule and monitoring.
- Hardware performance monitoring.

Disaster Recovery Controls
- Data backup.
- Software backup.
- Incident response procedures.
- Disaster recovery plan.
- Disaster recovery testing.

Computer operation Controls
- Service level agreement.
- Operations procedures.
- Procedures for hardware purchases and deployment.
- Hardware configuration standards and procedures.
- Network transmission control.
- Operation schedule.

IT Performance Measurement Controls
- Cost benefit analysis.
- Business case methodology.
- Cross charging IT cost to avoid waste of resources.
- Key performance indicators.
- IT score card reporting.

REVIEW QUESTIONS

1. What is the relationship between software change controls and systems development controls?

2. Who should approve the corporate disaster recovery plan?

3. How often should a disaster recovery plan be tested?

4. Who should the CIO report to?

5. What is the best approach to moving software to the production library?

6. What is the difference between an environment and a library?

7. What does an auditor see in an organization chart?

8. What is the drawback of parity check?

9. How often should a bank back up its transaction files and why?

10. What kind of system is the grandparent-parent-child backup approach used for?

CASE - Progressive Realtor

Shortly after your accounting firm received the notice of appointment as auditor of Progressive Realtors Ltd. (PRL), you, a manager in this Big Four accounting firm, made a visit to the company's office. You found that the company had a very sophisticated information system. At the time of that visit, you were introduced to Billy Chow, the manager of the Information Technology Division (ITD) of PRL. Billy had developed and progressively refined the systems in PRL during the last five years and is understandably proud of his achievements.

Transactions are keyed from batch vouchers and/ or coding forms by keying clerks in the user departments and subsequently their supporting documents are scanned for electronic storage. The information system edits the data for reasonableness and rejects whole batches if it finds errors. The accepted transactions will often be used to generate additional transactions automatically, e.g., interest charges, service charges, amortizations, depreciation, etc.

All major departments of PRL are provided with actual and budgetary information and reports, e.g., single and consolidated income statements and balance sheets, salesmen's commission statements, payroll registers, customer mortgage statements, etc. Important functions such as the mortgage system can be accessed from any one of 300 workstations.

Files are sometimes updated by the users with "non-essential" data issued by a user department clerk without hard copy documentation, e.g., a sales representative's address. The company uses a wide area network that is accessible from each of the ten branches in Canada. The annual IT budget is roughly $15,000,000. 65% of this sum is recovered through outside work, but the remaining portion represents about 15% of total company expenses. The IT department acts as a Web based application service provider (ASP) to other property management companies and individually operating property managers. This allows external companies and freelance property managers to logon to the property management system to service their own clients. The client data for these external parties is stored in PRL servers. The growth rate of the ASP business has been 15% annually over the last five years, and Billy expects the same rate of increase over the next three to five years.

The internal company operation including accounting and billing is supported by a combination of in-house developed systems and software packages. These systems do not produce user friendly management information reports and lack user generated reports with variable parameters. PRL has an internal auditor who has been with the company for ten years as a human resources specialist. He recently decided to pursue the Certified General Accountant designation and the company made him the internal auditor last year.

During your visit, the vice-president of property management described the Information Technology Division as Billy's "toy shop". Reports are delivered to users' network folders on schedule. However, changes are not easy. Billy is the one who pretty much decides what change requests will be worked on and the delivery dates. Billy takes ownership of the ITD and the systems and is not afraid to take the blame when things go wrong.

Mr. Chow further said: "I operate a production-oriented shop and have only highly trained professionals on board who know several modern programming languages. The dynamics of the operation require that each programmer works interactively with system administrators and users. Little time is therefore required, and indeed left, for documentation. Most of the programmers can help out when the systems administrators are either unable to interpret instructions or when they are off on a break. Sometimes, they work with our ASP customers online to troubleshoot.

"I pretty well consider myself on top of all problems, even though it means very long and irregular hours. I prefer to run my shop with as little interference from the other managers as possible, and for that matter from auditors. After all, I am a software engineer and designed a successful process control system for a Fortune 100 company before I came to PRL. You guys are so control oriented that you often forget to adapt to a new environment. Time is money in my shop and production is king. But if you have helpful practical suggestions, I am all ears."

A few days later, you had a meeting with PRL's president. He expressed concerns about coping with Billy.

"He has probably the most brilliant and intellectually independent mind of my managers and I feel I do not have the background, experience and, to be fully truthful, the desire, to exercise much control over the ITD. I trust him fully and prefer to give him a free hand. He attracts the brightest people and his shop is profitable. I would like you to provide me with the assurance I need to feel comfortable when the board of directors and especially the audit committee raise any questions. It is also important that I know what is going on. I know that auditability, as you guys call it, of the system is as much my responsibility and that of my managers, as it is yours. My problem is that I really don't know what auditability of the systems means. I guess what I am really saying is that you as my auditor are really responsible to my board of directors, the audit committee, and my managers, including me, for the auditability of the systems."

Required

Outline, for the client and your audit partner, how PRL can adequately control the activities of the Information Technology Division, including the ASP operation.

MULTIPLE CHOICE QUESTIONS

1. How does the Investor Confidence Rules affect IT governance? It
   a) requires management to certify internal controls.
   b) prohibits an accounting firm from providing consulting service to an audit client.
   c) requires the appointment of a chief risk officer.
   d) requires the appointment of a chief privacy officer.
   e) requires the rotation of auditors every five years.

2. In which environment is source code accessed the most?
   a) Production
   b) Development
   c) Testing
   d) Staging
   e) Audit

3. Which of the following is an internal control?
   a) Segregation of duties.
   b) The organization will hire only honest employees.
   c) Software change requests must be approved by the chief information officer.
   d) Source code must be compiled to object code before user acceptance testing.
   e) Information system risks are assessed annually.

4. Which environment should a program be sent to if user acceptance testing reveals an error?
   a) Development
   b) Testing
   c) Production
   d) Programmer
   e) Backup

5. Which is the most effective control over system administrators?
   a) Code of ethics
   b) Reference check
   c) Supervision
   d) Management review of activity log
   e) Performance appraisal

6. Who are responsible for IT governance?
   a) Chief financial officer
   b) Chief risk officer
   c) Chief auditor
   d) Senior executives
   e) Board of directors

7. Which of the following is a back-up procedure?
   a) Keeping transactions for seven years
   b) Compressing historical transactions
   c) Sending historical transactions offsite
   d) Keeping a duplicate of the master file
   e) Keeping the computer printouts and the master file

8. Which one is the correct one-to-one correspondence in number?
   a) Library and environment
   b) Programmers and testers
   c) Source code and object code
   d) Master file and transaction file

9. Which of the following library can be accessed by programmers extensively?
   a) Test
   b) Development
   c) Staging
   d) Production

10. Which of the following statements represents an undesirable practice?
   a) Appointing the chief auditor to the firm's IT steering committee
   b) Assigning accountants to systems project teams
   c) Hiring outside consultants occasionally to advise with respect to system development activities
   d) Appointing the chief information officer to the firm's IT steering committee

CHAPTER FOUR – SYSTMS DEVELOPMENT CONTROLS

You must be the change you want to see in the world. - Mahatma Gandhi

The average organization spends about half of its information technology (IT) budget in developing systems. Systems development is not trivial and most organizations do not do as well as they would like to. Many systems development projects are not completed on time and on budget and do not meet all user requirements. Organizations need to have a discipline in developing systems. Systems are developed more frequently these days as the life of a system is shorter. The life is shortened in a way by international competition which compels organizations to change to keep up with the industry. eBusiness has empowered small organizations to compete with multinationals. Small companies can change their systems more dynamically as they have less overhead and fewer organizational layers to go through; they are also more adventurous.

Twenty years ago, the average systems development project took two years to complete. Today, if implementation does not start one year from project initiation, the organization may be falling behind its competitors or customer expectation. It is important to maintain discipline and practice controls while speeding to meet business challenges in systems development.

EXAMPLES OF SYSTEMS DEVELOPMENT PROJECT SHOFTFALLS

Here is a list of systems development projects that did not succeed as expected or had significant bugs after implementation.

1. A Toronto company hired a large consulting firm to develop a leading edge system to increase market share. After a few months on the job, the new chief executive officer (CEO) terminated the project and wrote off millions of capitalized project cost. This was the chief operating officer's pet project. Managers approved invoices from the consulting firm without ensuring that the deliverables were acceptable. Users complained about the project progress and the usefulness of functions that had been delivered.

2. In June 2012, social workers in British Columbia, Canada said a new computer system that handled thousands of files for the Ministry of Social Development and the Ministry of Children and Family Development was plagued with problems and wasting valuable time. The $180-million Integrated Case Management System was designed to enable social ministries to share information, but an internal document obtained by the New Democratic Party says the system was prone to breakdowns and is almost impossible to use. Employees said they sometimes had to take hours to enter data or search clients' history, but information could get lost or even shredded in the process. The new system, launched just two months ago, was designed to replace 64 different databases.

3. In 2008, the Heathrow Airport Terminal 5 new baggage handling system produced wrong flight status information to the baggage crew. This resulted in bags not getting loaded to the right planes. One estimate was that this crisis cost the airlines £50m.

COMMON REASONS FOR SYSTEMS DEVELOPMENT PROJECT FAILURES

Here is a list of common pitfalls in managing systems development projects.

- The project is too big and therefore difficult to manage – A solution is to break it to more manageable projects that can be carried out concurrently with different project managers or successively if resources are limited.
- No senior management accountability thus leading to insufficient monitoring – An executive sponsor should be assigned to each project, who should also be the system owner.
- Insufficient project reporting to senior management – There should be a process for periodic reporting to the project sponsor and the IT steering committee.
- No post-implementation validation of project success – There should be an independent post-implementation review.
- Lack of project management skill thus leading to poorly coordinated projects – Large organizations should establish project management offices as centers of excellence in project management.
- Insufficient project planning thus leading to a project running off the wrong direction – An organization should have a standard for project planning. If you fail to plan, you plan to fail.
- Insufficient management and user signoffs thus leading to wrong deliverables or missed deliverables – An organization should require signoffs at multiple stages of a project.
- Insufficient business case thus leading to a system that is not cost effective – A business case should be required before the project sponsor signs off the project plan.
- Inadequate system design thus leading to a system that does not meet business requirements – An organization should have a standard and rigorous procedures for systems design.
- Inadequate requests for proposals for purchased systems thus leading to buying the wrong systems – An organization should charge the project sponsor with assigning business users to write the request for proposals (RFP) and for the RFPs to be approved by project sponsors.
- Changing user requirements thus leading to projects that are late or don't get finished – An organization's systems development methodology should not allow user requirements to be changed after signoff unless the project sponsor approves.
- Resistance to change thus leading to project delay – The systems development methodology should include a communication plan for the project to ensure the affected staff receives proper and timely information about how they will be affected.
- Inadequate testing thus leading to unreliable systems – The systems development methodology should require different stages of testing and signoffs.

- Inadequate training thus leading to ineffective use of a system – Training plans and signoffs evidencing receiving of training should be part of the systems development methodology.
- Lack of user involvement thus leading to systems that do not meet business requirements – An organization's systems development methodology should require detailed requirements to be signed off by the project sponsor. Frequent meeting with user representatives should be held to allow for status reporting and checkpoint reviews.
- No software change controls thus leading to effective programs – The software change controls discussed in the last chapter will help prevent this.
- Incorrect data conversion thus leading to systems with wrong opening data – An organization's systems development methodology should require user sign-off of data conversion.

ANNUAL SYSTEM DEVELOPMENT PLAN

Organizations have limited resources. Resources have to be allocated to desired projects based on the business cases and each project's congruence with the IT strategy. As part of the IT strategy, there should be an annual plan of systems development projects, i.e., what systems will be developed this year, next year, the year after, and year 4 etc. The annual plan should look forward at least three years and include current projects. The project management office (PMO) should be responsible for developing and monitoring this plan, i.e., monitoring the progress of systems development projects.

SYSTEMS DEVELOPMENT METHODOLOGY

Each organization should have a systems development methodology. The methodology should include the following.
- Definition of a systems development project versus a software change request. A systems development project is developing a new system or a major modification of an existing system, rather than an ad hoc or minor system change.
- Process for project initiation, business case preparation, project approval to proceed and project monitoring.
- Guidelines for system acquisition as well as managing vendors and consultants.
- Program naming convention.
- System documentation standard and format.
- Definition of each phase in systems development, the stakeholders and parties responsible:
    - Problem definition.
    - Feasibility study.
    - Project proposal including a business case.
    - System analysis.
    - Detail project plan.

- User requirements.
- System architecture.
- System design.
- Programming.
- System integration testing.
- User acceptance testing.
- Policies and procedures development.
- Update of the disaster recovery plan.
- Management approval to implement.
- Conversion.
- Implementation.
- Post-implementation review.
- Project monitoring and reporting, this occurs throughout the project.

The software change management controls that we talked about in the last chapter also apply to systems development projects because systems development requires software changes and implementation. In addition, a systems development project requires more controls related to project justification, project monitoring, documentation, testing, conversion, implementation, training and post-implementation review.

The key stakeholders that should sign off all or most of the above phases are the project sponsor, the project manager, the IT department, user area representatives, internal audit and the IT security function. Even though IT security may be part of the IT department, its sign-off should be separate from the sign-off of the chief information officer (CIO) or programming manager, mainly because of the internal control implication. IT security is a type of internal controls. The involvement and sign-off of internal audit are mainly to help ensure that adequate internals are built into the system and that the systems development methodology is followed. The systems development methodology is a collective internal control to ensure that systems are developed only based on authorized requests, accurately, on a timely basis, completely and efficiently.

PROBLEM DEFINITION

Before a systems development project commences, a business problem should be recognized and documented. The problem should be more than just an impulsive concern about operation. It should be a shortfall that has been sustained. A problem may also stem from a regulatory requirement, e.g., a reporting requirement from a regulator. A problem may be a requirement of a business strategy, e.g., to launch a new product. A problem may result from a directive or the law, e.g., a directive from the banking regulator or a new tax; in either case, a systems development project may have to be started to meet the directive or legal requirement. A system may be developed to seize a business opportunity, e.g., to expand market share. Whether the driver for a new system is a problem to address current shortcomings, to meet a legal or regulatory requirement, or to support new business direction, the need to justify the systems development project and manage it to successful implementation is the same. We will, in this chapter, refer to these three types of driver, as a problem.

A problem needs a champion unless it comes from the CEO or COO. The champion will solicit executive interest in the problem to a point where there is agreement that the problem has to be addressed potentially with a new system or a major system upgrade. The champion is likely someone who reports directly or indirectly to the executive with the biggest stake in the business area affected, i.e., the system owner. If there is no existing system to be replaced, the system owner would be the executive in charge of the area that benefits most or has most control over the new system, e.g., the chief financial officer (CFO) for an accounting system, the vice-president of mortgage lending for a system to support a new mortgage product.

The next step is to conduct a feasibility study.

FEASIBILITY STUDY

The problem now has corporate recognition. The question to answer is whether it is solvable with a new system or a major system upgrade. Is a system solution feasible? There are three feasibility aspects to address: financial, technical and organizational. The feasibility study should be performed by the champion. The output is a feasibility report to be submitted to the system owner.

Financial Feasibility

This is actually a high level business case. At this point, the champion is not ready to ask for money. S/he wants to see if the system development is financially affordable. This will involve understanding the financial atmosphere of the organization, e.g., is the organization facing significant financial pressure? It will also involve estimating the cost and benefit of the system without going into significant details. If the cost and benefit estimation indicates there is a convincing business case in light of the organization's financial health, financial feasibility can be demonstrated.

Technical Feasibility

The system required may be well ahead of the organization's IT infrastructure or skills. Although technology and skills can be purchased and the organization may have a lot of money, a quantum leap increases the risk of project failure and management may hesitate to approve such a project unless it is required by law or to survive in the business. This is what technical feasibility is about.

Organizational Feasibility

The organization may be financially healthy, the system may have strong payback, the organization may have solid infrastructure and highly skilled developers, the idea to develop a system to solve the problem at hand may still be shot down if the organization has other significant problems or priorities to deal with. For example, if the new system will clash with the corporate culture, require significant re-organization, sends a message to customers, shareholders and taxpayers that the organization is taking a major risk in IT and business direction, or if the system introduces a major labor relations problem, the project request may not be approved. That's what organizational feasibility is about.

PROJECT PROPOSAL

If the feasibility study is approved, the project champion should initiate the project to find an IT solution for the identified problem. A proposal will be prepared and approved at ascending levels. The proposal should include a problem definition and a statement that is based on preliminary analysis, that a new system or a major system change is required. It should state at a high level, how the problem will be solved. Major projects may need to be approved by the IT steering committee or perhaps even the board before commencement. The level of approval depends on the cost of the project. Cost, for this purpose, means initial cost + annual net cost. Annual net cost = annual gross cost – cost reductions that have no strings attached, e.g., based on a signed contract that produces cost reductions. It is not net of benefits like projected increased profit or projected cost reductions generated by automation or efficiency. The latter items are subject to risks and may not materialize. This is why it is the initial cost + annual net cost (net of cost reductions with certainty) that should be used to decide how high up the proposal needs to be approved at.

The project proposal should also include a project risk statement to help the approvers assess the risks of undertaking the project. The risk statement should describe the types of risks and their probability. The suggested time frame for the project, as well as a breakdown of the types of resources by amount should be stated.

The proposal should include a business case that is based on the organization's business case methodology for capital projects, including the application of capital budgeting techniques. The business case should address the cost of hardware, software, vendor fees, consultants and salary.

Cost justification is primarily the responsibility of the project sponsor. This is usually the executive accountable for the function that the proposed system will support. For an accounting system, the sponsor is probably the chief financial officer. The sponsor usually does not have time for day-to-day management of systems development projects so s/he typically designates a project manager. The sponsor or a delegate should develop the cost-benefit analysis by engaging business and IT management. At this stage there is no assurance that the project will go ahead, and a project manager may not have been appointed yet.

Intangible benefits should be described in the business case. Intangible costs should be addressed in the risk statement.

Business Case

The cost-benefit analysis should include only incremental cost. This means existing hardware generally should not be included. However, if the use of existing hardware, premises or management resources would result in another project having to make procurement or hiring, then the cost of such existing resources should be included in the cost-benefit analysis of the current project. The salary of existing programmers and other staff dedicated to the projects should be included as it varies with project requirements. The organization's capital budgeting and business case methodologies should be followed to take into account the time value of money and income tax effect.

Consider the time value of money. Expenses and revenue that occur in future periods should be discounted using the organization's expected rate of return from capital.

Consider the uncertainty of estimates. Future revenue, even if covered by a contract, bears some degree of uncertainty, and should be discounted based on factors such as the customers' reputation and the organization's track record in delivering the products and services. Estimated cost will usually occur, especially costs that are stipulated in contracts. Approval of IT expenditure should take into account the risk of future revenue, e.g., by discounting revenue estimates based on risk. Such discounting should be applied even if future revenue is based on a signed contract, because of the risk of a contract breach. Management should take into account the uncertainty created by new technology and large project size when estimating costs.

External costs that are stipulated in contracts will occur and can be taken at face amounts. Internal costs may be subjective depending on who is doing the estimation. Business units that provide internal services to a captive internal market have a tendency to overestimate their costs to insulate against unforeseen circumstances and unfavorable factors beyond their control. On the other hand, project managers and sponsors who feel strongly for a project would tend to lean towards the low end of a range of estimated cost and the high end of estimated revenue. Organizations should expect project managers and sponsors to negotiate competitive costs with internal and external service providers and hold the business units accountable for cost estimates. Decision making with respect to approving the initiation and continuation of a project should involve some discounting of revenue estimates and grossing up cost estimates, except for items that are locked in by contracts with reputable customers and vendors. The factors that should be considered in such discounting and gross-up include:

1. Remoteness of timing - The farther out the timing for estimates, the less reliable they are. For example, for each year out, a 1% discount of revenue and gross-up of cost can be applied. This discount is in addition to the discount for time value of money. It is intended to account for uncertainty related to the time remoteness.
2. Experience with the business and technology - For new ventures and emerging technology, the learning curve makes estimates less precise. Cost estimate should allow for this.

3. Project size - Large projects involve many stakeholders, multiple business units and sometimes different external parties. This increases the difficulty and error margin of estimates, not just in dollars but also in percentage. An organization can set strata of project sizes and apply an escalating rate for discounting revenue estimates and grossing up cost estimates.

The cost-benefit analysis should cover a maximum period three years, depending on the life of the new system. It should be updated at least annually.

Treat cost avoidance differently from cost reduction. Cost avoidance constitutes true savings. Cost reduction is difficult to materialize completely. It is easier to avoid giving than to take something back. A common category of cost reduction is expected salary savings. No managers enjoy firing people. So even if a department accepts that a new system will reduce the requirement for staff, managers will and should try to find ways to redeploy the surplus employees. However, in doing so, temporary assignments with little value may be created. It is important to take into account the restructuring and retraining expenses in estimating human resources savings that can accrue from using a new system.

Cost avoidance should reflect the new system's ability to prevent adverse incidents. To put a value to such preventive ability, business units should have been recording the costs of incidents. These include:
- Loss of assets
- Loss of revenue
- Legal liability
- Loss of productivity
- Time taken to rebuild systems and information
- Cost of increased paper based transactions during system outage
- Financial resources needed to reassure customers and mend customer relations

At the end of each phase of the project, the risk statement and business case should be reviewed and adjusted as necessary. In the case of cost overrun, the project manager should implement measures to prevent better control costs. Significant variances, e.g., 10%, should be reported to the parties who approved the project proposal to seek a "go – no go" decision.

Project Risk Statement

It is critical to perform risk assessment before devoting resources to develop a system. The proposal should include risk assessment and indication of how the risks will be mitigated. The project risk assessment should consider the common IT risk criteria that are discussed in Chapter Two.

1. Incomplete system implementation – This risk is quite high because there are numerous programs in a project. The main controls to mitigate this are system integration testing and user acceptance testing.
2. Unauthorized system implementation – This risk is also quite high for the same reason. The main control is sign-off of the test results and the conversion plan.
3. Inaccurate system development and implementation – This risk is high. Testing is the main mitigation.
4. Untimely implementation – This can be a common occurrence. The main mitigation includes a detailed project plan and monitoring by the project management office.
5. Implementing a system no one requested (occurrence) – This risk is quite low because a systems development project requires significant resources and if on one asks for the project, it is hard to find the resources. The main mitigation is the requirement for a project plan.
6. Inefficient system implementation – This risk is quite high because of the usually large size of a project and the variety of interfaces required. The main control is management monitoring of the project progress.

The risk of a project increases with the complexity of technology and scope of the project. For example, eBusiness and infrastructure integration projects are of high risk. When an organization conducts an enterprise resource planning (ERP) system project, the risk is very high because of the complexity of the system, the tendency to use consultants owing to lack of internal expertise, the need to manage software vendor relations, business process reengineering involved, changes in business functions, resistance to changes and the wide array of business functions affected.

SYSTEM ANALYSIS

Once the proposal for a solution has been approved, a project is initiated to seek the solution and the business sponsor will designate a project manager. At this time, a small project team should be assembled. The team, consisting of IT and business area staff, should define the project scope by analyzing the existing system to determine the extent to which the problem can be solved with existing system functions. Based on this analysis, the team will assess the extent of the new system and develop a detailed project plan. The result of the analysis phase is a detailed report that describes the effectiveness of the existing system. The following components should be included:

1. System overview in narrative and diagrams.

2. System users.

3. System deficiencies reported in the past. These deficiencies actually are the drivers for the new system.

4. Strong features of the system; these features should be repeated in the new system.

5. Expert developers and expert users of the system. These will be valuable resources in developing the new system.

This report should be signed off by the project sponsor. The next phase is to develop a detailed project plan.

PROJECT PLAN

The project plan should consist of the following.

- Project objectives.
- Project team.
- Business sponsor and project manager.
- Work breakdown structure – This is a detailed list of activities that have to be carried out to develop and implement the system. They are grouped by phase. For each phase and activity, the person(s) responsible for the work and for signing off should be stated. The timeframes should also be stated.
- Time table – This should not exceed two years. It is also called a Gantt chart. It shows the tasks under each systems development phase, timetabled ideally by week, showing the name of each team member responsible for each task during each week, the number of hours needed, as well as the deliverables and checkpoints for approval. Actual progress in terms of time spent and deliverables completed can be shown on the Gantt chart to be compared to the plan.
- Critical path diagram to show the tasks that have predecessors, i.e., a task that cannot start until certain tasks are completed. This diagram will help the project manager determine the impact of task slippage in terms of the ability to meet the project deadline. The critical path is the path of predecessor dependent tasks that together takes the longest elapsed time. Any delay of this path will delay the project; i.e., there is no slack time allowed.
- Responsibility of each team member.
- Approvals required.
- Incident notification contacts.
- Detailed risk assessment
- Risk mitigation plan

A project management software tool should be used to help ensure comprehensiveness of the project plan, its monitoring and reports. Studies show that the duration of a project should not exceed two years, for the following reasons:

- It is difficult to keep the team focused on a project for a longer period.
- After two years, the business environment may have changed so much that the solution is no longer competitive.
- Technology may have changed so much that the solution is no longer the best available given the cost the organization is willing to commit to.

The project plan must be signed off by the project sponsor.

Critical Path Diagram

The following is a simple example of a critical path diagram.

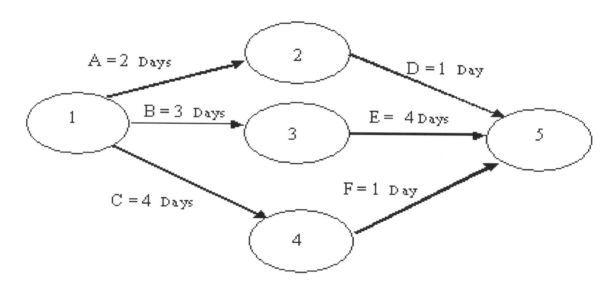

This diagram shows that tasks A, B and C are not dependent on each other; nor are D, E and F. The minimum duration of the project is seven days. Any delay in task B or E will delay the project. How about delay in task A? Well, it depends on how much delay. B to E is called the critical path because it is the longest path of predecessor dependent activities in terms of elapsed time, i.e., 7 days. A to D will take 3 days. Thus, A and D combined can be delayed for up to 4 days without delaying the project. A critical path diagram is useful to measure the impact of delay of certain activities on the project's timely completion. Well, if B is delayed, what should the project manager do? S/he should assign more resources to catch up and prevent further delay. If additional resources are not available, stakeholders should be informed and a revised deadline should be negotiated.

Project Team

The project team must be formed before the work stated in the work breakdown structure is carried out. Some team members may be assigned part time to the project from within the organization, some may be seconded full time to the project. Some may be hired as new employees for the project and then transferred elsewhere after the project. Some may be hired as term employees just for the project. Yet some may be consultants. Where team members are seconded from within the organization, the secondment agreement must cover a long enough period. A tricky arrangement is for someone to be assigned part time to the project. The agreement between the project manager and the line manager who supplies the team member must state the duration, the amount of time each week the person will be available to the project and how conflict in demand will be resolved. Consultant contracts must be supported by statements of work, statements of deliverables, checkpoints, provision for conflict resolution and provision for corrective action and remedy for non-performance.

Gantt Chart

This is a time table of the project activities grouped by phase indicating the time and deliverables expected of each team member. Project management software can be used to prepare this chart. Over the course of the project, actual time and deliverables can be input to the software and overlaid on the Chart to compare with the planned progress. Here is a simple example of a Gantt Chart.

	Week 1	Week 2	Week 3
User requirement: First draft	V D'Angelo – 10 hrs	T Cruise – 12 hrs	S Feng – 14 hrs
Second draft		B Zhou – 8 hrs	D Cullen – 3 hrs
Sign-off			C Nichols – 5 hrs

Project Management Skills

The Project Management Institute develops education and reference material for project managers. It also grants the Project Management Professional (PMP) designation upon successful completion of a uniform examination and confirmation of meeting the experience requirement. A PMP indicates possession of project management experience and knowledge. A good project manager also needs soft skills.

A project manager has to manage a project team with members who are not assigned to the project full time. When conflicting deadlines or pressure occur, those team members might be inclined to give priority to their full time jobs. Even before that, the project manager has to identify skilled people from the organization, negotiate their availability and in some way "attract" those people to join the team. Although the project manager can hire people, for cost effectiveness and knowledge availability, an effective project team should consist of existing employees and new hires.

A common risk in projects, especially systems development projects, is scope creep. That is, users keep changing their requirements. This can delay project completion. A project manager must be firm and not afraid to say no. User requirements must be frozen after sign-off by the project sponsor unless there is a huge gap. The project manager must also be organized as detailed planning and monitoring are important. The project manager must be knowledgeable about the business, pragmatic, a good listener, a good articulator and have overall knowledge about IT. S/he must be deadline conscious and lead by examples. S/he has to be good in holding and controlling meetings. Too many meetings are too long. Last but not least, the project manager must be good with people, to make people feel good in the head and the stomach. The adages "motivated staff are productive staff" and "respect must be earned and cannot be demanded" apply aptly in project management.

It seems like a project manager has to walk on waters; well, almost. Because it is such a demanding job, successful completion of a major project often will land the project manager a promotion…and the converse may also be true.

Where do project managers come from? Are they hired to run a project, transferred from the IT department or from the business unit? The answer is, it varies. It depends on the type of system, the availability of internal expertise, the technical knowledge required and the urgency. Many successful project managers did not come primarily from the IT area. One can safely argue that an experienced project manager for a building construction project can run an IT project well. There is more emphasis on management than IT. A large organization should have a project manager pool in the PMO. A project manager may run a large project only or several small projects simultaneously.

Before any system development work can start, the project manager must obtain detailed system requirements from the user area.

USER REQUIREMENTS

This is largely the responsibility of the business area sponsoring the system. Requirements should be detailed. It should state what transactions will be processed and how, what information is required in the solution, when it is required, who it has to be available to. It should also include what system functions are required to be used by whom. User requirements should state the reports and whether they have to be online. The frequency of processing should also be described. The availability of the system in percentage should be specified. The requirements should indicate the types and volume of transactions to be processed and the format of the transactions. The requirements should be reviewed by the project manager and the IT department to make sure that they are understandable to the technical people who will develop the system. User requirements should include provisions to comply with the associated policies and standards. How transactions will be processed includes defining what transactions will be processed online, in batches, centrally, in a distributed manner etc.

For systems that process financial information, the accounting department should review the user requirements to ensure that the organization's accounting principles are followed. The team preparing the user requirements should be aware of the organization's policies and standards that pertain to or address internal controls, to ensure that controls are included in the requirements. It is important at this time to state the information and audit trail that is needed to carry out management review and approval as well as independent checks. The team should also consider the need to refer the requirements to the law department.

Internal controls should be included in user requirements in two ways. First, they should be integrated in the business process and report requirements. Secondly, they should be pulled out as a separate section. This control section will help people who perform risk assessment to determine the adequacy of internal controls. The user requirements should include both automated and manual functions because the systems developers will need to know how people interface with the system. Even if a manual function requires no system interface, if it uses system produced information, it should be stated so the systems developers know how information will be used and this will help them in designing the system function and data format. The control matrix shown in the last chapter should be used as a frame of reference to compose internal controls that will be built into the system along with manual controls.

	Complete	Authorized	Accurate	Timely	Occur	Efficient
Input						
Processing						
Output						
Storage						

The user requirement document should be signed off by the project sponsor, the IT department including the responsible system architects and lead designer, the project manager, internal audit and IT security. Internal auditors should ensure that the user requirements include enough provision for audit trail and data file availability to support computer assisted audit techniques (CAAT). CAATs involve using computers to automate internal control testing and substantive testing. A common type of CAAT is to use a general data extraction tool to analyze data files for control testing or substantive testing. It is therefore important for internal audit to know that the needed data files will be available. Usually what is important to the auditors is important to management. If management keeps sufficient audit trail, the appropriate data files should be available and adequate for the auditors. Management has just as great a need as auditors to obtain reports from systems to perform data analysis.

User requirements should be detailed and account for input, processing, output and storage. Input will include the types of transactions to be processed, what information will be gathered, input form etc. Processing will include the functions to be performed, e.g., aging of accounts receivable in 30 days, 60 days; batch processing vs online processing; centralized processing vs distributed processing. Output should indicate the exact output screens and reports, whether reports will be regular or on demand, who can get what reports, hard copy or electronic, retention of data and reports etc. As far as storage, the user requirements should address where data will be stored, for how long and who are responsible.

The following questions must be addressed, at a minimum, in the user requirement document:

1. What will be recorded? In other words, what is a recordable transaction?
2. How will the transaction be recorded?
3. When will the transaction be recorded?
4. What system related internal controls will be necessary to ensure authorized, accurate, timely, complete and efficient execution and recording of transactions?
5. What system related internal controls will be necessary to ensure that only real transactions are recorded?
6. What input screens will be used?
7. What output and enquiry screens will be necessary?
8. What management and other ad hoc system queries will be necessary and available?
9. What reports will be produced and in what format? Will they be pushed to users or pulled by users?
10. When reports will be produced?
11. Details of each report and system enquiry and their layout.
12. What staff positions will input transactions and receive reports?
13. What staff positions will need to perform which system enquiries?
14. Whether each transaction or enquiry is needed to be input or invoked centrally or in distributed locations, and which locations?

Depending on the system, transactions include financial transactions like invoicing, finance related transactions like setting up a general ledger account, and non-financial transactions like setting up a user access profile.

In developing a new system to replace a current system, the project sponsor should charge the business unit representatives to go through a paradigm shift to streamline processes. A value chain should be established to ensure that each system function and related manual procedure adds value, and that the value added exceeds the cost of developing the function as well as the cost of exercising the function and related activities. This streamlining process is also called business process reengineering.

Here are the common steps an organization should follow in business process reengineering.

1. Build a cross functional team with experts in each business area involved.
2. Identify and agree on the business objectives.
3. Develop a value chain including applying activity based costing.
4. Benchmark the value chain with industry standards as well as known competitors' cost and system performance metrics.
5. Validate the value chain with testing and prototyping.
6. Establish performance indicators for subsequent measurement of the development process and the operational system.

Based on detailed user requirements, system developers can start the technical work. System architecture should be prepared to develop the system infrastructure. Meanwhile, system design can proceed to construct the software and database.

SYSTEM ARCHITECTURE

Based on user requirements, IT architects will define the network topology and required hardware. The documentation will be in diagrams, flowcharts and narrative. It is called system architecture. System architects are experienced and skilled in network design. They may be former programmers, former designers, hardware engineers, software engineers or people trained specifically in network management or database administration.

General controls should be included in the system architecture. Examples are firewall, network authentication, virus checking and redundant servers. Application controls are not required here as they will be addressed in system design.

Although the system architecture should be based on user requirements and internal controls should be specified in the user requirements, business unit people are not qualified and knowledgeable to think about the general controls that are usually technical in nature and are not directly tied to a transaction cycle. For example, users would not know whether a firewall is necessary. It is therefore important that system architects be trained in internal control concepts and techniques. System architecture must comply with the organization's policy and standards about hardware and system software configuration, e.g., security parameters. There should be a standard checklist followed by the architects. Because many infrastructure controls are of a security nature, it is important for IT security specialists to participate in this process.

The system architecture should be signed off by the project manager, the IT department including the programming manager, user representatives, system designers, internal audit and IT security.

SYSTEM DESIGN

Based on the user requirements, the assigned IT staff members can design the solution. The design should address the following.

- The input to be processed, including what data is required, the format, who it comes from, frequency, whether it is in batches or online.
- The edit and authorization checks to be performed on the input.
- The computerized processing functions, their sequence, frequency, input and output.
- The computer checks to be performed on processed data and results.
- The format of reports and whether they are online or in hard copy.
- The format of input and whether they are in batches or online.
- Whether reports are automatically sent or produced on request.
- The information needed for management and staff to perform review, checks, approval and reconciliation.
- The format, size and media for databases and files.
- The software tools required.
- Interfaces with external entities.

Design documentation will take the form of entity relationship diagrams (ERD), flowcharts, data dictionary, input screens, forms, report layouts and narrative. Application controls should be included in a more detailed form than those in the user requirement document. There should be cross-referencing of the system logic to user requirements. There are software engineering tools to draw the diagrams. The designers must review such diagrams for consistency with the user requirements.

System design must comply with the organization's policy and standards about hardware and system software configuration, e.g., security parameters. There should be a standard checklist followed by the designers.

The final deliverable of the design phase is pseudo code. This is a set of system processing activities almost in the form of computer programs. This is why it is called pseudo code. Some people call it programs in plain language. It is somewhat less detailed than computer programs, especially in input, output and data storage tasks. Pseudo code mainly addresses processing. Programmers will write programs based mainly on pseudo code. They will use narrative and diagrams described above as secondary references.

The design documentation package should be signed off by the project manager, user representatives, the programming manager, the assigned IT architects, internal audit and IT security.

Entity Relationship Diagram

Before system logic can be worked out, the designers should review the user requirements and understand the external and internal entities in a system. Examples of external entities are customers and banks. Examples of internal entities are departments.

An entity relationship diagram (ERD) shows the relationship between any two entities. The relationship is usually expressed in an action. The following is an example of an ERD.

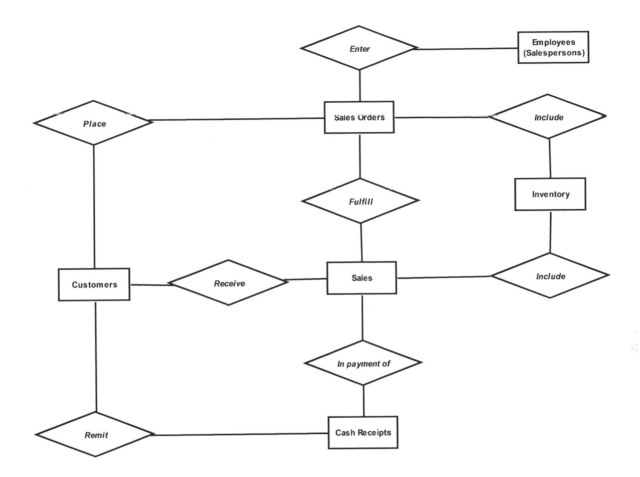

There are usually multiple ERDs in a system, in successive levels of details. Once the relationships of entities are defined, the designers can compose the database structure and select the database management system. The database structure will include the following:

- A data dictionary that defines how data is stored in each table and in what fields, data format, field lengths and order. There should be a table for each entity. Some entities have successively detailed tables.
- Database management system.
- Table layout.
- Table relationships.
- Access control lists defining which computer programs have access to which tables and which fields and the nature of access, e.g., read, update, delete.
- Database schemas, i.e., logical views for the application that define what each system function and user can access.
- The input forms, manual or online, to collect the data.

Flowchart

After defining relationships, the designers should study how data should flow between entities to satisfy user requirements. This includes defining the processes. Such definition should be in the form of narrative and flowcharts. Many of the procedures in a flowchart are internal controls, e.g., checking to see if a credit limit is to be exceeded. Here is an example of a flowchart.

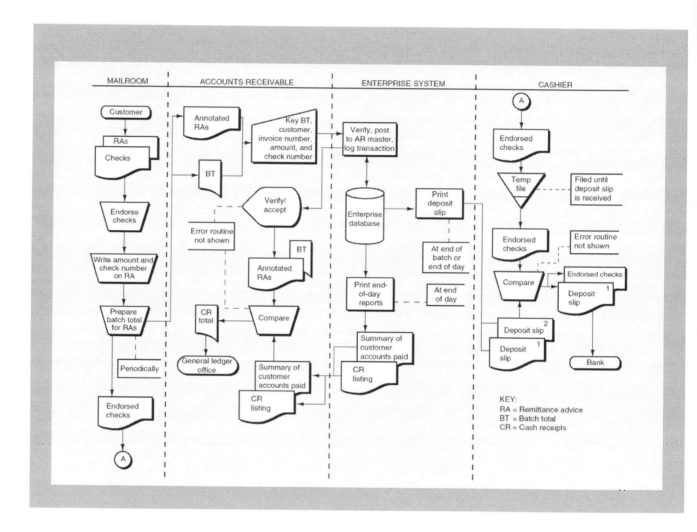

Although the system design should be based on user requirements and internal controls should be specified in the user requirements, business unit people may not be knowledgeable to think about the technical IT application controls such as database normalization and referential integrity checks. We will discuss these controls in Chapter Six. It is therefore important that system designers be trained in internal control concepts and techniques like the above, as well as security techniques like boundary checking of user inputs to prevent code injection and buffer overflow that can distort or misdirect system processing. We will talk more about the technical security controls referred to in the last sentence, in Chapter Eight.

Designers should use narrative to supplement the diagrams because the diagrams show the interfaces between processes but do not describe the processes in detail in terms of the system functions including internal controls. The narrative includes two levels. First in point form, it expands the user requirements to account for data layout and data table relationship, and also to describe the entities, documents and processes indicated in the diagrams. A question is, why bother repeating the information in the diagrams in the form of narrative? Diagrams provide an overview for programmers to understand the relationships between entities and processes. It is easier to use narrative to capture in more specific terms all the relationships and processes, so narrative should be cross checked to diagrams.

The second level of narrative is called pseudo code. It is in the form of program instructions but in plain English. This is actually the final reference source for programmers to write programs. Pseudo code is more detailed than the first form of narrative because it includes technical statements about how to data is read and updated. However, during programming, the programmers will find it useful to also study the diagrams when they have doubt about the pseudo code and also to debug programs. Debugging means working out program bugs that cause a program to malfunction. Pseudo code is less detailed than actual computer programs because it covers only input, processing and output. It does not specify data format, the form of input (manual or online) and the form of output.

The design documentation should be signed off by the project manager, the IT department including the programming manager, user representatives, system architects, internal audit and IT security. Internal audit should assess the adequacy of data format for computer assisted audit techniques. The design phase and the architecture phase can be carried out concurrently. However, during construction, the two teams should exchange information and material to ensure that they are compatible, i.e., the infrastructure will support the software.

PROGRAMMING

Once a system solution has been designed, programming can start. A team of programmers will divide the functions to work on, as assigned by programming managers. There should be a standard for program documentation, testing and naming. Each programmer should test his or her own programs one at a time and in a series. They should also swap programs for peer testing, as assigned by the programming managers. Where existing programs are needed to be used as the basis for change, programmers should apply to the change control coordinator for a copy of the programs that are used in operation, to ensure that changes are made from the current version. Programming is performed in the programmers' own libraries. Peer testing, also called string testing, is carried out in the development library, which is a library with common access by programmers in the project for read only. The systems development methodology should provide guidelines for constructing test cases which should be based on the system design documentation. There should be cross referencing of the test cases to the system design documentation. Every system function should be tested and all linked functions should be tested together.

The IT department should have a standard test bank for each application to ensure consistency of test data. The test bank should be updated periodically to reflect the comprehensiveness of real transactions. Testing for a system development project is more extensive than testing ad hoc program changes. Test results should be signed off by the programming manager and the project manager.

Software engineering tools can be used for code generation for routine functions. The configuration of these tools must be approved by management to ensure consistent coding conventions and documentation. The code generated must also be reviewed by the programmers with written indication of such review to ensure correctness. The use of objects (reusable code) should be subject to risk assessment and management approval to avoid blindly using previously written code. The project management office should maintain an inventory of these common objects and periodically test them.

Open source tools should be subject to the same level of due diligence as reusable objects and should be tested to the same rigor as locally developed programs. The organization should have a policy in adopting open source with respect to approval, types of application allowed, inventory and license violation. The time involved in adapting open source code should be tracked to assess the savings vs developing proprietary code. Open source means ready made programs in source code format available from vendors, trading partners or the IT community.

Programming standards and training should specify techniques to avoid security holes being programmed that will open back doors to hackers. For example, an input program must check the validity and length of values input to prevent buffer overflow (overflowing the real memory in the computer and therefore overwriting program instructions loaded in real memory that could then cause a system to misbehave or shut down). Programming standards and training should also address how each operating system service (function) or port is used in the system, in which programs and how these operating systems features are also used in other systems to assess the risk of system compromise if these components are abused by programs or hackers. A port is a channel used for computers on a network to exchange information for a particular application; an example of an application is a network game. A port is analogous to a radio channel.

Reusable code has to be periodically tested and traced to its source version. The source version should then be checked for changes and such changes should be reconciled to management sign-off. Reusable programs should be grouped by functionality and classified in terms of their sensitivity. Management approval should be required to reuse sensitive and powerful programs, in light also of the sensitivity of the application where reusable code will be imported to.

Programmers should be trained and instructed to use ample narrative within programs to make program instructions understandable to the authors and other programmers in the future to facilitate program updates. Narrative can be inserted in line within programs with suitable prefixes so the compiler knows that the narrative is not part of program instructions.

Tested and completed programs should be approved by the programming and project managers. How about user representatives? Shouldn't they sign off? Well, they most likely cannot read programs and so cannot sign off. Don't worry. They will get their chance to test the programs and sign off the system, as stated below. It is true that programming managers and the project manager also probably cannot understand programs. Why bother asking them to sign off? Well, there should be management sign off of this important phase of systems development. Programming managers will sign off on the strength of peer testing and general review of program documentation including program narrative. The project manager will sign off mainly on the strength of the programming managers' signoff. It is not just rubber stamping. It is accountability. The project manager should sign off at the completion of each phase.

SYSTEM INTEGRATION TESTING

It seems that one can never test enough, as soon as a system is implemented, bugs are discovered. The organization should have standards that guide in determining the extent of and responsibility for testing and how tests should be documented. In addition to testing done by programmers, the system should be tested by independent staff members, who are normally in the IT department but not programmers. It is important for non-programmers to do most of the testing so that they can be objective and think beyond the programs.

Testing must be done in a separate environment without being part of programming and operation. The programs being tested must have strict access control to avoid changes being made after testing without the knowledge of the tester, as that could invalidate the test results. Testing must be thoroughly documented. Testing of a system under development is more extensive than testing ad hoc program changes. There are more test cases and extensive test data compared to string testing. That's why this phase is called integration testing.

System integration test result should be signed off by the IT department, project manager, user representatives, internal audit and IT security.

USER ACCEPTANCE TESTING

After system integration testing, user representatives will perform their own testing. This will also include using operations procedures along with system testing and assessing the system's user friendliness and capability to process fluctuating transaction loads. User acceptance testing should focus more on user friendliness and procedures because automated functions have been extensively tested under system integration testing.

User acceptance test result should be signed off by the IT department, the project sponsor, user representatives, the project manager and internal audit.

SOFTWARE CERTIFICATION

Some programs are not just parts of an application. They are reusable code (program source or object code that can be used in other systems development projects) or utility programs (programs that can be used for housekeeping but critical functions like backup and archive). In addition to user signoff, these programs should receive certification in the organization for reuse. The criteria for certification should be broad yet detailed, broad in a sense that they take into account the needs of the organization across business units, detailed in that they are rigorous in terms of the extent of testing and documentation. Certification should be signed off by the project manager of the project that creates the reusable code and also by the PMO which maintains a repository of reusable code.

PROCEDURES DEVELOPMENT

Before system implementation, procedures should be developed or updated. These procedures should include:

- User procedures;
- Accounting procedures;
- Computer operations procedures;
- IT security procedures including user account management;
- Technical support procedures; and
- Data and program backup procedures.

Procedures can be developed once the user requirements are signed off. Procedures should be signed off by the user area representatives, project manager, project sponsor and internal auditors.

DISASTER RECOVERY PLAN UPDATE

You can recall from the last chapter that the disaster recovery plan (DRP) should contain a list of business critical systems to be recovered when the backup computing facility is activated. This list will change from time to time depending on business changes, new systems and system retirement. The DRP should be reviewed for every systems development project and updated accordingly.

TRAINING

Training is often put to the backburner. The risk is that systems are designed properly but improperly operated and used. Before system implementation, training material and a training plan should be prepared. Training sessions should be conducted for operators, technical support people and users. The affected employees should be required to be certified as trained.

CONVERSION AND IMPLEMENTATION

In most cases, data conversion is necessary before system implementation. Conversion should be planned and tested. Data conversion often is automated and the programs that convert data should be subject to rigorous testing. Implementation should usually occur immediately after conversion to avoid the need for multiple conversions. The following are common approaches. There should be a conversion plan. Conversion result should be reconciled with the source files to ensure accuracy and completeness. There are a number of risk based conversion approaches. It is the project manager's decision as to which approach to take. The decision will be based on the complexity of the system, tightness of deadlines and experience with the individual approaches etc.

Direct Cutover

All data from the old system is converted to the new system and the old system stops at the time the new system kicks in. This approach is quite risky because if the new system does not work properly, there will be service disruption and may be data loss. Customer impact could be significantly felt. However, technology advancement and competitive pressure continue to make this approach appealing. Technology advancement can make the fall back arrangement almost seamless; i.e., if the new system has a major glitch, processing can be automatically reverted to the old system. This approach is also called the big bang method.

Pilot Implementation

When the deadline is not tight and the risk of direct cutover is too high considering the complexity of the system, an organization may adopt a more conservative method of conversion and implementation. One such method is pilot implementation. Under this method, a small business unit, e.g., a branch, is selected for using the new system. This is a good way to test the water in a real environment. If the system does not work properly, the damage is limited. This is commonly used in financial institutions.

Parallel Implementation

This is the safest implementation method and also the most expensive. It involves running the old system in parallel with the new system. Everything is processed twice. It is costly and impractical for customer service systems. A modified version is to run only the backroom processing in parallel. That would lower the cost and inconvenience but also would provide less redundant safety margin as fully parallel conversion. Parallel conversion is more practical for accounting systems especially the general ledger systems where there is no customer interface, the transaction volume is low and the required degree of integrity is high. It is also more commonly used for a payroll system which tends to process transactions on a batch basis and there is no customer interaction. Parallel implementation is impractical for an online system because of the inconvenience posed to online business operation where time is of the essence.

Phased Implementation

This is similar to the pilot approach except that instead of selecting a unit to use the new system, the entire organization will use it but only selected functions will be turned on, and those corresponding functions of the old system will be turned off. If the replaced functions of the old system cannot be turned off, transaction adjustments will be made for the overlap, and that can be complicated. This may not be practical for enterprise resource planning systems that integrate many functions of the organization.

Conversion and Implementation Plan

The conversion and implementation plan should include the following:

- Old file names and versions to be converted.
- Names of new file and system versions.
- Dates of conversion and implementation.
- Approach (method) to conversion.
- Programs used to convert.
- Procedures and responsibilities.
- Tests to ensure completeness and accuracy.
- A checklist to ensure people, infrastructure, software, procedures and information are ready and have been implemented.
- User signoff.

The conversion plan and result should be signed off by the IT department, the project sponsor, the project manager, user representatives and internal audit.

SYSTEM DOCUMENTATION

The new system should come with detailed documentation that includes user requirements, project plan, progress reports, business case, management and user signoffs, system design, test cases, test results, conversion plan, conversion results, implementation plan, operations procedures, user procedures and maintenance procedures. Documentation should be prepared at each phase of the systems development project. At the end of development, the system documentation should be cataloged in the corporate system library. The library contains the system documentation of each system and should be maintained by the PMO.

PROJECT MONITORING AND REPORTING

Project progress must be monitored by the project manager and significant variances should be reported to the project sponsors, stakeholders and senior management. Most organizations today use project management software to create project plans, progress reports and variance reports. The PMO should have access to all of these reports to provide independent monitoring in addition to that performed by the project manager. Reports should include narrative progress reports, critical path diagrams and Gantt charts showing actual progress vs planned.

There should also be financial monitoring to see if the actual expenses incurred are consistent with the business case. A useful metric for this is earned value. An earned value demonstrates the extent of useful time spent on a project. Here is an example using earned value analysis.

1. The planned staff time for week 1 of a project is estimated to cost $10,000.
2. The planned deliverable in week 1 is completion of the entity relationship diagrams.
3. The actual staff time spent in week 1 is $12,500 including approved overtime.
4. Only 75% of the entity relationship diagrams is completed.
5. The earned value is 75% of planned cost, i.e., $7,500.
6. The cost variance is $5,000, unfavorable.
7. The project manager will have to talk to staff and find out the reason for the variance and find out why the overtime was approved.
8. Assuming the same rate of progress for this activity, the project will be over budget by at least $12,500/75% - 10,000, or $6,667. The schedule will be late by (5/75% - 5) days, or 1.67 days.
9. If the project manager can correct the "inefficiency", the cost overrun will still be the actual overrun to date, $5,000 and the schedule tardiness will be 1.25 days. The project manager may have to make other processes ahead of target in terms of efficiency to make up for the loss.

Project progress should be reported at least monthly to the project sponsor.

POST-IMPLEMENTATION REVIEW

Every system should be subject to a post-implementation review. The purpose is to assess whether the system is a success. Some projects might have finished on time and on budget but are not useful. The review should be done 3 to 6 months after implementation by someone who did not develop the user requirements, perform testing or develop the systems. Quite often, an internal auditor is a suitable person. The review should entail interviews with users, control walkthrough, assessing whether the project plan was carried out properly and assessing whether the business case was adhered to. Detailed project documentation will be reviewed. The review report should indicate the following:

- Total project development cost compared to budget cost.
- Any user requirements not included in the system or not functioning properly.
- Missing project documentation.
- Missing approval of project deliverables.
- Summary and details of user feedback.
- System and project management deficiencies.
- Recommendations for corrective actions for the current project and improvements for future projects.

Post-implementation review should be conducted by people independent of systems development and management for the project. Internal auditors and quality assurance staff members are often desirable candidates to carry out this review because of their objectivity. The report should be addressed to the system sponsor. Ideally, internal auditors who were not involved in the systems development audit in terms of reviewing project documentation during development should perform the post-implementation review. If such "independent" auditors are unavailable, even auditors who reviewed the system documentation during development are still reliable to perform the post-implementation review because they can draw on their knowledge gained during the project and also because auditors are trained to be objective.

Project or system deficiencies should be corrected immediately to the extent practical. For example, if certain sign-offs are missing, the responsible stakeholders should provide the sign-off even if it is tardy, such as a programming manager's sign-off, in order to complete the project documentation and acceptance of accountability. Another example is inadequate testing or training. Such findings should also be corrected as soon as possible. Some findings, however, are meaningless to correct retroactively. For example, if project meetings were held only monthly instead of bi-weekly as called for by the project plan, there is no point in holding the missed meetings because the project is done. A recommendation to address this would go along the line of strengthening future assurance that project meetings are held on a timely basis, perhaps implementing an email notification to the project sponsor with meeting minutes bi-weekly.

RAPID APPLICATION DEVELOPMENT

For simple applications or when the project deadline is very tight, the organization may decide to apply rapid application development techniques. These techniques are used to condense the systems development life cycle or bypass some of the phases. The use of these techniques must be approved by the project sponsor and the CIO.

Joint Application Development

This approach combines the user requirement phase with the system architecture and system design phases. Workshops are conducted to involve user representatives, system architects and system designers to design the system and architecture from a user perspective interactively. The benefit of this approach is that real time interaction can expedite the development process and avoid misunderstanding. Brainstorming can also make people more creative. The risks are as follows.

An aggressive party in the workshop may give undue influence to the others and dominate the workshop to such an extent that the other participants are constrained from making thorough and innovative contribution to the process. This can lead to systems specifications that are incompatible with the infrastructure, impractical to program or inefficient for programming. It can also lead to less than thorough user requirements if the user representatives are "overpowered" by the architects and designers.

Secondly, documentation may not be detailed. Even if user requirement definition, architecture design and software design are done in workshops, it is critical that project documentation indicates what the users expressed as their requirements and how these requirements are translated to architecture and design specifications. Throughout these workshops, such information should be documented. At the end of the workshops, detailed user requirements, architecture and design documents should be prepared.

Joint application development should include experienced moderators who ensure that each party participates actively and expressions are documented in a structured way. The moderator will also ensure that proper documentation is prepared and signed off. The moderator can come from the quality assurance department of the CIO division. The user requirements, design specifications and architecture must be separately signed off by the parties stated above under these respective headings.

Prototype

Applications that involve a new user environment and significant online user interfaces may benefit from prototyping. This means developing a working replica of the system before detailed development effort is expended. Input and output screens are developed before detailed design and architecture are prepared. This allows users to "experience" the new system or product in a somewhat virtual manner to assess user friendliness and practicality before the development team and stakeholders start to worry too much about detailed functions. Based on prototyping, system design can be more refined iteratively to suit user needs. Prototyping can also help users articulate their requirements. Should prototype be used on every project? The answer is no because it can be expensive to set up a prototype environment. Also, in most cases, users can articulate their requirements without "new experience", especially when the users are highly knowledgeable about the business that the system will support. Further, if user requirements are detailed and the business functions supported are not significantly "out of the ordinary", architecture definition and software design can be carried out directly from the user requirements.

Prototype can present a risk in that if the users are highly impressed, they may assume the designers know what they want and therefore be less thorough in writing the user requirements. A CEO once saw a prototype demonstration and asked when the system would be ready. This put a lot of pressure on the project manager and as a result, corners were cut to get the system ready ahead of schedule. Guess what suffered..., internal controls, documentation and training.

Organizations should set a policy and provide guidelines on the use of prototype so that systems development teams know when it can be used, what approval is required and what documentation has to be prepared. Tighter management reporting should be required for prototype projects. The internal audit department should be informed so it can help ensure that internal controls are not compromised by user enthusiasm in system appearance. The user requirements, design specifications and architecture should be signed off by the parties listed earlier under these respective headings.

End User Development

Today's employees are more IT savvy than ever before. Many are technically empowered to develop systems. It is therefore tempting for users to bypass the IT department and start writing programs and implementing the programs on their own computers or the local area network. Such temptation will even be higher if the IT department is overloaded or less responsive than what the users expect

End user development can in many cases deliver a system faster than going through the IT department because fewer people are involved and there is less communication. However, the system may be developed incorrectly because some users think they can program and have too much confidence in themselves. Further, testing may be significantly inadequate or not carried out at all. Documentation may not be prepared because the end user developers think they know how to use and maintain the system. If the system has to integrate with other systems, inadequate testing and documentation will affect system integrity and performance.

Experience shows that end user development cannot practically be prevented. Many organizations condone it and think it adds to the organizations' competitiveness if some users can "help themselves" to develop small systems. Such systems are more likely to meet the users' requirements. What organizations must do is to set a policy on end user development. The policy should define the types of users allowed to carry out end user development, e.g., the management information systems support staff within each business unit. The policy should also outline the following:

- Approval levels and stages of approval.
- End user development methodology and procedures.
- Types of systems that can be developed by users, e.g., only systems used for management information, not transaction processing systems.
- Programming tools allowed.
- Documentation required and checkpoints.
- Business case justification.
- Extent of testing.
- Naming convention for spreadsheets, queries, forms, database tables and system query code like structured query language (SQL).
- Backup of spreadsheets and SQL code.
- Documentation in terms of comments for spreadsheets and SQL code.

The end user development policy actually should be a mini version of the systems development methodology. End user developed systems should not be allowed to run on a network so as to prevent undue reliance by other business units and also contaminating the corporate systems.

SYSTEMS ACQUISITION

The foregoing material applies to systems being developed in house. When a new system is needed, the organization has three other options:

- Hire a firm to develop the system, outsourcing.
- Buy a system off the shelf.
- Buy a system and hire a firm to customize and implement.

Outsourcing Systems Development

This will occur usually when the organization does not have enough expertise in the type of system to be acquired. Here are the risks of this option.

- Selecting a firm that does not have enough expertise.
- Selecting a firm that is too expensive.
- Selecting a firm that is not stable and cannot finish the project.
- Miscommunicating user requirements to the firm, although this risk also applies to in-house development, communication between organizations is more challenging.
- Inadequate project oversight, as it is more challenging to manage a firm than your own staff.
- System ownership not properly defined.

To mitigate these risks, organizations should set a policy on systems development outsourcing. This policy should address the following.

- Defining criteria for outsourcing.
- Defining approval levels for outsourcing.
- Defining outsourcing procedures.
- Defining rules and criteria for single sourcing vs obtaining competitive bids.
- Procedures for qualifying vendors.
- Standard contract and review process.
- Ownership of source code and source code escrow arrangement. A source code escrow agreement involves placing the current source code with a third party. In the event of a contract breach or the developing vendor ceasing business, the user organization can access the source code to maintain the system.

If the user organization does not have the source code, it will have to continuously rely on the vendor. The lack of source code, from an auditor point of view, may be favorable because it reduces the risk of unauthorized program changes.

Buying a System off the Shelf

This usually applies to simple systems. The risk is fairly low because the system tends to be market proven. The user organization will not have the source code. Only minimal testing needs to be performed.

Buying a System to Customize to the Organization's Environment

A common scenario is the acquisition of an enterprise resource planning system like SAP or Oracle. The risk and internal control considerations for systems development outsourcing also apply here. An additional risk is integration with legacy systems, which will call for more testing than the previous two options.

ERP Acquisition and Implementation Considerations

Before an organization decides to buy an ERP, it should perform business process reengineering. Because of the wide scope of an ERP, an organization planning to implement such a system should seize the opportunity to review the business processes throughout the enterprise and establish a value chain of functions of activities at the same time weeding or streamlining the functions and activities that do not deliver value. An ERP should be used to automate and integrate efficient processes instead of magnifying inefficiency.

Because of the wide scope of an ERP, a detailed implementation plan should be prepared. Organizations that use the phased approach have to realize that the full benefit of the ERP will not be realized until all modules are implemented. An ERP presents a steep learning curve because of increased automation and integration as well as changes in business processes.

Advanced training is crucial. Just as it is important to have fully trained IT specialists to configure, test and implement an ERP, it is a good idea to have internal certification of ERP users before implementation.

Request for Proposals

When a significant system is to be obtained externally or developed by a consulting firm, the user organization should send out a request for proposals (RFP). The RFP should include detailed user requirements. Additional components of the RFP include the evaluation criteria, deadline for submitting bids and a standard contract. The law department and the internal auditors should be consulted. Internal auditors should review user requirements to help ensure that controls are adequately included. Proposals should be evaluated by the authors of the user requirements along with selected system designers and architects who can provide the technical advice in reviewing vendor submissions. The decision process and justification for vendor selection as a result of the evaluation of proposals should be thoroughly documented and signed off by the project sponsor. Pricing should account for at least half of the consideration in vendor selection.

The final contract should be signed only upon satisfactory testing. So after reviewing the vendor submissions, the project manager should sign a provisional contract with the vendor to test the system and the test criteria should be stated in the provisional contract.

SUMMARY OF SYSTEMS DEVELOPMENT AND ACQUISITION PHASES

1. At an organizational level, develop a three year systems development plan that is updated every year. This is part of the IT strategy. The systems development plan should include all current and planned projects. The start dates, checkpoints, end dates, deliverables and resource requirements should be included for each project. The CIO is responsible for this and the IT steering committee should approve. Internal and external auditors should be informed. The project management office should maintain this plan.

2. Problem recognition, which is a business unit responsibility, must be approved by the system owner(s) of the systems to be replaced and developed, before the development of each system.

3. Feasibility study, a business unit responsibility, must be approved by the system owner(s) of the systems to be replaced and developed, before the development of each system.

4. Project proposal, a business unit responsibility, must be approved by the level of management with financial authority to sign off the net cost of the project over the life time before netting the cost with operational savings. Operational savings may not materialize if circumstances change or the estimates are too liberal.

5. System analysis, a project manager responsibility, must be approved by the project sponsor.

6. Project plan, a project management responsibility, must be approved by the project sponsor and IT department.

7. User requirements, a business unit responsibility, must be approved by the project manager, IT department and project sponsor; should be signed off by internal audit and IT security. The IT architecture and design units must also sign off to make sure the user requirements can be expanded to architecture and design specifications.

8. System architecture, an IT department responsibility, must be approved by project manager. It must be signed off by the lead designer, internal audit and IT security.

9. System design, can be carried out concurrently with system architecture, is an IT department responsibility. It must be approved by project manager, user representatives, the system architects, internal audit and IT security.

10. Programming, an IT department responsibility, must be approved by the programming and project managers.

11. System integration testing, an IT department responsibility, must be approved by project manager, IT department. It must also be signed off by internal audit and IT security.

12. User acceptance testing, a business unit responsibility, must be approved by project manager, IT department and project sponsor. It should be signed off by internal audit.

13. Procedures development can be carried out concurrently with the above processes after system design. This is a project manager responsibility. It must be approved by the project manager, IT department and project sponsor. It should be signed off by internal audit.

14. Disaster recovery plan update, an IT department responsibility, can be carried out concurrently with the above process after system design. It must be approved by project manager, IT department and project sponsor.

15. Training can be carried out concurrently with the above process after system design. It is a business unit and IT department responsibility, it must be approved by project manager and project sponsor. Affected employees must be certified.

16. Conversion and implementation, a project manager responsibility, must be approved by the IT department and project sponsor. It should be signed off by internal audit.

17. Post-implementation review is a project sponsor responsibility. It must be signed off by internal audit and the project manager. The review should be done by someone independent of the systems development project.

MANAGEMENT CHECKLIST

1. Develop a systems development methodology that addresses systems development, systems acquisition and rapid application options.

2. Develop an end user development policy.

3. Ensure internal audit is involved in systems development.

4. Set procedures to inform the board and the IT steering committee about major projects.

5. Ensure that IT staff and appropriate user areas are trained on the systems development methodology.

6. Develop an annual systems development plan containing planned and active projects.

7. Establish a PMO to monitor and report on systems development projects.

8. Develop quality assurance metrics and procedures for systems testing, documentation, training and acceptance.

9. Establish a business case methodology as part of the systems development methodology that is consistent with corporate policies.

10. Prepare quarterly status reports on active projects measuring progress, cost and benefits.

AUDITOR'S INVOLVEMENT

The internal auditor should be closely involved in major systems development projects, from system proposal to post-implementation review. The concern about lack of objectivity or independence can be addressed as long as the auditor does not take part in decisions other than internal control definition and test plan development. It is true that an auditor could be less objective, or appear so, if s/he reviewed the test plan and subsequently reviewed test results or audited the system when it is in operation. However, the value delivered by the auditor in being proactive during systems development can most likely outweigh the loss or perceived loss of objectivity in doing the post-implementation review or auditing a system after implementation. In large organizations, different auditors can be used to take part in internal control advisory and subsequent auditing of systems in operation.

Internal auditors should be given the right to review documentation and sign off at each stage of development, before the next stage can begin. In order to be a corporate team player while maintaining objectivity, internal auditors should get involved as early as possible as it is easier to influence the project team before it has taken a position. If control issues cannot be resolved with the project manager, the auditors may have to elevate to executives including the CEO. At the end of each major project, there should be an internal audit report, and the findings should be addressed with a management action plan. Internal auditors should provide their own requirements to the project manager in terms of its ability to retrieve data for audit testing after system implementation.

At the end of the project, the internal audit department should provide a closing report to the project sponsor that lists all the findings and recommendations to date as well as the status of implementing the recommendations. This report is not the same as the post-implementation report. The post-implementation report is produced 3 to 6 months after implementation and it comments on the success of the project along with outstanding deficiencies in the system and management of the project.

The systems development phases of most importance to internal auditors is the user requirements phase, followed by architecture, design, system integration testing, user acceptance testing, conversion, implementation and procedures development. The user requirements stage is the most important because this is where internal controls and the auditors' data retrieval requirements should first be specified. These phases are also important to the external auditors. However, to the external auditors, the conversion phase is more important than the others because it affects financial statements integrity more directly.

External auditors should be informed of systems development projects although it is usually impractical for them to be closely involved. They should assess the impact of the new system on the financial statements. They can also advise on internal controls and should try to be proactive even if that means spending some time that is not billable. It would boost their image and make them appear more to be value adding. Meanwhile, they have to consider their independence and perceived independence. In other words, the shareholders' auditors should be proactive and assertive while keeping arms-length. This is especially important for public companies. The Sarbanes-Oxley Act restricts shareholders' auditors from providing systems development consulting to their audit clients.

External auditors should rely heavily on internal auditors in obtaining assurance that systems are developed with proper controls and data is converted properly. They should obtain a copy of all internal audit reports and the post-implementation report. External auditors should perform some direct testing of data conversion as this affects financial statements directly. They should also review the internal audit work papers.

INTERNAL AUDIT CHECKLIST

1. Review the systems development methodology and ongoing changes to ensure that it includes adequate provision for project management, system documentation and system testing.

2. Review the annual systems development plan to assess significance and select projects to be involved in.

3. Inform the CIO of the projects in which internal audit wants to participate by means of meeting attendance and sign-off of documents from an internal control perspective.

4. Inform the CIO of the projects for which internal audit would like to receive progress reports in order to assess the risk of implementation tardiness and the impact of upcoming implementation on internal audit assignments.

5. Establish a core team of auditors experienced in systems development auditing.

6. Develop a systems development audit methodology that is congruent with the systems development methodology.

7. To the extent practical, segregate duties between systems development auditing and auditing of existing systems to ensure objectivity.

8. Ensure the new system will be auditable, i.e., the data can be easily retrieved for audit testing.

9. Update the audit programs of operation unit audits to account for the internal controls in the new system.

10. Report periodically on systems development audit findings and trends to the audit committee.

EXTERNAL AUDIT CHECKLIST

1. Review the systems development methodology to assess the adequacy of systems development controls (project controls).

2. Review the annual systems development plan to assess significance to the financial statements.

3. Review the internal audit plan for the year to assess the degree of reliance to be placed on internal audit.

4. Review the internal audit reports on systems development audits and consider findings in formulating the financial statement audit approach.

5. For systems with significant financial statement implication, review the internal audit work papers.

6. Update audit programs to reflect new systems implemented in the current year.

7. For systems with significant financial statement implication, review and test the conversion result and audit trail.

8. Review user and accounting procedures to assess clarity and adequacy of internal controls.

9. Review any reports to the IT steering committee and the board.

10. For systems with significant financial statement implication, confirm that the sponsors have signed off.

CONCLUSION

Systems development is a major IT activity in most organizations. Even organizations that use purchased software packages often find the need to enhance the systems' functions or tailor the packages to their environments. Systems development may seem straight forward in that users are free to define their requirements and the IT department is expected to write programs to fulfill the requirements. In fact, it is a risky undertaking because of the need to coordinate expectation and understanding between users and stakeholders who may not be IT savvy and because of the increasing interaction between systems in today's globally competitive environment. Many organizations have failed to complete systems development projects and have produced the wrong systems in relation to their business needs. Organizations need to mitigate this risk by implementing a systems development methodology to be used consistently to ensure that the development of only duly requested systems is authorized, accurate, efficient and complete and that implementation is timely.

REVIEW QUESTIONS

1. What are the different phases of system testing and who are involved?

2. If an organization hires a firm to develop a system, how does the organization ensure that the system will be maintainable, i.e., changeable?

3. What is included in a request for proposals?

4. What are the pros and cons of buying a system?

5. What is a good use of the critical path diagram?

6. Who should sign off the user requirements and why?

7. When should internal controls be first included in a systems development project?

8. Who should the project manager report to?

9. Write a job advertisement for a project manager.

10. Who should be the sponsor of a student records system?

CASE - Internal Audit Report – Agriculture and Agri-Food Canada

For the following excerpt of an audit report on National Land & Water Information Service Project - System Under Development, of the Canadian Government, prepare an audit program that includes at least ten audit procedures that you think the audit team has used. Show the objective of each procedure. Do not be restricted by the findings and conclusion in this report.

Audit Report - National Land & Water Information Service Project - System Under Development Audit

Office of Audit and Evaluation
October 2008

Table of Contents

1.0 Audit Objectives

The overall objective of this "System Under Development" (SUD) audit is to provide management with independent assurance on the adequacy and effectiveness of key elements of the control framework for the National Land and Water Information Service Project (the "NLWIS Project" or "Project"). A SUD audit is a parallel or concurrent review of the relevant System Development Life Cycle (SDLC) stages of a project, as they are happening, to highlight risks/issues and provide necessary risk mitigation recommendations to the appropriate management.

During the audit planning phase, three risk areas and specific audit objectives were identified:

Project Governance: Assess project governance to ensure it demonstrates evidence of a well-defined structure of roles, responsibilities and authorities within which the Project operates, and within which all major decisions concerning the scope and objectives of the Project, including changes, are made.

Business Requirements: Assess the adequacy and efficiency of processes implemented to define record, update and manage business requirements in support of development efforts and the delivery of business solutions identified in the Project's business case.

Project Management: Determine whether NLWIS project management practices, processes and controls are consistent with industry best practices and relevant government and departmental policies.

2.0 Scope and Approach

Like any system in its development phase, the NLWIS Project environment is constantly changing as project activities, objectives, risks and controls evolve to reflect the stage of the Project, lessons learned and stakeholder needs/input and other changes in the operating environment. It is important to note that this audit reflects an assessment of project risks and controls during a specific period of project implementation. To the extent possible and to ensure relevance of audit findings, audit procedures were tailored to take account of the state of NLWIS project development.

The audit of the NLWIS Project was included in the Office of Audit and Evaluation's approved 2007-08 Internal Audit Plan. Audit planning began in June 2007 and culminated with the completion of a risk assessment and audit plan in October 2007. Audit field work, which included a review of key documents, process walkthroughs, limited substantive testing and extensive interviews, was conducted during the period November 2007 to January 2008. Synthesis and analysis of findings took place in February and March 2008. The audit was conducted with the assistance of professional staff from PricewaterhouseCoopers LLP.

Auditors were provided with unrestricted access to project documentation and personnel. We wish to express our appreciation to NLWIS management and staff for their assistance and cooperation in providing documentation and participating in interviews throughout the course of this audit.

The following chart outlines the three phases of the audit approach and key tasks within each phase:

Approach of NLWIS SUD Audit		
Phase 1 **Planning** **Jun 07-Oct 07**	**Phase 2** **Fieldwork** **Nov 07 - Jan 08**	**Phase 3** **Analysis & Reporting** **Feb 08 - May 08**
Project Initiation. Kick-off meeting. Obtain documentation. Develop interview list. Scan Document Interviews Conduct preliminary interviews Review key managerial controls and risk management processes. Risk assessment. Develop detailed audit plan and schedule.	Conduct audit program using the following techniques. Interview project personnel. Review documentation. Conduct process walk-throughs.	Analyze findings & synthesize issues. Prepare audit observations. Validate findings with management. Prepare draft audit report. Prepare final report with recommendations. Finalize all audit working papers. Obtain and review management response and action plans.

Audit criteria for this SUD audit were drawn from the following sources:

- COBIT (Control Objectives for Information and related Technology), a set of best practices for information technology management created by the Information Systems Audit and Control Association (ISACA), and the IT Governance Institute (ITGI);

- Treasury Board's Policy on Management of Information Technology (MIT), which promulgates the efficient and effective use of information technology to support government priorities and program delivery, increase productivity, and enhance service to the public;

- Treasury Board's Enhanced Framework for the Management of Information Technology Projects, which is designed to ensure that information technology projects fully meet the needs of the business functions they are intended to support, deliver expected benefits and are completed within their approved schedule, cost and functionality.

Sufficient audit work was performed and sufficient evidence gathered to support the conclusions contained in this audit report.

3.0 Background

The NLWIS Project is a $100 million Major Crown Project. Treasury Board's Policy on the Management of Major Crown Projects states that a project is deemed to be a Major Crown Project when its estimated cost will exceed $100 million and TBS assesses it as high risk.

The purpose of the NLWIS Project is to transform the way the Department of Agriculture and Agri-Food Canada (AAFC) uses geomatics by rationalizing the Department's geomatics investments (people, data, infrastructure, IT applications, services and management), and rolling these into an enterprise service.

NLWIS's cross-functional and geographically dispersed team has presented some challenges.

A project priority was to provide on-line access to detailed information about land, soil, water, air, climate and biodiversity using a combination of geospatial and business intelligence technologies. Information made available by this service will be developed in concert with other federal departments, provinces and territories and allow land managers to access multiple geospatial information services through a single web portal. The end product is an effective decision support tool to help local, regional and national land-use planners and managers assist the Canadian agricultural sector in making effective land management decisions.

The NLWIS Project lifecycle is comprised of the following phases to be implemented over the period from 2005/06 to 2008/09:

- Phase I: Single Window (build a new single Internet portal for applications, data and tools currently situated in various Web pages on the AAFC Online Web site);

- Phase II: Geographic Environment (build the infrastructure, procedures and processes for the new AAFC Geographic Information Services (GIS) enterprise system);

- Phase III: National Source for Agri-environmental Geospatial Information (provide national direct access to geospatial data, spatial functions and additional functionality through improved technology); and

- Phase IV: Integration of Information from Collaborating Organizations (develop new software tools and updated and standardized databases in order to provide value-added information, products and expertise for land-use decision support).

During the audit conduct phase (November 2007 to January 2008), the NLWIS Project was in its third year of development, with just over a year remaining in its lifecycle.

4.0 Audit Summary

The NLWIS Project is technically complex (i.e., cross-functional with a geographically dispersed team), involves many stakeholders from within and beyond AAFC, and has a $100 million budget.

This SUD audit assessed Project risks and controls during a specified period of time. Audit fieldwork occurred in year three of the Project life-cycle, November 2007 to January 2008, just prior to the NLWIS Executive Director's proactive initiation of a review of the overall health of the Project, followed by an aggressive 13-month action plan to address its findings.

Given the magnitude, complexity and stage in the NLWIS Project lifecycle, auditors expected to see and confirm a relatively mature control framework and a system development control infrastructure in place that reflects industry best practices and meets Government of Canada requirements.

Audit findings in the next section of the report are presented on an exception basis. That is, findings describe areas of weakness in the project controls that were examined in the course of this audit.

Notwithstanding the findings and recommendations within this report, the audit team found a number of areas of strength in the controls and control environment, in particular:

- The use of appropriate System Development Lifecycle (SDLC) Techniques;

- Consolidation of testing under a single manager;

- A focus on continuous improvement including a management-led review and follow-up action plan for the final year of the Project, "lunch and learn" sessions and "way forward" documents;

- Evolving governance structures to strengthen decision-making and accountability; and,

- Establishment of a Change Control Board which represents a significant enhancement to the change management process.

However, audit findings also indicate that, although there is evidence of improvement since the Project's start, during the time of the audit, established controls for project governance, business requirements and project management did not yet reflect the expected level of maturity nor industry best practices.

While management had initiated action on many of these issues at the time of the audit, there are a number of challenges that require attention. Unless addressed, these challenges increase the risk that the Project will not achieve one or more of its objectives related to value-for-money and/or service sustainability in a timely manner.

Challenges identified by the audit are summarized below:

Project Governance

- Steering Committee function and membership does not reflect best practices in terms of membership and stakeholder representation.

- Incomplete and/or dated documentation of roles and responsibilities of governance committees, project resources and stakeholders which has led to instances of confusion and inconsistency between observed and expected roles.

- Based on project organizational charts, the Quality Assurance function does not have the expected autonomy and independence.

- Duties amongst teams responsible for application development, architecture and business requirements are insufficiently segregated.

Business Requirements

- Business requirements are not effectively gathered and systematically prioritized within a sound governance framework. Specifically, business requirements are not:

- independently validated by the Quality Assurance function;

- clearly linked to user requirements or work breakdown structures; or

- linked to architecture/application designs or release deliverables that had been developed with active participation of key stakeholders.

- As of November 2007, the Project's business requirements document had not been validated or signed off by stakeholders.

Project Management

- The Project's change management process has compliance issues.

- The Project's risk management process was not effective throughout the Project lifecycle.

- The Project had limited capability to track and assess value-for-money as project reporting did not link expenditures to realized benefits.

- There is limited capability to forecast whether the Project will be delivered on time and within budget.

- There has been limited focus on planning for project completion and transition to the end-state.

It is important to note that this audit was conducted at a time of significant change in the senior management level of the NLWIS Project. Subsequent to the audit, proactive measures were taken to assess Project gaps and weaknesses and implement corrective measures. Nevertheless, sustained attention and further enhancements are required as the Project enters its final year.

5.0 Conclusions

Based on the audit findings, significant control weaknesses exist in the areas of project governance, business requirements and project management. Such weaknesses pose serious risks to the timely achievement of the NLWIS Project objectives and therefore require immediate attention to ensure successful project outcomes.

Source: www4.agr.gc.ca/AAFC-AAC/display-afficher.do?id=1233606529174&lang=eng#s1, accessed on June 20, 2012.

MULTIPLE CHOICE QUESTIONS

1. A company has hired a consulting firm to develop a system, but the consulting firm does not want to release the source code to the company? What would protect the company's interest in terms of the system's upgradeability and maintainability?
   a) Registration of the system
   b) Confidentiality agreement
   c) Non-compete agreement
   d) Source code escrow agreement
   e) Access control

2. Which risk goes up the most when an organization outsources systems development?
   a) System integrity
   b) System reliability
   c) System maintainability
   d) Unauthorized data access
   e) System responsiveness

3. Is which systems development phases are flowcharts prepared?
   a) User requirement
   b) Programming
   c) Design
   d) Procedures development
   e) Conversion

4. Which pair of activities can often be carried out concurrently?
   a) Training and procedures writing
   b) Testing and conversion
   c) User requirements development and system design
   d) Project planning and system design
   e) Design and programming

5. When internal auditors are asked by a project manager to provide user requirements to a system development project, they should
   a) refuse in order to maintain independence.
   b) provide as comprehensive requirements as possible by thinking like the business users to ensure the system is complete.
   c) address the system's auditability.
   d) address the system's disaster recovery capability.
   e) facilitate the user requirement workshops.

6. What is the relationship between systems development controls and software change controls?
   a) They are mutually exclusive.
   b) Software change controls depend on systems development controls.
   c) They are inter-dependent.
   d) Systems development controls depend on software change controls.
   e) For a system under development, software change controls should be applied before engaging systems development controls.

7. Which of the following concern is most common to systems development controls and software change controls?
   a) User requirement definition
   b) Testing
   c) Feasibility study
   d) Database design
   e) Emergency fixes

8. What is the correct sequence of system development documentation?
   a) System architecture, user requirements, flowcharts, programs.
   b) Project plan, test plan, user requirements, flowcharts.
   c) Entity relationship diagram, user requirements, Gantt chart, flowcharts
   d) Business case, feasibility study, test plan, user requirements.
   e) User requirements, entity relationship diagrams, system architecture, flowcharts.

9. How do user representatives sign off computer programs?
   a) Review of design documentation
   b) Review of user requirements
   c) Review of computer programs
   d) Testing
   e) Post-implementation review

10. Which phase is avoided when an organization purchases a software package rather than developing it in house?
    a) Defining information requirements
    b) Identifying alternatives
    c) Design
    d) Testing

CHAPTER FIVE – CONTROL AND AUDIT IMPLICATIONS OF EBUSINESS

"The advance of technology is based on making it fit in so that you don't really even notice it, so it's part of everyday life." – Bill Gates

In Chapter Two, we discuss the risk impact of information systems. We conclude that generally, business risks increase proportionally with the use of information systems. This relationship applies to inherent risk, control risk and audit risk. eBusiness involves more IT resources than traditional information systems so we can deduce that eBusiness increases inherent risk, control risk and audit risk.

In addition to discussing the risks of eBusiness, we will cover the legal aspects of IT. This is because organizations that engage more in eBusiness will find that they have more IT related intellectual property to protect, e.g., eBusiness model, search engine, commercial software and product information. These properties are also more available on the Internet and the risk of copyright infringement is higher. Organizations are more accessible via the Internet so the risk of unauthorized access to trade secret increases.

We will discuss eBusiness controls to mitigate risks. eBusiness is a new way of conducting business, rather than a new type of transactions. So eBusiness controls are classified as general controls. eBusiness differs from traditional computer system mainly in the area of infrastructure, so before talking about risks and controls, we should discuss the typical eBusiness infrastructure.

eBUSINESS INFRASTRUCTURE

In Chapter One, we discuss the five components of a system: infrastructure, software, procedures, people and information. Of these five components, the one that is most likely to be different between eBusiness and systems that do not use the Internet is infrastructure. Let's see what that entails and what the risks are. Most of the risks are addressed with access controls, which we will discuss in more details in Chapter Eight.

Servers

Customers know of eBusiness by the domain name, e.g., www.united.com. This domain name is attached to a server called a web server. This is the server that takes input from and relay output to customers.

A web server is common and often the first target of attack, because it is the first server accessed by external parties. It must be configured to withstand stressful traffic and abuse. On the other hand, its configuration should not be as tight as an internal server, otherwise the web server will not fulfill its role of being "opened" to the public. Common configuration parameters include logging as well as ports and services restrictions. A common type of attack on a web server is defacement. Sometimes, instead of defacement, a hacker might change or delete a price, an interest rate or some words in a user agreement. The latter will be less noticeable and the damage can be significant. Organizations should continuously monitor the web server for attacks and changes. A common practice is to frequently refresh the content from an offline version.

The traditional content of a web server consists of data in hypertext markup language (HTML). Increasingly, organizations use eXensible markup language (XML) to connect links to data and define the nature, format and rules of data, to facilitate eBusiness and particularly business-to-business eBusiness that involves a purchasing organization's system interfacing with a supplier web site directly. For example, an XML link may define that the underlying data table is a table of inventory items where the first field is an alphanumeric product number. Organizations that use XML need to ensure that the links that define data are correct.

A web server usually contains public information and is not used to process financial transactions. A customer transaction is then routed to an application server, a server that contains the programs for transaction processing. Even before that, when authentication is required, a customer request is directed to an authentication server that contains credentials for authentication. There is also a database server that contains master and transaction data. All the servers other than the web server should be behind firewalls and more rigorously protected than the web server.

Web Master

This is the person who designs the web site using web authoring software tools. S/he must be well trained, meticulous and have high integrity. The authoring software must be properly configured. Web site design must be thoroughly documented and its content update must be subject to rigorous change control procedures including pre-approval and post verification.

Web Hosting Software

This is the software on a web server that communicates with the browser in a user's computer. In a way, this is the web server's version of a browser. Like a browser, this tool can be configured in a number of ways. The organization should have a standard configuration checklist for the web hosting software to ensure consistency in audit trail and security.

Web Site Tracking Tool

Web sites used to generate revenue would find this tool essential. If misconfigured, the tool may produce inaccurate statistics or fail to capture and analyze traffic. This can result in incorrect charges for advertising. Organizations should periodically review the configuration and verify the statistics produced. This is a highly critical business system for web sites that generate advertising revenue. These sites should have sophisticated web traffic monitoring algorithms to detect click fraud and ensure that advertisers are charged correctly. For example, ten clicks on the same link within a minute should be discarded for calculating advertising charges.

229

Internet Addressing

There are four types of address:

- uniform resource locator (URL) at the application layer

- Internet Protocol (IP) address at the network layer

- media access control (MAC) address at the data link layer

- port at the transport layer

Every Internet transaction has to include these addresses in order for it to be routable. A URL is essentially a web site address like www.ontario.ca. An IP address is a numeric address consisting of four 8-bit bytes and in more advanced networks, four 32-bit bytes. A MAC address is hard coded address assigned to a network adaptor by the manufacturer, like a vehicle identification number. URLs and IP addresses can be assigned dynamically. In other words, a computer may be assigned different URLs or different IP addresses from time to time, however, the MAC address does not change. The MAC address is therefore crucial for a network to route traffic. It also provides a permanent audit trail of which computer was used to carry out an activity and this information is useful in establishing an audit trail and forensic investigations.

Traffic on the Internet is generally routed using IP addresses. Every device on the network is assigned such an address. Organizations should subscribe to enough IP addresses for its users and servers, although a device needs an IP address only when it is connected to the network. Workstations and laptops can be assigned temporary IP addresses. Servers should have permanent addresses in order to lessen change to the domain name servers, which we will discuss below. Organizations should try to hide its real IP addresses from the public to prevent attacks by using network address translation methods, i.e., translating an internal IP address to an external IP address and vice versa. IP addresses around the world are assigned, for a fee, by Internet Assigned Numbers Authority (IANA), a not-for-profit organization in the United States owned by Internet Corporation for Assigned Names and Numbers (ICANN), also a not-for-profit corporation in the United States. ICANN controls domain names to avoid duplication and keeps track of what organizations own what domains.

IP addresses are geographically assigned, i.e., there are ranges for Asia Pacific, North America, Latin America, Africa and Europe. Within each of these ranges, addresses are assigned by country and then grouped by region within a country. It is therefore easy to tell where an IP address is assigned to.

Most IP addresses are composed of four 8-bit bytes. When expressed decimally, an IP address can theoretically range from 000.000.000.000 to 255.255.255.255. There are 256 combinations of an 8-bit byte. For example, IP address 192.168.0.107 is assigned by my Internet service provider (ISP) to my computer right now at 10:46 pm on June 21, 2012.

The current 8-bit scheme can accommodate 4,294,967,296 addresses and is not enough so many organizations have to dynamically ration IP addresses hence limiting their networks. A new range, called IP Version 6, has been introduced to use four 32-bit bytes for each IP address. This can accommodate 340 undecillion addresses, or 340,282,366,920,938,000,000,000,000,000,000,000,000 addresses, and that means

49,402,201,933,934,200,000,000,000,000 per person in the world. Countries are asking for their blocks of this new range. For example, China has requested 32 billion addresses. Some large organizations and ISPs are adopting IP V6. An organization should keep track of what IP addresses have been assigned to what devices.

A port is a conventional "door" or mailbox used on the Internet to standardize the types of Internet data traffic. Common ports include port 80, which is used for web browsing, port 443, used for encrypted Internet traffic like eBusiness, and port 25, which is used for traditional email (not browser email) based on the simple mail transfer protocol, e.g., email via Microsoft Outlook. There are thousands of ports recognizable on the Internet. Although each port is intended for a specific application for consistency and seamlessness, an organization can configure its systems to use any of these ports internally for tailored applications. For example, Microsoft's MSN Messenger uses port 1863.

Domain Name Servers

This is a server that is used only in an IP environment. It translates URLs to IP addresses. A URL may be a domain name or an extension thereof (part of a domain), e.g., www.ontario.ca or www.cica.ca/itac. For the Internet to be universally operable, every URL is assigned an IP address.

A DNS uses a table to translate each URL to an IP address and vice versa. The "vice versa" occurs usually for research and investigate purpose. For example, if a network administrator finds that an IP address is causing an enormous amount of traffic load, s/he can look up the URL that uses the IP address and contact the system administrator. The table is supplied by ICANN and updated frequently. Large ISPs have very up-to-date tables.

A DNS also contains internal references for IP address translation in order to route traffic within an intranet and also to route traffic received from an ISP to internal servers and workstations. Small organizations may not have DNS and may instead rely on the ISP. For those with DNS, the tables may be less up to date and any URL that cannot be translated to an IP address is then deferred to the ISP for translation.

A DNS is a common target of hacking. If a DNS is down, traffic that needs the DNS for IP address resolution (translation) will be stopped. Worse, if the DNS table is changed by a rouge person, e.g., substituting a bank's IP address with that of a hacker site, a bank customer can be directed to the hacker site.

Organizations should have redundant DNS and place their DNS behind firewalls. Changes should be monitored. Periodic test of IP resolution should be performed. A DNS can be used by an organization to prevent employees from going to undesirable sites by routing those URLs to a static server that returns a warning message.

Some DNS are placed at the network perimeter mainly to find the IP addresses of deep URLs. A deep URL is one with suffices to the domain name, e.g., http://www.yorku.ca/yorkweb/cs.htm. If I key this in from a browser at home, my ISP may be able to resolve it to an IP address in York University. However, my ISP may not know which server hosts the document I am looking for. If York University has a DNS at the network perimeter, it can then take me to the appropriate server.

Internet Model

You have probably heard the term TCP/IP in relation to the Internet. Transmission Control Protocol (TCP) is a protocol that is used to deliver data from one network to another and it is important that all organizations including ISPs use this protocol to ensure seamless communication. TCP actually predated the Internet and was used by organizations to connect their proprietary networks. Internet Protocol (IP) was added to TCP to form the Internet. IP is used to identify the source and destination by means of the IP addresses. It is also used to break a message down to packets.

TCP has error control capability, i.e., when the packets are assembled at the destination, the headers are checked to assess completeness of transmission of a message. If incomplete, the receiving router will ask the sending router to resend the packets. TCP/IP structures data in five levels as follows, based on the Open System Interconnection model.

Layer	Main Functions	Hardware	Software	Addresses
5. Application	Lets a user compose data and presents data to the destination	Servers, PCs and smart phones	Web browser and Internet hosting software	URL
4. Transport	1. Breaks a message into packets for expedient transmission via the quickest paths. 2. Assign ports.	Servers, PCs and smart phones	Operating system	Port number
3. Network	Captures the IP address	Servers, PCs, smart phones, routers and switches.	Operating system	IP address and port number
2. Data link	1. Error detection and correction. 2. Captures the MAC address.	Servers, PCs, smart phones, routers and switches.	Operating system	IP address, port number and MAC address.
1. Physical	Data transmission	Circuits like phone line, cable, satellite.	Telecommunication software	IP address and port number

Every Internet message is generated at the application layer and lowered successively to the physical layer at which time it is broken into packets. The packets are transmitted on the chosen circuit and when a packet arrives at a destination or intermediate device like a switch or router, it is raised. In the case of a switch (discussed below), the packet is raised to layer 2, a router (discussed below) raises received packets to layer 3. When the packet arrives at a server or user device like a PC, it is raised to layer 5. The only direct communication between devices is at layer 1, the physical layer. That is, each device raises a packet from layer 1 to the appropriate layer desired for the device to manage data.

A simpler form of Internet communication than TCP is Uniform Datagram Protocol (UDP). UDP uses a smaller header and does not check for errors. UDP is used when speed is more critical. It is therefore more often used for video and audio streaming, this is why such streaming sometimes has low quality and precision compared to financial data. Secondly UDP is also used by a router to find a computer and direct content to the computer. If the computer cannot be found, the router will send a second request and a third request etc. until the set timeout period expires for that message.

Firewall

An organization that hosts a web site should have at least one firewall. It is better to have multiple firewalls. A firewall screens incoming traffic to determine what is admissible, e.g., by IP address or port. It can also prevent certain outgoing traffic. We will discuss firewalls in detail in Chapter Eight.

Router

A router is a device that connects two networks or network segments. Many of us have simple routers at home that connect the Internet modem to different devices like computers, printers and voice-over-IP boxes.

Data travels on networks in packets. A packet is a fixed group of bytes to facilitate efficient use of network transmission resources. For example, a long transaction or message may take longer to be transmitted if the network circuits are very busy. By segmenting every message or transaction to packets with fixed length, a message or transaction can be transmitted via different circuits and regrouped at the destination, hence increasing efficiency. A typical packet has 1,024 bytes.

For packets to be assembled at the destination, each packet must have control information, which is recorded in the packet header. Critical header information includes:

- source IP address
- destination IP address
- port number
- packet size
- ID and sequence number of the packet within the message to allow the destination network point to assemble the packets

The header information is then followed by the actual data, e.g., "Gerald Chan to be Superior Court judge".

The type of service can be used by the network to prioritize traffic, e.g., web surfing takes precedence over email. This is only practical internally as an organization cannot dictate how the ISP prioritizes traffic.

The more packets are used in a message, the more overhead is incurred and the slower the traffic is. However, the offset is that a small number of packets means each packet is longer and the chance of finding space on the Internet to deliver a long packet is lower and that means it takes longer to deliver. The packet size also depends on the length of messages. If there are a lot of short messages, it does not make sense to use a large packet size. A network can be configured to vary the packet size based on type of service or time of day.

A router plays a large role in determining which circuit a packet will travel on. It is, in a large sense, a traffic controller and director. Because it directs traffic, it can be used as a perimeter firewall. A router has its own operating system similar to a computer's operating system but less complicated. It has configuration parameters that can affect efficiency, audit trail and security. If a router is down, network traffic can come to a standstill. It is therefore important to have redundant routers.

A router uses simple network management protocol (SNMP) community strings to authenticate workstations and servers. An SNMP community string is a text string that acts as a password. It is used to authenticate messages that are sent between the management station (router) and the SNMP agent (a PC or server). The community string is included in every packet that is transmitted between the SNMP management station (router) and the SNMP agent. Organizations should use complicated SNMP strings, just as it is important to use complicated passwords.

Switch

A switch is similar to a router but less configurable, i.e., it has no operating system. It generally works at layer 2 and uses the MAC address to filter and forward traffic. Because most devices' MAC addresses are not broadcast externally, a switch tends to be used in internal networks. One exception is smart phone email traffic where the MAC addresses can be included and a switch can then be used to filter and forward such traffic. A switch is faster but has much less audit trail capability than a router. It is not recommended to replace a router for forwarding business transactions. A switch that connects with external network nodes operates at layer 3 and it has an operating system. A node is a network access point. A switch also uses SNMP community strings. A key difference between a switch and router is that a router can perform more logging than a switch.

Internet Routing

Here is how messages are routed on the Internet or Intranet. A message may be an Internet purchase transaction, a surfing request, an email message or an intranet transaction etc. A message is broken down into packets; a small message may take only one packet.

A DNS looks up the IP address for the destination URL and places it in every packet, which also contains the source IP address. The ISP will find the fastest route on the Internet to transmit the packet to the destination. When the packets arrive, they are assembled to form a message. To get the message to the destination server or computer, the destination network sends out a short UDP message to all connected devices to ask which device is assigned the destination IP address and then send the message to the determined device.

Internet and eBusiness Service Providers

An ISP is increasingly becoming as important to an organization as the utility company or telephone company. In fact, many organizations use their telephone companies as ISPs and some utility companies lease their fiber infrastructure to ISPs. An ISP's outage because of a virus attack or router problem can cripple eBusiness for an organization. It is important for user organizations to select reputable ISPs and include availability commitment and responsibility for outage in the contracts.

In addition to using ISPs, some organizations use eBusiness application service providers. An example of such a provider is J. P. Morgan's Order to Pay service that processes orders and payments. Another type of eBusiness service is a content delivery service that stores an organization's data close to customers to improve user friendliness and reduce bandwidth cost. Akamai, for example, operates almost 10,000 Web servers located near the busiest Internet network access points. These servers contain the most commonly requested Web information for some of the busiest sites like Certified General Accountants Association of Canada, Yahoo!, Monster and Ticketmaster. This approach is called edge computing, i.e., placing information on the edge of an organization's sphere of influence to make it easily accessible to customers. Edge computing increases the risk of information dispersal and data inconsistency. User organizations should have tight contracts with network service providers with respect to due diligence over information maintenance and access controls to prevent unauthorized change.

A somewhat similar computing approach involving service providers is cloud computing, whereby an organization stores information in an ISP's server to interact with information in local servers throughout the day to expedite transaction processing and reduce cost. Cloud computing increases the risk of unauthorized access because more devices are interfaced. User organizations should ensure that their contracts with the ISP provide for adequacy security. User organizations also have to review their firewalls, intrusion detection system and intrusion prevention system in light of the increased risk of cloud computing. We will talk about these access controls in Chapter Eight. The following is a recent incident that demonstrates the risk of cloud computing.

The dangers of using consumer cloud storage systems became clearer earlier this month, when a hacker claimed that he accessed presidential candidate Mitt Romney's Dropbox storage and email accounts using an easily cracked password. The apparent hack of Romney's accounts came on the heels of IBM's rollout of a bring-your-own-device (BYOD) policy that bans the use of Dropbox due to concerns that hackers could easily access sensitive information stored there. Such examples make it clear that it's risky to keep corporate data on consumer-oriented cloud storage systems, say IT executives and analysts. "IBM has the world's biggest BYOD program, and they just locked down Evernote and Dropbox because they discovered their future product plans and all sorts of really sensitive data was being beamed automatically out to these services," said Dion

Hinchcliffe, an executive vice president at IT consulting firm Dachis Group. Though companies are increasingly tightening their BYOD policies, most have yet to address the use of consumer apps and services such as cloud storage on mobile devices.

Source:
http://www.computerworld.com/s/article/9228147/BYOD_exposes_the_perils_of_cloud_storage?source=rss_security&utm_source=feedburner&utm_medium=feed&utm_campaign=Feed%3A+computerworld%2Fs%2Ffeed%2Ftopic%2F17+%28Computerworld+Security+News%29; accessed on June 20, 2012.

RISKS OF eBUSINESS

In Chapter Two, we examine the risks of IT and conclude that inherent risk, control risk and audit risk increase with the growing use of IT. eBusiness uses more IT compared to the conventional business model. Therefore, risks increase when eBusiness is used. Let's review the six risk criteria of incompleteness, unauthorized, inaccuracy, untimeliness, non-occurrence and inefficiency and see how they are affected by eBusiness.

Incomplete Transaction

eBusiness transactions are recorded at the point of sale, so the risk of a transaction not getting recorded is generally lower than that for a paper based transaction. However, because customers perform data entry, the risk of incomplete data is higher than that of a transaction entered by a customer service representative. There is also the concern that even though recording is instantaneous, the human action required, such as to arrange for shipment, may not be carried out because of some information falling through the crack. Overall, the risk of incomplete processing can be rated as moderate.

Unauthorized Transaction

The main concern about eBusiness is security. This translates to the risk of unauthorized transactions. It is widely recognized that this risk is higher than that in a non-Internet business environment.

Inaccurate Transactions

In eBusiness, customers perform the data entry. This affects accuracy because many customers are not good typists and they tend to be in a rush. The risk of inaccurate transactions is therefore high. Also, eBusiness transactions are more subject to hacking to change transactions for the benefit of the hacker or just to distort processing. For example, a hacker can change the interest rate table displayed to mislead customers. Another example is to change a transaction string while a transaction is in progress. The second example is described in more detail here.

Here is a hypothetical example of a web string built up by web server as a customer carries an online transaction:
www.chanman.com/orders/final&custID=112&num=55A&qty=20&price=10&shipping=5&total=205

This string shows that customer #112 is buying 20 units of product 55A at $10 each and the shipping charge is $5, yielding a sales amount to be charged to the credit card as $205 before sale tax. So far so good.

A hacker who gains unauthorized access to this string can edit it as

www.chanman.com/orders/final&custID=112&num=55A&qty=20&price=10&shipping=5&total=25

Now, the amount charged before tax is $25 and Chanman company is losing $200.

The web string is used to display the progress and result of a transaction to the customer and then ask the customer to confirm before giving out the credit card number. If an organization simply takes the result of this web string to charge the credit card, a string that has been altered by a hacker will lead to incorrect revenue. To mitigate this risk, organizations should recalculate the invoice amount behind the web interface before finalizing the transactions. Such recalculation is made by the application and it takes place in the application server.

Untimely Transactions

Customers buy on the Internet for convenience. Internet transactions are processed immediately and the risk of untimeliness is therefore lower than the conventional transaction model. The risk of untimely processing is therefore low.

Non-occurrence

Because of open access and the lack of paper trail, the risk of a recorded transaction not representing an actual business event is higher when eBusiness is used. The concern often extends beyond the transaction, to also the parties. Is the customer or the supplier real? We would therefore consider the risk of non-occurrence, i.e., information in the system not reflecting real transactions, to be higher than that for conventional transactions.

Inefficient Processing

Organizations offer eBusiness mainly for efficiency gain because transactions are recorded as they take place. Thus, naturally, the risk of inefficiency goes down. Organizations should be due diligent in ensuring there is adequate redundancy in data storage and hardware devices to minimize down time.

eBUSINESS CONTROLS

When an organization offers eBusiness, it should review the current general and application controls in relation to the increased risks. Usually, the following internal controls have to be expanded or added. These controls are in addition to the existing application controls in transaction processing systems because in most cases, eBusiness is a new or additional way of conducting business but the transaction processing should not differ significantly whether the order is placed online or in person.

- Boundary checking
- Digital certificate
- Digital signature
- Disaster recovery plan
- Edit checks
- Encryption
- Firewall
- Intrusion detection system
- Intrusion prevention system
- Online backup
- Recalculate transaction amount behind the web server to nullify change made by a hacker
- Redundant communication lines
- Redundant servers
- Web site refresh

Recalculation of transaction amount behind the server is discussed above. The other controls are covered in Chapters Three and Eight.

ELECTRONIC DATA INTERCHANGE

Electronic data interchange (EDI) predated the Internet. The Internet, however, has made EDI more affordable and widespread. EDI is a protocol that allows two organizations to exchange accounting documents like purchase orders and invoices without human intervention. Company A can send batches of purchase orders to companies B, C, D etc. Company A can also send invoices to companies X, Y, Z etc. Each of these companies can send purchase orders, invoices and other common transaction documents electronically so that the documents can be imported to the accounting systems of the recipient companies. This saves paper, postage and key entry. With lower transaction processing cost, companies can order more frequently and therefore keep less inventory. This means there are less average inventory and accounts payable, which also means a smaller balance sheet. Yes but, if less money is tied up in inventory, there is more cash, so why is the balance sheet smaller? Organizations that use EDI are progressive and they don't keep much idle cash. They will use the cash to expand, so the balance sheet is relatively smaller in relation to the income statement than organizations that do not use EDI. As an EDI organization expands by for example, opening more stores, its balance sheet will grow again; at least, in the short term, the balance sheet is smaller in terms of inventory, cash and accounts payable.

Inventory is less likely to be obsolete and the cost of storage is lower. The balance sheet is smaller and there is less substantive testing for auditors. Less substantive testing does not mean the audit is easier; the auditors have more internal controls, EDI controls, to test.

EDI can also be used for payments. Paying organizations send remittance advices to their banks. Their banks then distribute the remittance advices and funds to the banks of the payee organizations. The payees' banks in turn send the remittance advices to the payees and credit the payees' accounts. This avoids the risk of check bouncing.

In order for organizations to exchange transaction documents and have their systems interpret the documents, the format must be standardized. There are two common EDI transaction formats, American National Standards Institute (ANSI) for the United States and Canada, and EDI Standard for Finance, Administration, Commerce & Transportation (EDIFACT) for the rest of the world. Each organization using EDI needs a translation software tool to convert its own accounting system format to the common format and vice versa. The translation software can be developed in house or purchased from EDI software vendors. When installing the translation software, an organization will import its local data formats for the software to learn. Once imported, every time outgoing transactions are loaded to the EDI server, the software will convert the documents to the standard format. Also every time incoming transactions are received into the EDI server, the translation software will convert the format to the organization's own format.

The attractiveness of EDI is somewhat reduced by an increasingly sophisticated use of XML for web sites. If company A can automate its purchasing system to place orders on the web site of company B which is highly XML driven, company A may decide not to submit orders using EDI. Another trend in EDI is that two organizations that have a close business relationship may opt to use XML as the data standardization method instead of adopting ANSI or EDIFACT.

ANSI and EDIFACT accommodate a long list of business documents, categorised as follows:
- Air and motor
- Automotive transportation
- Delivery
- Engineering management and contract
- Financial
- Government
- Health services

- Insurance
- Manufacturing
- Material services
- Mortgage
- Ocean transportation
- Purchase order
- Product services
- Quality and safety
- Rail
- Tax services
- Warehousing

Risks of EDI

The risks of EDI include incomplete transmission, unauthorized transmission, inaccurate transmission (e.g., to the wrong parties), untimely transmission, transmitting documents that do not reflect real business transactions (non-occurrence) and inefficient transmission. These risks all relate to transmission because EDI is a transmission protocol. Transactions are already prepared before they reach the EDI server so the risks of inaccuracy and unauthorized transaction generation etc. are less relevant.

Incomplete Transmission

This risk is significant because of the large volume of documents. If the volume is small, an organization will likely not want to incur the overhead of EDI. Organizations should apply batch total verification and require acknowledgement from the recipient parties to confirm completeness.

Unauthorized Transmission

This can occur if the person invoking the transmission is not authorized or the batch job for scheduled transmission was set up without authorization. The impact is significant because one unauthorized click can send a lot of documents. The controls over this include mainly access control lists, passwords and management review of the transaction log.

Inaccurate Transmission

This risk is relatively low because EDI is used to transmit documents instead of generating the transactions. The preparation of a purchase order or invoice is independent of EDI, or in other words, the data going on a purchase order or invoice is not affected by the use of EDI.

241

The inaccuracy risk with EDI mainly has to do with translation to and from the ANSI or EDIFACT EDI format and maintaining the list of transmission destinations. The control would be to periodically test the translation software and validate the transmission destinations. Reconciling the transmission log totals to the application systems would also detect inaccurate transmission.

Untimely Transmission

The risk is quite low because EDI is much faster than using Canada Post or couriers. Timeliness would be impaired if the transmission schedule is incorrectly changed or set up. It could also occur if the person responsible for invoking the transfer forgets or is sick and there is no backup staff. To mitigate these risks, management should periodically review the transmission schedule and implement an incident response plan.

Transmitted Documents not Representing Real Transactions

This risk is moderate because EDI is used only for transmission, assuming there are strong controls in the application systems to mitigate the risk of non-existence. The risk is not low because of the powerful access capability of the person who invokes an EDI batch. If the transmission is automatically scheduled without human intervention, the risk of non-occurrence is low. We will discuss those controls in the next chapter, under Application Controls. In addition, management should implement access controls over the generated EDI files to prevent manual insertion.

Inefficient Transmission

Organizations adopt EDI for efficiency gain because there is savings in key entry, postage, paper and inventory level. To ensure the intended savings is achieved, organizations should minimize delays and check the accuracy of format translation. They should also monitor the transmission log and counter party acknowledgement to detect and address transmission delay.

EDI Controls

EDI is a transmission protocol so the internal controls should address data transmission. The transaction processing controls substantially do not change. Some of the transaction processing controls will change in form. For example, edit checks will be performed on transaction data when the transactions are read by the recipient organization's system instead of when data is entered by people. The following are the basic EDI controls that address data transmission.

- Acknowledgement of transfer completeness
- Batch total
- Digital signature
- EDI agreement with trading partners
- Encryption
- Transfer log and its review

The EDI agreement should describe the following:
- Digital signatures if any.
- EDI transmission standard and protocol, e.g., ANSI, XML, email transmission, browser based transmission, file transfer protocol (one organization sending files to another organization without using email or a browser, an inherently less secure approach with less audit trail).
- ISPs
- Legal credibility of transactions.
- Place and time of acknowledgement.
- Place and time of message receipt.

Some of the above are access controls, which we will discuss in Chapter Eight.

eXTENSIBLE BUSINESS REPORTING LANGUAGE

We have discussed HTML and XML as well as their control implications in this chapter. A similar Web enabled data format that is gaining momentum in large corporations is eXtensible Business reporting Language (XBRL). This technology is increasingly used by large corporations to format their financial statements for filing with securities regulators. XBRL enables the regulators and financial analysts to quickly analyze financial statements with their own software packages. It is also similar to the EDI standard in that every set of financial statements under XBRL is in the same format. The benefits are also similar to those of EDI. Each financial statement caption like fixed assets or accounts payable is assigned a standard tag. This way, securities commissions and stock analysts can easily use software to analyze financial statements.

The risk of XBRL is that an organization has not aligned its financial statement captions with XBRL, resulting in incorrect reporting. The effect of this risk includes incorrectly transmitted financial statements and financial statements not easily comparable to other industry participants' or to previous financial statements of the same organization. Internal controls would include a due diligence process for reviewing the mapping table, reviewing and approving any change to the mapping table and testing the conversion of native format to XBRL.

MOBILE EBUSINESS

Mobile devices are increasingly used in business transactions. Common examples are smart phones, laptops and radio frequency IDs (RFID). The risk implications are mainly related to security which will be covered in Chapter Eight. However, for RFID, the risks go beyond security and include the validity, completeness and accuracy of asset tagging.

Radio Frequency Identification

RFID is increasingly used in business and governments to track the whereabouts of equipment and inventory. Common applications include consumer products, toll roads, libraries and even hospital supplies. The benefit of technology application depends on the correctness and robustness of configuration as well as the reliability of the supporting and interfacing systems. This principle, of course, also applies to RFID.

Technical Aspects of RFID

Unlike bar code scanning, RFID does not require line of sight in order to be read. This makes its application more diversified and flexible. RFID technology basically comprises three components. These components include a tag, a reader and the system that records the information transferred by a reader. A tag, which can also be called a transponder, is a small device that is made up of an antenna and a microchip. The tag transmits frequencies to a reader which verifies and analyzes the information being transmitted. The reader then transfers the information to a server for further analysis and storage. An example of RFID applications is toll road usage tracking. The following diagram illustrates the data flow in an RFID application.

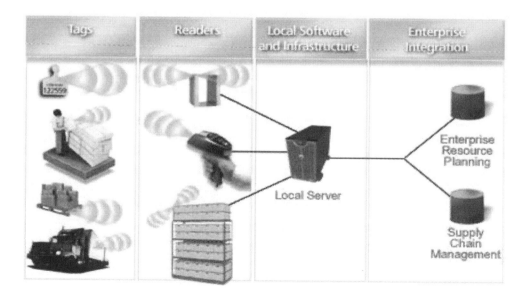

Source: Singapore Government web site

244

RFID Tags

A tag or transponder can be passive or active. An active tag has a battery that sends power to the microchip and allows the chip to send information to the reader. It can be tracked on an RFID network. A passive tag, which is less expensive, does not have a battery but it receives power from a nearby reader. Passive tags are less expensive. Active tags generally have the capability to receive "read" and "write" commands. In other words, they can receive information to be stored, in addition to their ID numbers, and transmit information to a reader. A passive tag can only transmit information. Some passive tags have their own batteries because the readers are too far like toll road metering.

Common Applications

RFID is increasingly used as an inventory control measure. By outfitting each product or case with a tag, a company can track the quantity and location. Some large retail chains require suppliers to outfit their products with RFID tags. Hospitals can use RFID to track supplies, inventory level, bed vacancy and patient status (e.g., check-in and check-out). Tags can also be given to nurses, doctors and other workers to act as access keys.

RFID is also increasingly used as transit tokens. For example, Hong Kong's Octopus system issues RFIDs in the form of a plastic card the size of a credit card. This card can be used for public transit and convenience store purchases. The value of the card can be reloaded in almost all convenience stores at denomination amounts of $50, $100, $150.

Credit cards are equipped with RFIDs that can be tapped on a merchant's reader for small purchases to be processed using a technology called near field communication (NFC). Two smart phones can be tapped on each other to exchange information. Contactless NFC tags will also be installed in smart phones to facilitate "wave and pay". NFC has shorter range than Bluetooth, about 20 cm. With NFC capability, phones and credit cards warrant more safeguarding. The "tap to send" and "wave to pay" features can be disabled by the phone owner.

"Joseph Krull has a chip in his shoulder. He is one of a small but growing number of people who have RFIS chips implanted in their bodies. Krull has a blown left pupil from a skiing accident. If he were injured in an accident and unable to communicate, an emergency room doctor might misinterpret his blown pupil as a sign of a major head injury and begin drilling holes to relieve pressure. Now doctors use the RFID chip to identify Krull and quickly locate his medical records on the Internet. Critics say such chips pose privacy risks because they enable organizations to use RFID to track users such as Krull. Retailers, for example, can track when he enters and leaves stores. Krull does not care. He believes the advantages outweigh the privacy concerns."

Source: Network World, April 4, 2005.

Risks Associated with RFID technology

One fairly wide concern about RFID is privacy. For example, if an organization attaches a tag to a consumer product, can the organization track where the product is used and perhaps who uses it? This concern is understandable as privacy breaches are often reported in the media. The risk and control implications of RFID, however, go beyond privacy. In fact, the basic reliability factors of completeness, accuracy, authorization, timeliness, occurrence and efficiency have to be considered as they can be compromised by less than adequately controlled deployment of RFID. Here are some specific risks in using RFID.

Privacy Breach

This often arises as organizations are increasingly empowered by technology to collect, store and analyze personal information or to analyze and infer customer purchasing pattern. This can lead to violation of privacy legislations and perceived lack of control over safeguarding customer personal information. As a result, the use of RFID may be resisted.

Given that RFID tags are so small and not noticeable, people are at risk of having tags sewn into clothing and being scanned unknowingly. Tags can also be placed in automobiles and other personal belongings and people can once again have their movements or actions tracked. The reason this is a major privacy risk and concern is that each tag usually is assigned a unique bar code. This can lead to the issue of identity theft. With so much information being passed through these small tags, the likelihood of interruption and corruption is high. As a result, identity theft is a much larger concern now that RFID is increasingly used.

An issue that is already being discussed is the implementation of RFID tags in employee ID cards. While companies claim it is for operational purposes, it essentially allows the employer to monitor every movement that the employee makes. Further, in some cases, the tags are implemented without the knowledge of the employee. It is a pressing issue that begs the question: What is acceptable and what is not? Organizations should ensure they comply with the relevant privacy regulation and communicate to employees that monitoring of business activities will be conducted without violating the relevant privacy regulations. Overall, RFID technology poses security and privacy threats in two main ways. First of all, if the technology falls into the wrong hands it can be used to track personal information and whereabouts. Given that the technology only needs a tag to be scanned for something to trigger, terrorist attacks could be conducted more easily. Another concern is employer tracking of employee actions and movements. Also, visitors or unauthorized employees can place readers to sniff information being transmitted.

Tracking or Interception by Hackers

Hackers and criminals can track the radio frequency and alter data being transferred. They can also intrude servers and change the table that correlates tags to assets or people. Reader configuration can be changed to redirect traffic or have their logs compromised.

Unauthorized Tag Removal

As a result, inventory movement cannot be tracked and asset will be overstated in the financial statements. Incorrect inventory positions can lead to inability to meet customer demands. Tags assigned to medical equipment or patients, if removed without authorization, can cause health hazards.

Incorrect Description of Asset Information in an RFID

If the information being tracked is incorrectly recorded in an RFID, it can lead to asset misstatement, the inability to satisfy customer demands or unnecessary funds tied up in inventory etc.

Tag Failure

A tag may fail because of faulty manufacturing, damage by environmental factors, incorrect installation or an expired battery. If this is not monitored, information tracking will be incomplete. The large number of RFIDs in most applications can make this risk significant.

Incorrect Expiry Dates

Tags that are attached to access passes, passports and perishable items must have expiry dates. If the date is incorrect, assets can be lost, hazardous food may be sold, or inappropriate access may be granted.

Activated Tags not Attached to Correct Objects being Tracked

A reader or server has no way of knowing whether the information described in a tag actually represents an object or the correct object intended to be tracked. This risk generally applies to the use of remote technology. It is particularly high for RFID because of its small size.

Failure to Attach Tags on Assets Being Tracked

An organization may fail to attach a tag on certain units that are intended to be tracked. This risk increases as the population of the units grows and manual effort is involved. The result will include understated inventory, incomplete information about individuals or denial of legitimate access.

Incomplete or Incorrect Data Transmission

This can occur because of faulty tags, reader malfunctions or communication line breakdown. Information stored on servers will therefore be incomplete or inaccurate. Updates from servers to active tags may also be lost resulting in inconsistent or inaccurate tracking.

Control Considerations

To mitigate the above risks, management should consider adopting the following control practices.

1. Review the RFID application project plans and system functions with the chief privacy officer to ensure compliance with privacy regulations.

2. Subject RFID systems and devices to rigorous integration and user acceptance testing.

3. Periodically perform network penetration testing to assess the exposure to hacker and worm attacks.

4. Perform regular physical check of devices.

5. Perform regular testing of data capture and tracking to ensure accuracy.

6. Frequently validate the inventory of activated RFID devices.

7. Regularly review reports of activation and deactivation to ensure tag movements are authorized.

8. Regularly review statistics about tag data transfer volume and delays.

9. Ensure servers have adequate intrusion detection and virus detection software.

10. Deploy network transmission integrity checking techniques like redundant data check or parity check.

11. Educate customers and employees about privacy risk and measures to protect their privacy when using RFID, e.g., removing RFID tag when a suit is sold and not carrying unused RFIDs around.

12. Perform cyclical and year end inventory count instead of relying only on the inventory information on RFID tags.

Financial Considerations in Using RFID

It is not hard for management to be sold on the benefits of RFID. The costs must also be comprehensively considered. They include the following:
- Tags
- Readers
- Servers
- Software
- Conversion from existing data
- Training
- Preventive maintenance
- Systems development and maintenance

In the rest of this chapter, we will discuss the legal issues that have either arisen or been accentuated with eBusiness, including privacy.

UNIFORM ELECTRONIC TRANSACTION ACT

This Act was passed in 2000. The purpose of the Act is to define the legal enforceability of eBusiness transactions. This Act aims to reduce the legal uncertainty associated with electronic communications and contracting.

There are four main points. First, the Act recognizes an electronic signature as legally binding. Secondly, the Act recognizes the interaction between electronic agents or between an electronic agent and a person as legally binding in constituting an offer or an acceptance. Thirdly, and most important to auditors, is that the Act puts the onus on merchants to put in place reasonable measures to prevent errors, that includes internal control. Fourth, the Act expects parties to have reasonable security, e.g., it states that a buyer is responsible for mistakes made by his or her browser or computer.

Electronic Signature

The Act defines electronic signature as "an electronic sound, symbol, or process attached to or logically associated with a record and executed or adopted by a person with the intent to sign the record." This is construed to mean more than a scan image of a handwritten signature. The Act expects parties to a transaction to be equipped with security procedures to verify electronic signatures. This means that the Act really means digital signature, when referring to electronic signature. A digital signature is composed using cryptography.

Errors Prevention

The Act says:

In an automated transaction involving an individual, the individual may avoid the effect of an electronic record that resulted from an error made by the individual in dealing with the electronic agent of another person if the electronic agent did not provide an opportunity for the prevention or correction of the error and, at the time the individual learns of the error, the individual:
(A) promptly notifies the other person of the error and that the individual did not intend to be bound by the electronic record received by the other person;
(B) takes reasonable steps, including steps that conform to the other person's reasonable instructions, to return to the other person or, if instructed by the other person, to destroy the consideration received, if any, as a result of the erroneous electronic record; and
(C) has not used or received any benefit or value from the consideration,
if any, received from the other person.

The Act gives the following example.

if Buyer sends a message to Seller ordering 100 widgets, but Buyer's information processing system changes the order to 1000 widgets, a "change" has occurred between what Buyer transmitted and what Seller received. If on the other hand, Buyer typed in 1000 intending to order only 100, but sent the message before noting the mistake, an error would have occurred which would also be covered by this section.

This means that a customer can cancel an eBusiness transaction if s/he has made a keying mistake and has not benefited from the service or good. On the other hand, if the customer's computer made a mistake in transmission or if a hacker has changed the transaction, the customer is not protected by this Act and would have to honor the transaction.

This section puts the onus on eBusiness merchants to put in place reasonably preventive controls, e.g., placing a limit on the number of books ordered per title, or alerting a securities trading customer that the number of shares of a common stock s/he wants to buy is the same as his or her current holding (in case the customer means to sell). We will discuss these controls in more details under in the next chapter.

PRIVACY

Many people refrain from using eBusiness because of their concern about privacy. The general public has never been more concerned about information privacy. The concern has been heightened in recent years by technology advances, identity theft and security breaches. The exponential increase in computing power allows organizations to store more and do more analysis of personal information, potentially breaching privacy.

Hackers are now more entrepreneurial. They are less interested in defacing a web site or sending a worm to bring down a web site without financial gain and running the risk of going to jail. They are more interested in stealing identity and selling to criminals.

Before we go further, let's be clear on what information privacy means. It means the confidentiality of personal information, not business information, although personal information can have business implication. For example, privacy does not apply to a company's business strategy. Privacy also does not apply to someone's telephone number if the number is listed, because it is no longer confidential. What is personal information in the context of privacy legislation? It is confidential information about a person collected from the person. The "personal" nature of information has to be interpreted in the context of where is it held and used. For example, my salary is not personal information when it is stored in the systems of my employer; this is because I did not provide my salary to the employer, my salary is set by the organization that employs me. However, my salary which I have given to my bank for a credit application is personal information in the bank.

Governments realize this concern and have established legislations to deal with it. The Federal Privacy Act applies to the United States Government and federal agencies. States have their own privacy acts. At the national level, the United States does not have a comprehensive act that applies to all businesses. Instead, it has privacy legislations for specific industries and types of transactions. Examples are the Health Insurance Portability and Accountability Act, Fair Credit Reporting Act and Electronic Communications Privacy Act.

Most privacy legislations in developed countries revolve around the Safe Harbour framework developed by European Union, that covers the following principles.

1.   Accountability.

2.   Identifying purpose.

3.   Consent.

4.   Limiting collection.

5.   Limiting use, disclosure and retention.

6.   Accuracy.

7.   Safeguards.

8.   Openness.

9.   Individual access.

10.   Challenging compliance.

An organization's privacy policy should cover these ten principles. Many large organizations post their privacy policies online. The privacy policy of the Bank of Montreal has been extracted and pasted later in this chapter.

Accountability

Each organization should

- designate someone in the organization to be accountable for compliance,

- protect personal information held by the organization or transferred to a third party, and

- develop and implement personal information policies and practices.

<u>Internal Controls</u>

1. Designating a senior employee to be accountable for privacy compliance. In a large organization, this person is called the chief information privacy officer.

2. Develop a privacy policy.

3. Provide this accountable person and the management team with privacy training.

Identifying Purposes

The organization must identify the reasons for collecting personal information before or at the time of collection. This includes the following procedures.

- Before or when any personal information is collected, identify why it is needed and how it will be used.
- Document why the information is collected.
- Inform the individual from whom the information is collected why it is needed.

<u>Internal Controls</u>

1. Indicate on forms and the web site the purpose of collection where personal information is collected.
2. Provide procedures to staff members collecting personal information to state the purpose when information is collected verbally or in free form of written communication.

Consent

Unless required by the Criminal Code or another statute, the organization must obtain consent from the person providing personal information at the time of request for the information and before disclosure. This includes the following procedures.

- Communicate in a manner that is clear and can be reasonably understood.
- Record the consent received.
- Never obtain consent by deceptive means.

- Do not make consent a condition for supplying a product or a service, unless the information requested is required to fulfill an explicitly specified and legitimate purpose.
- Explain to individuals the implications of withholding or withdrawing their consent.
- Ensure that employees collecting personal information are able to answer an individual's questions about the purposes of the collection.

Internal Controls
1. Indicate on forms and web sites that consent is requested and required where personal information is collected.
2. Provide procedures to staff members collecting personal information to obtain and document consent when personal information is collected verbally or in free form of written communication. Documentation can be in the form of recording the conversation.

Limiting Collection

The organization must limit the collection of personal information to the purpose for which the information is needed. This includes the following procedures.
- Not collect personal information indiscriminately.
- Not deceive or mislead individuals about the reasons for collecting personal information.

Internal Controls
1. Design forms such that personal information is collected only in consistency with the stated purpose.
2. Provide procedures and templates to staff members to collect only the personal information necessary for the stated purpose.

Limiting Use, Disclosure and Retention

The organization must not use or disclose personal information other than for the purpose of collection and must not retain personal information longer than needed for the purpose of collection. This includes the following procedures.
- Put guidelines in place for accessing, disclosing, retaining and destroying personal information.
- Keep personal information used to make a decision about a person for a reasonable period. This should allow the person to obtain the information after the decision and pursue redress.
- Destroy, erase or render anonymous information that is no longer required for an identified purpose or a legal requirement.

<u>Internal Controls</u>
1. Develop a retention schedule for personal information, based on purpose of collection.
2. Program retention duration in systems to automatically purge data where practical.
3. Provide procedures to employees who come across personal information to specify how the information can be used.
4. Provide procedures to employees who come across personal information to specify how the information can be disclosed and who to disclose to.
5. Configure web servers to be P3P compliant. Platform for Privacy Preferences (P3P) is a security protocol for web sites to declare how they will use the information collected through a browser, in accordance with their posted privacy policy. For example, if a privacy policy says that the organization will not use a cookie to change a customer's data in the PC, the web server logic should be internally certified by the organization that it will not use a cookie for that purpose. Once a web server is configured to be P3P compliant, a browser can check whether the web site is P3P compliant and if so, the browser's configuration can trust the web site more. For example, a browser can be configured to reject cookies from a web site that is not P3P compliant. How does a browser know that a web site is P3P compliant? P3P is like XBRL in a way. It is a standard for an organization to put its privacy policy in a compact form readable to only a browser. The compact privacy policy contains parameters about privacy, e.g., what kind of cookies and used and how they will be used.

Accuracy
The organization must implement internal controls to ensure the accuracy of personal information collected, disclosed and retained. This includes the following procedures.
- Keep personal information as accurate, complete and up to date as necessary, taking into account its use and the interest of the individual.
- Update personal information only when necessary to fulfill the specified purposes.
- Keep frequently used information accurate and up to date.

<u>Internal Controls</u>
1. Provide user friendly screens and procedures for capturing personal information.
2. Provide system edit checks such as date format check.
3. Display entered sensitive information like date of birth for user confirmation before recording.
4. Perform periodic verification of personal information with employees and customers.
5. Perform regular backup of personal information.

Safeguards

The organization must implement access controls over personal information. This includes the following procedures.
- Protect personal information against loss or theft.
- Safeguard the information from unauthorized access, disclosure, copying, use or modification.
- Protect personal information regardless of the format in which it is held.

Internal Controls
1. Use access control lists and user profiles to control access.
2. Require users to label documents and data files with sensitivity levels and provide guidelines for determining the sensitivity levels.
3. Use passwords.
4. Encrypt sensitive information like medical records.

Openness

The organization must make its privacy policy available to customers and external stakeholders. This includes disclosing the following:
- name or title and address of the person who is accountable for the organization's privacy policies and practices.
- name or title and address of the person to whom access requests should be sent.
- how an individual can gain access to his or her personal information.
- how an individual can complain to the organization.
- brochures or other information that explain the organization's policies, standards or codes.
- a description of what personal information is made available to other organizations (including subsidiaries) and why it is disclosed.

Internal Controls
1. Post the privacy policy on the web site.
2. Make the privacy policy available to customers on request.
3. Put the privacy policy on the organization's annual report.
4. Requires the CEO's approval of the privacy policy and any change thereof.

Individual Access

The organization must allow individuals who provided personal information access to the information they provided. This includes the following procedures.
- When requested, inform individuals if the organization has any personal information about them.
- Explain how such personal information is or has been used and provide a list of any organizations to which it has been disclosed.
- Give individuals access to their information.

- Correct or amend any personal information if its accuracy or completeness is challenged and found to be deficient.
- Provide a copy of the information requested, or reasons for not providing access.
- An organization should note any disagreement on the file and advise third parties where appropriate.

<u>Internal Controls</u>
1. Put on the web site and the annual report the procedures and contact names for customers and employees to view their own personal information.
2. Provide procedures to staff members to handle customers' and employees' requests for access, including the approval process.
3. Provide procedures for documenting access requests and their disposition.
4. Perform independent review of processed access requests to assess privacy compliance.
5. Provide privacy training to all employees.

Challenging Compliance

The organization must respond to challenges by stakeholders and privacy authorities about the organization's compliance with the respective privacy legislations. This includes the following procedures.
- Develop simple and easily accessible complaint procedures.
- Inform complainants of avenues of recourse. These include the organization's own complaint procedures and the privacy commissioner.
- Investigate all complaints received.
- Take appropriate measures to correct information handling practices and policies.

<u>Internal Controls</u>
1. Develop procedures for handling complaints from the privacy commissioner, customers and employees.
2. Provide procedures for documenting such complaints and their disposition.
3. Conduct periodic management review of outstanding complaints and complaints that have been addressed to assess privacy compliance.

Sample Privacy Policy

The following is the privacy policy of the Bank of Montreal, a major Canadian bank.

Your Privacy is our Priority

This Privacy Code outlines our commitment to you and is designed to comply with applicable Privacy legislation in Canada, which incorporates the following ten (10) principles:

- <u>Accountability</u>

- <u>Identifying Purpose</u>

- <u>Obtain Consent</u>

- <u>Limit Collection</u>

- <u>Limit Use, Disclosure and Retention</u>

- <u>Be Accurate</u>

- <u>Use Appropriate Safeguards</u>

- <u>Be Open</u>

- <u>Give Individuals Access</u>

- <u>Provide Recourse</u>

Other important information:

- <u>Respecting Your Privacy Preferences</u>

- <u>Scope</u>

- <u>Our Commitment to You</u>

- <u>Web Tools Statement</u>

1. Accountability

Each and every one of our employees is responsible for maintaining and protecting the personal information to which they have access. We have strict policies and procedures for protecting <u>personal information</u> and designated individuals within BMO Financial Group who are responsible for monitoring our compliance.

BMO Financial Group has a Chief Privacy Officer who oversees privacy governance including policy, dispute resolution, education, communications activities and reporting to our Board of Directors and Executive Management on enterprise-wide privacy matters. See <u>principle #10</u> for contact information.

2. Identifying Purpose

When you become a BMO Financial Group customer, or apply for additional products and services, we ask you for your personal information for the following purposes:

- to verify your identity and protect against fraud

- to understand your financial service requirements

- to determine suitability of products and services for you

- to determine your eligibility for certain products and services, or those of others, and offer them to you

- to set up and manage products and services you have requested, and

- to comply with legal or regulatory requirements

Your personal information may be verified with credit bureaus, credit insurers, registries, your employer, personal references and other lenders.

3. Obtain Consent

When you apply for a new product or service, we ask you for your consent to collect, use or disclose your personal information. You may, at any time, withdraw your consent as long as:

- you provide reasonable notice;

- we are not legally required to collect, use or disclose your information;

- withdrawing your consent does not impede our ability to fulfill your contract with us;

- it does not relate to a credit product we have granted you where we are required to collect and exchange your personal information on an ongoing basis with credit bureaus, credit insurers and other lenders.

4. Limit Collection

We only collect the information we need. We may ask you to provide the following personal information:

- Social Insurance Number (SIN) for tax reporting purposes as well as other government purposes, such as when opening an income generating account or a registered retirement investment. We do this in order to comply with the Canada Revenue Agency's income reporting requirements. We may also collect and use your SIN for administrative purposes, such as to ensure an accurate match between your personal information and your credit bureau information, or as an internal identification number to accurately identify customers having same or similar names.

- Financial Information to ensure that the advice we give is appropriate for you and/or the investments you purchase are suitable for your circumstances.

- Health Information is required for some of our insurance products to ensure that you are eligible for coverage.

- Contact Information such as your name, address, telephone number or email address.

You can choose not to provide us with certain information in some situations. However, if you make this choice, we may not be able to provide you with the product, service, or information you request. We may monitor or record our incoming or outgoing telephone calls with you for our mutual protection.

We will make certain that you are informed of the purposes listed above when you apply for any of our products or services. If a new purpose for using your personal information develops, we will ask you for your consent.

5. Limit Use, Disclosure and Retention

BMO Financial Group will only use or disclose your personal information for the reason(s) it was collected. Under no circumstances do we sell or give lists of our clients to other companies for their own use and, if we obtain client lists from other organizations, we require the organizations to confirm their compliance with all relevant privacy legislation.

Your personal information may be shared with other companies within BMO Financial Group for the purpose of marketing, including telemarketing, so that these companies can offer you a broader range of product and service solutions to meet your needs.

To ensure that you benefit from our full range of products and services, we will, with your consent, or as required by law or regulation, share your personal information amongst BMO Financial Group. Over time, we may buy new businesses or sell some of our businesses. Accordingly, personal information associated with any accounts, products or services of the business being purchased or sold will be transferred as a business asset to the new business owner.

We may use other companies to provide services on our behalf such as data processing, account administration and marketing. They will be given only the information needed to perform those services. We have contracts in place holding these companies to the same high standards of confidentiality by which we are governed. In some cases, these other companies may be located outside Canada and may be required to disclose information to government authorities, regulators or law enforcement under a lawful order made in that country.

Personal information may be released to legal or regulatory authorities in cases of suspected money laundering, insider trading, manipulative or deceptive trading, or other criminal activity, for the detection and prevention of fraud, or when required to satisfy the legal or regulatory requirements of governments, regulatory authorities or other self-regulatory organizations. Other reasons for the release of personal information include when we are legally required to do so (e.g. by court order) or to protect our assets. If we release personal information for any of these reasons, we keep a record of what, when, why and to whom such information was released.

BMO Financial Group has policies in place that govern the retention of your personal information so it will be kept only for as long as it fulfills its intended purpose or as legally required.

6. Be Accurate

We are committed to maintaining the accuracy of your personal information and ensuring that it is complete and up-to-date. If you discover inaccuracies in our data, or your personal information changes, please notify the branch or office where you do business immediately, so that we can make the necessary changes. When required, we will make our best efforts to advise others of any important amendments to your personal information that we may have released to them. If we do not agree to make the amendments that you request, you may challenge our decision. Recourse is described in principle #10.

7. Use Appropriate Safeguards

Your personal information is secure within BMO Financial Group, regardless of the format in which it is held. We have comprehensive security controls to protect against unauthorized use, access, alteration, duplication, destruction, disclosure, loss or theft of your personal information.

We maintain physical, electronic and procedural safeguards to protect your personal information. Examples of safeguards include restricted access to our information processing and storage areas, limited access to relevant information by authorized employees only, use of passwords, PINs and pass keys, firewalls and encryption of electronically transmitted information, and the use of secure locks on filing cabinets and doors.

We have agreements and controls in place with credit bureaus, credit insurers, other lenders and third party service providers requiring that any information provided by us must be safeguarded and used only for the sole purpose of providing the service we have requested the company to perform.

Within BMO Financial Group web sites, cookies or other information-tracking technologies may be used to improve the functionality or security of web sites, or to provide you with a more customized online experience. Please note that cookies cannot capture files or data stored on your computer. Refer to BMO's Web Tools Statement for further details regarding information-tracking technologies.

8. Be Open
BMO Financial Group's Privacy Code is available in our branches and offices as a printed brochure. From time to time, we may make changes to this policy and will inform you of changes, as required by law. The most up-to-date Privacy Code, is always available at www.bmo.com and the privacy link located at the bottom of the page.

9. Give Individuals Access

If you want to review or verify your personal information, or find out to whom we have disclosed it, please request this by contacting the branch or office where you do business. We may need specific information from you to enable us to search for, and provide you with, the personal information we hold about you. We may charge you a nominal fee depending on the nature of your request. However, we will advise you of the fee prior to proceeding with your request. There may be instances where we are unable to provide some of the personal information we hold about you and if we are unable, we will let you know the reason(s) why.

In most provinces you have the right to access and verify the personal information held about you by credit bureaus. We will provide you with the name and location of any credit bureau that has provided us with a report on you.

10. Provide Recourse

The branch or office where you do business is well equipped to handle any questions you may have about our Privacy Code. However, we want to hear from you if you have any further concerns. Please contact us at one of the following offices:

President and Chief Executive Officer
Personal and Commercial Banking Canada
BMO Financial Group
P.O. Box 1
1 First Canadian Place
Toronto, Ontario M5X 1A1
Call: 1 800 372-5111

Or

President and Chief Executive Officer
Private Client Group
BMO Financial Group
P.O. Box 150
1 First Canadian Place
Toronto, Ontario M5X 1H3

Or

Chief Privacy Officer
BMO Financial Group
P.O. Box 150
1 First Canadian Place
Toronto, Ontario M5X 1H3

Independent Oversight

Office of the Ombudsman
BMO Financial Group
55 Bloor Street West
Toronto, Ontario M4W 3N5
Call: 1 800 371-2541
Or
Fax: 1 800 766-8029

Or

Office of the Privacy Commissioner of Canada
Place de Ville, Tower B, 3rd Floor
112 Kent Street
Ottawa, Ontario K1A 1H3
Call: 1 800 282-1376
Or
Fax: (613) 947-6850

Respecting Your Privacy Preferences

BMO Financial Group fully respects your privacy preferences. Simply contact the branch or office where you do business to discuss the following options that are available to you:

- **Direct Marketing** - If you do not want to receive direct marketing communications, please ask us to remove the personal information about you from our marketing lists.

- **Sharing** - If you do not want us to share personal information about you among BMO Financial Group members (see Scope for list of members), request to opt out of this type of sharing. Please note that you cannot opt out of sharing your personal information where you have requested a product or service that is jointly offered by more than one member of BMO Financial Group or when the sharing is required by law or regulation.

- **Social Insurance Number (SIN)** - If you do not want us to use your SIN for administrative purposes as described in principle #2, with the exception of income tax reporting or other legal or regulatory purposes, request to opt out.

Source: http://www.bmo.com/home/about/banking/privacy-security/our-privacy-code; accessed on June 21, 2012.

INTELLECTUAL PROPERTY

Organizations that increasingly offer eBusiness tend to use and own more intellectual property. For example, a major Internet pure play company in the world has intangible asset that accounts for about 14% of its total asset. Its search engine gives it a significant competitive edge. Intellectual property is subject to the following risks:

- Inaccurate valuation because the property is obsolete, the associated legal agreement is flawed, or the business environment has deteriorated.
- Infringement thereby affecting the company's competitiveness.
- Loss of software and documentation resulting in a company's inability to apply the intellectual property.
- Incurring legal claims that the company has infringed on another company's intellectual property.
- Ownership dispute; for example, does a consultant have software copyright or does the company which hired the consultant have it?

Legal disputes and protection of intellectual property are increasingly prevalent. This has given rise to a new area of legal practice, intellectual property law. The legal implications affect financial statement presentation in terms of valuation and contingent liability.

Common Intellectual Properties

The following types of intellectual property are common in large companies, especially companies whose business increasingly rely on the Internet. They should be protected with rigorous contracts, code of business conduct, user education, registration with the appropriate government office, access control and monitoring.

- Patent, such as a search engine or an advanced computer chip. Technology companies own a lot of patents that keep them competitive. Many company acquisitions are carried out because of the value of patents at stake. A patent is granted only if it is invention in nature.
- Copyright, e.g., for software. Copyright does not have to be granted by the government. It can be registered with the government of origin. Registration is not necessary for copyright to be legally defensible, but registration enhances legal enforceability as it puts others on notice that the copyright has been accepted by the government.
- Trade secret, e.g., business plan, product strategy.
- Trademark, e.g., a well known domain name that has significant commercial value, like google.com. Another example of trademark is Apple computer. Trademark does not have to be registered to be defensible. For a trademark to be defensible, the owner must demonstrate that an alleged infringing party uses the same or highly similar name for the same or highly similar business. A trademark distinguishes the trademark owner from others like competitors in terms of reputation and goodwill. Trademark infringement is called "passing off". In order to sue for passing off, the trademark owner has to prove the following.

  1. The owner has acquired a reputation in association with the mark.
  2. The defendant has misrepresented to the public so as to cause deception or confusion between the owner and the defendant.
  3. Damage has been or likely will be caused to the owner.

Registration deters infringement and strengthens an organization's position to seek legal recourse; it is a moderately preventive control. Access control, which we will discuss in Chapter Eight, serves as a stronger type of preventive control as it prevents access by unauthorized parties. Monitoring of the use of intellectual property by employees and customers serves as a detective control, e.g., reviewing access logs and Internet activities related to or resembling the organization's intellectual properties. The latter is difficult and time consuming, but some reasonable effort should be taken. Employee education about safeguarding is also important.

Intellectual Property Controls

The following internal controls should be implemented to protect intellectual property.
- Registration with government intellectual property offices
- Inventory of intellectual property
- Access controls
- Confidentiality agreement with employees and consultants
- Management review of consultant activities
- Assignment of copyrights in consultant contracts
- Waiver of moral rights in consultant contracts
- Software license agreement
- Source code escrow agreement
- Digital right restriction by putting locks on document features like copying and printing.

Intellectual Property Registration

Registration of intellectual property deters infringement and puts the copyright owner in a better legal position to seek compensation for damage because a public and legal notice has been declared about ownership. In the United States, intellectual property can be registered with Copyright Office or the Patent and Trademark Office.

MANAGEMENT CHECKLIST

To ensure that eBusiness and EDI are effectively controlled including compliance with privacy legislations, management should apply the following minimum checklist.

1. Develop an eBusiness strategy that is congruent with the overall business strategy.

2. Obtain board approval of the eBusiness strategy.

3. Develop an eBusiness policy and standards that address authorization, accuracy, information sensitivity and security.

4. Develop an information privacy policy and post it on the web site.

5. Appoint a chief information privacy officer.

6. Review contracts with Internet service providers annually to ensure adequate provision for responsibilities, billing arrangements, security and privacy.

7. Train eBusiness developers, operators and managers on eBusiness and privacy legislations.

8. Ensure EDI arrangement with each trading partner is documented in the form of a contract.

9. Thoroughly test each new EDI interface.

10. Keep an accurate inventory of its intellectual property and periodically assess whether valuation is realistic and conservative. Periodically assess and test the protection mechanism for intellectual property.

AUDIT CHECKLIST

1. Review the list of intellectual property and reconcile to the general ledger.

2. Assess the valuation of intellectual property for conservativeness. For example, is it based on acquisition price or development cost? Is the property obsolete?

3. Enquire about the law department with respect to intellectual property registration and assess the degree to which intellectual property supports the company's business and growth. Assess management's awareness of such impact and whether the associated forward looking statements and assumptions in financial statements and forecasts are realistic.

4. Review the organization's eBusiness plan and strategy and assess whether eBusiness applications are congruent with the strategy and plan.

5. Review the organization's agreement with IT service organizations and consultants to assess the degree of protection of the organization's intellectual property right.

6. Review human resource policies, code of business conduct and standard job offer letters to assess the clarity of informing employees that the organization owns all rights to what an employee develops.

7. Review the adequacy of access controls over intellectual property.

8. Review the adequacy of access controls over software developed by vendors to which the company has only right to use, to assess the degree of protection against misuse or license violation.

9. Review agreements with trading partners related to commonly used tools and systems to assess the clarity of who owns the associated intellectual property.

10. Test the implementation of EDI as well as the translation from local formats to EDI format and vice versa.

11. Periodically test internal controls for compliance with privacy legislations.

12. Perform an annual risk and internal control assessment of eBusiness.

CONCLUSION

eBusiness is here to grow. Not many people will dispute this. While today's eBusiness customers are more at ease with the Internet than customers ten, twenty years ago, there remain significant risks with respect to transaction authorization, completeness of audit trail and privacy. In fact, the concern about privacy is higher now than ten, twenty years ago. Organizations that offer eBusiness have to be constantly aware of and regularly assess the risks of unauthorized, illegitimate, inaccurate, incomplete and untimely processing of transactions, as well as the need to protect information privacy. Those organizations that implement sufficient internal controls to mitigate these risks will not only serve as respectable corporate citizens, but also lay a solid foundation for business growth as customers are increasingly IT savvy and demanding with respect to information reliability, integrity and privacy.

SUMMARY OF MAIN POINTS

eBusiness Infrastructure

- Web server, application server, authentication server and database server. all require protection with firewalls and rigorous operating system configuration. The inner servers after the web server need more protection.
- Web master, the person who maintains the web server content, needs to be trained and controlled.
- Routers route traffic from workstations to servers and the Internet. They need to be tightly configured.
- Contracts with the ISPs should be detailed, reviewed regularly and monitored.
- Domain name servers have to be protected from hacker attack to redirect traffic.
- IP address subscription should be optimized to avoid running out of addresses while without paying for unnecessary addresses.

Privacy Principles

1. Accountability – an organization should designate someone to be accountable for privacy.

2. Identifying purpose – When collecting personal information, an organization should state the purpose.

3. Consent – personal information should be collected with consent.

4. Limiting collection – An organization should collect only the personal information needed for the purpose stated.

5. Limiting use, disclosure and retention – In relation to the personal information and the purpose for which it was collected.

6. Accuracy – An organization should put in place a process to ensure the accurate recording and transmission of personal information.

7. Safeguards – An organization should put in place a process to protect personal information.

8. Openness – An organization should be open about its privacy policy and practice.

9. Individual access – An organization should allow the owners of personal information to access the respective information.

10. Challenging compliance – An organization should be prepared to respond to challenges from privacy regulators and customers.

Uniform Electronic Transaction Act

This act is consistent with most eBusiness legislations in other jurisdictions. This Act has following main points.

- It recognizes human-machine interfaces as offer and acceptance.

- It recognizes digital signatures.

- It places the onus on merchants to implement reasonable internal controls to prevent errors made by customers.

Radio Frequency ID

RFID expedites transactions and helps organizations perform better tracking of assets. However, because of its mobility, the risks of unauthorized transactions, device tampering and privacy intrusion increase. To mitigate these risks, management should consider adopting the following control practices.

1. Review the RFID application project plans and system functions with the chief privacy officer to ensure compliance with privacy regulations.

2. Subject RFID systems and devices to rigorous system integration testing and user acceptance testing.

3. Periodically perform network penetration testing to assess the exposure to hacker and worm attacks.

4. Perform regular physical check of devices.

5. Perform regular testing of data capture and tracking to ensure accuracy.

6. Frequently validate the inventory of activated RFID devices.

7. Regularly review reports of activation and deactivation to ensure tag movements are authorized.

8. Regularly review statistics about tag data transfer volume and delays.

9. Ensure servers have adequate intrusion detection and virus detection software.

10.   Deploy network transmission integrity checking techniques like checksum and parity checks.

11.   Educate customers and employees about privacy risks and measures to protect their privacy when using RFID, e.g., remove the RFID tag when a suit is sold and do not carry unused RFIDs around.

12.   Perform cyclical and year end inventory count instead of relying only on the inventory information on RFID tags.

Electronic Data Interchange

- Electronic transfer of accounting documents using the ANSI or EDIFACT standard, including but not necessarily payments via banks.
- Each organization needs to buy or develop translation software to convert local format to ANSI or EDIFACT format and vice versa.
- Organizations should acknowledge completeness of transfers.
- EDI calls for strong access and reconciliation controls.
- EDI reduces the cost of ordering and therefore lowers inventory level and accounts payable, resulting in less obsolescence and lower cost of storage. A smaller balance sheet means less substantive testing but more control testing, mainly EDI controls.

Controls over Intellectual Property

1. Access control.

2. Contracts and service agreements.

3. Confidentiality agreement.

4. User education.

5. Management monitoring.

6. Registration with government office, e.g., registering patents.

REVIEW QUESTIONS

1. What is the similarity between privacy legislations and Uniform Electronic Transaction Act?

2. Which risk does eBusiness affect the most?

3. What is the consequence if a domain name server is hacked?

4. What are the audit implications of EDI?

5. What is the difference between URL, IP address and MAC address and what are the risk implications?

6. What are the risk implications of RFID?

7. What are the key controls to protect intellectual property?

8. How do you think the audit of Google differs from that of General Electric?

9. How does eBusiness affect the five system components of infrastructure, software, people, procedures and information?

10. Referring to the general controls discussed in Chapter Three, which types do you think are more affected by eBusiness?

CASE – Alibaba.com

Alibaba Group makes it easy for anyone to buy or sell online anywhere in the world. It is a family of Internet-based businesses that includes online marketplaces that facilitate business-to-business international and domestic China trade, retail and payment platforms, shopping search engine and distributed cloud computing services. The Group was founded in 1999 by Jack Ma, a pioneer who has aspired to help make the Internet accessible, trustworthy and beneficial for everyone. The privately held Alibaba Group reaches Internet users in more than 240 countries and regions. Alibaba Group, including its affiliated entities, employs more than 25,000 people in some 70 cities in Greater China, India, Japan, Korea, the United Kingdom and the United States.

The Alibaba Group companies and affiliated entities include:

Alibaba.com - Global e-commerce platform for small businesses

Alibaba.com is a global e-commerce platform for small businesses and the flagship company of Alibaba Group.

Founded in 1999 in Hangzhou, China, Alibaba.com makes it easy for millions of buyers and suppliers around the world to do business online mainly through three marketplaces: a global trade platform (www.alibaba.com) for importers and exporters; a Chinese platform (www.1688.com) for domestic trade in China; and a transaction-based wholesale platform on the global site (www.aliexpress.com) geared for smaller buyers seeking fast shipment of small quantities of goods. Together, these marketplaces form a community of more than 79.7 million registered users in more than 240 countries and regions.

As part of its strategy to transition into a holistic platform where small companies can build and manage their online business more easily, Alibaba.com also offers Chinese traders a wide array of business management software, Internet infrastructure services and export-related services directly or through companies it has acquired including HiChina and One-Touch, as well as educational services to incubate enterprise management and e-commerce professionals. Alibaba.com also owns Vendio and

Auctiva, providers of third-party e-commerce solutions for online merchants. Alibaba.com has offices in more than 70 cities across Greater China, India, Japan, Korea, the United Kingdom and the United States.
Alibaba.com is wholly owned by Alibaba Group.

Taobao Marketplace - China's popular C2C online shopping destination

Launched in 2003, Taobao Marketplace (www.taobao.com) is a popular consumer-to-consumer (C2C) online marketplace in China. Its mission is to foster a comprehensive e-commerce ecosystem that will provide partners and consumers with the best user experience possible. With more than 800 million product listings and more than 370 million registered users currently, Taobao Marketplace is one of the world's top 20 most visited websites*.

Taobao Marketplace is wholly owned by Alibaba Group.

* According to Alexa and DoubleClick Ad Planner by Google site rankings.

天猫 TMALL.COM

Tmall.com - China's B2C shopping destination with an extensive selection of quality brands and authentic products

Launched in April 2008, Tmall.com (www.tmall.com) is an online shopping landmark in China with an extensive brand selection. An open B2C platform, Tmall.com has established itself as the destination for authentic, quality products catering to

increasingly sophisticated Chinese consumers and is the most visited B2C online retail website in China*. In June 2011, it was separated from Taobao's C2C marketplace and became an independent business.

Tmall.com currently features more than 70,000 major multinational and Chinese brands from more than 50,000 merchants. It offers several product verticals with customized customer services, including Consumer Electronics mall; Book mall; Home Furnishing mall; Designer Footwear mall; Beauty mall; and Imported Goods mall. Brands with flagship retail storefronts on Tmall.com include UNIQLO, L'Oréal, adidas, P&G, Unilever, Gap, Ray-Ban, Nike and Levi's. Tmall.com set a record for highest single-day transaction volume during a special promotion on November 11, 2011, facilitating the sales of goods totaling RMB3.36 billion (US$531.76 million) on the day or an average of more than RMB38,000 (US$6,022.18) per second.

Tmall.com is wholly owned by Alibaba Group.

* According to Alexa site rankings.

eTao - Shopping search engine with comprehensive product and merchant information

eTao (www.etao.com) is a comprehensive shopping search engine in China in terms of product and merchant information. It was beta-launched by Taobao in October 2010 and became an independent business in June 2011. Its mission is to create a "one-stop shopping engine" which can address the problems faced by Chinese consumers before and after shopping online, assist them in making purchase decisions, and help them identify low-cost, high-quality merchandise on the Internet faster.

Features and services include product search, group buy search, movie ticket search, e-promotion platform and Tao Bar community. It currently showcases more than 1 billion product listings, more than 5,000 quality business-to-consumer merchants, 600 group shopping websites, and more than 200 million pieces of shopping-related information. eTao reflects product results from various major online shopping websites including

Taobao Marketplace, Tmall.com, Amazon China, Gome, Yihaodian, Nike China and Vancl.

eTao is wholly owned by Alibaba Group.

Alibaba Cloud Computing - Developer of advanced distributed cloud computing services

Alibaba Cloud Computing was established in September 2009 with the mission of building an advanced distributed cloud computing service platform. The company is committed to supporting the growth of Alibaba Group and the whole e-commerce ecosystem by providing a comprehensive suite of Internet-based computing services, which include e-commerce data mining, high-speed massive e-commerce data processing, and data customization.

Alibaba Cloud Computing is wholly owned by Alibaba Group.

China Yahoo! - Long-serving Internet Portal in China

Alibaba Group acquired China Yahoo! (www.yahoo.com.cn) in October 2005 as part of its strategic partnership with Yahoo! Inc. China Yahoo! is a long-serving Chinese-language portal with a focus on essential Internet services including news, email and search.

China Yahoo! is wholly owned by Alibaba Group.

Alipay - Commonly used third-party online payment platform in China

Launched in 2004, Alipay (www.alipay.com) is a commonly used third-party online payment solution in China. It provides an easy, safe and secure way for millions of individuals and businesses to make and receive payments on the Internet. It had more than 650 million registered accounts as of December 2011. On November 11, 2011, Alipay set a record for the highest daily number of transactions, facilitating 33.69 million transactions during the 24-hour period.

The preferred online payment tool of Internet merchants in China, Alipay provides an escrow payment service that reduces transaction risk for online consumers. Shoppers have the ability to verify whether they are happy with goods they have purchased before releasing funds to the seller.

Alipay partners with more than 100 financial institutions including leading national and regional banks across China as well as Visa and MasterCard to facilitate payments in China and abroad. In addition to Taobao Marketplace and Tmall.com, Alipay provides payment solutions for more than 460,000 merchants, covering a wide range of industries including online retail, virtual gaming, digital communications, commercial services, air ticketing and utilities. It also offers an online payment solution to help merchants worldwide sell directly to consumers in China and supports transactions in 12 major foreign currencies.

Source:

http://news.alibaba.com/specials/aboutalibaba/aligroup/index.html?tracelog=24581_foot_company_info, accessed on June 29, 2012

Required

1. Discuss the IT risks faced by Alibaba and the controls it should implement to mitigate the risks.

2. Discuss the IT risks faced by Alibaba's customers and the controls they should implement to mitigate the risks.

MULTIPLE CHOICE QUESTIONS

1. Which of the following violates the Personal Information Protection and Electronic Documents Act?
    a) A professor shares your grades with other professors in your university.
    b) A bank uses an employee's doctor notes to assess whether to approve the employee's loan application.
    c) A life insurance company asks about your medical history.
    d) A government job application form asks about your citizenship.

2. Which of the following has the most privacy impact?
    a) Intellectual property
    b) Cookie
    c) Sarbanes-Oxley Act
    d) Database management system
    e) Enterprise resource planning system

3. What does P3P automate?
    a) Privacy policy
    b) Password change
    c) Cookies
    d) Favourite web sites
    e) Web history blocking

4. Which type of controls does the Ontario Electronic Commerce Act affect the most?
    a) General
    b) Access
    c) Input
    d) Processing

5. If a bank does not post its privacy policy on its web site, which principle is it violating?
    a) Accountability
    b) Limiting use
    c) Openness
    d) Individual access

6. Which of the following is most likely to occur if a domain name server breaks down?
    a) Business transactions can be decrypted by unauthorized parties.
    b) Users will be spammed.
    c) Users transactions cannot be forwarded.
    d) User computers will be infected.

7. Which of the following types of intellectual property is infringed on when someone distributes purchased music to a large group of friends?
   a) Patent
   b) Trademark
   c) Copyright
   d) Goodwill

8. Which type of control does intellectual property registration belong to?
   a) Corrective
   b) Preventive
   c) Detective
   d) Restrictive

9. Which organization is subject to Federal Privacy Act?
   a) Internal Revenue Service
   b) Harvard University
   c) Boeing
   d) Good Samaritan Hospital
   e) Google

10. Which risk do EDI payments mitigate?
   a) Late payment
   b) Overpayment
   c) Underpayment
   d) Paying the wrong party
   e) Bounced checks

CHAPTER SIX – APPLICATION CONTROLS

"Drive thy business, let not that drive thee." - Benjamin Franklin

Every CEO would agree to the above statement. Driving means moving ahead with a plan. A driver has to know where to go, stop and turn as well as how to control the car. It is the last function, control, that keeps the car progressing in a direction that the driver wants. Driving a business requires controls to ensure that business goals are met efficiently and avoid just going through the motion.

We started our discussion of internal controls in Chapter Three, where we talked about how internal controls should be mapped to inherent risks for management to achieve a tolerable level of business risk. The tolerable level should be set where the cost of an extra control would exceed the cost of the risk if materialized, taking into account the probability of the risk. This is called a reasonable level of internal controls.

An internal control is an instruction, procedure or tool to mitigate an inherent risk. An internal control is not an essential business activity or procedure for a transaction to complete. This means internal controls are optional for individual transactions although the lack of internal controls in a transaction increases the risk with respect to fictitious transaction, incompleteness, inaccuracy, untimeliness, lack of authorization and inefficiency. In the long run, internal controls are not optional. A system that has insufficient controls is less and less reliable.

To ensure that risk mitigation is organized and coordinated effectively, management should correlate internal controls to provide sufficient redundancy to prevent risks from being ignored while avoiding significant duplication of effort. Such correlation is called a plan of internal controls. This plan should be documented and used as a basis for employee training.

Internal controls may be general in nature or specific to applications. A general control is one that is applied to an environment or multiple applications. An application control mitigates the risk of only one system application. It would appear that general controls are more cost effective. However, because applications differ in risks and environments, organizations cannot implement only general controls. Management should start with general controls until the cost of a control exceeds the monetary impact of the risk being mitigated. Then, if the residual risk is too high and it very much likely will be, application controls should be implemented. Although an application control applies to a specific application (system), the same technique can be used across applications. For example, a credit limit and a check limit both use the same technique, but applied in different contexts.

APPLICATION CONTROL DOCUMENTATION

Application controls should be documented in user requirements, design narratives describing work flows, entity relationship diagrams and system flowcharts during systems development. For an implemented system, controls are documented in programs, program narratives, system configuration parameters, policies and procedures. For each system, there should be a list of internal controls that can be cross referenced to the documents mentioned above. This list of controls will be used for control and risk assessment of the system as well as for references in audits, control assurance to regulators and training courses.

APPLICATION CONTROL OBJECTIVES

Regardless of the application, there are six generic control objectives. They are: completeness, authorization, accuracy, timeliness, occurrence and efficiency. Internal controls are designed and implemented to ensure that information is reliable.

Internal controls should be applied to each stage of a transaction cycle. The typical transaction cycle includes input, processing, output and data storage. Relating this cycle to the control objectives of completeness, authorization, accuracy, timeliness, occurrence and efficiency, management and auditors can use the following matrix to assess the adequacy of internal controls.

	Complete	Authorized	Accurate	Timely	Occur	Efficient
Input						
Processing						
Output						
Storage						

Management should complete this matrix for each system and subsystem and rate each cell as high, moderate or low. Another scale can simply be acceptable or unacceptable. A low rating is unacceptable and management must design and implement internal controls to raise the rating to moderate or high. When should controls be moderate versus high in reliability and sufficiency? This depends on the degree of inherent risk and materiality of the system. There are software tools to aid in risk and control assessments.

TYPES OF APPLICATION CONTROLS

Application controls can be preventive, detective or corrective. Preventive controls usually give the organization better value for money than detective and corrective controls. However, an organization cannot rely only on preventive controls, otherwise operation will be too constrained. Organizations have to supplement preventive controls with detective and corrective controls.

Here are some common application controls:
- Access controls.
- Aging analysis to estimate inventory obsolescence and uncollectible accounts.
- Automated notifications to management on rate changes, salary changes, new hires etc.
- Batch total to ensure completeness.
- Credit limits.
- Customer statements for customers to verify transactions.
- Data correlation to identify anomaly, e.g., to detect illegitimate transactions or kickbacks.
- Database controls.
- Displaying data entered for the data entry clerk to verify accuracy.
- Exception reporting of transactions for management or independent review.
- Hash total to ensure completeness.
- Input edit checks for accuracy.
- Input edit checks for completeness.
- Management review of significant transactions.
- Run to run control total to ensure completeness.
- Segregation of duties between incompatible functions, between systems and within a system.
- Signing authority limits.
- Validity check of input data by verifying to a table of acceptable values.

Access Controls

Access controls can occur at a general level or an application level. For example, a password can be used to restrict access to the network. Another password can be used to authenticate users of the payroll system. We will discuss access controls in Chapter Eight.

Batch Total

Batch total is a common application control to ensure completeness of data input and processing. Here is an example of how it works.
1. At the end of each business day, bank tellers batch checks deposited by customers and wraps the list of checks around a batch with a batch total. A batch may contain, say, fifty checks.
2. The checks are picked up by a bank van or aircraft (depending on remoteness) and transported to a regional data center.
3. The operators in each regional data center keys in the amount of each check to a check clearing machine which also reads the encoded bank, branch and account numbers. The operator also keys in the batch total compiled by a teller.

4. The check clearing machine produces a batch total and compares it to the entered batch total. If there is a difference, the batch will not be processed and the operator has to correct. The difference may be the result of a keying error by the teller or the operator or the result of a check getting lost in transit.

A batch total can be applied to amounts or quantities. It can be taken at any stage when source documents are transported to ensure that documents are received in entirety and subsequently entered to the system. This technique basically involves comparing two totals of the same population taken at different stages of the transaction recording cycle to ensure that transactions are recorded completely and accurately. A drawback of a batch total is that it does not detect offsetting errors. In the above example, if a $100 check was not entered to the check clearing system, but another $100 check was entered twice, the two batch totals will still agree and this error will not be detected. To detect offsetting errors, organizations can implement hash totals.

Hash Total

This is similar to batch total. However, instead of keeping track of an item count, a quantity or amount, it uses a numeric field that is not intended for calculation. For example, in the above example, instead of or in addition to totalling the amount of checks, the teller and the check clearing system can total the account number of each check. This way, if a check is lost in transit to the data center, the total of account numbers tallied by the teller and the check clearing system will not agree. But if a $100 check is entered as $200 and vice versa, neither the hash total nor the batch total will detect this offsetting error. This shows that batch total and hash total mainly address completeness and to some extent, accuracy, but other controls are needed to ensure accuracy, such as edit checks or displaying an amount on data entry for the data entry person to verify.

Run to Run Control Total

There are many programs and functions in a system that process transactions. A transaction, especially a batch mode transaction, often has to go through many functions before it is fully recorded. A system may pass, internal to the system, transactions in batches from function to function. Just as it is important to pass control totals when source documents are transported, it is useful for functions in a system to calculate "batch totals" within a system for the receiving function to verify that all transactions that should have been passed between system functions have been received. For example, in an enterprise resource planning system of a company with diversified business units, payroll transactions information is transmitted to work-in-progress inventory of the applicable business units. In addition, and the total of each day's payroll transactions applicable to a business unit is transmitted. The inventory system receiving the transmission of payroll information will first calculate a total of the payroll costs for the day being transferred and then compare the calculated total with the transmitted total. Once the two totals agree, the inventory system will apply to detailed data to work-in-progress inventory.

Segregation of Duties

The purpose of segregation of duties is to provide opportunities for errors to be detected and to reduce the opportunity for irregular practices or fraud. It is critical to segregate the duties of IT from businesses. This is segregation of duties at a general level. It is similarly important to segregate incompatible functions in the business and accounting areas. Two functions are incompatible if they satisfy the following criteria:

- Having one person performing both functions will unduly and significantly increase the risk of fraud.
- Having one person performing both functions will unduly and significantly increase the risk of errors not being detected.
- Assigning the functions to at least two persons will not significantly impair operations effectiveness.
- Assigning the functions to at least two persons will not significantly reduce operations efficiency.

Segregation of duties is therefore based on risk assessment. Where it is impractical to segregate duties because of staff constraint, the organization can mitigate the resultant risk with more rigorous exception reporting and management review. For example, in a small organization, because of a maternity leave, if the controller who approves invoices is told to also approve purchase orders for a month, the president can mitigate the increase in risk by reviewing all large payments at the end of each week for substantiating documents. Segregation of duties should be implemented via organization charts, job descriptions, training and access controls.

Edit Checks

Edit checks on data input are critical preventive controls to ensure that data input is correct and complete. The same techniques can be applied in processing. Why do we have to apply the same techniques to processing if input data is correct? Well, in processing, programs perform calculations to update data files. Before data files are updated, the calculated results should be validated to detect errors. For example, an invoice with a negative amount should be reviewed before the sales journal and the accounts receivable subsidiary ledger are updated. Here is a list of common edit checks.

- Check digit, last digit of a control number serves as a control digit to validate the number.
- Data format check, e.g., a date field should be yyyymmdd.
- Limit check.
- Missing data check, i.e., all mandatory fields are filled in.
- Range check.

- Sequence check
- Sign check.
- Validity check, by verifying data input to a table of acceptable values.

Input Controls

This is the first series of internal controls to be applied to a transaction, to ensure that input reflects real transactions, is complete, authorized, accurate, timely and efficient. Controls should be exercised to assess whether data input is supported by a legitimate business transaction, including internal operational transactions. An example is assessing whether hours entered reflect actual hours worked by verifying to time sheets or asking a supervisor to review hours entered. Input controls may be manual or automated, they may also be in real time or a delayed mode. An example of a real-time control is for the system to check the data entered before accepting it. An example of a delayed control would be validating the data after accepting entry but before processing. An input control must be applied before processing, otherwise the purpose of the control is nullified.

Input Controls to Ensure Completeness

Transactions are often not processed properly because data is input incompletely. Here are some controls to mitigate this risk.
- User friendly screen to avoid incomplete data entry.
- Make certain fields mandatory and enforcing this with a system feature.
- Procedures to indicate the requirement to enter all fields.
- Emphasize mandatory field entry in user training.
- Batch control total comparing the total of amount or quantity from source documents to the total of amount or quantity input to the system.
- Hash total comparing certain arbitrary numeric fields from source documents to the corresponding fields input to the system.
- Displaying input screen after data entry to the employee or customer and asking for confirmation.
- Document count control comparison before and after data entry.
- Audio repeating of data entered to the customer.
- Summary screen displaying total value of key fields entered for confirmation by the employee or customer.

Input Controls to Ensure Authorization

A user who has been granted access to a system for data entry can enter any data if there are no controls to restrict and detect the entry of data without authorization or the entry of invalid data. Here are some examples of application controls to ensure authorized data entry.

- Access to dormant bank accounts requires supervisor override. A bank classifies a deposit account as dormant when there has been no customer initiated transaction for two years. Any human initiated transactions like a deposit, withdrawal or transfer made to a dormant account should trigger an alert to the branch manager, and if the initiation is done by the branch manager, the alert should be directed to the area manager.
- Authorized documents for data input are made available to only restricted employees.
- Data entry in excess of a certain limit in transaction amount requires a supervisor's override, also called management override.
- Input of highly sensitive data requires the involvement of at least two employees.
- Online bank account creation by a customer is not fully processed until a client returns a signed form in hard copy.
- Online system displaying only human readable data and asking for the data to be entered along with the transaction data to confirm that data entry is performed by the authorized person, as opposed to being faked by a hacker's program. For example, the customer is shown a character string in different highly italicized fonts and asked to type in the string. This control is intended to prevent automated data entry engineered by a hacker.
- Online transaction input is routed to another employee to confirm with the customer before processing.
- Management overrides are logged and reported for more senior management review.
- Senior management review of management overrides is also logged for audit trail.
- Procedures require the examination of management authorization before data entry.
- System asking for a ticket number or authorization number before accepting data.
- System notifying the appropriate managers of certain sensitive data entered before processing to seek confirmation of authorization.

Input Controls to Ensure Accuracy

Data entry is error prone. This is one of the reasons organizations increasingly automate data capture at source. Automated data capture also saves time. Here are some input controls to ensure accuracy.

- Applying a check digit to validate the entry of a control number like a product number. The check digit is the last digit of the number. For example, for product number 123456, a check digit, say 7, is added to the end. When an employee enters 1234567, the system applies a formula to 123456 to calculate the last digit. If the calculated value is 7, the data entry is accepted because the number satisfies the formula. If the data entry person makes a mistake in that number, the last digit will highly likely to be a value other than 7 and the system will not accept it. The reliability of this method depends on the length of the number and the sophistication of the formula. This method only helps ensure valid, but not necessarily correct data entry. In other words, even if a number satisfies the formula, it may not be the intended number; for example, an employee may enter the product number for a bicycle instead of a tricycle. A common application of check digit is for the creation of bar codes for products. If a staff member enters an invalid product number, i.e., one that does not exist in the inventory system and if the number has been turned into a bar code, that product will require a cashier to call someone to go to the shelf to check the actual price because the bar code will not be accepted by the inventory system. A check digit formula can be applied by the system to check that the number entered to the bar code creation system is valid so that the code inscribed or labelled on products will be acceptable to the inventory system. It should be noted that a check digit actually forms part of the permanent document or record control number, unlike an error detection value to detect a data transmission error, which is discarded after verification of data transmission.

- Apply data reasonableness check, e.g., is the pay rate reasonable in relation to the staff classification?
- Apply a sign check to detect values that should not be negative.
- Limit check.
- Check for proper data format, e.g., date, numeric and alphanumeric.
- Detailed procedures for data entry to prevent mistakes.
- Display the data scanned to be confirmed by the person doing the scanning.
- Test bar codes for correctness before producing the codes, e.g., assign an employee to read the product description by scanning the bar codes before making the codes "official".
- Test the scanners for accuracy.
- Staff training to prevent mistakes.
- User friendly screen to prevent mistakes.

Input Controls to Ensure Timeliness

Information may be correct but useless because it is too late. Here are some input controls to ensure timeliness.
- A schedule to ensure timely data entry.
- Audible alarm to remind about data entry.
- Automated data capture.
- Data entry format printed on transaction documents.
- Email reminder for data entry.
- Incentive for early data entry.
- Metrics on timeliness of data entry.
- Place data entry as close to transaction origination as possible.
- Timeliness of data entry included in performance and outsourcing contracts.
- Use radio frequency identifier (RFID) to ensure timely data capture.

Input Controls to Ensure Occurrence

There is a risk that data entered to a system does not reflect real business transactions. To mitigate this risk, management should implement internal controls to validate data, preferably before it gets into the system. The controls can be automated or manual.

Automated controls usually entail checking input data to existing data or correlating data from different sources including source documents. Manual controls mainly involve vouching input data to source documents.

Here are some examples of input controls for occurrence, i.e., to confirm that the data entered reflects a real and genuine transaction.

- A cruise company checks for any existing and identical reservation to confirm that it is not a duplicate before reserving the seats.
- A documented procedure that requires the payroll administrator to check for management authorization and employee identification before setting up a new employee in the payroll system.
- A telephone company requires a second employee to call the customer back to confirm an order.
- An insurance company checks for effective coverage before accepting a claim.
- An online stock brokerage alerts a customer when the number of shares of a stock to be purchased equals the number of shares already held, to confirm that the customer actually wants to buy instead of selling.
- Check for existence of a purchase order and shipping documents before accepting invoice data for invoice generation.
- Check the serial numbers of computers entered for disposal.
- Reconcile EDI totals to source system totals before translation to ANSI or EDIFACT format.
- Validate the social insurance/security number upon data entry.
- Validate automated teller machine (ATM) card before allowing transactions to be entered.

Input Controls to Ensure Efficiency

The Internet has heightened global competition and organizations are under constant pressure to cut cost. Further, customers are increasingly demanding in terms of system response time. Here is a common list of input controls to ensure efficiency.

- Populate standing data based on a record key like an account number to minimize key entry.
- Use scanning to minimize data entry.
- Use turnaround documents to minimize data entry, e.g., a perforated payment stub initially printed as part of a bill.
- Automated positioning of the cursor to the next field where data entry is required.
- Highlight fields that have to be completed.
- Use hyperlinks for online help features to expedite frequently asked questions (FAQs).
- Use customized screens for users to input data.
- Increase the use of voice recognition for data entry.
- Equip mobile staff with handheld devices for data entry.
- Use RFIDs to capture information to reduce key entry.

Processing Controls

Reliable data input does not guarantee reliable information produced by the system. How data is processed has to be controlled. Increasingly, the input of one transaction can trigger multiple related updates to different systems without human intervention, such as in the case of an enterprise resource planning system (ERP). It is critical that there are sufficient processing controls to ensure transaction processing is legitimate (occurrence), authorized, complete, accurate, timely and efficient.

Processing Controls for Completeness

Here are some internal controls to ensure that transactions are processed completely.
- Batch total and hash total.
- Run-to-run control totals for the system to check the completeness of transactions passed from one program to another. These are automated batch totals.
- Network transmission controls such as parity checks and redundant data checks.
- Reconciliation from subsidiary ledger to the general ledger.
- Reconciliation from transaction journals to the subsidiary ledgers.
- Customer statements.
- Transaction receipts to confirm processing.
- Gap detection to alert management of potentially missing transactions.
- For systems where almost all of the master file records are expected to be updated in each cycle, e.g., payroll, have the system produce a report of any records that do not receive an update.
- A schedule of batch updates to ensure complete processing.
- Confirmation to customers to ensure each transaction is completely processed.

Processing Controls for Authorization

Even with authorized data entry, transactions may still be processed without authorization. For example, a programmer may alter a system function to cause unauthorized processing. Another example is the fulfilment of sales orders that exceed credit limits. Here are some controls to ensure that processing is authorized.
- Confirmation with customer after data entry but before processing to ensure authorization.
- Customers are informed of system generated transactions to ensure authorization.
- Establish and periodically review credit limits.
- Online confirmation with the line manager whose cost center is being charged to ensure authorization before the transaction is processed.
- Procedures require changes to transaction processing schedules or fee arrangement to be approved by customers and management.
- Produce an exception report on sales that have caused credit limits to be exceeded.
- Statistical analysis of processing results to identify unusual trend.

- System generated transactions that are out of the ordinary have to be approved by management before being finalized.
- System renewal of billing arrangement or contracts are approved by management and the customers before being finalized.
- Perform process logic check behind the web interface to detect unauthorized change by a hacker.

Processing Controls for Accuracy

Correct input of data may still lead to incorrect transactions if processing or data transcription is wrong. It is critical to have extensive processing controls to verify data transmitted, transcribed and calculated. The following are some key processing controls over accuracy.

- Display the final data to be processed before a transaction is recorded on the screen for user or customer confirmation.
- Data transmission controls like parity check and redundant data check.
- Sequence check and gap detection.
- Statistical checks to assess reasonableness of calculated amounts.
- Limit check.
- Run-to-run control totals.
- Batch and hash totals.
- Three way matching of the purchase order, receiving report and invoice before payment.
- Sign check of quantitative data items to detect negative value that is not right.

Processing Controls for Timeliness

Operation is often delayed because transactions are not processed promptly. This can result from human errors, oversight, system breakdown or network latency. Here are some key processing controls to address timeliness.

- A processing schedule to ensure timeliness.
- A schedule of month end closing.
- Aging of suspense items for follow-up.
- Database error recovery procedures; this will be further discussed later in the chapter.
- Email notification to operators to initiate processing.
- Management review of aged list of suspense items.
- Management review of process logs.
- Periodic analysis of transaction throughput time.
- Staff training.
- Survey with users about timeliness of processing.

Processing Controls for Occurrence

Here are some examples of processing controls to ensure that data is processed only based on real transactions.

- A bank system putting a "hold fund" flag on an account for deposits until the checks have cleared.
- Attach cameras to RFIDs for inventory tracking, to detect tampering or removal of RFID from inventory.
- Cash receipts that cannot be posted to a customer account are recorded in a suspense account for investigation.
- Confirm transactions with customers.
- Confirm with counter-parties before processing a swap. A swap is a two way hedge of a financial instrument like a bond or a commodity whereby each of two parties to the swap agrees to cover the variance between the market price and the swap price to "insure" the other party against downturn or upswing. For example, a deal between a nature gas producer and a retailer may agree a price of $3 per million BTU. If the market price goes to $4 per million BTU, the producer gets $4 from the open market but provides a $1 rebate to the retailer. Conversely, if the market price is $2, the retailer can buy it in the open market for $2 but has to pay the producer $1. What is the relevance to computer systems? Systems have been inappropriately used by rogue traders to falsify swaps to hide their unauthorized transactions.
- Direct payroll deposits are reconciled to the payroll transaction file before despatching deposits to the financial institution.
- Duplicate detection to avoid processing a transaction twice.
- System comparison of transactions that are identical in amount, date of service and vendor to prevent processing the same transaction twice.
- Disbursement system cross-referencing to purchase orders before paying invoices.
- Payroll system confirms employee eligibility before accruing vacation credit.
- Payroll system requests confirmation from the hiring manager before creating a file for a new employee.
- Sales system references to original invoice before granting a refund.

Processing Controls for Efficiency

A system's bottleneck often occurs after data entry. This may be the result of inadequate hardware or inefficient programs. The former is easily preventable. The latter requires rigorous programming practices, careful design of processing functions and detailed testing. Here is a common list of processing controls to ensure efficiency.

- Stress tests of a system before implementation to ensure it can handle unusually high loads.
- Schedule the update of non-essential information after business hours.
- Prioritize network traffic.

- Hash long files or messages to a short form when the files and messages have to be repeatedly compared to assure there is no change. Hashing means using an algorithm to reduce a long string of data to a fixed and much shorter length with such precision and uniqueness that there is no collision, i.e., virtually no two original message will result in the same hash. With a unique hash, the system can just pass this hash when it is necessary to see if a file has been changed. For example, if the system wants to see if a contract has been changed, instead of scanning the entire contract, it can just hash the contract at time interval 1 and store it, and then hash the contract at time interval 2, 3 etc. and compare the new hashes with the previous hash. This alleviates the need for the system to literally check every word and transmit the entire contract just for confirming there is no change. Hashing is not the same as compression as the actual message or file cannot be recreated from a hash.
- Use cloud computing to tap unused resources on the Internet spared by trading partners and ISPs.
- Use virtualization to maximize the hardware resources of servers. Virtualization involves using sophisticated system software like network smoothing software to enable the sharing of available hardware resources to a very granular level.
- Use application service providers (ASP) to optimize processing. An ASP is a service organization that provides and hosts systems for corporate clients to use so that the clients do not have to maintain and support their own systems.
- Use edge computing to place data at the edge of the supplier's reach as close to users as possible to minimize network time. Here is an example.

The Situation
Certified General Accountants Association of Canada (CGA-Canada) delivers a Program of Professional studies via a distance education format to 24,000 students in Canada, China and the Caribbean Islands. In 2003, CGA-Canada and its regional and territorial affiliates decided to transform the delivery of the program from a CD-based method to an online method. In partnership with the Canadian Institute of Financial Planners, an online education delivery platform called edNET was developed, allowing students to access interactive course material, work with self-testing exercises, submit term work, participate in threaded-discussion forums, and have access to additional material that complements the education/certification program.

The Challenge
The edNet system makes it possible for students to complete CGA studies from anywhere in the world, as long as they have an Internet connection. It also means that assignments, review questions and solutions, electronic lesson notes, and so forth are accessed through and posted to a central server.

Knowing that thousands of students would be trying to access the CGA-Canada server, the organization worried how service to its students would be affected if slowdowns and crashes occurred, especially at deadline times. CGA-Canada was also concerned about the strain on its Internet connection from the extra system load. It knew it needed to be proactive to ensure the success of its comprehensive, interactive online distance education program.

The Goal
CGA-Canada needed to meet three key requirements to enable an efficient and flexible online learning environment:
* *Avoid infrastructure buildout—CGA-Canada wanted to deliver a robust online experience without increasing its infrastructure or personnel.*
* *Support peak traffic load—The organization's site needed to scale to support peak traffic that could potentially overload its Internet connection.*
* *Ensure availability—CGA-Canada needed to ensure students could access course content and submit their essay-type assignments and quizzes 24x7.*

Why Akamai
Realizing it needed to quickly find a solution for its students spanning 18 time zones, CGA-Canada started considering its options. According to Gabriel Vitus, CGA-Canada's Director of Information Technology, "The most obvious solutions included adding more servers, installing load balancers, making staff available 24x7, or outsourcing or co-locating our Web site. But all of these solutions were deemed costly and unsatisfactory - they would only partially address the scalability and availability problems and would have required us to spend more on infrastructure and headcount." As a non-profit organization, CGA-Canada needed the most value for its money and determined that the Akamai solution could help it affordably solve the challenges associated with online delivery of education. In fact, CGA-Canada estimates the Akamai solution enabled it to reduce its infrastructure and staffing expenses by almost 40% in the first year.

Source: http://www.akamai.com/html/customers/case_study_cga_canada.html
Accessed on June 24, 2012.

Akamai is an Internet service provider that specializes in Internet performance acceleration. Akamai stores the content of the GGA course material on Akamai users around the world to make the information more readily available for viewing and downloading by users around the world. Akamai has the similar arrangement with other organizations like some large Internet portals.

Output Controls

Information is reliable only if output reflects real transactions and if it is complete, authorized, accurate, timely and efficient. This requires a combination of system tracking controls, validation checks, management reviews and reconciliations. Because output is increasingly electronic and accessed by users online, some traditional output controls like procedures for report distribution have been replaced with access controls.

Output Controls for Completeness

Incomplete information can lead to incorrect decisions and incorrect financial reporting. What is produced should be checked to ensure all transactions are reflected. Here are some key output controls over completeness.

- A checklist to be signed off once hard copy reports have been distributed.
- Batch and hash totals.
- Confirmation with users to ensure output is received.
- Detailed instructions for interpreting output.
- Highlighted key fields for users to check completeness.
- Management and independent review of processing logs.
- Parity check and redundant data check.
- Procedures to approve changes to distribution lists.
- Reconciliation between systems.
- Requiring users to sign for receipt of paper reports.

Output Controls for Authorization

Even if output is complete, it may be useless or misleading if it is not authorized. Similarly, reports that represent unauthorized transactions can be damaging to the organization. Here is a sample of output controls over authorization.

- A list of authorized users who can sign off reports.
- Guidelines for classifying reports by sensitivity.
- Management review and approval of reports.
- Guidelines for report retention to prevent unauthorized access.
- Guidelines for report shredding.
- Procedures for approval of changes to distribution lists.
- Procedures for approving ad hoc report requests.
- Procedures for management or customer approval of release of information.
- Procedures for securing reports pending pickup.
- Procedures for review and approval of reports.
- System requirement for user review and approval of reports with documented evidence of review and approval via the system.
- A list of authorized report recipients. This control is increasingly being replaced with access controls because more and more output is electronic and available on a "pull" basis. Users may get notification that the output is ready in the system.

Output Controls for Accuracy

Reports must be accurate to be useful. Many users do not realize that the programs used to process transactions are often different from those used in generating reports. This means accurate processing does not necessarily mean accurate output. Here are some key output controls over accuracy.

- Detailed instructions for generating ad hoc reports.
- Highlighting totals to make it easy to assess report correctness.
- Instructions for interpreting report.
- Locking key fields on electronic reports to prevent accidental overwriting.
- Parity check and redundant data check.
- Policies and guidelines on end user systems development to prevent incorrect reports.
- Providing users and customers with contact information for reporting discrepancies.
- Reconciliation between systems.
- Separating numerical columns with text columns to prevent misreading.
- Standards for report headings and labels to ensure consistency.

Output Controls for Timeliness

Information may be correct, complete and authorized. But unless it is timely, usefulness can be significantly compromised. Here are some key output controls to ensure timeliness.

- A schedule for producing periodic reports.
- Communicate the report schedule to users so they can question when reports are late.
- Ongoing output is deposited in users' network folders for retrieval.
- Parity check and redundant data check.
- Reconciliation to the general ledger.
- Reminder to users to consider generating ad hoc reports.
- Reminders to users to retrieve reports.
- Reports are generated in real time as much as possible.
- Requirement for users to confirm report receipts.
- User training on the importance of timely review of reports.

Output Controls for Occurrence

Output should be validated to ensure that it reflects real transactions. A transaction may be as simple as an information request. Here are some related controls.

- Accident claim reports are reconciled to traffic tickets.
- Attendance reports are spot checked to timesheets.
- Independent confirmation of insurance policies with customers.
- Invoices are matched to purchase orders.
- Managers receive notification of salary raises relating to their subordinates for confirmation.
- Managers review exception reports.
- Managers review payroll transaction reports.
- Sending monthly statements to customers.
- Signatures on printed checks are verified before despatch.
- Stock picking sheets are reconciled to purchase orders.

<u>Output Controls for Efficiency</u>

Often information output is difficult to use because the format is not user friendly, it is too detailed or too brief. Sometimes, the format of output is not user friendly or the procedures are not clear. Other times, output is too voluminous therefore wasting time to read and the cost of printing. Here are some output controls to ensure efficiency.

- Provide output electronically as much as possible in a pull mode, letting users retrieve output when needed, to avoid unnecessary printing and display.
- Condense output for ease of reading and searching.
- Use hyperlink on output to provide help instructions.
- Format output that can be easily read on mobile devices.
- Use edge computing to expedite output.
- Consolidate reports to ease reference.
- Hyperlink fields that require actions.
- Use online analytical processing to facilitate real time slicing and dicing by users. For example, by clicking a link and/or entering data, the system will analyze data to provide the desired information on screen. Online analytical processing means a user can input online parameters or click some icons and the system will analyze a mass of data to produce trend information, ratios, graphs or the specific answer to a question.
- Use voice response as much as practical.
- Obtain user feedback for improving the user friendliness of output.

Application Controls over Stored Information

Information in storage is subject to risks. It may not reflect real transactions because of subsequent manipulation after the initial information is placed in storage. It may be accessed without authorization. It may be changed inaccurately, etc. It is critical to have internal controls over stored information.

<u>Stored Information Controls for Completeness</u>

Stored information may be lost because of inappropriate access or storage media failure. Database maintenance can also affect information integrity. Here are some key internal controls to ensure completeness of stored information.

- Fixed asset verification.
- Frequent review of change logs.
- Periodic audit of database for completeness by vouching to source documents and correlating database tables.
- Periodic confirmation with customers and users.
- Periodically verify the user account list with managers.
- Physical inventory taking.
- Reconciliation between systems.
- Redundant data storage.
- Referential integrity (defined under Database below) checks built in databases.

Stored Information Controls for Authorization

Information stored may be accessed without authorization. The retention of records may go beyond the authorized time periods. Here are some key controls to mitigate the risk of lack of authorization.

- Acceptable use policy. We will discuss this further in Chapter Twelve.
- Assigning data ownership to managers to authorize appropriate controls and access requests.
- Privacy policy.
- Privacy policy compliance checking by doing periodic spot checks.
- Privacy policy training.
- Procedures require approval of changes to record retention schedules.
- Procedures require approval of changes to stored data.
- Procedures require approval of data deletion.
- Procedures specify the process for gaining access to stored data.
- User screens to remind about the need to obtain authorization to share information.

Stored Information Controls for Accuracy

Information stored may, overtime, become inaccurate because of media damage or out-of-date procedures. Accidental change can also affect accuracy and integrity. Here are some key internal controls to mitigate these risks.

- Confirmation with employees and customers.
- Database referential integrity check.
- Frequent cross-checking and synchronization of databases.
- Periodic checking of contract information to the latest signed contracts.
- Periodic data tests for unauthorized change.
- Periodic inventory taking of fixed assets.
- Periodic reconciliation between systems.
- Regular review of stored information for obsolescence.

Stored Information Controls for Timeliness

Information stored is not effective if it is not timely. How so? The issue is availability, e.g., is the information available when needed? Is it relevant to the need in terms of the time period it represents? Here are some key controls.

- Conduct user survey about system responsiveness.
- Frequent update of retention schedules.
- Keep track of the dates of updates to assess information currency.
- Label files with expiry dates.
- Regular confirmation with users.
- Regular database synchronization.
- Regular review for currency.

- Regular tests of system availability.
- Regular tests of system queries for responsiveness.
- User instructions for ad hoc reporting and system queries.

Stored Information Controls for Occurrence

Stored information may not reflect real transactions resulting from invalid transactions or change to information after it is initially stored. This risk can also materialize if update or deletion transactions are not processed. Here are some controls to mitigate this risk.

- Changes to dormant account balances are reviewed by managers.
- Confirm patent with the government patent office.
- Inventory list is periodically reconciled to physical count.
- Location and assignment of fixed asset are periodically confirmed.
- Periodically confirm that employees on payroll are still employees.
- Periodically purge old data that is no longer required for statutory and management purposes.
- Reconcile the online service catalog to the corporate master list.
- Update databases to reflect organizational changes.
- Verify real estate holdings with the land title offices.
- Vouch recurring charges to contracts.

Stored Information Controls for Efficiency

With exponentially increasing computer power, organizations are storing more information than ever before. Even with the per unit cost decreasing, massive storage can amount to a significant amount of financial outlay. Here are some controls to ensure efficiency of data storage.

- Maintain an archive to store infrequently accessed information offline.
- Educate users to storage business information only on servers to avoid duplication.
- Normalize database to reduce redundancy. We will discuss this in more detail later.
- Use electronic vaulting to optimize the process for data backup.
- Maintain and frequently review the data backup schedule to avoid excessive storage.
- Use compression to save storage space.
- Maintain a schedule to periodically cull unneeded data.
- Provide graphic on demand to avoid storing complicated graphic images.
- Design a scheme to charge users for storage to deter resource hoarding or wasting.

Additional Controls for Enterprise Resource Planning System

An ERP system is an integrated accounting system so the above controls apply. In addition, because of integration and highly automated nature of an ERP, change control is very important. We don't mean just change over program instructions. In fact, for a purchased ERP like Oracle or SAP, the organization does not have the source code so software change control is less critical. However, the vendor provides flexibility for adaptation to the organization's business environment by means of configuration, i.e., setting of codes, rules and parameters. It is critical that changes to these rules, codes and parameters be subject to a rigorous process of pre-approval and verification before implementation. They should also be periodically reviewed for validity and currency.

DATABASE

Databases are increasingly used in organizations to facilitate data sharing for real time transactions and data mining. However, as is common when efficiency is to be gained, risk can go up. The sharing of data files (tables) increases the potential access points and the complexity of software. Thus, organizations need to implement controls to mitigate the additional risks. The typical databases used today are relational, object oriented and a hybrid of relational and object oriented models. Relational is the most popular model for systems that process primarily numerical and text data. This allows any two tables with a common field to interrelate and provides a lot of flexibility. In a database, a data file is called a table. A table is visually similar to an Excel spreadsheet. Common relational database management systems are Microsoft's Structured Query Language (SQL) Server and Oracle. Microsoft also has a mini version of relational database management system called Microsoft Access. An object oriented database stores graphical, video, sound and object oriented programming code. An object oriented program is a piece of reusable object code that often contains standard data like font and color. It can also contain holders for users to input data, thus combining code and data in one object with the data portion being dynamic. When data is changed, a new object can be created. Where the extent of graphic and sound data is limited and such data is often used in conjunction with text and numbers, a relational object oriented database model can be used.

Most business applications use the relational database model.

Database Components

A database is a collection of tables for sharing among applications. A table is also called a file. It consists of fields (attributes) and records. It can be pictured like an Excel spreadsheet where the columns denote the fields and the rows indicate the records.

To control the sharing of tables, the database is driven by a database management system (DBMS). The database management system is a system software product that controls the interfaces of and access to tables. Common database management systems are SQL Server, Oracle, DB2, Dbase, and Microsoft Access. A DBMS also has a data query facility, e.g., structured query language (SQL), which is the data query facility of SQL Server. The data query facility, or data query language, can be used by transaction processing programs for processing transactions and providing results to standard user queries like an account balance enquiry. It can also be used to perform ad hoc queries by coding tailored commands. The most common command type is to select fields, from tables, where (criteria). SQL is also used by programs to insert, update and delete records.

Another component of the database is a data dictionary. The purpose of the data dictionary is to keep track of the tables in a database, what each table contains in terms of fields, the format of each field, and the relative location of the fields in a table. Programs that access a table will come to the data dictionary first to find references to the needed tables and fields. The data dictionary must be kept current.

All hardware and software must be managed and controlled by people. The person who controls the database is called the database administrator (DBA). This person configures the database management system, updates the data dictionary and grants rights to programs and users to access tables. The access rights are defined in the DBMS. The database administrator has full control of the database. So it is important not to assign more duties to this person. For example, s/he should not be also a system administrator who controls the operating system.

Risks of Database Systems

A database improves efficiency and data redundancy. However, data sharing between applications increases the risk of unauthorized access and update errors. The more programs that can update a table, the more likely errors will occur. Also, because more system software is used in a database environment, the risk of incorrect software configuration (incorrect parameters) increases. Database applications often are operated in a distributed network. In that case, there are multiple copies of a database geographically dispersed. It is important to ensure that updates are synchronized. It is just as important to ensure time synchronization, by for example, operating a time server. Because a database consists of many tables that are shared between applications, there is also a risk of data inconsistency between tables when data is repeated unnecessarily, e.g., a customer address shows up in multiple tables but is represented inconsistently. This risk results from data redundancy. There is also the risk of concurrent updates, i.e., one transaction overwriting the result of a previous transaction.

Risk of Concurrent Updates

In a database environment, programs sometimes contend for the same table and field in terms of reading and writing. Although technically, the hardware will not allow two programs to update a field at the same time, just as it would be impossible for two full size cars to enter a single car garage, there is a risk of updates performed by two programs almost concurrently that could impair data integrity. Here is an example.

I deposit a $1,000 check at an ATM to a joint checking account. Less than a second later, my wife transfers $2,000 from the checking account to a savings account using eBanking. Before these transactions, the checking account balance is $5,000. Here is what could likely happen.

1.   My transaction reads the $5,000 balance and updates it to $6,000.
2.   My wife's transaction reads the $5,000 balance (after my transaction has read it but before my transaction finishes) and calculates a new balance of $3,000.
3.   My wife's transaction finishes after mine, so it overwrites the new balance as $3,000.
4.   In fact, the correct balance should be $4,000.

This is called concurrent update. That is, two transactions update the same field of the same record without knowing about each other. In other words, the left hand doesn't know what the right hand is doing. To prevent this kind of data inconsistency, organizations should configure database management systems to enforce record locking.

Database Anomalies

A table consists of fields and records. A record (row) represents an entity like an employee. A field (column) indicates an attribute about the record, e.g., job title. A table can be very long or very short. For example, all the payroll information can be contained in one table. This will make the table very long and difficult to manage. More specifically, it will present anomalies for record addition, deletion and updates. Here are three examples.

If all payroll information is in one table, it would make sense for the primary key to be the employee number. One of the fields is likely the position number. A position number should be unique for human resources tracking. Sometimes a position is vacant and there will be no associated employee number. Let's say the organization has created a new position that has not been filled. That position cannot be added to the table because the primary key is nil. This is called addition anomaly.

A similar problem is presented if the organization wants to delete a position because it is no longer needed. Because the primary key is the employee number, the organization cannot delete the position as long as the associated employee information has to be kept for income tax purpose. This is called deletion anomaly.

A third problem: If all the payroll information is in one table and the primary key is a combination of the employee number and pay period number, there is a record for every pay period in conjunction with every employee. The employee's address has to be in the system and since there is only one table, the address has to be a field in this table. Because an employee will occupy roughly 26 records per year for an organization that pays bi-weekly, the address will appear 26 times. If it is realized that the address is wrong, the organization has to correct the address on multiple records. Data entry is prone to errors so this risk of data inconsistency is increased. Recording the address on multiple records is called data redundancy. This problem is also called update anomaly. Database anomalies can be corrected using normalization. Normalization also reduces data redundancy.

Database Control

The purpose of database controls is to ensure that data access is authorized and that database table integrity is maintained. Integrity means completeness and consistency with other connected tables. We will describe the controls that should be implemented in a database environment to ensure reliability and integrity of information.

1. Segregate the duties of the database administrator (DBA) from other functions.

2. Assign and train backup DBAs.

3. Configure the database management system (DBMS) to enforce the following:
    - Record locking (described below)
    - Referential integrity (described below)
    - Detection and resolution of deadlock (described below)
    - Logging
    - Normalization (described below)
    - Synchronization between locations and environments to ensure consistency of content and clocks. Clock synchronization is critical to ensure transactions are time stamped correctly for audit trail and for prioritization of updates and interest calculation (e.g., 11:59 pm vs 12:00 am).
    - producing alerts on direct updates, i.e., updating not through an authorized program like ATM, to detect unauthorized data change.
    - passwords
    - producing alerts on table creation and deletion, to detect unauthorized data creation or deletion.

4. Rotate the duties of database administrators among different environments to increase the opportunity for error detection and reduce the risk of improper practices.

5. Establish procedures for database administration.

6. Establish procedures and authorization levels for approving access profiles for programs and users.

7. Periodic verification of the currency of the data dictionary.
8. Establish user procedures for data query to ensure correct applications and interpretation.

9. Establish error recovery and rollback procedures for database corruption or processing halts resulting from network outage, transaction errors or other unexpected occurrences. The DMBS has to recognize when processing was halted or failed and apply data integrity checks to compare before and after images and reconcile and reconstruct the differences to prevent data loss.

10. Configure the database query facility to prevent someone from running queries to deduce information that the person cannot otherwise obtain directly. For example, someone who does not have access to salary information of specific employees should be disallowed by the system to run successive queries to narrow down to the desired information. Database controls should be enforced in the DBMS to prevent queries that rule out the majority of the population or that focuses on a small part of the population unless the program or the user performing the query already has direct access to the small part being focused or that has not been ruled out. A more detailed description of this example is as follows:

> An employee wants to find out how much a female lawyer makes in a firm. If there are only two female lawyers and they have about the same rank and seniority, that person can first query the average compensation of a lawyer. Then he can query the average compensation of a male lawyer. The results of these two queries will give that person almost what he wants to know.

Record Locking

We have discussed the risk of concurrent update using the bank deposit example, where the withdrawal transaction is not aware of the deposit transaction and vice versa, leading to an incorrect balance. The principle internal control to mitigate this risk is record locking. Here's how it works.

When a transaction reads a record with intent to update it, the transaction should send a flag to the DBMS so the latter can lock the field where update is intended, and deny it from being read by another transaction that wants to use the information in the field to update that record or other records until the first transaction has finished. The purpose is to preserve information integrity. Other transactions that want to read the record just for information can be allowed to read the record being updated by the first transaction. The reason for the previous sentence is that when users query information they should realize that such information is subject to change.

Record locking can lead to a deadlock scenario, i.e., multiple transactions needing to access the same fields of a record for the purpose of updating the record. A deadlock can lead to a standstill as each transaction has to wait for the other transactions to finish. This is further explained below.

Deadlock

When inter-dependent transactions lock multiple records, the system can come to a halt. Here is an example.

▶ I enter an ATM transaction to transfer $1,000 from a joint checking account to a joint savings account.

▶ Before this transaction, the checking account and savings account balances are $5,000 and $3,000.

▶ At the same time, my wife uses eBanking to transfer $2,000 from our joint savings account to our joint checking account.

▶ My transaction starts first, so it locks the checking account balance after having read it; but before it reads the savings account balance, my wife's transaction reads the savings account balance and locks it.

▶ Now my transaction cannot read the savings account balance and my wife's transaction cannot read the checking account balance, so neither transactions can progress.

To resolve deadlock, the DBMS will release all the locks but one. As for which lock to leave engaged, the DBMS can use a first-come-first-finish method or the least impact method. Under the least impact method, the DBMS will calculate the optimal system delay (the least) and decide on which locks to cancel. The DBA can choose either method by selecting the respective parameters in the DBMS configuration.

Referential Integrity

Every table must have a primary key in order for each record to be identifiable. A primary key is a field or a combination of contiguous fields in a table that has a unique value from record to record, i.e., the value is never the same between records. Common primary keys are account number and student number. Sometimes, in order to uniquely describe each record, a table has to combine two or more contiguous fields as a composite primary key, e.g., employee_number and client_number can be the primary key in a table that shows the hours worked by each employee for each client. In this case, using either field separately as a primary key does not uniquely identify every record.

Often, the primary key of one table is included in another table as a field other than the primary key. For example, an invoice record should contain a stock ID field. In this case, the stock ID is called the foreign key. A foreign key is a field in a table that satisfies the following conditions:

a. It is not the primary key of the table.
b. It is the primary key of another table.
c. It must not have a null value.

This means if an invoice does not have a stock ID, it is invalid. This is a good control to avoid billing customers that cannot be traced to goods sold. In this case, the stock ID is the primary key in the inventory table where each record contains information about each stock item.

The DBMS should be configured to check tables for referential integrity, i.e., to check that every record does not have null value for the foreign keys.

Normalization

A normalized table reduces data redundancy by breaking tables to smaller tables, i.e., fewer fields. Tables will be more modular and granular. There are different degrees of normalization. The optimum degree is sixth. A sixth degree normalized table is absolutely free of redundant data. For business applications, third degree normalization is sufficient to avoid the anomalies described above.

A table that is not normalized consists of multiple records pertaining to the same entity and does not have a primary key. For example, if all payroll data is in one table, that would be the case. Keep in mind that a table showing columns and rows is only for human legibility. In computer storage, a table consists of a long string of 0 and 1. If there are multiple occurrences of the same data fields for an employee in a table without a primary key, the DBMS will have trouble determining where the information for one employee ends and where the next employee shows up in the table. Not only does a long table include redundant data as described above, data access can be inefficient as it takes the DBMS longer to find out where the next record begins by analyzing every data field for every record.

The following is an example of a table that is not normalized.

Table 6.1 - Unnormalized Payroll Table

Emp Num	Pay-per	Pay-date	Last_name	First_name	Dep num	Dep_name	Gross-pay	Netpay
123	1	Jan . 15, 2011	Chan	David	1	Accounting	8,500	5,200
	2	Feb. 15, 2011	Chan	David	1	Accounting	8,500	5,200
456	1	Jan. 15, 2011	Cullen	John	2	IT Security	9,500	5,800
	2	Feb. 15, 2011	Cullen	John	2	IT Security	9,500	5,750
789	1	Jan. 15, 2011	Ferrigni	Pat	3	Supply Chain	8,700	5,700
	2	Feb. 15, 2011	Ferrigni	Pat	3	Supply Chain	8,800	5,800
790	1	Jan.15, 2011	Williams	Maria	1	Accounting	8,000	5,000
	2	Feb. 15, 2011	Williams	Maria	1	Accounting	8,000	5,100

In the above table, there is no primary key. The field that looks like a primary key is the employee number. However, the record for each occurrence of the employee number has repeated occurrences of the fields in the other values, e.g., the two pay periods, where the name appears twice. This means it is difficult for the DBMS to know how long the record is, or how many instances of repeated occurrences. Keep in mind this is a simple table in terms of the number of rows for ease of reading. Regardless of the length, the DBMS, unlike a person, cannot just read the entire page or pages at a glance, it has to parse every byte. So without a primary key, this table is difficult to understand for the DBMS.

First Degree Normalization - The above table can be converted to first degree normalized by inserting a primary key. The primary key has to be able to uniquely identify every record, i.e., every row. It is easy to see that the key can be composed by combining the emp_num and pay_period fields, to yield the following table.

Table 6.2 – First Degree Normalized Payroll Table

Emp Num	Pay-per	Pay-date	Last_name	First_name	Dep num	Dep_name	Gross-pay	Netpay
123	1	Jan . 15, 2011	Chan	David	1	Accounting	8,500	5,200
123	2	Feb. 15, 2011	Chan	David	1	Accounting	8,500	5,200
456	1	Jan. 15, 2011	Cullen	John	2	IT Security	9,500	5,800
456	2	Feb. 15, 2011	Cullen	John	2	IT Security	9,500	5,750
789	1	Jan. 15, 2011	Ferrigni	Pat	3	Supply Chain	8,700	5,700
789	2	Feb. 15, 2011	Ferrigni	Pat	3	Supply Chain	8,800	5,800
790	1	Jan.15, 2011	Williams	Maria	1	Accounting	8,000	5,000
790	2	Feb. 15, 2011	Williams	Maria	1	Accounting	8,000	5,100

The primary key is shaded. A first degree normalized table is a table that has a primary key. A first degree normalized table has a drawback in that not every field depends on the entire key. For example, the employee name depends on the employee number but not the pay period number. The employee name therefore appears multiple times between records. This is data redundancy. Such data redundancy can be reduced with further normalization.

Second Degree (2NF) Normalization – A first degree normalized table can be upgraded to second degree by removing partial dependency, i.e., by making every field fully dependent on the primary key. In the example above, we can break Table 6.2 into the following tables by making every non-key field dependent on the entire key and not just part of the key.

In Table 6.2, the first non-key field, pay-date, depends on pay-period but not emp_num. It therefore does not depend on the entire primary key and creates data redundancy, i.e., pay_date values are duplicated across records. This field must be removed from the table and put in another table with pay_period as the key so that eventually, Table 6.2 will be second degree normalized.

Last-name, first-name dept_num and dept_name depend on emp-num but not on pay_period. This is why the values for these four fields are repeated between records. To help make Table 6.2 a second degree normalized table, we should remove these four fields and put them in a separate table with emp_num as the key.

Dept_ num and dept_name depend on the employee number but not on the pay period. So we have to remove dept_num and dept_name and put them in another table with emp_num as the primary key.

The remaining fields in Table 6.2 depend on the entire key so they can stay there.

The 2NF tables with limited sample data are shown on the following page.

Table 6.3 – Pay Periods

Pay-period	Pay-date
1	Jan . 15, 2010
2	Feb. 15, 2010

Table 6.4 – Employee

Emp_num	Last_name	First_name	Dept_num	Dept_name
123	Chan	David	1	Accounting
456	Cullen	John	2	IT Security
789	Ferrigni	Pat	3	Supply Chain
790	Williams	Maria	1	Accounting

Table 6.5 – Pay Period Details

Emp_Num	Pay-period	Gross-pay	Net_pay
123	1	8,500	5,200
123	2	8,500	5,200
456	1	9,500	5,800
456	2	9,500	5,750
789	1	8,700	5,700
789	2	8,800	5,800
790	1	8,000	5,000
790	2	8,000	5,100

The repeated values in Table 6.5 are attributable to the nature of the data instead of data redundancy. That is, although gross_pay seldom changes from period to period, because it could change and is part of transaction trail, we have to keep track of the data for every period.

Table 6.4 has repeated data, dept_num and dept_name. The repetition of dept_num is natural because there can be more than one employee in a department. However, dept_name does not have to have repeated data. What's wrong with repeated data? It means data redundancy. Data redundancy wastes storage, increases lookup time and can lead to data inconsistency, e.g., different dept_names for the same dept_num. Table 6.4 has data redundancy because there is transitive dependency, i.e., dependency between two non-key fields. This redundancy can be fixed by turning any table with transitive dependency into a third degree normalized table by removing the transitive dependencies.

A second degree normalized table is a table that has no partial dependency, i.e., every non-key field depends on the entire primary key.

Third Degree Normalized Table – A third degree normalized (3NF) table is a table where every non-key field depends on nothing but the entire primary key, i.e., there is no transitive dependency (dependency between two non-key fields). The following tables are 3NF. Tables 6.6 is the same as Table 6.3. Table 6.8 is the same as Table 6.5.

Table 6.6 – Pay Periods

Pay-period	Pay-date
1	Jan . 15, 2010
2	Feb. 15, 2010

Table 6.7 – Employee Names

Emp_num	Last_name	First_name	Dept_num
123	Chan	David	1
456	Cullen	John	2
789	Ferrigni	Pat	3
790	Williams	Maria	1

Table 6.8 – Pay Period Details

Emp_Num	Pay-period	Gross-pay	Net_pay
123	1	8,500	5,200
123	2	8,500	5,200
456	1	9,500	5,800
456	2	9,500	5,750
789	1	8,700	5,700
789	2	8,800	5,800
790	1	8,000	5,000
790	2	8,000	5,100

Table 6.9 – Department

Dept_num	Dept_name
1	Accounting
2	IT Security
3	Supply Chain

Table 6.4 has been split into tables 6.7 and 6.9.

Six Sigma

More and more organizations are applying the Six Sigma discipline as a standard to increase accuracy in transaction processing. Six Sigma means up to 3.4 defects per million, or 99.99966% correct. This target can be applied to any process of repeated transactions but it is more common in manufacturing processes or medical treatment systems where an extremely low frequency of defects is critical. There is applicability in accounting systems. An organization that wants to achieve Six Sigma will set up a project that involves defining the problems, measuring the risks, analyzing alternatives, designing controls and verifying results. Such an organization will achieve Six Sigma in evolution. Every large organization or organization that uses a high degree of automation in its business should assess the applicability of Six Sigma and if deemed applicable, carry out a project to achieve it. The project will require internal controls designed and implemented in the respective systems. What does "applicability" mean?

Management has to consider the cost of the controls and measurement of compliance. Well, with or without Six Sigma, every organization should assess risks and implement internal controls. Then Six Sigma becomes the degree of precision, or the extent of tolerable residual risk. Although 99.99966% accuracy is too demanding for most organizations, the Six Sigma culture should be adopted by every organization and this culture cannot sustain without strong internal controls. An organization can, over time, move towards Six Sigma. The Six Sigma concept should be applied to minimize transaction errors and also control breakdown. The latter will require controls over controls, i.e., monitoring controls.

TESTING APPLICATION CONTROLS

Application controls rest on general controls. A general control weakness that cannot be compensated for with other general controls will soften the foundation of application controls. If the impact of a general control weakness can be confined to certain applications, the external auditor can justify extending the testing of the related application controls to seek high application control assurance to mitigate the low general control assurance. Normally, the external auditor needs only moderate general control and application control assurance because the opinion of the audit is on the financial statements, not on internal controls. Moderate control reliance means moderate control risk, which is consistent with the AICPA guideline that auditors should seek to assess control risk at below maximum. Increasingly, public companies ask their shareholders' auditors to express an opinion on the internal controls that support financial statements and for that opinion to accompany the CEO's certification to the securities regulator that internal controls supporting financial statements are reliable. In such a case, the shareholders' auditors will seek high control assurance.

However, if general controls are significantly weak and the weaknesses are widespread, such as the lack of segregation of duties between the IT department and most business units, the external auditors may find it impractical to rely on even application controls because the foundation is extremely soft. In this case, the external auditor may resort to performing a substantive audit. If the client is a public company, the opinion on internal controls will have to be qualified or withheld; and that can be as devastating as a qualified financial statement audit opinion. A public company will do almost everything within its might to avoid this, i.e., to be really proactive in designing controls and asking the external auditors to test internal controls early in the year to allow time for correction.

Application controls can be tested by observation, review of documentation, confirmation with third parties and data analysis. Before testing, auditors should review the organization's documentation and identify the key application controls available and then assess whether these controls are sufficient to mitigate the business risks. If internal controls look good and adequate on paper, auditors should carry out test procedures.
These procedures can involve interviews, observation, review of system documentation, review of transaction trail, using test data, using computer assisted audit techniques, confirmation and data analysis. Here are some common test procedures.

- Review and verify bank reconciliation.
- Review the rejected transaction log and follow up for correction.
- Use test data to test input control and processing controls.
- Review the production schedule, i.e., the daily or weekly schedule of batch updates and confirm by reviewing computer operations audit trail.
- Review user procedures for correctness of instructions.
- Ask staff members questions to confirm their understanding of instructions.
- Observe segregation of duties.
- Review the DBMS configuration to assess the adequacy of provision for database integrity.
- Review the data dictionary and confirm with actual table layout.
- Send confirmation to customers to see if they have received the customer statements.
- Observe the mailing of customer statements.
- Perform data correlation to obtain evidence of controls, e.g., cross referencing invoices to receiving reports.

For a financial statement audit, application controls should be tested after obtaining assurance on general controls, around the midpoint of the year or shortly afterwards. There is no point in testing internal controls sooner as many controls cannot be practically tested without transactions. Control testing is also called the interim audit.

Upon obtaining moderate assurance on application controls, the audit team can go away and come back close to year end to start the substantive testing, i.e., auditing transactions for substantiation. Substantive testing is what directly supports the audit opinion.

At the pre-year-end or year-end stage of the audit where substantive testing is the focus, little control testing is carried out. The auditors merely perform a limited update of control testing. How can the auditors place reliance on controls for the whole year when the bulk of control testing was applied to the first half of the year? When the auditors start the pre-year-end audit phase, they should ask the CIO for a list of system changes since the interim audit. The auditors should then assess the financial statement significance of the changes. Where a financial statement assertion area is affected by one of these changes, the auditors should test the controls in that area to the same extent as control testing conducted during the interim audit. Otherwise, the auditors can conclude that controls have not changed significantly and justify performing a limited update of control testing. But how do the auditors know the list of system changes is complete and accurate? This is why software change controls are important. During interim audit, the auditors concluded that software change controls were reliable. When they come back at the pre-year-end phase, they will update the testing of software change controls to the same extent as that carried out during the interim audit. This allows them to place at least moderate reliance on software change controls. With reliable software change controls, the auditors can rely on the list of system changes, because software change controls ensure that system changes are authorized, recorded, tracked and reported to management.

Test Data

This is a quick way to test input controls and to some extent, processing controls. The increasing number of eBusiness systems makes this method practical, as the auditor does not have to ask the client to make arrangement for access to the system. Test data should be comprehensive to be reliable. When a system is not available on the Internet, the auditor will need to ask for access. The client often has reservation about the auditor putting test data through a live system. Therefore, the client might provide a test version of a system. How does the auditor know the test version has all the functions of the live system and no more?

Using a Test Version of a System in Auditing

The auditor should take the following steps to obtain assurance that the test system represents the live system. Depending on the significance and complexity of the system being tested, not all of the following procedures are necessary. For example, if code comparison reveals no discrepancy, that procedure alone is enough.

- Ensure that software change controls merit moderate reliance. If software change controls are reliable, the audit trail supporting software version movement should be reliable. The auditor can then review the audit trail to assess the currency of the test system and the currency of the live system and account for any difference in assessing the reliability of the test system for testing application controls.
- Observe the creation of the test system to gain assurance that it was created from the live system. If the client or auditee copies the live system to a test environment for you, review the operating system audit trail to confirm that the full live system has been copied.
- Perform code comparison between the live system and the test system.
- Reconcile totals of the test system to the live system.

Limitations of Test Data

Although test data can be used to directly test controls, there are drawbacks. The first is the uncertainty that the test system reflects the live system. Secondly, test data conveys only point in time assurance. Testing using test data should be repeated regularly. Manual controls cannot be tested using test data, e.g., bank reconciliation. Auditors should supplement test data procedures with reviewing transaction audit trail for control compliance and using computer assisted audit techniques.

Control Deficiency

How does the auditor deal with control deficiencies? Here are the common steps.

1. Look for compensating controls. In an organization, seldom are only the needed controls implemented. By design or as processes evolve, some redundant or complementary internal controls have been implemented. This provides room for the external auditors to find compensating controls. An example of a compensating control is that the chief financial officer (CFO) reviews all payments over a certain amount the day after the payment to ensure adequate supporting documentation. The control deficiency being compensated for is that when one of the dual check signatories goes on vacation, checks are signed by only the other signatory.

2. If there are insufficient compensating controls, the auditor should assess the need to rate application controls in that system as low.

3. This means the auditor will conduct much more substantive testing, in the case of a financial statement audit.

4. The control deficiency should be included in the management letter with recommendations for improvements. In making recommendations, the auditor should keep in mind general cost effectiveness without doing detailed analysis. Detailed cost analysis is management's responsibility.

MANAGEMENT CHECKLIST

1. Adopt a consistent set of application controls throughout the organization subject to variation between applications because of the nature of transaction processing (e.g., batch vs online) and materiality. For example, there must be monthly reconciliations signed off by managers; the format of a bank reconciliation may differ from that of a credit card reconciliation, but the requirement for extent of documentation and sign-off should be consistent.

2. Require each system owner to submit a control compliance report annually.

3. Document the internal controls for each business critical system in the same format.

4. Include internal control training as part of new managers' training.

5. Establish a secondment program for people to join the internal audit department for short term assignments and vice versa to increase internal control awareness in the organization.

6. Provide a semi-annual report to the audit committee on overall internal controls reliability in the organization.

7. Ensure that internal control recommendations from auditors are addressed promptly.

8. Include internal control compliance in the performance contracts of executives.

9. Assess the applicability of Six Sigma and initiate a project to achieve it if deemed practical.

10. Include the criteria and measurement of completeness, authorization, accuracy, timeliness and efficiency in each business unit's performance evaluation process.

INTERNAL AUDIT CHECKLIST

1. Include internal control testing in every audit.

2. Perform a risk and control assessment of every business critical system at least bi-annually.

3. Provide at least semi-annual internal control reliability reporting to the audit committee.

4. Include internal control courses in every auditor's training plan.

5. Provide trend reporting to management on common controls across departments and functions, e.g., reconciliations. Assess the trend in light of the need for better communication, procedures, monitoring and training.

6. Conduct internal control training for auditee staff and managers.

7. Establish a process for following up on reported control deficiencies.

8. Ensure that every reported control deficiency is supported by adequate work papers.

9. Provide quarterly internal control trend reporting to senior management.

10. Conduct internal control testing to support the audit of the financial statements.

EXTERNAL AUDIT CHECKLIST

1. For each general control deficiency, assess the implication on application control.

2. When testing application controls, consider the following factors:
   - period of coverage
   - direct evidence from system configuration
   - direct evidence from system logs
   - credibility of people being interviewed
   - credibility of documentation supplied by auditee staff members or managers

3. When using a test system, review audit trail and perform reconciliation to the live system to obtain assurance that the test system is the same as the live system.

4. Assess the impact of application control deficiencies on the extent of substantive testing.

5. Review internal audit work papers as a basis for relying on its testing of application controls.

6. Prepare control test techniques to test multiple controls for audit efficiency, e.g., when checking paid invoices to receiving reports, also assess timeliness of recording.

7. Assess the client's consistency in using application control techniques across applications. For example, are the same edit check techniques used in payroll and inventory? If not, assess justification.

8. For controls over changes to standing data like pay rates and credit limits, test the detective controls to detect changes, in addition to testing controls for pre-approval and accuracy of input. Changes to standing data bear higher risks than transaction data changes because of the long ranging impact.

9. Structure the audit programs such that there is a good mix of preventive and detective controls to be tested. For example, the percentage of detective controls should not be extremely lower than that of preventive controls.

10. For each detective control tested, also test the related corrective controls.

CONCLUSION

Application controls should be tested on every financial statement audit after testing and gaining assurance on general controls. A moderate level of assurance on general controls and application controls will enable the external auditors to limit substantive testing.

Internal audits mainly focus on internal controls and application controls are usually extensively tested. Other special purpose audits like providing control assurance on a service organization to corporate customers address mainly internal controls including application controls.

Computing power doubles annually. Organizations continue to empower customers and employees with technology by allowing direct access and automated transactions as well as by streamlining the manual review and approval process. This often leads to removing preventive controls to achieve efficiency. To avoid an unacceptable level of risk, management should design and implement rigorous exception reporting system functions and tracking mechanisms for exceptions to be addressed.

Sarbanes-Oxley Act requires CEOs to certify internal controls supporting financial statements annually. Application controls are directly related to financial statements. We will therefore see more rigorous documentation of application controls by management and more thorough testing of application controls by the external auditors who are often called on to express an opinion on internal controls for Sarbanes-Oxley reporting.

SUMMARY OF MAIN POINTS

- Application controls rest on general controls.
- If general controls are substantially weak, the financial statement auditors may choose to simply walk through application controls instead of detailed testing and adopt a substantive audit approach. Even with a substantive audit approach, auditors place some reliance on internal controls unless the auditors test every transaction. Even if the auditors test every transaction, there is a risk of hidden transactions. So there is always some reliance, probably low reliance on internal controls. This is why auditors should at least walk through internal controls. Walkthrough means taking one or two transactions per key control to verify the control. The result of the walkthrough, i.e., presence (with very limited assurance because there is only walkthrough instead of detailed control testing) or absence of controls will influence the auditors in focusing their substantive testing. Even in a substantive audit approach, the extent of substantive testing will differ depending on the result of control walkthrough, e.g., it can range from testing, say 10% of the transactions, to say 25% of the transactions. In other words, a lower detection risk will be tolerated if controls are largely absent as a result of the walkthrough.
- If general controls are reliable, a moderate level of application controls should be sought for the financial statement audit.
- In the audit of a public company in Canada or the United States, the shareholders' auditors are often asked to provide an opinion on internal controls that support the financial statements, in addition to the traditional financial statement audit opinion. In such a case, the shareholders' auditors will seek high control assurance on the internal controls that support financial statements, which means most general controls and most application controls.
- Internal auditors usually seek a high level of assurance and therefore will do more testing.
- Application controls should include an optimum mix of preventive, detective and corrective controls. Preventive controls are preferred, but not all major risks can practically be mitigated with preventive controls, otherwise, the environment may be too tight and therefore not competitive; e.g., it is impractical to require every transaction, regardless of amount, to be pre-approved by management. Hence, detective controls should be put in place to detect significant errors or irregularities and corrective controls are necessary to correct these errors and irregularities.

314

Common Application Controls

- Edit checks – Applied at input stage, e.g., checking for negative amounts.
- Batch total – Comparing one total accumulated to another total accumulated later in the transaction input phase, to check input completeness. Batch total can also be applied by comparing total input to total output.
- Hash total – Similar to batch total, but the total is applied to a field normally not intended for computation, e.g., check number. This avoids offsetting errors, e.g., a $100 check goes missing but another $100 check recorded as $200.
- Run-to-run control total – Similar to batch total but accumulation and comparison are done by programs within the system, to check the completeness of data passed from one program to another.
- Reconciliation.
- Management review of exceptions.
- Management review of transactions either before or after processing. Some transactions may be impractical or not cost effective for pre-approval, in which case post-approval may mitigate the risk.
- Customer statements.
- Limit check, e.g., checking customer orders to credit limit.
- Monitoring of open items, such as unbilled shipments.

Edit Checks

Edit checks on data input are critical preventive controls to ensure that data input is correct and complete. The same techniques can be applied in processing. Why do we have to apply the same techniques to processing if input data is correct? Well, in processing, programs perform calculations to update data files. Before data files are updated, the calculated results should be validated to detect errors. For example, an invoice with a negative amount should be reviewed before the sales journal and the accounts receivable subsidiary ledger are updated. Here is a list of common edit checks.

- Check digit to validate data entry of a control number like a product number.
- Data format check, e.g., a date field should be yyyymmdd.
- Limit check.
- Missing data check, i.e., all mandatory fields are filled in.
- Range check.
- Sequence check
- Sign check.
- Validity check, by verifying data input to a table of acceptable values.

Database Controls

More and more systems use databases. In such a system, there need to be internal controls to ensure data integrity when multiple files (tables) are shared by multiple applications. Here are the common database controls.

- Record locking to avoid concurrent update, i.e., two transactions trying to update the same record concurrently leading to a later transaction nullifying the first transaction.
- Referential integrity to avoid null value for critical fields.
- Detection and resolution of deadlock caused by conflicting record locks to avoid the system being hung.
- Logging of access to database especially changes, to facilitate error recovery.
- Normalization to reduce data redundancy and inconsistency.
- Synchronization between locations and environments to ensure consistency of content and clocks. Clock synchronization is critical to ensure transactions are time stamped correctly for audit trail and for prioritization of updates and interest calculation (e.g., 11:59 pm vs 12:00 am).
- Producing alerts on direct updates, i.e., updating not through an authorized system function like ATM, to detect unauthorized data change.
- Producing alerts on table creation and deletion to detect unauthorized data creation or change.

Common Application Control Test Procedures

- Review and verify bank reconciliation.
- Review the rejected transaction log and follow up for correction.
- Use test data to test input control and processing controls.
- Review the production schedule, i.e., the daily or weekly schedule of batch updates and confirm by reviewing computer operations audit trail.
- Review user procedures for correctness of instructions.
- Ask staff to ascertain their understanding of instructions.
- Observe segregation of duties.
- Review the DBMS configuration to assess the adequacy of provision for database integrity.
- Review the data dictionary and confirm with actual table layout.
- Send confirmation to customers to see if they have received the customer statements.
- Observe the mailing of customer statements.
- Perform data correlation to obtain evidence of controls, e.g., cross referencing invoices to receiving reports.

REVIEW QUESTIONS

1. What is the difference between redundant data check and referential integrity check?

2. What is the difference between batch total and hash total?

3. Describe an example of what can go wrong if concurrent update is allowed.

4. Describe a technique that can be used as a general control and an application control.

5. A common football tactic is to surround the quarterback of the opposing team. Draw an analogy between this and internal control.

6. Which risk do edit checks mainly address?

7. Give an example of a weakness in general control that will lead to seeking high assurance on application controls.

8. What is the drawback of test data?

9. What is the external auditors' justification for skewing internal control testing towards the first half of the year?

10. What are the similarity and difference between batch total, hash total and run-to-run control total?

CASE – Electronic Order-to-Pay System

The following is a quote from J. P. Morgan's web site:

J.P. Morgan offers the premier Order-to-Pay service for global commerce that automates purchase order delivery, invoice and payment processing, and discount management. By connecting buyers with their suppliers across a secure settlement network, the service automates transaction processing and optimizes working capital.

Order-to-Pay is available as a complete solution suite or through any combination of modules. Some benefits you can expect from our best-practice approach include:

Electronic Invoicing and Payment

- *Eliminate paper and reduce processing costs by 50% or more.*

- *Automatically validate invoice data before posting for payment.*

- *Dramatically improve on-time payment performance, with top performers close to 100%.*

Working Capital Optimization

- *Capture four times the savings with advanced discount capture features and invoice automation.*

- *Generate double-digit, annualized cash returns, risk-free.*

- *Maintain or extend "days payables outstanding" through enforcement of terms policy and payment optimization techniques.*

Supplier Management

- *Extend portal to small, mid-size and large suppliers for transaction visibility and self-service.*

- *Transact with tens of thousands of existing suppliers with no enrolment effort.*

- *Simplify master vendor file management.*

Benchmarking and Performance Measurement

- *Benchmark results against a set of Key Performance Indicators.*

- *Forecast objectives for process automation, working capital optimization and supplier management.*

- *Analyze results and compare them against your stated objectives.*

Total Settlement

- *Total Settlement is an electronic payment solution that can process all payment types - check, automated clearing house, card and wire - via a single Web-based interface.*

- *Total Settlement is an ideal solution for organizations looking to eliminate paper from their treasury operations and automate their entire order-to-pay operations in a phased approach.*

***End of quote from J. P. Morgan web site.

Source:
http://www.jpmorgan.com/cm/ContentServer?c=TS_Content&pagename=jpmorgan%2Ft s%2FTS_Content%2FGeneral&cid=1284675875617&source=DirectURL_whyordertopa y; accessed on June 25, 2012.

A generic order-to-pay system involves the following steps.

1. Business users generate purchase requisitions through an in house ERP system or a system hosted by a service organization.
2. The system routes the purchase requisitions to management for approval.
3. Management approves online.
4. The system generates purchase orders for review by purchasing agents (employees of the user organization.)
5. Purchasing agents approve POs online.
6. System sends POs to EDI server.
7. EDI server computes batch totals and converts POs to EDI format.
8. EDI server sends out POs.
9. Upon inspection of goods, users retrieves the PO from the system and checks the "received" box.
10. System marks the "received" field on the PO table for that PO with a value indicating "received", e.g., 1. Before that, the value may be 0, i.e., not received. This is not the quantity or amount received. It is just an arbitrary value to indicate whether the PO has been receipted or not.
11. Invoices are sent to the user organization or the service organization for processing by EDI.
12. The accounts payable system matches the PO number on the invoice to the PO file to confirm receipt of goods.
13. If goods have been received, the invoice is scheduled for payment to take advantage of cash discounts and avoid penalty.
14. If goods have not been received, the invoice is recorded in a pending file and the system sends a query to the PO contact for follow-up.
15. Payments are made by EDI.

Required

What internal controls do you expect an organization hosting an order-to-pay system to implement to ensure that transaction processing is authorized, accurate, complete and timely. What controls do you expect a user organization to implement?

MULTIPLE CHOICE QUESTIONS

1. Which one of the following examples best depicts a preventive control within the expenditure business cycle?
A. The accounts payable manager reviews a list of outstanding accounts payables balances for old or unusual items.
B. The purchasing manager reviews a listing of purchase orders issued and follows up on errors noted (e.g., prices, quantities, etc.).
C. The purchasing manager reviews purchase orders for accuracy before the orders are placed.
D. The chief accountant reviews an exception report listing purchase orders issued to vendors not included on the Company's authorized vendor listing.
E. Access control lists for the purchasing and accounts payable systems.

2. When auditing a retail giant that opens its inventory system to major suppliers for automatic replenishment, which type of controls do you test the most?
A. Input
B. Processing
C. Output
D. Access
E. Data storage

3. Which risk does database normalization reduce?
A. Concurrent update
B. Obsolete data
C. Data redundancy
D. Data incompleteness
E. Data leakage

4. Generally accepted auditing standards say that auditors should try to assess control risk at below maximum. This means:
A. a low range.
B. a high but not maximum level.
C. a minimum level.
D. the median point.
E. a moderate or medium range.

5. What is an auditor's primary concern when reading an organization chart?
A. Clarity of reporting relationship
B. Flattening of organization
C. Extent of distribution
D. Employee names
E. Segregation of duties

6. The mail room sends remittance advices to the accounts receivable department and the checks to the cashier's department. The cashier's department compares checks to deposit slips. With reference to these processes, what control is missing?
A. Bank reconciliation
B. Batch total of the checks and remittance advices
C. Credit limit check
D. Joint signatures
E. Check endorsement

7. Which type of controls is increasingly taking the place of a traditional output control of monitoring the distribution of reports to different buildings?
A. Input control
B. Edit checks
C. Access control
D. Processing control
E. Management control

8. An employee in the receiving department keyed in an incoming shipment and inadvertently omitted the purchase order number. The most appropriate input control to employ to detect this error is a:
A. batch total.
B. missing data check.
C. sequence check.
D. reasonableness check.

9. When an auditor finds a significant control deficiency, s/he should first
A. conduct substantive testing.
B. ask management to sign for risk acceptance.
C. look for compensating controls.
D. report to the audit committee.

10. An auditor comes across a lot of management overrides when testing application controls. S/he should:
A. test the logging and review of such overrides.
B. be pleased that there are so many management controls.
C. not trust the system.
D. recommend that such overrides not be permitted

Chapter 7 – Computer Assisted Audit Techniques

The first rule of any technology used in a business is that automation applied to an efficient operation will magnify the efficiency. The second is that automation applied to an inefficient operation will magnify the inefficiency. – Bill Gates

In Chapter Two, we discuss inherent risk, control risk and detection risk. We go through the attributes of IT as they relate to risks. For example, increasing electronic audit trail increases the risk of unauthorized access. Another example is the speed and power of computers, which could decrease the risk of delay. Generally, the factors that affect inherent risk also affect control risk and detection risk in the same direction. We concluded that information technology (IT) generally increased inherent risk, control risk and detection risk. Detection risk can be decreased with automation, i.e., to use computers to automate the audit process, taking advantage the inherent accuracy and speed of computers. Further, increasing affordability and portability of storage devices allow auditors to analyze more data and therefore increase audit coverage and correspondingly decrease detection risk. With the use of computer assisted audit techniques, the need to sample has gone down. The techniques used to automate audit procedures are called computer assisted audit techniques.

Today's computer assisted audit techniques take advantage of the exponential growth of computing power and the user friendliness of personal computer (PC) based systems. There are five types of computer assisted audit techniques (CAAT); the first three types receive more attention as they serve to automate audit testing and analysis.
- General audit software
- Integrated test facility
- Embedded audit module
- Audit scheduling
- Electronic work papers

GENERAL AUDIT SOFTWARE

General audit software (GAS) is the most popular type of CAAT, accounting for more than 90% of total CAAT applications. The most popular GAS tool is Audit Command Language (ACL), developed by ACL Inc. in Vancouver, Canada.

A GAS is similar to Microsoft Access in a way. It provides commands for auditors to import data files that are in a variety of format such as Excel, database and a text file with columns and rows. After importing, the user can use a number of "ready made" commands to analyze data by writing short formulae and combining formulae using the drag and drop features. This is why it is called general audit software. The word "general" may belittle the power of this tool. Because of the "general" nature, auditors can perform a variety of analyses and correlations. The extent of analysis is limited to the source data available.

GAS products usually come in versions that can run on a standalone PC, a local area network (LAN) or an IBM Z series server (mainframe).

Common GAS functions are:
- Data import.
- Data export, e.g., exporting analyzed data to Excel for easy graphing.
- Joining files.
- Merging files.
- Data extraction based on criteria (formulae).
- Aging
- Duplicate identification.
- Gap identification.
- Fraud analysis.
- Statistical profiling (analytical review)
- Statistical sampling.
- Regression analysis.

File Import

A data file is necessary in order to use GAS. Common data file (table) formats are text, Excel, dbf. Dbf is a generic database format. Most database tables can easily be saved as dbfs. Most GAS products like ACL can take a data file in just about any format. Data files that are in Excel and dbf can be recognized by a GAS usually automatically without the auditor defining the fields. Text files have to be defined field by field. Data files from an IBM Z series server can be exported from the source computer into a text file which can then be imported to a PC based GAS.

File Export

Analyses performed with a GAS tool usually generate new files. One drawback about most GAS products is that they come short in graphical and formatting capability like Excel. Often auditors will find it useful to export analyzed files to Excel for more user friendly presentations.

Joining

In the last chapter, we discussed normalization as a control process to reduce data redundancy. This helps to ensure data integrity. However, because normalization creates more tables with fewer fields, sometimes it is necessary to join tables for temporary data correlation, e.g., comparing accounts receivable balance to the credit limit, or comparing the sum of accounts receivable and current order to the credit limit. In auditing, it is also often necessary to compare fields between tables to assess transaction integrity. GAS tools allow a user to join any 2 tables and combine the fields into 1 table as long as the 2 tables have a common primary key.

Merging

Sometimes an auditor needs to perform the same analysis on multiple tables that have identical fields in the same order and format, e.g., several monthly transaction tables. In this case, the auditor may wish to combine the tables and perform the analysis only once. The merge function allows auditors to combine tables that have identical fields in the same order and that have the same format. For example, you may have downloaded twelve monthly files of journal entries but want to analyze them in one pass. You can merge these files and then perform the data analysis.

Extraction

GAS allows an auditor to extract fields from a table into a new table based on any combination of criteria (formulae) defined by the auditor using the drag and drop of standard operands like =, >, <, (,), AND, OR and field names. An example of a criterion is gross_pay > 10000. This is a very useful and versatile function as it allows the auditors to perform tests by means of data correlation and select questionable items for vouching or confirmation etc. Here are some common tests.

- Compare the sum of invoice and account balance to credit limit.
- Select high pay amounts for confirmation.
- Select high receivable amounts for confirmation.
- Obsolescence test by reviewing the date of last sale.
- Cross-reference invoices to receiving reports and purchase orders.
- Compare inventory cost to sale price.
- Check for the system's compliance with inventory costing methods like first-in-first-out, last-in-first-out or average costing by verifying the calculation of cost of sales for selected invoices.
- Look for negative amounts that are usually wrong.
- Verify commission calculation.
- Check for dormant account classification. A bank classifies a deposit account as dormant when there has been no customer initiated transactions for two years. Any human initiated transactions like a deposit, withdrawal or transfer made to a dormant account will trigger an alert to the branch manager. An auditor can look at the dates of the last two transactions, if the date of the second last transaction is two year or more apart from the date of the last transaction, the auditor should flag the account in the audit work papers and then vouch to the management alert that should have been triggered by the last transaction. Dormant accounts are common targets for frauds because the account holders are usually people who do not keep track of the accounts, e.g., senior citizens who live abroad.

Aging

This function allows the auditor to age based on a date. The most common application is accounts receivable. The auditor can define the age brackets like 30 days and 60 days. The output will be the number of records and total dollar value that falls within each bracket.

Duplicate Identification

Some records should not have duplicate values on certain fields, e.g., the social insurance or social security number. GAS allows auditors to select a field and look for duplicates in the table across records. The output will then be used to present to management for correction.

Gap Detection

This is the opposite of duplicate identification. It looks for gaps. An example of audit test is to detect gaps in purchase order numbers or invoice numbers which should be in sequence.

Fraud Analysis

GAS has statistical analysis functions that can be used to detect fraud. An increasingly used function is called Benford Analysis, based on the Benford Law.

Benford Law

Dr. Frank Benford was a physicist in General Electric Company. He enjoyed playing with numbers. In 1938, he stated that in a large series of natural numbers , the probability of the first digit being "1" was higher than that being "2" and the probability of the first digit being "2" was higher than that being "3", etc., and the first digit was least likely to be "9". This theory also applies to the second digit and the successively less significantly leading digits. That is, the probability of the second digit being "1" is higher than it being "2", and the probability of that digit being "2" is higher than that being "3" etc. The less significant the digit, the less it complies with Benford Law. The longer the number (i.e., number of digits in each number) and the larger the population, the more applicable Benford Law is. This theory was also stated by Simon Newcomb, an astronomer, in 1881. However, Newcomb did not perform the extensive research and proof that Benford carried out.

The Benford distribution holds true only for naturally progressing numbers like invoice amount, quantity, age, numerical invoice numbers and check numbers. It does not apply to arbitrarily assigned numbers like social security number, social insurance number and retail sales price. Social insurance numbers and social security numbers are not necessarily sequentially assigned as they were designed to satisfy a check digit algorithm, i.e., not every 9-digit number can be used as a social insurance number or a social security number. Retail sales prices are arbitrarily assigned and retailers often set the prices to start with the digit "9" in order to stay within a low number of digits so customers don't think the products are too expensive.

Benford performed massive numerical analysis to empirically prove this theory and eventually developed a formula to calculate the probability. He derived the following formula for calculating the probability of a number starting with a particular string of digits "n":

$$Log_{10}(1 + 1/n)$$

For example, the probability of a number starting with 314 is $LOG_{10}(1 + 1/314)$, or 0.14%. This means, for any number with at least three digits regardless of whether there is a decimal point and where the decimal is, the probability of that number, in the long run, starting with 314 is only 0.14%.

Let's see what the probability of a number starting with 1 is. It would be $LOG_{10}(1 + 1/1)$, or 30.1%. We can calculate the probability of the first digit being 2 to be 17.6% and the probability of the first digit being 9 to be 4.6%.

We can use this formula to calculate the probability of the second digit being 1. For the second digit to be 1, the first digit can be anywhere from 1 to 9. This means we should calculate the probabilities of a number starting with 11, 21, 31, 41, 51, 61, 71, 81, 91 and sum these probabilities. This yields 11.4%. Similarly, we can calculate the probability the second digit being 2 to be 10.9%.

You can see that for the first digit, the probability of a higher order digit (closer to 9) decreases exponentially from 1 to eventually 9. This distribution also applies to the second digit but the slope is much less steep.

The Benford first digit distribution can be graphed as follows along with a table of the probability from 1 to 9.

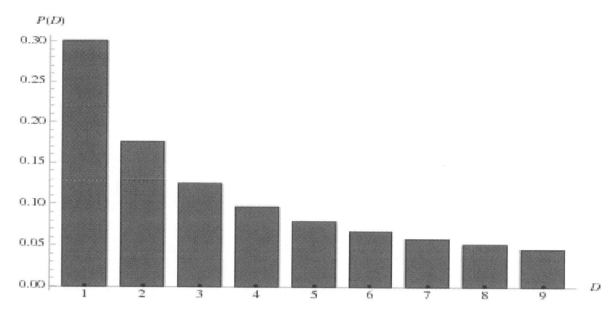

This graph shows the following probabilities of the first digit being 1, 2, 3…..9.

1	30.1%
2	17.6%
3	12.5%
4	9.7%
5	7.9%
6	6.7%
7	5.8%
8	5.1%
9	4.6%

The probability of the first digit being 0 is not calculated because the first digit will then default to the next digit that is not 0.

Common Sense Reasoning of the Benford Law

Most people might think that the probability of a digit being of any value is uniform. For example, in throwing a dice, the probability of each throw is 1/6. However, this thinking does not apply to naturally progressive numbers. When you throw a dice or toss a coin, each throw or toss is not affected by previous or future throws and tosses. However, in a naturally progressive number, the occurrences are inter-dependent. You cannot have two invoices bearing the same number. A 10 year old child will not be 10 years old next year.

Why does "1" have the highest chance as the first digit? Here is a simple example. A child is one year old before turning two. After the age of 9, a child becomes 10 years old and the first digit is "1" again. Then the person becomes 20 years old, etc. Most people won't reach the age of 90. This is an example of why "9" has the lowest chance of being the first digit.

Another example is numerical invoice number. The first invoice would be 1, then 2, and 3...etc. After invoice # 999, it will take 1,001 new sales for the invoice number to have a first digit being "2", and it will take much longer for "9" to claim the first digit again.

Yet another example is the Dow Jones index. It closed today on June 25, 2012 at 12,503 (a 138 point drop today, ouch). It will take a 60% increase for "2" to claim the first digit. A 60% increase of the Dow Jones index seems to be a dream that some investors may never see it. Although a 21% drop will let "9" claim the first digit, it is hard for "9" to keep that title because a 1 % rise will give the first digit back to "1". Benford Law applies to natural numbers, and the numbers do not have to be always progressive, they can fluctuate naturally like the Dow Jones index.

Next time you go out of town by road, place a bet with a companion that the next population sign will have a number starting from 1 to 3. At the end of an 8-hour ride, you will likely have won enough money to treat dinner.

Practical Applications of Benford Law

Benford analysis is useful to assess whether a group of natural numbers representing a particular object includes fictitious items. For example, Internal Revenue Service (IRS) and Canada Revenue Agency (CRA) can use it to review tax returns for overstated expenses like entertainment, maintenance and repairs or for understated business income. Some taxpayers with rental properties might be tempted to overstate repair expenses. Their greed might take them to try to claim $10,000. Psychology tells them that if the amount goes to five digits, it is more alarming or it might cross the threshold for tighter auditing. So they might report a seemingly random number like $9,276. Well, if a large number of tax returns show repair expense in the $9,000 range or if a taxpayer consistently uses that range or the $8,000 range year after year, the tax department's monitoring system should take note of this and apply tighter audit procedures like asking for supporting documents and authenticating the documents. There are similar applications in corporate fraud detection, consumer fraud detection, as well as analytical review for external and internal audits.

Statistical Profiling

A GAS can calculate statistical parameters like a mean or a median. It can plot numerical distribution, stratification and variance etc. to help an auditor assess the normality of a population of number, e.g., does it fit the normal (bell curve). Many business transaction amounts follow the normal distribution and the Benford distribution. These two statistical distributions have different units of measurement. The normal (bell) curve applies to most natural numbers. For example, extremely low and extremely high invoice amounts would fall at the left and right tails of the curve. Instead of measuring the entire amount or quantity, the Benford Law is applied to leading digits, i.e., it doesn't care about the value of the number, it focuses on the frequency of leading digits.

Statistical Sampling

A GAS can calculate the sample size as well as assessing sample findings in relation to the sample size and required statistical parameters like confidence level and precision (standard deviation). The assessment can tell the auditor whether the population is reliable or whether additional sampling is necessary.

One might argue that with the growing power of hardware and GAS, auditors often can test the entire population so sampling will be used less. That is true only if the entire test can be automated, i.e., it does not require manual vouching or observation. Many tests will require manual involvement; so statistical sampling is still valuable in audits, more so for large organizations.

The statistical sampling functions include physical unit sampling and dollar unit sampling. An example of physical unit sampling is to sample invoices for vouching regardless of the invoice amount. An example of dollar unit sampling is to treat every dollar in the population of invoices as a unit and select these units to be in a sample. When a dollar unit is selected, the entire invoice is pulled. Dollar unit sampling gives bias towards large dollar items. Both physical sampling and dollar unit sampling are used to test for attributes, so they are also called attribute sampling

Attribute Sampling

Audit applications of statistical sampling mainly use attribute sampling. That is, audit tests are designed to ascertain whether something is right or wrong, or whether a control is in place or not. That something or a control is an attribute. The outcome is yes or no. This applies to both control testing and substantive testing. GAS packages have ready to use functions for attribute sampling. Attribute sampling, whether it is applied to a physical unit like an invoice or a transaction, e.g., for control testing, or whether it is applied to dollar values (dollar unit sampling) for substantive testing, uses the binomial mathematical distribution. The binomial distribution is an approximation of the normal distribution.

Variable Sampling

Unlike attribute sampling, variable sampling is used to measure value, for example, estimating the saltiness of sea water in a region. In auditing, it can be used for some substantive tests like estimating inventory value. There is no right or wrong outcome. Variable sampling is based on the normal distribution, i.e., the bell curve. However, in most audit applications including substantive testing, attribute sampling can be used for estimation. This is because the auditor's job is to attest to what management presents. Auditors can use attribute sampling to confirm whether the figures presented by management are correct. In this case, there are two attributes, right or wrong. It is true that when an account balance is wrong, it is important to estimate how wrong; i.e., how much off is a $10,000 book balance from actual? Well, we can treat every dollar in that balance as a unit and still use attribute sampling to confirm whether each dollar is right. We will discuss this more below under dollar unit sampling. GAS tools are not easy to use for variable sampling. There are statistical analysis software tools like Statistical Analysis System (SAS) that can do that. When the unit of measurement of attributes is reduced to be very small, like every dollar, the binomial distribution closely approximates the normal distribution. In other words, when the unit of measure is small, attribute sampling can be used to achieve the general purpose of variable sampling.

Confidence Level

A GAS package can calculate the sample size based on a specified confidence level and tolerable error rate. Because of the law of large numbers, the population size is irrelevant unless it is small, in which case, sampling may not be necessary. When the population size exceeds 10,000, there is negligible impact on the sample size given the same confidence level, tolerable error rate and tolerable sample errors. But how much confidence level should the auditor specify? This depends whether it is for control testing or substantive testing. The confidence level for control testing can be lower for external auditors because only a moderate level of control assurance is needed. Auditors often wonder how the confidence level affects sample sizes.

Suppose a population consists of 1,000 invoices of which 970 are approved. The infraction rate is 3%. Draw a random sample of 100 invoices. Obviously, the most probable sample result will consist of 3 unapproved invoices. But there could be 4 unapproved invoices, 5 or more, or even 30; although the probability gets lower as the number of sample errors increases from 3. Similarly, the probability of finding no, 1 or 2 unapproved invoices increases in that order. We can accept that the most probable sample error rate is the same as the population error rate; but just how likely is this? How likely is it that the sample will produce no errors, i.e., causing the auditor to think that the population contains no error when in fact there is a 3% error rate?

This likelihood can be calculated as follows:
970/1,000 x 969/999 x 968/998 x …. X 871/901 = .04035, or 4.04%.

In other words, the chance of drawing an error free sample of 100 from a population of 1,000 with a 3% error rate is 4.04%, very unlikely. Let's interpret this from another direction. Suppose a random sample of 100 invoices from a population of 1,000 invoices reveals that all 100 invoices have been approved. We can conclude with 95.96% confidence that the population error rate is not higher than 3%. And yet another way of interpretation is that, if we want 95.96% confidence level and will not tolerate any sample errors, we need a sample of only 100 given a population of 1,000 and given that we are willing to tolerate a population error rate of up to 3%. Well, in reality, a confidence level meaningful to people should be close to a round number. To be conservative, we must round it down in making a conclusion. We can say that if we find no errors in a sample of 100 invoices from a population of 1,000 invoices, we are 95% confident that there are no more than 30 errors in the population, or that the population error rate is not more than 3%.

What if we found 1 error in the sample of 100 invoices? How can we conclude? Well, let's calculate the probability of finding 1 error as follows. We cannot use the above simple formula because the error may be in the first invoice sampled, the second invoice sampled....or the last invoice sampled. The probability of the error being in the first invoice sampled is calculated as follows.

30/1,000 x 970/999 x 969/998 ..... x 872/901, or .00138976, or 0.139%.

Similarly, the probability that the error will be in the second invoice sampled is calculated as

970/1,000 x 30/999 x 969/998 .... x 872/901, or .00138976, or 0.139%

Therefore, by deduction, we can simply multiple either of the above result by 100 to get the probability of finding 1 error in a sample of 100 invoices from a population of 1,000 invoices that contain 30 unapproved invoices. The result is 13.9%, much higher than the probability of finding no errors. This makes sense because the actual population error rate is 3%, so the likelihood of the sample error rate approaching the population error rate increases.

What is the probability of finding not more than 1 error in the sample of 100 invoices from a population of 1,000 invoices that contains 30 unapproved invoices? The answer is obtained by adding the probability of finding no errors and the probability of finding 1 error, i.e., 4.04% + 13.9%, or 17.94%. Thus, we can conclude that given an unknown population error rate and given that the population contains 1,000 items, by sampling 100 items and finding 0 or 1 error, we are 82.06% confident that the population error rate does not exceed 3%. In other words, given a confidence level of 82%, a sample error rate of not more than 1%, a population size of 1,000 and a sample size of 100, the upper error limit in the population is 3%.

But what if the population increases? Should the sample size increase accordingly? Let's see. Using the formula for finding no error in the sample and still drawing a sample of 100 invoices out of 10,000 invoices, the probability of finding no errors can be calculated as 9,700/10,000 x 9,699/9,999 x 9,698/9,998 ..... x 9,601/9,901, or 4.68%. This is higher than the probability of finding no errors from a population of 1,000 items that contains the same error rate, which we calculated earlier to be 4.04%. That is, given a large population size, if we keep the same sample size, the confidence level at which we can conclude that the population error does not exceed a certain rate is lower, i.e., we are less confident. This makes sense, because if we sample less in relation to the population, we have less convincing evidence and thus are less confident. This means that if we want to keep the same confidence level and if the population error rate does not change, but the population has increased, the sample size should also increase, but not increasing proportionally. The reason we say that the sample size does not have to increase in proportion to the increase in population size is that by keeping the same sample size in spite of a ten fold increase in the population size, we have compromised only 0.64% in confidence, from 95.96% to 95.32%.

What if the population has now grown to 1,000,000 items? If the population error rate is still 3% and we still draw a random sample of 100 items, what is the probability of finding no errors in the sample? This is calculated as follows.

970,000/1,000000 x 969,999/999,999 x 969,998/999,998 …. x 969,901/999,901, or 4.76%.

Note that this is very close to the probability of finding no errors from a sample of 100 items drawn out of a population of 10,000 items that contains a 3% error rate, which is 4.68%. Thus, we can say that after 10,000 items, the population size does not significantly affect the sample size. In fact, once the population size hits 1,000,000, any increase will not affect the sample size.

The above formula for calculating probability is clumsy even with a computer. It is easy to see that as the population size increases, the probability of finding no error in each item changes little. That is, the value of a fraction changes less as the numerator and the denominator approach infinity. There is a big difference between ¾ and 4/5. There is negligible difference between 9,700/10,000 and 9,701/10,001, it is .97 vs .970003. Thus, as the population increases, e.g., exceeding 10,000, one can use a simpler formula for calculating the probability of finding no error in a sample, by simply treating the problem as a problem of sampling with replacement, i.e., ignoring the effect of the change in population size.

Thus, the probability of finding no errors in a sample of 100 invoices from a population that has a 3% error rate can be calculated as .97^100, or .047553, or 4.76%. This is the same probability under the sampling without replacement method for population sizes over 1,000,000, and very close to the probability under the sampling without replacement method for a population size of 10,000, which is 4.68%. In practice, the sampling with replacement formula can be used for simplicity when the population size exceeds 10,000, which is very common in audits. The sampling with replacement method is based on the binomial mathematical distribution.

Using the binomial distribution, we can calculate the probability of finding 1 error in a sample of 100 invoices when the actual population error rate is 3% to be 0.03*0.97^99*100, because the error may be on the first invoice, the second invoice, the third invoice etc. The probability is .14707, or 14.71%.

What is the probability of finding 2 errors in the sample? Well, the 2 errors may be on the first 2 invoices in the sample of 100, may be the first and third invoices, the first and fourth invoices....or the last 2 invoices. The number of combinations of n in a population of N is calculated as N!/(N-n)!/n!. For example, the number of combinations of any 2 numbers in a population of 100 numbers is calculated as 100!/(100-2)!/2!, or 100!/98!/2!, or 100 x 99 x 98.... x 1 / (98 x 97 x 96... x 1) / (2 x 1), or 4,950. This means there are 4,950 sequences of these 2 errors to appear in the sample of 100 invoices. Thus, to calculate the probability of finding 2 errors in the population, we should take .03*.03*.97^98*4950, or .225153, i.e., 22.52%. Note this is higher than the probability of finding 1 error because the actual population error rate is 3%. The probability of the sample error rate being the same as the population error rate is the highest probability, higher than the probability of finding an error rate in the sample that differs from the actual population error rate.

Let's calculate the probability of finding 3 errors in the sample. It will be .03*.03*.03*.97^97*(100*99*98)/(3*2), or .227474, or 22.75%. Note that this is just slightly higher than the probability of finding 2 errors in the sample, whereas the probability of finding 2 errors is significantly higher than the probability of finding 1 error. This is because the probability of finding a number of errors that more closely resembles the actual population error rate changes less as the number of errors approaches the actual population error rate.

Auditors should use computer assisted audit techniques to automate the above procedures.

Well, if the probability of finding the same extent of errors in the sample as the actual population error rate is 22.75% when the actual error rate is 3%, we can conclude, if we find 3 errors in a sample size of 100, that the population error rate is 3%, with only a confidence level of 22.75%. Any conclusion with such a low confidence level is not going to be significant. Fortunately, auditors are concerned about higher error rates, not lower. A more meaningful conclusion is derived using cumulative probability. The fact that the auditor found 3 errors means that s/he could as well have found 0, 1 or 2 errors. Hence, by adding up the probabilities of finding 0 error, 1 error, 2 errors and 3 errors and taking the complement, the auditor can reach the confidence level that the population error rate is not more than 3% (3 out of 100). This confidence level = 100% - (4.68% + 14.71% + 22.52% + 22.75%) = 35.34%, still very low. Well then, what is the next step? If a population error rate of 3% is acceptable, what is the confidence level? The auditor now has to either raise the tolerable population error rate and the confidence level correspondingly, or increase the sample size and do more testing. By increasing the sample size and doing more testing and finding no more errors, the auditor can achieve a higher confidence level than 35.34% and that can gradually be increased towards an acceptable level.

So the above analysis shows that the confidence level, sample size, tolerable error rate in the population and tolerable number of sample errors are interdependent. When an auditor wants to determine any of these four parameters, s/he inputs the other three. For example, if the sample size is determined based on zero errors in the sample and the auditor finds one error, s/he has the following options:

1. Increase the sample size to do more testing.
2. Lower the confidence level, not a good idea, as doing so may mean low reliance.
3. Increase the tolerable error rate in the population, also not a good idea because that means increasing materiality.

For option 1, the auditor can now change the tolerable sample errors from 0 to 1, or even 2 or 3 if s/he is prepared to encounter more errors in the testing and thereby use larger sample sizes.

For option 2, the auditor can calculate the new and lower confidence by changing the sample errors to 1 and leaving the tolerable population error rate unchanged and the sample size unchanged, and click on confidence level to get the new confidence level to see if it is within the acceptable range.

For option 3, the auditor can calculate the new and higher estimated error rate in the population by changing the sample errors to 1 and leaving the sample size and confidence level unchanged, then click on the tolerable population error rate and see if the new rate is still within an acceptable range.

In other words, by inputting three of the following parameters, the fourth parameter can be solved. If we tighten confidence level, sample size will go up, tolerable error rate will go up, or the tolerable number of sample errors will go down. Again, the four parameters are:

*   Confidence level in %.
*   Tolerable population error rate in %, also called the upper error limit.
*   Tolerable number of sample errors. This increases with sample size.
*   Sample size.

Upper Error Limit

This is the maximum population error rate for the specific attribute that the auditor is willing to tolerate at a specified confidence level. The specified confidence level is prescribed by the accounting firm or the audit department for the nature of population and test. The confidence level for substantive testing should be higher than that for control testing in a financial statement audit, because the audit opinion is on the financial statements and not on internal controls. The confidence level for substantive testing when controls do not deserve moderate reliance would be even higher.

Determining the Sample Size

This is one of the first steps before sample selection. How large should the sample size be? Accounting firms and internal audit departments usually have standard sizes in audit programs. The standard sample sizes can be overridden by auditors given authorization and justification. How do the firms and audit departments determine sample sizes?

It is based on the upper error limit, desired confidence level and the number of sample errors that will be tolerable. Statisticians have made this process easy by calculating the upper error limit (UEL) factor. An upper error limit factor for a specified confidence level and a certain number of sample errors = the upper error limit in % multiplied by the sample size. Given this factor, the auditor can calculate the sample size. Here is a table of common UEL factors.

Sample errors	85% confidence		90% confidence		95% confidence	
	UEL	PGW	UEL	PGW	UEL	PGW
0	1.90	0	2.31	0	3.00	0
1	3.38	.48	3.89	.58	4.75	.75
2	4.73	.35	5.33	.44	5.30	.55
3	6.02	.29	6.69	.36	7.76	.46
4	7.27	.25	8.00	.31	9.16	.40
5	8.50	.23	9.28	.28	10.52	.36

When no error is found in the sample, the most likely error in the population is also zero. However, one cannot conclude with a high confidence that there are no errors in the population because as we saw earlier, the most likely probability is generally less than 50%. Therefore, there is a need to calculate a buffer, called the basic precision. This is similar to standard deviation in variable sampling. In attribute sampling, standard deviation is not applicable because the variation cannot go in the negative direction, i.e., there is no error level below zero. The table above shows the common sample error sizes, confidence levels, UEL factors and the widening of the UEL factors as more sample errors are found. That is, if more sample errors are found and the sample size is not increased, the UEL should go up. The widening magnitude is called the precision gap widening (PGW).

For example, if the auditor wants 90% confidence and is willing to tolerate 1 sample error, the UEL factor is 3.89. If the auditor is willing to tolerate a UEL of 5% in the population, the sample size is calculated as 3.89 divided by 5%, or 3.89/.05, or 77.8. Because you cannot select .8 of an item, the sample size should be rounded up to 78. GAS can do all that. In other words, sample size = UEL factor / UEL.

Sample Findings Evaluation for Physical Unit Sampling

Suppose the auditor has now found no more than 1 error, the auditor can now confirm that the population error rate is not higher than 5%. What if the auditor finds 2 errors? Well, s/he goes to the sample error column and locate the UEL factor for 2 errors, still holding a 90% confidence level. The UEL factor is now 5.33, because the sample size is only 78, the auditor can determine the revised upper error limit in the population by dividing 5.33 by 78, i.e., 5.33/78, or .06833. The revised population upper error limit is now 6.83%. The auditor will then have to ask whether this is acceptable. If this is not acceptable, the auditor should test more, but how many more. Well, to maintain a 5% maximum population error rate at 90% confidence level, the auditor will calculate the new sample size as 5.33/.05, or 107. The auditor will have to select 29 more items and hope to find no more errors. If more errors are found, the auditor may likely have to conclude that the population is not reliable for the attribute being tested. Alternatively, the auditor can relax the confidence level by moving to the left and then select the appropriate UEL factor for the actual sample error number and determine the upper population error rate to see if it falls within the predetermined acceptable level of 5%. Or the auditor can again expand the sample size and hopes to find no more errors....

What do we do with the PGW factor? Because it measures incremental change in precision, it applies more to continuous sampling instead of discrete sampling like physical unit sampling. PGW is useful for dollar unit sampling.

Dollar Unit Sampling

Dollar unit sampling is more appropriate for substantive testing where the sample size and findings should be related to materiality. Dollar unit sampling can use the attribute sampling method. Now, the population is the total dollar amount of all of the items. The sample size determination method is the same as that for physical unit sampling. However, because every dollar is treated as a unit, when a dollar is sampled, it does not make sense to pull just one dollar. When a dollar is included in a sample, the entire item or transaction is pulled. One can easily see that this method biases towards large dollar items and that should be so. Doing so helps to optimize audit effort, e.g., confirming a $10,000 account with a customer takes the same effort as confirming a $100 account, but the former provides much more audit assurance.

Evaluating physical unit sampling result seems pretty easy. That method needs some adjustment for evaluating dollar unit sampling result. For example, if a $100 account does not exist, it has less serious implication than a $10,000 not existing. This is how dollar unit sampling result should be evaluated.

Let's say the sample size is based on 90% confidence level, an upper population error limit of 5%, i.e., 5 % of the population monetary total, which should equate to materiality, and up to 1 sample error. The tolerable sample error of 1 does not mean $1, it means 1 x sampling interval. What is the sampling interval? It is the average dollar unit gap between sample items. If the population has $1,000,000 and 100 items are selected, the sampling interval is $10,000. This also means that the average value of an account is $10,000. A tolerable sample size of 1 means that if we find no more than $10,000 of error in the sample, we are comfortable.

Let's say we find one account to be $5,000 instead of the book value of $50,000, what does that mean? Is the error still 1 and should we be satisfied?

We now know the actual error is $45,000 and management should adjust for that. But because this is only from a sample, there are likely more errors. We should calculate the most likely error. In physical unit sampling, the most likely error is the sampling error rate multiplied by the population total. In dollar unit sampling, the most likely error is also calculated as the population error rate multiplied by the population error total. If the sample size is 100 and 1 account is wrong, the sample error rate is 1%. However, this account is not entirely wrong, it is only wrong by 90% (45,000/50,000). This means the sample error rate is 0.9%. If the population total is $1,000,000, the most likely error is 0.9% x 1,000,000, or $9,000. This is the same as multiplying the extent of error of each error by the sampling interval, i.e., 90% x 10,000. However, because the actual error is $45,000 and greater than the most likely error, we have to substitute the calculated most likely error with the actual error. Why so? This is because the item that is wrong is a very large item. In dollar unit sampling, often, an item being selected is greater than the sampling interval. We cannot ignore the actual error.

After calculating the most likely error, the auditor should calculate the probable error, or the upper error limit in dollars. This is done as follows.

1. Take the basic precision factor, i.e., the UEL factor at zero sample error and 95% confidence level, and multiply it by the sampling interval. In the case of a sampling interval of $10,000, this yields $23,100. This is the upper error limit when no sample errors are found.

2. For each sample error, calculate the percentage of error. For example, if an account with a book value of $10,000 has been verified as $8,000, the error is 20%. This means the item is 20% tainted. Multiply the error % of each sample error by the average sampling interval and sum each weighted error. The sum is the most likely error in $ for the population. This is the amount that should be adjusted by the client, unless this total is less than the actual error total, in which case, the actual error total has to be used for adjustment/correction.

3. For each sample error, multiply the PGW factor by the % of error and the sampling interval. For example, for the first error, the PGW is .58, so we take .58 x 20% x $10,000 = $1,160. If there is a second error, the PGW for the second error is .44, as per the table above. Sum the weighted $ of the PGW for all errors. The errors should be ranked in descending order before multiplying the error % in each erroneous item by the PGW.

4. Add the result from steps 1, 2 and 3 to arrive at the upper error limit in dollar terms for the population.

5. Compare this to materiality. If it exceeds materiality, the population is not reliable for the assertion being tested. The auditor may want to expand the sample size or lower the confidence level. For a financial statement audit, lowering the confidence level may not be practical.

Overstatement vs Understatement

In substantive testing, some errors may be understatements and some may be overstatements. Should they be offset? Yes, but they are not offset at the actual error level. Here is an example.

In accounts receivable confirmation, two errors are found. An account recorded as $10,000 has been confirmed to be $8,000; another account recorded as $8,000 has been confirmed to be $10,000. The auditor cannot conclude that there is no error and no adjustment is required. Doing so would be negligent because these are just sample results and not all the actual errors. Instead, the following steps should be followed.

1. Compute the most likely errors of overstatement and understatement separately. For the overstated account, the error is 25%, i.e., 2,000/8,000, and based on average sampling interval of $10,000, the most likely error is $2,500. For the understated account, the error is 2% and the most likely error is $2,000.

2. Net the most likely overstatement and most likely understatement, yielding a net overstatement of $500. This is the amount that should be adjusted by the client.

3. Compute the upper error limits of overstatements and understatement separately. For each upper error limit, offset it with the most likely error of the opposite direction. For example, if the upper error limit for overstatement is $40,000, it should be reduced by the most likely error of understatement, $2,000, to arrive at the upper error limit of $38,000. Offset the upper error limit of understatement with the most likely error of overstatement. The rationale is that the upper error limit of overstatement or understatement is a conservative estimate to begin with and it should be reduced by most likely errors in the other direction; i.e., if we know there is actually an understatement, then the upper error limit for overstatement can be relaxed.

338

4. The upper error limits for overstatement and understatement should each be compared to materiality to assess the reliability of the audit assertion.

5. In terms of the order of error, i.e., first error, second error, third error etc. for PGW calculation, separate overstatements from understatements. For example, if the first error is $2,000 understatement, the second error is $3,000 overstatement, the third error is $1,000 understatement and the fourth error is $1,500 overstatement, treat the $2,000 understatement as the first error for PGW calculation, treat the $1,000 understatement as the second error for PGW calculation for understatement; similarly, treat the $3,000 overstatement as the first error for PGW calculation, and then treat the $1,500 overstatement as the second error for PGW calculation.

A GAS package will automate most of the above steps. However, the auditor still has to select the confidence level, UEL and tolerable sample errors. Based on results, the GAS will evaluate the findings and tell the auditor whether the results are within the auditor's UEL and confidence level. If not, the auditor will have to increase the sample, relax the UEL or relax the confidence level. The latter two options are not desirable. Another alternative is for the auditor to conclude that the population is not reliable and perform other audit procedures to meet the audit objective.

Source File Authenticity

The data files used in GAS can be downloaded from the client's system directly or provided by the client. In some cases, the client may perform reformatting or extraction when providing a file to the auditors. For example, if the auditors cannot run the GAS on the client's mainframe environment because of lack of access, tools or expertise, the client may format the file to ASCII (PC format) for columner text for the auditors. When the client provides the files to the auditors, the auditors should perform some due diligence to ascertain that the files are what the client purports them to be. Even when the auditors can directly download the files, they should perform some procedures to ensure that they are accessing the right system.

Here is a list of procedures the auditor should carry out to ensure s/he is using the right files.

1. Study the data dictionary to identify the correct tables (files) required in relation to the audit objectives.

2. Reconcile file totals to live production reports and ledgers.

3. Observe the file generation by the client.

4. Review the operating system logs generated when the client extracted or downloaded the files, e.g., IBM's Job Control Language for mainframe computers (Z Series servers).

5. Review the programs used by the client to extract the files.

6. Perform some ordinary transaction online enquiry before and after downloading the files and verify the results of enquiries to ascertain you are accessing the correct system and files.

7. If still uncertain about the files' authenticity, expand your CAAT testing and vouch to source documents and vice versa. For example, selecting more source documents and vouch to the files.

Regression Analysis

This is a useful technique for analytical review. It measures the relationship between a dependent variable and a number of independent variables. For example, if interest revenue is the dependent variable and expressed as x, observations over a period of months can collect enough data to plot the relationship of $x = f(y, z)$. F in this case is the function, and a function can be as simple as a sum or a product of the independent variables. F may be the sum of a constant and a number of independent variables. Y and z in this case are the independent variables. A relationship where there is a constant may be expressing salary as a relationship with sales, in which case some sales department employees will always get paid regardless of sales. GAS can be useful in plotting relationships. The auditor does not need to know the relationship beforehand. S/he just has to collect a sufficiently large sample of observations of independent variable dependent variable values. There can be as few as one independent variable. If an independent variable has no bearing on the dependent variable, the coefficient will be zero or a conspicuously strange value. The auditor should test the derived equation on some specific observations to validate the plotted correlation. A common group of observations is a period of time units or a set of transaction documents like an invoice whose values depend on other variables like prices or costs.

Common GAS Tests

GAS provides a lot of versatility to auditors. Testing is limited only to the availability of source data files. It can be used to test controls, substantiate transactions and perform analytical review.

Control Testing

GAS can be used to test application controls because these controls are applied to data. The audit trail of such controls should be captured in the data files. GAS can also be used to test general controls in some cases, e.g., by analyzing the access log. Even when a control does not leave a trail, GAS can be used to test that control by looking for exceptions. For example, a control that rejects the entry of negative inventory quantity but does not leave a trail of the rejection can be tested by looking for negative quantity of processed orders. If the auditor does not find any negative quantity, s/he can conclude that the control has worked. Some auditing theorists argue that GAS cannot truly be used to test such a control because it may just be that no one entered any negative quantity. Although this argument is right, for practical purpose, the auditor can benefit from the assurance gained from this GAS test result if the test covers the entire or a majority of the population. If no negative quantity is found, the reliability of order processing is highly assured. Some might argue that this then becomes a substantive test. Well, in auditing, many tests have a dual purpose, control and substantive.

Here are some common control tests using GAS:
- Compare account balance to credit limit.
- Look for negative values to confirm edit checks.
- Check access logs for currency.
- Compare access profiles to payroll tables to identify departed employees still with active access profiles.
- Match receiving reports to invoices.
- Select pay rate changes and vouch to management approval.
- Select loans for vouching to approval and collateral.
- Check journal entries and other large transactions for approval.
- Check travel expense claims for approval.
- Look for credit check confirmation indicator on processed sales.
- Check government purchase orders to the list of vendors of record to ensure that the vendor is approved.
- Check write-offs for approval.

Substantive Testing

The quantitative and comparison functions of GAS make it ideal for substantive testing. Further, supporting documents are increasingly digital which facilitate vouching using a GAS. Here are some common substantive tests.
- Age accounts receivable.
- Check for inventory obsolescence by looking at date of last sale.
- Verify invoice calculation.
- Verify government medical insurance claims for compliance with legislation and regulation.
- Verify cost of sales in relation to the costing method like FIFO or LIFO.

- Select accounts for customer confirmation.
- Compare physical and perpetual inventory file details.
- Compare payroll to telephone directory to detect ghost employees.
- Verify depreciation calculation.
- Check payments for cash discount calculation.

Analytical Review

The computational capability of GAS enables a variety of analytical review. Just as increasing computing power makes data mining more practical, financial correlation for audit purpose is easier with automation. Here are some examples.
- Interest revenue over interest expense on a branch by branch basis.
- Interest revenue over non-interest revenue on a branch by branch basis.
- Non-interest revenue over non-interest expense on a branch by branch basis.
- Budget variance analysis.
- Store sales analysis.
- Calculating inventory turnover.
- Analysis of travel expense in relation to payroll expense
- Sales returns analysis.
- Standard cost variance analysis.
- Benford analysis.

The above ratios can be compared between periods or units or a combination. For example, in banks, a useful analytical review application is to compare the first three ratios between branches on a monthly basis, between branches of a certain size group on a monthly basis and between branches and the bank-wide average on a monthly basis.

The Role of ACL in Internal and External Audits

ACL can be used to carry out the above tests. It is widely used in internal and external audits. Its customer base includes:

- Over two-thirds of the Global 500 companies,

- 89% of the Fortune 500,

- 98 of the Fortune 100,

- All Big 4 accounting firms,

- Hundreds of national, state, provincial and local governments

- Over 14,700 organizations in more than 150 countries

Source: www.acl.com/customers, accessed on June 26, 2012.

Here is a brief description of how a major Canadian financial services company has used ACL.

Investors Group has used ACL to:

- Perform sample valuations on consultant commission fees and compare them to annual sales records to ensure they are accurate and error-free,
- Review client records for cash deposits over $10,000 to comply with reporting mandated by the Canadian Proceeds of Crime (Money Laundering) and Terrorist Financing Act,
- Develop a list of common suppliers and vendors and the relative expenditures of both Mackenzie and Investors Group, as part of back-office operations integration. Following this analysis, Investors Group developed a preferred list of suppliers, resulting in overall corporate savings of $600,000.
- Continuously monitor mutual fund trading activity to ensure ongoing compliance with a wide variety of industry regulations, and
- Develop and implement effective fraud detection controls testing which has helped to prevent any problems with fraud or compliance violations within the company

Source: http://www.acl.com/customers/story.aspx?Story=3, reprinted with permission from ACL Inc.

Brief Technical Guide to Using ACL

Here is a brief technical guide in using ACL. The ACL software package comes with a more detailed user guide.

<u>Creating an ACL File</u>

To use ACL, an ACL file must be created. It can be a blank file as a start. This is not a data file, but rather, a file of ACL test documentation including linkage to data files. An ACL file normally includes the ACL analysis work papers for an audit or a section of an audit.

After installing ACL, the auditor should select File, New to create an ACL file. The file can be named ABCsales. All ACL files carry the suffix of ACL. Now this file is empty. As ACL analyses are carried out, ABCsales.ACL will begin to grow. It is essentially a work paper file of ACL tests.

Importing Data Files

Because ACL is a GAS package, it is useful only when there are data files to be analyzed. A data file, as mentioned in the last chapter, is the same as a table. ACL can take data files in a variety of formats, including the following common formats, listed in the order of degree of ACL compatibility:
- DBF, data base file.
- Excel
- Text with delimiters, i.e., a text file with defined columns.

The PC and LAN versions of ACL have the same capability in accepting data file formats. There is also a Z series server version of ACL. Z series servers store data in the Extended Binary Coded Decimal Interchange Code (EBCDIC) format, whereas personal computers, most mid size computers and LAN servers use American Standard Code for Information Interchange (ASCII). EBCDIC uses 8-bit bytes and ASCII uses 7-bit bytes. EBCDIC therefore allows for more symbols on the keyboard. For example, the letter A is represented using an ASCII byte of 1000001, the EBCDIC representation is 11000001.

A Z series server data file is generally not recognizable to an operating system that uses ASCII. There is therefore a need to use utility programs to convert EBCDIC to ASCII.

When the PC or LAN version of ACL is used to analyse a Z series server data file, the auditors can ask the client or auditee to convert the file to ASCII, in a text file format. It is important that the auditor performs due diligence to ensure the file is genuine and complete. Such due diligence can take the form of being present during the conversion, examining the Z series server's Job Control Language (operating system log), and reconciling the file to ledgers etc.

A data file in DBF or Excel format is immediately recognizable to the PC or LAN version of ACL. A data file in text delimited format can be imported, but the auditor will have to define each field, its format (numeric, alphanumeric, date etc.) and its starting position and length to ACL.

The import of a data file is performed by selecting Data, Select, and identifying the source, i.e., whether it is from a disk or ODBC (Open Database Connectivity, i.e., a LAN where the server is not of the same hardware as the client computer, e.g., a LAN that allows client computers to access a midframe computer like IBM AS 400). In today's environment, the choice of source is most likely a disk. A disk can be a local drive, a portable drive or a network drive. Once the type of source is chosen, ACL will prompt the auditor to identify the file on the drive. ACL will then recognize the file as DBF, Excel or text and ask the auditor to name the data file within ACL. The auditor can use the same file name as the source file. The data file in ACL will be suffced with .FIL. FIL stands for filter. If the file is not a DBF or Excel file, the auditor will have to define the file layout. ACL will prompt the auditor and guide step by step.

Even if the file is DBF or Excel, the auditor should check the data type of each field to ensure that a field that will be used for calculation is represented in a numeric form and a field that will be used as a primary key is in alphanumeric form. This can be performed using the following steps:
1. Open the data file.
2. Select, Edit, Input File Definition.
3. Click on the desired field.
4. Check the data type and change it to numeric or ASCII respectively depending on whether the field is needed for calculation or used as a primary key. ASCII is the choice above numeric. ASCII in this case means alphanumeric.
5. Click the check mark to save.

Extraction

This is the most common function in ACL. It allows an auditor to extract records based on one or more conditions (equations). Here are the procedures.
1. Go to Data, Extract.
2. Click on the If box.
3. Select operands and operators to build equations. An equation can have a number or an input ASCII (alphanumeric) value. The latter has to be enclosed with " ". A date value also can be included in an equation. The format for a date value input by the auditor to an equation is `yyyymmdd` or `yymmdd`, depending the data field that you are trying to compare with, as to whether that field uses a 4-digit year or 2-digit year. A date field, under Input File Definition described above, has the data type of date, not numeric or ASCII. Multiple equations can be combined in an expression by selecting the AND, OR, and NOT operators.
4. Once the expression has been defined, the auditor should name the output file. If the auditor wants the output file to be stored in the same folder as the file being analyzed, s/he needs to type in the new file name only. If the auditor wants the new file to be stored in a different folder, s/he should click on the To box and find the folder.
5. With the Use Output File box checked, the output file will be displayed right away. Otherwise it will stay in the background and the auditor will have to go to Data, Select to find the output file.
6. Now, the auditor can click the check mark to start the extraction process.
7. At completion of the extraction process, the file history will first be displayed. The file history shows a trail of everything that was done to the file being analyzed. The criteria (expressions) for analysis/extraction, date and time are shown. The auditor can click on the x mark at the top right corner to close the file history. Then the output file will be displayed. The file history is automatically saved.

Export

ACL is versatile in data analysis but not great in data formatting or graphing. To make up for this shortfall, an auditor can export a file to Excel. This is done by selecting Data, Export and then selecting the type of file format, e.g., Excel.

Join

In data analysis, it is often necessary to join two files so that more fields can be meaningfully compared as a basis of extraction. For example, an invoice file can be joined to an inventory file to check for any sales that are below cost. Two files can be joined as long as they have the same key, even though they have different fields. In fact, the fact that two files have different fields is a common reason for joining the files. The procedures are as follows.

1. With one of the files open, preferably, the primary file, i.e., the file to which another file will be joined, select Data, Join.
2. On the right hand pane, select the secondary file. A file must have been imported to ACL in order to be joined.
3. Select the primary file key and the secondary file key. The two keys must be of equal length; they don't have to have the same name.
4. Select the fields from the primary file and the fields from the secondary file to be joined. Avoid using Select All because ACL will show the fields alphabetically, i.e., the key will likely not be shown as the first (leftmost) field in the output file. You should click the fields, including the key(s) one by one in the order in which you want them appearing in the output file.
5. Unless you want to find out whether any records in the secondary file do not have a corresponding key-match with the primary file, you do not have to select the secondary key as a displayed field in the output file.
6. Make sure you check the box "presort file" for both the primary and the secondary files.
7. If you check the Use Output File box, the output file will be shown right away after the history, otherwise, it will stay in the background.
8. In the To box, name the output file.
9. You can click the If box to perform a conditional join, i.e., combining the Join function with an extraction.
10. The default join criterion is that all secondary records that have a corresponding key match with the primary file will be included. You can expand or change that by clicking the More box and selecting the following:
    - Include all primary records regardless of a match
    - Include all secondary records regardless of a match
    - Include all primary records and all secondary records
    - Include only unmatched records
11. Go back to the Main section and click OK, joining will start.

Merge

Sometimes you might find it useful to merge two files that have identical layout. For example, you might want to merge twelve monthly transaction files and perform one set of analysis instead of analyzing each monthly file. ACL lets you merge two files at a time. In the above example, you can keep merging until all twelve monthly files are combined. For two file to be merged, it must have the same key with the same key name as well as the same field names with the same length and data format. The procedure is to go to Data, Merge and then select the primary file, primary key, secondary file and secondary key. Make sure the presort box is checked.

Analysis Functions

On the main menu, under Analysis, there are a number of functions as follows.

Total – This allows the auditor to total a selected field.

Count – This provides a record count.

Statistics – This calculates statistical parameters like mean, median, standard deviation etc.

Profile – This provides more statistical parameters like min, max and distribution.

Stratify – This provides a summary breakdown based on specified grouping of numerical fields, e.g., # of accounts < $5,000 each, between $5,000 and $10,000, and > $10,000.

Classify – This provides a summary breakdown of different classification, i.e., the field used for classification is alpha-numeric, e.g., # of invoices for each customer.

Histogram – This is the graphical format of stratify.

Aging

This function allows the auditor to age receivables and perhaps also inventory. The procedures are as follows.
1. Go to Analyze, Age.
2. Select the field to be aged.
3. Define the brackets, e.g., 0, 30, 60.
4. Click OK.

Benford

This function was explained in detail earlier. To exercise it, go to Analyze, Benford, and select the numerical field to be analyzed. Make sure the field represents a natural number. You can select the number of leading digits to analyze, e.g, the first digit, the first 2 digits or the first 3 digits. You cannot select a digit without also selecting the digit(s) to the left. ACL will then calculate the actual numbers of occurrences vs the Benford expected numbers of occurrences and the variances are reported as Z statistics. A Z statistic of 1 or lower is acceptable. Here is an example of analysis result of analyzing only the first leading digit.

Leading Digit	Actual Count	Expected Count	Zstat Ratio
1	23	68	6.428
2	22	40	2.997
3	26	28	0.325
4	25	22	0.607
5	31	18	3.132
6	25	15	2.517
7	24	13	2.981
8	31	11	5.747
9	18	10	2.299

As you can see, the Z statistics for the leading digit being 8 or 9 are quite high. This is consistent with the Benford Law that as the leading digit increases towards 9, the probability is lower. From the above analysis, we know that there should be more amounts starting with the digit 1 and 2, and that some amounts starting with the digits 5, 6, 7, 8 and 9 are quite likely doctored. But we don't know which amounts are wrong or fictitious. At least, this leads the auditor to conduct more testing on those ranges of amounts.

Gap

This function enables the auditor to look for gaps in a number sequence. The field to be analyzed can be numeric or alphanumeric, although a gap in an alphanumeric sequence is less meaningful and may not be cause for alarm. The procedures are as follows.
1. Go to Analyze, Gap.
2. Select the field to be analyzed.
3. Click OK.

Duplicate

This function is the converse of gap. The procedures are similar.

<u>Sampling</u>

This function allows the auditor to determine sample sizes, select samples and evaluate findings.

Sample Size Procedures

1. Go to Analyze, Sample.
2. Select Sample Size.
3. Select Monetary or Record. Monetary means dollar unit sampling as explained above, whereas Record means every record stands an equal chance of selection regardless of the value of the record.
4. For monetary sampling, input the confidence level in % without typing in the % sign. Input the population monetary value and materiality. The number of errors expected is optional and in most cases would not make a difference to the sample size unless a large number in relation to the population value is specified. Note that the auditor should be guided by the organization's statistical sampling policy when using this function; s/he will need knowledge of statistical sampling instead of blindly following the ACL parameters. For example, the auditor has to be able to relate materiality to errors found.
5. For record sampling, input the confidence level, population and upper error limit, i.e., the maximum error rate the auditor is willing to tolerate given the specified confidence level. The expected error rate is optional; it is assumed to be zero in the sample. If specified, a non-zero value will increase the sample size as the value increases. This is because the auditor will have to test more if the auditor thinks the population is flawed. If the number of errors found in the sample exceeds what the auditor has specified, the auditor should test more or conclude that the findings indicate the population is not reliable for the objective in terms of the tolerable error rate in the population. In the latter case, the auditor may want to perform supplementary audit procedures.

Sampling (Selection) Procedures

This function selects a sample from a population based on specified parameters. Here are the procedures.
1. Go to Analyze, Sampling, Sample.
2. Check off the MUS or Record box. MUS stands for monetary unit sampling.
3. If the MUS box is checked, select a numerical field to be sampled on.
4. Under Sampling Parameters, select Fixed Interval, Cell or Random. Interval means sample selection will be based on a fixed interval. For example, if the population value is $1,000,000 and the interval is $10,000, every 10,000th dollar will be selected and the record that consists of that specific dollar will be selected. The interval was determined under the Sample Size function described above. The auditor may also enter a starting point, i.e., the first dollar or record to be selected

even though the desired interval has not been reached. The starting point must be lower than the interval. For MUS, the auditor may also specify a cut-off value. If so, any record with a value equal to or more than the cut-off value will be selected. This might be puzzling because doesn't the interval serve this purpose? Well, if an auditor wants every account with $1,000 or more to be selected but wants to use a higher interval to limit the number of accounts, cut-off has its place. Let's say the cut-off is $1,000 and the interval is $2,000. In this case, every account with a balance of $1,000 or more will be selected. Smaller accounts may also be selected if the account consists of the every 2,000th dollar. ACL will adjust the number of accounts to be selected overall to account for the arbitrary inclusion of all accounts over $1,000; in other words, if such a cut-off parameter is specified by an auditor when the average sampling interval is $2,000, ACL will reduce the number of accounts under $1,000 that will be selected to meet the overall sampling coverage based on the confidence level and UEL specified by the auditor, regardless of the chosen selection method of interval or random. The random selection method means that ACL will not follow the fixed interval method in selecting but instead, will select the items at random to meet the overall sample size calculated based on confidence level and UEL.

In MUS sampling, the auditor can also choose the cell method for selection. This means that the population value will be divided into a number of cells based on the interval value. For example, if the population has $1,000,000 and the interval is 10,000, there will be 100 cells. Each cell will occupy $10,000. Within each cell, a random dollar will be selected and the account that carries that dollar will by default be selected. This method provides more randomness than the fixed interval method.

To achieve complete randomness, the auditor can select the random method of selection. In this case, given the above parameters, 100 random dollars will be selected from the population. The account that carries each of these dollars will by default be selected.

Regardless of the method of selection and type of sampling, the auditor should name the output file and indicate where it is to be stored. The default location is the folder where the population is located.

5. The auditor can use the Evaluate function under sampling to evaluate the findings. Input the confidence level in percentage without putting in the % sign, input the sample size and the number of errors found. The software will tell you what the upper error limit is. The upper error limit is the maximum error rate, given the specified confidence level, that could occur in the population. The auditor can then compare this to materiality. If it equals or exceeds materiality, the auditor should extend the sample size, perform supplementary procedures or form a reserved opinion about the population being tested.

INTEGRATED TEST FACILITY

In the last chapter, we discussed using test data to verify application controls. A drawback of test data is that it provides only point-in-time assurance. Because of the client's involvement in setting up the test environment, repeated testing may not be practical. Another drawback is the reliability of the test system. Is it the same as the live system? An integrated test facility (ITF) can overcome these problems.

An ITF is really a test branch or department in the live system. For example, a bank can set up a test branch in the banking system where auditors hold different types of accounts. This is a phantom branch. Because it is in the live system, all the transactions going through it are subject to the same processing functions as the real transactions, including the despatch of customer statements and the referral of exceptional transactions to the branch manager for approval. The branch manager in this case could be an audit manager. The main advantage of this tool is that the auditor can put in test data anytime s/he wants. The system is live and the auditor does not have to worry about whether the system is up-to-date. There is one caution, however. The test transactions must not get to the general ledger and not be included in reporting to external agencies like the banking regulator. This is easy, just don't tell the GL and the external reporting systems about the test branch number.

Here are some ITF tests:
- Test input edit checks.
- Test exception reporting.
- Test the timeliness of invoicing.
- Test the completeness of customer statements.
- Test access controls.
- Test sequence checking.
- Test credit limit.
- Test system warning.
- Test interest calculation.
- Test account application approval.

EMBEDDED AUDIT MODULE

GAS can be used for control testing, substantive testing and analytical review. ITF is used for only control testing because there is no real data. An embedded audit module (EAM) is somewhat similar to ITF in that it is part of the live system. However, EAM works with real data so it can be used to perform control testing, substantive testing and to a limited extent, analytical review.

An EAM is a module, i.e., a set of computer functions built into the live transaction processing system at the request of the auditors, usually internal auditors. Its main function is to inspect transactions being processed and apply analytical functions to those transactions that are of audit interest. Some would argue that what is important to auditors should be important to management. In that case, there is no need for an EAM as these functions should produce analytical information for management. This is a good point. Ideally, that would be the case.

When auditors are involved in a systems development project and want to see some analytical functions included in the new system that would be useful for audit engagements, the auditors will try to convince management to have these functions included in user requirements. If the auditors fail to convince management due to time constraint, budget constraint or a difference in opinion, the auditors may resort to insisting on these functions as audit requirements. In such a case, the analytical functions would be available for auditor access only. Or the auditor department may raise a system enhancement project to include these features in the system after initial implementation.

Another reason for an EAM is to provide for continuous sampling. For example, an EAM may copy every 10th loan or every loan granted to someone under 21 years of age that exceed $100,000 to an audit file for auditors to remotely access.

An EAM function normally copies transactions that satisfy certain criteria to audit files that auditors can access remotely at any time. Here are some examples of functions.
- Real time sampling.
- Reporting on direct database updates, i.e., changing data without the support of a transaction.
- Benford analysis.
- Reporting on management override; i.e., a management online approval to override a system warning or rejection.
- Emergency software changes.
- Frequent entertainment claims by an employee.
- Unusual loans.
- Large loans.
- Large accruals.
- Large refunds.

Because an EAM inspects all live transactions, it is also called continuous auditing. ACL has a continuous auditing module that applies most of the traditional ACL functions. The difference is timing, i.e., these functions are carried out as transactions are processed.

AUDIT SCHEDULING SOFTWARE

Effective use of audit resources is a popular topic in auditing symposiums and conferences. Indeed, many internal audit executives consider it a critical success factor for their departments. Also, audit committees are becoming more interested in the cost effectiveness of the audit department. As a result, internal audit executives are often asked to explain and justify how they have used their resources. Together, these developments have heightened the interest of many audit executives in objective risk analysis approaches to scheduling audit assignments, as opposed to more traditional and subjective methods.

Before discussing improved methodology, let's consider what is meant by effective audit resource management and why it is necessary. Compared with the managing of audit quality - which is aided by generally accepted audit standards, along with sound hiring practices, training and internal quality assurance procedures – the management of audit resources is less process driven and involves more ad hoc decisions. Also, this aspect of audit management is less likely to be consistent among organizations because of differences in corporate culture, audit committee directives and regulatory requirements.

Why is sound audit resource management important? Through analysis, internal audit executives may find that "mandatory" audit coverage accounts for only a small share of their available resources. Management often allocates the remaining audit resources based on materiality, its own subjective assessment of inherent risk and control risk, senior management concerns and visibility of the units to be audited.

Further, although all internal audit executives will agree that they have a responsibility to auditees to deliver quality findings and assurance, they don't always realize that auditees have the right to expect effective, if not optimal, use of audit resources. Auditees have this right because they contribute to the company's profit, part of which supports the audit department.

It is clear, then, that audit executives and auditees would both benefit greatly from more effective deployment of audit resources. Neither group, however, are well served by a haphazard scheduling approach.

Scheduling Made Simple

Here is a dynamic modeling technique that offers a simple yet comprehensive method of scheduling that applies to all auditable units. The logic in this method lends itself to frequent applications, allowing continual adjustment of the audit schedule. This model would be useful to audit executives shopping around for an audit scheduling software tool to assess whether the tools address the following process and factors. Alternatively, an audit department can develop its own software to apply this model. This approach has been formulated primarily for application in internal audit departments, but external auditors may find it useful in selecting clients' business units for more in-depth testing and analysis.

353

Risk Factors

Use the following risk factors to support the risk assessment of each auditable unit. Assign a weight on a scale of say, 1 to 5 to each factor. In order to achieve consistency of risk assessment among auditable units, use only one weight scale for the organization. In other words, if a factor is assigned a weight of 5, apply that weight to all units, which might include branches, head office departments, systems and data centers. The weights should be reviewed annually and adjusted to reflect any significant changes in operation and business strategy. Here are the common risk factors.
1. Vulnerability to fraud
2. Transaction complexity
3. Significance of information processed
4. Materiality
5. Contribution to company profit
6. Recent system changes
7. Staff turnover
8. Control risk

The first seven factors reflect inherent risk. More detailed inherent risk can be addressed in individual audits.

For example, the risk of vulnerability to fraud may be assigned a weight of 3 and the risk of transaction complexity may be assigned a weight of 4.

Risk Rating

Rate each risk factor on a scale of, say, 1 to 5. Unlike the weight for each risk factor, the rated value can vary from unit to unit. Again, the company can tailor the scale to suit its operation. Apply the same scale, however, to all units. For a rate scale of 1 to 5, 1 would be the highest risk rating for each risk factor. Next, the weighted total risk score for each unit can be calculated as follows:

Weight of risk factor #1 x rated value + weight of risk factor #2 x rated value....+ weight of risk factor #8 x rated value.

For example, the Toronto Branch may be rated 3 for vulnerability to fraud and rated 2 for transaction complexity; the Toronto Data Centre may be rated 2 for vulnerability to fraud and rated 4 for transaction complexity. The weighted risk scores for the Branch and the Data Centre are therefore (3 x 3 + 4 x 2) and (2 x 3 + 4 x 4) respectively, or 15 and 22 respectively. Based on this, the data center has priority over the branch for audit scheduling.

Scheduling Criteria

The following criteria can be used to schedule audits.
1. Risk score calculated above
2. Resources required to audit the unit
3. Time since last audit
4. Available resources

Scheduling Logic

The following process can be used to apply the risk scores to the scheduling criteria.

1. For each audit entity (system, unit or function), determine the person days required to audit, weighted by staff grade level. For example, if an audit requires 10 days of an auditor at grade 8, 5 days of a senior auditor at grade 10, and 1 day of a manager at grade 12, the number of weighted person days will be 10 x 8 + 5 x 10 + 1 x 12 = 142. This assumes that a higher staff grade is attached to a higher salary scale. If the converse is true, for the purpose of this exercise, the audit department can reverse the grade structure.

   Using the data center and branch example, if the data center takes 20 person days of auditor time, 10 person days of a senior auditor and 5 days of the manager to complete, the total weighted person days equal 20 x 8 + 10 x 10 + 5 x 12, or 320. If the branch takes 15 days of auditor time, 2 days of a senior auditor and 1 day of manager's time, the weighted person days equal 15 x 8 + 2 x 10 + 1 x 12, or 152 days.

   Based on this, the branch audit is more economical.

2. To arrive at the raw audit payoff score, divide the total risk score of each unit by the number of weighted person days required. An audit that is more resource intensive, with other factors constant, therefore, receives less priority in terms of scheduling.

   The raw audit payoff scores for the branch and the data center are 15/152 and 22/320 respectively, or .097 and .069 respectively. The branch audit seems to deserve more priority in audit scheduling.

3. Determine the time since the last audit for each unit.

   Let's say the branch was last audited 13 months ago and the data center was last audited 23 months ago.

4. Convert the time gap to points as follows:

0 to 6 months	= 1 point
6 to 12 months	= 2 points
12 to 18 months	= 3 points
18 to 24 months	= 4 points
Over 24 months	= 5 points

Based on experience, the organization may change the range and point scale. The same scale, however, should be applied to all units. This means branches, data centers and corporate departments will be subject to the same scale.

The time gap scores of the branch and the data center are 3 and 4 respectively.

5. To arrive at a time-adjusted payoff score, multiply the number of points for each unit by the raw audit payoff score.

The time adjusted payoff scores for the branch and the data center are 3 x .097 and 4 x .069 respectively, or .296 and .275 respectively.

6. Prioritize audits based on the time-adjusted payoff scores. If a unit has been selected for the second time within a year, it may not be necessary to perform a full audit.

The branch still has priority over the data center for audit scheduling.

The above steps can be performed as often as practical to achieve audit scheduling based on current risk and resource requirements.

One might argue that if the available weighted person days amount to 330 days and 152 days are spent to audit the main branch, the remaining resources are not enough for the data center audit and hence idle. Well, this would hardly be the case, because there are usually many more auditable entities for consideration to be subjected to this risk assessment process for audit scheduling. Further, since this model can be scheduled to run as often as possible, like monthly, optimal use of audit resources can be highly achieved. An organization can also include linear programming mathematical techniques to optimize the allocation of available resource days after the time adjusted pay-off scores have been calculated.

ELECTRONIC WORK PAPERS

This is by no means a new idea. However, many internal audit departments and small accounting firms have not embraced it. I developed an electronic audit work papers package in a major Canadian bank in 1989 using a word processor. Today's tools are much more user friendly and efficient. The entire audit file can be stored electronically with proper indexing and cross referencing. The benefits of electronic work papers include ease of preparation, ease of storage, ease of sharing (more than one person can read and comment simultaneously), ease of backup and ease of update (no eraser marks and use of different color pens). Disadvantages, like any new tool, include development and training cost.

Large accounting firms have their own packages. Internal auditors and smaller accounting firms can purchase a reasonably affordable commercial product. ACL also has its own version. Here is how an electronic audit work paper file can be prepared, reviewed, updated and stored.

1. The package includes audit programs for standard financial statement assertion areas and operation areas like cash, inventory, sales, data centers. These audit programs can be tailored to an organization's industry and environment. In fact, large accounting firms have standard audit programs for each industry.

2. There are forms for audit planning that conform with accounting institute requirements and the Institute of Internal Auditors recommendations, including the audit planning memorandum and engagement letter etc.

3. There are forms for audit budgeting by hours and auditor that can be updated with actual numbers and linked to the billing system.

4. There are tools and forms for risk assessment and analytical review.

5. There are internal control questionnaires that are fillable by auditors. The questionnaires can be linked to documentation like narrative description, flowcharts and customized audit programs. Based on answers in the yes, no, or cardinal ranking boxes checked by the auditors, the software can assess control risk as high, moderate or low. It can then produce an audit program for control testing.

6. The auditor tests controls and brings up the internal control questionnaire to input updated control information. The software then performs control risk assessment and produces an audit program for substantive testing.

7. The work paper software can be linked to general audit software packages, e.g., for statistical sampling and for inputting analysis results from a general audit software package.

8. Substantive audit programs are linked to standard forms for documenting test results.

9. Based on test results entered, the software can assess materiality and recommend an audit conclusion for the area.

10. Source documents including contracts and legal letters can be scanned and the software can import and link the scanned documents to the audit work paper file.

11. The audit work paper file is stored on a network with time stamps for access and updates. There will be concurrent update controls to prevent two people from updating a schedule simultaneously.

12. Reviewers can make review notes on a review note schedule for auditors to respond.

13. The audit work papers will be subject to daily backup with offsite storage.

The above description is based on the audit of financial statements. Commercial or proprietary tools can be developed along a similar line for internal audits.

AUDIT CHECKLIST

We are not providing a management checklist in this chapter because the material in this chapter is intended primarily for auditors. Internal auditors and external auditors have pretty much the same need for computer assisted audit techniques (CAAT). We are therefore providing a summary checklist for both internal auditors and external auditors.

1. Document consideration to use CAAT in each audit and justify why CAAT is not used.

2. In systems development auditing, document CAAT requirements in terms of data availability.

3. For each business critical system, assess CAAT applicability and the types of CAAT.

4. Include CAAT in each auditor's training plan.

5. Build a technical CAAT team in the audit department or the accounting firm.

6. Develop a CAAT documentation standard for each type of CAAT.

7. Use CAAT to perform organization wide analytical review not tied specifically to individual audits to identify risky areas for further audit work and management attention.

8. Include standard confidence levels, tolerable sample error sizes and upper error limits in the organization's audit methodology for different systems.

9. Keep track of CAAT audit hours and audit findings from CAATs to assess CAAT effectiveness.

10. External auditors should use internal auditors as much as possible to apply CAATs as the latter is closer to the organization's systems and has more resources. External auditors should rigorously review the internal audit work papers.

CONCLUSION

Our life is increasingly affected by digitization. This helps to enhance consistency, convenience and comfort. Car diagnosis is so computerized today that a mechanic's hands are less dirty and drivers are better educated on what went wrong. Computers facilitate micro surgery to improve precision and limit bleeding. Auditors should consider every meaningful opportunity to automate their work, from electronic work papers to using rigorous analytical review, etc., in order to reduce audit cost and risk.

SUMMARY OF MAIN POINTS

Main Types of Computer Assisted Audit Techniques

- General audit software – Most versatile, can be used for analytical review, control testing and substantive testing.
- Integrated test facility – This is an automated test data environment, mainly used by internal auditors for control testing.
- Embedded audit module – Also called continuous auditing, subjects transactions to certain audit tests automatically; the most common application is sampling.
- Audit scheduling.
- Electronic work papers.

General Audit Software

This is similar to Microsoft Access but it is tailored for auditors. It allows auditors to perform a variety of data analysis on client's data files. Here are the common functions:
- Data extraction based on criteria (formulae).
- Aging
- Duplicate identification.
- Gap identification.
- Fraud analysis.
- Statistical profiling
- Statistical sampling.
- Regression analysis.

Common CAAT Tests

Here are some common control tests:
- Compare account balance to credit limit
- Look for negative values to confirm edit checks
- Check access logs for currency

- Compare access profiles to payroll file to identify departed employees still with active access profiles
- Match receiving reports to invoices
- Select pay rate changes and vouch to management approval
- Select loans for vouching to approval and collateral
- Check journal entries and other large transactions for approval
- Check travel expense claims for approval
- Look for credit check confirmation indicator on processed sales
- Check purchase orders to the list of authorized vendors
- Check write-offs for approval

The quantitative and comparison functions of CAAT tools make them ideal for substantive testing. Further, supporting documents are increasingly digital which facilitate vouching using a general audit software package. Here are some common substantive tests.

- Age accounts receivable
- Check for inventory obsolescence by looking at date of last sale
- Verify invoice calculation
- Verify government medical insurance claims for compliance with legislation and regulation
- Verify cost of sales in relation to the costing method like FIFO or LIFO
- Select accounts for customer confirmation
- Compare physical and perpetual inventory file details
- Compare payroll to telephone directory to detect ghost employees
- Verify depreciation calculation
- Check payments for cash discount calculation

Analytical Review

The computational capability of GAS enables a variety of analytical review. Just as increasing computing power makes data mining more practical, financial correlation for audit purpose is easier and easier with automation. Here are some examples.

- Interest revenue over interest expense on a branch by branch basis
- Interest revenue over non-interest revenue on a branch by branch basis
- Non-interest revenue over non-interest expense on a branch by branch basis
- Budget variance analysis
- Store sales analysis
- Inventory turnover
- Travel expense over payroll expense
- Sales returns
- Standard cost variance analysis
- Benford analysis

<u>REVIEW QUESTIONS</u>

1. How does the use of computer assisted audit techniques mitigate detection risk?

2. State an argument that general audit software has limited application in control testing. Also argue against this.

3. What risk does Benford analysis mainly address?

4. Describe the relationship between GAS and sampling?

5. Why is an embedded audit module often called a continuous auditing tool?

6. In which industries is integrated test facility more applicable? Why?

7. Why is attribute sampling more applicable in auditing than variable sampling is?

8. What risks are analyzed by audit scheduling software?

9. How do IT trends affect computer assisted audit techniques?

10. What is the relationship between confidence level, population size, sample size and precision?

CASE - Canadian Building Supplies Ltd.

Canadian Building Supplies Ltd. (CBS), a client of yours, has recently installed a sales/order entry system.

Nature of Business

CBS is a wholesale distributor of building products. It has a head office, branches and 4 separate warehouses. Each warehouse has significant inventory levels and approximately 2,500 different items. Annual sales are $80 million and the accounts receivable balance is $25 million. There are 5,000 customer accounts.

The Computer Installation

The data center is located in head office. The accounting system can be accessed by accounting, order entry and warehouse staff members. The latter two functions are decentralized.

Computer Environment Controls

Historically, the computer operation at CBS has been well controlled. A review of the existing environment or general computer controls has revealed that controls over implementation, program and data files, physical operations and the operating system are adequate.

The Sales/Order Entry System

The system was designed to speed up the order entry processing/shipping function, and improve inventory and accounts receivable management. Clerks take orders over the phone or from salespeople's files. Input includes customer numbers, product numbers, quantity, special shipping instructions and branch location code. The system edits the input data for correct format, valid dates, valid customer, product and location codes. It also checks credit limits and inventory availability.

For all orders clearing the edits and system checks, a sales order is produced in two copies. A computer file of outstanding sales orders is created. The warehouse clerks take the orders and fill them. One copy of the sales order serves as the packing slip. The other copy is sent to accounting for filing by customer number.

The following action results when a transaction fails a system check:
- Invalid product number, customer code, location code or date is immediately identified to the operator for re-entry.
- Where the product is not available at the location identified, the inventory files of other locations are searched. If the product is available at the alternate location, a sales order is produced with instructions to ship the items that are available at the current or alternate warehouse.
- Where inventory is not available at any location, a record is created in the back-order file and a print-out of the order is sent to the purchasing department for follow-up.
- Where the credit limit is exceeded, the order is printed out in the accounting department for credit override approval.

When an order is complete and shipped, the warehouse clerk keys in this information and the order is flagged as shipped on the outstanding sales order file. In the case of a partial shipment from a warehouse, the clerk codes the order as partial and indicates the items shipped. This is noted on the outstanding order file and when these items have been shipped, the system changes the code on the outstanding order file to "complete".

For orders for which inventory is not available, a back order is created and identified on the outstanding order file. When all items other than the back-ordered items are keyed in as shipped, the system codes the order complete and it enters the billing cycle.

At the end of each day, the outstanding order file is processed and all shipments coded complete enter the billing system which creates invoices and updates the accounts receivable and sales files. Cyclical counts of inventory are carried out by designated warehouse clerks who adjust records as required directly on the system.

In order to carry out the credit checks at the input stage of the sales order system, the program accesses the price file, prices the order and calculates the total. It then accesses the receivable file to obtain the current balance, adds the order value and compares the total to the credit limit. To save processing time, only orders in excess of $1,000 are subject to the credit check.

If a customer account is not on file, the order is printed out at the accounting office printer and a credit investigation is done by credit clerks. When the customer is approved for credit, the credit clerk goes to the system and creates the customer file with the appropriate credit limit. The order is sent back to the sales order clerks for processing in the normal fashion.

The credit manager can approve sales over the credit limit. She receives these sales order copies and reviews them. When she authorizes a sale over the credit limit, she signs the order copy and resubmits it to the sales order clerks. With a special code, she can bypass the credit check and the order is processed normally. At the end of each week, a report of unfilled and filled orders is produced. On Monday morning, the warehouse managers review the report.

Cash Receipts

Payments on account are received by a cash receipts clerk who posts the payments to accounts receivable. He prepares a bank deposit slip in duplicate, and gives the payments and original deposit slip to a messenger who makes the bank deposit. Another clerk checks the stamped bank deposit slip to the accounts receivable total credits for the day. A daily cash listing is printed on the accounting office printer so that the cash receipts clerk can respond to any customer queries.

At month end, the following reports are printed:

        Accounts Receivable Aged Trial Balance
        Sales Analysis - by warehouse
                    - by salesman
                    - by product
        Inventory Adjustment listing
        Cash Receipts listing

These listings are used to update general ledger control accounts. Accounts receivable are reconciled to the general ledger by a clerk who is independent of the accounts receivable, inventory and cash receipts functions.

Required

The existing CBS Computer system is capable of supporting your audit software package. Using a general audit software package, suggest five tests for each of the following and indicate what data you will need from the systems to perform the tests.
(i)   the accounts receivable file
(ii)   the inventory file.

Indicate the respective audit objective for each test.

MULTIPLE CHOICE QUESTIONS

1. Which of the following numbers can be tested with the Benford Law?
A. Social insurance number
B. Student number
C. Store prices
D. Store inventory value for a product
E. Class size

2. How large does a population have to be for there to be negligible impact on the sample size as the population increases?
A. 10,000
B. 100
C. 1,000
D. 3,000,000

3. Which of the following information is useful in assessing inventory obsolescence?
A. Unit cost
B. Price
C. Quantity on hand
D. Economic order quantity
E. Date of last sale

4. Which type of audit procedures does Benford analysis most directly support?
A. Substantive testing
B. Control testing
C. Analytical review
D. Audit planning

5. Which type of computer assisted audit techniques requires test data?
    A. General audit software package
    B. Statistical analysis software
    C. Embedded audit module
    D. Integrated test facility

6. A small company claims that its sales order system will not process an order if it exceeds the customer's credit limit. Which is the most effective audit tool for external auditors to test this control?
   A. Analytical review
   B. General audit software package
   C. Test data
   D. Observation

7. Which CAAT tool is the most popular?
   A. General audit software package
   B. Embedded audit module
   C. Integrated test facility
   D. Statistical analysis software

8. Which GAS function helps an auditor to determine disbursement checks that are not accounted for?
   A. Dump
   B. Gap
   C. Join
   D. Profile

9. A test approach used to validate processing by setting up a fictitious company or branch in an application for testing transaction processing is called
   A. snapshot.
   B. test data.
   C. transaction tagging.
   D. integrated test facility.
   E. embedded audit module.

10. Which of the following computer assisted audit techniques is most useful in statistical sampling?
    A. Test data
    B. Integrated test facility
    C. General audit software package
    D. Embedded audit module

CHAPTER EIGHT – COMMON ACCESS CONTROLS

The only real security that a man can have in this world is a reserve of knowledge, experience and ability. - Henry Ford

SECURITY THREATS

In Chapter Two, we discuss the risk factors related to completeness, authorization, accuracy, timeliness, occurrence and efficiency. We also reviewed some examples of what have gone wrong with information systems. One type of mishaps particularly related to authorization is security breach. Here is a common list.

- Hacking
- Hardware theft
- Identity theft
- Inappropriate use of IT resources
- Internal breach
- Sniffing
- Software theft
- Spoofing
- Virus
- Worm

To mitigate these risks, an organization must implement preventive and detective access controls tailored to the environment. These controls can take the forms of software, instructions, procedures and physical devices.

Hacking

Every computer is hackable to some extent, unless it is turned off. This is a smokeless crime and the identity and source of hackers are often concealed. Here is a list of common payloads:

- Obtain system information to perform further crime like identity theft.
- Obtain sensitive customer or business information to achieve malice like blackmail or to embarrass people.
- Obtain sensitive information just for curiosity. The risk is that the suffering organization has no control as to how the hacker uses the information.
- Deface a web site.
- Change a web site's information, e.g., changing a customer agreement to make the organization liable for something which the organization has disclaimed in the agreement, or changing an advertised price or interest rate.
- Bring down or jamming a web site.

A hacker can install a rootkit in a computer after first obtaining root-level access, either by exploiting a known vulnerability or by obtaining a password using password cracking or social engineering. Once a rootkit is installed, it allows a hacker to mask the ongoing intrusion and maintain privileged access to the computer by circumventing normal authentication and access controls. Rootkits are commonly used in setting up and hiding malicious software, or injecting malicious software in otherwise normal programs.

Rootkit detection is difficult because a rootkit may be able to subvert the software that is intended to find it. Detection methods include file integrity monitoring and intrusion detection systems. Removal can be complicated or practically impossible, especially in cases where the rootkit resides in the kernel; reinstallation of the operating system may be the only available solution to the problem. The kernel is the core of an operating system that directly controls the allocation of the central processing unit (CPU) functions and random access memory (RAM). The CPU is the core hardware of a computer that performs calculation and data comparison without the aid of software.

A common hacking technique is to inject SQL code in an Internet transaction session. This means a hacker will key in some SQL code (program instructions) in fields that ask for data input to process a transaction like a Web order. A successful SQL injection may allow an attacker to spoof identity, collect information, and tamper with or destroy existing data. Spoofing means hiding one's identity by using another identifier to pretend to be the owner of that identifier, e.g., using someone else's IP address in place of the hacker's to hide the hacker's traceability. A more detailed example of SQL injection follows.

Consider a web application that allows users to change their passwords and asks for following inputs:

UserID: 'chand'
Old password: Soccer99
New password: Potash9999
The resulting SQL executed by the database then is:
        UPDATE usertable SET pwd='Potash9999' WHERE
                userid='chand';
This changes the pwd value in the user table for the user 'chand'.

Now, if the user provides the following special input instead:
UserID: 'chand' OR userid = 'admin'
Old password: Soccer99
New password: Potash9999
The resulting SQL executed by the database then is:
        UPDATE usertable SET pwd='Potash9999' WHERE
                userid='chand' OR userid = 'admin'
This changes the pwd value in the user table for the user 'admin', a commonly used ID for system administrators. It is true that the hacker would have to know admin's old password. That may not be difficult if the admin password is simple or has not been changed for a long time. Some large organizations that are not security conscious use a common password for the admin accounts of multiple servers to facilitate staff backup.

Hacking can be prevented and detected using a combination of access controls like firewall, strong passwords, intrusion detection system, intrusion prevention system, security training to programmers, vulnerability assessment, penetration testing (ethical hacking), rigorous testing of programs, inclusion of security practices in programming standards, and encryption. We will discuss these controls later.

Hardware Theft

As computing devices become smaller, they are subject to a higher risk of theft. The loss of hardware often also means the loss or disclosure of information. Organizations should provide users with notebook computer locks. It should educate users about the risk of theft and preventive measures. Networks should enforce passwords and encryption to minimize damage in case a device is stolen. Accurate inventory can aid in disabling the network access capability of lost devices.

Inappropriate Use of IT Resources

Today's employees are highly empowered in terms of IT tools. Every office employee in a medium to large organization has access to the Internet, email, a powerful PC, a large network folder and an office software suite that includes Microsoft Access. These tools help in commit wrongdoing, e.g., using the tools for non-work purposes to a significant extent or using the software to break the law, violate organizational policies, in harassment or in a way that will expose the organization to bad reputation or legal liability. It is critical for organizations to state clearly what uses are not acceptable. Research studies have shown that a large percentage of Internet traffic in a typical blue chip corporation is not for work purpose.

Why is this a security concern? Excessive use of IT resources for non-work purposes could affect system availability. Installation of unlicensed software can expose the organization to legal liability and introduce viruses or worms. Access to indecent web sites like child pornography or terrorist sites can incriminate an organization.

Identity Theft

Increasing personal information is stored electronically that can be accessed via a network. This is why criminals are more and more interested in stealing identities to enter into contracts, make purchases or cross borders using the stolen identities. The increasing number of social media sites escalates this risk.

Identity theft may be achieved using a combination of malicious acts including hacking, shoulder surfing and social engineering. Social engineering means someone posing as a legitimate party asking for seemingly benign information and then step by step gaining security intelligence about the organization and the intelligence will then be used to aid in identity theft. For example, a visitor to major high tech company was able to enter an open office area on a Friday afternoon where documents, unlocked notebooks and memory sticks were lying on desks and some on the floor. The visitor politely asked to go to the washroom when sitting in the waiting area of the company. The security guard let the visitor in without asking him to sign the log and wear a visitor badge. After coming out of a washroom, the visitor followed employees through three levels of physical security. In this case, social engineering was achieved because employees were not well trained to follow procedures and challenge strangers. A common instruction to employees is to never hold the door open for anyone you don't know or anyone you know should not have access to the area behind the door.

An increasingly common method in identity theft is phishing. This means sending email to people to entice them to release their personal information or to entice them to access a hacker site that can tap their personal information. I just received an email claiming to be from RBC Royal Bank with the subject line "Sign-in Protection Activation". The text of the email is as follows.

RBC Royal Bank Customer,

Your account was recently accessed from a location we're not familiar with. Please review the activity details below:

Location: Germany
Time: Today at 12:10am EST
Location estimated based on IP=87.118.101.175

"That was me."   "That was NOT me."

If anything looks unfamiliar, RBC will help you secure your account to prevent people in the future from accessing your account without permission.

Royal Bank Online Security

Right off the bat I knew this was from Royal Bank. First, the name of Royal Bank in Canada is RBC Financial Services. Secondly, I know banks don't send unsolicited email to customers to ask them to perform a function on the web site. Thirdly, the signature line just says Royal Bank Online Security, which is too brief to be business like. Fourthly, the two links provided do not point to Royal Bank web sites.

Organizations should educate their employees and customers about phishing, i.e., do not click on links embedded in emails that you don't expect or recognize and do not respond to such emails. A phish is an email purporting to be from a legitimate organization asking for identity or account information as part of social engineering.

Internal Breach

A 2008 FBI survey indicated that 25% of security breaches occurred within organizations. This is probably a conservative number because organizations tend to report external intrusion more than internal breaches. Insiders have an edge because they don't have to beat the firewall and they know the people, the organization's culture and systems.

It was reported in New York City media in September 2010 that a software engineer of an IT giant company used his internal clearances to access user accounts, including the information of four minors. This is just one of many types of breaches. Other common breaches include internal hacking, password cracking and copying information from an unattended computer.

Spam

The extent of junk mail is not just a nuisance. It is a security threat. Employees may receive so many spam messages that they may not read carefully before clicking on a link or opening an attachment, therefore getting infected with a virus or allowing a hacker to install a malicious program. Employees may also give out sensitive information. Some employees may delete work related messages because they think the messages are spams. Organizations should take measures such as installing a spam filter program to keep spams out.

Sniffing

One way to gain unauthorized access to information is to sniff it in transmission. This can be done using one of the following common methods:

- Installing a sniffing program on a networked computer.
- Connecting a sniffing device to a router or switch.
- Connecting a sniffing device to a circuit.
- Connecting a computer with a sniffing program or a sniffing device to a wireless channel.

The sniffed data will then be analyzed and deciphered to achieve the goal of gaining unauthorized access to information. Wireless networks are more vulnerable.

Wireless Network

A wireless network increases the risk of sniffing because data travels in the air. It is also slower and subject more to interference by noise pollution and physical barrier. A typical wireless connection in an office uses wireless routers to connect workstations and portable devices to a local area network. A wireless router is also called an access point. The access point broadcasts its availability to a range of distance and computers and other devices can then connect to the access point. The access point is connected in a wired mode to a server. It is critical for an access point to require strong authentication for connection by user devices.

Software Theft

Software theft is harder to prevent and detect because it is less visible. Software theft can lead to legal liability if the licensed software is used by unauthorized parties. It can also lead to loss of competitiveness; imagine a software giant having the source code of its flagship product exposed! Software theft can be prevented with access controls, employee education and stringent procedures covering software update, storage and distribution.

Spoofing

This means obtaining access using false identity. It is not the same as identity theft as spoofing does not really use the stolen identity to commit a crime or obtain financial gain. Spoofing is used by hackers to hide the source of hacking. It can also be used by someone to send email under a pretended email address. For example, John Doe could send out email as Mary Amato without actually using Mary's email address. A simple way is for John to change the displayed name connected to an email address other than Mary's to Mary Amato.

Spoofing is also used by hackers to hide their IP addresses to fool firewalls and make it difficult for the police to track them down. Rigorous firewall and intrusion detection systems can serve to mitigate this risk.

A hacker can also spoof the media access control address to beat any MAC address filtering by routers and to implicate someone else. Strong encryption for wireless networks, rigorous firewall configuration as well as hardened work station and server operating systems parameters can serve to mitigate this risk.

Organizations can prevent email spoofing using advanced email checking techniques like digital signatures and adopting sophisticated firewall rules. User education would also help.

Virus

This is a common threat. A virus is a program on its own or is attached to a legitimate program. A virus can be contracted when the program is triggered, unless the subject exposed to the virus is equipped with the proper anti-virus software tool. Common channels of contamination are email attachments, downloading programs and program sharing. Even a Word or Excel macro is a program so it can be virus borne.. A virus may be a malicious program on its own or it may be a useful program that also contains malicious code, in which case it is called a Trojan. Here are the common payloads.

- Erase an operating system file causing the computer to misbehave or shut down.
- Copy or erase a password.
- Try to logon to a system using a user ID and guess the password, thereby locking out the user because of unsuccessful password attempts.
- Erase data.
- Log key strokes and send them to a hacker site.
- Copy sensitive data and sending it to a hacker site.
- Plant a logic bomb to act up based on certain conditions or at a certain date to cause the above damage.
- Pick an email address from the infected computer's address list to send a strange email along with a copy of the virus to other addresses on the address list, thus causing confusion or panic and spreading the virus.
- Disable the operating system's security settings.

A virus spreads mainly by sending a copy of itself by email. The common ways of getting infected are:
- Clicking on an email attachment or a URL that contains the virus.
- Opening a file that contains the virus.

Common solutions are to use frequently (daily) updated anti-virus software, user education about avoiding strange email and blocking program files that come in as email attachments.

A computer virus is actually equivalent to a bacterium rather than a biological virus. It requires a subject's action to spread, i.e., to click on the virus or virus borne program file. There is a specific cure for it; anti-virus software is analogous to anti-biotic, although the former is preventive and the latter corrective.

Worm

This is similar to a virus, but is more stubborn and it spreads faster. It is more difficult to address than a virus. To help understand its resilience, one could equate it to a biological virus. A biological virus is easier to contract than a bacterium as it is smaller and lighter so can travel more in the air and one can contract it just by being sneezed on or by touching a door handle and later touching the lip.

A worm travels on a network and can infect any computer that is on the same network. When a computer is on the Internet, it is widely exposed to worms. However, just like virus infection of a human body, a healthier person is less susceptible to viruses or bacteria infection. A perfectly healthy computer is immune to worms. What does this mean?

Once a worm enters a computer, it looks for the vulnerability that the worm was written to exploit. A common type of vulnerability is a security hole in a system software product like the operating system that opens a back door to worms and hackers. If the vulnerability is found, the worm will release its payload which commonly generates a high volume of meaningless but resilient packets to clog up the computer and the network. It could also disable anti-virus software and other security measures. The high volume of packets will achieve denial of service. Imagine someone programming a computer to call your phone continuously!

Worms are written to exploit system vulnerabilities. When the hacker community publishes a vulnerability in, say, a commercial operating system, hackers will get on to write and propagate a worm to exploit the vulnerability. Zero day exploits, i.e., worms that are written within a day from the publicizing of vulnerabilities, are increasingly common. This leaves little time for the software vendor to develop and distribute fixes (patches). Common solutions to worms are to patch (update) system software and to reinstall anti-virus software. Anti-virus software can only remove worms from the hard disk. To prevent reinfection, the computer must be patched with the latest fix that closes the security hole that the worm is exploiting.

It is widely believed that worms are sometimes used in business and government espionage. A recent example is Flame. Its discovery was announced on 28 May 2012 by Budapest University of Technology and Economics, which considered Flame to be the most complex malicious software (malware) ever found. This is a targeted worm, which makes it difficult for anti-virus vendors to study it. Flame can spread to other systems over a local network or via USB stick. It can record audio, screenshots, keyboard activity and network traffic. The program also records Skype conversations and can turn infected computers into Bluetooth beacons which attempt to download contact information from nearby Bluetooth-enabled devices. This data, along with locally stored documents, is sent on to one of several command and control servers that are scattered around the world. The program then awaits further instructions from these servers. According to estimates by Kaspersky, a Russian security company in May 2012, Flame had initially infected approximately 1,000 machines, with victims including governmental organizations, educational institutions and private individuals. At that time 65% of the infections happened in Iran, Israel, Sudan, Syria, Lebanon, Saudi Arabia, and Egypt, with most targets within Iran. Flame has also been reported in Europe and North America. Flame supports a "kill" command which wipes all traces of the malware from the computer. The initial infections of Flame stopped operating after its public exposure. Flame is an uncharacteristically large program for malware at 20 megabytes. The malware uses five different encryption methods to store collected information. This worm was digitally signed using a false certificate purportedly from Microsoft.

Source: http://en.wikipedia.org/wiki/Flame_(malware), accessed on June 27, 2012.

ACCESS CONTROLS

In Chapter Three, we talk about general controls as internal controls that are applied to a multitude of systems. General controls should be implemented as the control foundation on which application controls will sit. One of the major types of general controls is access control. Access controls can also be implemented at an application level. Some access control tools can be deployed at a general level and an application level, e.g., passwords. Access controls are also called security. In this chapter, we will discuss access controls that are commonly used in an organization, whether they are applied at a general or application level. In the next chapter, we will explore more technical access controls for specific operating system platforms such as z/OS (mainframe), Windows and Unix.

Access controls mitigate the risk of unauthorized transactions, unauthorized change to information and unauthorized viewing of information. They also support software change control and segregation of duties, e.g., by prohibiting a programmer from implementing programs without testing. Access controls also support application controls by, e.g., preventing unauthorized change to electronic bank statements that would compromise bank reconciliations.

There are three objectives in implementing access controls. They are integrity, confidentiality and availability. Integrity calls for access controls to prevent and detect unauthorized change. Confidentiality means no unauthorized viewing. Availability assurance will require access controls to mitigate the risk of system outage. You might wonder why we talk about availability here, since the controls against system outage are discussed in Chapter Three under disaster recovery planning and backup. The link between security and availability mainly has to do with hackers and viruses. These two malicious agents often cause computers to lose their functions.

How are these three objectives related to the control criteria of completeness, accuracy, authorization, timeliness, occurrence and efficiency? These six criteria are affected by access controls that ensure integrity and availability. A system without integrity will most likely produce inaccurate information. A system that is not consistently available will lead to untimely processing. A system that has no access controls will be vulnerable to a lot of unauthorized transactions.

Why don't we just use the six control criteria above as a frame of reference to discuss access controls, instead of focusing on confidentiality, integrity and availability? First, the six control criteria do not address confidentiality and availability. Secondly, access controls address mainly authorization and occurrence and have less direct impact on completeness, accuracy, timeliness and efficiency.

The three access control criteria are confidentiality, integrity and availability. Further, every access control will perform one of the following five functions:

- Identification
- Authentication
- Authorization
- Logging
- Monitoring

Each process may address multiple objectives and the extent to which each objective is met depends on the access control that falls into a process. Let's use a common system, automated teller machine (ATM), to demonstrate these five processes.

1. You insert your card to be identified.
2. Your personal identification number (PIN) is used to authenticate you.
3. Your daily withdrawal limit is used for authorization.
4. Your transaction is logged.
5. Try to use your card at ten locations on the same day, guess who will leave you a voice mail message before the end of the day....that's monitoring.

In the rest of this chapter, we will discuss the common access controls, i.e., access control techniques that can be applied at a general level and an application level. These controls are common to many operating environments and applications. Access controls may be manual, procedural, physical or logical. A manual access control involves mainly human review or authorization. A procedural access control involves mainly policies, standards or procedures. A logical access control relies mainly on software, e.g., a password.
A physical access control relies mainly on hardware, e.g., a surveillance camera.

ACCESS CONTROLS POLICIES, STANDARDS AND PROCEDURES

Procedures are instructions for users to interface with a system and interpret system information. Procedures are based on policies, which contain mandatory statements about governance, expected behavior and adopted principles. Policies are less fluid than procedures as the latter are used to guide day to day operations. Procedures are written to comply with policies. Because procedures are for people to use, they do not apply to automated functions. How then, do automated functions comply with policies? That compliance is achieved in two ways. First, policy requirements should be included in systems development user requirements and design specifications that we discuss in Chapter Four. The extent of such compliance, however, is often questionable. For example, how long should a password be? To address this, standards can be created. Standards sit between policies and procedures. They also sit between policies and system specifications. Standards are changed more frequently than policies but less frequently than procedures and system requirements. This does not mean that a change in a standard will not get propagated to a procedure or system requirement. What it means is that procedures and system requirements are sometimes changed even when there is no change to the associated policies or standards. For example, how functions are carried out by a system or manually may not be the result of a change in a policy or a standard. It may be the result of a user change request for a system.

Access controls are commonly called information security, especially in the mind of IT people and users. It is often auditors who think of security as access controls because auditors want to tie security to risks and other types of controls. Let's not be hung up about terminology here.

As stated in Chapter Three, internal controls should start at the policy level. Controls that require manual compliance are in the form of procedures and standards. Controls that require system compliance are in the form of system functions. Controls that are implemented by configuring system software like the operating system and a database management system (DBMS) are set in security standards. Procedures, standards and system functions are based on policies. Some procedures are developed based on policies. Some procedures are developed based on standards which in turn are developed based on policies. The need for a standard depends on the technical nature of policy compliance and the extent of automation. Computer systems logic and configuration are not based on procedures which are manual in nature, instead, they are carried out based on standards.

Information Security Policy

An organization should have an overall information security policy to define the overall security strategy and risk tolerance. This policy will tell employees why information security is important in the organization given the nature of information processed, who is accountable for the information security function, who are responsible for information security and the responsibilities of users. This policy should address infrastructure, software, people and information.

For infrastructure and software, the policy should state the corporate protocol for obtaining approval for security infrastructure and software installation. It should also state the requirements for due diligence security review and testing of infrastructure and software, by referencing to the systems development methodology and software change procedures.

The policy addresses the people component of a system by stating accountabilities and responsibilities. Responsibilities will be codified in standards and procedures. The information component is addressed in the policy by means of providing criteria for defining ownership and assessing risks.

The information security policy as well as supporting standards, guidelines and procedures should be posted on the intranet. New items and significant changes should be communicated to employees by email. There should be training on new policies or procedures to key IT employees and the affected employees in other areas.

The information security policy will need to be supplemented by security standards that address specific risk management and control areas. Examples of standards are password and firewall standards. The following is an example of a corporate information security policy, the Canadian Government's. Only the main body of the policy is shown here.

Treasury Board of Canada Secretariat

www.tbs-sct.gc.ca

Policy on Government Security

1. Effective date

1.1 This policy takes effect on July 1, 2009.

1.2 It replaces the 2002 *Government Security Policy* and the 2004 *Policy for Public Key Infrastructure Management in the Government of Canada.*

2. Application

2.1 This policy applies to:

- All departments within the meaning of Schedules I, I.1, II, IV and V of the *Financial Administration Act* (FAA), unless excluded by specific acts, regulations or Orders in Council.

3. Context

3.1 Government security is the assurance that information, assets and services are protected against compromise and individuals are protected against workplace violence. The extent to which government can ensure its own security directly affects its ability to ensure the continued delivery of services that contribute to the health, safety, economic well-being and security of Canadians.

3.2 Security begins by establishing trust in interactions between government and Canadians and within government. In its interactions with the public when required, the government has a need to determine the identity of the individuals or institutions. Within government, there is a need to ensure that those having access to government information, assets and services are trustworthy, reliable and loyal. Consequently, a broad scope of government activities, ranging from safeguarding information and assets to delivering services, benefits and entitlements to responding to incidents and emergencies, rely upon this trust.

3.3 In a department, the management of security requires the continuous assessment of risks and the implementation, monitoring and maintenance of appropriate internal management controls involving prevention (mitigation), detection, response and recovery. The management of security intersects with other management functions including access to information, privacy, risk management, emergency and business continuity management, human resources, occupational health and safety, real property, material management, information management, information technology (IT) and finance. Security is achieved when it is supported by senior management - an integral component of strategic and operational planning - and embedded into departmental frameworks, culture, day-to-day operations and employee behaviours.

3.4 At a government-wide level, security threats, risks and incidents must be proactively managed to help protect the government's critical assets, information and services, as well as national security. Advice, guidance and services provided by lead security agencies support departments and government in maintaining acceptable levels of security while achieving strategic goals and service delivery imperatives.

3.5 The management of security is most effective when it is systematically woven into the business, programs and culture of a department and the public service as a whole.

3.6 Deputy heads are accountable for the effective implementation and governance of security and identity management within their departments and share responsibility for the security of government as a whole. This comprises the security of departmental personnel, including those working in or for offices of Ministers or Ministers of State, and departmental information, facilities and other assets.

3.7 Ministers of the Crown, ministers, and Ministers of State are responsible for the security of their staff and offices as well as the security of sensitive information and assets in their custody, as directed by the prime minister.

3.8 This policy is issued under section 7 of the FAA.

3.9 Treasury Board has delegated to the President of the Treasury Board the authority to amend directives that support the policy in the following subject areas:

- Departmental security management
- Identity management
- Information and identity assurance
- Individual security screening
- Physical security
- IT Security
- Emergency and business continuity management
- Security in contracting

3.10 This policy is to be read in conjunction with the *Foundation Framework for Treasury Board Policies*, the *Directive on Departmental Security Management* and the *Directive on Identity Management*.

4. Definitions

4.1 For definitions of terms used in this policy, refer to Appendix A-Definitions.

5. Policy statement

5.1 The objectives of this policy are to ensure that deputy heads effectively manage security activities within departments and contribute to effective government-wide security management.

378

5.2 The expected results of this policy are:

- Information, assets and services are safeguarded from compromise and employees are protected against workplace violence;

- Governance structures, mechanisms and resources are in place to ensure effective and efficient management of security at both a departmental and government-wide level;

- Management of security incidents is effectively coordinated within departments and government-wide;

- Interoperability and information exchange are enabled through effective and consistent security and identity management practices; and

- Continuity of government operations and services is maintained in the presence of security incidents, disruptions or emergencies.

6. Requirements

6.1 Deputy heads of all departments are responsible for:

6.1.1 Establishing a security program for the coordination and management of departmental security activities that:

a. Has a governance structure with clear accountabilities

b. Has defined objectives that are aligned with departmental and government-wide policies, priorities and plans; and

c. Is monitored, assessed and reported on to measure management efforts, resources and success toward achieving its expected results;

6.1.2 Appointing a departmental security officer (DSO) functionally responsible to the deputy head or to the departmental executive committee to manage the departmental security program, and identifying an executive to participate in setting government-wide security and identity management direction and to represent the deputy head to TBS on all departmental security and identity management activities related to this policy;

6.1.3 Approving the departmental security plan that details decisions for managing security risks and outlines strategies, goals, objectives, priorities and timelines for improving departmental security and supporting its implementation;

6.1.4 Ensuring that managers at all levels integrate security and identity management requirements into plans, programs, activities and services;

6.1.5 Ensuring that all individuals who will have access to government information and assets, including those who work in or for offices of Ministers and Ministers of State, are security screened at the appropriate level before the commencement of their duties and are treated in a fair and unbiased manner;

6.1.6 Ensuring that their authority to deny, revoke or suspend security clearances is not delegated;

6.1.7 Ensuring that when significant issues arise regarding policy compliance, allegations of misconduct, suspected criminal activity, security incidents, or workplace violence they are investigated, acted on and reported to the appropriate law enforcement authority, national security agency or lead security agency;

6.1.8 Informing TBS of their department's activities related to the development of national or international security and identity management standards, as those activities relate to this policy.

6.2 Deputy heads of lead security agencies are responsible for:

6.2.1 Providing departments with advice, guidance and services related to government security, consistent with their mandated responsibilities;

6.2.2 Appointing an executive or executives to coordinate and oversee the provision of support services to departments and to represent the deputy head to TBS in this regard; and

6.2.3 Ensuring that the security support services provided help government departments achieve and maintain an acceptable state of security and readiness and that those services remain aligned with government-wide policies, priorities and plans related to government security.

- A list of lead security agencies and details on the nature and scope of their responsibilities under this policy are found in Appendix B-Responsibilities of Lead Security Agencies.

6.3 Monitoring and reporting requirements

Within departments

- Deputy heads are responsible for ensuring that periodic reviews are conducted to assess whether the departmental security program is effective, whether the goals, strategic objectives and control objectives detailed in their departmental security plan were achieved and whether their departmental security plan remains appropriate to the needs of the department and the government as a whole.

By departments

- Deputy heads are responsible for reporting periodically to TBS, on the status and progress of implementation of this policy and on the results of ongoing performance measurement.

Lead security agencies

- In additional to monitoring and reporting on their departmental security program Deputy heads of lead security agencies are also responsible for:
- Ensuring that periodic reviews are conducted to assess the effectiveness of their security support services to ensure they continue to meet the needs of departments and the government as a whole; and
- Reporting on their activities under this policy through current government reporting mechanisms, e.g., Management, Resources and Results Structure (MRRS), departmental performance reports (DPR) and reports on plans and priorities (RPP).

Government-wide

- TBS is responsible for:
  - Monitoring compliance with this policy and the achievement of expected results in a variety of ways, including but not limited to MAF assessments, Treasury Board submissions, DPRs, RPPs, results of audits, evaluations and studies, and ongoing dialogue and committee work; and
  - Reviewing and reporting to Treasury Board on the effectiveness and implementation of this policy and its directives and standards at the five-year mark from the effective date of the policy. Where substantiated by risk analysis, TBS will also ensure an evaluation is conducted.

7. Consequences

7.1 The deputy head is responsible for ensuring appropriate remedial actions are taken to address issues regarding policy compliance, allegations of misconduct, suspected criminal activity or security incidents, including denying, revoking or suspending security clearances and reliability status, as appropriate.

7.2 If the Secretary of the Treasury Board determines that a department may not have complied with any requirement of this policy or its supporting directives or standards, the secretary of the Treasury Board may request that the deputy head:

7.2.1 Conduct an audit or a review, the cost of which will be paid from the department's reference level, to assess whether requirements of this policy or its supporting directives have been met; and/or

7.2.2 Take corrective actions and report back on the outcome.

7.2.3 Consequences of non-compliance with this policy and its supporting directives and standards or failure to take corrective actions requested by the secretary of the Treasury Board may include recommending to Treasury Board that measures deemed appropriate in the circumstances be imposed.

(End of excerpt from Government of Canada Security Policy)

Information Security Standards and Procedures

An information security policy is at a corporate, high level and generally is not enough for day to day operations and system configuration. Standards and corporate procedures should be developed to take the information security policy to a lower level as a basis for defining system requirements, guiding employee behavior, educating customers, configuring system software and writing operation procedures. Each subsidiary standard or corporate procedure should address a specific subject such as password and firewall. Organizations can refer to professional sources like Control Objectives for Business and Information Technology (COBIT) and International Standards Organization (ISO) as benchmarks to assess the comprehensiveness of their security standards. ISO 17779 provides guidelines and a framework for organizations to implement information security. Standards should be supplemented with local procedures that fit each division and computing platform. In addition to standards, there are corporate security procedures for certain areas where there is little fluctuation among operating areas, such as procedures for reporting loss of equipment. The following is a common list of security standards and corporate procedures that large organizations should have.

- Anti-virus.
- Appropriate use of information and information technology.
- Cryptography.
- Data center.
- Disposal of data, media and equipment.
- eBusiness.
- Email.
- Firewall.
- Information classification.
- Intrusion detection and prevention.
- Loss reporting.
- Mobile computing.
- Password.
- Patching.
- Routers.
- Servers.
- Software design.
- Virtual private network.
- Wireless.
- Workstations.

Anti-virus Standard

Anti-virus software is widely deployed in organizations. Tools are controlled by people. Anti-virus software is effective only if IT people properly deploy it and users do not mess around with it. The anti-virus standard should dictate the layers of anti-virus software, the approval for deployment and changes as well as the need to regularly update the virus list (dat file in the anti-virus software tool). Layering means how many levels of anti-virus software protection an email message or a file is subjected to before being opened.

Appropriate Use of I & IT

This security standard should instruct employees as to what kinds of use of I & IT resources are not acceptable in order to support a strong security infrastructure and comply with the overall information security policy. Here is a common list of what is considered unacceptable.

- The use of corporate IT resources for personal purpose to a significant extent.
- Use personal IT resources to conduct corporate business, unless approved by a manager.
- Access, display, download, create, distribute or store any software, graphics, images, text, music, video or other data which are offensive and conducive to a poisoned work environment.
- Use the corporate network for sharing files such as music files, video clips, digital image files or software programs, unless for corporate business.
- Streaming audio or video from the Internet, unless for corporate business purposes.
- Use corporate resources to play games.
- Operate a private business or political activity.
- Misrepresent the organization's views on a matter.
- Discredit others in the organization through electronic communications.
- Send anonymous messages or impersonating others.
- Send chain letters or spams.
- Use offensive, threatening or abusive language in electronic communications.
- Use IT resources to discriminate against or harass, threaten or intimidate other employees or to create a hostile or humiliating work environment.
- Perform unauthorized network scans on, or conduct unauthorized access attempts to corporate systems, applications or services, or spreading viruses or malicious code to other systems.

Employees should be educated about this standard upon joining the organization and reminded periodically. For example, a login script can be implemented to pop up a reminder that requires acknowledgement periodically when an employee logs on to the network. This standard should be enforced with system controls such as using a web filtering software system to deny web sites that fall into the above categories and track the types and extent of Internet use. Frequent Internet users should be flagged for reporting to managers who can then assess appropriateness in relation to job requirements.

Cryptography Standard

The Internet has raised security concern in that sensitive information transmitted may be intercepted in the public domain. To mitigate this risk, information can be encrypted. Even information in storage may be viewed by unauthorized individuals when role based access rules are circumvented. Encryption can fill this void.

Encryption is based on the mathematical technique of cryptography. It uses a rigorous algorithm and numeric keys. The effectiveness of encryption depends on the robustness of the algorithm and the length of the keys. The cryptography standard should dictate when encryption and encryption related security measures are necessary. It should also define the stakeholders and configuration requirements of the public key infrastructure (PKI). We will describe PKI in more details later. This standard should also specify the strength of algorithms and length of keys.

What is the difference between cryptography and encryption? Cryptography means using mathematics in computer programs to disguise information to achieve security. Encryption means scrambling information with a secret key so that only the authorized people can read the information. Encryption is an application of cryptography. Other common applications include digital signatures, message digest and digital certificates. We will discuss these later.

Data Center Security Standard

A data center carries a high degree of security risk because of the concentration of servers, information transmission and information storage. It attracts a lot of hacker attention. The data center security standard should specify the physical security measures for location of equipment, access levels, locks and surveillance systems etc., commensurate with the significance and mass of servers, data storage and data communication facilities. It should address the location of building site selection and building construction to provide adequate disaster prevention and security breach prevention.

Procedures for Disposal of Data, Media and Equipment

These procedures should instruct management and staff as to the approval levels for disposing of different types of equipment, the disposal log, review of the log, updating inventory records, backing up information and sanitizing the storage media before disposal to prevent the leakage of sensitive information. The organization should adopt a robust disk sanitizing software product that prevents the information from being recovered. Such a product is independent of the operating system in the device being cleansed so that even the operating system logs and configuration parameters are erased.

Where data is stored in an old medium to which the disk wiping software does not apply, the organization should set requirements as to how the medium is disposed of. Examples of such requirements include shredding and sending the medium to a trusted contractor for destruction.

eBusiness Security Standard

We discuss eBusiness infrastructure in Chapter Five and the need to secure the infrastructure. The infrastructure should include security devices. The eBusiness security standard should document the requirements in building the eBusiness infrastructure and provide guidance for mapping the risks of eBusiness to security features.

Email Security Standard

Email is a business critical system because business communication with colleagues, business partners and to a less extent, customers, is done predominantly through email. Just remember what you did last time the email system was down. Being an easy and far reaching tool, email can be abused. Employees may use it to send indecent or illegal material. They may use it for personal purpose to a significant extent, e.g., to such an extent that the majority of email messages are for personal purpose. Organizations should have a standard to tell employees what is not acceptable. The standard should also say when email is not appropriate, e.g., when sending highly sensitive material. Confidential material should be encrypted and the organization should provide a standard tool and procedure for this.

Firewall Standard

Every organization that hosts a web site should have a firewall to protect its systems against intrusion. Large organizations should have multiple firewalls deployed across business units and in a layered approach to protect the network as the information gets deeper in the organization. A firewall is a security device with rules set by the hosting organization that define what is allowed in and what is allowed out. The firewall standard should provide criteria for locating firewalls, the types of firewall (e.g., rule based vs artificial intelligence), the generic rules, and guidelines for writing specific rules. It should also provide requirements for firewall software update and firewall administration. The logging requirement and associated independent review should also be stated. This standard should define the following:
- Extent of logging
- Log retention
- Change control approval and documentation with respect to rules and configuration
- Firewall administration responsibilities and approval
- Types and location of firewall
- Types of systems supported by firewalls
- Layers of firewall
- Reporting of rule infractions

Information Classification Standard

Information is the most important component of a system. The extent of infrastructure and software depends on the volume and criticality of information to be processed. Access controls are designed to mitigate the risk of information integrity and confidentiality. Risk assessment should be consistent throughout the organization. An organization should have a standard that guides managers to classify information based on availability, integrity and confidentiality. Standard labels like levels 1, 2, 3; top secret, secret, confidential; or high, medium, low should be used. Procedures, education, reminders and ideally automated tools should be implemented to support this standard.

The standard should prescribe the level of confidentiality, the place of storage and the channel of transmission that require encryption. It should also state when information should not be sent by email. For example, employee health information should not be sent by Internet email; password reset should be sent in an encrypted email; security diagrams should be encrypted in storage.

Intrusion Detection and Prevention Standard

Firewalls are important preventive controls. We discussed in previous chapters that preventive controls are not enough because fool-proof prevention is impractical in order to ensure flexibility and effectiveness of the business environment. Preventive controls should be supplemented with detective controls. The detective complement of a firewall is an intrusion detection system. This device scans allowed traffic and develops a pattern for assessing the likelihood of intrusion. It then either alerts systems administrators to take protective or preemptive actions, or if configured accordingly, the system will take the preemptive actions automatically. When the tool, usually a more advanced tool, is capable of taking preemptive actions automatically, it is called an intrusion prevention system. The intrusion detection and prevention standard contains similar guidance to that in the firewall standard. It states where intrusion detection and prevention systems should be installed, the types of systems (rule based vs artificial intelligence), criteria for rules and device administration as well as support requirements.

Procedures for Reporting Loss of Equipment

As equipment and storage media become more portable, they are subject to a higher risk of theft and loss. The loss of hardware results in the cost of replacement, information may be lost if there is no backup. Even with backup, sensitive information may be disclosed. Although it may be too late to prevent such disclosure or information loss, management should be informed immediately to assess the implication and take remedial measures such as informing stakeholders, changing business plans, changing system configuration information so that the leaked intelligence cannot be used against the organization and taking the lesson learned to strengthen procedures. Employees should be instructed on how to report losses and what immediate security measures to take to minimize damage.

Mobile Computing Standard

Employees are increasingly provided with smart phones and laptops. Quite often employees use these devices to send personal email and surf the net for personal purposes. This poses the risks of virus infection, clogging the network with personal messages and exposing the organization to liability if illegal material is sent. To mitigate these risks, an organization should have a standard that defines what types of mobile computing is allowed in the organization and that no personal devices are to be connected to the organization networks unless approved by management. These requirements should be supported by network configuration and monitoring tools. For example, the standard should say that messages sent over mobile devices for business purpose must be encrypted. The standard should cover inventory tracking of mobile devices. It should also address laptop computer deployment with respect to justification, approval process, physical security, operating system configuration and inventory tracking.

The "bring you own device" (BYOD) trend is developing. This means letting employees in their own devices like a smart phone for synchronization with the corporate network. While this may appeal to young and IT literate workers, it increases the risk of virus infection, compromise of sensitive information and hacking because the security of the personal devices may not be compatible with the corporate network in terms of security requirement. Organizations should perform a rigorous risk and benefit assessment before allowing this. If this is allowed, there should be a process for monitoring the use of new tools by employees that have not been rolled out by the organizations.

Password Standard

A password is probably the most common access control. We all have different passwords for different systems. The strength of a password depends on its length, change frequency, complexity and place of storage. The password standard should specify these parameters in relation to the risk of information being protected.

Patching Standard

A worm exploits a computer's software vulnerability, mainly a vulnerability in the operating system. An essential solution to worm infection is to patch the vulnerabilities by installing the fixes released by software vendors. It is important for a large organization to have a standard to specify when patching is to be done, how to prioritize patches when deadlines are tight, how to test the patches etc.

Router Standard

A router is a device that connects two networks or network segments. Many of us have simple routers at home that connect the Internet modem to different devices like computers, printers and voice-over-IP boxes. Routers are necessary for wide area networks and therefore also the Internet. A router has its own operating system which can be configured with different options of parameters. A router also has an address table that governs how data is forwarded, through which circuit and to which IP address. The router standard should indicate the following:

- Authorization framework for parameters and routing table changes.
- Standard configuration parameter values.
- Extent of logging.
- How to locate.
- Periodic review.
- Redundancy, i.e., provision of backup routers.

Server Standard

A server must be physically and logically secured. The standard should specify the physical security necessary depending on the sensitivity of information processed. It should also provide standard configuration parameters for the operating system; which is often called the "standard image". This standard should also provide for inventory tracking.

Software Design Security Standard

Many large organizations have strong infrastructure security but have neglected the need for robust application functions to fend off intruders. This is especially risky against unauthorized access by employees because they don't have to beat firewalls. Application access controls by means of robust design and programming is like homeland security, which is in addition to border control and necessary.

The software design security standard should specify techniques to avoid security holes being programmed that will open back doors to hackers. A back door is a path that leads one to privileged computer resources bypassing the normally required authentication and authorization checks exercised by the relevant applications, operating system and DBMS. Programmers should be required to check the validity and length of values input to prevent buffer overflow (overflowing the real memory in the computer and therefore overwriting program instructions loaded in real memory that could then cause a system to misbehave or shut down). Checking the validity and length of input will also prevent a hacker from injecting System Query Language (SQL) code to query user identity or related information.

Virtual Private Network Standard

Telecommuting is increasingly used to support a mobile work force. Some employees are allowed to work from home. Many organizations give employees remote access to the network to perform system functions that they can perform when they are in the office;

one of the reasons for this is to ensure business goes on in the event of a disaster, public transit strike or pandemic. Remote connections increase the risk of unauthorized access because people in the office cannot see who is accessing the network.

Virtual private network (VPN) is a technology that allows people to access an organization's network through the Internet and perform the functions that can be performed as if the person were in the office. That is, the network can be accessed virtually privately using encryption and enhanced authentication. This is not the same as web browsing or eBusiness. In web browsing or eBusiness, the user is restricted to what the web server allows; whereas through a VPN, a user can access everything that s/he can access in the office, e.g., checking pay statements, submitting expense reports and approving journal entries.

The VPN standard should specify the security structure for VPN, the extent of encryption, the depth of authentication, the approval process for users, the applications that are available through a VPN, the logging process, and the monitoring of usage. Some organizations have found that a large number of VPN users have not used the service. Keeping a list of VPN users who don't need the service wastes money and increases security exposure as it unnecessarily increases the number of virtual access points.

Wireless Standard

Organizations increasingly deploy wireless networks to increase flexibility and efficiency. Wireless data transmission is more susceptible to sniffing than wired communication.

The Institute of Electrical and Electronic Engineers (IEEE) has published wireless security standards which have been adopted by network service providers including phone companies and many large organizations. An organization should have a wireless standard to define where wireless can be deployed, the approval process for users to get on the wireless network, applications that are open to the wireless network and which IEEE standard should be followed and when. The latest IEEE wireless security standard is 802.11i, which calls for the Wi-fi Protected Access (WPA) 2 protocol. WPA2 mainly uses an advanced symmetric encryption algorithm that requires a key length of at least 128 bits for authentication and encryption, called Counter Mode and Cipher Block Code Message Authentication Protocol. The actual key used for message encryption is a derivative of the access point's assigned key, a random number generated by the access point, as well as the MAC addresses of the access point and the remote device.

Workstation Security Standard

A workstation must be physically and logically secured. The standard should specify the physical security necessary depending on the sensitivity of information processed. It should also provide standard configuration parameters for the operating system; which is called the "standard image". The standard should also require inventory tracking.

COMMON ACCESS CONTROLS TECHNIQUES

An information security policy sets the corporate, high level and mandatory requirements for access controls. Compliance with the policy is achieved by infrastructure, software and people. People are guided not only by the policy, but also by standards and procedures. Compliance with the security policy and standards by means of infrastructure and software is achieved by implementing automated security techniques and tools. Here is a list of common access control techniques.

- Access card

- Access control list

- Access log

- Active directory

- Anti-virus software

- Biometric

- Boundary checking

- Challenged response

- Compliance scanning

- Cryptography

- Disabling unnecessary system software features

- Disk wiping

- File blocking

- File integrity monitoring

- Firewall

- Honeypot

- Intrusion detection system

- Intrusion prevention system

- Locks

- Management or independent review

- Password

- Patching

- Personnel security screening

- Security education

- Single sign on

- Spam filtering

- Staff termination or transfer checklist

- Standard operating system configuration image

- Two factor authentication

- User profile

- Virtual private network

- Vulnerability assessment

- Web filtering

- Web site refresh

We will discuss each of these below.

Access Card

Building and computer room access should be controlled with access cards that contain electronic information to identify the card holder and the facilities that can be accessed. The access control system should be capable of deactivating a card that has been lost or is no longer needed. A change in access privilege such as adding a floor should be done by physically verifying the card and the card holder's identity. Card holders should be required to sign a form upon card issuance committing to inform management when the card is lost and committing not to share the card without management approval. The access control system should track all card usage. Access cards should be coded to indicate the departments where the employees work, the employee classification and the premises where access is to be allowed. Such coding allows the organization to deactivate access privilege with a few clicks for an employee or a group of employees, e.g., locking out unionized employees during a strike. An access card prevents unauthorized access and it is a general control as it is applied to physical facilities instead of specific information systems. The security assertions addressed are confidentiality and availability.

Access Control List

Users should be allowed access based on their job requirements. This applies to the breadth and depth of access. Breadth means the extent of information and depth means whether the access is read only, write, delete or all. A system has to be told who to allow access to what and to what depth. This telling is by means of an access control list (ACL). An ACL should first define the system resource, which may be a file, database table, system function, workstation, router, server or web site. It will then specify who can access the resource and to what depth. "Who" does not have to be a person, it can be a program or system function. For example, the payroll query function cannot update the payroll master file (table). An ACL can be expressed as a matrix with the Y-axis denoting users or programs and the X-axis indicating the depth of access. The parties having the right to access can be indicated in the cells. One can understand ACL better by going to a Windows computer, and finding Windows Explorer, and then right click on a folder and file, going to Security, to see who can access that object (folder or file) and the type (depth) of access. If this is your personal computer, you can define who can access the folder and the type of access, e.g., read, write, delete. The parties having access rights can be the administrator, the owner of the file or folder (who created it), any user names (that has a profile in the computer) and guest (everyone else).

ACL can be applied to any object. Common ACLs are applied in applications, operating systems, firewalls and routers. The subject, i.e., the party with access privilege, may be a user, a computer program, a system function, a job class or a user group. For example, a common ACL is one in a payroll system to restrict the system access to create employee profiles to the payroll administrators. An example of a general control using ACL is to allow only certain computers to go through a router by programming the MAC or IP addresses of the authorized computers on the router.

An ACL is a preventive control as it allows access only based on authorization. It can be applied at a general or application level and satisfies the confidentiality, integrity and availability security assertions.

Access Log

Logging is one of the five security processes. Activity logging allows the events to be reviewed and validated. It also provides a trail for investigation if necessary. Applications, operating systems and other system software products like firewalls should be configured to provide automatic logging. The extent of logging depends on the sensitivity of information. For example, a government system that processes alimony and child support payments should be configured to log all read and write transactions.

The medium used for logging should be reviewed frequently to make sure it is not full. In fact, the system should alert system administrators when the medium capacity is approaching the full mark so that the log can be archived and refreshed. Logs should be reviewed regularly and analyzed with automation to identify exceptions. An example of a log we can all relate to is the access record of entry to a building. The logging system must enforce review and keep track of the logs that have not been reviewed. Managers should be sent automated reminders to complete the reviews. Organizations should procure reporting software to translate technical logs to user friendly information to facilitate management review and such translation should be validated periodically.

An access log is a detective control and it requires review to detect irregularities. It can be applied at a general or application level and satisfies the security assertion of confidentiality, integrity and availability.

Active Directory

This hierarchical access authentication and authorization structure has replaced the primary domain controllers and backup domain controllers for the Windows operating system. It has the following features:
- Central location for network administration and security
- Information security and single sign-on for user access to networked resources
- The ability to scale up or down easily
- Standardizing access to application data
- Synchronization of directory updates across servers

Active Directory stores all information and settings for a deployment in a central database. It allows administrators to assign system security policies as well as to deploy and update software. Active Directory networks can vary from a small installation with a few computers, users and printers to tens of thousands of users, many different network domains and large server farms spanning many locations. Active Directory contains information about users, user groups, roles and access privileges etc. It is a formal structure of ACLs along with user authentication credentials. Active directory is a preventive control and it supports all security criteria.

Anti-virus Software

This is a "must have" internal control in every organization. The main reason viruses cause less headache for management today than say, a decade ago, is that anti-virus software is more rigorous. The software includes the virus detection and cleansing software engine and a user interface. Virus detection is performed mainly by comparing the suspected virus to a virus signature file in the software. The virus signature file, called a dat file, contains the signature of each active virus, i.e., a virus that is known to have propagated and still has a significant potential to travel in the Internet community. So what is a signature?

A virus signature is in some ways similar to a human signature. To be more precise, it consists of an almost unique identification of the virus. However, unlike human signatures, a virus signature is not created by the virus writer. It is not an agent that allows the virus to multiply. A virus multiplies by way of sending itself to different computers either by email or another widespread Internet channel.

When a virus propagates, anti-virus software vendors study the virus as to what damage it can do and how the damage is done. It looks for a sequence of bits in the virus that can uniquely identify it. In some ways, this sequence is like DNA. The length of this sequence should be long enough to prevent false positive but also not too long so as to quickly trap a virus. This sequence is called the signature. The vendor then adds this signature to the signature file that contains thousands of virus signatures, i.e., for the viruses that are still active. The anti-virus software vendor also updates the repository of virus description available on its web site that talks about the extent of propagation and pay load (damage) of each active virus.

Anti-virus software vendors make the signature file available for download by its customers. In fact, most vendors have configured the anti-virus software to check the vendor's site to download the latest file. The customary practice is daily checking.

When a virus is found, the software will remove the virus from the infected file. The anti-virus software tool can also be configured to quarantine the infected instead of removing the virus to allow the user organization to study the infected file for, e.g., forensic purpose. How does the anti-virus software know there is a virus? Well, every program file, including a Word or Excel macro, will be scanned for comparison with the signatures. If there is a match, that program file or macro is deemed to be infected and the virus removal or file quarantine action will be engaged. This happens in the background and is usually transparent to the user.

Organizations should have a standard configuration for anti-virus software and instruct users not to change the settings. Anti-virus software should be installed at multiple layers for redundancy to achieve defense in depth. In a large organization, there should be three layers, which have to do with the fact that viruses mainly infect by email.

Anti-virus should be installed on the Internet email server to scan all incoming Internet mail. It should also be installed on the local email servers to scan internal email and Internet email that has passed the Internet email server. The latter will provide redundancy, i.e., an extra level of protection in case the Internet email server anti-virus software is not up to date. Finally, anti-virus software should be installed on every server and every workstation. This is to detect any virus that does not come through by email or that comes in by email and has somehow bypassed the Internet email server and the local email servers virus scanning. Why is a server other than an email server at risk? Well, if the server accepts file transfers, it is at risk. A non-email server is also at risk because it may get infected from software installation.

Virus writers and hackers have solicited users and organizations about their interest in anti-virus software and posted faked anti-virus solution and dat files. Organizations should download dat files only from authorized sources and such downloading should be centralized to prevent users from being hoaxed.

Although anti-virus software detects viruses, it is a preventive control as it stops a virus from infecting a computer. Because the email system is common to all employees, anti-virus software protects the infrastructure and is a general control. Anti-virus software addresses the authorization stage of the access control cycle and supports the confidentiality, integrity and availability attributes of security, because a virus can cause confidential information to be leaked, change information or bring down a system.

Biometric

This authentication method is increasingly used despite privacy concerns. For example, in Japan, a large number of ATMs use biometric. Many PCs and laptops are equipped with fingerprint authentication for login.

Organizations should assure users such as customers and employees that the biometric will be secured and used only for the purpose of authenticating the user in the specific system disclosed when the biometric was captured. To apply this method, the organization first has to capture the biometric. The biometric will then in recorded in a user profile and stored in a secure authentication server. When the user shows his or her biometric, e.g., palm print, the capturing device will digitize the image and send it to the server for comparison. If there is a match, the user is allowed access. Biometric should be encrypted when not in use. When a device needs to access a biometric, it sends an encryption key to decrypt the information. The server must be hardened to prevent hackers from swapping credentials.

Advancing technology is reducing the chance of false positives or false negatives to a negligible degree. Capturing devices must be capable of detecting artificial images of biometrics, e.g., a plastic finger. For example, in addition to reading the finger print pattern, the device can check the temperature, humidity and pulse of the finger.

Biometric is a preventive control as it serves the authentication function. It can be applied as a general or application level. The security attributes being supported are confidentiality, integrity and availability, depending on the system capability of the resource being protected with biometric authentication. The relevant security process is authentication.

Boundary Checking

This web based control is used to prevent SQL injection and buffer overflow. It restricts the length of data input to prevent insertion of commands that will cause system misbehavior. Here is an example of SQL injection.

Boundary checking is a preventive control as it prevents invalid data input. It is usually applied at an application level because such checking has to be part of the application's web interface. It covers the authorization stage of the access control cycle and addresses mainly the integrity security attribute.

Challenge Response

Sometimes when we register as a user on a web site, we are asked to choose or compose a security question and provide the answer. Later on if we have to access the web site to obtain sensitive information, we might be asked to provide the same answer. If our answer differs, our request is denied. This method of authentication is called challenge response. Another application of challenge response is to ensure that the access is being attempted by a human being as opposed to an automated agent like a robotic tool. In this application, the user is asked to read some letters in skewed, disproportional or italicized fonts and type it in a box. The challenge response method can be applied at the application or general level. It is a preventive control and supports all three security attributes of confidentiality, integrity and availability because the system being protected may contain confidential information, information that must not be compromised and be a critical system that must be available all the time. The relevant security process is authentication.

Compliance Scanning

An organization's security policies and standards should be implemented in hardware and system software consistently using standard images across the enterprise. Every computer should be configured using a baseline of minimum security parameters. Certain sensitive servers can surpass the minimum configuration. System configuration should be scanned periodically using software tools for compliance with policies and standards. The scanning should be performed by people who have no system administration responsibility in order to be objective. Compliance deviations should be reported to management and followed up for correction.

Compliance scanning is a detective control and it can be applied at an application or general level depending on the scope of the system software being scanned. It covers the authorization stage of the access control cycle and addresses all three security attributes of confidentiality, integrity and availability. The relevant security process is monitoring.

Cryptography

Cryptography is a technique to code and scramble data to prevent it from being read or changed without authorization. It enables information to be stored or sent across communication networks without losing confidentiality or integrity. Cryptography uses complicated algorithms and numeric keys. Its effectiveness depends on the rigor of an algorithm, the length of the keys and the security over the keys against unauthorized use. The common applications of cryptography are message digest, data encryption, digital signature and digital certificate. Each of these mathematical applications can be used in a variety of business scenarios.

Message Digest

Usually, cryptography is used to protect confidentiality so that only the intended recipients can read the data and that is achieved with data encryption. Where confidentiality is not the only concern and integrity must be preserved, a form of cryptographic function called message digest can be used. A message digest is a hashed version of a document or a message, determined using a hashing algorithm.

When the recipient wants assurance that a long document or message has not been changed along the way, a message digest can fulfill this need. The sender's computer uses a hashing algorithm to compute a message digest and sends it along with the document or message. The recipient's computer uses the same hashing algorithm to compute the message digest and compares it to the message digest received. If there is no difference, the recipient has assurance that the document or message has not been changed along the way, say, by a hacker.

The hashing algorithm computes a fixed length message digest from an original data string. The length of the digest depends on the algorithm and ranges from 128 bits to 512 bits, regardless of the length of the original data string. Because most documents or messages are longer than 512 bits, in theory, some different documents or messages will be hashed to the same message digest; i.e., the relationship is many to one. This lack of uniqueness casts some concern with respect to the reliability of a message digest, i.e., how does one know that a message digest for a document is actually the true message digest or is it really the message digest of another document? The proximity to uniqueness, or the reliability, of a message digest depends on its length. A 512 bit digest is more reliable than a 128 bit digest. However, the longer the digest, the slower the process is in hashing. Another factor in reliability is the sophistication of the algorithm. The current hashing algorithms use hash lengths of up to 512 bits. Common hashing algorithms are Secure Hash Algorithm and Message Digest. To prevent a hacker from changing the document in transit and substituting the hash, both must be sent using different channels that are highly difficult for a hacker to link the two objects.

Even with a 128 bit hash, this means the number of different hash values is 2^{128}, or 340,282,366,920,938,000,000,000,000,000,000,000,000. Although there is no theoretic uniqueness in a message digest, with such a large number of hashes, it is extremely unlikely that two different documents prepared at random will be hashed to the same value. If it is unlikely for two documents to have the same hash, it is even less likely for three or four...documents to have the same hash. This cryptographic process is irreversible, i.e., a message digest cannot be used to recreate the original document or message, so as to prevent hackers from doing reverse engineering to determine the actual document or message from the message digest. Here is a situation where the inability to recreate a document or message from a hash would be useful.

An organization makes frequent use of a long document or software tool that it has downloaded from another organization or network. The user organization wants to be assured that the document or software has not changed. The source organization or network can send a message digest to the user organization instead of sending the lengthy document, especially if the document is highly confidential. The user organization can then compare it to the message digest originally received along with the document or software some time ago. In this case, even if a hacker can intercepts the message digest, s/he cannot create the actual document or software. Well, if the hacker intercepts and changes the message digest, the user organization will notice the difference and follow up with the software vendor to clarify. Nothing is lost.

A key property of a hashing algorithm is that it must be structured such that a minor difference between two plain text data strings, when hashed, will produce two hashed strings that are different, but not necessarily just different in a minor way like the original data strings. This property makes it difficult for a hacker to reverse engineer.
A message digest algorithm should have the following properties:
1. Every bit of the hashed value is influenced by every bit of the plain text value.
2. If any bit of the plain text changes, every output bit has a 50% chance of changing.
3. Given a hashed value and its corresponding original plain text, it should be computationally infeasible to find another plain text string with the same hashed value.

Message digest is a preventive control and can be applied at a general or application level. If it is to be used in email, it is a general control. If it is used for secure transaction transmission, it is an application control. It prevents spoofing and covers the authentication stage of the security cycle. The security attribute addressed is integrity.

COMMON BUSINESS APPLICATIONS OF MESSAGE DIGEST

Now, you understand the mechanics of a message digest. What are the business applications? There are two common applications.

An organization that wants to post a critical document on the Internet or deliver it to another party and may be concerned that the document might be changed by a third party or altered because of network noise or errors. A message digest can be used to confirm that the document has not been changed. The posting or sending organization will compose a message digest of the document before delivering it. It can then deliver the document and the message digest separately. The recipient can then recompute the message digest using the same algorithm and verify with the message digest received. If the two message digests match, there is assurance of the integrity of the document. If the document is posted on a web site, the posting organization can download it and recompute the message digest, and then compare it with the message digest computed before posting. The two message digests should match. This is a good technique to periodically check the integrity of web site content to detect even a minor but critical change by a hacker, e.g., a key word in a contract or system description. Comparing two message digests is faster than comparing two copies of web site content.

The second application of a message digest is actually related to the first one. Instead of or in addition to ensuring integrity, the sender of a message may want to assure the recipient that the message is actually sent by him or her, not by someone who pretends to be the legitimate sender. As we discussed earlier, it is not difficult for a technical person to send out email as someone else. This is called email spoofing. To mitigate this risk, a message digest can be composed and then encrypted to form a digital signature. The digital signature will be sent along with the message. The recipient can then verify the digital signature to confirm that the message actually came from the purported sender. We will discuss digital signatures in more details later in this chapter. Confirming that a message was actually sent by the purported sender makes the message unrepudiatable, i.e., the sender now cannot deny having sent the message because the digital signature has been verified by the recipient.

Data Encryption

When sensitive information is transmitted in an inadequately secured channel or stored in a less than secure place, the information sender, owner or custodian may wish to encrypt it to prevent unauthorized viewing. When encryption is used, an algorithm transforms plain text into a coded equivalent, known as cipher text, for transmission or storage. The coded text is subsequently decoded (decrypted) at the receiving or retrieval end and restored to plain text.

Encryption uses an algorithm and a key to turn plain text into coded information which cannot be decoded without the same algorithm and the appropriate key. A key is used to make encryption unique to the same user or a small group of users. The purpose of encryption is to enable only the authorized users to read the data, so the encryption algorithm must be reversible, i.e., what is encrypted must be decryptable to the authorized parties. Because of decryptability and most encryption algorithms are commonly accessible, a key is necessary, in addition to the algorithm, to prevent encrypted data from being decrypted by just anyone.

The key is randomly generated by encryption software and it consists of a bit string that generally ranges from 56 bits to 2,048 bits. Like a password, the longer the key and the more frequently it is changed, the more difficult it is for an intruder to break the encryption. Safeguarding the key is also critical; for example, a key recorded in a computer without strong password protection serves little value in protecting the stored data; a similar weakness is to store a smart card holding the key in the same bag with the computer.

There are two types of encryption algorithm: symmetric and asymmetric. A symmetric algorithm uses the same key to encrypt and decrypt. An asymmetric algorithm uses a pair of keys, one key to encrypt and the other key to decrypt.

Encryption would be invaluable when a computer or a disk falls into the wrong hands, to keep the data protected. News about credit card numbers being exposed to hackers by merchants points to the importance of stored data encryption. Some companies store credit card numbers in plaintext.

Individual files or folders can be encrypted. Organizations are increasingly deploying hard drive encryption software that encrypts the entire hard disk instead of leaving it to the user to decide what files to encrypt. A pass phrase should be configured to invoke the decryption. Portable devices like removable disks and USB keys can be purchased with encryption software resident in the devices.

Encryption software should be configured to allow a limited number of pass phrase attempts before the pass phrase is invalidated and hence the data cannot be decrypted. There should be a key recovery process to guard against legitimate failure to enter the correct pass phrase, administered within the organization. If a thief steals a laptop and fails to enter the right pass phrase, say, after five trials, the disk becomes useless.

Encryption prevents unauthorized viewing and can be applied at a general or application level depending on what is encrypted. It addresses the confidentiality security attribute. The relevant security process is authentication.

Symmetric (Private) Key Encryption

In symmetric key algorithms, the same key is used to encrypt and decrypt the data. This private key must be kept secret for the information to remain secure; thus, a different shared key is required for each pair of users. Using the same key at both ends simplifies the process, however, that makes it very important to safeguard the key. A symmetric key typically ranges from 56 to 256 bits long.

A major drawback of using symmetric keys is that the number of keys to maintain can be unwieldy. Here is an example.

Two people who communicate with each other using encryption can use the same key. Three people who communicate secretly with each other should not use the same key, otherwise, the value of encryption starts to erode. For three people, Al, Bill and Cherry to use unique symmetric keys, Al will need 2 keys, one for communicating with Bill and another for communicating with Cherry, Bill and Cherry will also need 2 unique keys each; however, there is some overlap, because the 2 keys used by Al can also be used by Bill and Cherry, i.e., the key between Al and Bill is the same as the key between Bill and Al. So for a group of 3 people, we need 3 keys. For a group of 4 people, we need 6 keys, so far the number is quite manageable. The formula for calculating the number of keys needed is (n x n - n) / 2, with n being the number of parties in the group. For an organization with 60,000 employees who communicate with each other using encrypted email, the number of keys is 1,799,970,000; it can be difficult to manage. This formula is based on combinatorial mathematics because a symmetric key is used by two parties and since both parties have to know the same key, order does not matter, so it is the number of combinations of 2 in a group of n users that determines the number of keys needed, not the number of permutations.

The above analysis seems to suggest that symmetric key encryption is impractical. That is not true. Temporary keys are often used to encrypt data that travels on the Internet, for example, for eBusiness. Because such a key expires as soon as the user logs off or exits the web site, there is no need to maintain a large file of keys and the key management overhead described above does not apply. Common symmetric key encryption protocols include Data Encryption Standard (DES, 56 bit key), Triple DES (56 bit key applied three times), Wi-fi Protected Access (128 bit or 256 bit key) and Secure Socket Layer (128 bit dynamic key). Secure Socket Layer is used in eBusiness.

Asymmetric (Public) Key Encryption

The other major type of algorithm in popular use is public key encryption, which is based on a pair of keys: a private key and a public key. Something encrypted with one of the keys can be decrypted only with the other key. Generally, the public key is used to encrypt data and the private key to decrypt. The two keys with equal length but different values are generated by the same algorithm simultaneously and therefore mathematically related. However, the algorithm is asymmetric, so knowing one key is no help in being able to derive the other. A user wanting to receive confidential information can therefore freely announce his or her public key, which then is used by the senders to encrypt data. The data can be decrypted only by the holder of the corresponding private key. The private key is usually stored on the hard disk. It can be stored in a memory disk or a smart card. It is not memorized because the user is not asked to key it in.

The public key system reduces the number of keys to be managed because each user needs only two keys regardless of the number of parties involved in communication. Compare this with the symmetric key system, where a unique key has to be used to communicate with each person. The number of keys needed for a group of n parties to communicate with each other using the public key system can be calculated as 2n. So for an organization with 60,000 employees, only 120,000 keys have to be managed, as opposed to 1,799,970,000 under the symmetric key system.

In a public key system, it is critical to ensure that the public key is authentic and really belongs to its announced owner. A public key can be attached to a digital certificate, which serves to authenticate the public key. We will discuss digital certificate in more detail later in this chapter.

Asymmetric keys are typically 512 to 2,048 bits long. They are longer than symmetric keys because to prevent a hacker from deriving the private key from the pubic key, more rigorous mathematics is used. Public key (asymmetric) algorithms are therefore slower to execute than symmetric-key algorithms. Common asymmetric algorithms are RSA (Rivest, Shamir and Adleman) and Diffe Hellman.

Public-Key Infrastructure

A public-key infrastructure (PKI) is the underlying technical and institutional framework that allows public key encryption technology to be deployed widely within an organization and between organizations. It includes policies and procedures, the infrastructure to manage keys, key users, key owners and the key recovery process in case of loss of a key. A common tool to manage keys and key owners is a key directory. There are commercial software packages for such a tool. Often keys are shared between organizations, so it would help to have a standard protocol for key management and searching. One such protocol is Lightweight Directory Access Protocol (LDAP). It is called "lightweight" because it is easier to implement and migrate than earlier directory protocols like X500.

PKI is a general control as it applies to multiple applications. It is also a preventive control as it helps preserve confidentiality and integrity. The security process of authentication is covered.

Digital signature

The public key system also allows the sender of a message to digitally sign the message by using his or her private key. The recipient can authenticate this signature by using the sender's public key. Digital signatures are difficult to counterfeit and easy to verify, making them superior to handwritten signatures. A digital signature is established by creating a message digest of an electronic communication, which is then encrypted with the sender's private key. A recipient who has the sender's public key can verify that the digest was encrypted by the sender and therefore also find out whether the message has been altered by a third party. Here's how it works.

1. David wants to send a message to Elaine, "Will you marry me?"

2. Elaine has told David to digitally sign messages about their relationship so she knows they are really from him.

3. David's computer will first create a message digest of the actual message.

4. The message digest is then encrypted using the David's private key to form the digital signature.

5. The digital signature is now sent along with the message.

6. When Elaine receives the message and the digital signature, her computer also creates a message digest by hashing the actual message using the same algorithm.

7. Elaine's computer uses David's public key to decrypt the digital signature. Because the digital signature was created by encrypting the message digest using David's private key, by decrypting the signature, Elaine should arrive at the message digest created by David's computer. Now Elaine has the message digest David composed.

8. In step 6, Elaine had also independently composed a digest of the received message.

9. Elaine's computer then compares the independently computed message digest with the decrypted digital signature. The two should match. It they do, Elaine's computer has confirmed that the digital signature is genuine, or that the message was actually sent by David. If there is no match, Elaine's computer will alert that the digital signature cannot be verified and the inference then, is that the message was not sent by David.

One might ask, why bother creating a hash of the message for digital signature? Why doesn't David just encrypt the message with his private key to create the digital signature? Then Elaine can decrypt the digital signature using David's public key and compare the decrypted value to the actual message received. That will work too and it avoids the step of creating the message digest. The drawback is that now the digital signature is as long as the message, which is burdensome on the transmission network. A message can be ten pages long and creating a signature that long does not make economical sense. Keeping the length of the digital signature to a reasonable minimum is the main reason for hashing. Digital signatures have legal recognition in Canada and the United States.

Digital signatures can be applied to email messages, other forms of electronic communication, software downloading and software distribution. The purpose is to provide assurance that the source is authentic and the content has not been changed during transmission. Programs and data files can be digitally signed to enable the users to authenticate the files for origins and authors.

A digital signature can be classified as an application control or a general control depending on the scope of implementation. It addresses the security criterion of integrity. The relevant security process is authentication.

Some organizations use digital signature and encryption to authenticate and protect DNS lookup requests and IP address values, for internal IP addresses tied to highly sensitive servers.

Digital Certificate

A digital certificate is an electronic business card used on the Internet to certify that a web site being visited or the party conducting eBusiness is who s/he or it claims to be. It is generally used in secure Internet connection. When a user accesses a web site that requires encryption, a digital certificate is transmitted by the web site to the user. The user's browser can then confirm the authenticity of the digital certificate and stores the certificate on its hard disk for future reference. The digital certificate includes, among other information, the certificate owner's public key and the digital signature of the organization that issued the digital certificate.

Most digital certificates of large organizations are issued by independent organizations. This is analogous to an education certificate issued by a university to a graduate. A certificate issuer is called a certificate authority (CA). To assure the certificate holder and other users that the certificate was actually issued by the CA, the CA digitally signs the certificate. Two major CAs in North America are Verisign and Entrust.

A CA charges a fee for the certificate and exercises due diligence to assess the authenticity of the web site including a limited security review, interviews with management, financial review as well as confirmation and collaboration with third party information like industry regulators, to ascertain that the organization requesting a certificate is who it claims to be and that the server where the certificate will be placed is owned by the web hosting organization and secured. The CA also provides the software for key generation and processing. A CA may be internal. For example, a government may issue certificates to servers for secure intranet, or to users for authenticating the users. Most organizations that conduct eBusiness with customers engage external CAs. Where the data being transmitted between the web site and users are less sensitive but still encrypted, the web site may use a self issued certificate. For example, many universities use self issued digital certificates. The organization still has to purchase the commercial tool to generate the certificate and the asymmetric keys. Sometimes when you access a university web site for its hosted web based email system, you might get a warning from your browser that the digital certificate cannot be authenticated. People who access such an organization frequently usually ignore such warning, and that may be OK when you are not providing credit card, financial or other sensitive information. Such a self-issued certificate cannot be authenticated because the user's browser does not have the web site's public key to verify the signature or because the certificate has not been digitally signed.

404

A digital certificate typically contains the following information:

1. Serial Number: Used to uniquely identify the certificate.
2. Subject: The person, or entity identified.
3. Signature Algorithm: The algorithm used to create the CA's digital signature.
4. Issuer: The entity that verified the information and issued the certificate.
5. Valid-From: Valid-To: The expiration date. The date the certificate is first valid from. A certificate is seldom longer than one year. The longer a certificate is for, the higher the risk that the certificate owner's authenticity has deteriorated without the knowledge of the CA, in which case, the certificate is misleading.
6. The web site's public key.
7. The CA's web site.
8. Issuer's (CA's) digital signature.
9. The algorithm used to hash the digital certificate to produce the digital signature.
10. It may also contain the CA's public key.

How does a browser use a web site's digital certificate? Upon downloading the digital certificate, the browser will check whether the certificate is the same as that stored on the hard disk. If so, it has authenticated the certificate before and the certificate has not changed. If not, it will verify the CA's digital signature. Most browsers have the public keys of major CAs like Verisign and Entrust. As stated above, a public key is used to verify a digital signature.

How is the digital signature verified? The user's browser uses the CA's public key to decrypt the signature to arrive at the message digest of the digital certificate. It then uses the hashing algorithm stated in the certificate to hash the certificate to form a message digest. The two message digests are then compared. If they agree, the CA's digital signature has been verified and the digital certificate is deemed to be authentic.

Once the web site's digital certificate has been verified, the browser uses the web site's public key for secure eBusiness. Some web sites require users to have digital certificates. Organizations that give their employees remote access to corporate systems through a virtual private network (VPN) may require employees to use personal digital certificates issued by the organization.

Another example where user digital certificates are required is secure electronic transactions (SET). Under SET, a bank issues digital certificates to customers and merchants for the purpose of authenticating the merchants in credit card transactions. We will discuss VPN and SET in more detail later in this chapter.

A digital certificate prevents malicious web site spoofing or redirecting as it assures the user that the user is accessing the web site s/he intends to access. It can be applied at a general or application level depending on the business scope of device that is being certified. It covers the authentication stage of the security cycle and addresses the confidentiality and integrity security attributes depending on the access capability of the device being certified.

eBusiness Encryption

Secure Socket Layer (SSL) is the de facto encryption standard for eBusiness encryption. Here's how it works.

1. A user accesses a web site that requires encryption. Encryption is enforced by the web site, not a user.
2. The browser downloads the digital certificate from the web site.
3. The browser checks the hard disk to look for an identical digital certificate.
4. If there is a match to a stored digital certificate, the browser trusts the web site and goes to step 13.
5. If there is no match, e.g., this is the first time the web site is visited from the computer being used, the browser checks the downloaded digital certificate to determine the identity of the CA and reads the certificate's digital signature and the CA's public key.
6. The browser retrieves the CA's public key from a file in the browser. If the browser does not have the CA's public key, the browser goes to the CA's web site to download it. The browser compares the independently obtained CA public key to the one stated on the digital certificate (if it is stated). If there is a difference, it does not continue to authenticate the certificate and it alerts the user that the certificate cannot be authenticated; the browser does not continue with the transaction. If the browser has the CA's public key or if the downloaded CA's public key does not conflict with the CA's public key on the digital certificate, the browser proceeds to step 8.
7. If there is no matching certificate in the hard disk and the downloaded certificate is not signed, the browser gives the same warning to the user as in the last step. If the user decides to ignore the warning, the unsigned certificate is stored in the hard disk, and the browser continues with the transaction.
8. The browser uses the CA's public key to decrypt the digital signature.
9. The browser uses the hashing algorithm stated in the digital certificate to hash the digital certificate.
10. The browser compares the decrypted digital signature with the hash.
11. If the two match, the browser has authenticated the digital certificate and trusts the web site. The certificate is stored on the hard disk.
12. If the hash computed by the browser does not match the decrypted digital signature, the browser warns the user that the site is not trustworthy and leaves it up to the user to decide to proceed or not. If the user wants to proceed, the following steps are carried out by the browser.
13. The browser generates a 128 bit symmetric key.
14. The browser uses the web site's public key to encrypt the 128 bit symmetric key.
15. The browser sends the encrypted symmetric key to the web site.
16. The web site uses its private key to decrypt the 128 bit symmetric key.
17. All data transfers between the browser and the web site are encrypted and decrypted using the 128 bit symmetric key.
18. If the web site asks the browser whether it has a digital certificate issued by the web site for the user, i.e., a customer (consumer's digital certificate), the browser looks up the user's digital certificate and provides it to the web site. This certificate is

seldom used and its main purpose is to authenticate the user. It is impractical as it creates overhead for the merchant and makes eBusiness less portable for customers. If the web site does not require a user digital certificate, the process goes to step 17.

19. If the user has a customer digital certificate issued by the merchant's web site, it sends the certificate to the merchant. The merchant which issued the customer digital certificates should require the customers to use pass phrases to activate the digital certificates every time they are used.

20. The merchant's web site then authenticates the customer's digital certificate with the customer's public key which was generated by the merchant's web site and kept there.

21. The communication between a merchant and a financial institution when transmitting the credit card and charges information is similar to the SSL communication between a merchant and a customer.

22. When the web site is closed by the user or when the user logs off from the web site, the 128 bit symmetric key is discarded by the browser and the web site.

Because of the short life and the length of a 128 bit symmetric key used in eBusiness, it is believed that such a key has not been broken by hackers. There are 2^{128} different values of a 128 bit key, or 340,282,366,920,938,000,000,000,000,000,000,000,000 different keys. It is estimated that it would take a powerful computer a million years to break a 128 bit key. Why don't the web site and the browser just use the web site's public key for data encryption? There are two reasons.

First, an asymmetric algorithm is much slower than a symmetric algorithm and the system performance impact is significant considering the large amount of data being transmitted; e.g., someone can stay on a web site to do account enquiry, make purchases or trade stocks for hours.

Secondly, even if the browser can encrypt data using the web site's public key and the web site can decrypt it using its private key, what key will the web site use to encrypt data to be sent to the browser? A typical browser is not capable of generating a key pair. Even if it can, a web site will have to keep track of the public keys of numerous and an uncontrollable number of users because anyone can access a web site to make purchases.

How do you know a web site has enabled encryption? There are two ways. First check the URL at the top to see if it starts with https, if so, there is encryption. The letter "s" stands for secure. Secondly, look for a lock at the top of the screen.

eBusiness encryption is a preventive control. It is an application control because encryption is enabled by the merchant on an application by application basis. The security assertion of confidentiality is addressed and the relevant security processes are authentication and authorization.

Email Encryption

In most large organizations, the email security policy or standard provides criteria for securing email by means of encryption and digital signature. The corporate email system should support it. For example, the security policy may say that information rated as "medium" sensitive must be encrypted when sent outside the organization by email. Email messages generated by a corporate email system like Microsoft Outlook and destined for a similar email system, i.e., email applications using the Simple Mail Transfer Protocol (SMTP) like Outlook, can be encrypted using public keys. They can also be digitally signed using private keys. There are four degrees of security when sending email.

An email message can be sent:
in plain text,
encrypted,
digitally signed or
encrypted and digitally signed.

Let's explain the process for email encryption and signature.
1. Frank wants to send an encrypted and signed message to Gail.
2. Frank's computer is equipped with software to generate an asymmetric pair of keys.
3. Gail's computer is equipped with software to generate an asymmetric pair of keys.
4. Frank's computer generates the key pair and stores both keys on the hard disk.
5. Frank's computer sends the public key to the organization's PKI directory for sharing with other users.
6. Frank can also send the public key by email to friends or post it on a web site.
7. Gail will also perform the last three steps.
8. If Frank wants to encrypt an email message to Gail, Frank's computer encrypts the email with Gail's public key. The email program fetches Gail's public key from the PKI directory.
9. If Frank wants to digitally signs an email message to Gail, Frank's computer prompts Frank for a pass phrase.
10. If the pass phrase is accepted, Frank's computer creates a message digest of the email message and encrypts it using Frank's private key to form a digital signature.
11. Frank's computer then sends the encrypted and signed email message to Gail. The signed message of course includes the digital signature.
12. When Gail opens the message, the computer realizes it is encrypted. It prompts Gail for a pass phrase.
13. If the pass phrase is accepted, Gail's computer decrypts the message with Gail's private key.
14. Gail's computer also recognizes that the email message is digitally signed.
15. Gail's computer creates a message digest from the email message.
16. Gail's computer fetches Frank's public key from the PKI directory and uses that key to decrypt the digital signature. The decrypted digital signature now becomes the message digest that Frank's computer composed before sending the message.

17. Gail's computer compares the message digest it has computed with the decrypted digital signature.
18. If the two values match, Gail's computer is assured that the email was actually sent by Frank and it has not been altered along the way.
19. If there is no match, Gail's computer alerts Gail that the digital signature cannot be verified. There should be a link for Gail to click on to find out what the alert means.

How does an email program like Outlook generate encryption keys? The answer is it doesn't. It can only apply the keys in encryption and digital signatures. The keys are generated by encryption software which can be ported to Outlook. Large organizations will buy and implement the software as part of their public key infrastructure (PKI). A small organization may buy encryption software that does not require a PKI, e.g., Pretty Good Privacy, which allows two users or organizations to exchange and authenticate their public keys respectively. Public keys should not be exchanged in plain text Internet email otherwise they are subject to man-in-the-middle attack, as explained below. PGP uses an even more rigorous process of encryption than what is described above. It generates a session key like an eBusiness SSL session key for encrypting and decrypting email. It lets the sender encrypt the session key with the recipient's public key and sends the encrypted session key along with the encrypted email.

The above process does not apply to Web mail like Yahoo, Hotmail or university provided email accounts over the Internet. The encryption used for web mail is based on the SSL protocol, like that used in eBusiness. A web mail operator may enforce encryption for the entire session or only for the password. Digital signatures are generally not available in Web mail. This is because to enforce digital signatures, the sender and the recipient have to each possess a key pair, private key and public key. As we discussed under eBusiness encryption, it is impractical for a web site to require customers to have a key pair.

Not only does SMTP encryption prevent unauthorized viewing, it mitigates the risk of accidentally sending sensitive email to the wrong party. For example, if one wants to send an encrypted email message to david.c.chan@ontario.ca, but inadvertently types david.chan@ontario.ca, and the sender does not have David Chan's public key, the email program will notify the sender that the public key cannot be found; this should alert the sender to correct the address. On the other hand, if the sender does not bother to encrypt the email message, it will go to David Chan instead by mistake, instead of being sent to David C Chan.

The importance of email in terms of confidentiality is sometimes underestimated. It is no longer used just for message transmission. Instead, it is increasingly used to transmit business transaction data like insurance policy applications. Email is a business critical system.

Email encryption is much less frequently used than eBusiness encryption for two reasons. First, unlike eBusiness encryption which is invoked by the merchant and requires no action by the customer, email encryption other than web mail requires the sender to invoke encryption or digital signature and that usually involves a couple of extra clicks and a pass phrase. Secondly, the recipient may not have encryption software installed or a key pair. Because most recipients do not have email encryption software installed, the default practice of senders is to send plain text email even if the sender has encryption capability. It is important for organizations to remind users to encrypt and digitally sign highly sensitive email and to refrain from sending such information by email if encryption is impractical. There should be criteria to define sensitivity. Sensitivity, for the purpose of deciding whether to use encryption, mainly has to do with confidentiality. Examples of highly confidential information are health information, business plans, contracts and documents related to litigations.

Email encryption is a preventive control to preserve confidentiality. Because the email program is not specific to any application, email encryption is a general control. The relevant security processes are authentication and authorization.

Person in the Middle Attack

This is a risk in sharing public keys. In the above example, Frank and Gail share their public keys by going through the corporate PKI. This is safe. But if Frank and Gail work in organizations that don't have PKI, they may send their public keys in plain text email. That's risky. The plain text public key can be intercepted by a hacker and replaced with the hacker's public key. By doing so, the hacker can intercept all subsequent encrypted email messages between Frank and Gail. Here is what can happen.

1. Frank sends his public key to Gail by email and vice versa.
2. Hank the hacker intercepts both emails and replaces the public keys with his.
3. Frank sends an encrypted email to Gail asking "will you marry me?" Frank encrypts the email using what he thinks is Gail's public key.
4. Hank intercepts the email and decrypts the email using his private key because Frank was actually using Hank's public key that Frank thought was Gail's.
5. Hank reencrypts the email using Gail's public key, which Hank has earlier intercepted and kept.
6. Gail is thrilled and sends back a quick reply, encrypted using what she thinks is Frank's public key (but it is actually Hank's), saying "sure!"
7. Hank intercepts the email and decrypts it using his private key because the email was actually encrypted using Hank's public key.
8. Hank changes the email to say "not a chance!".
9. Hank reencrypts the message with Frank's public key, which Hank has earlier intercepted and kept.
10. Frank is now depressed and calls in sick for a week!

A PKI will mitigate this risk because public keys are centrally managed and authenticated. If two parties want to exchange public keys directly, the keys should not be sent in plaintext email.

Secure Electronic Transaction

This is an eBusiness encryption protocol that hides the credit card number from the merchant and the order details from the credit card issuing financial institution to preserve privacy. It requires a customer to be issued a digital certificate by the financial institution. This increases the cost of the credit card issuing financial institution and decreases the portability of the customer because the customer then always has to use the same computer for eBusiness or has to install the digital certificate on any other computer which the customer wants to do eBusiness using the same credit card. Secure Electronic Transaction (SET) serves to reduce credit card fraud. A common cause of credit card fraud is weak security in merchants' servers. SET is not popular because of the high overhead on financial institutions and inconvenience to customers. It is not widely used in North America.

This is how SET works.

1. A customer receives a "personal" digital certificate from the credit card issuing financial institution or an ePayment vendor like Paypal. The customer stores it on the hard disk. The financial institution or ePayment vendor may require the customer to protect it with a password or pass phrase, i.e., to use a password or pass phrase to activate the certificate every time it is used.
2. When the customer buys something on a web site, s/he sends his or her digital certificate to the merchant, which sends it to the financial institution. S/he also downloads the merchant's and the financial institution's digital certificates.
3. The customer's browser hashes the purchase order and the credit card (or payment order) information separately to form two message digests.
4. The customer signs the message digests to form the composite digital signature.
5. The digital signature is sent to the merchant which in turn forwards it to the financial institution.
6. The customer uses the merchant's public key to encrypt the purchase order and s/he uses the financial institution's public key to encrypt the payment information. The merchant forwards the payment information to the financial institution or ePayment vendor.
7. The merchant and the financial institution use the customer's public key to decrypt the digital signature.
8. The merchant and the financial institution independently computes the message digests of the purchase order and payment order respectively.
9. The independently computed message digests are then compared to the message digests in the decrypted digital signature.
10. Now the merchant and the financial institution/ePayment vendor have authenticated the purchase and credit/ePayment card information separately and independently.

Credit Card and Debit Card Encryption

The PIN is verified by the bank card chip. The smart card hashes the PIN and compares it to the stored hash. The transaction is encrypted with a symmetric key resident in the chip and the Bank's server. Each card has a unique symmetric key.

Wireless Network Encryption

Wireless transmission of confidential information should be protected with strong encryption. An insecure wireless connection exposes users to eavesdropping. Here are some examples:
1. Email can be intercepted to be read or changed.
2. A hacker who hijacks a session can replace a user's credential with false information that leads to the destination server rejecting the user's access attempts, thereby causing denial-of-service.
3. An unauthorized person can logon to a wireless network that is not secure and use the resources including free connection to an ISP.

Wireless security standards are evolving in the Institute of Electrical and Electronic Engineers (IEEE) 802.11 series, with 802.11i being the latest practical standard. These standards mainly address encryption. This is because the main risk of wireless traffic is eavesdropping. The encryption protocol that meets 802.11i is Wi-fi Protected Access (WPA). Here's how it works.

1. A device authorized to access an access point is installed with the access point's ID, called a service set ID (SSID), a static 128 bit symmetric key and the encryption software.
2. The access point sends challenge response text to the accessing PC or laptop (device).
3. The device encrypts the challenge response text and the SSID and sends it to the access point.
4. The access point decrypts the text and compares to the plain text that it sent out earlier and verified the SSID.
5. If there is match, the device is allowed connection.
6. The access point and the device generate a new 128 bit symmetric key for each packet exchanged. The packet keys are encrypted using the static key for each device.

More security conscious organizations have implemented WPA2 which uses 256 symmetric keys. In addition to complying with 802.11i, an organization may want to augment security with public key authentication by installing digital certificates on access points and devices.

WPA2 mainly uses an advanced symmetric encryption algorithm that requires a key length of at least 128 bits for authentication and encryption, called Counter Mode with Cipher Block Code Message Authentication Protocol. The actual key used for message encryption is a derivative of the static authentication key, random values generated by the access point and the remote device, as well as the MAC addresses of the access point and the remote device.

Messages transmitted using smart phones can be protected with encryption. For example, the Blackberry Enterprise Server (BES) model of Research in Motion (RIM) integrates the device with corporate email. It uses Triple DES or Advanced Encryption Standard to encrypt information between a Blackberry device and an enterprise server in a corporate customer. A different symmetric key is assigned to each Blackberry by the enterprise server. An enterprise server is operated by a corporate customer for its employees and customers and the organization can choose to change the symmetric key as often as possible without involving RIM. Blackberry Messenger (BBM) emails are encrypted using a common key controlled by Research In Motion (RIM) for all Blackberry devices and are therefore less secured than BES emails. A user organization may choose to assign its own common BBM symmetric key for the organization, for BBM emails within the organization, which, effectively, is more secure than relying on the common RIM BBM encryption key. However, internally encrypted BBM email is much less secure than BES email. RIM cannot decrypt BES mail because it does not have the keys.

Other smart phones can also be connected to corporate email systems using other software such as Microsoft Exchange Active Sync, but encryption may be less consistently applied because the exchange server or user PC connected to the smart phone may not enforce encryption. I think that BES provides the best security and best central control of smart phone connection to corporate email in terms of seamlessness and consistency. The BES model is also believed to make better use of battery life by using more streaming of email messages to alleviate the load on the hardware in the smart phone to holding and manipulating long messages.

Smart phones connected to web mail accounts use the SSL protocol just like using a smart phone to browse the Web.

Encryption is also used for mobile payments. For example, a smart phone containing an RFID can be used to wave at a reader like a small credit card terminal and sends the credit card number and expiry date in an encrypted form to the reader within 20 cm. The technology used is called near field communication which is about a decade old but has only recently been adopted for mobile payment. The phone downloads the reader's public key and uses it to encrypt credit card data.

Wireless encryption is a preventive control that preserves confidentiality and integrity. It can be applied at a general or an application level. The relevant security processes are authentication and authorization.

Limitation of Encryption

Encryption cannot prevent file deletion. Role-based access controls are important. Another limitation is that it relies on the encryption key, so there must be a process for key recovery in the event the key or the associated pass phrase cannot be obtained either because of human memory lapse, accidental deletion, misplacement of a smart card holding the key, or the departure of the staff members holding the key or pass phrase. Most encryption software tools include a feature for an encryption administrator to use a special key to recover a user key. Such a special key should be kept offline under joint custody.

How Encryption Works with Other Access Controls

Encryption is often used with other techniques. Examples include:
Encrypting a password hash
Requiring a strong password or pass phrase to protect an encryption key
Using a token or a smart card to activate an encryption key
Encrypting biometrics.

However, other technologies can be limited because encryption is used. The purpose of encryption is to prevent unauthorized disclosure. That means encrypted data can be read only with the proper keys and algorithms. Encrypted traffic therefore may not be subject to full inspection by other security mechanisms like firewalls, anti-virus software and intrusion detection systems. To enable these mechanisms to function effectively, network traffic has to be decrypted before the business applications process the data. The point of decryption reflects a risk based trade-off between confidentiality and the need to weed out malicious traffic.

Audit Checklist for Cryptography

To assess the effectiveness of cryptographic applications, auditors should carry out the following procedures.

1. Review the organization's information security policy to determine whether it provides sufficient guidance in information classification and application of cryptography.

2. Review and test the encryption software to assess whether it adequately supports the information security policy and information classification.

3. Review the PKI responsibilities, policies and procedures.

4. Review LDAP implementation and test the procedures, access controls and management monitoring.

5. Review the points of decryption and assess whether data custodians and owners are aware of the need for compensating controls.

6. Review user procedures and interview selected users to determine whether encryption is effectively applied.

7. Review contracts with CAs to assess whether responsibilities and obligations are clearly understood.

8. Where applicable, review the external control assurance report on CAs.

9. Review procedures and infrastructure controls for wireless networks to assess whether encryption provides comparable security to wired networks.

10. Review procedures and infrastructure controls for mobile devices to assess whether encryption provides comparable security to workstations.

Disk Wiping

The growth of electronic information is increasing organizations' exposure to loss. Unlike paper documents where massive access can be quite conspicuous, a large quantity of confidential information can be scanned by unauthorized people without notice in seconds. It is critical that users realize the importance of safeguarding information on computers. In this digital world, it is not enough to just tell users not to store confidential information electronically.

Many people think that deleting files and even emptying the recycle bin will permanently remove the files. Computer forensic specialists have proved that files can be recovered even after a disk has been reformatted. It is therefore crucial for an organization to adopt a fool proof tool for disk wiping and enforce its use. Such a tool should be applied to computers that are reassigned, sold, donated or returned to the lessor. A common product is called Blancco, which is adopted by many large organizations and governments. Applying Blancco to a disk seven times will render the data unrecoverable by even forensic data recovery tools. Similar data removal tools should be applied to smart phones. For example, Research In Motion supplies a tool to corporate customers to remotely wipe Blackberries and other smart phones.

Disk wiping prevents the unintended disclosure of confidential information. It can be applied at a general or an application level depending on the scope of the disk. The relevant security process is authorization.

415

Chapter 8 – Common Access Controls

File Blocking

Anti-virus software is never current no matter how frequently it is updated by anti-virus software vendors. This is because a vendor knows about a virus only after the virus has surfaced. To address the window of exposure created by new viruses that are not yet included in anti-virus software, organizations should adopt a practice of blocking executable (program) files in channels like email and downloading. A virus is a program, that's why blocking program files can help to guard against new viruses.

Very few employees have a need to receive programs by email. Most employees don't even need to download programs. An organization can block such file attachments and downloading, based on common file extensions such as .exe., .vbs., .com. Security conscious organizations on average block about 25 file types.

File Integrity Monitoring

We often check our work files using Windows Explorer and review the date of last change to ensure we are using the up-to-date files, e.g., when writing reports. In a corporate network, the high volume of files makes it impractical for someone to check for changes. Organizations should use tools to frequently check sensitive files for changes. This technique is similar to source code comparison discussed in Chapter Three. Because of the large file sizes, most large organizations can use hashing to check for file changes. You will recall from discussion above that a minor change to a file will change the hash, and that the size of a hash is much smaller than that of the source file. Thus, by hashing files in different time frames and comparing the hashes, an organization can find out whether a file has been changed and if there is change, the organization should seek the audit trail to support it. A good application is to check for changes to web site content to detect minor but critical changes made by a hacker. Another application is to check operating system files to detect rootkits.

File integrity monitoring is a detective control. It can be applied at a general or application level depending on the scope. It addresses the security objective of integrity and covers the process of monitoring.

Firewall

A firewall is a device used to protect a network from other networks. Any organization that hosts a web site, i.e., that exposes its network to the Internet, should have a firewall. Large organizations typically have many networks deployed horizontally and vertically. Horizontal deployment means putting firewalls at Internet entry points and vertical deployment achieves defence in depth by placing firewalls behind each Internet entry point at multiple layers.

A firewall's main function is to screen data traffic and the result of screening is either to accept the data or block it. It can be applied to both incoming and outgoing traffic, although the risk of incoming data is obviously higher.

A firewall screens data traffic basically using rules. Each rule will say what is allowed or what is to be rejected. A firewall can be configured to accept all traffic unless otherwise stated, in which case the rules are rejection rules. If the firewall is configured to reject all, the rules will be "allow" rules. Here is an example of an "allow" rule, that allows web surfing on the web server that bears the destination IP address, from anywhere.

Type	Source IP Range	Initiation Ports	Destination IP	Destination Ports
Allow	Any	80	142.107.93.143	80

Suppose the organization wants to block access from an IP range to the web server regardless of the type of access, it can implement the following firewall rule.

Type	Source IP Range	Initiation Ports	Destination IP	Destination Ports
Block	135,135.135.x	Any	142.107.93.143	Any

The above range includes IP addresses from 135.135.135.000 to 135.135.135.255, a total of 256 IP addresses under the current and gradually phased out IP address numbering scheme, IP v4. The number 256 equals 2^8, i.e., the last range of the number, each range consists of an 8-bit byte. Under the new IP address numbering scheme, this range would include 135.135.135.0 to 135.135.135.4294967296, i.e., 4,294,967,297 addresses.

A common hacking technique is IP spoofing, i.e., a hacker using an IP address of an innocent party. For example, a hacker may use an internal IP address of an organization to hack into the organization. An organization can mitigate this risk by blocking internal IP addresses from coming in. However, this has to be judicially applied. It is because a bank employee is usually allowed to do eBanking from work. The firewall then, can block all incoming traffic bearing internal IP addresses where ports 80 and 443 are not used. Port 80 is used for web surfing and port 443 is used for encrypted web surfing including eBusiness. Another way to allow employees to use the Internet to perform banking transactions or purchase transactions with the employing organization is to route all such traffic within the intranet.

There are basically three successively sophisticated ways a firewall can screen and block data: packet filtering, proxy and stateful inspection. These three methods can be applied cumulatively, i.e., a stateful inspection firewall can also use packet filtering and proxy filtering.

A firewall can be a router, an appliance with built in firewall software, a server with installed firewall software or simply a software tool installed on a PC. A PC firewall is also called a personal firewall. Personal firewalls can be freely downloaded from the Internet, but users should be cautious about the source, as the firewall may consist of a virus. Large organizations should not use freely downloadable firewalls and should not let employees do that, by removing the local administer privilege of employees to their PCs, so they cannot install software.

A firewall prevents hacking. Because it applies to the network, it is a general control. The security assertion addressed is integrity and the relevant security processes are authorization and logging.

Packet Filtering Firewall

This firewall inspects every packet and compares the packet against a set of rules to determine whether the packet is acceptable. For example, a certain range of IP addresses can be programmed in a rule for rejection. The rules can be applied to each packet using "and" or "or". The firewall can also filter based on the MAC address (mainly for internal firewalls and wireless routers).
Because a router operates on layer 3 of the Internet model, it is not capable of deciphering port numbers so it can usually be used only to filter IP addresses. A packet filtering firewall in the form of an appliance or server can inspect data at layer 4 and therefore also filter by port.

Proxy Firewall

A proxy firewall usually takes the form of a server with firewall software installed. In addition to packet filtering, a proxy firewall can check for malicious software and hide the internal IP addresses. A proxy firewall appears to the public as an internal host server and it appears to internal users as an external site. A proxy firewall operates on layer 5, the application layer and hence is privileged to all data in a packet.

Here is how IP address hiding works. Say an organization subscribes to IP addresses 123.123.000.000 to 123.123.255.255, in total 256^2 IP addresses, or 65,536 IP addresses. The organization will name its proxy firewall with IP address of say, 123.123.0.1. All the internal IP addresses can be numbered from 10.3.0.0 to 10.3.255.255. The 10.x.x.x range of IP addresses has been reserved by ICANN for internal use. Any organization can use this internally and Internet service providers (ISPs) know that such a range is not valid as routable external addresses. When a proxy firewall is used, an organization actually does not have to assign externally IP addresses to its computers and instead, and it only has to assign internal IP addresses. However, the downside is that if the proxy firewall is not functioning, traffic will come to a halt because ISPs cannot understand internal IP addresses; so the usual method is to still assign external IP addresses to computers but use the proxy firewall to mask the external IP addresses as internal IP addresses. What is the point in even using internal IP addresses if the only IP address outsiders see is the firewall's? Well, the firewall has to know which computer to route traffic to.

Stateful Inspection Firewall

Both packet filtering and proxy firewalls use rules to screen data traffic. A stateful inspection firewall, also operating at Layer 5, inspects the entire series of packets for a message instead of each packet in isolation. This requires more computing power. Every packet inspected is checked for context within the message to see if the packet is suspicious or invalid. For example, the firewall can check whether a packet bears the same session ID as the current session in which the packet is trying to join to detect a hacker trying to inject data to an otherwise genuine eBusiness transaction. A session ID is an ID assigned by a web server to a user upon the user initiating connection with the server. It helps the web server keep track of user activities for problem solving, customer relationship management, and knowing what a user has requested so the requested information can be provided to the right user. A stateful inspection firewall can also check the relationship between components in a packet, e.g., checking the length of all packets for a session within a certain time slot for port 443 (eBusiness), or for port 25 (SMTP mail) to assess whether the traffic is legitimate; a session sending an usually large volume of data for a stock trading transaction is suspicious. A stateful inspection firewall takes the form of a server or an appliance. An appliance is a security appliance that comes preloaded with software. Its size is like that of a digital video disk player.

Personal Firewall

An increasing number of personal computer (PC) users are installing personal firewalls on their computers. This can be downloaded as freeware or purchased by an organization to be installed on workstations and laptops. Modern operating systems include this as an essential feature. Personal firewall operates at layer 5 so is privileged to all incoming data. A personal firewall generally operates in a silent mode because an organization may not turn on all of the alert options so as not to confuse users and also to conserve resources and hence maintain a high level of system efficiency. A personal firewall is the last firewall gate because by now, the traffic has passed more than one corporate firewall.

Because a personal firewall affects only one computer, an organization has a lot of choice in terms of tailoring the configuration to computers that contain highly sensitive information and are of high risk.

Critical Properties of a Firewall

For a firewall to be effective, it should have the following characteristics.

1. It should not be remotely configurable. That is, the change in configuration and rules should be done on site to prevent the firewall from being abused by a hacker. In the event that remote administration is absolutely necessary, e.g., when the premises cannot be accessed, rigorous two factor authentication should be used. Two factor authentication means using something the user knows and something the user possesses; ATM is a simple example. The firewall should be configured to send alerts to management when it is remotely managed.

2. It should log all traffic and the log should be analyzed using data mining software to detect anomaly.

3. The log should be monitored to avoid being full.

4. A firewall should be configured to fail close. That is, if for any reason, the firewall fails, e.g., the log is full, no traffic can go through. A firewall should be configured to deny all traffic by default, i.e., only the traffic that satisfies a rule is allowed.

5. After the first rule of global allow or global deny, rules should be put in to reject or allow based on criteria. A global deny rule will still admit traffic if there is a subsequent "allow" rule. Traffic that meets the "allow" conditions will be admitted. Similarly, rules that follow the global allow rule will determine what traffic will be admitted or denied. An organization that places a global deny rule will save time and be more secure in defining what should be denied.

6. After the global rule, rules will be exercised sequentially; so rule placement has to be careful, especially for deny rules. For example, after the global rule, if the next rule is to deny all access from IP addressed in a certain country, all such access will be denied even if there is a later rule to admit email traffic from that country. This is because a deny rule after the global rule will essentially drop the traffic. The same does not hold true for an "accept" rule, because accepted traffic does not go pass the firewall immediately, it is subject to further rules. This means the more rules there are, the slower the network will be; so it is important to periodically review firewall rules and remove unneeded ones.

   Here is an example.
   - A general rule to deny all is put in place.
   - A more specific rule allows access from any IP address to any IP address as long as certain ports are used, e.g., port 80, port 25 (SMTP mail) or port 443.
   - A lower level specific rule can be put in place to block certain IP addresses.

7. Firewall rules should be subject to the change control procedures that discussed in Chapter Three.

8. A log retention schedule should be approved by management and audited periodically for effective compliance. Firewall logs are analyzed by intrusion detection systems and intrusion prevention systems. They are also used in forensic investigations.

9. Firewall logging should be monitored to avoid the log getting full and the resultant logging failure.

Firewall Placement

Theoretically, a firewall should be placed on the outermost edge of an organization's network. However, it is often impractical to do all of the screening at that outside location in order to avoid unnecessary performance degradation of the network.

A large organization should have multiple layers of firewall. This approach is called defence in depth. In addition, an organization needs to deploy at least one firewall at each network entry point; that is, installing firewalls horizontally. It is not unusual for a large organization to have tens of firewalls installed vertically and horizontally. While it is easier to understand the need for horizontal firewall placement, the vertical placement, i.e., defence in depth, warrants more discussion. Here is an example.

A bank may place a packet filtering firewall in front of each web server or a cluster of horizontal web servers. We say a cluster because seldom is one web server enough to handle all the incoming web traffic, so a cluster is used for load balancing and redundancy. Behind the web servers, the bank can place another layer of firewalls to inspect traffic before the application servers are accessed.

The rules in the external firewalls are less rigorous than those in the inner firewalls. This is because the web server should not contain confidential information. The rules will be targeted more at preventing denial of service attacks, defacement and change of critical information like posted interest rates.

When a transaction request needs to get past the web server, e.g., an eBanking transaction, the web server will direct the request to an authentication server to authenticate the customer. The transaction is then subject to screening by an internal firewall, which has more rigorous rules and most likely is more advanced, e.g., a proxy firewall. The area between an external firewall and the first internal firewall is called a demilitarized zone (DMZ). In military terms, a DMZ is the frontier between two countries where military activity is not permitted. It is not as safe as homeland.

The common network devices situated in the DMZ are web servers, external email servers and external domain name servers.

An external email server takes Internet email into the organization and vice versa. Because of the high volume of external network traffic, placing the external email server in the DMZ will lessen the traffic congestion in the interior network. Further, this server is also a common attack target. Although the server should be rigorously configured to prevent attack and is behind a packet filtering firewall, when it is attacked, the effect is somewhat limited because the internal network is not compromised. The worst result of such an attack is the organization's inability to receive or send Internet email temporarily. Although email messages could be compromised, an organization can install anti-virus software and use encryption to protect messages.

A web server is typically in the DMZ for the same reason as placing an external email server in the DMZ. The web server is the most common target of attack and it should be kept away from the internal network to protect homeland. At the same time, there should be reasonable protection, by means of placing it behind a packet filtering firewall.

An external DNS translates deep URLs to local IP addresses. Because the deep URL is received from an ISP without IP address resolution, the external DNS has to be placed at the network perimeter, i.e., the DMZ. It cannot be in front of the web server because the latter is the first server to receive incoming data traffic.

Honeypot

An organization may install a server that appears to process business transactions but does not. It is usually placed right behind the DMZ to attract hackers. The organization can use this server to capture hacker activities and analyze and learn from them to strengthen its security.

Intrusion Detection System

A firewall is critical to blocking malicious web traffic. It is not fool proof. Highly skilled and determined hackers will craft attacks that look very much like legitimate requests or transactions. For example, a hacker may piggyback on a web transaction and once inside the network, the extra code will generate widespread attack. This is where an intrusion detection system (IDS) is useful to mitigate the risk.

An IDS inspects data traffic that has passed firewalls and checks for anomaly. An anomaly is usually determined in aggregate, e.g., studying the pattern of traffic over a period and comparing the pattern to a base that has been built up and determined to be normal. A common anomaly is a surge is traffic from a range of IP addresses. Even though every session satisfies all the firewall rules for acceptance, the overall pattern is concerning. When an IDS determines an anomaly, it sends an alert to a security analyst, who will assess the alert based on established procedures. The procedures may call for escalation to management, collaborating with trading partners, IT service providers or security agencies as well as taking actions to block the traffic by placing a rule on the exterior firewall etc. Similar to a firewall, an IDS can use rules or mathematical modelling to identify anomalies. For example, if a worm attack is going around in the community, a rule can be placed on an IDS to look for a packet of certain size and of a certain sequence (similar to a virus signature) that arrives in a high frequency. An IDS that uses mathematical modelling is similar to stateful inspection firewall blocking; it studies traffic pattern and measures it against a baseline to detect rogue traffic. The baseline should be updated over time. This is also somewhat similar to neural network that learns from doing.

An IDS can be placed on a network to scan all traffic that passes the network point or it can be connected to a server to inspect all traffic that has entered the server. The former is more economical while the latter can be more granular but is less timely because the traffic is already in the server. Organizations should use a mix of both. Certain highly sensitive servers should have their own IDS.

An IDS should be placed at each critical juncture of the internal network. With respect to its relationship to horizontal firewalls, there might be an IDS for several horizontal network access points. An IDS can also be placed behind a server or a cluster of servers, in which case the IDS is called a host based IDS. An IDS addresses the security assertion of integrity and the relevant security process is authorization.

The rules (also called signatures) and criteria for anomaly determination should be updated regularly to prevent obsolescence that slows down data analysis and also to account for new threats. Software and security vendors send information about new threats to their customers. Some not-for-profit organizations also provide security alerts. One of them is Carnegie Mellon Software Engineering Institute. Organizations should be careful about interpreting security alerts from black hat sites which are hosted mainly for hackers. Although these sites provide some good information about security threats, there are sometimes hoaxes and the solutions may contain viruses.

Intrusion Prevention System

An intrusion prevention system (IPS) is really a highly automated IDS. Some people call it an IDS on steroid. It can be configured to alert a security analyst to take preventive action or it might take the action automatically. An immediate action taken by IPS without the judgement of a security analyst is usually sending an instruction to the firewall administrator to put in a firewall rule to block further traffic of that nature, or if the IPS is connected to a firewall, to insert such a rule to the firewall directly.

An IPS can take preventive actions on its own or send alerts to a security analyst. Usually, the less urgent anomalies or rule infraction will cause an alert to the security analyst. Also, if the likelihood of false positive is high, the IPS should be configured to treat those scenarios by sending alerts to the security analyst to investigate before taking pre-emptive actions. A security analyst may have to contact the intruding organization to confirm whether the traffic is the result of an error, miscommunication, misunderstanding or an actual attack. There should be guidelines to help the security analyst, and to help that person to even decide whether to contact the "intruding" organization, as doing so may tip off the intruder. The incident response procedures we discuss in Chapter Three apply here. The procedures should address the need to document everything and make sure the audit trail is captured, which might be needed to investigate the incident and for forensic purpose. The criteria for escalation to different levels of management for decisions on network adjustment, new firewall rules to block traffic to fend off intrusion and forensic investigation should be clearly stated in the incident response procedures and such decisions and communications should be thoroughly documented. An IPS encompasses all the functions of an IDS. In addition, it has the ability to block traffic of the same pattern or anomaly. Most large organizations deploy a combination of IDS and IPS.

One might question the need for an IPS if the firewall is made stronger. Well, the rules and analysis performed at the firewall level cannot be too exhaustive, otherwise, it will slow down network traffic. The IPS will look at "iffy" scenarios and pattern. In other words, if a traffic stream (transaction) has a fairly high probability of being malicious, say more than 15%, it should be caught by a firewall. The rest is then left to the IPS. A firewall slows down the network but an IPS does not, because an IPS only inspects a copy of the network traffic passed on by the firewall, not the original.

An IPS should be placed at each critical juncture of the internal network. With respect to its relationship to horizontal firewalls, there might be an IPS for several horizontal network access points. An IPS can also be placed behind a server or a cluster of servers, in which case the IPS is called a host based IPS. A host based IPS detects malicious traffic that has just entered a server. The risk is higher because the traffic is already in the server. Analysis has to be quick so that remedy can be taken before deep damage is done. A host based IPS augments network IPS and is intended for highly critical servers. It has rules and analyses that can be tailored to the application supported by the host.

The rules and criteria should be updated regularly to prevent obsolescence that slows down data analysis and also to account for new threats. Software and security vendors send information about new threats to their customers. An IPS addresses the security assertion of integrity and the relevant security process is authorization.

Lock

Physical facilities should be restricted with access cards. The access cards will unlock the door. In addition, sensitive equipment should be secured with robust locks that can be opened with smart cards or keys that cannot be duplicated without notifying the key manufacturer. Laptops should be issued with locks that will work when the laptops are docked or loose. There should be instructions given to laptop users to lock their laptops to fixtures while unattended, and organizations should periodically patrol for compliance.

For a highly sensitive device or room, a lock that requires both keys or combinations should be deployed.

A lock prevents unauthorized access and it can be a general control or an application control depending on the scope of deployment. The security assertions supported are integrity and availability.

Management and Independent Review

Organizations continue to empower employees and customers with technology to expedite transaction processing. This results in a shift of manual to automated controls. While expediting transaction processing by giving users automated tools and direct access, an organization can mitigate the resultant risk of unauthorized transactions by using technology to perform rigorous analysis to produce exception reports for management to review. The reviewer, in some cases, may not be the manager of the user being reviewed. That's acceptable if the reviewer is independent of the process being reviewed and knowledgeable about the process. Here are the common access controls that involve exception reporting as well as management and independent review.

- Review repeatedly unsuccessful access attempts to assess the extent of policy compliance and user education as well as the practicality of the access controls.

- Periodic review of access rights to confirm appropriateness.

- Pre-approval of user profile and access control list changes and then verify the implemented changes to the pre-approvals.

- Pre-approval of firewall rule changes and then verify the implemented changes to the pre-approvals.

- Network layout changes, pre-approve and post-review.

- Review of access logs to identify anomaly.

- Review of security incidents to ensure correction plan is in place.

- Review of summarized intrusion detection and prevention system reports to ensure mitigation actions have taken place.

- Review of system administration event log, in the form of exception reports generated using software to let management know of suspicious system administrator activities.

Management and independent review can be a preventive or detective control depending on the timing of review. It addresses mainly the authorization phase of the security cycle and the integrity security criterion. It can be applied at an application or general level.

Access controls also support management and independent review by preventing change to information that is subject to review, e.g., by preventing a treasury analyst from changing electronic bank statement information to hide reconciling items.

Password

This preventive control to authenticate users is simple and inexpensive. Its strength depends on the length, complexity and frequency of change. A password should be the first line of authentication. For more sensitive systems, two-factor authentication or biometric should be used to replace or augment passwords. Two factor authentication means requiring the user to provide something specific that s/he knows and something specific that s/he possesses, e.g., ATM card and the PIN.

Aside from being too short or too static, the risk of a password being disclosed, which is a control risk, depends on whether the password is stored or transmitted in plain text. A system should not store or transmit passwords in plain text. Here's how passwords should be stored and transmitted to avoid unauthorized disclosure.

A password entered is hashed by the computer that receives the password. Every operating system has this function. The hashing algorithm for creating a message digest can be used for password hashing. MD5 is commonly used to hash passwords.

The hashing algorithm hashes a password to a fixed length regardless of the original length of the password. An example of a hash is d3ccf205c702f315aad3b435b51404ee. The original password may be much shorter than this value. Next time you enter the password, the operating system (e.g., Windows) will hash the password using the same algorithm and then compare the hash with the hash stored in the computer. If they match, you are in. As long as you have not changed your password and key it in correctly each time, the hashed value will match the hash that is in storage in the hard disk. Once you change your password, a new hash is calculated to replace the stored hash. Because hashing is one way, someone who locates your password in the hard disk will see only the hash. If that person thinks that is the plain text password, it won't work. That is, if an unauthorized person keys in the hash as your plain text password under your ID, the system will hash that to a different value and try to match it with the hash stored, the two will not match so access will be denied.

If the hashing algorithm converts every password to a fixed length hash value, what is the point of using long password? Well, let's bear in mind that the hash is irreversible. This means a hacker cannot derive the actual password from the hash. S/he has to try different plain text passwords to try to match to the hash. So the longer a password, the more combinations a hacker has to try.

What if you are accessing a remote system like eBusiness? The password should be hashed by the remote server. Well, if the server does not have your original (real) password, how can you retrieve your password if you forget it? You could retrieve it from your personal notes stored in a secure place. Failing that, the server won't be able to tell you what the password is. This is why the help desk standard practice is to first verify your identity by asking you some challenge questions like your mother's maiden name or the model of your first car, answers to which you have provided before and are registered in the system. After that, the help desk will reset your password and the system should require you to change that reset temporary password to one that you can easily remember and meets the organization's password standard. A good password is one that you can easily remember but is difficult to be guessed by others; it should be a secret.

Passwords should be sufficiently long but not so long that people will be tempted to write them down. They should be subject to syntax check for a combination of digits and letters. They should be changed regularly. Users should adopt different passwords for different systems. This alleviates the risk of exposing your records in all systems that you access when your password is compromised.

Important Password Characteristics

Here is a list of key characteristics of a reliable password.

- Users must not disclose their passwords.

- Users must know who to contact if they forget the passwords or if the passwords don't work.for assistance with their password.

- Initial passwords should be communicated to the user directly in person, by telephone or through an encrypted channel.

- The password owner, on first login, must change the initial password.

- A password should contain at least 8 characters.

- A password should contain at least a digit, an upper case letter and a lower case letter.

- Passwords must be chosen so that they are easy enough to remember but not easily guessed by someone else, e.g., Tigeryear05.

- Passwords must not include easily identifiable personal information about the owner; e.g., names of family members, pets, birthdays, anniversaries or hobbies.

- Passwords must not be any words, phrases or acronyms that are part of the broadly recognized culture in the organization, e.g., diversity.

- Passwords must not be the same as all or part of a user's login id, actual last or given names, or a common nickname.

- Passwords must not be blank. The use of NULL passwords is prohibited.

- A mechanism should be in place to ensure that passwords are not reused within a number of cycles. For example, the last ten passwords cannot be reused.

- Vendor set default passwords must be changed upon installation.

- Regular users should change their passwords at least every ninety days.

- System administrators must change their passwords at least every thirty days.

- Password changes should not involve the use of easily recognized patterns, e.g. changing "nflpool01" to "nflpool02".

- Documented procedures must be in place to mitigate risk in the event of password loss, change or emergency modification.

- Passwords must be changed immediately if they have been or are suspected to have been compromised.

- Passwords must not be displayed while being entered but must be represented on the screen by a special character such as an asterisk.

- The system should disable the user after a number of consecutively incorrect password entries, e.g., five. The user will then have to call the help desk for password reset.

- Passwords must be hashed.

Most of the above rules can be enforced by computers. User education is also important.

A question often asked by people is why a bank requires its employees to change passwords but does not impose that on customers. Most people think it is because a bank does not want to inconvenience customers. Well, that may be true to some extent. The main reason is that a customer's password allows the customer access to only his or her information, whereas an employee's password allows access to corporate or customer information. The accountability is different. Banks, however, should encourage customers to change their passwords frequently.

A password is a preventive control for authentication that supports the assertions of confidentiality, integrity and availability.

Password Cracking

If passwords are stored in hash, how does a hacker steal a password and use it? Well, such a person will first capture the hashed passwords that s/he wants to use. Such capture can be done by accessing the computer that holds the passwords along with the user IDs or by sniffing unencrypted network traffic.

The hacker will now try to hash a number of values and then compare each hash to the hashed password that is being attempted for cracking. If there is a match, the hacker knows the real password. The hacker will use the same hashing algorithm as that used by the system in question. This is not difficult, as there are only a handful of commercially used algorithms. The hacker will also research to find out the organization's password policy with respect to length, syntax and case sensitivity. Now, the hacker will use the process of elimination as follows. It will be done with software. There are numerous password cracking software tools available as free software or for a nominal price.

The hacker will first hash the common names and words that satisfy the password policy and compare each hashed value to the hashed password. If s/he knows about the password owner, this task is easier. For example, the hacker can hash the names of the owner, his or her pets, friends, family members, street names, sports celebrities or words that describe hobbies.

If the above does not produce a match, the hacker can hash dictionary words. If that still does not work, the hacker will conduct a brute force attack. This means s/he will hash all the permutations of characters (with replacement) that satisfy the password policy and compare each hash to the hashed password. Eventually, there will be a match. But that eventuality may take so long that the hacker will give up, even though the process is automated. Or the process will take so long that the cracked password has been changed by the user.

A hacker does not have to compute the hashes for every cracking attempt. There are pre-computed tables of hash values in circulation in the hacker community or available in password cracking software tools.

So how long does it take to crack a password? It depends on the length and complexity of the password? It also depends on the power and number of computers used. A high end password cracker run on a powerful PC can computer up to 2.8 billion hashes a second. There are 76,927,928,940,573 combinations of 8-character, case sensitive, alphanumeric passwords. This means that such a random password takes less than four hours to crack.

However, most users select passwords that are easy to remember and therefore also easy to crack than a random password. Who would use $%*9Mczz as a password? Studies have shown that a user selected eight-character alphanumeric, case sensitive password takes an average of 16 minutes to crack. Note that the work can be distributed over many computers to further speed up the time to crack. Well, the above cracking time is slightly longer if the hacker does not know the organization's password policy. For example, without knowledge that a system requires a password length of 8 characters, the hacker will have to try all passwords from say, 6 to 8 characters.

Advanced password algorithms use a salt to complicate the hashing. Here is how it works.

1. A user creates a password.

2. The password algorithm generates a random bit string, called a salt.

3. The password algorithm applies the salt to the password to create a hash.

4. The salt is stored separately from the hashed password but linked to the user account.

5. When the user uses the password again, the system retrieves the salt and uses it to hash the password. The hash is then compared to the stored hashed password to authenticate the user.

6. Common salt lengths are 12, 48 and 128 bits. A 12 bit salt can, on average, increase the password cracking time by 2,000 times, assuming the hacker knows the length of the salt but cannot locate the salt. The salt generates different hash values for identical passwords. However, once created or changed, a password will always have the same hash because the salt for the password is then statically stored. Not only does a salt make cracking much harder, it reduces the risk implication of a user selecting the same password for different systems because the salt is then independently derived by each system.

Some have said that passwords are now more a deterrent than a strong access control against determined hackers. As computing power doubles annually, passwords are increasingly crackable. This is why more and more organizations are opting to use pass phrases instead of passwords. Pass phrases are longer and easier to remember; and it can often be meaningful and unique to the owner, i.e., easy to remember but hard to guess. An example of such a pass phrase is "My son will be a Supreme Court justice."

A consolation factor to password cracking is that organizations can rely on other access controls to protect the server that contains password hashes, e.g., by hardening the server in terms of tightening the operating system parameters, patching the computer rigorously with security updates, putting servers behind firewalls, installing host based intrusion detection and prevention systems, educating users to compose hard-to-crack passwords, encrypting password hashes when the server is inactive, encrypting password transmission and enforcing password rules to prevent cyclical passwords.

Patching

We discuss Internet worms earlier in this chapter. A worm is sent by a hacker using the power and speed of the Internet to infect computers to cause denial of service or to disable certain security features to make it easier to hack into the network. A worm exploits a vulnerability in an operating system or other system software like a database management system. This is a backdoor. Once the vendor realizes a backdoor is left open, it will send out a patch to its customers to install. For example, Microsoft issues patches at least monthly.

There are software products used to test and install the patches. Such a product automates the installation across an organization's network so that, for example, a network with 50,000 computers can have a patch installed within a day. Time is of the essence as software vendors and user organizations race with the hackers.

What if a computer is turned off when a patch is rolled out? Well, corporate networks should be configured such that at connection, the network will check the patch level of the user computer and install the patch if required. This is even before the computer accesses other sites so as to prevent worm infection.

Patches should generally be tested before being rolled out unless a patch is intended to address a zero day exploit. A zero day exploit is an exploit written to be a worm on the day the backdoor is publicized. This leaves little room for the software vendor to react. Organizations, in that scenario, should send out emails to employees to be cautious about opening emails and accessing web sites, and to look out for strange messages and computer viruses.

Patching prevents Internet worms and hacking. It is a general control as the process can be applied to the whole organization. It addresses the security cycle of monitoring and supports the security assertion of integrity and availability.

Personnel Security Screening

People form one of the five components of a system. Some have said that people are often the weakest link in the chain of information processing as they can make mistakes and may not be trustworthy. Many IT staff members handle sensitive information so rogue or dishonest employees can hurt an organization and its customers. It is an increasingly common control for organizations to conduct personnel security screening of new hires including a combination of criminal record check, driving record check and credit check, depending on the job function. Personnel security screening prevents the hiring of rogue employees and ethically questionable consultants. It is a general control because the same procedures apply regardless of where the employee or consultant works in the organization. The security assertions supported are confidentiality and integrity and the security cycle addressed is authorization.

Security Education

To extend our argument that people often constitute the weakest link in the chain, it is important that their behavior supports the organization's access controls. They have to be educated on what is right and what is wrong in terms of controlling the assets and information in their possession.

A large organization should have a security education program that consists of classroom courses, web based training, posters and email reminders. Courses should range from general security to specific topics tailored to different job functions. Security education should include the following mandatory training:
1. New staff training.
2. New manager training.
3. Annual security training for IT managers.
4. Training for IT employees to address system design, architecture, programming, testing and computer operation (including operating system administration).
5. Business user training for user requirement composition to address security.
6. Training on new security policies, procedures and systems for technical IT people and technical IT managers.
Optional training that is current and fun should be offered on the organization's intranet including quizzes to encourage employees to keep up to date with the organization's security policies.

Security education prevents rogue behavior or inappropriate handling of information. It is a general control as the employees being trained in a program may come from different departments. The security cycle addressed is authorization and the assertions include confidentiality, integrity and availability.

Single Sign-on

We all have passwords to manage. I have ten different passwords. Wouldn't it be nice if I could use the same password for everything. I don't mean using the same value for all passwords. I mean using a password that is connected to all the systems I access regularly and once I key in the password, I have access to all the systems for which I am permitted. Well, that is not possible because my employer is not my bank etc. Most of my passwords are for connection to systems hosted by my employer. Wouldn't it be nice if I could log on to a portal once and it then makes all the other systems available to me based on my access profile? Well, that is the trend.

A single sign-on (SSO) system also presents a single point of failure so the risks of unauthorized access and loss of availability go up. The authentication requirement must be stronger than that for a typical system. For example, if a user name and a password allows someone to access seven systems which formerly required different logons and have different levels of sensitivity, the authentication requirement for single sign-on should be based on the system with highest sensitivity, not an average of the former

432

authentication requirements for the seven systems. This means, if the password lengths required formerly ranged from 6 characters to 12 characters, the new single sign-on password length should be at least 12 characters, may be even stronger. Why even stronger? It is because if someone compromises that password, s/he has access to all systems.

An organization that adopts single sign-on should use two-factor authentication. SSO is particularly suitable to government operation to let citizens access all the services they are entitled to and have registered for, especially for people who are less IT literate. Canadian governments are progressive in this area and there is ongoing development for expanding SSO within some large governments.

SSO is a preventive general control. It address the security process of identification and authentication. The security objectives of confidentiality, availability and integrity are supported.

Spam Filtering

Spam is more than a nuisance and productivity distracter. It slows down the network and can lead to denial-of-service. Employees should be educated about how to recognize and deal with spams. As well, an organization should install spam filtering software, which may be part of the anti-virus software package. Spam filtering is a preventive general control and addresses the security assertions of availability. The security cycle of authorization is covered.

Staff Termination or Transfer Checklist

Many organizations have experienced information compromise, system damage or sabotage by staff members who are terminated or who resign on ill accord. This is why it is becoming a common practice to terminate the access right of employees as soon as such a situation arises. Even for harmonious parting, it is critical that an employee's access rights be terminated on a timely basis. In addition, IT assets should be reclaimed immediately. Every organization should have a checklist to help ensure this takes place and the checklist should be part of the exit process administered by the line manager and monitored by the human resources department. This checklist should also apply to staff transfers. Some items on the checklist may not apply to transfers but the onus should be on human resources to indicate why such items are not applicable. Technology continues to improve management's ability to keep track of IT assets assigned so that they can be recovered. For example, Research In Motion has just announced its Mobile Fusion offering that will provide the following mobile device management capabilities for all supported mobile devices:

- Asset management
- Configuration management
- Security and policy definition and management
- Secure and protect lost or stolen devices (remote lock, wipe)

- User- and group-based administration
- Multiple device per user capable
- Application and software management
- Connectivity management (Wi-Fi, VPN, certificate)

The staff termination and transfer security checklist prevents rogue behavior and asset loss and it is a general control. The security cycle covered is authorization and the security assertions are confidentiality and integrity.

Standard Operating System Configuration Image

The operating system provides the foundation for access controls. There are many ways to configure an operating system including the browser to make services available, constrain services and ration resources. Loose configuration can open the doors to hackers and network worms. It can also lead to the loss of audit trail. An organization should have a standard image of what parameters should be turned on and what options should be activated for every PC and server. All PCs and servers should be configured according to standard images and the images should be reviewed periodically. Exceptions require management approval. Servers and workstations, including connected laptops should be periodically scanned for compliance with the standard configuration image. Applying a rigorous standard image of the operating system is called "hardening".
Using a standard image prevents system vulnerabilities. This is a general control because the images should apply to all computers. The security assertion addressed is confidentiality and integrity and the security cycle is authorization. The standard image should specify what services and ports are open, the extent of logging and the password configuration (how long, how complicated and when change is required).

The standard image for a browser should include the security settings such as acceptance of mobile code like Active X and Java, acceptance of unsigned code, acceptance of cookies, checking for a web site's P3P compliance and activation of a popup blocker. The standard image of a browser is harder to control because a user can often change the settings. This risk can be addressed in the security policy to tell users what they should not change.

Two Factor Authentication

In our discussion of passwords earlier, we conclude that passwords are becoming less reliable against hackers. This is why organizations are increasingly implementing two factor authentication, which requires something the user knows and something the user possesses. A common example is ATM. A two factor authentication system can tolerate a weaker password like a PIN. Of course, the stronger of both factors the better security is achieved. There are two other common methods for two factor authentication.

A system may require a personal digital certificate to be installed in a user computer which is activated with a pass phrase. The certificate and the pass phrase are the two factors. Another method is to give users a token that looks like a memory stick and displays a pass code that changes every minute. The pass code is synchronized between the token and the authentication server. A user has to key in this dynamic pass code and a static password to gain entry to a system.

Two factor authentication can be a general control or an application control, depending on the scope of implementation. It prevents unauthorized access and supports the security objective of confidentiality, integrity and availability. It is commonly used in virtual private network explained below. An increasing number of banks in Asia and Europe require two factor authentication for eBanking.

User Profile

We have discussed access control lists earlier in this chapter as a preventive control to restrict the information and system functions a user can access. Another way to exercise such a restriction, often at a less granular level but also to supplement access control lists, is by putting parameters in a user profile or a group profile. A group profile is a profile that applies to a group of users, e.g., all the users in department X.

Here are the common parameters that can be set in a user profile.
- The environments that the user ID can access, e.g., development, test or production.
- Time of day, day of week and day of month on which access is allowed.
- The group that the user belongs to.
- Expiry date.
- Special privileges that can override access control lists in the system or environment; e.g., a system administrator privilege classification has total access to a server regardless of access control lists. This would include installing programs on the server or workstation in which the user has a special privilege, or the so called system administration right. An "auditor" classification can have read access to all files in a server. "Auditor" here does not just mean internal auditors or external auditors. It means someone charged with the responsibility to perform ongoing data checking.
- Password expiry date.
- Last password change date.

User profiles should be used along with access control lists to prevent inappropriate access. A user profile is a preventive application control and it addresses the security objectives of authentication and authorization. The reason this is an application control is that a user may have different profiles for different systems.

Virtual Private Network

An organization often finds it necessary or desirable to allow employees and contractors to access the organization's network as if they were within the premises. There are basically two ways to do this. One is to set up the systems that need to be accessed remotely as an eBusiness server and the user would access it just like an eBusiness site. Another way is to give the user blanket access to the network and the user then has the same degree of access to system functions as if s/he were in the office. The former is easier to control and the risk is lower. For example, many organizations have set up a web based mail server to allow employees to access corporate email from remote sites. We have discussed the web based access method to specific systems under eBusiness encryption. The second method is called virtual private network (VPN).

An example of a VPN application is to allow employees to work at home in the event of a disaster or a major disruption to city traffic. The organization would give the employee VPN access instead of setting up a web server for each of the application for any of three reasons. First, the frequency and user base for accessing a specific application may be too low to web enable the application. Secondly, the application may be too old to be web enabled, thus an employee can access it once admitted to the VPN using non-Web software as if s/he were in the office. Thirdly, the employee may need to access a variety of applications concurrently; thus letting him or her into a VPN would be more expedient than requiring the employee to log onto different applications via a browser.

Because a VPN allows a user blanket access to the network as if s/he were in the office, a high level of authentication requirement is adopted. It should use two factor authentication. A VPN typically goes through the Internet, so the entire data stream should be encrypted. Such encryption is similar to eBusiness encryption.

VPN prevents unauthorized access. It is a general control because it merely lets the user into the network. Once admitted, the user is still subject to the application level authentication like a user ID and a password for each application to which the user has been authorized to access. The security objectives supported are confidentiality, integrity and availability.

Vulnerability Assessment

We talked about the importance of installing patches from software vendors to close security loopholes left open during software product launch or implementation. Sometimes a patch does not reach a new computer because the computer was not registered in the network when the patch was applied or because the patching for that computer failed while the network was disrupted. Also, a patch may be undone because of errors by system administrators or the malicious effect of a worm. Another scenario is that even if all the patches have been applied, a security hole has been created by a system administrator in error by changing a number of parameters or created by an application in error to activate certain powerful operating system features that are seldom needed. Organizations should periodically review the configurations of operating systems and other system software to identify vulnerabilities and close them. This can be done by manually reviewing the configurations in the system, using scanning software to analyze the configurations or by trying to hack into a system. All three methods can be engaged in a progressive manner. Trying to hack into a system is also called ethical hacking or penetration testing. Some security firms, including the Big Four accounting firms, offer penetration testing services.

Here are the common steps involved in penetration testing.

1. Obtain senior management approval.

2. Map the network, i.e., studying the network to identify entry points including IP addresses. One might argue that this does not simulate hacking because a hacker would not have this information. If the penetration tester wants to be more objective and to simulate an actual hack more closely, s/he may decide not to rely on internal documentation of the network and instead, use external scanning, Internet research and social engineering.

3. Probe the network by using automated commands like ping to find out what ports are open on each web server.

4. Use security scanning software to scan web server for loopholes, e.g., unpatched operating system.

5. Try to hack into a system to view confidential information. There are automated tools available on the Internet and within the hacker community.

6. Obtain system administrator IDs and passwords of servers.

7. Obtain firewall, IDS and IPS rules.

8. Inject a small amount of bogus traffic to test the firewall and intrusion prevention system. There are automated tools available on the Internet and within the hacker community.

9. Shows attempts and ability to cause denial-of-service attack, defacement or changing data.

10. Report deficiencies to management and make recommendations for improvements.

Vulnerability assessment detects system software security weaknesses and it is a general control because it applies to the network. The security assertions addressed are confidentiality, integrity and availability. The security process covered is monitoring.

Web Filtering

The Internet can be abused by employees to watch movies, listen to music or even visit indecent web sites such as sites that display pornography. An organization should monitor the use of the Internet by employees and make employees aware that monitoring takes place. Inappropriate use can cause harassment, legal liability and productivity loss.

Organizations should filter web traffic to prevent abuse. For example, web sites in the nature of social media, gambling, pornography, weaponry, hate and terrorism can be blocked. So should web sites that transmit a lot of video. Some organizations block Youtube and Facebook. During the Olympics and World Cup Soccer tournament, an employer may even want to block certain sports sites. A U. S. research firm conducted a survey about Internet usage in large corporations recently and found that about half of the usage was not for corporate purpose.

Most employers condone personal use of the Internet, just as they condone personal use of the office telephone. However, excessively personal use should not be tolerated. Excessive users can be identified with web traffic monitoring. Organizations should implement software tools to monitor web traffic by employers and also to block undesirable sites. Such tools usually block sites based on URLs, IP addresses and also content by recognizing and analyzing the text and graphics. A web filtering software tool is seldom fool proof. A pornographic site that transmits such material not too explicitly may escape detection. This is why it is also important to report on high frequency Internet users and ask the managers to justify.

In addition to site blocking, such a tool can report on the number of attempts to each category that have been blocked and the computers that generated the attempts so the organization can consider following up with the management of the employees using those computers. In addition, the tool can be configured to report on the extent of traffic by computer to sites that are allowed, e.g., stock trading sites.

Web filtering prevents unauthorized use of the Internet and it addresses the security criteria of integrity and availability. Integrity is relevant because an undesirable web site is more likely to contain worms that can infect the organization's network. Availability is relevant because excessively personal use can slow down the network. Another aspect of integrity is related to the organization's reputation and legal liability. Imagine the consequence of employees going to a child pornography site and the organization is seen to condone it; or the consequence of a lot of employees going to sites that facilitate the exchange of unlicensed software or music. Web filtering is a general control because it is not related to any particular business application. The security process covered is monitoring.

Web Site Refresh

In the early days of the Internet, a common way of hacking is to deface a web site. This is easily noticeable and a standard solution is to disconnect the web server and reload the content from a backup and offline computer. The vulnerability that allowed the defacement also has to be closed by patching or shutting down some services and ports.

Instead of defacement, a hacker may change a small part of a web site that can have a significant effect, e.g., changing a posted interest rate on a bank web site. Organizations have learned that it is a good practice to reload the web content from an offline computer periodically, perhaps several times a day, to nullify any unauthorized change. The offline version must also be checked regularly for currency and correctness.

Web site refresh is a corrective general control and it covers the security cycle of monitoring.

MANAGEMENT CHECKLIST

1. Appoint a chief information security officer reporting to the CIO.

2. Set up an information security committee as a subordinate committee to the IT steering committee. The chief information security officer should be the chair.

3. Develop an information security strategy that supports the IT strategy.

4. Perform annual security risk assessment of the organization to assess inherent risk, control risk and residual risk. This assessment should include security testing such as vulnerability assessment.

5. Ensure that access control assessment is part of the systems development methodology.

6. Establish an information security policy as a corporate umbrella for access controls.

7. Develop information security standards for each technology platform such as database management system, eBusiness and cryptography. These standards can be used by individual business units to develop tailored procedures.

8. Develop corporate information security procedures to ensure consistent handling of security threats and incidents.

9. Conduct security check for new hires to sensitive positions including consultants.

10. Establish a security education program to ensure awareness of security policies, standards and procedures. This program should require employees to take annual refresher courses within the organization, e.g., online courses.

11. If the organization hosts eBusiness, it should establish network security monitoring procedures and tools to monitor for hacking attempts and network worms.

12. Periodically monitor the Internet traffic generated by employees to prevent inappropriate use including excessive use for personal purpose.

13. Assess the cost effectiveness of each common access control like password, encryption, lock and firewall. The purpose is to determine whether the controls are accepted, complied with, effective and generate the intended risk mitigation. This can be done by surveying users, reviewing system configuration and testing.

INTERAL AUDIT CHECKLIST

1. Review the information security strategy annually to assess congruence with the IT strategy.

2. Review management's annual information risk assessment, or perform it directly.

3. Test the access controls in major data centers annually.

4. Encourage auditors to pursue the Certified Information Systems Security Professional designation.

5. Include access controls in the recurring audits of existing applications.

6. Include access controls in systems development audits with respect to the review of user requirements, system specifications, system architecture and pre-implementation testing.

7. Include access control testing in the recurring audit of operational units, e.g., management of user profiles on a need to know basis and security background check of employees in sensitive positions.

8. Conduct an annual security audit of the eBusiness infrastructure.

9. Ensure that access controls are assessed annually for business critical systems.

10. Conduct annual assessment of the effectiveness of security policies and standards.

EXTERAL AUDIT CHECKLIST

1. Review the IT security skills and training plan of the internal audit department to assess adequacy and currency.

2. Review the internal audit plan to assess adequacy of access control coverage.

3. Review internal audit files for data center audits and business critical application security.

4. Test access controls at the general and application levels.

5. Review the reports of vulnerability assessments conducted by the client.

6. Assess the organization's compliance with the Payment Card Industry security standard. We will discuss this further in Chapter Eleven.

7. Assess the relevance and reliability of access controls in supporting financial reporting.

8. Meet with IT steering committee annually to assess its concern about any access control deficiencies and assess the adequacy of the corrective action plan.

9. Review the chief IT security officer's annual report to the IT steering committee and CIO to assess the financial statement significance of control deficiencies.

10. Conclude on the adequacy of access controls at the general and application levels.

CONCLUSION

Access controls should be implemented at a general level and an application level. Management should assess the inherent risks with respect to authorization, occurrence and timeliness and then design general access controls as much as practical. The remaining risk should be mitigated with application level access controls until the residual risk is tolerable.

Access controls are implemented mainly to address the authorization and occurrence criteria. From the perspective of an IT specialist, the three common access control objectives are confidentiality, integrity and availability. For auditors, these can be tied to authorization and occurrence. Each access control serves one of the following five roles: Identification, Authentication, Authorization, Logging and Monitoring. Access controls support organization controls by enforcing segregation of duties, they support software change control by restricting access to source and object codes, they also support management and independent controls by preventing changes to exception reports and audit trail.

SUMMARY OF MAIN POINTS

Access controls should take the forms of policies, standards procedures, system configuration, management review, independent review, exception reporting, system screening, access control rules and systems tools like passwords. Here is a list of common access controls.

- Access card – identification and authentication, preventive.

- Access control list – authorization, preventive.

- Access log – logging, detective.

- Anti-virus software – authorization, preventive.

- Biometric – authentication, preventive.

- Boundary checking – authorization, preventive.

- Challenge response – authentication, preventive.

- Compliance scanning – monitoring, detective.

- Digital certificate – authentication, preventive.

- Digital signature – authentication, preventive.

- Disabling unnecessary system software features – authorization, preventive.

- Disk wiping – authorization, preventive.

- Encryption – authorization, preventive.

- File blocking – authorization, preventive.

- File integrity monitoring – monitoring, detective.

- Firewall – authorization, preventive.

- Hashing – authorization, preventive.

- Honeypot – authorization, preventive.

- Intrusion detection system – authorization, detective.

- Intrusion prevention system- authorization, preventive.

- Lock – authorization, preventive.

- Management or independent review – monitoring, detective.

- Password – authentication, preventive.

- Patching – authorization, preventive.

- Personnel security screening – authorization, preventive.

- Security education – authorization, preventive.

- Single sign-on – identification and authentication, preventive.

- Spam filtering – authorization, preventive.

- Staff termination or transfer checklist – authorization, preventive.

- Standard operating system configuration images – authorization and logging, preventive.

- Two factor authentication – authentication, preventive.

- User profile – authentication and authorization, preventive.

- Virtual private network – authentication and authorization, preventive.

- Vulnerability assessment – monitoring, detective.

- Web filtering – authorization, preventive.

- Web site refresh – authorization and monitoring, detective.

REVIEW QUESTIONS

1. What is the relationship between privacy and access control?

2. Who should the chief information security officer report to and why?

3. Why is email encryption not very commonly used?

4. What are the relationships between access controls and other internal controls?

5. Which technique is used both in a password control and a digital signature? How?

6. How is defence in depth achieved?

7. What is the difference between hashing and encryption?

8. Where should an intrusion detection system be placed in relation to a firewall and why?

9. How does encryption affect anti-virus software tools and what should an organization do to address the effect?

10. What security risk can materialize if a domain name server is compromised?

CASE – Global Products Inc.

Global Products Inc. (GPI) is a Web based catalog mail-order company. GPI's head office is located in Calgary, Alberta. It is changing its marketing strategy and investing $3 million in promotion, staff, and technology that it uses to sell its 4,500 catalog items using the Internet.

Your firm has been the auditor of GPI for the past two years. The company's CIO, Jackie Chan, has asked the engagement partner to comment on a proposal received from WPMI, an eBusiness infrastructure development company, to provide the software and training that will enable GPI to integrate its sales systems, inventory and billing. The integrated system will also use electronic data interchange (EDI). It will allow instant access by all warehouses, customers and vendors. Jackie intends to approve this proposal, and he would like your comments on the viability and risks of the proposed system. He would also like you to tell him what internal controls, in particular security controls he should implement in GPI and demands from WPMI.

The engagement partner has asked you to draft a letter to the client addressing the client's request for comments. Before you prepared the letter, you interviewed the client's staff and have taken the following notes.

1. WPMI will provide its eBusiness platform to GPI for processing Web orders, including performing credit card verification, inventory availability check and committing inventory

2. GPI's current accounting and business software is outdated and, therefore, cannot handle the increasing customer demands. WPMI recommends replacement of GPI's current software with a package called InterCom. This software will enable GPI to post its catalog, receive sales orders as well as to update inventory, shipping status, credit check and billing instantaneously. It will provide management with daily sales reports. WPMI will supply and install the software as part of its proposal. The web site will be hosted by WPMI. InterCom will run on GPI servers. Intercom is a back end accounting system that will interface with the WPMI eBusiness platform.

3. WPMI recognizes that all of the data in GPI's current accounting system will need to be converted to work with InterCom. WPMI proposes to write a special conversion system that will take the database from GPI's existing accounting system and convert it to InterCom's format. WPMI wants to review the existing GPI source code as a basis for writing the conversion system. WPMI intends to perform the conversion on a weekend on GPI premises, so that no employees will be using the current accounting system at the time of conversion and no work days will be lost.

4. A client of WPMI is suing the company over credit card information leakage.

5. Each day, GPI will access WPMI's system and the orders will be downloaded to GPI's computer system. The orders will be processed on GPI's computer system and automatically posted to GPI's to the sales and accounts receivable systems.

6. InterCom's inventory module will track quantities of stock, and inventory will be updated to reflect the items ordered as customer's orders are processed. The program will send an electronic message to the purchasing clerk when quantities fall below a predetermined point. The clerk then prepares purchase orders and sends them out using WPMI's EDI interface.

7. InterCom can recognize RFID and update inventory based on that.

Required

Prepare a letter to Jackie Chan to describe the information risks of this proposal. Also describe the access controls that GPI should implement and demand from WPMI.

MULTIPLE CHOICE QUESTIONS

1. Which of the following provides the strongest protection against hackers?
   a. Operating system
   b. Access control list
   c. Firewall
   d. Virtual private network

2. Which of the following would be the most appropriate task for a systems administrator to perform?

   a. Configure the operating system.
   b. Develop access control lists.
   c. Develop a checklist for operating system configuration.
   d. Set a password policy.

3. Which of the following is most likely to change with technology?
   a. Security standard
   b. Security procedure
   c. Security configuration
   d. Security training

4. Which of the following technologies would conflict with encryption the most?
   a. Virtual private network
   b. Digital certificate
   c. Anti-virus software
   d. Password

5. Which of the following is the most effective solution for preventing external users from modifying sensitive and classified information?
   a) Security standards
   b) Intrusion detection system
   c) Access logs
   d) Firewall

6. eBusiness encryption uses
   a. asymmetric keys
   b. symmetric keys.
   c. session keys only.
   d. asymmetric keys and symmetric keys.

7. When a firewall log is full, the firewall will:
   a. let all traffic through
   b. either let all traffic through or deny all traffic depending on its configuration.
   c. deny all traffic.
   d. simply stop logging without affecting traffic screening.

8. Which of the following best protects the authenticity of an electronic document?
   a. Encryption
   b. Digital certificate
   c. Digital signature
   d. Checksum

9. Which is the most appropriate inference from a penetration test that cannot get through the network?
   a. The network is fool-proof.
   b. The test is deficient.
   c. There is no bad news about the network.
   d. The network is commercially reliable.

10. Which of the following generates an SSL encryption key?
    a. Browser
    b. Web server
    c. ISP
    d. Database server

CHAPTER NINE – OPERATING SYSTEM ACCESS CONTROLS

Security is, I would say, our top priority because for all the exciting things you will be able to do with computers – organizing your lives, staying in touch with people, being creative – if we don't solve these security problems, then people will hold back.

- Bill Gates

The access controls we discussed in the last chapter apply to pretty much all systems and infrastructure. In this chapter, we will go over the access control parameters and architecture at an operating system level and review the security relationship between operating systems and access control software tools. We will cover the following common platforms:

- Windows
- Mac OS X
- Unix
- IBM Z Series (mainframe) servers

For each platform, an organization should have a standard image for each desktop, laptop and server as a baseline. Exceptions should be approved by management. There should be less room for exceptions for desktops and laptops as these devices are not application specific. Common controls in a standard image include disabling certain ports and services and the ability to update the system registry. A common restriction is to take away a user's ability to install software by not giving the user local administration privilege.

WINDOWS

Windows security has been improving with successively new versions mainly to address the growing threat from hackers. Our discussion of Windows security will cover the workstation and server levels. It will be structured around the three security processes of authentication, authorization and logging. The other two common security processes of identification and monitoring are not operating system specific and our discussion in the last chapter is sufficient.

Authentication

Windows allows users to configure a password policy with respect to length, syntax, number of allowable attempts and expiry date. A password is hashed to a 128-bit value. Windows uses salting only for offline authentication, mainly for laptops. Salting is performed for offline access because the user cannot be authenticated by a server. For example, someone who travels with a laptop might want to do some work at home or in a hotel. Without access to Active Directory, the person will be authenticated based on the password hash stored on the laptop. This is how offline authentication works.

1. A network user creates a password.
2. Windows hashes without a salt and stores the hash on the server.
3. Windows hashes with a salt using the full user name as the salt and stores the salted hash on the laptop or desktop.
4. When the user logs in online, the server hash is used.
5. When the user logs in offline, the laptop or desktop hash is used.

This salt is not as strong as a hash that uses a random salt as discussed in the last chapter.

What can a user access when logging in offline? A user can access cached email messages and everything on the local hard drive. Organizations generally do not allow users to use a computer offline without a password.

Windows also supports biometrics, e.g., a thumb print mouse.

Authorization

Windows supports user profile settings, access control lists, security alerts and network security settings. These are all controlled by the system administrator in accordance with organization policies. Most employees do not have full access to their computers because the systems administrator has locked down the computer using the user access control feature of Windows. Windows facilitates security configuration and alerts settings in the Action Center, previously called Windows Security Center (pre-Windows 7).

The Action Center has the following security features.

1. It allows the user to schedule Windows updates so that updates will be downloaded and implemented automatically. Organizations usually disable this function and instead, let the domain controller (server) oversee this function.

2. Internet options – we will discuss these under a separate heading.

3. Firewall configuration for the Windows firewall.

4. Full disk encryption using 128-bit Advanced Encryption Algorithm.

5. Microsoft Security Essential, which is the Windows anti-virus software.

6. Data Execution Prevention feature that prevents buffer overflow by marking certain memory pages intended for data as non-executable.

7. Protected Media Path to protect digital rights management through denying access to digitally righted material by unauthorized applications. This prevents the copying of programs that can only be executed.

8. Locking down users to prevent them from installing programs.

9. Defining user access rights as guest, folder owner, administrator (full access), and specific user (requiring a logon account).

10. Defining access control lists for folders and files.

Logging

Windows logs key activities in an event log. Event logs are special files that record significant events on your computer, such as when a user logs on to the computer or when a program encounters an error. Whenever these types of events occur, Windows records the event in an event log that you can read by using Event Viewer. Advanced users might find the details in event logs helpful when troubleshooting problems with Windows and other programs.

Event Viewer tracks information as follows.

- **Application (program) events.** Events are classified as *error*, *warning*, or *information*, depending on the severity of the event. An error is a significant problem, such as loss of data. A warning is an event that isn't necessarily significant, but might indicate a possible future problem. An information event describes the successful operation of a program, driver, or service. This includes commands exercised at the command line and the execution of Windows systems commands, such as those carried out by systems administrators. A driver is a system program kept within Windows to support a device like a printer. A service is a feature in Windows that performs certain system transactions; an example is remote procedure call, which accesses the operating system instructions of a remote computer like a server or a connected workstation.

- **Security-related events.** These events are called *audits* and are described as successful or failed depending on the event, such as whether a user trying to log on to Windows was successful.

- **Setup events.** These events include the set-up of user profiles, access control lists, connected devices, installed applications etc. In other words, the creation, deletion or change of any Windows resources, users and applications are recorded.

Active Directory

This hierarchical access authentication and authorization structure has replaced the function of the primary domain controller and backup domain controller in authentication and authorization. It has the following features:

- Central location for network administration and security
- Information security and single sign-on for user access to networked resources
- The ability to scale up or down easily
- Standardizing access to application data
- Synchronization of directory updates across servers

Active Directory (AD) stores all information and settings for a deployment in a central database. It allows administrators to assign policies as well as to deploy and update software. AD networks can vary from a small installation with a few computers, users and printers to tens of thousands of users, many different network domains and large server farms spanning many locations.

Internet Explorer Security Features

Internet Explorer security settings can be configured for each of four zones: Internet, intranet, trusted sites and restricted sites. Trusted sites are sites that the user has almost full trust, e.g., a trading partner's site. Restricted sits are sites that are trusted and also that are seldom used and these site, by nature of their service, can cause significant damage to the user's system. Most users should have no restricted sites activated. For each of the four zones, a user can set the security configuration. The security parameters for Internet and restricted sites should be significantly tighter than those for intranet and trusted sites. For each zone, a user can select the default level, which provides about medium security, or to customize the setting. A user without system administrator right, i.e., an ordinary user, can still change the Internet Explorer security setting.

If a user selects the custom option, s/he can further define one of three parameters for the following browsing features. The three parameters are enable, disable or prompt. The browsing features supported by the custom option are:

1. Run .NET Framework reliant components not signed with Authenticode. Running such software components presented by a web site carries a significant risk, which the user, in this case, has the option to always accept, always deny, or decide that when prompted. The last option allows the user to assess the reliability of the web site and the application being used and decide whether to accept the running of an unsigned .NET Framework reliant software component. The .NET Framework is a collection of software tools for Windows application development, allowing for programming language interoperability, i.e., a program can include instructions written in other programming languages. Authenticode is Microsoft's tool for software distributors to digitally sign the software and for user browsers to verify the digital signatures. It is a high risk for a user to select the enable option for running .NET Framework reliant components not signed with Authenticode. The security risk of .NET is somewhat mitigated by the fact that these components usually are run in the sandbox. The sandbox is an enclosed area in Windows that does not allow access to local files and input functions, it is like an operating system within the operating system.

2. Run .NET Framework reliant components signed with Authenticode. This type of software is safer because it is digitally signed.

3. Accepting or rejecting mobile code such as ActiveX control components. ActiveX control is a framework for writing reusable code. Users should configure the browser to not accept unsigned ActiveX components automatically. ActiveX components usually are not run in the sandbox and therefore riskier than .NET components.

4. Enabling or disabling popup blocker. A popup is a new window automatically opened without your interaction. This can be distracting and if the user clicks on an icon in the new window, malicious software may be downloaded or run in real time. A lot of popups are used in advertising. Windows Explorer's popup blocker blocks popup. There is a message at the top of the screen to tell you that a popup is being blocked. If the user expects a web based program to load and nothing comes up, the user can check the popup blocker message and allow that popup. Although this poses some inconvenience, it prompts the user to think twice before allowing the popup and be more alert in using the content and functions presented by popups

A user can also specify the privacy settings by selecting a range from high to low. High is the safest and most restrictive. These settings mainly affect cookies. Here is the list of options:

1. Save cookies from any site.

2. Block third party cookies from site that don't comply with P3P.

3. Block third party cookies that save information that can be used to contact you without your consent.

4. Block first party cookies that save information that can be used to contact you without your consent.

5. Block cookies from any site that is not P3P compliant.

6. Block cookies from any site that saves information that can be used to contact you without your consent.

7. Block all cookies from any site. Existing persistent cookies, i.e., cookies already on your hard disk can still be read by the web sites that created them.

MAC OS X

OS X has the versatility of Unix and also the GUI looks and feels of Windows. The system commands in OS X are actually Unix commands. OS X has all the security features that Windows has. Its web browser is called Safari, which is used in Mac desktops, iPad and iPhone. Safari has similar security features to Internet Explorer. OS X has its own version of active directory. It supports full disk encryption using a 256-bit key.

UNIX

This open source operating system predated Windows. Open source means the source code is available to the public. Windows is not open source. Unix provides a lot of flexibility to users and systems administrators in configuring security. Common versions of Unix includes Linux for PCs, HP-UX for HP servers, AIX for the IBM AS400 mid-range servers and Solaris for Sun servers. Unix has its own version of active directory.

Authentication

A main difference between Unix and other operating systems is the way passwords are managed.

1. Password hashes are hidden from users because no one has a need to read them. The authentication server, of course, has access. Unix separate the hash from the user account in different files. To link the two, the user account file has a pointer called a shadow that points to the file with the hash and the location of the hash. This places the hashes a step more removed from the account IDs and therefore more difficult to compromise.

2. A salt ranging from 48 to 128 bits is added to the password for hashing, depending on configuration, Twelve bits of this bit string are hashed to form the first two bytes of the password hash.

3. Unix is quite sensitive to special characters like ^, @ and # and may interpret them as commands. Users should be cautioned to avoid these characters in passwords.

Authorization

Unix uses the following simple convention for data resource access control. It allows a file or directory to be defined as readable, writable (including deletion) and executable by the owner, anyone in the owner's user group or anyone else. A typical access control list is rwxr_x__x. This means the owner can perform all three functions, a group member can read and execute and anyone else can only execute. Execution means being able to run the program or use the function. Well, don't you have to read the program to run it? Not really, when we use ATM, we don't get to read the object code. If the file or directory contains only non-executable data, like a document, the third byte for each user type is set to "-". Of course, the superuser, i.e., a system administrator, has full access to all data on the server.

Logging

Unix provides a large number of log files that can be configured by the system administrator. The most widely used and versatile is syslog. Syslog provides messages indicating what actions are being done on what resources by whom. It also indicates the priority of the message that requires system administrator action.

IBM Z SERIES (mainframe) SERVERS

These servers used to be called mainframe computers because of their large size in memory and disk storage. As PC based servers grow in size, the fast computing that was once the monopoly of mainframes is now affordable using PC based servers, although there is still some difference in speed and power between these two types of computers; the difference is becoming narrower and narrower.

However, the architecture is different between PC based servers and Z series servers, as is the data format at the operating system level. For data representation, PC based servers use American Standard Code for Information Exchange (ASCII), which is more user friendly. Z series servers use Extended Binary Coded Decimal Interchange Code (EBCDIC), which involves a larger character set and therefore can accommodate a keyboard with more special keys. It is less user friendly, i.e., the data representation is less English like. The operating system used in Z series servers is z/OS. Z/OS is viewed by some as a more secure system than Windows and Unix mainly because it is a less popular target for hackers. However, in closer analysis, z/OS has fewer security features than Windows and Unix because its predecessors, Multiple Virtual Storage and Virtual Memory, were developed before the Internet and therefore not fully designed to mitigate today's hacking risks.

Z/OS is highly capable in supporting real time networks. A main reason is that real time networks were used by large organizations like banks well before the Internet. This enabled organizations to operate real time transaction systems that were geographically dispersed many years before the Internet was commercialized. Within z/OS, Structured Network Architecture (SNA) provides the network architecture to connect terminals (including z/OS emulated PCs) to servers, including TCP/IP support. Z/OS supports PKI and SSL.

Another component of z/OS, Customer Information Control System (CICS), provides the software framework for programs to develop online real time systems that process customer transactions, like banking transactions. It is not a programming language. CICS is somewhat similar to .NET but it is more "close", i.e., it is not a collection of tools, but rather, a software structure with commands for programmers to use and it is very rigid.

Z/OS also supports systems development and production batch jobs via its Time Sharing Option (TSO). TSO allows programmers to submit programs for execution. It provides a text editor for changing Job Control Language (JCL). JCL is the z/OS equivalent to

Windows commands like copy, regedit or ipconfigsys; these are operating system commands that can be input in free form at the command line prompt. JCL also provides an operating system log.

Z/OS native security is viewed by many to be acceptable for systems development and local processing but leaving quite a bit to be desired for real time transaction processing. It provides user profile restriction for developers and program files. It also provides file protection via passwords. Its access control list function is less robust than those in Windows and Unix.

CICS provides additional security by restricting access from individual workstations. It also provides restriction of access by end users like bank customers but leaves passwords optional. CICS also cannot protect resources from external access, i.e., access by parties or objects not defined within the scope of CICS implementation in the environment, e.g., hackers or a user from another application that does not use CICS or is not within the same CICS environment.

A typical CICS user in a financial institution is a teller or an ATM, but not a bank customer. To CICS, a user is the workstation, ATM or the web server session ID that has been assigned to the customer at that moment. To address the security shortfall of CICS, IBM offers an external security manager called Resource Access Control Facility (RACF) as an optional add-on to z/OS. RACF sits on z/OS and can interface with CICS, TSO or the OS directly.

RACF

RACF can be installed in a distributed manner. For example, a provincial or state government can host a RACF environment in each ministry or department, with the provincial or state environment as the master control. Policies are implemented at the global environment with certain parameters changeable in local environments.

RACF provides user authentication, resource access control, security logging and audit reporting. It is much more granular than operating system security. For example, it makes available 254 security levels (labels) that can be assigned to each resource object. A label indicates the users or objects that can access a resource and how. A resource object may be a data table (file), a program, a workstation, an ATM or another network device. In addition, RACF allows the RACF administrator to set up user profiles that dictate user access privileges. Resource profiles can be discrete or generic. Similarly, user profiles can be individual or group. A generic profile is like a group profile. A discrete or individual profile overrides a generic or group file in the event of conflict. Similarly, a user profile overrides a resource profile where there is a conflict, e.g., a user profile with the user class of Special has full access to all data files irrespective of the resource profiles. A user may also be a program or a system function. For example, RACF can define what data the payroll "add" function has access to and the extent of access.

An organization can set a default access profile for all resources which can be overridden with specific access profiles. For example, the default profile may say that only the owner can change and delete and everyone can read. There is a risk in this because unless a specific access profile is created for a sensitive data table, everyone can read it. This default profile is called universal access authority (UACC). If the RACF administrator does not specify a value for UACC, the system assigned value is NONE, which means no one has access; a very safe approach, but may be too inflexible.

RACF IDs can be revoked automatically by the system once certain parameters are met. A RACF administrator can also manually revoke a user ID. Revocation does not mean deletion. A revoked ID can be revived. Revival is manual and is done by a RACF administrator. Examples of conditions for revoking user IDs are password attempt failures, departure from or transfer within the organization, and system abuse.

In addition to resource and user profiles as well as the universal access authority setting, the RACF administrator can set global options for each installation and for a local domain of installations. In conflict, global installation options will override the local environment domain options. The options are mainly for authentication and audit trail. Here is the list of common options:

- Activate auditing for access attempts by class.

- Activate auditing for security labels.

- Activate checking for previous passwords and password phrases.

- Activate or deactivate auditing of access attempts to RACF-protected resources based on installation-defined security levels.

- Control change intervals for passwords and password phrases.

- Control mixed-case passwords.

- Establish password syntax rules.

- Gather and display RACF statistics.

- Limit unsuccessful attempts to access the system using incorrect passwords.

- Log RACF events.

- Protect devices.

- Require that all work entering the system, including users logging on and batch jobs, have a security label assigned.

- Warn of password expiry.

RACF is a policy repository system. When access is requested by a system as part of transaction processing or by a user as part of ad hoc batch job, z/OS enquires RACF for the access policies for the data resource and the user and then grants permission or deny it. It is z/OS that contains the engine for access granting and denial based on policy settings in RACF.

CONCLUSION

PC and PC based server security continues to be improved by their vendors. Recently made available features include full hard disk encryption, application firewall and integrated malicious software features including anti-virus. In security, the weakest link is people, including people's commitment to define strong policies and comply with policies. Organizations should have tight operating system images for desktops and servers across the enterprise to comply with their policies. User access rights should be limited to their job functions and users should not be given administrator privilege to their desktops and laptops. System administrators should be controlled with thorough reference check, criminal record check before hiring and periodically thereafter, rotation of duties among servers, limiting the servers they support, limiting their other duties and regular management review of the system logs using software products to turn system logs into meaningful management reports.

MANAGEMENT CHECKLIST

1. Require system administrator to use longer and more complicated passwords than ordinary users. Require them to change passwords more frequently.

2. Secure server rooms with two-factor authentication.

3. Periodically assess the security features and follow a plan to enable and configure them in accordance with risk assessment and the security policy.

4. Develop policies and standard images for security features.

5. Periodically scan operating system and security feature parameters for policy compliance.

6. Establish patching procedures and monitor for compliance.

7. Disable employee access to the administrator account in their PCs.

8. Perform periodic review of the Active Directory configuration for compliance with the security policy.

9. Establish procedures for full disk encryption key recovery.

10. Conduct an annual review of operating system security for each operating system platform and report on overall security policy compliance.

AUDIT CHECKLIST

1. Perform a risk assessment of each operating system platform taking into account the applications supported, the size of the installed base and the degree of geographical distribution.

2. Review the organization's policy on operating system configuration and administration.

3. Review the audit trail of management monitoring of system administrators' activities.

4. Review Active Directory implementation and configuration to assess the adequacy of authentication and authorization infrastructure.

5. Review the patching procedures to assess adequacy.

6. Review patching audit trail to assess timeliness and completeness.

7. Confirm that ordinary users do not have local administrator access right to their computers.

8. Review the organization's policy about background check for system administrators and confirm that the policy is followed.

9. Review the organization's policy for disk encryption and verify compliance, including the control over recovery keys.

10. Test the operating system and RACF security features.

SUMMARY OF MAIN POINTS

1. Differences between operating systems in terms of access controls mainly have to do with authentication, authorization and logging.

2. Windows salts passwords for offline access. The user name is the salt.

3. Unix stores a 12-bit salt as the first two bytes of the hash. This, to some extent, reduces the value of the salt.

4. Unix uses a shadow file to point to the actual password hash, which is stored in a separate file. This reduces the risk of password cracking.

5. An operating system mainly logs the program events, security events and setup events.

6. Ordinary users without local administration privilege can change browser security and privacy settings. This means more monitoring and education are required.

7. Anti-virus software, firewall and full hard drive encryption now come standard with commercial PC operating systems.

8. Ordinary users should not be given local administration privilege so that they cannot install software.

9. Management should install software to decipher system logs to produce meaningful management reports.

10. z/OS has weaker security than Windows and Unix because its predecessors, Multiple Virtual Storage and Virtual Memory, were developed well before the Internet and not designed to mitigate the risk of hacking. RACF should be installed to provide commercial grade security for Z series servers.

REVIEW QUESTIONS

1. What are the purpose and functions of Active Directory?

2. What is a common way to prevent users from installing unauthorized software?

3. What is the purpose of the shadow file?

4. What is the purpose of the sandbox?

5. What type of access does a Special user in RACF have?

6. What are the three types of events recorded in the Windows Log?

7.   What is the function of the password salt and how long is the Unix salt?

8.   What are the CICS security deficiencies?

9.   What OS components does RACF interface with?

10.   Where is the Windows salt stored?

CASE – Data Center Security

The following is a list of audit findings on operating systems controls in a large organization. The auditee was the Department of Information Technology (DIT).

DIT did not fully restrict the use of privileged access rights to individuals based on their job function. Unauthorized use of privileged access rights could compromise the integrity of unemployment data and deny its availability. Our review of privileged access rights disclosed:

a) DIT did not restrict the security administration privilege to only security administrators.

b) DIT did not restrict the operations support privilege to only those individuals responsible for system maintenance and operations. This privilege allows individuals to manage all files. This privilege also provides full access, such as read, copy add, delete or modify to these same files.

c) DIT did not prohibit all users from having multiple incompatible privileged access rights.

DIT did not properly secure unemployment data and operating system files. As a result, DIT could not ensure that confidential unemployment data and critical operating system files were protected from unauthorized access and use. Our review of access to the third party service provider's mainframe computer system disclosed:

a) DIT did not restrict access to data files. The default system access allows all users to read and copy confidential employer and employee data, such as employee name, data of birth, social security number and wage earnings without DIT knowledge.

b) DIT granted its development staff, operations support staff and the third party service provider's staff unnecessary modify access to application data files. Modify access allows users to bypass established controls and make unauthorized changes to data.

c) DIT did not restrict access to operating system files. DIT granted its development staff, operations staff and the third party service provider's staff modify access to the operating system files. These files contain codes that define system operation and system security. Inappropriate access to operating system files could adversely affect the availability of information systems to users.

DIT had not established effective security administration and monitoring over the third party service provider's mainframe computer system. As a result, DIT could not ensure that it would detect the unauthorized use of privileged access circumventing security and controls. Our review of security administration and monitoring disclosed:

a) DIT assigned individuals primarily responsible for system development the incompatible duties of security administration. The security administration privilege allows administrators to manage user accounts and assign access to system resources. Without proper segregation of duties, there is a risk that these individuals could grant themselves or others inappropriate access.

b) DIT did not assign the responsibility for security monitoring to an individual independent of the security administrator function. Consequently, DIT cannot ensure that the system administrator is performing only appropriate and authorized activities. The security monitoring and security administrator functions are incompatible and should be performed by independent individuals.

c) DIT did not define the system administrator duties and authority in the security administrator's position descriptions. Without defined duties and authority, DIT cannot evaluate security administrators or establish accountability for the security of the third party service provider's mainframe computer system.

d) DIT did not ensure that security administrators were adequately trained to effectively perform their job responsibilities. The security administrator's position descriptions did not identify the necessary knowledge, skills and abilities needed to effectively perform security administrator duties. Without identifying the necessary knowledge, skills and abilities, DIT management cannot ensure that security administrators receive appropriate training.

e) DIT did not have a strategy to monitor the privileged access of system administrators. As a result, DIT cannot be assured that its monitoring practices will deter or detect misuse of privileged access.

f) DIT had not developed and implemented complete security reports to monitor the privileged access to all user accounts. In addition DIT had not developed and implemented policies and procedures for monitoring security on the mainframe computer system. Security reports should identify the critical security activities to be monitored, which user accounts will be monitored, and the process for using and maintaining security reports.

DIT did not fully develop and maintain complete security requirements for the mainframe security system. Consequently, DIT did not properly configure the security system and effectively protection critical system resources.
Although DIT and the third party service provider have made recent efforts to document the security requirements and settings of the security system, our review of DIT's efforts disclosed:

a) DIT did not clearly define its security administration role and responsibility in these security requirements. The agreement with the third party service provider stipulated that the State was responsible for security administration. However, our review of the security requirements and DIT's practices indicated that DIT had not assumed responsibility for security administration.

461

b) DIT had not established policy and procedures to administer the third party service provider's security system. As a result, significant aspects of the security requirements of privileged access, resource access management and segregation of duties were not well defined or were missing. Policy and procedures would provide direction to the security administrator and facilitate development of complete security requirements.

c) DIT did not sufficiently understand the functions of the security system or the strategy used to configure it. According to DIT, documentation that explained the State's initial strategy to configure the mainframe security system had been missing for several years. Maintaining complete and accurate documentation will help ensure that DIT security administrators understand the strategy used to configure the system.

d) DIT did not ensure the appropriateness of detailed security requirements and settings used to configure the third party service provider's security system. DIT did not explicitly agree to most of the third party provider's recommended security settings that were placed into operation. Although DIT recently documented these security settings, DIT should evaluate the appropriateness of the settings, revise where necessary, and document its agreement with the third party service provider.

Required

1. For each finding, assess whether the solution requires system configuration, management review, policy change, procedure change, or a combination.

2. For each finding, recommend a solution. For each solution that requires system configuration, state the solution in the z/OS and Windows environments.

MULTIPLE CHOICE QUESTIONS

1. Which operating system is RACF applicable to?
   a. Windows
   b. Unix
   c. z/OS
   d. Mac OS

2. A salted password is?

   a. easier to crack.
   b. less visible.
   c. harder to crack.
   d. encrypted.

3. Which of the following pairs is most closely related?
   a. Single sign-on (SSO) and access control list
   b. Single sign-on and two factor authentication
   c. RACF and Mac
   d. Salt and access control list

4. Which of the following is run in a sandbox?
   a. Active X
   b. RACF
   c. .NET components
   d. SSO

5. Which operating system uses CICS?
   a. z/OS
   b. Windows
   c. Mac OS
   d. Unix

6. Which operating system uses a string like rw–x--- in an access control list?
   a. z/OS
   b. Windows
   c. Mac OS
   d. Unix

7. Which Internet zone is the safest?
   a. Restricted
   b. Trust
   c. Internet
   d. Intranet

8. Which cookie will still work even with the highest Internet Explorer privacy setting?
    a. Persistent and being used
    b. All persistent
    c. Existing session
    d. Session cookies from trusted sites

9. What is the longest encryption key supported by Mac OS?
    a. 128
    b. 256
    c. 64
    d. 512

10. Who would be a frequent user of TSO?
    a. Bank customer
    b. Programmer
    c. RACF administrator
    d. Database administrator

CHAPTER TEN – CONTROL AND AUDIT IMPLICATIONS OF OUTSOURCING

If you deprive yourself of outsourcing and your competitors do not, you're putting yourself out of business. – Lee Kuan Yew (first prime minister of Singapore)

Information technology (IT) outsourcing has been on the rise in the last twenty years. It has slowed down because there is a finite number of functions in an organization that can be outsourced. The main reason for outsourcing is to cut cost. However, some companies later realize that the short term cost savings has led to long term loss of competitiveness related to disappearing skills within the organizations.

Information technology is the most common function being outsourced because it is not a core competency in most organizations. Another reason for outsourcing information technology is that it is harder to build expertise in house, compared to the effort to develop employees in administrative and clerical duties. Other common areas being outsourced are call center, payroll and accounting. For example, some banks have outsourced payroll; companies in some industries and governments outsource systems development, network management and computer operations; many technology companies have outsourced their call centers; some utility companies have outsourced IT, accounting, payroll and accounting.

While outsourcing in most cases brings short and medium term savings, it increases risks. It increases inherent risk because the business process has changed. Even if the changes are all positive, inherent risk can increase because employees have to get used to the new processes. Change, by nature, brings risk, because of uncertainty and the learning curve. Another reason for the increase in risk is that some business processes are now carried out by a vendor and therefore the uncertainty of reliable processing increases.

If inherent risk goes up, so does control risk. This is because control activities are part of business activities. Detection risk also goes up because the auditors have to understand the new processes; secondly, some of the audit trail is now in the service organization and may not be easily accessible to the auditors.

Outsourcing to foreign countries where the cost of labor and professional salaries are lower, is increasing. The CIO Magazine reported the following in July 2012.

Mega-deal outsourcing deals--those contracts with a value of $1 billion or more-picked up in the second quarter of 2012, according to the quarterly Global TPI Index. Five mega-deals were signed during the quarter compared with just one each in the second quarter of 2011 and the first quarter of 2012. All five were awarded outside of the mature U.S. and Western European markets-three of them in India and Brazil. (*Source: http://www.cio.com/article/711727/Mega_IT_Outsourcing_Deals_Move_Offshore?sourc e=CIONLE_nlt_insider_2012-07-24_default*).

If an organization outsources to a foreign company or the subsidiary of a foreign company, the information may be subject to foreign law. The organization has to take into account the implication of foreign legislation in its outsourcing decision.

CONTROL IMPLICATION

Management should conduct a risk assessment before deciding to outsource to assess whether the savings will outweigh the increase in risks and to determine the actions to minimize the outsourcing risks. These actions include the following:

1. Assess the risk vs benefit of outsourcing, including the risk of unreliable processing, system unavailability, loss of intellectual property, loss of skills, and privacy.
2. Develop a detailed business case.
3. Adopt a rigorous process for vendor selection.
4. Negotiate a detailed contract that protects the organization financially, operationally and legally and that provides for ongoing system availability.
5. Develop a contingency plan to continue operation and competitiveness in the event the service organization cannot be relied on any more.
6. Ensure that the outsourcing contract does not inhibit the organization from performing effective audits.
7. Develop a process to monitor the outsourcing contract for compliance with respect to system reliability, internal controls, system availability and privacy protection. Monitoring should also include ensuring that invoices are supported by delivered results.
8. Train employees to work with the outsourced processes.
9. Include the internal control expectations and requirements for the processes being outsourced in the outsourcing contract, to ensure that internal controls do not deteriorate as a result of outsourcing.
10. Obtain approval from the board of directors before outsourcing.

AUDIT IMPLICATION

Internal audit implications can be addressed by management's due diligence in contracting with the service provider to ensure that control expectations and audit requirements are met, including the right of audit and a process for monitoring internal controls in the service organization.

With respect to the audit of financial statements, the effect of outsourcing has to be addressed more structurally because of the more rigid audit requirements and generally accepted auditing standards. When an organization has outsourced a significant financial function, the shareholders' auditor faces an increase in audit risk because some significant internal controls and audit trail have been outsourced. However, regardless of the extent of outsourcing, the user organization always has access to the transaction records because the transactions pertain to the user organization. An analogy is when an accountant prepares an income tax return for a taxpayer, the taxpayer always owns the income tax return and data.

There are four options for the shareholders' auditor to address this increase in audit risk.

1. Identify compensating controls within the client to provide the same assurance as that could be provided from the outsourced controls. When the function outsourced is not complicated, e.g., payroll, the auditor can often find enough input and output controls to provide the necessary control assurance. Even processing controls can be tested from within the client without going into the service organization, e.g., most user organizations have online access to the outsourced payroll system.

2. Test the controls in the service organization. This is possible if the contract includes the right of audit.

3. Rely on an independent control assurance report on the service organization.

4. Take a primarily substantive audit approach. This would be necessary if the first three options are not available or practical. This option is always possible because regardless of the extent of outsourcing, the user organization owns and has access to transaction records.

We will discuss option 3 in more detail below.

Independent Control Assurance Report

There are two auditing standards that guide external auditors in obtaining the necessary audit evidence to support the financial statement opinion when a client has outsourced a process that materially affects the financial statements. The first is Statement of Auditing Standard (SAS) 70, *Service Organizations*. The second standard is Statement on Standards for Assurance Engagements (SSAE) 16, *Reporting on Controls at a Service Organizations*.

SSAE is a series of assurance standards to be used for non-financial statement audit engagements where the auditor is required to provide an independent opinion. Such engagements are called assurance engagements. Quite often, an assurance opinion provides a basis of reliance for the external auditors in conducting a financial statement audit.

In preparing and relying on an independent control assurance report, it is important for all parties to understand their roles as follows:
- A service organization is an organization that provides IT services for a fee.
- A user organization is an organization that procures IT services.
- A service auditor is an accounting firm hired by a service organization to provide an independent control assurance opinion on the services offered.
- A user auditor is the shareholders' auditor of a user organization.

SAS 70

This audit standard is to be followed when an audit client has outsourced a process that materially affects the financial statements. Here are the key requirements.

1. Obtain an understanding of the services provided by the service organization. This may require interaction with the service organization.

2. Determine whether adequate substantive audit evidence is available within the client, and if not, obtain such evidence from the service organization.

3. Enquire management as to whether the service organization has reported non-compliance with laws and regulations as well as uncorrected misstatements that affect the client, and if so, determine the effect on audit risk.

4. When a user auditor includes reference to the work of a service auditor to support a qualified opinion, the user auditor's report will also indicate that such reference does not diminish the user auditor's responsibilities for the opinion.

5. The auditor may rely on service auditors' reports issued under standards developed Under SSAE 16. When relying on such a report, the shareholders' auditor of a user organization (user auditor) may not refer to this report in the user organization financial statements opinion. This is consistent with the practice that shareholders' auditors do not mention outside experts used in carrying out an audit, in the audit opinion. However, if the financial statements audit opinion is qualified largely as a result of a qualified SSAE 16 report, the user auditor may attribute the qualified financial statement opinion to the qualified SSAE 16 report. For example, if the financial statement audit opinion is qualified because of a going concern issue caused by the loss of the year's financial transactions after the audit is completed, and the SSAE 16 report is qualified due to failed backup procedures, the financial statement audit opinion can refer to the qualified SSAE 16 report.

SSAE 16

These two standards guide the external auditors of a service organization to conduct a review and tests of the organization's internal controls with respect to services provided to the organization's customers, and to opine on such internal controls. The external auditors are specifically hired by the service organization to express an opinion on the controls defined by the organization, and they may also be the auditors of the organization's financial statements. AICPA requires that such auditors (service auditor) be licensed to practice public accounting.

The purpose of such an assurance engagement is to provide comfort to the shareholders' auditors of the user organizations (user auditor) . However, the report is addressed to the user organizations because the service auditor has no contractual obligation to the user auditor.

SSAE 16 provides for two types of internal control assurance engagements. The first type, Type 1, covers internal control design and provides point-in-time assurance. The second type, Type 2, covers internal control operational effectiveness and covers a period. Both standards state that a period must be at least six months. Although the maximum length is not stated, there is no point for such a period to exceed a year because the purpose of this type of assurance engagement is to support the financial statement audit of user organizations. A type 1 report does not mean that the internal controls stated will only be tested for a day. Many controls involve the build-up of procedures and design work so the auditors will likely need to review the associated activities for many days. A type 2 report requires that every control be tested throughout the period of six months or more. An example of a type 1 report control that requires testing for more than a day is a disaster recovery plan. For the auditor to opine on this control, the audit work includes more than reading and assessing the plan. It also includes reviewing the test results and the test likely has taken more than one day to complete.

SSAE 16 requires the auditor to opine on the correctness of system description, the adequacy of internal control procedures to support each stated control objective, and the comprehensiveness of internal control objectives.

Assurance Engagement Initiation

1. Once a service organization decides to hire an accounting firm to express an opinion on its internal controls that support its services, for the purpose of providing an assurance report to its customers' shareholders' auditors, the service organization enters into an engagement agreement with the accounting firm. The accounting firm, in this context, is called the service auditor.

2. The service organization and the service auditor agree to perform the engagement in accordance with SSAE 16, based on the service auditor's understanding of the written system description used in providing the services.

Assurance Engagement Planning

1. The service organization describes the systems used to perform the services.

2. The service auditor reviews the system description to assess its correctness. If the auditor finds that the system description is materially incorrect or incomplete, it should ask the service organization to correct.

3. If the service organization uses another service organization for a significant service in relation to the service provided to the primary service organization, the scope of the assurance engagement must include the secondary service organization.

4. If the service organization refuses to correct the system description, the service auditor should take one of the following actions.

   a) Describe the material inconsistency or misstatement of fact in the assurance report.
   b) Withhold the assurance report until the matter is resolved.
   c) Withdraw from the engagement.

   The extent of incorrectness of the system description should be a critical factor in deciding whether to continue with the engagement. If the description is grossly incorrect, the service auditor should withdraw from the engagement.

5. The service organization develops internal control objectives and control procedures to support the system description. Internal control procedures may be manual or automated.

Internal Control Assessment

1. The service auditor reviews the internal control objectives in relation to the system description.

2. The service auditor assesses the appropriateness and completeness of the control objectives.

3. If the control objectives are considered materially inappropriate or incomplete, the service auditor should suggest to the service organization that the objectives be corrected or expanded.

4. If the service organization refuses to correct a significant misstatement in control objectives, the auditor should inform the service organization that the opinion will be qualified.

5. The service auditor assesses the appropriateness and adequacy of the internal control procedures for each stated internal control objective.

6. If the service auditor finds a material weakness in internal control procedures, it suggests that the client correct.

7. If the service organization refuses to correct or replace a significant misstatement in internal control procedures, the auditor should inform the service organization that the audit opinion will be qualified.

8. The service auditor reviews any recent internal audit work papers pertaining to the internal controls and discusses the work papers and related reports with the internal auditors.

9. The service auditor conducts testing of control procedures using sample sizes that will yield high assurance. This requires more extensive testing than testing internal controls in a financial statement audit because the auditor will be

470

expressing an opinion on internal controls. In a typical financial statement audit, the auditor seeks only moderate assurance as control testing is only a method to reduce substantive testing and the auditor's opinion is on the financial statements, not on internal controls. Even though the service auditor achieves high assurance in its testing, the user auditors can place only moderate internal control reliance on the independent control assurance report because the controls are somewhat generic, i.e., applying to all organizations that use the system subject to the assurance report. When the user auditors adapt such internal controls to their clients' environments, there is often some loss of relevance, hence the originally high assurance from the control assurance report may likely be reduced to moderate.

10. If the service auditor finds a material weakness in internal control procedures, it suggests that the service organization correct.

11. If the service organization refuses to correct or replace a significant misstatement in control procedures, the auditor should inform the service organization that the audit opinion will be qualified.

12. The service auditor concludes on test results and the internal control objectives.

13. The service auditor decides whether the results warrant an unqualified opinion.

14. If the service auditor becomes aware of non-compliance with laws and regulations, fraud, or uncorrected errors attributable to the service organization that are not clearly trivial and may affect one or more user organizations, the auditor should determine whether the matter has been communicated appropriately to the affected user organizations. If the matter has not been so communicated and the service organization is unwilling to do so, the auditor should take one of more of the following actions:
    - Obtain legal advice about the consequence of different courses of action.
    - Communicate with the board of directors and the chief executive officer.
    - Communicate with third parties, for example, a regulator.
    - Qualify the audit opinion.
    - Withdraw from the engagement.

Management Response to Control Deficiencies

If the service auditor assesses that an internal control procedure is deficient in design or is not operated reliably, the service organization has the following options to address this.

1. Correct the control procedure. This option may not be practical if the control procedure is found to be deficient because it has not been operated reliably for a significant part of the period under review. The control procedure may not be correctable retroactively, e.g., password protection. An example of a control procedure that can be retroactively corrected is source code comparison. If it has not been compared in the first six months

when the procedure calls for monthly comparison, the service organization can do the retroactive comparison as long as the historical record of source code versions are available.

2. Replace the internal control procedure. This may not be practical for the same reason indicated above, i.e., the new control procedure cannot mitigate the risk caused by the failure of the control deficiency because the new control procedure cannot address the deficiency retroactively. Management may find an existing control that can replace the failed control if the replacement control can be tested retroactively.

3. Cancel the assurance engagement or make it a control assurance review provided only to service organization management without the intent to provide the report to user organizations.

4. Accept a qualified opinion.

Audit Reporting

Letter of Representation

Before issuing the audit report, the service auditor must obtain a letter of representation from the service organization. The letter of representation includes the following items:

1. Confirmation that the system description is correct.
2. Confirmation that the service organization has provided the auditor with all relevant information and access agreed to in the engagement letter.
3. Confirmation that the service organization has disclosed to the auditor any of the items listed below to the client's best knowledge.
   - Non-compliance with laws and regulations, fraud, or uncorrected deviations attributable to the service organization that may affect one or more user entities.
   - Internal control deficiencies.
   - Any events subsequent to the period covered by the system description up to the date of the auditor's report that could have a significant effect on the report.

Audit Report

The audit report should include the following items.

1. A title that clearly indicates that the report is an independent service auditor's assurance report.

2. System description.

3. The part of the system description that is not covered by the audit opinion.

4. If the system description refers to the need for complementary user entity controls, the audit report must state that the auditor has not evaluated the suitability of design or operating effectiveness of such user organization internal controls, and that the

control objectives stated in the audit report can be achieved only if complementary user organization controls are suitably designed or operated effectively, along with the controls at the service organization. An example of such a control procedure is user organization review of certain exception reports, which requires very timely review in order to be effective.

5. If services are performed by a subservice organization, the nature of activities performed by the subservice organization as described in the service organization's system description should be stated. It should also be stated whether the auditor has tested the subservice organization's internal controls.

6. The criteria (assertions) for specifying the internal control objectives as well as the control objectives.

7. If the audit covers a period, a list of audit procedures should be included. This allows the user auditors to reconcile to their own audit programs to assess the comprehensive of audit coverage in the service auditor control testing.

8. A statement that the service organization is responsible for:
   - preparing the system description, internal control objectives and internal control procedures;
   - providing the services as described in the system description.

9. The extent of reliance on the service organization's internal auditors should be stated.

10. A statement that the service auditor's responsibility is to express an opinion on the system description, the adequacy of internal controls to support the stated control objectives, and the comprehensiveness of control objectives.

11. A statement that the engagement was performed in accordance with SSAE 16.

12. A statement of the limitation of controls and the risk of projecting to future periods any evaluation of the operating effectiveness of controls.

13. A statement to indicate any material change in internal control procedures from the previous assurance engagement.

14. An opinion to state whether, in all material aspects,
   a) The description fairly presents the service organization's system that had been designed and implemented as at a specified date (type 1 report) or throughout the specified period (type 2 report);
   b) The controls related to the control objectives were suitably designed as at a specified date (type 1 report) or throughout a specified period (type 2 report);
   c) The controls tested operated effectively throughout the specified period (for type 2 report only);
   d) The control objectives are adequate in relation to the system description (SSAE 16 only).

Distribution of the report is restricted to the service organization, the user organizations and the user organizations' external auditors.

Subsequent Events

Events or transactions sometimes occur subsequent to the point in time or period of time covered by the service auditor's report but prior to the date of the report, that have a material effect on the system or control objectives, or that require adjustment or disclosure in the report. In performing an attest engagement, an auditor should consider information about subsequent events that comes to his or her attention. Two types of subsequent events require consideration by the auditor.

The first type consists of events that provide additional information with respect to conditions that existed at the point in time or during the period of time covered by the service auditor's report. This information should be used by the auditor in considering whether the subject matter or assertion is presented in conformity with the criteria and whether it affects the presentation of the subject matter, the assertion, or the service auditor's report. An example of this type of event is that a disaster recovery test carried out subsequent to the report period failed because data backup in the report period was done incorrectly. The auditor should assess the significance of this control failure and consider qualifying the report. If the control failure is not significant, there is no need to disclose this subsequent event in the audit report.

The second type consists of those events that provide information with respect to conditions that arose subsequent to the point in time or period of time covered by the audit report that are of such a nature and significance that their disclosure is necessary to keep the subject matter from being misleading. This type of information will not normally affect the audit report if the information is appropriately disclosed by the service organization. An example is the collapse of the data center.

Although the service auditor has no responsibility to detect subsequent events, s/he should inquire of the service organization as to whether they are aware of any subsequent events, through the date of the audit report, that would have a material effect on the subject matter or assertion. The representation letter ordinarily would include a representation concerning subsequent events. The service auditor has no responsibility to keep informed of events subsequent to the date of the audit report; however, s/he may later become aware of conditions that existed at that date that might have affected the audit report had s/he been aware of them.

Sample Report

To the board of directors of XYZ Company

We have examined the accompanying description of the stated internal control objectives of the ABC system of XYZ Company and the control procedures designed to achieve those objectives, and have performed tests of the effectiveness of those control procedures during the period from January 1, 2011 to December 31, 2011. Our examination was made in accordance with Canadian Standards for Assurance Engagements, and accordingly included such tests and other procedures as we considered necessary in the circumstances.

In our opinion, the control procedures included in the accompanying description were suitably designed to provide reasonable, but not absolute, assurance that the stated internal control objectives described therein were achieved, and the control procedures operated effectively from January 1, 2011 to December 31, 2011.

The description of stated internal control objectives and procedures at XYZ Company is as of December 31, 2011, and information about tests of operating effectiveness of specific controls covers the period from January 1, 2011 to December 31, 2011. Any projection of such information to the future is subject to the risk that, because of change, the description may no longer portray the control procedures in existence. The potential effectiveness of specific control procedures at XYZ Company is subject to inherent limitations and, accordingly, errors or fraud may occur and not be detected. Further, the projection of any conclusions to future periods, based on our findings, is subject to the risk that changes required because of the passage of time, may alter the validity of such conclusions.

This report in intended for the use of the customers of XYZ Company and their auditors, potential customers and regulatory authorities.

Craig and Feng
Certified Public Accountants
April 25, 2012

MANAGEMENT CHECKLIST

1. Perform a risk analysis before deciding to outsource.

2. Perform a cost benefit analysis before deciding to outsource.

3. Obtain approval from the board of directors before outsourcing.

4. Review the outsourcing contract with company lawyers before committing.

5. Ensure that the outsourcing contract includes at least one of the following:
    a. right of audit
    b. annual independent control assurance report
    c. written control assurance checklist from the service organization at least semi-annually.

6. Review the service organization's financial stability before committing.

7. Obtain reference checks about the service organization before committing.

8. Follow the organization's signing authority levels before awarding the contract.

9. Designate an executive to own each outsourcing contract and monitor vendor compliance including monitoring processing reliability, system availability, internal control compliance, privacy protection, incident management and invoice substantiation.

10. Perform annual review of each contract for compliance and satisfaction.

INTERNAL AUDIT CHECKLIST

The above material provides clear guidance to user organization management, service organization management, user auditor and service auditor to deal with outsourcing arrangement and the review of controls in a service organization. Internal auditors of a user organization can play a valuable role to help management to address the risk of outsourcing. I provide an internal audit checklist below.

1. Review all outsourcing contracts to assess inherent risk and control risk.

2. If the inherent risk or control risk is material, the auditors should determine whether the contract provides the user organization with right of audit.

3. If right of audit is available, the auditors should request management approval to assess and test the internal controls in the service organization and report the results of assessment and testing to management.

4. Review the service organization control assurance report to assess its impact on the risk of outsourcing and ensure management is aware of such risk.

5. Follow up with management on any qualified service organization report to ensure that management will take that into account in contract management and renewal consideration.

6. Review the invoices from the service organization to ensure consistency with the contracts.

7. Review any internal control checklists submitted by the service organization to assess their effect on the user organization's inherent risk and control risk and provide appropriate reporting to management.

8. Provide assistance to the shareholders' auditors to help them assess the risk of outsourcing and obtain the necessary control assurance.

9. Provide assistance to the shareholders' auditors to help them conduct substantive testing in relation to the activities outsourced.

10. Assist management in assessing the risks of potential outsourcing and assessing the risk of the vendor selection process.

EXTERNAL AUDIT CHECKLIST

This checklist is intended for the shareholders' auditors of a user organization to address the control assurance gap created by outsourcing.

1. Assess the financial statement materiality of the business process that has been outsourced.

2. Assess the impact of outsourcing on the organization's ability to meet regulatory requirements such as privacy legislations and public company reporting requirements.

3. Look for compensating controls in the organization to replace the controls that have been outsourced for audit reliance.

4. Review the outsourcing contract to assess the availability of audit right and control assurance report from the service organization.

5. Review the impact of outsourcing on the client's intellectual property and its valuation.

6. Follow SAS 70 to address the control assurance gap.

7. Engage a computer audit specialist to review any independent control assurance report on IT outsourcing.

8. Assess the comprehensiveness of internal control test procedures disclosed in an independent control assurance report in relation to the accounting firm's methodology and the client's transactions.

9. Assess the qualification of the auditors preparing the independent control assurance report.

10. Assess the implication of a qualified independent control assurance opinion on the financial statement audit.

CONCLUSION

Outsourcing is the rise and there is no indication that the trend will reverse. Management has to balance the risk with potential savings. Internal auditors should lend their internal control and risk assessment expertise to help management in outsourcing decisions and in contract management. External auditors need to ensure that management is aware of the effect of outsourcing on audit evidence and audit trail availability, particularly in relation to the audit of financial statements.

SUMMARY OF MAIN POINTS

1. A service organization is an organization that provides IT services for a fee.
   A user organization is an organization that procures IT services.
   A service auditor is an accounting firm hired by a service organization to provide an independent control assurance opinion on the services offered. This accounting firm may also be the financial statement auditor of the service organization.
   A user auditor is the external auditor of a user organization.

2. When an external audit client has outsourced a financially material function, the external auditors are faced with a control assurance gap. It is only a control assurance gap because the outsourcing organization always has access to financial records regardless of the extent of outsourcing. Thus, a substantive audit is always possible.

3. To bridge the control assurance gap, the external auditors should successively consider the following options:
   - Look for compensating in-house controls.
   - Seek to rely on an independent control assurance report.
   - Seek to test controls in the service organization.
   - Resort to a substantive audit.

4. To consider the above options, external auditors are guided by SAS 70.

5. If a service organization offers an independent control assurance report, that report and the audit work to support it must be prepared in accordance with SSAE 16.

6. SSAE 16 requires the opinion to address the correctness of system description, the adequacy of internal controls to support each stated control criterion, and the comprehensiveness of internal control objectives.

7. A Type 1 independent control assurance report provides point in time assurance. A Type 2 report covers a period of at least six months.

8. To address a control deficiency in an independent control assurance audit, a service organization has the following options:
    - Correct the control deficiency if not too late.
    - Replace the control with another control if not too late.
    - Stop the audit and deal with the repercussion with the user organizations.
    - Accept a qualified report.

9. The independent control assurance report must disclose material changes in internal controls from the previous year and material subsequent events.

10. Internal audit should play a proactive role in helping management assess the risk of outsourcing, preparing clauses in the contract to address risks and control compliance, and regularly assessing the service organization's contract compliance.

REVIEW QUESTIONS

1. What is the effect of outsourcing on the role of internal auditors?

2. What is the effect of outsourcing on inherent risk, control risk and detection risk?

3. What is the role of the service auditor?

4. What is the difference between SAS 70 and SSAE 16?

5. What is the difference between a Type 1 report and a Type 2 report?

6. Who are the audiences of a service organization control assurance report and why?

7. Can the shareholders' auditor of a service organization also be the "service auditor" in the context of SSAE 16? Why or why not?

8. What are the options to the shareholders' auditors of an organization that has outsourced and which one is the most desirable?

9. Why do you think a Type 2 control assurance report has to disclose the audit tests?

10. What level of control assurance is provided by a type 2 control assurance report and why?

CASE

Study the following excerpt of a sample SSAE 16 Type 1 report. Describe the audit procedures you would carry out to obtain assurance on the internal controls, assuming the audit is carried out to support a Type 2 audit opinion.

Source of report: www.sas70exam.com. Permission granted by MacDonald Page & Co, LLC.

ABC, INC.
PAYROLL PROCESSING SERVICES

TO THE MANAGEMENT OF ABC, INC.
ANYTOWN, MAINE

We have examined ABC, Inc.'s description of their payroll processing services as of December 31, 2010 (the "description"), and the suitability of the design of controls to achieve the related control objectives stated in the description.

In Section II, ABC, Inc. has provided an assertion about the fairness of the presentation of the description and suitability of the design of the controls to achieve the related control objectives stated in the description. ABC, Inc. is responsible for preparing the description and for the assertion, including the completeness, accuracy, and method of presentation of the description and the assertion, providing the services covered by the description, specifying the control objectives and stating them in the description, identifying the risks that threaten the achievement of the control objectives, selecting the criteria, and designing, implementing, and documenting controls to achieve the related control objectives stated in the description.

Our responsibility is to express an opinion on the fairness of the presentation of the description and on the suitability of the design of the controls to achieve the related control objectives stated in the description, based on our examination. We conducted our examination in accordance with attestation standards established by the American Institute of Certified Public Accountants. Those standards require that we plan and perform our examination to obtain reasonable assurance about whether, in all material aspects, the description is fairly presented and the controls were suitability designed to achieve the related control objectives stated in the description as of December 31, 2010. An examination of a description of a service organization's system and the suitability of the design of the service organization's controls to achieve the related control objectives stated in the description involves performing procedures to obtain evidence about the fairness of the presentation of the description of the system and the suitability of the design of the controls to achieve the related control objectives stated in the description.

Our procedures included assessing the risks that the description is not fairly presented and that the controls were not suitably designed to achieve the related control objectives stated in the description. An examination engagement of this type also includes evaluating the overall presentation of the description and the suitability of the control objectives stated therein, and the suitability of the criteria specified by the service organization and described in Section III. We did not perform procedures to determine the operating effectiveness of controls for any period. Accordingly, we express no opinion on the operating effectiveness of any aspects of ABC, Inc.'s controls, individually or in the aggregate. We believe that the evidence we obtained is sufficient and appropriate to provide a reasonable basis for our opinion.

Because of their nature, controls at a service organization or subservice organization may not prevent, or detect and correct all errors or omissions in processing or reporting transactions. Also, the projection to the future of any evaluation of the fairness of the presentation of the description, or conclusions about the suitability of the design or operating effectiveness of the controls to achieve the related control objectives is subject to the risk that controls at a service organization or subservice organization may become inadequate or fail.

In our opinion, in all material respects, based on the criteria described in ABC, Inc.'s assertion in Section II,
a) The description fairly presents the payroll processing services that were designed and implemented as of December 31, 2010
b) The controls related to the control objectives stated in the description were suitably designed to provide reasonable assurance that the control objectives would be achieved if the controls operated effectively as of December 31, 2010.

The information included in Sections I and IV of this report is presented by ABC, Inc. to provide additional information to user organizations and is not a part of ABC, Inc.'s description of controls placed in operation. The information in Sections I and IV has not been subjected to the procedures applied to the examination of the description of the controls related to the payroll processing services and, accordingly, we express no opinion on it.

This report is intended solely for the information and use by the management of ABC, Inc., user entities of the payroll processing services as of December 31, 2010, and the independent auditors of such user entities, who have a sufficient understanding to consider it, along with other information including information about controls implemented by user entities themselves, when obtaining an understanding of user entities information and communication systems relevant to financial reporting. This report is not intended to be and should not be used by anyone other than these specified parties.

We have prepared the description of ABC, Inc.'s payroll processing services (the "description") for user entities of the system as of December 31, 2010, and their user auditors who have a sufficient understanding to consider it, along with other information, including information about controls implemented by user entities themselves, when obtaining an understanding of the user entities' information and communication system relevant to financial reporting. We confirm, to the best of our knowledge and belief, that

A. The description fairly presents the payroll processing services made available to user entities of the system as of December 31, 2010. The criteria we used in making this assertion were that the description

(i) presents how the system made available to user entities of the system was designed and implemented to process relevant transactions, including
   1. the classes of transactions processed.
   2. the procedures, within both automated and manual systems, by which those transactions are initiated, authorized, recorded, processed, corrected as necessary, and transferred to the reports presented to user entities of the system.
   3. the related accounting records, supporting information, and specific accounts that are used to initiate, authorize, record, process, and report transactions; this includes the correction of incorrect information and how information is transferred to the reports provided to user entities of the system.
   4. how the system captures and addresses significant events and conditions, other than transactions.
   5. the process used to prepare reports or other information provided to user entities of the system.
   6. specified control objectives and controls designed to achieve those objectives.
   7. other aspects of our control environment, risk assessment process, information and communication systems (including the related business processes), control activities, and monitoring controls that are relevant to processing and reporting transactions of user entities of the system.

(ii) Does not omit or distort information relevant to the scope of the payroll processing services, while acknowledging that the description is prepared to meet the common needs of a broad range of user entities of the system and the independent auditors of those user entities, and may not, therefore, include every aspect of the payroll processing system that each individual user entity of the system and its auditor may consider important in its own particular environment.

B. the controls related to the control objectives stated in the description were suitably designed as of December 31, 2010, to achieve those control objectives. The criteria we used in making this assertion were that
   (i) the risks that threaten the achievement of the control objectives stated in the description have been identified by the service organization; and
   (ii) the controls identified in the description would, if operating as described, provide reasonable assurance that those risks would not prevent the control objectives stated in the description from being achieved.

ABC, INC. BACKGROUND

Founded in 1957, ABC, Inc. is a leading payroll processing service provider located in Anytown, Maine. ABC, Inc. is the leading provider of HR, payroll, and tax services to financial institutions, schools, and small and medium size business. ABC, Inc. has about 300 employees who service approximately 150,000 clients throughout New England. ABC, Inc. is committed to providing a secure outsourced business solution to each client and strives to form strong partnerships with clients to achieve a seamless partnership.

PAYROLL PROCESSING SERVICES

ABC, Inc.'s payroll processing services are designed to assist companies in processing their payroll transactions by streamlining the process to improve client productivity. ABC, Inc. manages the payroll tasks that include payroll processing, W2 preparation and tax reporting. ABC, Inc. payroll processing services uses custom developed software supported by a Windows 2003 network. Transmission of payroll data is performed using encoded FTP via SSL / SSH or Pretty Good Privacy (PGP) encrypted files via FTP. The Payroll Processing Manager oversees the payroll processing services and reviews each client contract to verify that appropriate services and support is being provided.

This section can include any relevant information about the company that is not part of the description of controls presented in Section II.

ORGANIZATIONAL STRUCTURE

ABC, Inc. has a formal organizational structure with functional areas and a reporting hierarchy. The senior management at ABC, Inc. includes the President / Chief Executive Officer (CEO), Treasurer and Chief Financial Officer (CFO), Chief Security Officer (CSO), and Payroll Processing Manager. A formal organizational chart is in place that includes the Payroll Processing department and identifies responsibility areas.

The Payroll Processing Manager has oversight responsibilities for the payroll processing services. Within the department, positions include the Payroll Processing Manager, Payroll Processing Assistant Manager, and Payroll Processing Associates. Formal job descriptions are in place for Payroll Processing department employees. The job descriptions include key responsibilities, service standards, and client service expectations.

EMPLOYMENT MANUALS

An employee manual is in place to document company policies including acceptable use and confidentiality. The employee manual is available to all employees on ABC, Inc. network. The CEO reviews the employee manual on an annual basis at year-end and makes updates as necessary. Employees are required to sign an acknowledgement of receipt of the employee manual at the time of hire.

EMPLOYEE HIRING PROCEDURES

ABC, Inc. has a formal recruiting process for each new employee. The Human Resource Manager obtains applicable reference checks and performs a documented criminal background check for each new employee prior to their start date. A new hire checklist is used for the new employee to ensure that required hiring steps have been performed. ABC, Inc. also has formal termination procedures, which include a termination checklist with assigned tasks to be completed upon the employee's termination. Tasks are assigned to the Human Resource department, the employee's supervisor and IT-related employees, as applicable.

ORIENTATION AND TRAINING

ABC, Inc. holds company-wide meetings on a quarterly basis to communicate company information including new policies. The Payroll Processing department holds monthly meetings to discuss issues from the previous month. Additionally, on-going job-related training is provided to each employee in the Payroll Processing department.

STAFF PERFORMANCE

Formal annual performance evaluations are conducted by a member of senior-management for each employee, which includes feedback provided by the employee's direct supervisor. Annual evaluations are added to each employees HR folder. *In addition to Organization and Administration, other sections included in Section II typically are Customer Servicing, Computer / Daily Operations, Software Change Management, Logical Security and Physical Security.*

CLIENT CONTROLS

In order for ABC, Inc.'s clients to benefit from the controls described in this report, ABC, Inc.'s clients must determine whether the following controls are in place and functioning. Furthermore, the following list of controls addresses only those controls relating to payroll processing services. *This list is not intended to be a complete listing of the controls that provide a basis for the assertions underlying the accounting records.* ABC Inc.'s clients, through their agreements with ABC, Inc. have selected unique levels of services, and therefore, not all user control considerations may apply to each client. Payroll processing clients are expected to setup the following controls:

USER ACCESS CONTROLS

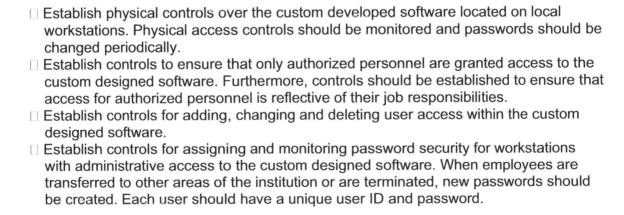

- ☐ Establish physical controls over the custom developed software located on local workstations. Physical access controls should be monitored and passwords should be changed periodically.
- ☐ Establish controls to ensure that only authorized personnel are granted access to the custom designed software. Furthermore, controls should be established to ensure that access for authorized personnel is reflective of their job responsibilities.
- ☐ Establish controls for adding, changing and deleting user access within the custom designed software.
- ☐ Establish controls for assigning and monitoring password security for workstations with administrative access to the custom designed software. When employees are transferred to other areas of the institution or are terminated, new passwords should be created. Each user should have a unique user ID and password.

CHANGE MANAGEMENT

☐ Establish controls to ensure that patches are applied after appropriate approval from an authorized employee is granted and testing has been performed.

☐ Establish controls to ensure that changes to institution parameters are requested by authorized individuals and that a review of completed institution parameter changes is performed.

☐ Establish controls to ensure that support requests are submitted by authorized individuals and are followed up on a timely basis.

NETWORK SECURITY

☐ Implement firewalls or other equivalent security devices to protect network systems that are connected to ABC, Inc. from public networks.

☐ Establish controls to ensure changes to institution parameters are requested from authorized individuals and that a review of completed institution parameter changes is performed.

☐ Implement a process to review and install operation system-level patches on workstations running the custom developed payroll processing software.

DISASTER RECOVER PLANNING

☐ Review the applicability of ABC, Inc.'s disaster recovery plan and the results of the annual disaster recovery plan testing.

☐ Develop a comprehensive business continuity plan that corresponds to ABC, Inc.'s disaster recovery plan.

The plan should identify procedures that minimize the potential downtime that could be experienced if a disaster was declared at either ABC, Inc. or their own organization.

DESCRIPTION OF CONTROL OBJECTIVES AND EVALUATION OF INTERNAL CONTROLS

INTRODUCTION

Application of internal controls at ABC, Inc.'s user organizations is necessary to achieve many of the control objectives listed in this report. Therefore, it is critical to evaluate each user organization's internal control structure in conjunction with ABC, Inc.'s internal control structure as described in this report. There may be additional control objectives and related internal controls that are appropriate for the payroll processing services that are not identified in this report.

ORGANIZATION & ADMINISTRATION

CONTROL OBJECTIVE 1: Controls provide reasonable assurance that through the recruiting, hiring, evaluation and training processes, employees possess the necessary skills and conform to organizational policies and ethics.

CONTROLS SPECIFIED BY ABC, INC.
COMMENTS

A formal organizational chart that establishes proper delegation of authority is used.
    No exceptions noted.

Each employee is assigned responsibilities based on formally defined job descriptions.
    No exceptions noted.

The Employee Manual is reviewed annually by the CEO for applicable updates.
    No exceptions noted.

Company policies are documented in an employee manual and made available to each employee.
    No exceptions noted.

Employees receive and sign acknowledgement of the Employee Manual at the time.
    No exceptions noted.

A formal hiring process exists including reference checks and criminal background checks for each new employee.
    No exceptions noted.

A formal new hire checklist is used as part of the hiring process.
    No exceptions noted.

A formal terminated employee checklist is used to ensure that each required step is completed upon termination.
    No exceptions noted.

Annual evaluations are performed for each employee by senior management.
    No exceptions noted.

Ongoing internal job related training is provided to each employee.
    No exceptions noted.

Company wide meetings are held on a quarterly basis to communicate new information including new or updated policies.
    No exceptions noted.

MULTIPLE CHOICE QUESTION

1. Which of the following firms can conduct an SSAE 16 assurance engagement?
   A. IBM
   B. McKinsey & Co.
   C. KPMG
   D. Microsoft

2. Which is an option that is always available to the shareholders' auditor of a corporation that has outsourced?

   A. Take a primarily substantive audit approach.
   B. Rely on compensating controls in the client.
   C. Test the internal controls of the service organization.
   D. Rely on an independent internal control assurance report.

3. Which requirement forms a key difference SSAE 16 audit opinion and a financial statement audit opinion?
   A. One of these standards does not allow a point-in-time assurance report.
   B. One of these standards requires the service auditor to opine on the adequacy of internal control objectives.
   C. They differ on the extent of control testing.
   D. They differ on the extent of audit procedures disclosure.

4. From an organization risk perspective, which is the greatest risk factor of outsourcing to an offshore location?
   A. Threat to local economy
   B. Higher cost
   C. Challenge by Internal Revenue Service
   D. Contract dispute resolution
   E. Impact of foreign legislation

5. Which option is always available to the management of a service organization if a service auditor cannot rely on a stated internal control?
   A. Replace the internal control
   B. Fix the internal control
   C. Remove the internal control objective
   D. Stop the engagement

6. What level of control assurance can the user auditor derive from a service organization control assurance report?
   A. High
   B. Moderate
   C. Low
   D. Moderate for a period report

7. What is the period of testing for internal controls in a type 1 control assurance report?
   A. One day
   B. Three months
   C. One or more days
   D. At least six months

8. Which of the following internal control deficiencies is most correctable by a service organization in an independent control assurance engagement?
   A. Weak password
   B. Lack of testing of disaster recovery plan
   C. Back-up not stored offsite
   D. Late management review of staff absence record

9. The disclosure of audit procedures in a type 2 report helps
   A. service organization management to assess the comprehensiveness of control testing.
   B. user organizations to assess the comprehensiveness of control testing.
   C. user organization auditors to assess the comprehensiveness of internal control testing.
   D. the shareholders' auditors of the service organization to support its financial statement audit opinion.

10. What should the service auditor do if the internal controls pertaining to a control objective are inadequate?
    A. Withdraw from the engagement.
    B. Qualify the audit opinion.
    C. Provide an adverse opinion.
    D. Delay the report.

Chapter 11 – SysTrust and Payment Card Industry Control Assurance

The most important thing for a young man is to establish credit – a reputation and character. – John D. Rockefeller

Organizations continue to increase their reliance on information systems. Aside from traditional outsourcing, there are arrangements for organizations to share information systems and trading partners to share information. As a result, there is increasing demand on organizations operating information systems to provide assurance to external stakeholders. In this chapter, we will discuss two common types of such assurance reports, other than those in an outsourcing agreement, which was discussed in the last chapter. The two types of non-outsourcing IT control assurance engagements we will discuss in this chapter are:

- SysTrust, and
- Payment Card Industry security assurance

SYSTRUST

An organization that hosts an information system used by business partners like suppliers, corporate customers or affiliates may be demanded to provide internal control assurance with respect to the system. To ensure that such an engagement provides consistent assurance from organization to organization, Canadian Institute of Chartered Accountants (CICA) and American Institute of Certified Public Accountants (AICPA) developed the trust services standard to guide this type of internal control assurance.

Under the trust service standard, this type of internal control assurance is called SysTrust. The trust service standard starts with defining the following five trust services principles:

1. Security – The system is protected against unauthorized access.

2. Availability – The system is available for operation and use as committed or agreed.

3. Processing integrity – System processing is complete, accurate, timely, and authorized.

4. Confidentiality - Information designated as confidential is protected as committed or agreed.

5. Privacy – Personal information is collected, used, retained, disclosed, and destroyed in conformity with the commitments in the entity's privacy policy and the applicable privacy legislation.

The first three principles must be subscribed to by the service organization in order for a SysTrust engagement to commence. The confidentiality and privacy principles are optional.

The trust services principles and criteria of security, availability, processing integrity, confidentiality and privacy are organized into four broad areas:

1. *Policies* – The entity has defined and documented its policies relevant to the particular principle. The term *policies* as used here refers to written statements that communicate management's intent, objectives, requirements, responsibilities and standards for a particular subject.

2. *Communication* – The entity has communicated its defined policies to responsible parties and authorized users of the system.

3. *Procedures* – The entity has put in place operation procedures to achieve its objectives in accordance with its defined policies.

4. *Monitoring* – The entity monitors the system and takes action to maintain compliance with its defined policies.

Once a service organization has decided to go ahead with a SysTrust engagement, it will hire an accounting firm to perform such control assessment and testing. The accounting firm must be licensed by AICPA to perform the SysTrust engagement. Usually, only large accounting firms are licensed.

The Trust Services model was developed initially for an engagement type called Web Trust. In the early days of the eBusiness, consumers had concerns about security and whether the merchants would deliver the goods upon payment. AICPA and Canadian Institute of Chartered Accountants (CICA) saw the need to come up with a control assurance standard for eBusiness merchants to comply with and obtain a Web Trust seal from an accounting firm to place on their web sites if they pass the control standards upon an independent audit. WebTrust is now out of favor because more consumers are used to eBusiness and knowledgeable about recognizing whether a site uses encryption by looking for the lock. On a smaller scale, some certificate authorities (CA) provide malicious software protection assurance by reviewing a site's controls against malicious software and if a site is deemed to have such protection, a CA will give the site a security seal for a fee, to be placed on the web site. An example is Verisign's Trust Seal.

SysTrust was actually "invented" after Web Trust but it is based on the same control principles. The criteria are more detailed because a system is more complicated than a web site. SysTrust is widely adopted in North America.

Drivers for a SysTrust Audit

When an organization wants independent assurance about a system hosted by another organization, the user organization(s) may ask for a SysTrust audit. Sometimes, the initiative is taken by the service organization. When the initiative is taken by the user organizations, it may be driven by the following concerns.

- Remoteness of user organizations.
- Potential conflict of interest between the service organization and a user organization
- System complexity
- Frequent system failure
- Frequent evidence of unauthorized access
- Loss of data integrity
- Serious maintenance problems

Internal Control Criteria

Within each principle, there are internal control criteria that must be met by the service organization by designing and operating internal control procedures, which may be automated or manual. An internal control criterion is similar to an internal control objective. Unlike a control assurance engagement under SSAE 16, a SysTrust engagement has little flexibility in terms of the internal control criteria. That is, the criteria in the SysTrust model are mandatory unless a service organization deems it inapplicable to the system being audited and the SysTrust auditor agrees, e.g., there is no use of the Internet. The SysTrust model also provides a long list of illustrative internal control procedures for each criterion which the service organization could adapt. The service organization can also develop its own control procedures to address the criteria. To support each criterion, the service organization must document the internal control procedures and demonstrate their effectiveness at a point in time or during the specified period of at least six consecutive months, as chosen by engagement.

We have listed below the internal control criteria. For the first criterion, we have also listed the illustrative internal control procedures. The criteria are grouped by principle.

Security Principle and Supporting Criteria

The security principle refers to the protection of the system from unauthorized access, both logical and physical. Limiting access to the system helps prevent potential abuse of the system, theft of resources, misuse of software, and improper access to, or use, alteration, destruction, or disclosure of information. Key elements for the protection of the system include permitting authorized access based on relevant needs and preventing unauthorized access to the system in all other instances.

1.0 Policies: The entity defines and documents its policies for the security of its system.

1.1   The entity's security policies are established and periodically reviewed and approved by a designated individual or group.

Illustrative Controls:
- Written security policy, addressing both IT and physical security, has been approved by the IT standards committee and is implemented throughout the company.
- As part of the periodic risk assessment process, the security officer identifies changes to the IT risk assessment based on new applications and infrastructure, significant changes to applications and infrastructure, new environmental security risks, changes to regulations and standards, and changes to user requirements as identified in service level agreements and other documents. The security officer then updates the security policy based on the IT risk assessment.
- Changes to the IT security policy are approved by the IT standards committee prior to implementation.

1.2   The entity's security policies include, but may not be limited to, the following matters:
a) Identifying and documenting the security requirements of authorized users.
b) Classifying data based on its criticality and sensitivity and that classification is used to define protection requirements, access rights and access restrictions, as well as retention and destruction requirements.
c) Assessing risks periodically.
d) Preventing unauthorized access.
e) Adding users, modifying the access levels of existing users, and removing users who no longer need access.
f) Assigning responsibility and accountability for system security.
g) Assigning responsibility and accountability for system changes and maintenance.
h) Testing, evaluating, and authorizing system components before implementation.
i) Addressing how complaints and requests relating to security issues are resolved.
j) Identifying and mitigating security breaches and other incidents.
k) Providing for training and other resources to support its system security policies.
l) Providing for the handling of exceptions and situations not specifically addressed in its system security policies.
m) Providing for the identification of and consistency with applicable laws and regulations, defined commitments, service level agreements and other contractual requirements.
n) Providing for sharing information with third parties.

1.3   Responsibility and accountability for developing and maintaining the entity's system security policies, and changes and updates to those policies, are assigned.

2.0   Communications: The entity communicates its defined system security policies to responsible parties and authorized users.

2.1   The entity has prepared an objective description of the system and its boundaries and communicated such description to authorized users.

2.2   The security obligations of users and the entity's security commitments to users are communicated to authorized users.

2.3   Responsibility and accountability for the entity's system security policies as well as changes and updates to those policies are communicated to entity personnel responsible for implementing them.

2.4   The process for informing the entity about breaches of the system security and for submitting complaints is communicated to authorized users.

2.5   Changes that may affect system security are communicated to management and users who will be affected.

3.0   Procedures: The entity has put in place operation procedures to achieve its documented system security objectives in accordance with its defined policies.

3.1   Procedures exist to
a) identify potential threats of disruption to systems operation that would impair system security commitments and,
b) assess the risks associated with the identified threats.

3.2   Procedures exist to restrict logical access to the defined system including, but not Limited to, the following matters:
a) Logical access security measures to restrict access to information resources not deemed to be public.
b) Identification and authentication of users.
c) Registration and authorization of users.
d) The process to make changes and updates to user profiles.
e) Distribution of output restricted to authorized users.
f) Restriction of access to offline storage, backup data, systems and media.
g) Restriction of access to system configuration, superuser functionality, master passwords, powerful utilities and security devices.

3.3   Procedures exist to restrict physical access to the defined system including, but not limited to, facilities, backup media and other system components such as firewalls, routers and servers.

3.4   Procedures exist to protect against unauthorized access to system resources.

3.5   Procedures exist to protect against infection by computer viruses, malicious code and unauthorized software.

3.6   Encryption or other equivalent security techniques are used to protect user authentication information and the corresponding session transmitted over the Internet or other public networks.

3.7   Procedures exist to identify, report and act upon system security breaches and other incidents.

3.8   Procedures exist to classify data in accordance with classification policies and periodically monitor and update such classification as necessary.

3.9   Procedures exist to provide that issues of non-compliance with security policies are promptly addressed and that corrective measure are taken on a timely basis.

3.10 Design, acquisition, implementation, configuration, modification and management of infrastructure and software are consistent with defined system security policies to enable authorized access and to prevent unauthorized access.

3.11 Procedures exist to provide that personnel responsible for the design, development, implementation and operation of systems affecting security have the qualifications and resources to fulfill their responsibilities.

3.12 Procedures exist to maintain system components, including configuration consistent with the defined system security policies.

3.13 Procedures exist to provide that only authorized, tested and documented changes are made to the system.

3.14 Procedures exist to provide that personnel responsible for the design, development, implementation, and operation of systems affecting availability and security have the qualifications and resources to fulfill their responsibilities.

4.0   Monitoring: The entity monitors the system and takes action to maintain compliance with its defined system security policies.

4.1   The entity's system security is periodically reviewed and compared with the defined system security policies.

4.2   There is a process to identify and address potential impairment to the entity's ongoing ability to achieve its objectives in accordance with its defined system security policies.

4.3   Environmental, regulatory and technological changes are monitored and their effect on system security is assessed on a timely basis and policies are updated for that assessment.

Availability Principle and Supporting Criteria

The availability principle refers to the accessibility to the system, products or services as advertised or committed by contract, service level or other agreements. It should be noted that this principle does not, in itself, set a minimum acceptable performance level for system availability. The minimum performance level is established through commitments made by mutual agreement (contract) between the parties.

1.0   Policies: The entity defines and documents its policies for the availability of its system.

1.1   The entity's system availability and related security policies are established and periodically reviewed and approved by a designated individual or group.

1.2   The entity's system availability policies include, but may not be limited to, the following matters:
(See criterion 1.2 under the Security Principle.)

1.3   Responsibility and accountability for developing and maintaining the entity's system availability and related security policies, as well as changes and updates to those policies, are assigned.

2.0   Communication: The entity communicates the defined system availability policies to responsible parties and authorized users.

2.1   The entity has prepared an objective description of the system and its boundaries and communicated such description to authorized users.

2.2   The availability and related security obligations of users and the entity's availability and related security commitments to users are communicated to authorized users.

2.3   Responsibility and accountability for the entity's system availability and related security policies as well as changes and updates to those policies are communicated to entity personnel responsible for implementing them.

2.4   The process for informing the entity about system availability issues and breaches of system security and for submitting complaints is communicated to authorized users.

2.5   Changes that may affect system availability and system security are communicated to management and users who will be affected.

3.0   Procedures: The entity has put in place operation procedures to achieve its documented system availability objectives in accordance with its defined policies.

3.1   Procedures exist to (1) identify potential threat of disruptions to systems operation that would impair system availability commitments and (2) assess the risks associated with the identified threats.

3.2   Measures to prevent or mitigate threats have been implemented consistent with the risk assessment when commercially practical.

3.3   Procedures exist to provide for backup, offsite storage, restoration and disaster recovery consistent with the entity's defined system availability and related security policies.

3.4   Procedures exist to provide for the integrity of backup data and systems maintained to support the entity's defined system availability and related security policies.

3.5   Procedures exist to restrict logical access to the defined system including, but not limited, the following matters:
(See criterion 3.2 under the Security Principle.)

3.6   Procedures exist to restrict physical access to the defined system including, but not limited to, facilities, backup media and other system components such as firewalls, routers and servers.

3.7   Procedures exist to protect against unauthorized access to system resources.

3.8   Procedures exist to protect against infection by computer viruses, malicious code and unauthorized software.

3.9   Encryption or other equivalent security techniques are used to protect user authentication information and the corresponding session transmitted over the Internet or other public networks.

3.10   Procedures exist to identify, report and act upon system availability issues and related security breaches and other incidents.

3.11   Procedures exist to classify data in accordance with classification policies and periodically monitor and update such classifications as necessary.

3.12   Procedures exist to provide that issues of non-compliance with system availability and related security policies are promptly addressed and that corrective measures are taken on a timely basis.

3.13   Design, acquisition, implementation, configuration, modification and management of infrastructure and software are consistent with defined system availability and related security policies.

3.14   Procedures exist to provide that personnel responsible for the design, development, implementation and operation of system affecting availability and security have the qualifications and resources to fulfill their responsibilities.

3.15   Procedures exist to maintain system components, including configuration consistent with the defined system availability and related security policies.

3.16   Procedures exist to provide that only authorized, tested and documented changes are made to the system.

3.17   Procedures exist to provide that emergency changes are documented and authorized.

4.0   Monitoring: The entity monitors the system and takes action to maintain compliance with its defined system availability policies.

4.1   The entity's system availability and security performance is periodically reviewed and compared with the defined system availability and related security policies.

4.2   There is a process to identify and address potential impairments to the entity's ongoing ability to achieve its objectives in accordance with its defined system availability and related security policies.

4.3   Environmental, regulatory and technological changes are monitored, and their effect on system availability and security is assessed on a timely basis, policies are updated for that assessment.

Processing Integrity Principle and Supporting Criteria

The processing Integrity principle refers to the completeness, accuracy, validity, timeliness and authorization of system processing. Processing integrity exists if a system performs its intended function in an unimpaired manner and free from unauthorized or inadvertent manipulation. Completeness generally indicates that all transactions are processed or all services are performed without exception. Validity means that transactions and services are not processed more than once and that they are in accordance with business values and expectations. Accuracy means that key information associated with the submitted transaction remains accurate throughout the processing of the transaction and that the transaction or service is processed or performed as intended. The timeliness of the provision of services or the delivery of goods is addressed in the context of commitments made for such delivery. Authorization means that processing is performed in accordance with the required approvals and privileges defined by policies governing system processing.

1.0   Policies: The entity defines and documents its policies for the processing integrity of its system.

1.1   The entity's processing integrity and related security policies are established and periodically reviewed and approved by a designated individual or group.

1.2   The entity's processing integrity policies include, but may not be limited to, the following security matters:
(See criterion 1.2 under the Security Principle.)

1.3   Responsibility and accountability for developing and maintaining the entity's system processing integrity and related system security policies, changes, updates and exceptions to those policies are assigned.

2.0 Communications: The entity communicates its documented system processing integrity policies to responsible parties and authorized users.

2.1 The entity has prepared an objective description of the system and its boundaries and communicated such description to authorized users.

 a) The terms and conditions by which it conducts its e-commerce transactions including, but not limited to, the following matters:
  (i) Time frame for completion of transactions
  (ii) Time frame and process for informing customers of exceptions to normal processing of orders or service requests
  (iii) Normal method of delivery of goods or services, including customer options, where applicable.
  (iv) Payment terms, including customer options, if any.
  (v) Electronic settlement practices and related charges to customers.
  (vi) How customers may cancel recurring charges, if any.
  (vii) Product return policies and limited liability, where applicable.

 b) Where customers can obtain warranty, repair services, and support related to the goods and services purchased on its web site.

 c) Procedures for resolution of issues regarding processing integrity. These may relate to any part of a customer's e-commerce transaction, including complaints related to the quality of services and products, accuracy, completeness, and the consequences for failure to resolve such complaints.

2.2 The processing integrity and related security obligations of users and the entity's processing integrity and related security commitments to users are communicated to authorized users.

2.3 Responsibility and accountability for the entity's system processing integrity and related security policies, and changes and updates to those policies, are communicated to entity personnel responsible for implementing them.

2.4 The process for obtaining support and informing the entity about system processing integrity issues, errors and omissions, and breaches of systems security and for submitting complaints is communicated to authorized users.

2.5 Changes that may affect system processing integrity and system security are communicated to management and users who will be affected.

3.0   Procedures: The entity has put in place operating procedures to achieve its documented system processing integrity objectives in accordance with its defined policies.

3.1   Procedures exist to (1) identify potential threats of disruption to systems operations that would impair processing integrity commitments and (2) assess the risks associated with the identified threats.

3.2   The procedures related to completeness, accuracy, timeliness and authorization of inputs are consistent with the documented system processing integrity policies. If the system is an e-commerce system, the entity's procedures include, but may not be limited to, the following matters:
   a) The entity checks each request or transaction for accuracy and completeness.
   b) Positive acknowledgement is received from the customer before the transaction is processed.

3.3   The procedures related to completeness, accuracy, timeliness and authorization of system processing, including error correction and database management, are consistent with documented system processing integrity policies. If the system is an e-commerce system, the entity's procedures include, but may not be limited to, the following matters:
   a) The correct goods are shipped in the correct quantities in the time frame agreed upon, or services and information are provided to the customer as requested.
   b) Transaction exceptions are promptly communicated to the customer.
   c) Incoming messages are processed and delivered accurately and completely to the correct IP address.
   d) Outgoing messages are processed and delivered accurately and completely to the service provider's (SPs) Internet access point.
   e) Messages remain intact while in transit within the confines of the SPs network.

3.4   The procedures related to completeness, accuracy, timeliness and authorization of outputs are consistent with the documented system processing integrity policies. If the system is an e-commerce system, the entity's procedures include, but are not necessarily limited to, the following matters:
   a)   The entity displays sales prices and all other costs and fees to the customer before processing the transaction.
   b)   Transactions are billed and electronically settled as agreed.
   c)   Billing or settlement errors are promptly corrected.

3.5   There are procedures to enable tracing of information inputs from their source to their final disposition and vice versa.

Security related criteria relevant to the system's processing integrity

3.6   Procedures exist to restrict logical access to the defined system including, but not limited to, the following matters:
        (Refer to criterion 3.2 under Security.)

3.7   Procedures exist to restrict physical access to the defined system including, but not limited to, facilities, offline storage media, backup media and systems, and other system components such as firewalls, routers and servers.

3.8   Procedures exist to protect against unauthorized access to system resources.

3.9   Procedures exist to protect against infection by computer viruses, malicious code and unauthorized software.

3.10   Encryption or other equivalent security techniques are used to protect user authentication information and the corresponding session transmitted over the Internet or other public networks.

Criterion related to execution and incident management used to achieve objectives.

3.11   Procedures exist to identify, report and act upon system processing integrity and related security breaches and other incidents.

Criteria related to the system components used to achieve objectives.

3.12   Procedures exist to classify data in accordance with classification policies and periodically monitor and update such classifications as necessary.

3.13   Procedures exist to provide that issues of non-compliance with system processing integrity and related security policies are promptly addressed and that corrective measures are taken on a timely basis.

3.14   Design, acquisition, implementation, configuration, modification and management of infrastructure and software are consistent with defined processing integrity and related security policies.

3.15   Procedures exist to provide that personnel responsible for the design, development, implementation and operation of systems affecting processing integrity and security have qualifications and resources to fulfill their responsibilities.

Change management related criteria applicable to the system's processing integrity.

3.16   Procedures exist to maintain system completeness, including configurations consistent with the defined system processing integrity and related security policies.

3.17   Procedures exist to provide that only authorized, tested and documented changes are made to the system.

3.18   Procedures exist to provide that emergency changes are documented and authorized.

3.19   Procedures exist to protect the system against potential risks that might impair system processing integrity.

3.20   Procedures exist to provide for restoration and disaster recovery consistent with the entity's defined processing integrity practices.

3.21   Procedures exist to provide for the completeness, accuracy and timeliness of backup data and systems.

4.0   Monitoring: The entity monitors the system and takes action to maintain compliance with the defined system processing integrity policies.

4.1   System processing integrity and security performance are periodically reviewed and compared with the defined system processing integrity and related security policies.

4.2   There is a process to identify and address potential impairments to the entity's ongoing ability to achieve its objectives in accordance with its defined system processing, integrity and related security policies.

4.3   Environmental, regulatory and technological changes are monitored, their impact on system processing integrity and security is assessed on a timely basis, and policies are updated for that assessment.

Confidentiality Principles and Criteria

The confidentiality principle refers to the system's ability to protect the information designated as confidential, as committed or agreed. Unlike personal information, which is defined by regulation in a number of countries worldwide and subject to the privacy principles, there is no widely recognized definition of what constitutes confidential information. In the course of communicating and transacting business, partners often exchange information they require to be maintained on a confidential basis. In most instances, the respective parties wish to ensure that the information they provide is available only to those who need to access to complete the transaction or to resolve any questions that may arise. To enhance business partner confidence, it is important that the business partner be informed about the entity's system and information confidentiality policies, procedures and practices. The entity needs to disclose its system and information confidentiality policies, procedures and practices relating to the manner in which it provides for authorized access to its system and users and shares information designated as confidential.

1.0   Policies: The entity defines and documents its policies related to the system protecting confidential information, as committed or agreed.

1.1   The entity's system confidentiality and related security policies are established and periodically reviewed and approved by a designated individual or group.

1.2   The entity's policies related to the system's protection of confidential information and security include, but are not limited to, the following matters:
(refer to criterion 1.2 under the Security Principle.)

1.3   Responsibility and accountability for developing and maintaining the entity's system confidentiality and related security policies, as well as changes and updates to those policies, are assigned.

2.0   Communications: The entity communicates its defined policies related to the system's protection of confidential information to responsible parties and authorized users.

2.1   The entity has prepared an objective description of the system and its boundaries and communicated such description to authorized users.

2.2   The system confidentiality and related security obligations of users and the entity's confidentiality and related security commitments to users are communicated to authorized users before the confidential information is provided. This communication includes, but is not limited to, the following matters:
a) How information is designated as confidential and ceases to be confidential. This includes the handling, destruction, maintenance, storage, backup, distribution and transmission of confidential information.
b) How access to confidential information is authorized and how such authorization is rescinded.
c) How confidential information is used and shared.

d) If information is provided to third parties, disclosures including any limitations on reliance on the third party's confidentiality practices and controls. Lack of such disclosure indicates that the entity is relying on the third party's confidentiality practices and controls that meet or exceed those of the entity.

e) Practices to comply with applicable laws and regulations addressing confidentiality.

2.3   Responsibility and accountability for the entity's system confidentiality and related security policies as well as changes and updates to those policies are communicated to entity personnel responsible for implementing them.

2.4   The process for informing the entity about breaches of confidentiality and system security and for submitting complaints is communicated to authorized users.

2.5   Changes that may affect confidentiality and system security are communicated to management and users who will be affected.

3.0   Procedures: The entity has put in place operation procedures to achieve its documented system confidentiality objectives in accordance with its defined policies.

3.1   Procedures exist to (1) identify potential threats of disruption to system operation that would impair confidentiality commitments and (2) assess the risks associated with the identified threats.

3.2   The system procedures related to confidentiality of input, processing and output are consistent with the documented policies.

3.3   The system procedures provide that confidential information is disclosed to parties only in accordance with the entity's defined confidentiality and related security policies.

3.4   The entity has procedures to obtain assurance or representation that the confidentiality policies of third parties to whom information is transferred and upon which the entity relies are in conformity with the entity's defined system confidentiality and related security policies and that the third party is in compliance with its policies.

3.5   In the event that a disclosed confidentiality practice is discontinued or changed to be less restrictive, the entity has procedures to protect confidential information in accordance with the system confidentiality practices in place when such information was received, or obtains customer consent to follow the new confidentiality practice with respect to the customer's confidential information.

System security related criteria relevant to confidentiality

3.6   Procedures exist to restrict logical access to the system and the confidential information resources maintained in the system including, but not limited to, the following matters:
(Refer to criterion 3.2 under the Security Principle.)

3.7   Procedures exist to restrict physical access to the defined system including, but not limited to, facilities, backup media and other system components such as firewalls, routers and servers.

3.8   Procedures exist to protect against unauthorized access to system resources.

3.9   Procedures exist to protect against infection by computer viruses, malicious code and unauthorized software.

3.10   Encryption or other equivalent security techniques are used to protect transmission of user authentication and other confidential information passed over the Internet or other public networks.

Criterion related to execution and incident management used to achieve the objectives

3.11   Procedures exist to identity, report and act upon system confidentiality and security breaches and other incidents.

Criteria related to the system components used to achieve the objectives

3.12   Procedures exist to provide that system data is classified in accordance with the defined confidentiality and related security policies.

3.13   Procedures exist to provide that issues of non-compliance with defined confidentiality and related security policies are promptly addressed and that corrective measures are taken on a timely basis.

3.14   Design, acquisition, implementation, configuration, modification, as well as management of infrastructure and software are consistent with defined confidentiality and related security policies.

3.15   Procedures exist to help ensure that personnel responsible for the design, development, implementation and operation of systems affecting confidentiality and security have the qualification and resources to fulfill their responsibilities.

3.16   Procedures exist to maintain system components, including configuration consistent with the defined system confidentiality and related policies.

3.17   Procedures exist to provide that only authorized, tested and documented changes are made to the system.

3.18   Procedures exist to provide that emergency changes are documented and authorized.

3.19   Procedures exist to provide that confidential information is protected during the system development, testing and change processes in accordance with defined system confidentiality and related security policies.

4.0   Monitoring: The entity monitors the system and takes action to maintain compliance with its defined confidentiality policies.

4.1   The entity's system confidentiality and security performance is periodically reviewed and compared with the defined system confidentiality and related security policies.

4.2   There is a process to identify and address potential impairments to the entity's ongoing ability to achieve its objectives in accordance with its system confidentiality and related security policies.

4.3   Environmental, regulatory and technological changes are monitored, and their impact on system confidentiality and security is assessed on a timely basis. System confidentiality policies and procedures are updated for such changes as required.

Privacy Principle

The privacy principle focuses on protecting the personal information an organization may collect about its customers, employees and other individuals. Some personal information is considered sensitive. Laws and regulations in most developed countries define the following to be sensitive personal information:

- Date of birth
- Personal ID number like a social insurance number
- Consumer purchase history
- Finance
- Medical or health condition
- Offence or criminal conviction
- Sexual preference
- Trade union membership

There are no privacy control criteria specified in the Trust Services Standard. We have discussed the privacy internal controls in Chapter Five. The Trust Services Standard contains generally accepted privacy principles, which are consistent with the privacy principles discussed in Chapter Five.

Disclosure Related to E-commerce Systems

For an e-commerce system, the organization has to make the following disclosures in connection with the Trust Services Principles. The respective control criteria in the related principles are quoted below, with an emphasis on disclosure.

Security and Availability

1. The security and availability obligation of users and the entity's security commitment to users are communicated to authorized individuals.

2. The process for informing the entity about breaches of system security and for submitting complaints is communicated to authorized users.

3. Changes that may affect system security are communicated to management and users who will be affected.

Processing Integrity

1. The entity has prepared an objective description of the system and its boundaries and communicated such description to authorized users. If the system is an e-commerce system, additional information provided on its web site includes, but may not be limited to, the following matters:

2. The processing integrity and related security obligations of users and the entity's processing integrity and related security commitments to users are communicated to authorized users.

3. The process for obtaining support and informing the entity about system processing integrity issues, errors and omissions, and breaches of system security and for submitting complaints is communicated to authorized users.

4. Changes that may affect system processing integrity and system security are communicated to management and users who will be affected.

Confidentiality

1.   The process for informing the entity about breaches of confidentiality and system security and for submitting complaints is communicated to authorized users.

2.   Changes that may affect confidentiality and system security are communicated to management and users who will be affected.

Privacy

The organization must disclose its privacy policy and procedures to support the ten generally accepted privacy principles discussed in Chapter Five, including the contacts for obtaining access and complaints. The following information must be disclosed.

*   Purpose of collection of personal information.
*   What consent means and how it is given.
*   How personal information will be used.
*   Who personal information may be shared with.
*   Security over personal information.
*   Who to contact for questions, complaints and access to personal information.
*   Privacy policy.

Process of a SysTrust Engagement

1.   An organization hosting a system used by other organizations decides to secure a SysTrust opinion on the system's reliability. This is called the service organization.

2.   The service organization prepares the system description to be consistent with the contract of service. The description should include infrastructure, software, procedures, people and information.

3.   The service organization selects up to both of the optional principles, i.e. confidentiality and privacy.

4.   The service organization reviews the SysTrust criteria and decides which ones do not apply. Provide justification for those that do not apply, e.g., the system is not connected to the Internet.

5.   The service organization develops internal control procedures (manual and automated) to support each criterion, using the illustrative controls in the SysTrust model as guidance.

6.   The service organization decides on whether the assurance sought will be at a point in time or for a period of six or more consecutive months.

7. The service organization hires a large accounting firm licensed by AICPA to perform a SysTrust assurance engagement. The accounting firm is now called the service auditor.

8. The service auditor reviews the system description for consistency with the contract of service, and to assess its comprehensiveness and correctness.

9. If the service auditor has a significant concern about the system description, it should ask the service organization to correct. If the service organization does not address the concern to the accounting firm's satisfaction, the firm should withdraw from the engagement.

10. The service auditor reviews the list of control criteria excluded by the hosting organization and assesses the appropriateness of rationale. If the service auditor does not agree with the service organization and the latter does not address the disagreement to the service auditor's satisfaction, the service auditor should withdraw from the engagement if the criteria affected are part of a mandatory principle. If the criteria affected are part of confidentiality or privacy, the service auditor can continue with the engagement but agrees with the service organization to exclude such optional principles from the scope.

11. The service auditor reviews the internal control procedures (manual and automated) for each criterion and assess their adequacy to address the criterion.

12. If the service auditor is not satisfied that a criterion is adequately supported by internal control procedures, it should raise with the service organization for correction. If the service organization cannot correct to the accounting firm's satisfaction, the service auditor should withdraw from the engagement if the criterion affected is part of a mandatory principle, or makes sure the service organization understands that the opinion will be qualified. If the criterion affected is part of confidentiality or privacy, the service auditor can continue with the engagement but agree with the service organization to exclude such optional principles from the scope.

13. If the service auditor is satisfied that there are sufficient stated internal controls to support each criterion, the service auditor conducts control testing with the aim of achieving high assurance.

14. If a significant control deficiency is found, the service auditor presents to the client and informs the client that the control is not reliable. If the client does not correct the control retroactively and does not come up with a compensating control for the auditor to test, the service auditor will have to qualify the opinion, unless the control deficiencies affect only the privacy and confidentiality principles, in which case, the assurance opinion can still be unqualified if the affected principles are removed.

Sample System Description

The following is an illustrative system description suggested by AICPA.

Background

XYZ Co. Pension Services (XPS), based in New York, New York, with offices across North America, manages and operates the Pension Administration System (PAS) on behalf of pension plan sponsors who are XPS's customers. The plan members are the employees of XPS's customers who are enrolled in the pension plan. XPS uses PAS for recordkeeping of pension-related activities.

Infrastructure

PAS uses a three-tier architecture, including proprietary client software, application servers, and database servers. Various peripheral devices, such as tape cartridge silos, disk drives, and laser and impact printers, are also used.

Software

The PAS application was developed by programming staff in XYZ Co.'s Information Technology Department (XITD), Systems Development and Application Support area. PAS enables the processing of contributions to members' pension plans and withdrawals at retirement, based on plan rules. PAS generates all the required reports for members, plan sponsors, and tax authorities. PAS also provides a facility to record investments and related transactions (purchases, sales, dividends, interest, and other miscellaneous transactions). Batch processing of transactions is performed nightly. PAS provides a facility for online data input and report requests. In addition, PAS accepts input from plan sponsors in the form of digital or magnetic media or files transmitted via the telecommunications infrastructure.

People

XPS has a staff of approximately 200 employees organized in the following functional areas:
1. Pension administration includes a team of specialists that set up pension rules, maintain master files, process contributions to PAS, report to plan sponsors and members, and assist with inquiries from plan members.
2. Financial operations is responsible for processing withdrawals, depositing contributions, and investment accounting.
3. Trust accounting is responsible for bank reconciliation.
4. Investment services is responsible for processing purchases of stocks, bonds, certificates of deposits, and other financial instruments.

5. XITD has a staff of approximately 50 employees who are dedicated to PAS and its related infrastructure and are organized in the following functional areas:
- The help desk provides technical assistance to users of PAS and other infrastructure as well as plan sponsors.
- Systems development and application support provides application software development and testing for enhancements and modifications to PAS.
- Product support specialists prepare documentation manuals and training material.
- Quality assurance monitors compliance with standards and manages and controls the change migration process.
- Information security and risk is responsible for security administration, intrusion detection, security monitoring, and business-recovery planning.
- Operational services performs day-to-day operation of servers and related peripherals.
- System software services installs and tests system software releases, monitors daily system performance, and resolves system software problems.
- Technical delivery services maintains job scheduling and report distribution software, manages security administration, and maintains policies and procedures manuals for the PAS processing environment.
- Voice and data communications maintains the communication environment, monitors the network, and provides assistance to users and plan sponsors in resolving communication problems and network planning.

Procedures

The pension administration services covered by this system description include
1. pension master file maintenance,
2. contributions,
3. withdrawals,
4. investment accounting, and
5. reporting to members.

These services are supported by XITD, which supports PAS 24 hours a day, 7 days a week. The key support services provided by XITD include
1. systems development and maintenance,
2. security administration and auditing,
3. intrusion detection and incident response,
4. data center operations and performance monitoring,
5. change controls, and
6. business recovery planning.

Data

PAS data consists of the following:
1. Master file data
2. Transaction data
3. Error and suspense logs
4. Output reports
5. Transmission records
6. System and security files

Transaction processing is initiated by the receipt of paper documents, electronic media, or calls to XYZ Co.'s call center. Transaction data is processed by PAS in either the online or batch mode and is used to update master files. Reports are available either in hard copy or through a report-viewing facility to authorized users based on their job functions. Pension statement and transaction notices are mailed to plan sponsors and members.

Period of Coverage

The service auditor and the service organization may decided to issue a point-in-time report or a report that covers a period. The following factors should be considered in deciding which type of report to issue.

- The anticipated users of the report and their needs.
- The need for contiguous coverage between reports.
- The degree and frequency of change in each of the system components.
- The cyclical nature of processing within the system.
- Historical information about the system.

AICPA requires that if a period is to be covered, it should not be less than six consecutive months.

Subsequent Events

Events or transactions sometimes occur subsequent to the point in time or period of time covered by the service auditor's report but prior to the date of the report, that have a material effect on the system or control objectives, or that require adjustment or disclosure in the report. In performing an attest engagement, an auditor should consider information about subsequent events that comes to his or her attention. Two types of subsequent events require consideration by the auditor.

The first type consists of events that provide additional information with respect to conditions that existed at the point in time or during the period of time covered by the service auditor's report. This information should be used by the auditor in considering whether the subject matter or assertion is presented in conformity with the criteria and whether it affects the presentation of the subject matter, the assertion, or the service auditor's report. An example of this type of event is that a disaster recovery test carried out subsequent to the report period failed because data backup in the report period was done incorrectly. The auditor should assess the significance of this control failure and consider qualifying the report. If the control failure is not significant, there is no need to disclose this subsequent event in the audit report.

The second type consists of those events that provide information with respect to conditions that arose subsequent to the point in time or period of time covered by the practitioner's report that are of such a nature and significance that their disclosure is necessary to keep the subject matter from being misleading. This type of information will not normally affect the audit report if the information is appropriately disclosed by the service organization. An example is the collapse of the data center.

Although the service auditor has no responsibility to detect subsequent events, s/he should inquire of the service organization as to whether they are aware of any subsequent events, through the date of the audit report, that would have a material effect on the subject matter or assertion. The representation letter ordinarily would include a representation concerning subsequent events. The service auditor has no responsibility to keep informed of events subsequent to the date of his or her report; however, s/he may later become aware of conditions that existed at that date that might have affected the audit report had s/he been aware of them.

Illustrative Report

The following is an illustrative report provided by AICPA.

To the management of ABC Company, Inc.:

We have examined management's assertion that during the period [*month, day, and year*] through [*month, day, and year*], ABC Company, Inc. (ABC Company) maintained effective controls over the _____ [*type or name of system*] system based on the AICPA and CICA trust services availability, security, processing integrity, and confidentiality criteria to provide reasonable assurance that
1. the system was available for operation and use, as committed or agreed;
2. the system was protected against unauthorized access (both physical and logical);
3. the system processing was complete, accurate, timely, and authorized; and
4. information designated as confidential was protected by the system as committed or agreed based on the AICPA and CICA trust services security, availability, processing integrity, and confidentiality criteria.

ABC Company's management is responsible for this assertion. Our responsibility is to express an opinion based on our examination. Management's description of the aspects of the _____ [*type or name of system*] system covered by its assertion is attached. We did not examine this description, and accordingly, we do not express an opinion on it.

Our examination was conducted in accordance with attestation standards established by the American Institute of Certified Public Accountants and, accordingly, included (1) obtaining an understanding of ABC Company's relevant controls over the availability, security, processing integrity, and confidentiality of the _____ [*type or name of system*] system; (2) testing and evaluating the operating effectiveness of the controls; and (3) performing such other procedures as we considered necessary in the circumstances. We believe that our examination provides a reasonable basis for our opinion. Because of the nature and inherent limitations of controls, ABC Company's ability to meet the aforementioned criteria may be affected. For example, controls may not prevent or detect and correct error or fraud, unauthorized access to systems and information, or failure to comply with internal and external policies or requirements. Also, the projection of any conclusions based on our findings to future periods is subject to the risk that changes may alter the validity of such conclusions.

In our opinion, management's assertion referred to above is fairly stated, in all material respects, based on the AICPA and CICA trust services security, availability, processing integrity, and confidentiality criteria.

[*Name of CA firm*]
Chartered Accountants

PAYMENT CARD INDUSTRY SECURITY STANDARD

The Payment Card Industry (PCI) Security Standard was introduced in 2004 by American Express, Diners Club, Discover Card, JCB International, MasterCard, and Visa to prevent credit card theft. These credit card issuers expect merchants, information technology (IT) service organizations and financial institutions to comply with the standard. The standard is maintained by the PCI Security Standard Council (PCISC) whose membership includes the six major credit card issuers.

Credit card issuers (e.g., Visa and MasterCard) require large merchants and IT service organizations to obtain annual external validation of compliance. For example, Visa requires a merchant or eBusiness service provider that processes 20,000 eBusiness Visa transactions or a merchant that processes more than 1 million Visa transactions to obtain annual external validation of compliance with the PCI Security Standard. Failure to comply may lead to penalty imposed by the card issuer.

Requirements of the Standard

The PCI Security Standard has the following twelve high level requirements. These requirements are not intended to be taken just literally. Each organization has to assess the requirements in relation to its processing environment to determine the extent of implementation. The literal meaning should be used only as a baseline. In other words, in a large environment, the organization has to go beyond the literal requirements.

1. Install and maintain firewall and router configurations to protect cardholder data.

2. Do not use vendor supplied defaults for system passwords and other security parameters.

3. Protect stored cardholder data.

4. Encrypt transmission of cardholder data across public, open networks.

5. Use and regularly update anti-virus software on all systems commonly affected by malware.

6. Develop and maintain secure systems and applications.

7. Restrict access to cardholder data on a need-to-know basis.

8. Assign a unique ID to each person with computer access.

9. Restrict physical access to cardholder data.

10. Track and monitor all access to cardholder data and network resources.

11. Regularly test security systems and processes.

12. Maintain a policy that addresses information security.

The above requirements apply to an organization's cardholder data environment, i.e., the IT environment and systems that process and store credit card transactions. PCISC has provided the following guidelines on each of the above requirements. I have added some explanatory notes to these guidelines.

Firewall Configuration

1. There must be a formal process for approving and testing firewall connections as well as changes to configuration of firewalls and routers.

2. There must be current network diagrams with connections to cardholder data, including wireless connections.

3. There must be a firewall at each Internet connection as well as between a demilitarized zone (DMZ) and an internal network.

4. Groups, roles and responsibilities for logical management of network components must be defined.

5. Document with business justification the use of all services, protocols, and ports allowed, including documentation of security features implemented for those protocols considered to be insecure. Examples of insecure services, protocols, or ports include but are not limited to file transfer protocol, Telnet, POP3 (Internet email) and Internet Message Access Protocol (IMAP). IMAP is a common Web mail protocol that allows users to access email on a remote server.

6. Review firewall and router rules semi-annually.

7. Restrict external network access to the cardholder data environment (CDE). CDE is defined as an area of computer system network that processes cardholder data or sensitive authentication data and those systems and segments that are directly attached to or support cardholder processing, storage, or transmission.

8. Restrict inbound and outbound traffic to that which is necessary in CDE.

9. Secure and synchronize router configuration files.

10. Install perimeter firewalls between any wireless networks and the cardholder data environment, and configure these firewalls to deny or control any traffic from the wireless environment into the cardholder data environment.

11. Limit inbound traffic to IP addresses in the DMZ.

12. Implement stateful inspection firewalls.

13. Place system components that store cardholder data in an internal network zone, segregated from the DMZ and other untrusted networks.

14. Do not disclose private IP addresses and routing information to external parties.

15. Install personal firewall software on any mobile and/or employee-owned computers with direct connectivity to the Internet (for example, laptops used by employees), which are used to access the organization's network.

Vendor Supplied Defaults

1. For wireless environments connected to the cardholder data environment or transmitting cardholder data, change wireless vendor defaults, including but not limited to default wireless encryption keys, passwords, and SNMP community strings.

2. Develop configuration standards for all system components to comply with industry accepted system hardening standards.

3. Implement only one primary function per server to prevent functions that require different security levels from co-existing on the same server.

4. Enable only necessary and secure services as well as protocols, etc., as required for the function of the system.

5. Remove all unnecessary functionality, such as scripts, drivers, features, subsystems, file systems, and unnecessary web servers.

6. Protect and restrict all system administrative access not carried out at the server with strong cryptography.

7. Shared hosting providers must protect each entity's hosted environment and cardholder data.

Protect Stored Cardholder Data

1. Implement a data retention and disposal policy that includes:
   _ Limiting data storage amount and retention time to that which is required for legal, regulatory and business requirements.
   _ Processes for secure deletion of data when no longer needed.
   _ Specific retention requirements for cardholder data
   _ A quarterly automatic or manual process for identifying and securely deleting stored cardholder data that exceeds defined retention requirements.

2. Do not store the card verification code or value (the 3-digit or 4-digit number on the back of the card) used to verify card-not-present transactions. This code is a hash of the card number and expiry date.

3. Do not store the PIN. The PIN is hashed and stored in the credit card chip only.

4. Do not display the entire credit card when confirming to a customer or the third party. The maximum digits to be displayed are the first 6 and the last 4.

5. Do not store credit card numbers in easily recognizable plain text.

6. Document the encryption key management process.

Develop and Maintain Secure Systems and Applications

1. Ensure that all system components and software are protected from known vulnerabilities by having the latest vendor-supplied security patches installed. Install critical security patches within one month of release.

2. Separate development, test and production environments with appropriate segregation of duties.

3. Do not use production data for testing or development.

4. Test security patches.

5. Have fall-back procedures.

6. Develop systems to prevent SQL injection and buffer overflow.

Assign a Unique ID to Each Person with Computer Access

1. Incorporate two-factor authentication for remote access to the network by employees, administrators, and third parties.

2. Set passwords for first-time use and reset to a unique value for each user, requiring a change immediately after the first use.

3. Immediately revoke access of any terminated users.

4. Remove or disable user IDs after 90 days of inactivity.

5. Enable accounts used by vendors for remote access only during the time period needed. Monitor vendor remote access.

6. Do not use group, shared, or generic accounts and passwords.

7. Change passwords at least every 90 days.

8. Require a minimum password length of 7 alphanumeric characters.

9. Do not allow reuse of the last 4 generations of passwords.

10. Lock out users after 6 unsuccessful password attempts for 30 minutes or until reactivated by the system administrator.

11. Lock the screen after 15 minutes of inactivity.

12. Control addition, change and deletion of user profiles.

Restrict Physical Access to Cardholder Data

1. Use video cameras and/or access control mechanisms to monitor individual physical access to sensitive areas. Review collected data and correlate with other entries. Store for at least three months, unless otherwise restricted by law.

2. Restrict physical access to publicly accessible network jacks. For example, areas accessible to visitors should not have network ports enabled unless network access is explicitly authorized.

3. Restrict physical access to wireless access points, gateways, handheld devices, networking/communications hardware, and telecommunication lines.

4. Develop procedures to easily distinguish between onsite personnel and visitors, especially in areas where cardholder data is accessible.

5. Make sure visitors are:
   - authorized before entering an area where cardholder data is processed or maintained;
   - given a physical token that expires and identifies the visitor as such;
   - asked to surrender the token when leaving the area.

6. Use a visitor log to maintain a physical audit trail of visitor activity. Document the visitor's name, the firm represented, and the onsite personnel authorizing physical access on the log. Retain this log for a minimum of three months, unless otherwise restricted by law.

7. Store media back-ups in a secure location, preferably an off-site facility, such as an alternate or back-up site, or a commercial storage facility. Review the location's security at least annually.

8. Physically secure all media

9. Classify media based on information sensitivity.

10. Send the media by secured courier or other delivery method that can be accurately tracked.

11. Properly maintain inventory logs of all media and conduct media inventory counts annually.

12. Shred, incinerate, or pulp hardcopy materials so that cardholder data cannot be reconstructed.

13. Render cardholder data on electronic media unrecoverable so that cardholder data cannot be reconstructed.

Track and Monitor All Access to Cardholder Data and Network Resources

These guidelines apply to merchants and eBusiness service organizations which are required to provide annual validation of PCI Security Standard compliance. They also apply to financial institutions.

1. Establish a process for linking all access to system components to individual users.

2. Secure audit trails so they cannot be altered.

3. Review logs for all system components at least daily. Log reviews must include those servers that perform security functions like intrusion detection systems, firewalls, intrusion prevention systems, authentication and authorization.

4. Retain audit trail history for at least one year.

Regularly Test Security Systems and Processes

These guidelines apply to merchants and eBusiness service organizations which are required to provide annual validation of PCI Security Standard compliance. They also apply to financial institutions.

1. Test for the presence of wireless access points and detect unauthorized wireless access points on a quarterly basis.

2. Run internal and external network vulnerability scans at least quarterly and after any significant change in the network. The external scans must be done by a PCI approved scanning vendor.

3. Perform external and internal penetration testing at least once a year and after any significant infrastructure or application upgrade or modification. These penetration tests must include the network and application levels.

4. Use intrusion-detection systems, and/or intrusion-prevention systems to monitor all traffic at the perimeter of the cardholder data environment as well as at critical points inside the cardholder data environment, and alert personnel to suspected compromises. Keep all intrusion-detection and prevention engines, baselines, and signatures up-to-date.

5. Deploy file-integrity monitoring tools to alert personnel to unauthorized modification of critical system files, configuration files, or content files; and configure the software to perform critical file comparison weekly.

<u>Maintain a Policy That Addresses Information Security</u>

These guidelines apply to merchants and eBusiness service organizations which are required to provide annual validation of PCI Security Standard compliance. They also apply to financial institutions.

1. Include an annual process that identifies threats, vulnerabilities and results in a formal risk assessment.

2. Review the security policy annually.

3. Develop daily operational security procedures.

4. Develop usage policies for critical technologies (for example, remote access technologies, wireless technologies, removable electronic media, laptops, tablets, personal data/digital assistants, e-mail usage and Internet usage) and define proper use of these technologies.

5. Ensure that the security policy and procedures clearly define information security responsibilities for all personnel.

6. Assign to an individual or team the following information security management responsibilities:
   - Establish, document, and distribute security policies and procedures.
   - Monitor and analyze security alerts and information, and distribute to appropriate personnel.
   - Establish, document, and distribute security incident response and escalation procedures to ensure timely and effective handling of all situation.
   - Administer user accounts, including additions, deletions, and modifications.
   - Monitor and control all access to data.

7. Implement a formal security awareness program to make all personnel aware of the importance of cardholder data security.
   - Education personnel upon hiring and annually.
   - Require personnel to acknowledge at least annually that they have read and understood the security policy.

8. Screen potential personnel prior to hire to minimize the risk of attacks from internal sources.

9. If cardholder data is shared with service providers, maintain and implement policies and procedures to manage service providers, to include the following:
   - Maintain a list of service providers.
   - Maintain a written agreement that includes an acknowledgement that the service providers are responsible for the security of cardholder data the service provider possesses.
   - Ensure there is an established process for engaging service providers including proper due diligence prior to the engagement.
   - Maintain a program to monitor service providers' PCI DSS compliance status annually.

10. Create an incident response plan to be implemented in the event of system breach. Ensure the plan addresses the following, at a minimum:
    - Roles and responsibilities as well as communication and contact strategies to be deployed in the event of a compromise including notification of the payment brands.
    - Specific incident response procedures.
    - Business recovery and continuity procedures.
    - Data back-up processes.
    - Analysis of legal requirements for reporting compromises.
    - Coverage and responses of all critical system components.
    - Reference or inclusion of incident response procedures in the payment brands.
    - Test the plan annually.
    - Designate specific personnel to be available on a 24/7 basis to respond to alerts.
    - Provide appropriate training to staff with security breach response responsibilities.
    - Include alerts from intrusion detection, intrusion-prevention, and file integrity monitoring systems.
    - Develop a process to modify and evolve the incident response plan according to lessons learned and to incorporate industry developments.

MANAGEMENT CHECKLIST

This checklist is intended for the management of an organization that hosts a system to be used by other organizations and also an organization that processes a large volume of credit card transactions.

1. Document the system descriptions and internal controls of systems used by other organizations.

2. Develop a process to monitor for system effectiveness regularly in order to assure user organizations.

3. If a SysTrust audit is pursued, assign ownership to an executive.

4. If a SysTrust audit is pursued, consider adopting the optional principles of privacy and confidentiality.

5. If a SysTrust audit is pursued, assess the applicability of control criteria and document control procedures for each criterion.

6. Assess the organization's need to comply with the PCI Security Standard.

7. If the PCI Security Standard is applicable, set up a project to achieve compliance.

8. If the PCI Security Standard is applicable, assign an executive to be accountable for compliance.

9. Perform an internal PCI compliance check regularly.

10. Select the PCI compliance external auditor in accordance with guidelines from the PCI Security Council whose membership includes the major credit card issuers.

INTERNAL AUDIT CHECKLIST

1. Develop expertise in the SysTrust principles and control criteria.

2. Develop expertise in PCI Security Standard.

3. Ensure that the SysTrust control criteria and the relevant control procedures are subject to annual testing in audit assignments.

4. Ensure that the PCI Security Standard is addressed comprehensively on an annual basis in internal audits.

5. Conduct SysTrust training seminars for management.

6. Provide advice to management as to the pros and cons of SysTrust in relation to a CSAE 3416 or SSAE 16 control assurance opinion.

7. Ensure that the control procedures cover infrastructure, software, people, information and procedures.

8. Assess management's justification of any control criteria deemed not to be applicable in a SysTrust review.

9. Meet with the SysTrust and PCI executives regularly to assess the organization's readiness for compliance.

10. Document internal control test results thoroughly for external auditors' review.

EXTERNAL AUDIT CHECKLIST

This checklist is intended for the external auditors who perform a SysTrust audit.

1. Review the service organization's system description for correctness and comprehensiveness in relation to the services offered through the systems.

2. Assess the service organization's justification of any control criteria deemed by the organization to be not applicable.

3. Review the control procedures for each control criterion to assess comprehensiveness.

4. Test control procedures.

5. Consider the relevance of any compensating control procedures supplied by the service organization to address control deficiencies in terms of the validity and sufficiency of the period of effectiveness.

6. If a period is to be covered, ensure that it covers at least six months.

7. Ensure that material subsequent events are disclosed in the SysTrust audit report.

8. Ensure that any outsourcing performed by the service organization that has a material effect on the system involved is supported by appropriate written control assurance from the second tier service organizations.

9. If an optional principle is not met because of control deficiencies, inform the service organization of its option to remove that principle from the report.

10. Rely on internal control testing by the internal auditors as a basis for limiting direct testing.

CONCLUSION

Technology trends like cloud computing, edge computing and software as a service increase the need for system operators to provide assurance to system users about information reliability. The two commonly comprehensive system assurance frameworks are SSAE 16 and SysTrust. The former caters to shareholders' auditors of user organizations, while SysTrust is intended to provide direct assurance to user organization management. SysTrust is highly structured and focuses primarily on policies and monitoring. SysTrust adoption is expected to grow because more organizations are relying on systems hosted by other institutions to carry out their business.

The Payment Card Industry Security Standard is also gaining prominence as more merchants, financial institutions and eBusiness service providers realize that they need to be serious about preventing credit card fraud. In the process of complying with the PCI standard, many organizations have come to realize that their networks and security infrastructures have significant holes. The success of the PCI framework can be measured by comparing credit fraud statistics over time as more organizations come to comply with this standard.

SUMMARY OF MAIN POINTS

1. A SysTrust audit is intended to provide assurance to user organizations of a system hosted external to the organizations that the system is reliable from the perspective of security, processing integrity, availability, confidentiality and privacy protection.

2. SysTrust is similar to SSAE 16 in that all three are to provide assurance on a system hosted by one organization that is used by other organizations.

3. SysTrust differs from SSAE 16 in that its main audience is management of the user organizations, not shareholders' auditors of the user organizations.

4. SysTrust also differs from SSAE 16 in that it is based on a rigid set of internal control criteria for each of the principles of security, processing integrity, availability, confidentiality and privacy. SSAE 16 provide the standard for an internal control assurance report to address control objectives set by management in relation to the system description. There is more flexibility in SSAE 16.

5. The confidentiality and privacy protection principles are optional.

6. A firm must be licensed by CICA or AICPA specifically for SysTrust in order to perform a SysTrust audit.

7. A SysTrust audit can provide point-in-time assurance or assurance over a period.

8. PCI Security Standard applies to all merchants, IT service organizations and financial institutions that process credit card transactions electronically. Large merchants and IT service organizations are required to provide annual independent validation of compliance.

9. The complexity of an organization's networks will affect the extent of details to which the PCI security standard is applied.

10. The PCI Security Standard applies only to the Cardholder Data Environment, a network environment where a substantial quantity of cardholder data is stored or processed.

REVIEW QUESTIONS

1. Map the SysTrust principles to the control matrix we discussed in Chapter Six.

2. How does SysTrust differ from SSAE 16 in terms of the comprehensiveness of assurance?

3. What are the management options to avoid a qualified SysTrust audit opinion when a significant control deficiency is found?

4. What does the SysTrust audit opinion cover?

5. What parties can benefit from a SysTrust audit report?

6. What kinds of organizations are held to comply with the Payment Card Industry Security Standard?

7. What kinds of organizations are required to provide an annual external validation of compliance with the PCI Security Standard?

8. According to the PCI Security Standard, what kinds of access should be monitored?

9. How does the PCI Security Standard affect the financial statement audits of large retail merchants?

10. How does the PCI Security Standard affect the profit of large retail merchants?

CASE – Independent Electricity System Operator

The Independent Electricity System Operator (IESO) works at the heart of Ontario's power system, connecting all participants – generators that produce electricity, transmitters that send it across the province, retailers that buy and sell it, industries and businesses that use it in large quantities and local distribution companies that deliver it to people's homes. Every five minutes, the IESO forecasts consumption throughout the province and collects the best offers from generators to provide the required amount of electricity. This allows hydro companies and their industrial customers to see price fluctuation based on supply and demand. As a result, they can shift consumption away from peaks in demand to times when the price is lower.

The IESO monitors the system and identifies what is required to maintain reliability in the future, reporting on these recommendations through regular publications. In its quarterly 18-month forecasts of the growth in demand for electricity, the IESO assesses whether there will be adequate generation and transmission facilities. In addition, the IESO prepares the semi-annual Ontario Reliability Outlook, which reports on the progress of interrelated generation, transmission and demand-side projects underway to meet Ontario's reliability requirements.

The IESO co-ordinates emergency preparedness for the province's electricity system and played a key role in managing the restoration of power following the August 2003 blackout.

The IESO continues to work with other stakeholders to evolve the market for the benefit of all. Further enhancements will strengthen the market, enhance reliability and provide Ontarians with greater access to information about their power system.

IESO is a not-for-profit corporate entity established in 1998 by the Electricity Act of Ontario. It is governed by an independent Board whose members are appointed by the Government of Ontario. Its fees and licences to operate are set by the Ontario Energy Board and it operates independently of all other participants in the electricity market.

The IESO has full statute-based authority for establishing, monitoring and enforcing reliability standards in the province. All the companies that make up the power system in Ontario must meet the IESO's standards.

Source: http://www.ieso.com/imoweb/siteShared/whoweare.asp?sid=bi, *accessed on July 2, 2012.*

Required

Describe how the SysTrust model can be applied to IESO.

MULTIPLE CHOICE QUESTIONS

1. Which of the following is an optional SysTrust principle?
   A. Confidentiality
   B. Security
   C. Processing integrity
   D. Availability

2. Who is the primary audience of a SysTrust report?
   A. Service organization management
   B. Shareholders' auditors of service organization
   C. User organization management
   D. Shareholders' auditors of user organization(s)

3. Who is responsible for developing control procedures in a SysTrust audit?
   A. External auditors
   B. Service organization management
   C. Internal auditors
   D. User organization management

4. Which SysTrust principle addresses application controls the most?
   A. Security
   B. Confidentiality
   C. Processing integrity
   D. Availability

5. Which of the following differs the most between SysTrust and SSAE 16?
   A. Flexibility in internal control objectives
   B. Level of control assurance
   C. Qualification of auditor
   D. Requirement for system description

6. Which organization is most likely exempted from obtain external scanning for compliance with the PCI Security Standard?
   A. Sony
   B. Amazon
   C. Boeing
   D. Walmart

7. What kind of access to cardholder data must be monitored by Best Buy?
   A. All
   B. Update
   C. External
   D. Create

8. Who make up the PCI Security Council?
   A. Large banks
   B. Major credit card issuers
   C. Large online merchants
   D. Federal Reserve Board

9. What is the maximum credit card number data that can be displayed to a customer or a merchant?
   A. First 6 and last 4
   B. First 6
   C. Last 4
   D. First 10
   E. First 4 and last 4

10. How is a credit card PIN verified?
    A. Comparing the keyed PIN to the database
    B. Comparing the keyed in value to the hash of the credit card number
    C. Comparing the hash of the keyed in value to the hash in the bank's database
    D. Comparing the hash of the keyed in value to the hash stored in the credit card chip

Chapter 12 – Computer Crime

Technological progress is like an axe in the hands of a pathological criminal. –

Albert Einstein

Computer crime has increased in volume, impact and variety in the last decade mainly because of the Internet. There are broadly speaking, two types of computer crime: crime causing fairly immediate damage like hacking, and crime that is fraudulent in nature like am email scam. In either case, the crime may be committed on IT resources or it may use IT as a tool to achieve the criminal intent.

Here is a list of recently publicized computer crimes.

- In June 2011, Spanish police reported that it had arrested three members of a local Anonymous group in three separate cities, claiming they were responsible for the hacking attacks against the PlayStation Store. Anonymous is a group initiating active civil disobedience and spread through the Internet while staying hidden. The police alleged that these three individuals were leaders of a the group, and considered them to be some of the masterminds behind the attack. In addition to being charged with the PlayStation store hacks, these three were accused of leading hacks against government websites of a number of countries, two Spanish banks, an Italian energy company, and the website of the Spanish Electoral Board.

- One of the biggest frauds in financial services history was carried out by a 31-year-old trader in Société Générale's Paris headquarters, Jerome Kerviel. The trader took massive fraudulent directional positions – bets on future movements of European stock indices, without his supervisor's knowledge, the Bank said. Because he had previously worked in the trading unit's back office, he had in-depth knowledge of the control procedures and evaded them by creating fictitious transactions to conceal his activity. The fraud was discovered on January 20, 2008. Société Générale (SocGen), one of the largest banks in Europe, started to unwind the positions the next day just as global equity markets were tanking on fears of a U.S. recession. "It was the worst possible time," says Janine Dow, senior director for financial institutions at the Fitch ratings agency in Paris. SocGen, which also announced a nearly $3 billion 2007 loss related to U.S. mortgage-market woes, had to seek a $5.5 billion capital increase.

- On August 18, 2011, Toronto police arrested and charged a man on 38 charges for ATM skimming. The man identified was arrested after evidence was seized from a house. The suspect was identified on a surveillance tape. According to police, the suspect had installed at least 38 skimming devices on ATMs in financial institutions across the Greater Toronto Area. These skimming devices, installed in the card slots of ATMs, can be used to obtain personal information from ATM cards. The ATM skimming business nets over a billion dollars annually.

Here are the common types of computer crime that are not quite fraudulent in nature and that cause immediate damage.

- Altering a public computer system like a bank system without approval – Main control is a firewall.

- Deliberately spreading viruses and worms – Main controls include anti-virus software and patching.

- Email interception – Main control is encryption.

- Hacking – Main control is a firewall.

- Sabotage of computer equipment – Main control is physical security.

- Spreading, uploading or storing child pornography – Main control is web filtering.

- Theft of computer equipment – Main control is physical security.

- Theft of information – Main control is encryption.

- Theft of software – Main controls include access control list, digital rights control and management monitoring.

The following is a list of common computer frauds.

- ATM skimming – Main controls include user education and a surveillance camera.

- Changing computer system information to hide defalcation – Main controls include a firewall and access control lists.

- Computer scam – Main control is user education.

- Email interception – Main control is encryption.

- Gaining unauthorized access to systems to transfer funds – Main control is an access control list.

- Identity theft – Main controls include user education and access control lists.

- Producing fictitious transactions – Main controls include segregation of duties and management review.

These lists are just common examples of information technology (IT) crime. A lot of other crimes can be committed with the aid of computers, e.g., lapping, by adjusting accounts receivable data. This chapter is not intended to discuss all business crime and accounting fraud. It focuses on IT crime and fraud. However, for the non-IT crime, many system controls can be used to prevent or detect them. These controls have been discussed in chapters 3, 6 and 8.

Computer crime is committed because of temptation and opportunity. An opportunity to a criminal is created when internal controls are weak. Temptation is present when vulnerable assets are easily accessible.

INTERNAL CONTROLS

Here are the common internal controls against computer crime.

- Access control list

- Access log

- Chief ethics officer

- Code of business conduct

- Digital certificate

- Digital rights monitoring

- Digital signature

- Encryption

- Exception reporting

- File blocking

- File integrity monitoring

- Firewall

- Intrusion detection system

- Intrusion prevention system

- Locks

- Management and independent review

- Password policy

- Password system configuration to comply with the password policy

- Security check for sensitive positions including criminal record check

- Security education

- Segregation of duties

- Web filtering

- Web site refresh

- Whistle blowing policy

Many of these controls are covered in Chapter Eight and Chapter Nine. We will describe the others below.

Chief Ethics Officer

Large organizations increasingly have an executive titled chief ethics officer. This is part of setting the tone at the top. This new position was created by many organizations to deter fraud by raising the awareness of ethics. Some organizations also include a compliance function in this position. Governments are also increasingly instituting such a function. The following is an excerpt of an article from National Post that describes this function, on June 19, 2004.

"Proponents who believe in it say that a corporation with a chief ethics officer treats the issue seriously enough to dedicate a senior management position to it. The chief ethics officer deals with fostering and maintaining integrity and ethical behaviour, handles internal complaints about business practices and often is responsible for part of the regulatory and compliance work. The last component of the job description has grown increasingly onerous since the passage of the Sarbanes-Oxley Act.

In Canada, similar work falls on the shoulders of the corporate secretary or a compliance-tasked vice-president. But supporters of the chief ethics officer say the position also allows for increased dialog with potential whistleblowers who might be too intimidated to speak with a chief executive officer or a corporate secretary."

It must be clear to management that the chief executive officer (CEO) has ultimate responsibility for ethics. The chief ethics officer's job is to create a work environment where people frequently think about ethics, have good understanding of what is ethically acceptable and feel comfortable about coming forward and raising concerns. The chief ethics officer owns and administers the whistle blowing policy that tells people under what conditions they can go to the chief ethics officer to report suspected improper act and that there will be no reprisal as a consequence.

Code of Business Conduct

One of the first tasks of a chief ethics officer is to document a code of business conduct and establish a process for communication to everyone in the organization and regular reminder about the code. The code tells employees and consultants what not to do when engaging in organization business or using organization resources. It addresses the following common topics:

- Unacceptable use of organization resources like surfing inappropriate sites or running a side business.
- Conflict of interest with suppliers, superiors, colleagues and subordinates.
- Avoiding fraud or potentially criminal activities.
- Reporting improper conduct, fraud or crime to the chief ethics officer following prescribed procedures.
- Respecting license restriction of software provided by the organization.
- Avoiding using personal software on organization computers.
- Avoiding using organization resources for personal purposes in a significant way.
- Acknowledging that employer activities in the organization or while conducting organization business are subject to monitoring by the organization.
- Respecting the confidentiality of organization information.

The code of business conduct should be supplemented with a policy on acceptable use of IT resources. This policy should state the types of unacceptable use of IT resources. Here is a common list of what is considered unacceptable.

- The use of corporate IT resources for excessive personal use.
- Using personal IT resources to conduct corporate business, unless approved by a manager.
- Accessing, displaying, downloading, creating, distributing or storing any software, graphics, images, text, music, video or other data which are offensive and conducive to a poisoned work environment, e.g., pornography.
- Using Internet sites for sharing files such as music files, video clips, digital image files or software programs, unless for corporate business.
- Streaming audio or video from the Internet, unless for corporate business purposes.
- Using corporate resources to play games.
- Operating a private business or political activities.
- Misrepresenting the organization's views on a matter.
- Discrediting others in the organization through electronic communications.
- Sending anonymous messages or impersonating others.
- Sending chain letters.
- Using offensive, threatening, abusive language in electronic communications.
- Using IT resources to discriminate against or harass, threaten or intimidate other employees or to create a hostile or humiliating work environment.
- Performing unauthorized network scans on, or conducting unauthorized access attempts to corporate systems, applications or services, or spreading viruses or malicious codes to other systems.

533

Employees should be educated about this policy upon joining the organization and reminded periodically. For example, a login script can be implemented to pop up a reminder that requires acknowledgement periodically when an employees logs on to the network. This policy should be enforced with system controls such as using a web filtering software system to deny web sites that fall into the above categories and track the types and extent of Internet use. Frequent Internet users should be flagged for reporting to managers who can then assess appropriateness in relation to job requirements.

Exception Reporting

Exception analysis can range from fairly simple tracking of account status like customers whose accounts get very close to the credit limits, to complicated multi-variable regression analysis and simulation to find insider trades or tax frauds. Large organizations like banks, securities regulators, insurance companies and governments use statistical analysis including data mining tools to detect insider trades, tax frauds, insurance frauds, defalcation and loan frauds. For example, Benford analysis is used by income tax departments to help in selecting questionable tax returns for audit. Statistical Analysis Software (SAS) is used by many large organizations to help them in customer relationship management systems and fraud detection. The following is a quote from the SAS web site, http://www.sas.com/solutions/fraud/index.html, accessed on July 3, 2012.

> *Banks, insurance companies, health care organizations and government entities are all seeing an increase in the incidence and sophistication of fraud, waste and abuse activities, fuelled in large measure by the financial turmoil gripping the world's economy. To fight fraud effectively, organizations must continually improve the monitoring of transactions across multiple accounts and systems. SAS® Enterprise Financial Crimes Framework provides a technology infrastructure that integrates fraud detection, alert management, network analysis and case management – giving organizations the upper hand in detecting fraud in any form, at any touch point.*

Statistical analysis is a powerful tool in that when numbers deviate from the norm, they require attention. For example, if the material cost of an aircraft deviates significantly from historical cost, it doesn't take an aeronautic engineer to suspect that something may be wrong.

When the population is large enough to form a base for comparison, even simple analytical review can lead to discovery of significant fraud. For example, a bank can calculate the following ratios every month for each branch and then compare the ratios for each branch to the overall ratios for the bank:

Interest revenue / non-interest revenue

Interest revenue / interest expense

Non-interest revenue / non-interest expense

Interest revenue / loan total

Interest expense / deposit total

Non-interest revenue / transaction volume

To be more granular, each branch's ratios can be compared to the ratios of the region or city; or each branch's ratios can be compared to the ratios for the types of branches, e.g., main branches, large commercial branches, urban branches, suburban branches and rural branches. The ratios should also be compared from period to period. There can also be correlation between ratios as the ratios between ratios should also be fairly stable. For example, if the interest revenue / non-interest revenue remains fairly stable but interest revenue / interest expense has decreased, there may be some significantly non-performing or fictitious loans. A fraudster may not think that the difference between 2.3 and 2.4 is not significant; however, if the historical difference in the last year has ranged from 2.28 to 2.32, 2.4 would be a significant deviation. Software tools can be used to query even much longer periods and much larger populations.

EVIDENCE

Evidence is crucial in any forensic investigation. Without credible evidence, prosecution, pursuit of compensation and disciplinary action will not be successful. There are four types of evidence in IT forensic.

1. Physical evidence includes tangible objects that can be physically carried into a court. Examples include a hard disk accompanied by a printout of its content and a phone log. Physical evidence speaks for itself.

2. Documentary evidence includes recorded information such as audio or video recording. Documentary evidence requires the collaboration of an expert witness.

3. Testimonial evidence includes testimony made under oath by witnesses as well as confessions and hearsay evidence. Examples include a security expert's opinion and a computer technician's statement of what s/he read or saw when fixing a computer.

4. Demonstrative evidence includes charts, graphs and computer reconstruction of data that expert witnesses or lawyers can use in testimonies or cross examinations.

When handling evidence, a forensic auditor must ensure the following:

- Evidence is not altered, damaged, contaminated or destroyed in the investigation procedures. Simply viewing data using a word processor can destroy important audit trail. This is why the entire hard disk should be imaged to an offline medium and data should be analyzed from the a copy of the image.

- No malicious software is permitted to infect or corrupt the subject computer, the auditor's computer or other computers on the subject's computer's network.

- All possible relevant evidence extracted from the subject's computer or network is fully preserved.

- An unbroken chain of custody is established, documented and maintained.

- The privacy and confidentiality of all data on the subject's computer and networks are properly maintained.

FORENSIC SOFTWARE

A popular forensic investigation software tool is Encase. It is used by police and large organizations like banks, large companies and governments. Here are the common functions.

- On site or remote imaging of a disk and RAM with MD5 or SHA-1 hash to preserve integrity. The hash is performed before imaging, after imaging and periodically to ensure that the entire disk has been imaged and the image has not been changed.

- File analysis to look for evidence.

- Data recovery from deleted files.

- Investigation case documentation organization.

- Investigation work papers and report templates.

Encase applies the Locard exchange principle, which says that every contact leaves a trace.

Investigations should also use other more focused tools for functions like searching email and archive files. Discovery Accelerator is one such tool. It is important that these tools be run from highly secured computers like offline computers in order to prevent tampering with the evidence.

FORENSIC INVESTIGATION PROCEDURES

The following are some common computer forensic investigation procedures.

1. Assess the situation and understand what type of incident or crime is to be investigated.

2. Obtain senior management approval to proceed with an investigation. The level of management should be several levels above the target individuals being investigated to avoid conflict of interest or abuse of the investigation process. For example, if the chief financial officer (CFO) wants the controller investigated, the organization's policy should require that the CFO's supervisor approves this before investigation begins.

3. Carry out procedures to "freeze" audit trail, e.g., sending a court order to the Internet service provider (ISP) to provide access to the suspect's Internet data, copying emails, imaging hard disks, identifying remote storages and imaging the relevant disks and RAM. In some cases, a warrant is necessary. The organization's lawyers should be consulted with respect to police involvement.

4. Apply packet sniffing.

5. Review system logs.

6. Determine the equipment and software needed to carry out the investigation.

7. Apply special software like Encase to recover erased data.

8. Avoid shutting down the suspected computers, connect uninterrupted power supply (UPS) to keep the computer on, so as to prevent loss of data or system audit trail. If UPS is not available and the computer has to be moved, unplug it instead of using the operating system to shut it down; unplugging will involve less interference with the audit trail.

9. Scan imaged drives and copied emails for viruses.

10. Back up the evidence.

11. Use the organization's PKI key recovery process to decrypt files. If that does not work, use password cracking software to obtain the password for the encryption key.

12. Boot the captured or suspected computers with an external boot disk instead of using the computer's operating system to avoid loss of audit trail.

13. Document all sequence of events, all interviews, time spent by each investigator and the work performed by each investigator.

14. Maintain arm's length with the people being investigated, the requester of the investigation, the approver of the investigation and people who provide information to investigators, to avoid conflict of interest.

15. Continuously assess the need to communicate with the law department, senior management and the police.

16. Do not communicate information about the investigation using post mail or an unencrypted electronic medium.

17. Be a patient listener, ask open questions, make others comfortable in talking to you, take copious notes.

18. Safeguard the investigation files with encryption and physical measures.

19. Keep all evidence, including electronic media for a case all together as complete audit trail, with proper cross references to source, date, sequence of events etc.

20. Dispose of unneeded electronic evidence by using the organization's approved data wiping software and standard procedures, including if necessary, corporate approved vendors for media storage, backup and destruction.

MANAGEMENT CHECKLIST

1. Appoint a chief ethics officer.

2. Establish a code of business conduct including a whistle blowing policy.

3. Establish a policy on acceptable use of IT resources.

4. Obtain employee acknowledgement of understanding of the code of business conduct and the policy on acceptable use of IT resources regularly.

5. Establish a policy on reference check for new hires.

6. Establish a policy for conducting security check including criminal record check for positions that handle sensitive information or vulnerable assets.

7. Large organizations should establish a forensic investigation function.

8. Ensure the audit committee is made aware of all computer crime committed against the organization.

9. Ensure that the applicable labor unions are consulted with respect to the development and changes of the code of business conduct.

10. Establish a protocol for informing the police of criminal activities in or against the organization, involving the security and law departments. The protocol should include procedures for providing audit trail, evidence and information to the police with respect to management approval, warrants and court orders; e.g., what documents and information can be provided to the police without a warrant or court order.

INTERNAL AUDIT CHECKLIST

1. Obtain training in computer forensic investigation and keep staff training up-to-date. Encourage staff members to obtain relevant professional designations like Certified Fraud Examiner.

2. Develop an audit program for computer forensic investigation.

3. Establish a protocol with management for requesting forensic investigations, conducting investigations, reporting as well as for working with the security department, the law department and the police.

4. Establish a suite of forensic investigation tools.

5. Ensure that audit committee is informed of computer crime.

6. Perform organization wide analytical review to identify areas more vulnerable to fraud.

7. Include analytical review in every audit assignment to detect fraud.

8. Include a questionnaire in every assignment to probe management about its suspicion or detection of computer crime.

9. Review the organization's staff turnover list to identify functions that control sensitive information or vulnerable assets that have been occupied by the same persons or persons who have not taken vacation for years. Escalate the audit of these functions.

10. Review organization charts to identify functions with weak segregation of duties that involve the approval or control of sensitive information or vulnerable assets. Escalate the audit of these functions.

EXTERNAL AUDITOR CHECKLIST

1. Review last year's internal control recommendations and confirm corrective actions to assess the client's vulnerability to computer crime.

2. For internal control deficiencies not corrected, perform substantive testing to detect material computer crime.

3. Ensure the calculation of materiality takes into account the risk of computer crime.

4. Ensure that computer crime is communicated to the audit committee.

5. Review the client's internal investigations of computer crime to assess control deficiency and financial statement impact.

6. Review the client's filings with regulators about computer crime.

7. Meet with the chief ethics officer, chief auditor, CIO and CFO to review the list of reported crimes to assess internal control deficiency and materiality.

8. Perform analytical review to identify significantly unusual trend.

9. Review off-balance sheet system transaction fluctuation to identify fraudulent trend. Because these transactions do not affect the balance sheet, they may be paid less attention by management in ongoing review and therefore may be attractive to fraudsters.

10. Assess the implication of reported or suspected computer crime on materiality, management credibility and contingent liability.

FORENSIC INVESTIGATION CHECKLIST

When computer crime is highly suspected or has occurred, depending on the crime's scale and impact, management may want to order a forensic investigation. The objective of such an investigations includes:

- Confirming that crime has been committed within or on the organization.
- Collecting evidence and linking it to suspects.
- Collecting evidence to provide to the police or to support a civil litigation.
- Determining the people who committed or assisted in committing the crime.
- Root cause analysis with recommendations to improve internal controls.

A typical IT forensic assignment includes the following activities.

1. Determine the suspects, suspected computers and storage media.

2. Capture information from the suspected computers and storage media without leaving a trace on the computers and media, more importantly, without distorting the audit trail in the computers and media.

3. Decrypt the data files.

4. Determine the content of computer files.

5. Compare the content of computer files to known reference files or documents.

6. Determine the time and sequence in which the files were created or changed.

7. Recover deleted files.

8. Look for key phrases or key words.

9. Study and analyze source code.

10. Link evidence, analyses, interview notes and assessments in a case work paper file.

11. Encrypt analyses and evidence other than source data.

12. Physically protect the work paper file.

13. Logically protect the work paper file without tampering with source data or distorting the audit trail of source data.

14. Keep a copy of the work paper file and captured data offsite.

15. Determine the internal control weaknesses that let the fraud or crime occur.

16. Make recommendations to tighten internal control weaknesses.

17. Provide a report to senior management.

18. Provide information to law enforcement agencies with appropriate review by the organization's lawyers.

CONCLUSION

As the world is becoming more computer literate and organizations increasingly rely on computers, cyber crimes and computer related frauds are taking up a larger and larger portion of overall crimes. It doesn't take long for criminals to realize that a few clicks can land them much more money than holding up a bank. Identity theft is also growing, which can serve as the portal to other crimes like stealing real estate, obtaining business secret, money laundering and transferring money from the victim's bank accounts.

Shareholders' auditors have to assess the risk of crime and fraud in planning and carrying out every audit. Internal auditors should devote a significant portion of their resources to detect fraud and respond to management requests to investigate. Internal audit departments of large organizations should be equipped with forensic accounting and auditing tools and selective auditors should receive specialized training. All auditors should have computer forensic awareness as part of their annual training programs. Forensic investigators should use a disciplined investigation program and rigorous tools so that their findings can stand up in court. They should follow closely the organization's policy on appropriate use of IT resources and privacy to avoid contaminating evidence or taking actions that can be challenged by the defense counsel. The law department should be involved; and where the criminal law is highly suspected to have been broken by the suspect, the police should be informed and involved.

SUMMARY OF MAIN POINTS

1. Opportunity has to be present for computer crime to occur. Opportunity is created by internal control deficiency.

2. Two types of computer crime: crime that is not mainly deceitful like hacking, and computer fraud. Shareholders' auditors are more concerned about computer fraud as it carries more uncertainty.

3. IT resources may be the target of computer crime. IT resource may be used to commit a crime.

4. Preventing computer crime starts with appointing a chief ethics officer as well as educating employees and customers on what behavior and activities are unacceptable.

5. The CEO is ultimately accountable for ethics. The chief ethics officer is a facilitator.

6. ID theft is a common computer crime that can lead to other crimes.

7. Internal auditors should address the risk of computer crime in every audit.

8. Shareholders' auditors should assess the risk of computer crime in audit planning and perform analytical review to identify significant computer crime.

9. Every large organization should establish a computer forensic investigation function to perform forensic investigations based on management requests, suspicions from control deficiencies and proactive scanning of employee IT network activities for anomalies

10. IT forensic assignments should involve obviously technical IT specialist, but also investigators with business and financial experience, the law department, labor union representatives and the police (for computer crime).

REVIEW QUESTIONS

1. What is the shareholders' auditors' responsibility for computer fraud detection?

2. What is the internal auditors' responsibility for computer fraud detection?

3. What are common computer crimes committed against financial institutions and retailers?

4. Who do you think the chief ethics officer should report to and why?

5.   What computer crimes can result from identity theft?

6.   What internal controls can organizations implement to prevent system alteration?

7.   What are some system controls that can prevent or detect disbursement fraud?

8.   What technology do you think the police and securities commissions use to detect insider trading?

9.   How can a bank use analytical review to detect fictitious loans?

10.   What is the relationship of Encase and Blancco?

CASE – Deloitte & Touche LLP v. Carlson, 2011 WL 2923865 (N.D. Ill. July 18, 2011), U. S. District Court, State of Illinois.

Source: *http://blog.internetcases.com/2011/07/27/computer-fraud-and-abuse-act-case-against-hard-drive-destroying-director-goes-forward/, accessed on July 3, 2012.*

Defendant had risen to the level of Director of a large consulting and professional services firm. After defendant left the firm to join a competitor, he returned his work-issued laptop with the old hard drive having been replaced by a new blank one. Defendant had destroyed the old hard drive because it had personal data on it such as tax returns and account information.

The firm sued, putting forth a number of claims, including violation of the Computer Fraud and Abuse Act (CFAA). Defendant moved to dismiss for failure to state a claim upon which relief can be granted. The court denied the motion. Defendant argued that the CFAA claim should fail because plaintiff had not adequately pled that the destruction of the hard drive was done "without authorization." The court rejected this argument.

The court looked to Int'l Airport Centers LLC v. Citrin, 440 F.3d 418 (7th Cir. 2006) for guidance on the question of whether defendant's alleged conduct was "without authorization." Int'l Airport Centers held that an employee acts without authorization as contemplated under the CFAA if s/he breaches a duty of loyalty to the employer prior to the alleged data destruction.

In this case, plaintiff alleged that defendant began soliciting another employee to leave before defendant left, and that defendant allegedly destroyed the data to cover his tracks. On these facts, the court found the "without authorization" element to be adequately pled.

<u>Required</u>

1. What else could Carlson have done to keep his personal information from Deloitte when the laptop was returned?

2. How do you think Carlson communicated with the other employee whom he was alleged to have solicited to leave Deloitte?

3. What are some steps you think Deloitte might have used to find evidence of Carlson's loyalty breach or improper system activities?

MULTIPLE CHOICE QUESTIONS

1. Which address is most useful in a forensic investigation?
    a. IP
    b. MAC
    c. URL
    d. Email

2. If a forensic auditor inspects a computer containing a critical file that is known to be highly encrypted but currently opened, what should the auditor do immediately?
    a. Pull the plug on the computer.
    b. Perform an orderly shutdown of the computer.
    c. Make an immediate shadow volume copy of the entire hard drive.
    d. Browse the open file.

3. Which medium should a forensic investigator target if a workstation's hard disk has been thoroughly wiped by a fraudster using Blancco, say ten times?
    a. Firewall log
    b. Network drive
    c. Anti-virus log
    d. Sandbox

4. What computer crime does a firewall mitigate against?
    a. Hacking
    b. Identity theft
    c. Virus spreading
    d. ATM skimming

5. Which of the following techniques or tools is most useful to detect a bank loan fraud committed by a branch manager?
    a. Benford analysis
    b. Firewall
    c. Segregation of duties
    d. Discovery Accelerator

6. Which of the following crime is most commonly committed with ID theft?
   a. Hacking
   b. Virus spreading
   c. Loan fraud
   d. Child pornography

7. When of the following events must be reported to police?
   a. Employee found to be sending hate propaganda.
   b. A customer sent email to other customers to discredit the company.
   c. Many child pornography pictures found in an employee's shared network drive.
   d. A vendor has overbilled by $1 million and been paid.

8. When an auditor images an employee's hard disk and performs data analysis, what is the most relevant objective?
   a. Connecting suspect to evidence
   b. Connecting evidence to traces
   c. Obtaining testimony
   d. Determining network breach

9. If a forensic auditor comes across an opened file that seems to contain criminally implicating information, what is the next step?
   a. Pull the plug.
   b. Study the file.
   c. Power down the computer.
   d. Image the hard disk.

10. What type of evidence is most readily prepared using Encase?
    a. Physical
    b. Demonstrative
    c. Testimonial
    d. Documentary

Glossary

Access control list	A list of users or programs that are authorized to access a specific resource like a file, indicating the type of access, e.g., read, write.
Access point	A wireless router connected to a wired network.
ACL	Audit Command Language, the most popular general audit software tool.
Action Center	A Windows facility for security configuration and repository of security settings.
Active Directory	Active Directory serves as a central location for network administration and security. It is used for authenticating and authorizing all users and computers within a network of Windows domain type, assigning and enforcing security policies for all computers in a network and installing or updating software on network computers.
Active X	ActiveX control is a framework for writing reusable code. Users should configure the browser to not accept unsigned ActiveX components automatically. ActiveX components usually are not run in the sandbox and therefore riskier than .NET components.
Advanced Encryption Standard	An advanced symmetric standard that uses algorithms that require 128-bit or 256-bit keys.
Architecture	The design and layout of a system's infrastructure.
ASCII	American Standard Code for Information Interchange is the de factor personal computer data format; some people use it to refer to only alphanumeric data.
Attribute sampling	Sampling of items to confirm the presence of attributes, e.g., approved or not approved.
Asymmetric encryption	A pair of related keys are used. Something encrypted with one key can be decrypted only with the other key.
Audit risk	The risk of an audit with a favorable conclusion when the financial records or internal controls do not warrant such a conclusion. For a financial statement audit, audit risk = inherent risk x control risk x detection risk.

Authenticode	Authenticode is Microsoft's tool for software distributors to digitally sign the software and for user browsers to verify the digital signatures. It is a high risk for a user to select the enable option for running .NET Framework reliant components not signed with Authenticode.
Back door	A hole in software left open by accident or intent to allow an alternate method to access a system. A backdoor by design allows system administrators to perform quick fixes.
Batch total	A control total of an amount or quantity taken at one point of a transaction cycle for a batch system and agreed to another control total of the same batch of transactions taken at a later point to confirm completeness of processing.
Benford Law	A statistical distribution that indicates that the leading digits of a natural number are more likely to be a low order digit like 1 or 2 than being a high order digit like 9 or 8.
Bit	A binary digit that is 0 or 1. A bit is not standalone, it is part of a byte. The number 1 can be represented with a byte with the value 0000001. All data in a computer is in bits and bytes. The letter "a" takes the digital byte of 1000001.
Boundary checking	Checking that the data input in a Web application does not exceed the field length expected by the application, to prevent buffer overflow.
Buffer overflow	A hacking technique to put in more data than requested in an Internet application to overflow the buffer of real access memory (RAM) allocated to the requested input and therefore overwrite some data in RAM allocated to other applications, causing havoc.
Business impact analysis	Analysis of disaster or business interruption scenarios and their impact on an organization's business. The purpose is to decide on the scope of a disaster recovery plan.
Business process reengineering	A rigorous and detailed review of the business processes throughout the enterprise to establish a value chain of functions of activities at the same time weeding or streamlining the functions and activities that do not deliver value.
Byte	A collection of bits. A computer may use 7-bit or 8-bit bytes. A 7 bit byte can represent a number as high as 128. A large number will take more bytes. A byte is also used to represent a character, so my last name will take 4 bytes.

Certificate authority	An organization that issues digital certificates, usually for a fee.
Challenge response	Asking pre-arranged security questions of the user to help authenticate the access attempt.
Check digit	Using the last digit of a control number like a product number to validate data entry. The check digit is a derivative of the preceding digits. This control helps ensure valid, but not necessarily control numbers.
CICS	Customer Information Control System (CICS) provides the software framework in IBM Z series severs for programmers to develop online real time systems that process customer transactions, like banking systems. It is not a programming language.
Click fraud	Clicking on a commercial link without the intent to learn about or buy the product or service. The intent here is mainly to cause a company to pay more for online advertising in an unfair manner.
Cloud computing	Using distant servers or servers in other networks to share hard disk and memory to optimize performance.
COBIT	Control Objectives for Business and Information Technology, published by Information Systems Audit and Control Association.
Code comparison	A software change control that compares source code between periods to detect changes in order for the changes to be reconciled to audit trail. Where an organization does not have source code, e.g., a purchased package, object code can be compared.
Cold site	An alternate disaster recovery site that is available in several days to a week. It takes time for the organization to arrange hardware and software to be moved into the site.
Compliance scanning	Use security software to scan system configuration for compliance with security standards.
Concurrent update	Two processes or transactions updating the same record almost concurrently. For example, the first transaction reads the opening balance and updates it. Before the first update, the second transaction reads the balance. The second transaction finishes after the first, and therefore overwrites the changes made by the first transaction. This is a database anomaly and can be prevented with record locking.

Confidence level	The percentage of confidence that the sample result correctly reflects the population characteristics.
Control risk	The risk of an internal control being improperly designed, implemented or carried out.
Critical path diagram	It shows the planned elapsed time of predecessor dependent activities. The path of contiguous and predecessor dependent activities with the longest planned cumulative elapsed time is called the critical path. There is only one critical path in a project. A delay in the critical path will delay the project.
Cryptography	An area of mathematics that is applied to protecting data by scrambling data. It can also be used to produce digital signatures to authenticate electronic messages and files.
Customer relationship management system	A system that uses data mining to find out who the valuable customers are. For example, many affinity card systems include customer relationship management systems.
Data anomaly	This exists when inconsistent changes to a database can be made. For example, when a customer moves, the customer address has been updated in some tables but not in others.
Data dictionary	A master table in a database that defines what data is in each table, the format of data, what programs and users have access to which field and the type of access, e.g., read or write.
Data Encryption Standard	A common and old encryption algorithm using a 56-bit key. Considered to be insecure for eBusiness.
Data mining	Quantitative analysis of a large mass of data including transaction data and external data to determine patterns. This is commonly used in customer relationship management systems, risk analysis and executive information systems.
Data redundancy	Keeping repetitive data in a database that increases the risk of data anomaly.
Database administrator	The person responsible for planning, organizing, controlling and monitoring a database and the database management system.
Database management system	This is a system software tool that manages data sharing in a database by allocating data table access to computer programs and users.

Database synchronization	A database control to compare the content of copies of databases distributed over servers and networks to ensure they are synchronous including time synchronization.
Deadlock	An application coming to a halt as a result of multiple record locks that lock out contending transactions. The database management system has to be configured to detect this and then release all locks but the first one in progress in order to allow the affected transactions to be completed.
Defence in depth	Placing multiple layers of firewalls in a network to successively protect inner servers and provide for redundancy.
Detection risk	The risk of audit procedures failing to detect a significant transaction error. For internal auditors, detection risk also means the risk of test procedures failing to detect a significant control deficiency.
Development library	A library of programs being used in peer testing. Peer testing is also called string testing.
Digital certificate	An "electronic business card" about a user or a web site that is used by the other party on an Internet transaction to authenticate the user or web site.
Digital rights monitoring	Using technology like digital locks to prevent the copying of software and data, including the disallowing of viewing of object code when a software package is used.
Digital signature	It is an encrypted hash of a message to allow the recipient to verify that the message was actually sent by the purported sender.
Direct cutover	Converting the old system to the new system in one pass, without any overlap between running the old and new systems. This is risky but the trend because of competitive pressure and advanced technology that enables operation to revert to the old system in real time if necessary.
Distributed computing	A system that splits processing between central servers, intermediate servers and remote workstations. An example is ATM.
Disaster recovery plan	A plan to ensure that the organization can resume operation of business critical systems in the event of a significant interruption of the data center.

DMZ	Demilitarized zone is the network space between an external firewall and an internal firewall. Medium sensitive servers that do not contain financial information can be placed there. It is created as part of defence in depth.
Dollar unit sampling	Attribute sampling using each dollar in the population as a sample item, hence assessing whether each dollar satisfies the prescribed attributes, e.g., correct or not.
Domain name server	This is a server that is used only in an IP environment. It translates URLs to IP addresses.
Earned value	An earned value demonstrates the extent of useful time spent on a project. It is calculated as the percentage of work completed multiplied by the planned cost of the entire work. The difference between actual cost incurred to date and the earned value represents a cost variance. If the earned value is less than the actual cost, the project will likely go over budget.
EBCDIC	Extended Binary Coded Decimal Interchange Code is the data format of IBM Z series server.
Echo check	A receiving node sends back what it receives to the sending node for the sending node to verify accuracy of transmission.
Edge computing	A service performed by an network service organization to store a web site's data close to customers to reduce data traffic. For example, the eLearning material of an organization that is accessed world wide can be stored in service organizations at different corners of the world for quick access.
Electronic data interchange (EDI)	Transmitting common business documents in electronic batches, e.g., purchase orders.
Electronic vaulting	Online transfer of data to a backup server without using computer tape.
Embedded audit module	A computer assisted audit technique that subjects real transactions to a set of rules in the system designed by auditors in order to test the transactions in real time and perform real time audit sampling.
Encryption	Using an algorithm and a digital key to scramble data which can be decrypted using the same algorithm and an appropriate key.

End user development	User areas developing their own systems instead of going through the IT department. This must be controlled in terms of approval, testing and documentation.
Enterprise resource planning system	An integrated accounting system that updates multiple journals and ledgers based on one transaction, thereby minimizing paper, key entry and phone calls etc. It also enables comprehensive, real time enquiries. Common products are SAP and Oracle.
Entity relationship diagram	This diagram shows the relationship between entities and it shows the cardinality. For example, the relationship between invoice and product number is many to many. This diagram is part of database design.
Environment	The hardware or network segment that holds a software library.
Error detection value	The amount of redundant data sent along with a transmitted packet that will be used by the receiving node to verify complete and accurate transmission.
Exploit	A worm written to exploit a security hole like a back door.
Exposure	Quantified risk in relation to the value of asset or information at risk, i.e., risk x materiality.
File integrity monitoring	Using hashing algorithms to check the change in file size change.
Firewall	A security device placed on a network to filter out unacceptable Internet traffic.
Foreign key	An alphanumeric field in a table that is the primary key in another table. A foreign key is a field that must not be blank in order to preserve data integrity. An example is the supervisor ID of an employee. Every employee must have a supervisor.
Gantt Chart	A time table for a project, in calendar form showing the tasks across time lines, people assigned to tasks, person days required and deliverables. The chart should also accommodate the display of actual progress vs planned progress.
General audit software	An audit software tool that allows auditors to extract data and analyze it based on criteria.

Hardening	Disabling unnecessary services (features) and ports of an operating system or similar system software package in accordance with the organization's baseline configuration image to prevent system attacks.
Hash total	A control total of a numeric field that is neither an amount nor a quantity, taken at one point of a transaction cycle for a batch system and agreed to another control total of the same batch of transactions taken at a later point to confirm completeness of processing. This control is used in addition to or instead of batch total to catch offsetting errors. For example, the field totalled may be the account number.
Hashing	The irreversible scrambling of data using an algorithm; commonly used in digital signature formation, password protection and data integrity checks.
Honeypot	A trap set to detect, deflect, or in some manner counteract attempts at unauthorized use of information systems.
Hot site	An alternate disaster recovery site that is available within an hour of notice. It has all the hardware, software, work stations and backed up data.
HTML	Hypertext Markup Language is the primitive coding scheme for constructing static web pages that links a string of clickable text to a file to provide the desired information to the web user.
Index sequential access method	A database access method that uses an index like the table of content in a book to facilitate locating records.
Inherent risk	The risk of an undesirable event.
Integrated test facility	A test branch in an organization that can be used by auditors to put in test transactions that are subjected to live processing without updating the general ledger.
Intrusion detection system	A sensor or a server with appropriate software to analyze traffic that has gone through firewalls to detect potential intrusion for assessment by security specialists.
Intrusion prevention system	A sensor or a server with appropriate software to deny traffic that has gone through firewalls but that is determined to be part of a hacking scheme.

Investor Confidence Rules	This is sometimes called CSOX, Canada's rules that require public companies to certify internal controls to their provincial securities regulators.
ISO	International Standards Organization defines industry standards to promote quality. ISO 17779 is a security standard.
IT governance	The oversight responsibility for the strategic management of the IT function and resources. IT governance should cover IT planning, organization, acquisition, implementation, delivery, monitoring and evaluation.
Job Control Language	The operating system commands and log for z/OS; z/OS is IBM's operating system for mainframes (Z Series servers).
Joint application development	This approach combines the user requirement phase with the system architecture and system design phases. Workshops are conducted to involve user representatives, system architects and system designers to design the system and architecture from a user perspective interactively.
Kernel	The kernel is the core of an operating system that directly controls the allocation of the central processing unit (CPU) functions and random access memory (RAM).
Law of large numbers	A theorem that describes the result of performing the same experiment a large number of times. According to the law, the average of the results obtained from a large number of trials should be close to the expected value, and will tend to become closer as more trials are performed.
LDAP	Lightweight Directory Access Protocol is a modern protocol for managing and exchanging PKI directories.
Local area network	A network of PCs in a building connected to a server.
MAC address	Media access control address is a hard coded serial number of a computing device, like a vehicle serial number, used to uniquely trace the activities of a device.
Man-in-the-middle attack	A hacker intercepts the exchange of public keys and replaces them with his or her key and then subsequently uses his or her key to decrypt intercepted emails.
Message digest	A hash of a message to form a digital signature or to verify data integrity.

Near field communication	Short range wireless transfer of data within 20 cm. This is increasingly used for mobile payments of small amounts.
.NET	The .NET Framework is a collection of software tools for Windows application development, allowing for programming language interoperability, i.e., a program can include instructions written in other programming languages.
Node	A network connection point like a router or a server.
Normal distribution	This is called "normal" because it reflects the pattern of most natural numbers like invoice amounts and household income. It is also called the bell curve.
Normalization	Reducing the number of fields in database tables to a reasonable minimum to avoid data redundancy and make the database more modular.
Object code	Computer programs that have been compiled from the programming language format to computer or machine language understandable to the operating system. Only object code can be processed by a computer for calculation and transaction processing. Object code is usually linked as one object, e.g., software that we download is in one .exe file.
Open source	Ready made programs in source code format available from vendors, trading partners or the IT community.
OSI model	Open System Connection model defines Internet network traffic in five layers to standardize data transfer on the Internet. The five layers are physical, data link, network, transport and application.
P3P	Platform for Privacy Preferences (P3P) is a security protocol for web sites to declare how they will use the information collected through a browser, in accordance with their posted privacy policy. For example, if a privacy policy says that the organization will not use a cookie to change a customer's data in the PC, the web server logic should be internally certified by the organization that it will not use a cookie for that purpose.
Packet	A fixed block of data transmitted over a network. A message is usually broken into several packets so each packet can find the fastest route to travel. At the destination, the packets are regrouped to form the message.
Parallel implementation	Operating the old and new systems in parallel until the new system is stable. This system conversion method is more suitable to batch systems.

Parity check	Using the last bit of a byte as a check bit for the receiving node to detect whether any bits in a byte has been turned on or off as a result of bad communication or hacker interception.
Password cracking	A hacker using password hash tables or trial and error to hash a number of passwords to try to find a hash that is identical to the stolen hashed password, with the intent of determining the real password.
Patching	Installing a security fix from a software vendor, e.g., Microsoft.
Payload	The damage done by a virus or worm on a computer; in a way, like the punch line of a joke.
Payment Card Industry Security Standards	A set of security standards established by the Payment Card Industry Security Standards Council made up of major credit card issuers like MasterCard and Visa, that apply to merchants, financial institutions and IT service organizations that process credit card transactions electronically.
Penetration testing	A control procedure whereby an organization hires a consultant or assigns technical staff members to try to hack into the organization, to test the network security.
Personal information	Information about a person provided by the person, e.g., my salary information in my bank.
Personal Information Protection and Electronic Documents Act	Canada's privacy act that applies to any business and not-for-profit organization that is not substantially funded by a government and where there is no comparable provincial privacy legislation applicable to the private sector.
Phased implementation	A risk based system implementation approach where selected functions will be turned on, and those corresponding functions of the old system will be turned off.
Phishing	An email trying to trick a reader to click on a link to provide login credentials.
Pilot implementation	Implementing a new system in a selected store or branch to test the water.
Port	A channel used for computers on a network to exchange information for a particular application; an example of an application is a network game. A port is analogous to a radio channel.

Post-implementation review	An independent review of a system development project at completion to assess to extent to which cost and benefit comply with the business case, the adequacy of signoff and documentation and the level of user satisfaction.
Primary key	An alphanumeric field in a table that uniquely identifies records, e.g., customer number.
Privacy	Confidentiality of personal information, to protect the information owner from having the personal information used inappropriately at the detriment of the information owner.
Private key	This is the one of the key in a key pair generated by an asymmetric encryption algorithm that is kept private in a user or a web site system; used to decrypt messages and compose digital signatures.
Production library	The library of programs actually used in transaction processing. This is the master and official version of the programs in a system.
Project management office	The corporate office that keeps an inventory of systems development projects, monitors progress, maintains the systems development methodology and techniques, maintains and controls the reusable code, and supplies project managers to projects. It is the center of excellence in systems development.
Project sponsor	An executive who owns a system development project and will be accountable for the project's success. This is usually the system owner when the system is implemented.
Prototype	This means developing a working replica of the system before detailed development effort is expended. Input and output screens are developed before detailed design and architecture are prepared.
Public key	This is the one of the key in a key pair generated by an asymmetric encryption algorithm that is released to other parties, for use to encrypt messages and decipher digital signatures.
Public key infrastructure	PKI is a set of policies, procedures and software to manage the public key directory and enable users and systems to use the asymmetric encryption method in an organization and with other organizations.

557

RACF	Resource Access Control Facility is IBM's add on security software for z/OS.
Radio frequency ID	A portable device that can be attached to a physical asset to transmit information about the asset using radio wave to a reader for recording in system. A common example is a toll road transponder. Another example is a tag attached to a pallet of soft drinks to keep inventory up to date.
Random access method	The database hashes the primary key to determine the physical location of a record when the record is created and subsequently accessed. The hashing algorithm must be sophisticated enough to prevent collision, i.e., two records being hashed to the same location.
Rapid application development	For simple applications or when the project deadline is very tight, the organization may decide to apply rapid application development techniques. These techniques are used to condense the systems development life cycle or bypass some of the phases.
Record locking	A database control to lock the field of a record to prevent it from being read by a transaction that intends to use the field's information to update the field or other fields in the record, when there is already a transaction in progress to update that field, to avoid the result of the first transaction from being overwritten by the second transaction.
Redundant data check	A method of transmission verification that involves sending extra data that is a derivative of the actual message for the receiving node to verify accurate transmission.
Regression analysis	Correlative analysis of a hypothesized dependent variable and one or more independent variables to estimate a relationship.
Request for proposals	A request to prospective vendors to propose a system to address an organization's user requirements. The request may be posted on a web site and open to the public or may be sent to a list of vendors that the organization thinks will be interested in proposing.
Residual risk	This is the risk remaining after implementation of internal controls. Residual risk should be acceptable if theoretically the cost of the next control will exceed the cost of the risk to be mitigated.

Reusable code	Programs that can be reused in other applications, e.g., boundary checking or sorting.
Risk registry	A corporate repository of inherent and residual risks segmented by business area indicating the risk owners, the risk weights and risk ratings, to facilitate ongoing risk assessment.
Rootkit	A program used by a hacker to obtain root access to the operating system to bypass security.
Router	A network device that connects workstations to a server. It can connect workstations to a modem. A router usually has one or a few input connections and many more output connections.
Run-to-run control total	A control total for a batch system prepared and verified by the computer without human interaction.
Salt	Extra bits added by a password management system to a raw password to arrive at a more complicated password, to make it harder for password cracking.
Sandbox	An enclosed area in Windows that does not allow access to local files and input functions, it is like an operating system within the operating system.
Sarbanes-Oxley Act	A United States Act passed in 2002 after the collapse of some big public companies like Enron. This Act was proposed by Senator Paul Sarbanes and Congressman Michael Oxley, to tighten financial control over public companies. The Act requires the CEO of a public company to certify internal controls that support financial statements to Securities Exchange Commission. It also restricts shareholders' auditors of public companies in performing non-audit services to their audit clients in order to maintain objectivity.
Secure Electronic Transaction	Under SET, a bank issues digital certificates to customers and merchants for the purpose of authenticating the merchants in credit card transactions. The merchant does not see the credit card number and the bank does not see the order information other than the amount.
Secure Socket Layer	SSL is the encryption method used in eBusiness, using a 128-bit symmetric key generated by a browser and sent to the web site encrypted with the web site's public key.

Session ID	A session ID is an ID assigned by a web server to a user upon the user initiating connection with the server. It helps the web server keep track of user activities for problem solving, customer relationship management, keeping track of what a user has requested so the requested information can be provided to the right user and web site visit pattern management system etc.
Single sign on	Using strong authentication to allow a user to access a number of systems via the same password or two factor authentication parameters. This enhances the efficiency of user authentication.
Six Sigma	An excellence standard to achieve a defect rate of not more than 3.4 per million.
SNA	Within z/OS, Structured Network Architecture (SNA) provides the network architecture to connect terminals (including z/OS emulated PCs) to servers, including TCP/IP support.
Sniffing	Unauthorized tapping of network traffic.
SNMP community string	A text string that acts as a password. It is used to authenticate messages that are sent between the management station like a server or a router and the device (the SNMP agent) like a workstation. The community string is included in every packet that is transmitted between the SNMP manager and the SNMP agent. All devices assigned to a management station have the same community string as the management station's.
Software change management system	A system that keep track of the versions of programs during development, testing and in production. It keeps track of the updates and retrievals of programs in the development, test, user acceptance (staging) and production environments.
Social engineering	Using seemingly benign approaches to obtain information about one's identity or an organization's network in order to perform hacking.
Source code	Compute programs written in a programming language. It has to be compiled to object code (computer or machine language understandable to the operating system).
Source code escrow	A source code escrow agreement involves placing the current source code with a third party. In the event of a contract breach or the developing vendor ceasing business, the user organization can access the source code to maintain the system.

Spoofing	Disguising one's IP or email address to mislead the message recipient or network monitoring system.
SQL	Structured query language is the de facto common language for creating, updating, deleting and querying records and tables in a database.
SQL injection	A hacking technique to put in SQL instruction in an eBusiness data input field, thus causing unexpected system functions.
SQL Server	Microsoft's database management system
SSID	The ID of an access point that has been configured in an authorized remote device to authenticate the device.
Staging library	The library that holds programs being used for user acceptance testing.
Standard image	An approved and consistent set of configuration that applies to all PCs and servers in the organization.
Storage access network	A network dedicated to performing and storing data backup. It is a cross-department, cross site network that processes the online transfer of data and provides a means for business areas to retrieve backed up data online.
String testing	Testing of several programs at a time by a peer programmer. This is the second phase of testing.
Switch	A network device that connects workstations to a server. Unlike a router, it has no operating system so logging and rules for connection are more limited.
Symmetric encryption	The same key is used to encrypt and decrypt. The two parties must trust each other and have a secret way to share the key.
System administrator	A system administrator is someone who controls a server. This is a critical IT position and must be rigorously controlled.
System integration testing	Testing the entire or the majority of a system together before implementation. This is done by independent testers who do not have other IT roles and it uses a massive data bank.
System software	Software that interfaces between the operating system and applications to perform common resource management functions like database management.

TCP/IP	Transmission Control Protocol/Internet Protocol is the Internet's protocol that allows seamless data transfer.
Three-tier network	A network that involves workstations, application servers and database servers.
Threat	A general description of a risk without quantification, e.g., a snow storm.
Time server	A server in a network that keeps the official time. Servers can connect to the time server to synchronize their time. Time synchronization is critical in organizations that rely largely on online transactions carried out in distributed regions.
Triple DES	A much improved symmetric encryption algorithm that uses three 56-bit keys in iteration to achieve an estimated effective key length of 112 bits. Why not 168 bits? Well, the iterations make it easier for hackers to deduce the keys and this compromise has effectively reduced the key strength to 112 bits.
Trojan	A program that performs a useful function but also contains a hidden function that compromises security.
Two factor authentication	Using something a user knows and something a user has to authenticate a user, e.g., ATM.
User acceptance testing	Testing performed by user representatives to confirm a system's reliability and user friendliness, including the testing of user procedures. This is the last phase of system change testing.
UDP	A simpler form of Internet communication than TCP. UDP uses a smaller header and does not check for errors. It is used when speed is more critical.
Unit testing	Testing a program or several programs performed by the person who wrote the program(s). This is the first phase of systems change testing.
Upper error limit	UEL is the maximum error rate for the specific attribute that the auditor is willing to tolerate at a specified confidence level.
Upper error limit factor	Upper error limit in % multiplied by the sample size. A table of UEL factors allows auditors to calculate the sample size based on the number of tolerable sample errors and the UEL %.

Variable sampling	Sampling of items to estimate the value of the population, less used in auditing.
Virtual private network	Using encryption and two factor authentication to allow a user to access a corporate network via the Internet to protect data transmission and authenticate the user.
Virtualization	Using system optimization software to reallocate disk space and real memory in servers to maximize performance, thereby reducing the number of servers.
Virus signature	This is the "DNA" of a virus. It is a unique combination of bits in the virus. It is rare for two objects to have the same combination of bits. Thus a signature can uniquely identify a virus for detection.
Virtual Sequential Access Method	VSAM is IBM's index sequential access software tool used for legacy systems.
Vulnerability	The extent of risk as a result of a control failure or absence, for example, an operating system is vulnerable if is not updated regularly.
Vulnerability assessment	An exercise whereby an organization's security staff reviews the network and operating system configuration to identify security holes, including where necessary, penetration testing.
Warm site	An alternate disaster recovery site that takes a day or two to be available. It usually has hardware and backed up data. But the software has to be brought up to date.
Web site refresh	Regularly refreshing a web site's content from a backup version to nullify any change by a hacker.
Wide area network	A collection of local area networks.
Wifi Protected Access	WPA is the most secured encryption protocol for wireless access to a local area network. It complies with the latest IEEE (Institute of Electrical and Electronic Engineers) standard 802.11i.
Worm	A malicious program that travels on the Internet that will infect computers on the Internet or the same local area network where the worm is travelling. Typical damage is sending many packets of data to tie up the network. It does not require any action by a victim to infect a computer. The effective mitigation is to patch computers to prevent infection.

	EXtensbile Business Reporting Language is a tailored type of XML to let organizations present their financial statements in a form that can be analyzed by software without human keying of the information.
	EXtensible Markup Language is an extension of HTML to describe the data behind each link. This facilitates eBusiness especially business to business eBusiness. It enables the application triggered by a browser, or even an organization's purchasing system to process the data behind a link with little or no manual interpretation and clicking.
Zero day exploit	An exploit that is written to be a worm on the day a backdoor is publicized, thus leaving very little time for software vendors to react.